A TEXT BOOK OF

TELECOMMUNICATION NETWORKS AND MANAGEMENT

For

Semester - I

FINAL YEAR (BE) DEGREE COURSE ELECTRONICS AND COMMUNICATION ENGINEERING

Strictly As Per the New Revised Syllabus of
Dr. Babasaheb Ambedkar Marathwada University, Aurangabad
(2009-2010)

Dr. P. W. WANI
M.E., Ph.D.
Professor, E & TC Dept.,
Government College of Engineering
PUNE.

R. C. JAISWAL
M.E. (E & TC)
Assistant Professor, E & TC Deptt.,
Pune Institute of Computer Technology,
Dhankawadi, **PUNE.**

NIRALI PRAKASHAN
Advancement of knowledge

N2666

TELECOM NETWORKS AND MANAGEMENT (BE - E & C - BAMU) ISBN: 978-93-83525-92-8
First Edition : October 2013
© : Authors

The text of this publication, or any part thereof, should not be reproduced or transmitted in any form or stored in any computer storage system or device for distribution including photocopy, recording, taping or information retrieval system or reproduced on any disc, tape, perforated media or other information storage device etc., without the written permission of Authors with whom the rights are reserved. Breach of this condition is liable for legal action.

Every effort has been made to avoid errors or omissions in this publication. In spite of this, errors may have crept in. Any mistake, error or discrepancy so noted and shall be brought to our notice shall be taken care of in the next edition. It is notified that neither the publisher nor the authors or seller shall be responsible for any damage or loss of action to any one, of any kind, in any manner, therefrom.

Published By : **Printed at**
NIRALI PRAKASHAN Repro Knowledgecast Limited
Abhyudaya Pragati, 1312, Shivaji Nagar, India
Off J.M. Road, PUNE – 411005
Tel - (020) 25512336/37/39, Fax - (020) 25511379
Email : niralipune@pragationline.com

DISTRIBUTION CENTRES
PUNE

Nirali Prakashan
119, Budhwar Peth, Jogeshwari Mandir Lane
Pune 411002, Maharashtra
Tel : (020) 2445 2044, 66022708, Fax : (020) 2445 1538
Email : niralilocal@pragationline.com

Nirali Prakashan
S. No. 28/25, Dhyari,
Near Pari Company, Pune 411041
Tel : (020) 24690204 Fax : (020) 24690316
Email : bookorder@pragationline.com

MUMBAI
Nirali Prakashan
385, S.V.P. Road, Rasdhara Co-op. Hsg. Society Ltd.,
Girgaum, Mumbai 400004, Maharashtra
Tel : (022) 2385 6339 / 2386 9976, Fax : (022) 2386 9976
Email : niralimumbai@pragationline.com

DISTRIBUTION BRANCHES

NAGPUR
Pratibha Book Distributors
Above Maratha Mandir, Shop No. 3, First Floor,
Rani Jhanshi Square, Sitabuldi, Nagpur 440012,
Maharashtra, Tel : (0712) 254 7129

BENGALURU
Pragati Book House
House No. 1, Sanjeevappa Lane, Avenue Road Cross,
Opp. Rice Church, Bengaluru – 560002.
Tel : (080) 64513344, 64513355,
Mob : 9880582331, 9845021552
Email:bharatsavla@yahoo.com

JALGAON
Nirali Prakashan
34, V. V. Golani Market, Navi Peth, Jalgaon 425001,
Maharashtra, Tel : (0257) 222 0395
Mob : 94234 91860

KOLHAPUR
Nirali Prakashan
New Mahadvar Road,
Kedar Plaza, 1st Floor Opp. IDBI Bank
Kolhapur 416 012, Maharashtra. Mob : 9855046155

CHENNAI
Pragati Books
9/1, Montieth Road, Behind Taas Mahal, Egmore,
Chennai 600008 Tamil Nadu, Tel : (044) 6518 3535,
Mob : 94440 01782 / 98450 21552 / 98805 82331, Email : bharatsavla@yahoo.com

RETAIL OUTLETS
PUNE

Pragati Book Centre
157, Budhwar Peth, Opp. Ratan Talkies,
Pune 411002, Maharashtra
Tel : (020) 2445 8887 / 6602 2707, Fax : (020) 2445 8887

Pragati Book Centre
Amber Chamber, 28/A, Budhwar Peth,
Appa Balwant Chowk, Pune - 411002, Maharashtra,
Tel : (020) 20240335 / 66281669
Email : pbcpune@pragationline.com

Pragati Book Centre
676/B, Budhwar Peth, Opp. Jogeshwari Mandir,
Pune 411002, Maharashtra
Tel : (020) 6601 7784 / 6602 0855

PBC Book Sellers & Stationers
152, Budhwar Peth, Pune 411002, Maharashtra
Tel : (020) 2445 2254 / 6609 2463

MUMBAI
Pragati Book Corner
Indira Niwas, 111 - A, Bhavani Shankar Road, Dadar (W), Mumbai 400028, Maharashtra
Tel : (022) 2422 3526 / 6662 5254, Email : pbcmumbai@pragationline.com

www.pragationline.com info@pragationline.com

Preface ...

It gives us great pleasure to bring out the book on **'Telecommunication Networks and Management'**. This text is designed to explain the various types of Telecommunication Networks in use today.

The book is written mainly for the Final Year (BE) Students of Electronics and Communication Engineering Course of Dr. Babasaheb Ambedkar Marathwada University, Aurangabad for the subject **"Telecommunication Networks and Management"**. It is written strictly as per the revised syllabus 2009 of Dr. Babasaheb Ambedkar Marathwada University, Aurangabad. Also additions as per recent discussion of the subject is done so that students will get knowledge of latest trends in Telecommunication Networks and Management.

We have divided the subject into small units so that the topics can be arranged and understood properly. The topics within the units have been arranged in a proper sequence to ensure smooth flow of **'Telecommunication Networks and Management'** subject.

This book gives the theoretical and practical knowledge of the different Telecommunication Networks and their Management issues.

Nirali Prakashan put the book, what we thought of into reality. Our sincere thanks to Shri. Dineshbhai Furia, Shri. Jignesh Furia and Shri. M. P. Munde. The books could be completed in time, due to sincere and hard work of Nirali Prakashan's staff namely Mr. Malik Shaikh, Mrs. Prajakta, Miss Pallavi Kumari Mrs. Sonal and Miss Chaitali Takale. We thank them all.

Valuable suggestions from our esteemed readers to improve the text will be most welcome and highly appreciated.

9th **October, 2013**   **Authors**
Pune.

Syllabus ...

1. **Introduction to Switching and Telecom Networks** (06 Hours)

   Introduction to crossbar and electronics exchange, Types of networks, Network design issues, Design tools, switching technologies (circuit switching and packet switching).

2. **Broadband Telecom Networks** (06 Hours)

   ISDN, Basic structure, ISDN Interfacing and functions, transmission structure Protocol architecture, Narrow band and Broadband ISDN

3. **Frame Relay and ATM** (08 Hours)

   Frame Relay introduction, Protocol, architecture frame, mode call control, LAPF core Protocol, frame Relay congestion control.

   ATM, ATM Protocols, Public ATM networks, ATM cells their details and transmission, AAL, Traffic congestion and control.

4. **Broadband Access and Routing Technologies** (07 Hours)

   DSL, ADSL, Cable modems, WLL, Optical wireless, Leased lines. Routing Algorithms for shortest path centralized routing, Distributed, Static and dynamic routing.

5. **QOS and Reliability Issues of Telecom Networks** (05 Hours)

   Delay, Jitter, Throughput/Bandwidth, Crosstalk/Interference Issues, Network reliability and survivability Issues, Network protection mechanisms.

6. **Telcom Network Management** (08 Hours)

   Telcom network operation and maintenance, Traffic management, Management of Transport Networks, Configuration management, Fault management, Security, Network planning support, Network management using SNMP: Object management, management Information base, traps.

***

Contents ...

1. **Introduction to Switching and Telecom Networks** — 1.1 - 1.66

2. **Broadband Telecom Networks** — 2.1 - 2.54

3. **Frame Relay and ATM** — 3.1 - 3.92

4. **Broadband Access and Routing Technologies** — 4.1 - 4.76

5. **QOS and Reliability Issues of Telecom Networks** — 5.1 - 5.96

6. **Telcom Network Management** — 6.1 - 6.88

***

Unit I

INTRODUCTION TO SWITCHING AND TELECOM NETWORKS

1.1 Introduction to Switching and Telecom Networks

Telecommunication networks carry information signals among entities which are physically (geographically) far away. Such an entity may be a human being attending a telephone, computer, fax machine, etc. For communication between any two entities like a call or data transfer, many more entities might be invoked.

If it is telephonic conversation, the one who initiates the call is the **calling subscriber** and the one for whom the call is made is called the **called subscriber.** For other information transfers, the two communicating entities are called the **source** and **destination.**

Communication is realised only when any entity in one part of the world can communicate with any other entity in rest of the world. Such connectivity in telecommunication networks is achieved by the use of switching systems. In this unit, we will be studying telephone basics, switching, signalling, that is basics of establishing a connectivity between a source and destination.

1.1.1 Evolution of Telecommunications

Telegraphy was introduced in 1837 in Great Britain and 1845 in France. In March 1876, Alexander Graham Bell demonstrated long distance communication, the possibility of telephony. And this invention was put to use almost immediately.
Graham Bell demonstrated point-to-point telephone connection.

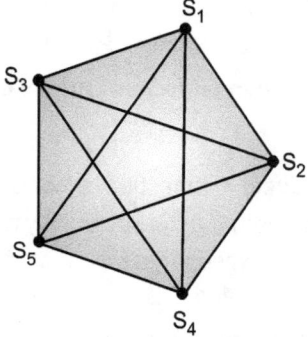

Fig. 1.1: Point-to-Point links in a network

If it is a network of five subscribers, individual links are amongst all. To establish a connection, calling subscriber chooses appropriate link with the called subscriber. To draw attention of called subscriber before information exchange can begin, some form of signalling is required with each link. If called subscriber is engaged, suitable indication should be given to calling subscriber by signalling.

As in Fig. 1.1, there are five subscribers (entities) and ten point-to-point links.

In order to connect 1st entity to all others, $(n - 1)$ links are required (e.g. 1-2, 1-3, 1-4, 1-5).

Because of this 2nd entity is already connected to first.

Therefore, to connect 2nd entity to all others, $(n - 2)$ links are required. (e.g., 2-3, 2-4, 2-5). Similarly, for 3rd, $(n - 3)$ links are required and so on.

$$\therefore \text{Total number of links} = (n - 1) + (n - 2) + \ldots + 1 + 0$$

$$= \frac{n(n-1)}{2}$$

Such networks with point-to-point links among all the entities are known as **fully connected networks.** Because of individual links, total number of links becomes too large even for a small number of subscribers.

e.g. for 50 subscribers, we need 1225 links.

As a result of this, implementation of telephony on a large scale demanded telephone sets, pairs of wires and also the switching system/switching office/exchange.

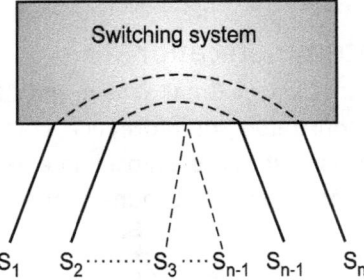

Fig. 1.2: Interconnection with an exchange

In such systems, there is no direct connection among the subscribers, but instead, all subscribers are connected to the exchange (switching system). When a subscriber initiates a call, a connection is established between the two at the exchange. e.g. as in Fig. 1.2, connection between S_1 and S_n and S_2 and S_{n-1}. In such a system, only one link per subscriber is required between the subscriber and the exchange. This limits the total number of links equal to total number of subscribers to that exchange.

Now, signalling is required to draw attention of the switching system/exchange to establish or release a connection. The exchange should also be able to detect if called subscriber is busy and if so, that should be indicated to the calling subscriber. These functions performed by an exchange in establishing and releasing connections are known as **control functions.**

Early and very basic exchanges or switching systems were manual, or needed operator. These had many limitations, so **automatic exchanges** came into existence. They are classified as below.

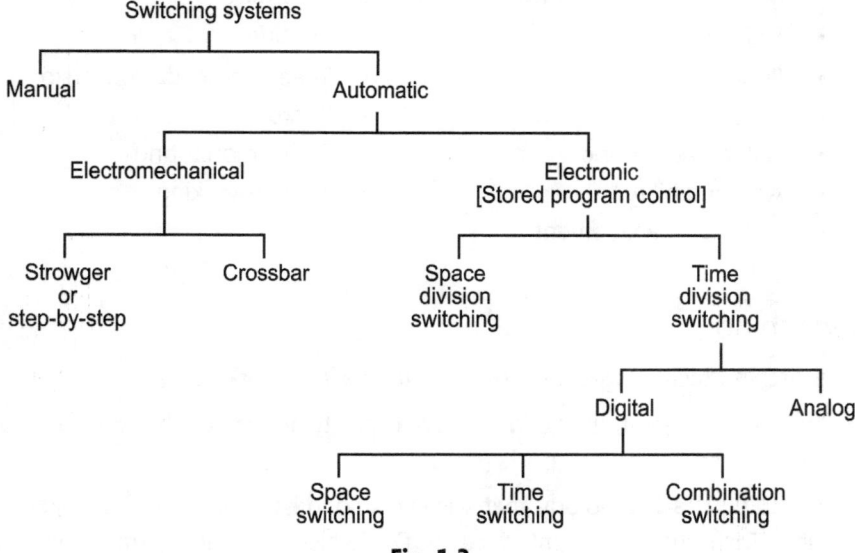

Fig. 1.3

- In Strowger systems, the control functions are performed by circuits associated with the switching element in the system. (For details of Strowger and Crossbar refer to appendix).

- Crossbar systems have hard-wired control subsystems which use relays and latches. But these have limited capability and it is impossible to modify them to provide additional functionalities.

- In electronic systems, control functions are performed by **computer** or **processor.** So these are called as **SPC (Stored Program Control)** systems. New functions, fascilities can be easily added by changing or modifying control program.

- In space division switching, a dedicated path is established between the calling and the called subscribers for the entire duration of the call.

    This technique can be used in Strowger and Crossbar systems.

    An electronic exchange may use crossbar switching matrix for space division switching.

1.2 Network Functions

1. Networks should be constructed to share (hardware and software) resources and to improve cost-effectiveness.
2. Networks should be administered by specialised staff and maintained properly for increasing efficiency of the network.
3. In view of guaranted and reliable communication of telecommunication data, the study of the following network functions are essential.
   - Switching
   - Flow control
   - Security
   - Failure monitoring
   - Accountability
   - Network management
   - Routing
   - Speed and code conversion
   - Backup
   - Traffic monitoring
   - Internetworking

1.2.1 Switching

1. Switching technologies are crucial to the new network design.
2. Switches are great, they add network capacity and speed, but they are not a cure-all.
3. *Switching* is a technology that alleviates congestion in Ethernet, Token Ring, and Fiber Distributed Data Interface (FDDI) LANs by reducing traffic and increasing bandwidth.
4. Such switches, known as *LAN switches*, are designed to work with existing cable infrastructures so that they can be installed with minimal disruption of existing networks.

Layer 2 Switching:

1. Layer 2 switching is hardware based, which means it uses the Media Access Control (MAC) address from the host's network interface cards (NICs) to filter the network. Switches use Application-Specific Integrated Circuits.
2. Layer 2 switching provides the following: Hardware-based bridging (MAC), Wire speed, High speed, Low latency, Low cost. Layer 2 switching is so efficient because there is no modification to the data packet, only to the frame encapsulation of the packet, and only when the data packet is passing through dissimilar media (such as from Ethernet to FDDI).
3. Use layer 2 switching for workgroup connectivity and network segmentation (breaking up collision domains). This allows you to create a flatter network design and one with more network segments than traditional 10BaseT shared networks.

4. Layer 2 switches have the same limitations as bridge networks. Remember that bridges are good if you design the network by the 80/20 rule: users spend 80 percent of their time on their local segment.
5. Broadcast and multicasts, along with the slow convergence of spanning tree, can cause major problems as the network grows. Because of these problems, layer 2 switches cannot completely replace routers in the internetwork.

Layer 3 Switching:

1. The only difference between a layer 3 switch and a router is the way the administrator creates the physical implementation. Also, traditional routers use microprocessors to make forwarding decisions, and the switch performs only hardware-based packet switching.
2. The benefits of layer 3 switching include the following: Hardware-based packet forwarding, High-performance packet switching, High-speed scalability, Low latency, Lower per-port cost, Flow accounting Security, Quality of service (QoS).

Layer 4 Switching:

1. Layer 4 switching is considered a hardware-based layer 3 switching technology that can also consider the application used (for example, Telnet or FTP). Layer 4 switching provides additional routing above layer 3 by using the port numbers found in the Transport layer header to make routing decisions.
2. Layer 4 information has been used to help make routing decisions for quite a while.
3. The largest benefit of layer 4 switching is that the network administrator can configure a layer 4 switch to prioritize data traffic by application, which means a QoS can be defined for each user. For example, a number of users can be defined as a Video group and be assigned more priority, or band-width, based on the need for video conferencing.

Multi-Layer Switching (MLS):

1. Multi-layer switching combines layer 2, 3, and 4 switching technologies and provides high-speed scalability with low latency.
2. It accomplishes this high combination of high-speed scalability with low latency by using huge filter tables based on the criteria designed by the network administrator.
3. Multi-layer switching can move traffic at wire speed and also provide layer 3 routing, which can remove the bottleneck from the network routers.
4. There is no performance difference between a layer 3 and a layer 4 switch because the routing/switching is all hardware based.

1.2.2 Routing

1. Term *routing* refers to selecting paths in a computer network along which to send data.
2. Routing directs forwarding, the passing of logically addressed packets from their source network, toward their ultimate destination through intermediary nodes; typically hardware devices called routers.
3. The routing process usually directs forwarding on the basis of routing tables which maintain a record of the best routes to various network destinations.
4. Thus, constructing routing tables, which are held in the routers' memory, becomes very important for efficient routing.
5. *Routing* is the act of moving information across an internetwork from a source to a destination.

Routing Components:

1. Routing involves two basic activities: determining optimal routing paths and transporting information groups (typically called packets) through an internetwork.
2. In the context of the routing process, the latter of these is referred to as packet switching. Although packet switching is relatively straightforward, path determination can be very complex.

Path Determination:

1. Routing protocols use metrics to evaluate what path will be the best for a packet to travel.
2. A metric is a standard of measurement, such as path bandwidth, that is used by routing algorithms to determine the optimal path to a destination.
3. To aid the process of path determination, routing algorithms initialize and maintain routing tables, which contain route information. Route information varies depending on the routing algorithm used.
4. Routing algorithms fill routing tables with a variety of information. Destination/next hop associations tell a router that a particular destination can be reached optimally by sending the packet to a particular router representing the "next hop" on the way to the final destination.
5. When a router receives an incoming packet, it checks the destination address and attempts to associate this address with a next hop. Fig. 1.9 depicts a sample destination/next hop routing table.

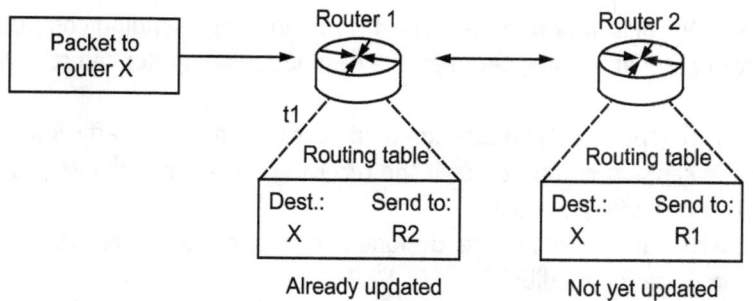

Fig. 1.4: Destination/Next Hop associations determine the Data's Optimal Path

6. Routing tables can also contain other information, such as data about the desirability of a path. Routers compare metrics to determine optimal routes, and these metrics differ depending on the design of the routing algorithm used.
7. Routers communicate with one another and maintain their routing tables through the transmission of a variety of messages.
8. The routing update message is one such message that generally consists of all or a portion of a routing table.
9. By analyzing routing updates from all other routers, a router can build a detailed picture of network topology.
10. A link-state advertisement, another example of a message sent between routers, informs other routers of the state of the sender's links.
11. Link information can also be used to build a complete picture of network topology to enable routers to determine optimal routes to network destinations.

1.2.3 Flow Control

1. In communications, the process of adjusting the flow of data from one device to another to ensure that the receiving device can handle all of the incoming data.
2. This is particularly important where the sending device is capable of sending data much faster than the receiving device can receive it.
3. In computer networking, **flow control** is the process of managing the rate of data transmission between two nodes.
4. This should be distinguished from congestion control, which is used for controlling the flow of data when congestion has actually occurred.
5. Flow control mechanisms can be classified by whether or not the receiving node sends feedback to the sending node.

6. Flow control is important because it is possible for a sending computer to transmit information at a faster rate than the destination computer can receive and process them.
7. This can happen if the receiving computers have a heavy traffic load in comparison to the sending computer, or if the receiving computer has less processing power than the sending computer.
8. Modern data networks are designed to support a diverse range of hosts and communication mediums.
9. Consider a 200 MHz Pentium-based host transmitting data to a 25 MHz 80386/SX. Obviously, the Pentium will be able to drown the slower processor with data.
10. Likewise, consider two hosts, each using an Ethernet LAN, but with the two Ethernets connected by a 28.8 Kbps modem link.
11. If one host begins transmitting to the other at Ethernet speeds, the modem link will quickly become overwhelmed. In both cases, *flow control* is needed to pace the data transfer at an acceptable speed.
12. Request/reply flow control requires each data packet to be acknowledged by the remote host before the next packet is sent. Sliding window algorithms, used by TCP, permit multiple data packets to be in simultaneous transit, making more efficient use of network bandwidth.

1.2.4 Speed and Code Conversion

1. In digital telecommunication networks allowing devices using different communication codes or operating at different speed for communications.
2. This generally involves the buffering the data.
3. In telecommunication, a **buffer** is a routine or storage medium used in telecommunications to compensate for a difference in rate of flow of data, or time of occurrence of events, when transferring data from one device to another.
4. Buffers are used for many purposes, such as (a) interconnecting two digital circuits operating at different rates, (b) holding data for use at a later time,
   (c) allowing timing corrections to be made on a data stream, (d) collecting binary data bits into groups that can then be operated on as a unit, (e) delaying the transit time of a signal in order to allow other operations to occur.

1.2.5 Security

1. In telecommunication, **communications protection** is the application of communications security measures to telecommunications systems in order to: (a) deny unauthorized persons access to sensitive unclassified information of value, (b) prevent disruption of telecommunications services, or (c) ensure the authenticity of information handled by telecommunications systems.

2. **Communications security:** Measures and controls taken to deny unauthorized persons information derived from telecommunications and ensure the authenticity of such telecommunications. Communications security includes cryptosecurity, transmission security, emission security, traffic-flow security, and physical security.

- **Cryptosecurity:** The component of communications security that results from the provision of technically sound cryptosystems and their proper use. This includes insuring message confidentiality and authenticity.
- **Emission Security:** Protection resulting from all measures taken to deny unauthorized persons information of value which might be derived from intercept and analysis of compromising emanations from crypto-equipment, automated information systems (computers), and telecommunications systems.
- **Physical Security:** The component of communications security that results from all physical measures necessary to safeguard classified equipment, material, and documents from access threat or observation there of by unauthorized persons.
- **Traffic-Flow Security:** Measures that conceal the presence and properties of valid messages on a network. It includes the protection resulting from features, inherent in some cryptoequipment, that conceal the presence of valid messages on a communications circuit, normally achieved by causing the circuit to appear busy at all times.
- **Transmission Security:** The component of communications security that results from the application of measures designed to protect transmissions from interception and exploitation by means other than cryptanalysis (e.g. frequency hopping and spread spectrum).

1.2.6 Backup

1. This is ability to react the component failure.
2. This may include sending alarms and rerouting traffic to avoid the failed components.
3. Backup systems differ from fault-tolerant systems in the sense that backup systems assume that a fault *will* cause a data loss event and fault-tolerant systems assume a fault *will not*.
4. Backups are typically that *last* line of defense against data loss, and consequently the least granular and the least convenient to use.
5. Since a backup system contains at least one copy of all data worth saving, the data storage requirements are considerable. Organizing this storage space and managing the backup process is a complicated undertaking.

1.2.7 Failure Monitoring

1. The ability to keep track of which components are working.
2. This is very important issue in traffic monitoring of network.
3. Detecting network path anomalies generally requires examining large volumes of traffic data to find misbehavior.
4. We observe that wide-area services, such as peer-to-peer systems and content distribution networks, exhibit large traffic volumes, spread over large numbers of geographically-dispersed endpoints.
5. This makes them ideal candidates for observing wide-area network behaviour. Specifically, we can combine passive monitoring of wide-area traffic to detect anomalous network behavior, with active probes from multiple nodes to quantify and characterize the scope of these anomalies.
6. This approach provides several advantages over other techniques: (1) we obtain more complete and finer-grained views of failures since the wide-area nodes already provide geographically diverse vantage points; (2) we incur limited additional measurement cost since most active probing is initiated when passive monitoring detects oddities; and (3) we detect failures at a much higher rate than others since the services provide large volumes of traffic to sample.
7. The term network monitoring describes the use of a system that constantly monitors a computer network for slow or failing systems and that notifies the network administrator in case of outages via email, pager or other alarms.
It is a subset of the functions involved in network management.
8. While an intrusion detection system monitors a network for threats from the outside, a network monitoring system monitors the network for problems due to overloaded and/or crashed servers, network connections or other devices.

1.2.8 Accountability

1. The ability to keep track of traffic level possibly by type of usage.
2. For short-term process, it can be useful for dynamic routing and flow control.
3. For long-term process like network designing whether capacity may be productively increased or decreased.

1.2.9 Internetworking

1. Performing the functions needed to communicate with and across other networks.
2. An *internetwork* is a collection of individual networks, connected by intermediate networking devices, that functions as a single large network.

3. Internetworking refers to the industry, products, and procedures that meet the challenge of creating and administering internetworks.
4. Fig. 1.5 illustrates some different kinds of network technologies that can be interconnected by routers and other networking devices to create an internetwork.

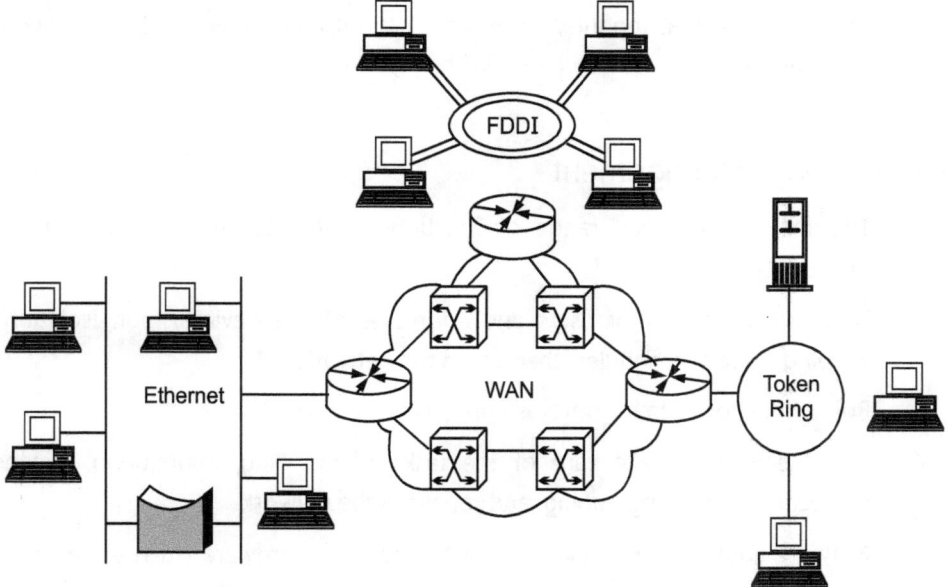

Fig. 1.5: Different Network Technologies can be connected to create an Internetwork

5. Implementing a functional internetwork is no simple task. Many challenges must be faced, especially in the areas of connectivity, reliability, network management, and flexibility.
6. Each area is key in establishing an efficient and effective internetwork.
7. The challenge when connecting various systems is to support communication among disparate technologies.
8. Different sites, for example, may use different types of media operating at varying speeds, or may even include different types of systems that need to communicate.
9. Because companies rely heavily on data communication, internetworks must provide a certain level of reliability.
10. This is an unpredictable world, so many large internetworks include redundancy to allow for communication even when problems occur.
11. Furthermore, network management must provide centralized support and troubleshooting capabilities in an internetwork. Configuration, security, performance, and other issues must be adequately addressed for the internetwork to function smoothly.

12. Security within an internetwork is essential. Many people think of network security from the perspective of protecting the private network from outside attacks.

13. However, it is just as important to protect the network from internal attacks, especially because most security breaches come from inside. Networks must also be secured so that the internal network cannot be used as a tool to attack other external sites.

1.2.10 Network Management

1. This includes a broad range of functions related to the management of the network.

2. Maintaining the list of users and addresses of the devices, fault isolation and keeping track of scheduled changes to the network.

3. Role of network administrator is important.

4. This means they take care of the tasks of installing, configuring, expanding, protecting, upgrading, tuning, and repairing the network.

5. Network administrators take care of the network hardware (such as cables, hubs, switches, routers, servers, and clients), as well as network software (such as network operating systems, e-mail servers, backup software, database servers, and application software).

6. Most importantly, network administrators take care of network users by answering their questions, listening to their troubles, and solving their problems.

1.3 Centralized Network

- The source data is located at central location.
- Other clients or terminals can access this centralized data.
- Following are the examples of the centralized networks.

    (1) Stock quotation and information system.

    (2) Bank credit card system.

    (3) Components distribution system.

    (4) ATM (Automatic Teller Machines) System.

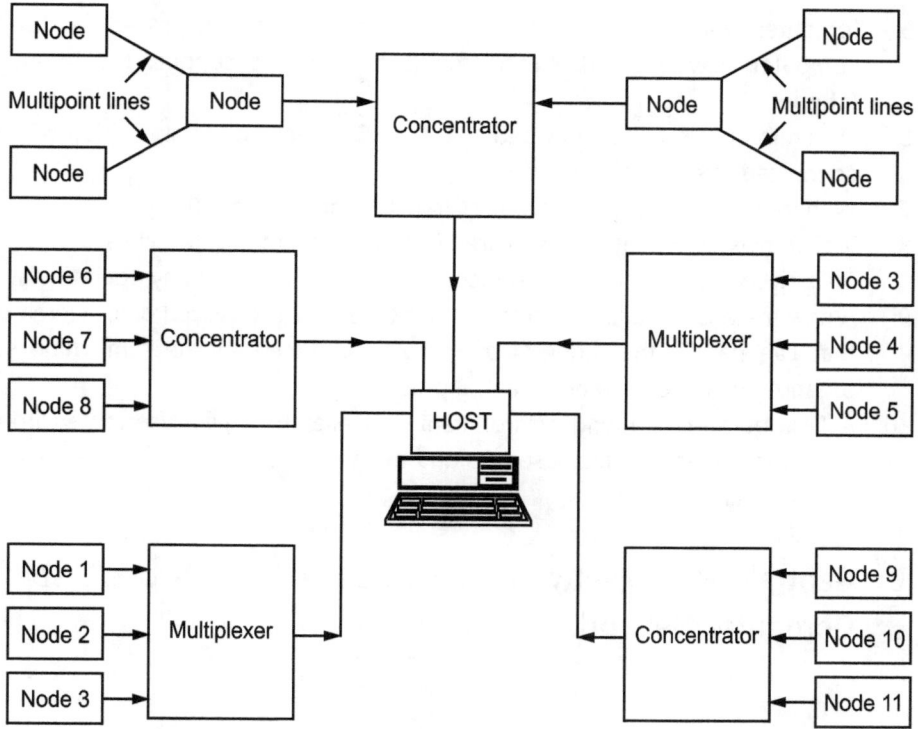

Fig. 1.6: Typical Centralized Data Network

- Centralized network can be a part of any complex network.
- In centralized network, different networks performing similar activities are linked.
- Tree topology is implemented in the centralized data network.
- In centralized network, cost effectiveness is achieved using concentrators and multiplexers.
- Nodes (also called as terminals) can be connected to central site directly or indirectly (i.e. through multiplexers and concentrators).

1.4 Distributed Computer Networks

1. A distributed computing system is immediate growth from centralized computer systems and client/server computer systems, as shown in Fig. 1.16.
2. Distributed computing is basically client/server computing.
3. Data is not located in one server, but in many servers.
4. These servers might be at different areas, connected by WAN links into enterprise networks that join the many standalone and autonomous computer systems in workgroups, departments, and divisions of an organization.

5. Computer Networks built with Web technologies are also called as distributed computer networks. Distributed computer networks support the Intranet and Internet.
6. Dynamic information provided by the Back-end database systems can be connected to these Web servers.
7. Web technologies add new features to distributed computing.
8. Web browsers like internet explorer, Netscape communicator, Netscape Navigator are universal clients that can connect with Web servers with any operating system.
9. A new trend is to build intranets in which all data is centralized on clustered servers that can handle the requests of many, many users at the same time so that organizations need powerful central processing systems.
10. A Distributed-computing environment is similar to a client/server environment, except that there are many servers and many clients who access any one of those servers at any time.

1.4.1 Centralized Network/Client-Server Network/Distributed Computer Network

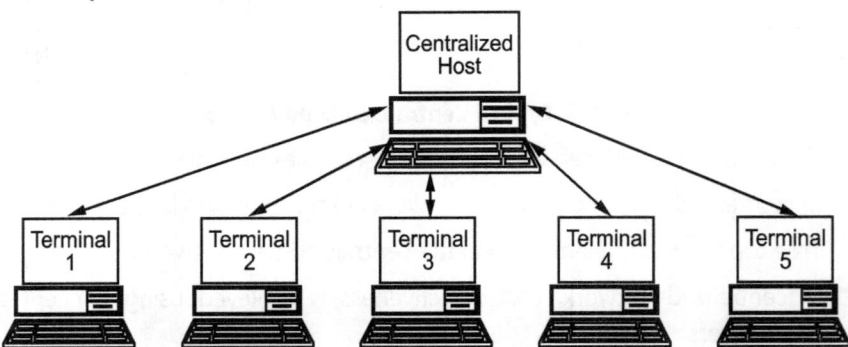

Fig. 1.7: Centralized Computer Network

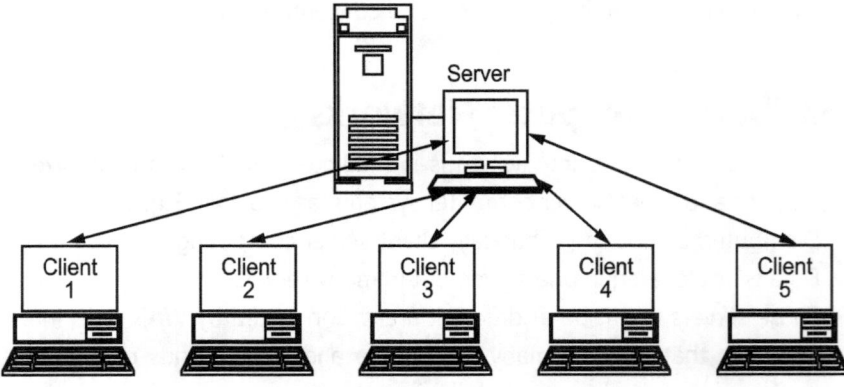

Fig. 1.8: Client-Server Configuration

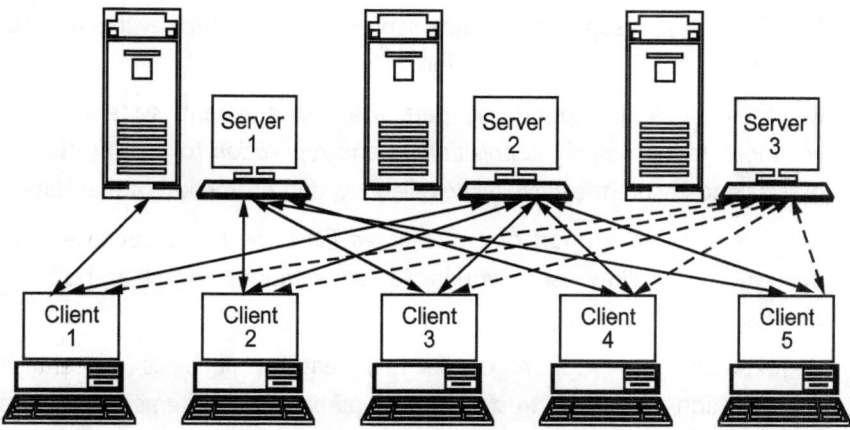

Fig. 1.9: Distributed Client Computing

1.4.2 Advantages and Disadvantages of Distributed Computer Networks

1. The distributed computing model supports access to data already located at diverse sites.
2. Databases are replicated to other locations so that users at those locations can access data locally instead of using expensive WAN link to access centralized data at corporate places.
3. Distributing data in distributed computer networks provides protection from local network failure. If one site goes down, users can still access data at other sites.
4. In distributed computer networks, Distributing data requires complex replication and synchronization over LAN or WAN links that requires more management and supervision. Skilled managerial activities are expected.
5. Next step is to have distributed systems built with TCP/IP protocols and Web technologies or network applications that promote distributed computing.
6. The target is to make the data computing as simple as possible.

1.4.3 Needs of Distributed Computer Networks

1. The network *platform* that supports a variety of multivendor products and TCP/IP protocol support due to its wide acceptance.
2. Real-time connection-oriented methods or communication systems are required to communicate with Servers.
3. Requirement and support of a directory naming service which keeps track of resources and information and where they are located.

4. Requirement and support of a time service to synchronize events among different servers that hold related information.

5. Requirement and support of database management systems that support advanced features such as *partitioning* and *replication* to provide the distribution of data and ensure the availability, reliability, and protection of that data.

6. Requirement and support of a *distributed file system* that operates in a peer-to-peer mode to allow users working at workstations to act as both clients and servers.

7. Requirement and support of Security features such as authentication and authorization, as well as trust relationships between systems so users can access multiple servers and databases without the need to prove their identity every time they access a remote resource.

1.5 Voice Networks

1.5.1 Analog Voice Network

1. Public switched telephone networks are communication systems that are available to the public to allow users to interconnect communication devices.

2. Public telephone networks within countries and regions are standard integrated systems of transmission and switching facilities, signaling processors, and associated operations support systems that allow communication devices to communicate with each other when they operate.

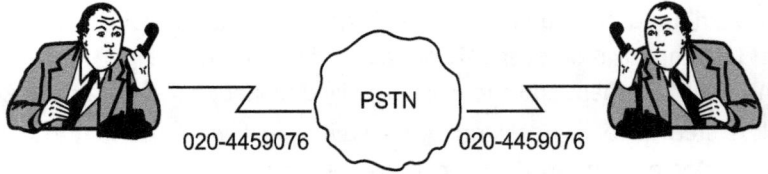

Fig. 1.10: Typical Analog Voice Network

3. A telephone call may consist of an ordinary voice transmission using a telephone, a data transmission when the calling party and called party are using modems, or a facsimile transmission when the two parties are using fax machines.

4. Where a telephone call has more than one called party, it is referred to as a conference call.

5. Calls are usually placed through a network (such as the Public Switched Telephone Network) provided by a commercial telephone company.

6. If the caller's wireline phone is directly connected to the calling party, when the caller takes their telephone off-hook, the calling party's phone will ring.

7. This is called a hot line. Otherwise, the calling party is usually given a tone to indicate they should begin dialing the desired number.
8. In some cases, the calling party cannot dial calls directly, and is connected to an operator who places the call for them.
9. Preceding, during, and after a telephone call is placed, certain tones signify the progress and status of the telephone call.
10. A **dial tone** signifying that the call is ready to be placed either:
    - a ringing tone signifying that the calling party has yet to answer the telephone.
    - a busy signal (or engaged tone) signifying that the calling party's telephone is being used in a telephone call to another person.
11. Status tones such as STD notification tones (to inform the caller that the telephone call is being trunk dialed at a greater cost to the calling party), minute minder beeps (to inform the caller of the relative duration of the telephone call on calls that are charged on a time basis), and others a tone (sometimes the busy signal) to signify that the called party has hung up.

1.5.2 Digital Voice Network

1. Above discussion is related to the typical analog voice network. Let us discuss the digital voice network.

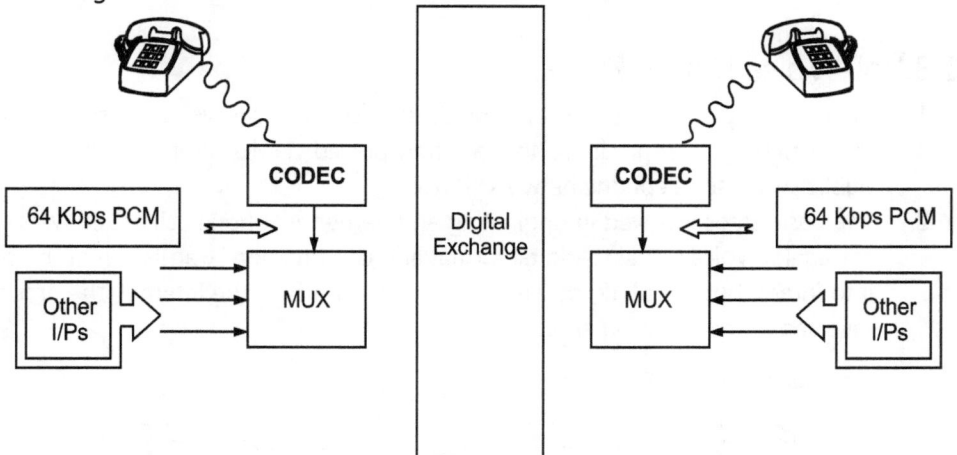

Fig. 1.11: Typical Digital Voice Network

2. Generally, above network is commonly referred to as a T1 line or circuit.
3. That circuit was developed to relieve cable congestion in metropolitan areas by providing a transport mechanism for 24 digitized voice conversations to be simultaneously carried over one cable.

4. To do so, each voice conversation is digitized using a technique called pulse code modulation (PCM).
5. Under PCM, an analog voice conversation is digitized at 64 Kbps.
6. To provide information that enables one conversation to be distinguished from another and switched into and out of a group of conversations, framing bits must be added to the T1 data flow.
7. Those framing bits operate at 8000 bps and carry control information, error-detection information, and a limited data-link capability.
8. This capability, for example, enables two private branch exchanges (PBXs) to communicate with one another while transporting 24 voice conversations on a T1 circuit interconnecting the PBXs.
9. The 24 channels, each operating at 64 Kbps, result in an operating rate of 1.536 Mbps.
10. When the 8 Kbps framing information is added to the T1 line, its operating rate becomes 1.544 Mbps.
11. Communication carriers also offer low-speed digital services operating at data rates from 2.4 Kbps upto 56 Kbps, using time-division multiplexers to group multiple low-speed digital circuits onto a 64 Kbps circuit.
12. The 64 Kbps circuit, in turn, is connected to a channel on a carrier's T1 line, which represents the basic backbone infrastructure used for transporting voice, data, and video across entire country.

1.5.3 VoIP Voice Network

1. Internet telephony refers to communication services like voice, facsimile, and/or voice-messaging applications that are transported via the Internet, rather than the public switched telephone network (PSTN).
2. The basic steps involved in originating an Internet telephone call are conversion of the analog voice signal to digital format and compression/ translation of the signal into Internet protocol (IP) packets for transmission over the Internet; the process is reversed at the receiving end.

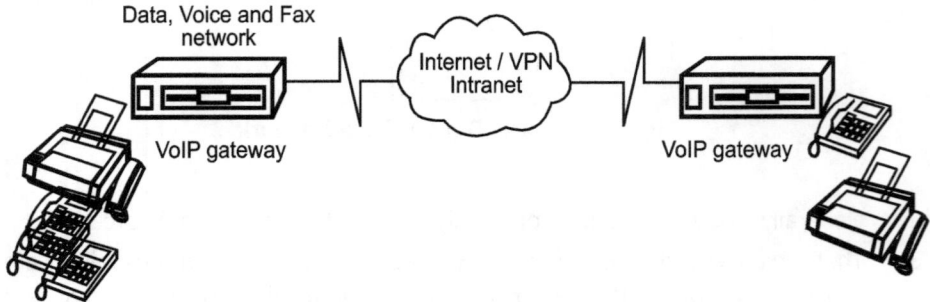

Fig. 1.12: Typical VoIP network (voice network) with VoIP Gateway

3. Initially, convert the dialed number to an IP address.
4. Secondly, establish connection to remote gateway.
5. Thirdly, rend voice over the data network.
6. Finally, receive voice over the data network at receiver end.
7. This feature allows VoIP to operate over Frame Relay and ATM networks autonomously.
8. More importantly, VoIP operates over typical LANs to go all the way to the desktop.
9. In this sense, VoIP is more of an application than a service, and VoIP protocols have evolved with this in mind.
10. VoIP protocols fall into two general categories: centralized and distributed.
11. In general terms, centralized models follow a client/server architecture, while distributed models are based on peer-to-peer interactions.
12. Both architectures have advantages and disadvantages.
13. Distributed models tend to scale well and are more resilient (robust) because they lack a central point that could fail.
14. Conversely, centralized call control models offer easier management and can support traditional supplementary services (such as conferencing) more easily, but they can have scaling limits based on the capacity of the central server.
15. Hybrid and networking models being developed also offer the best of both approaches.
16. The strong pressures driving the integration of voice and data networks have resulted in various solutions to the problem, each with its own strengths and weaknesses. Three general approaches exist:
    - Voice over IP
    - Voice over ATM
    - Voice over Frame Relay

1.6 Integrated Networks

1. Integrated networks involve the digitization of the telephone network, which permits voice, data, text, graphics, music, video, and other source material to be transmitted over existing telephone wires.
2. The emergence of Integrated networks represents an effort to standardize subscriber services, user/network interfaces, and network and internetwork capabilities.

3. Integrated networks applications include high-speed image applications.

4. Additional telephone lines in homes to serve the telecommuting industry, high-speed file transfer, and videoconferencing.

5. A network consisting of an integrated telephone, IP or video system. Also called as Converged Communications or Multi-service Networks.

6. The convergence of data, voice, and video onto a single network offers enterprises attractive opportunities for reducing communication costs and complexities as well as enabling progressive productivity gains.

7. IP Communications system delivers enterprise-class solutions for IP telephony, unified messaging, IP video and audio conferencing, IP video broadcasting, and contact centers.

8. Integrated solutions dramatically improve operational efficiencies, increase an organization's productivity, enhance customer satisfaction, and enable a collaborative workforce.

1.6.1 Key Benefits of Integrated Networks

- Smooth network migration strategy.
- Simplified system configuration and management.
- Reduced operational costs.
- Advanced packet network capabilities.
- Scalability.
- High reliability.

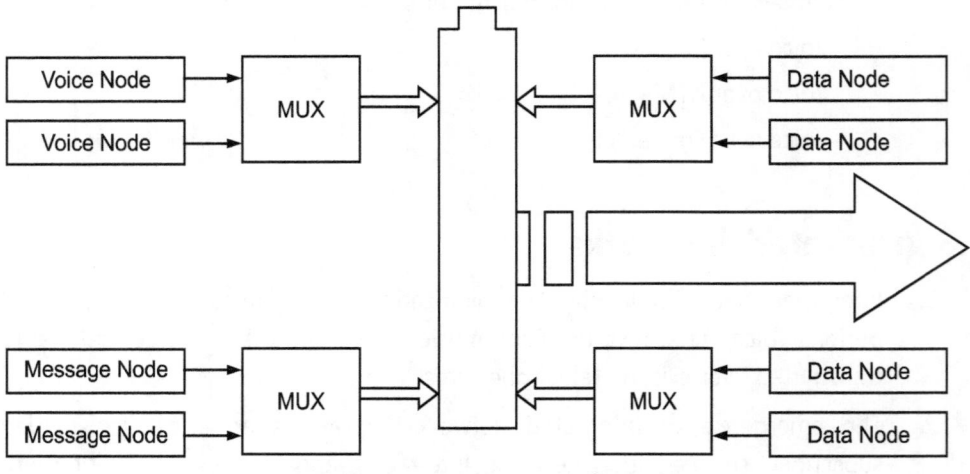

Fig. 1.13: Typical Integrated Network

1.7 LAN, WAN, MAN and Internet

1.7.1 Local Area Network (LAN)

1. Networks used to interconnect computers in a single room, rooms within a building or buildings on one site are called Local Area Network (LAN).
2. LAN transmits data with a speed of several megabits per second (10^6 bits per second). The transmission medium is normally *coaxial cables*.
3. LAN links computers, i.e., software and hardware, in the same area for the purpose of sharing information.
4. Usually LAN links computers within a limited geographical area because they must be connected by a cable, which is quite expensive.
5. People working in LAN get more capabilities in data processing, work processing and other information exchange compared to *stand-alone computers*.
6. Because of this information exchange, most of the business and government organizations are using LAN.

Major Characteristics of LAN

1. Every computer has the potential to communicate with any other computers of the network.
2. High degree of interconnection between computers.
3. Easy physical connection of computers in a network.
4. Inexpensive medium of data transmission.
5. High data transmission rate.

Components of LAN:

1. Workstations:
- In LAN, a workstation refers to a machine that will allow users access to a LAN and its resources while providing intelligence on board allowing local execution of applications.
- It may allow data to be stored locally or remotely on a file server.
- Obviously, diskless workstations require all data to be stored remotely, including that data necessary for the diskless machine to boot up.
- Executable files may reside locally or remotely as well, meaning a workstation can run its own programs or those copied off the LAN.

2. Servers:
- A server is a computer that provides the data, software and hardware resources that are shared on the LAN.
- A LAN can have more than one server; each has its unique name on the network and all LAN users identify the server by its name.

- **Dedicated Server:** A server that functions only as a storage area for data and software and allows access to hardware resources is called a dedicated server. Dedicated servers need to be powerful computers.

- **Non-Dedicated Server:** In many LANs, the server is just another work station. Thus, there is a user networking on the computer and using it as a workstation, but part of the computer also doubles up as a server. Such a server is called a non-dedicated server. Since, it is not completely dedicated to serving. LANs do not require a dedicated server since resource sharing amongst a few workstations is proportionately on a smaller scale.

- **Other Types of Servers:** In large installations, which have hundreds of workstations sharing resource, a single computer is often not sufficient to function as a server.

Some of the other servers have been discussed here under:

- **File Server:** A file server stores files that workstations can access and it also decides on the rights and restrictions that the users need to have while accessing files on LAN.

- **Printer Server:** A Printer server takes care of the printing requirement of a number of workstations.

- **Modem Server:** It allows LAN users to use the modem to transmit long distance messages. Server attached to one or two modems would serve the purpose.

3. Clients:

- A client is any machine that requires something from a server.
- In the more common definition of a client, the server supplies files and sometimes processing power to the smaller machines connected to it.
- Each machine is a client.
- Thus, a typical ten PC local area network may have one large server with all the major files and databases on it and all the other machines connected as clients.
- This type of terminology is common with TCP/IP networks, where no single machine is necessarily the central repository.

4. Nodes:

- Small networks that comprise of a server and a number of PC.
- Each PC on the network is called a node.
- A node essentially means any device that is attached to the network. Because each machine has a unique name or number (so the rest of the network can identify it), you will hear the term node name or node number quite often.

5. Network Interface Cards:

- The Network Interface card, or LAN adapter, functions as an interface between the computer and the network cabling, so it must serve two masters.
- Inside the computer, it controls the flow of data to and from the Random-Access Memory (RAM).
- Outside the computer, it controls the flow of data in and out of the network cable system.
- An interface card has a specialized port that matches the electrical signaling standards used on the cable and the specific type of cable connector.
- One must select a network interface card that matches your computer's data bus and the network cable.
- Token ring LANs require token ring NICs, Ethernet LANs require Ethernet NICs, etc.
- The peripheral component interface bus (PCI) has emerged as a new standard for adapter card interfaces.
- It is advisable to put PCI-equipped computers and using PCI LAN adapters wherever possible.
- Software is required to interface between a particular NIC and an operating system called as **Network Interface Card Driver**.

6. Connectors:

- Connectors used with TP included RJ-11 and RJ-45 modular connectors in current use by phone companies.
- Occasionally other special connectors, such as IBM's Data Connector, are used.
- RJ-11 connectors accommodate 4 wires or 2 twisted pairs, while RJ-45 houses 8 wires or 4 twisted pairs.

7. The Network Operating System:

- The Network Operating System software acts as the command center, enabling all of the network hardware and all other network software to function together as one cohesive, organized system.
- In other words, the network operating system is the very heart of the network.
- It can be client-server or Peer-to-Peer Network Operating System.

Advantages of LAN:

1. The reliability of network is high because the failure of one computer in the network does not effect the functioning for other computers.
2. Addition of new computer to network is easy.

3. High rate of data transmission is possible.
4. Peripheral devices like magnetic disk and printer can be shared by other computers.

Uses of LAN:

Following are the major areas where LAN is normally used:

1. File transfers and Access
2. Word and text processing
3. Electronic message handling
4. Remote database access
5. Personal computing
6. Digital voice transmission and storage
7. Office automation
8. Factory automation
9. Distributed Computing
10. Fire and Security Systems
11. Process Control
12. Document Distribution.

1.7.2 Wide Area Network (Wan)

1. The term Wide Area Network (WAN) is used to describe a computer network spanning a regional, national or global area.
2. For example, for a large company the head quarters might be at Delhi and regional branches at Mumbai, Chennai, Bangalore and Kolkata.
3. Here regional centers are connected to head quarters through WAN.
4. The distance between computers connected to WAN is larger. Therefore the transmission media used are normally telephone lines, microwaves and satellite links.

Characteristics of WAN:

Following are the major characteristics of WAN.

1. Communication Facility:

- For a big company spanning over different parts of the country, the employees can save long distance phone calls and it overcomes the time lag in overseas communications.

- Computer conferencing is another use of WAN where users communicate with each other through their computer system.

2. Remote Data Entry:
- Remote data entry is possible in WAN. It means sitting at any location you can enter data, update data and query other information of any computer attached to the WAN but located in other cities.
- For example, suppose you are sitting at Chennai and want to see some data of a computer located at Delhi, you can do it through WAN.

3. Centralized Information:
- In modern computerized environment, you will find that big organizations go for centralized data storage.
- This means if the organization is spread over many cities, they keep their important business data in a single place.
- As the data are generated at different sites, WAN permits collection of this data from different sites and save at a single site.

Examples of WAN:
1. SMDS
2. X.25
3. Frame relay
4. B-ISDN

Difference between LAN and WAN:
1. LAN is restricted to limited geographical area of few kilometers. But WAN covers great distance and operate nationwide or even worldwide.
2. In LAN, the computer terminals and peripheral devices are connected with wires and coaxial cables. In WAN, there is no physical connection. Communication is done through telephone lines and satellite links.
3. Cost of data transmission in LAN is less because the transmission medium is owned by a single organization. In case of WAN the cost of data transmission is very high because the transmission media used are hired, either telephone lines or satellite links.
4. The speed of data transmission is much higher in LAN than in WAN. The transmission speed in LAN varies from 0.1 to 100 megabits per second. In case of WAN, the speed ranges from 1800 to 9600 bits per second (bps).
5. Few data transmission errors occur in LAN compared to WAN. It is because in LAN, the distance covered is negligible.

1.7.3 Metropolitan Area Network (Man)
1. A Metropolitan Area Network (MAN) is a bigger version of a Local Area Network (LAN) and usually uses similar technology.

2. A MAN can cover a group of corporate offices or a town or city, and can be either privately or publicly owned. A MAN can support both data and voice, and may be related to the local cable television network (CATV).
3. A MAN employs one or two cables, and does not contain switching elements, which simplifies the design.

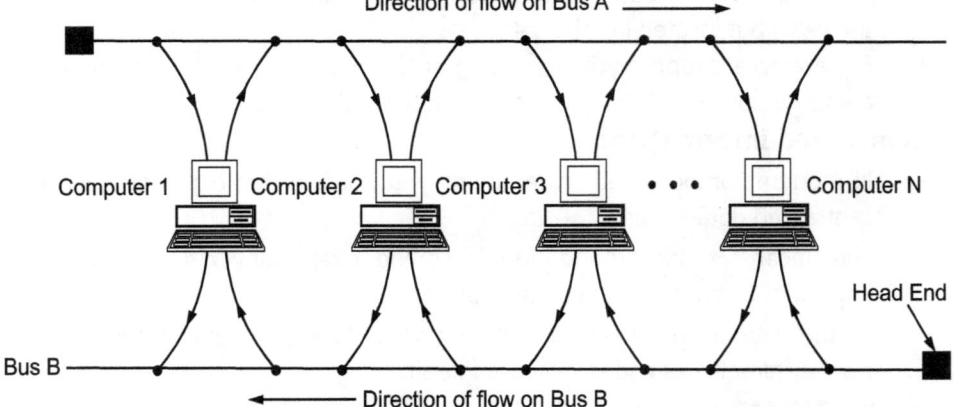

Fig. 1.14: Typical MAN Network (also known as 802.6 DQDB network)

4. A standard has been adopted for MANs called *Distributed Queue Dual Bus* (DQDB) and is defined by IEEE 802.6.
5. DQDB consists of two unidirectional buses (cables) to which all of the computers on the network are connected.
6. Each bus has a *head-end* that initiates transmission activity.
7. In the following diagram, traffic that is intended for a computer to the right of the source computer uses the upper bus, while traffic intended for a computer to the left uses the lower bus.
8. The network is based on fiber-topic cable in a dual-bus topology, and traffic on each bus is unidirectional, providing a fault-tolerant configuration.
9. Bandwidth is allocated using time slots, and both synchronous and asynchronous modes are supported.

1.7.4 Internet

1. Internet is the extensive, worldwide computer network available to the public. An internet is a more general term for any set of interconnected computer networks that are connected by internetworking.
2. The Internet, or simply the Net, is the publicly available worldwide system of interconnected computer networks that transmit data by packet switching using a standardized Internet Protocol (IP) and many other protocols.
3. It is made up of thousands of smaller commercial, academic, and government networks.

4. It carries various information and services, such as electronic mail, on-line chat and the interlinked web pages and other documents of the World Wide Web.
5. Hypertext is viewed using a program called a web browser which retrieves pieces of information, called "documents" or "web pages", from web servers and displays them, typically on a computer monitor.
6. One can then follow hyperlinks on each page to other documents or even send information back to the server to interact with it.
7. The act of following hyperlinks is often called "surfing" or "browsing" the web. Web pages are often arranged in collections of related material called "web sites."
8. Although the English word *worldwide* is normally written as one word (without a space or hyphen), the proper name World Wide Web and abbreviation WWW are now well-established even in formal English.
9. Typical network schematic is shown in Fig. 1.15.
10. Function of webserver is to host website (web pages).
11. Function of proxy server is to provide internet connectivity to the different machines with private IP addresses.

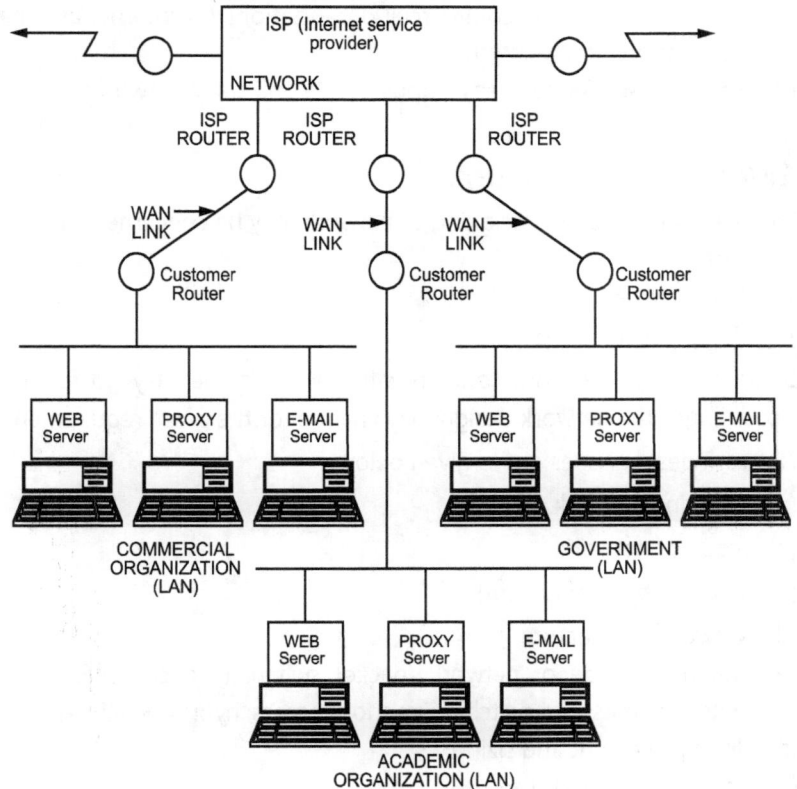

Fig. 1.15: Typical Internet Connection Components

12. E-mail server is used to provide different E-mail accounts for E-mail transactions.
13. Thus, Routers are used to interconnect different LANs to form Internet.
14. Organization's **Router** and ISP's **Router** are interconnected to form Internet.
15. Customer router to ISP router link can be of –
    (a) Dial-up-line
    (b) Leased line
    (c) ISDN line, etc.
16. LAN Technology can be of –
    (a) Ethernet (802.3 or CSMA/CD) Technology
    (b) Token Ring (802.5) Technology
    (c) Token Bus (802.4) Technology
17. Thus, internet consists of the following groups of networks:
    (a) Backbones: Large networks that exist primarily to interconnect other networks.
    (b) Regional networks: Connecting for example, Universities and colleges.
    (c) Commercial networks: Providing access to the backbones to subscribers and networks owned by commercial organizations for internal use that also have connections to the Internet.
    (d) Local networks, such as campus – wide university networks.

1.8 Network Design Issues

1. The person involved in designing of network may be concerned with
   - Cost
   - Performance
   - Manageability.
2. Some one may be more concern with cost or some may go for manageability. Accordingly, the network design may change for the given requirements.
3. Network design issues are as given below.
   (a) Justifying network.
   (b) Scope of network.
   (c) Manageability of network.
   (d) Network architecture.
   (e) Switching mode of network (packet switching, circuit switching, VC packet switching, message switching, random access, hybrid switching).
   (f) Node placement and sizing.
   (g) Link topology and sizing.
   (h) Routing protocol selection.

1.8.1 Justifying Network

1. Justified network is the start of Network designing.
2. Some applications may be best satisfied by individual point-to-point connections to handle specific telecommunication requirements.
3. Some network application requirements are in such a way that they do not fit into any general network requirement or
4. It may be possible that a private network already exists within organisation to satisfy the requirements.
5. Most networks are designed using existing communication channels usually leased from a common carrier.
6. The common carrier is in a better position to achieve and then share, a greater economy of scale and may be better able to maintain reliable service through experienced communication engineers on staff.

1.8.2 Scope of Network

1. There are many ways of successfully dividing the responsibility of network function among all parties involved, including those parts of the organization building the network, and the vendors providing external functions.
2. Data transferred should be received by receiver without packet loss.
3. If packet loss occurs, it must be recovered back by any mechanism and responsibility should be defined and taken by that particular head.
4. The geographic scope of network must also be considered. It might be assumed that a corporate network should satisfy all the needs of the corporation and hence extend to all corporate locations.

1.8.3 Manageability of Network

1. Manageability is very important design consideration for designing the Network.
2. It concerns with different points related to communication between service provider and entire network structure.
3. Allows consolidation of multiple applications on a single system while maintaining required service levels. This allows users to integrate multiple applications on a single server.
4. The tight integration between the software and its management tools helps ensure ease of use, complete compatibility with the software system and a one stop, fully tested environment for users. Provides a cost saving alternative to third-party network managers.

5. Provision of centralized industry-standard services in a secure manner.
6. Reduction of duplication of effort and simplifies data delivery.
7. Significantly simplifies management of network configurations, while providing administrators with improved access to some of the more advanced networking features in the different platforms.
8. Allows consolidation of multiple applications on a single system while maintaining required service levels. This allows network users to integrate multiple applications on a single server.
9. System upgradation and network management also plays an important role. Since the system can be upgraded while the system is still running, downtime is reduced significantly. In the case of an upgrade failure, you can quickly fall-back to the original environment with a simple reboot, thereby eliminating the downtime for the production environment associated with normal test and evaluation processes.
10. Network manageability implementation significantly reduces installation time, configuration complexity, and administrative resources, while improving deployment scalability. Servers should be easily reprovisioned or retasked to a different service based on demand.
11. Network manageability study allows for more flexible installation methods for software developers and better system control for system administrators.
12. It enables organizations to deliver an integrated set of management tools that support and promote World Wide Web technology.
13. It makes administration easier. Enhances manageability of the environment by ensuring the accuracy of this important system setting across all systems.
14. Significantly simplifies network configuration set up.
15. Simplifies monitoring and measurement of application status.
16. Often slack is left in the network even though it increases the cost, in order to make the network more robust and more easily managed.
17. Slack should be added only where it actually enhances performance and gain is measured against the added cost.

1.8.4 Network Architecture

1. In computing, **network architecture** is the design of a computer network.
2. In telecommunication, the term **network architecture** has the following meanings:

- The design principles, physical configuration, functional organization, operational procedures, and data formats used as the bases for the design, construction, modification, and operation of a communications network.
- The structure of an existing communications network, including the physical configuration, facilities, operational structure, operational procedures, and the data formats in use.

3. With the development of distributed computing, the term **network architecture** has also come to denote classifications and implementations of distributed computing architectures.

4. For example, the applications architecture of the telephone network PSTN has been termed the Advanced Intelligent Network.

5. There are any numbers of specific classifications but all lie on a continuum between the dumb network (e.g. Internet) and the intelligent computer network (e.g. the telephone network PSTN).

6. Other networks contain various elements of these two classical types to make them suitable for various types of applications.

7. Another issue relating to the overall architecture of the network is whether to decompose the network into subnetworks for the sake of design and operation.

8. Also network architecture decides whether network is considered as a single mesh or not.

9. If it is considered as single mesh, it becomes more difficult to design and to operate but might function more efficiently because of the additional option available to share capacity among all nodes.

10. For example, this Network architecture is drawn for those who are involved in the planning and design of a Telecom network infrastructure.

11. Consultants, system architects, and information technology (IT) professionals who are responsible for the planning stages of application or infrastructure development across multiple projects will benefit from the information in this sample network architecture.

12. Others who would likely benefit include:

    - Architects and planners who are responsible for driving the architecture efforts for their organizations.
    - Business analysts and decision makers who have critical business objectives and requirements that need IT support.

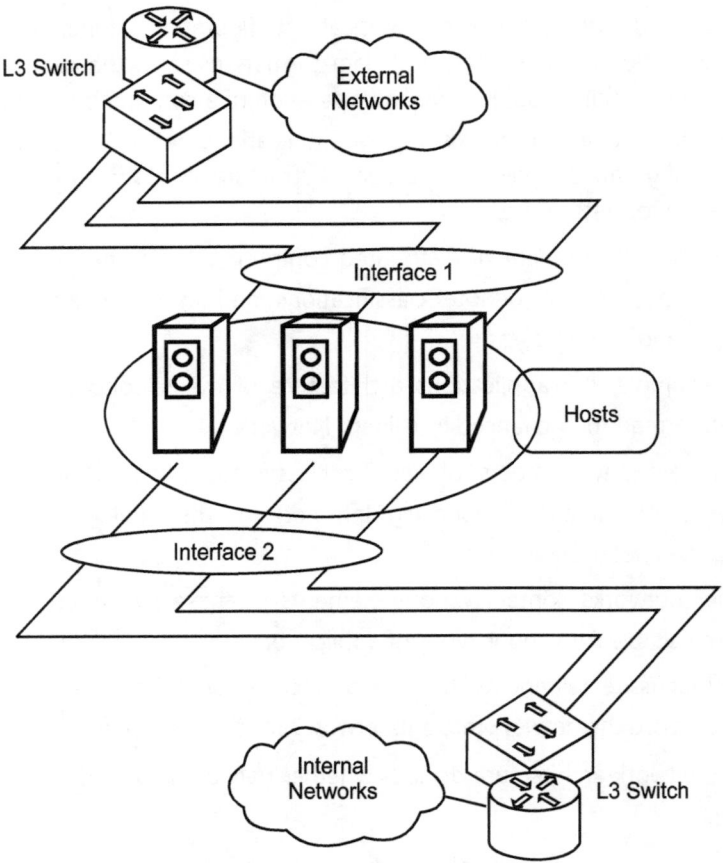

Fig. 1.16: Example figure for network architecture implementation

13. It is important to understand that there are many ways to design even the simplest of network architectures; it is not a precise art.
14. The information presented in Fig. 1.16 is designed to provide insights and examples to help you complete a network architecture design that fits your needs.
15. The introduction of the simple scenario provided fictional data to illustrate the process that was followed in the network architecture design.
16. The design processes are documented in the "Network Architecture Design" and "Network Architecture Design" sections of Fig. 1.16, which also discuss the detailed design decisions by including samples of the data generated in the actual design processes.
17. All data generated by the design team is provided in the Implementation Guides; the reason for this separation is that this data will usually be unique to each instantiation and therefore only relevant in the context of a specific implementation.

18. The design is based on a combination of the specific requirements, environment, budgets, and preferences of the organization's design team.
19. There is no single "right" answer, only one that meets an organization's requirements in a timely and affordable manner.
20. Once the architectural design is in place, there are many device-specific factors that can affect the selection of physical devices to fulfil the network architecture requirements.

1.9 Switching Techniques

1. Historically, most communication systems have started with point-to-point links which directly connect together the users wishing to communicate using a dedicated communications circuit.
2. As the distance between users increases beyond the length of the cable, the connection between the users was formed by a number of sections which were connected end-to-end in series to form the circuit.
3. The connection between the users (A and D) in Fig. 1.17 (i.e. A and D) is represented by a series of links (AB, BC, and CD), each link connects two entities known as nodes.
4. For a point-to-point circuit (also known as a permanent circuit), the nodes are patch panels, which provide a simple connection between the two links (i.e. the two transmission circuits).

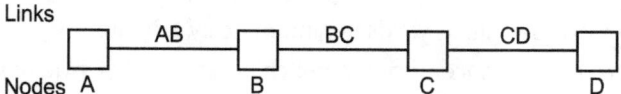

Fig. 1.17: A connection between two systems A and D formed from 3 links

5. As the number of connected users increased, it has become infeasible to provide a circuit, which connects every user to every other user, and some sharing of the transmission circuits (known as "switching") has become necessary.
6. To accomplish this goal, the data communications network has evolved.
7. A network is a set of nodes that are interconnected to permit the exchange of information.
8. Three switching techniques have been proposed for building networks:
   - Circuit switching
   - Message switching
   - Packet switching (Both datagram and virtual circuit).

9. Each allows sharing communication facilities among multiple users (end systems), and each uses equipment located at the nodes (intermediate systems) to replace the patch-panels used in a point-to-point connection.
10. Packet switching is most often used for data communication.
11. Most networks consist of many links (see Fig. 1.18) which allow more than one path through the network between nodes.
12. A data communications network must be able to select an appropriate path for each required connection.

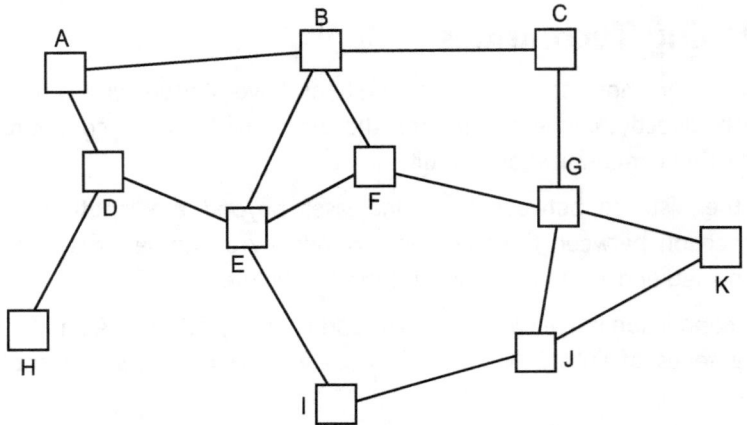

Fig. 1.18: A mesh of network nodes (A-K) connected by links

13. Any of the three approaches (circuit switching, message switching, and packet switching) could yield minimum delay in a particular situation, though situations where message switching yields minimum delay are rare.
14. The relative performance of circuit switching and packet switching depends strongly on the speed and "cost" of establishing a connection.

1.10 Circuit Switching

1. Circuit switching is the most familiar technique used to build a communications network.
2. It is used for ordinary telephone calls.
3. It allows communications equipment and circuits, to be shared among users.
4. Each user has sole access to a circuit (functionally equivalent to a pair of copper wires) during network use.
5. Consider communication between two points A and D in a network. The connection between A and D is provided using (shared) links between two other pieces of equipments, B and C.

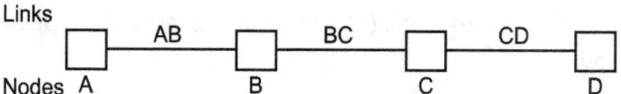

Fig. 1.19: A connection between two systems A and D formed from 3 links

6. Network use is initiated by a connection phase, during which a circuit is set up between source and destination, and terminated by a disconnect phase.

7. These phases, with associated timings, are illustrated in Fig. 1.20.

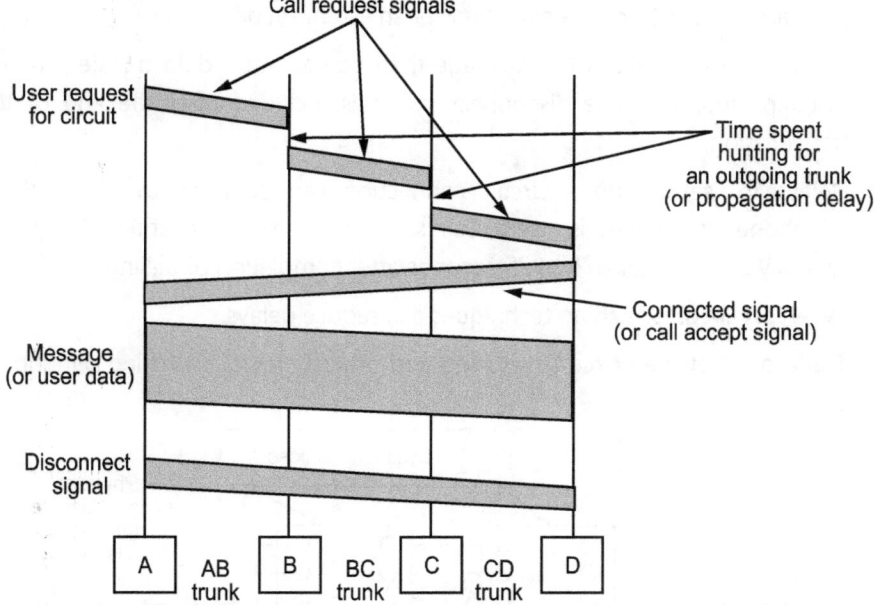

Fig. 1.20: A circuit switched connection between A and D

8. (Information flows in two directions. Information sent from the calling end is shown in plain and information returned from the remote end is shown in dots).

9. After a user requests a circuit, the desired destination address must be communicated to the local switching node (B).

10. In a telephony network, this is achieved by dialing the number.

11. Node B receives the connection request and identifies a path to the destination (D) via an intermediate node (C).

12. This is followed by a circuit connection phase handled by the switching nodes and initiated by allocating a free circuit to C (link BC), followed by transmission of a call request signal from node B to node C.

13. In turn, node C allocates a link (CD) and the request is then passed to node D after a similar delay.
14. The circuit is then established and may be used.
15. While it is available for use, resources (i.e. in the intermediate equipment at B and C) and capacity on the links between the equipment are dedicated to the use of the circuit.
16. After completion of the connection, a signal confirming circuit establishment (a connect signal in the diagram) is returned; this flows directly back to node A with no search delays since the circuit has been established.
17. Transfer of the data in the message then begins. After data transfer, the circuit is disconnected; a simple disconnect phase is included after the end of the data transmission.
18. Delays for setting up a circuit connection can be high, especially if ordinary telephone equipment is used. Call setup time with conventional equipment is typically of the order of 5 to 25 seconds after completion of dialing.
19. New fast circuit switching techniques can reduce delays.
20. Trade-offs between circuit switching and other types of switching depend strongly on switching times.

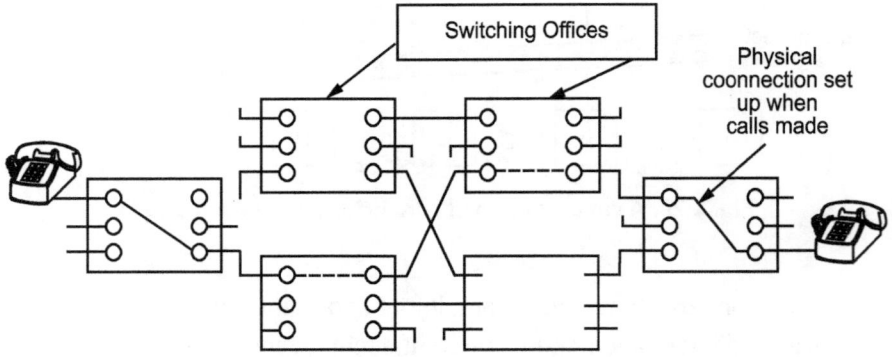

Fig. 1.21: Typical example of circuit switching network (Telephone Communication System)

21. In telecommunications, a **circuit switching** network is one that establishes a dedicated circuit (or channel) between nodes and terminals before the users may communicate.
22. Each circuit that is dedicated cannot be used for other users until the circuit is released and a new connection is set up.

23. If no actual communication is taking place in a dedicated circuit then that channel still remains unavailable to other users.
24. Channels that are available for new calls to be set up are said to be idle.
25. In Circuit Switching networks, when establishing a call a set of resources is allocated for this call.
26. These resources are dedicated for this call, and cannot be used by any of the other calls.
27. Circuit Switching is ideal when data must be transmitted quickly, must arrive in sequencing order and at a constant arrival rate.
28. There for when transmitting real time data, such as audio and video, Circuit Switching networks will be used.

1.11 Packet Switching

1. Packet switching is similar to message switching using short messages.
2. Any message exceeding a network-defined maximum length is broken up into shorter units, known as packets, for transmission; the packets, each with an associated header, are then transmitted individually through the network.
3. The fundamental difference in packet communication is that the data is formed into packets with a pre-defined header format, and well-known "idle" patterns which are used to occupy the link when there is no data to be communicated.
4. Packet network equipment discards the "idle" patterns between packets and processes the entire packet as one piece of data.
5. The equipment examines the packet header information and then either removes the header (in an end system) or forwards the packet to another system.
6. If the out-going link is not available, then the packet is placed in a queue until the link becomes free.
7. A packet network is formed by links, which connect packet network equipment.

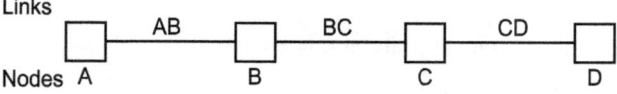

Fig. 1.22: Communication between A and D using circuits which are shared using packet switching

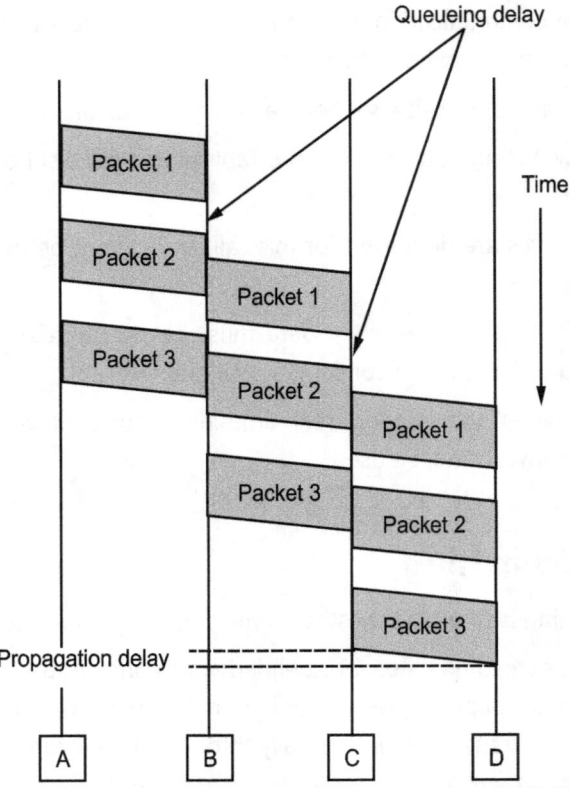

**Fig. 1.23: Packet-switched communication between systems A and D
(The message in this case has been broken into three parts labelled 1-2-3)**

There are two important benefits from packet switching

BENEFIT 1:
- The first and most important benefit is that since packets are short, the communication links between the nodes are only allocated to transferring a single message for a short period of time while transmitting each packet.
- Longer messages require a series of packets to be sent, but do not require the link to be dedicated between the transmission of each packet.
- The implication is that packets belonging to other messages may be sent between the packets of the message being sent from A to D. This provides a much fairer sharing of the resources of each of the links.

BENEFIT 2:
- Another benefit of packet switching is known as "pipelining".
- Pipelining is visible in Fig. 1.23.
- At times, packet 1 is sent from B to C, packet 2 is sent from A to B, packet 1 is sent from C to D, packet 2 is sent from B to C, and packet 3 is sent from A to B, and so forth.

- This simultaneous use of communications links represents a gain in efficiency, the total delay for transmission across a packet network may be considerably less than for message switching, despite the inclusion of a header in each packet rather than in each message.

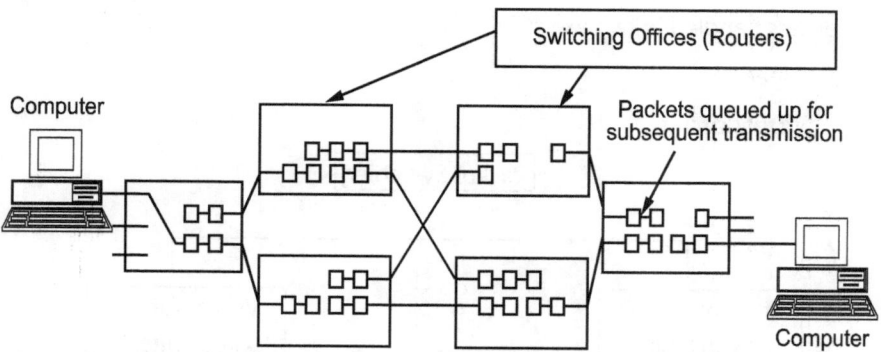

Fig. 1.24: Typical Example of Packet Switched Network (With this technology, individual packets are sent as need be, with no dedicated path being set up in advance. It is upto each packet to find its way to the destination on its own)

The Internet is based largely on packet switching and the Net is basically a huge connectionless network joined together. By transmitting data in packets, the same data path can be shared among many users in the network.

Table 1.1: Comparison between Circuit Switching and Packet Switching

Parameter	Circuit switched	Packet Switched
Call set requirement	Required	Not required
Dedicated physical path requirement	Yes, it is required	No, it is not required
Whether each packet follows the same path (route)	Yes, it follows the same path (route)	No, it does not follow the same path (route)
Bandwidth Available for Transmission	It is fixed here	It is dynamic here.
Congestion can occurs at	At setup time	On every packet
Whether Bandwidth Wastage?	Yes	No
Store and Forward transmission is	Not available	Yes, it is available
Transparency in System	Yes, it is present	Not present
Charge applied	Per unit time	Per unit packet

1.12 Packet Switched Network in Detail

1. Station breaks long message into packets.
2. Packets sent one at a time to the network.
3. Packets handled in two ways:
   - Datagram
   - Virtual circuit

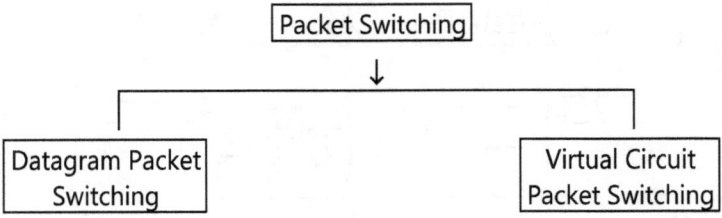

1.12.1 Datagram Packet Networks

- **Each packet treated independently.**
- **Packets can take any practical route.**
- **Packets may arrive out of order.**
- **Packets may go missing.**
- **Receiver is responsible to re-order packets and recover from missing packets.**

1. Two basic approaches to packet switching are common: The most common is datagram switching (also known as a "best-effort network" or a network supporting the connectionless network service).
2. **This is what is used in the network layer of the Internet.**
3. Datagram transmission uses a different scheme to determine the route through the network of links.
4. Using datagram transmission, each packet is treated as a separate entity and contains a header with the full information about the intended recipient.
5. The intermediate nodes examine the header of a packet and select an appropriate link to an intermediate node, which is nearer the destination.
6. In this system, the packets do not follow a pre-established route, and the intermediate nodes (usually known as "routers") do not require prior knowledge of the routes that will be used.
7. A datagram network is analogous to sending a message as a series of postcards through the postal system.

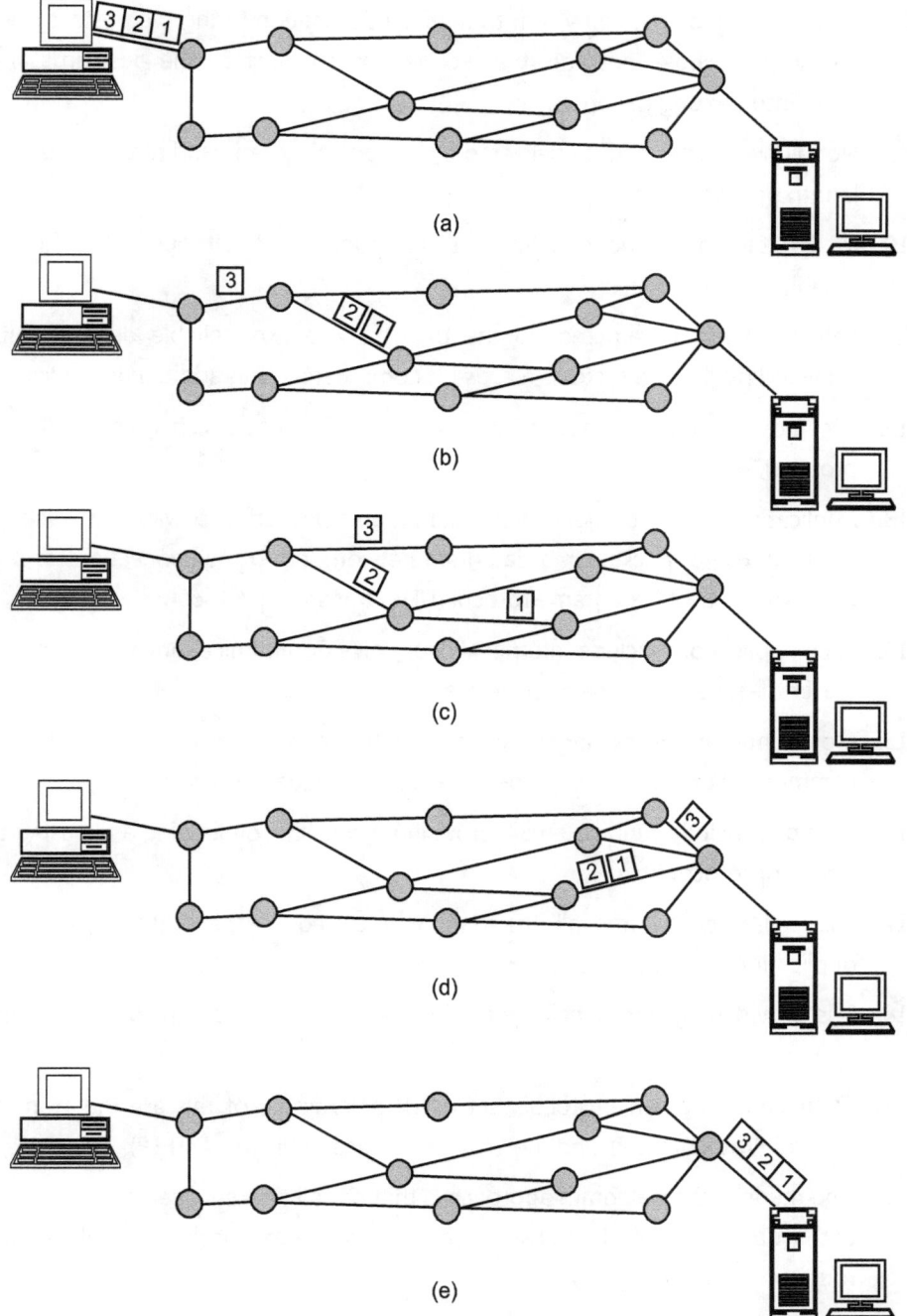

Fig. 1.25: Packet flow in Typical Datagram Packet switched network

8. Each card is independently sent to the final destination (using the postal system). To receive the whole message, the receiver must collect all the postcards and sort them into the original order.

9. Not all postcards need be delivered by the postal system, and not all take the same length of time to arrive.

10. In a datagram network, delivery is not guaranteed (although they are usually reliably sent).

11. Enhancements, if required, to the basic service (e.g. reliable delivery) must be provided by the end systems (i.e. user's computers) using additional software.

12. The most common datagram network is the Internet which uses the IP network protocol.

13. Applications, which do not require more than a best effort service can be supported by direct use of packets in a datagram network (using the connectionless protocol or known as User Datagram Protocol (UDP) transport protocol).

14. Such applications include Internet Video, Voice Communication, messages notifying a user that she/he has received new email, etc.

15. Most Internet applications need additional functions to provide reliable communication (such as end-to-end error and sequence control).

16. Examples include sending email, browsing a web site, or sending a file using the file transfer protocol (ftp).

17. This reliability ensures all the data is received in the correct order with no duplication or omissions.

18. It is provided by additional layers of software algorithms implemented in the End Systems.

19. Connection-oriented protocols are used for example of this are the Transmission Control Protocol (TCP), and the Trivial File Transfer Protocol (TFTP).

20. One merit of the datagram approach is that not all packets need to follow the same path (route) through the network (although frequently packets do follow the same route).

21. This removes the need to set-up and tear-down the path, reducing the processing overhead, and a need for Intermediate Systems to execute an additional protocol.

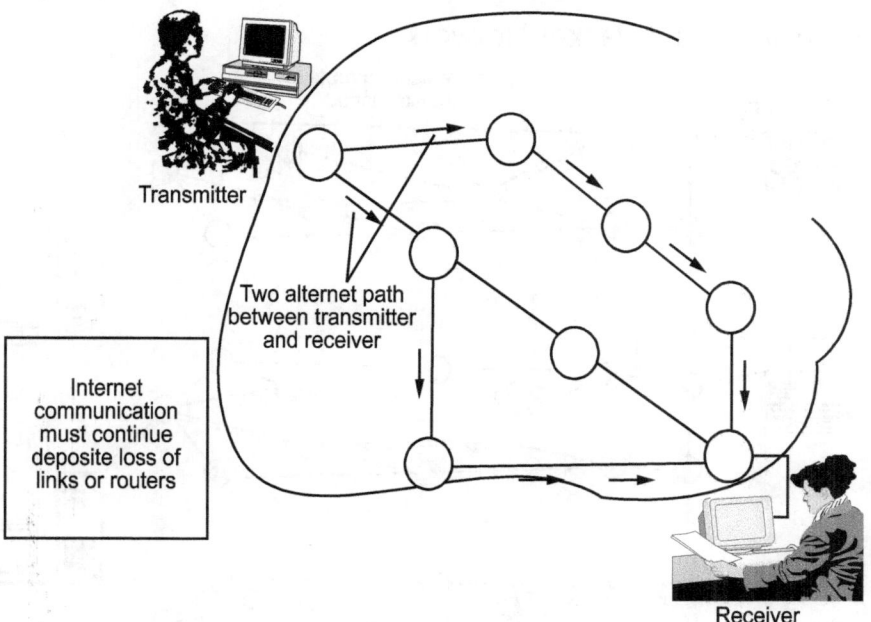

Fig. 1.26

22. Packets may also be routed around busy parts of the network when alternate paths exist.

23. This is useful when a particular intermediate system becomes busy or overloaded with excessive volumes of packets to send.

24. It can also provide a high degree of fault tolerance, when an individual intermediate system or communication circuit fails.

25. As long as a route exists through the network between two end systems, they are able to communicate.

26. Only if there is no possible way to send the packets, will the packets be discarded and not delivered.

27. The fate (success/failure) of an application therefore depends only on existence of an actual path between the two End Systems.

28. This is known as "fate sharing" - since the application shares the "fate" of the network.

1.12.2 Virtual Circuit Packet Network

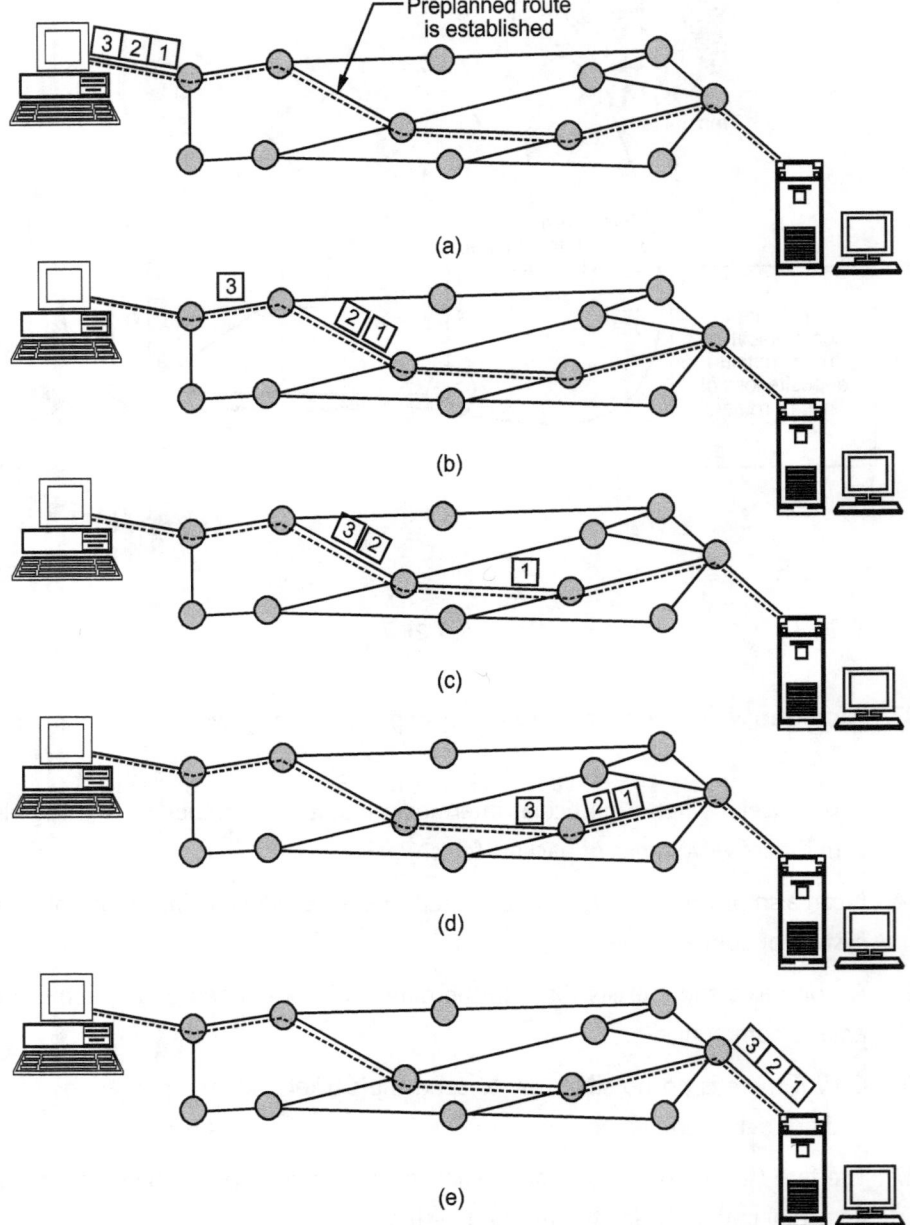

Fig. 1.27: Packet flow in Typical Virtual circuit Packet switched network

A. Pre-planned route established before any packets sent.
- All packets follow the same route.
- There is a connection establishment (Like Circuit Switching).

> B. Call request and call accept packets establish connection (handshake).
> C. Each packet contains a virtual circuit identifier instead of destination address (i.e. No routing decisions required for each packet).

1. A virtual circuit is a logical circuit created within a shared network between two network devices.
2. Two types of virtual circuits exist: switched virtual circuits (SVCs) and permanent virtual circuits (PVCs).
3. SVCs are virtual circuits that are dynamically established on demand and terminated when transmission is complete.
4. Communication over an SVC consists of three phases: circuit establishment, data transfer, and circuit termination.
5. The establishment phase involves creating the virtual circuit between the source and destination devices.
6. Data transfer involves transmitting data between the devices over the virtual circuit, and the circuit termination phase involves tearing down the virtual circuit between the source and destination devices.
7. SVCs are used in situations in which data transmission between devices is sporadic, largely because SVCs increase bandwidth used due to the circuit establishment and termination phases, but they decrease the cost associated with constant virtual circuit availability.
8. PVC is a permanently established virtual circuit that consists of one mode: data transfer.
9. PVCs are used in situations in which data transfer between devices is constant.
10. PVCs decrease the bandwidth use associated with the establishment and termination of virtual circuits, but they increase costs due to constant virtual circuit availability.
11. PVCs are generally configured by the service provider when an order is placed for service.

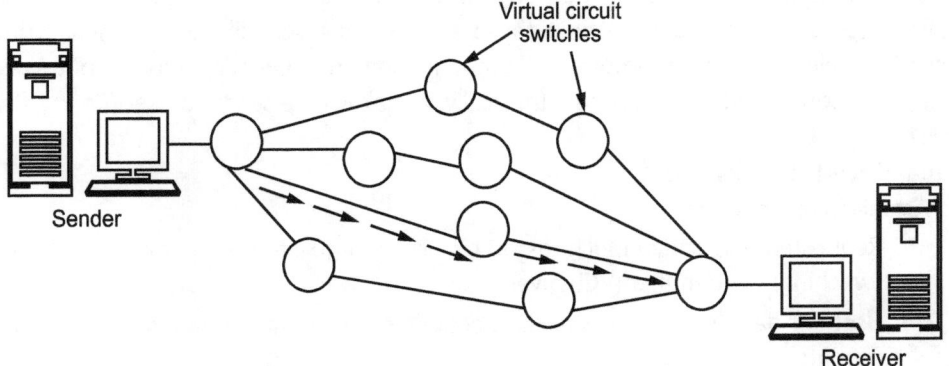

Fig. 1.28: Typical Virtual Circuit Switched Packet Network

12. An initial setup phase is used to set up a route between the intermediate nodes for all the packets passed during the session between the two end nodes.
13. In each intermediate node, an entry is registered in a table to indicate the route for the connection that has been set up.
14. The packets passed through this route, have short headers, containing only a virtual circuit identifier (VCI).
15. Each intermediate node passes the packets according to the information that was stored in its table, in the setup phase and according to the packets header content.
16. In this way, packets arrive at the destination in the correct sequence.
17. This approach is slower than Circuit Switching, since different virtual circuits may compete over the same resources.
18. As in Circuit Switching, if an intermediate node fails, all virtual circuits that pass through it are lost.
19. The most common forms of Virtual Circuit networks are X.25 and Frame Relay, which are commonly used for public data networks (PDN).

Thus, in Virtual Circuits –
- **Network can provide sequencing and error control.**
- **Packets are forwarded more quickly.**
- **No routing decisions to make.**
- **Less reliable.**
- **Loss of a node losses all circuits through that node.**

1.12.3 Datagram (DG) Service and Virtual Circuits (VC) Service

The service defines what the user must do to obtain service and what can be expected, while the implementation defines how the network responds to the user requests and manages network operations in order to meet those expectations. As will become clear from the discussion below and the examples, DGs may implement DG or VC service, but since VC implementation provides VC service intrinsically, it makes little sense to use VCs to offer DG service.

Virtual Circuit (VC) Service:
Virtual circuits must be –
- Requested explicitly, much as a circuit is requested and initialized in circuit switching; VC identifier (VCI) given;
- Used for data transmission: packets containing the data are sent, referring to VCI for routing;
- Explicitly terminated, returning VCI to pool.

VCs offer guarantees that the packets sent –

- Arrive in the order sent.
- With no duplicates or omissions.
- With no errors (with high probability).

Regardless of how they are implemented internally.

Datagram (DG) Service:

DG service offers no real guarantees. Packets, while they may belong together logically at a higher level, are not associated with one another at the network level. There is no setup or teardown request, just the request to send the datagram packet.

A datagram may
- Arrive at the receiver before a datagram sent earlier by the sender.
- Arrive in a damaged state (and most likely be discarded).
- Be delayed arbitrarily long (unless some expiration mechanism causes it to be discarded).
- Be duplicated.
- Be lost.

DGs are a "best-effort" service.

Examples:
- VC/VC - SNA (Simple Network Architecture), Tymnet
- VC/DG - Arpanet
- DG/DG - DNA (Digital Network Architecture)

1.12.4 Datagram (DG) Vs Virtual Circuits (VC)

Table 1.2

Parameters	Datagram (DG) Network	Virtual Circuit (VC) Network
Requirement of Circuit Setup	It is not needed here	It is needed here
Routing of Packet	Each packet is routed independently	Route is chosen when VC setup is over and all packet follows the same.
Router failure	None	Less probability
If router fails	Packets are lost during the crash	All VCs that passed through the failed router are terminated
Achievement of Quality of service	It is difficult here	It is easy if enough resources can be allocated in advance for each VC.
Congestion control	It is difficult over here	It is easy if enough resources can be allocated in advance for each VC.
Examples of network	TCP/IP internet network	Example X.25, Frame Relay and ATM networks

Summary of Circuit Switched/Message Switched/ DG Packet Switched/VC Packet Switched

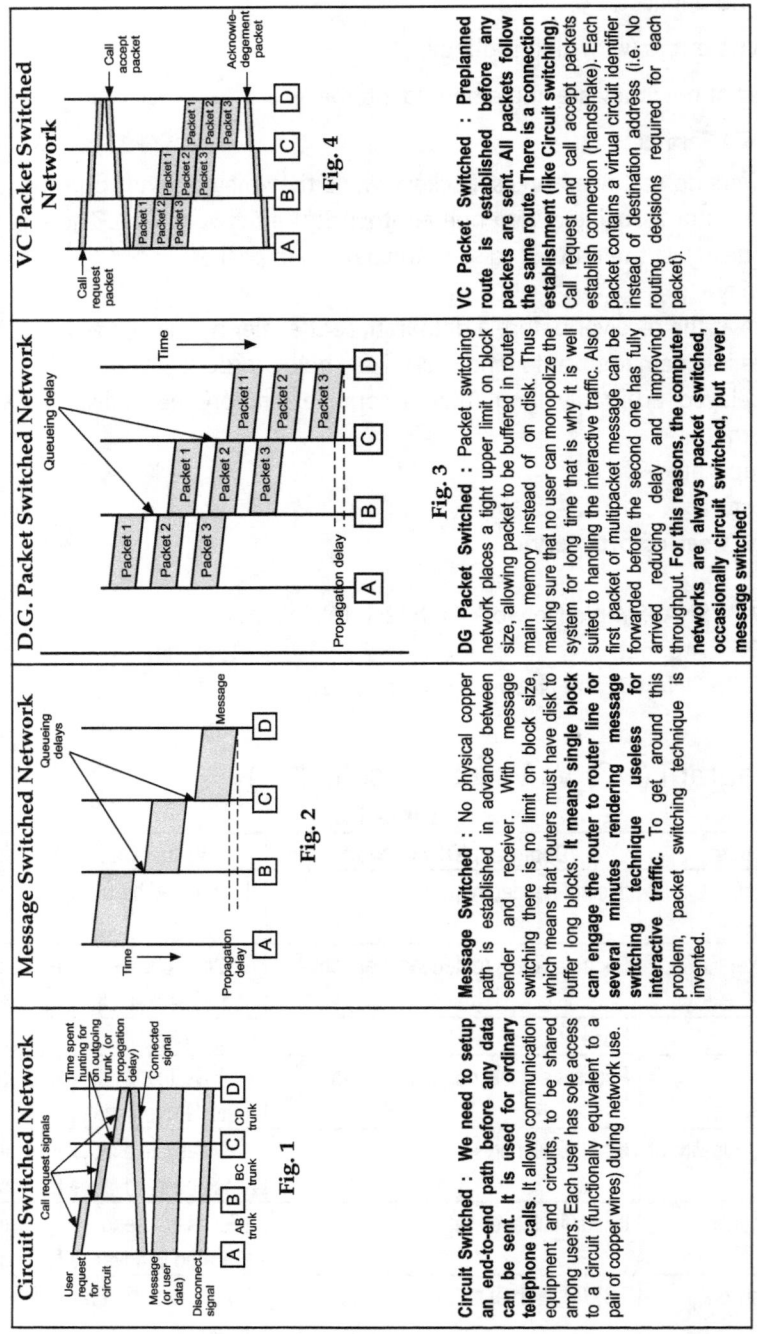

Circuit Switched Network (Fig. 1)

Circuit Switched : We need to setup an end-to-end path before any data can be sent. It is used for ordinary telephone calls. It allows communication equipment and circuits, to be shared among users. Each user has sole access to a circuit (functionally equivalent to a pair of copper wires) during network use.

Message Switched Network (Fig. 2)

Message Switched : No physical copper path is established in advance between sender and receiver. With message switching there is no limit on block size, which means that routers must have disk to buffer long blocks. **It means single block can engage the router to router line for several minutes rendering message switching technique useless for interactive traffic.** To get around this problem, packet switching technique is invented.

D.G. Packet Switched Network (Fig. 3)

DG Packet Switched : Packet switching network places a tight upper limit on block size, allowing packet to be buffered in router main memory instead of on disk. Thus making sure that no user can monopolize the system for long time that is why it is well suited to handling the interactive traffic. Also first packet of multipacket message can be forwarded before the second one has fully arrived reducing delay and improving throughput. **For this reasons, the computer networks are always packet switched, occasionally circuit switched, but never message switched.**

VC Packet Switched Network (Fig. 4)

VC Packet Switched : Preplanned route is established before any packets are sent. All packets follow the same route. There is a connection establishment (like Circuit switching). Call request and call accept packets establish connection (handshake). Each packet contains a virtual circuit identifier instead of destination address (i.e. No routing decisions required for each packet).

1.13 Data in Support of Network Design

1. The complex part of network designing is assembly of input data.
2. While collecting the data, balance must be struck between the amount of information available with a realistic amount of effort and sufficient detail needed to support quantitative analysis.
3. The data to be collected should be current (updated or latest) or recent data for reliale network design.
4. One way to reduce both time and effort in collecting data is to build upon existing automated sources of information. For example, attached host on network may maintain accounting information used to bill for host services which can be used as sources of traffic requirements.
5. It is important to distinguish between static data and dynamic data.
6. It is also important to be prepared to deal with inconsistencies in the data and not to attempt to obtain an unrealistic degree of precision.
7. In some cases, there may be outright errors in the data. It is important to apply some consistency checks to the data to assure, atleast gross integrity.
8. In some cases like voice networks, it is desirable to filter the data relatively from odd location to avoid overburdening the network design.
9. Also data requirements for small applications without any accounting records may be handled approximately.
10. It is also essential that the data collection process be flexible enough to handle situation where data supplying node is removed from its place.
11. This indicates network design process must be able to function with incomplete and approximate data inputs.
12. Also by understanding the network design process itself and in particular, the sensitivity of specific design decisions to changes data, we must try to minimise effects of approximations.
13. In practice, each database (general) may include information specific to the applications and network at hand.
14. A network design procedure which demands data that is if unavailable then that procedure is of no use or useless.

1.13.1 Location of Data

1. The information needed to describe the locations in the networks is normally discussed under this section.

2. Important information in the database concerns the set of locations involved in the network.
3. It includes sources and destinations of requirements and candidate locations for network devices such as switches, multiplexers, etc.
4. It is also possible to maintain multiple views of the network during the design process.
5. Also an important design decision is the on-net or off-net decision, where the choice is made as to which locations to serve via. permanent facilities as opposed to dial-in or not to serve at all.
6. Also by including two sites inside the same building/apartment as different locations, we can keep track of links between them.
7. Links between geographically separate locations, there can be the problem of dealing with private facilities with untariffed cost that are difficult to obtain or even estimate.
8. If selection of correct location is wrong when network design may be severely affected.
9 Practically to retain flexibility, the original "raw" data should be collected and maintained on the basis of large set of locations.
10. Thus, data is useful as input to network design algorithm.
11. For location representation, identifiers should be there and it is best to use mnemonic identifier externally and then convert them to numbers for internal representation in network design algorithm.
12. Each location should have a set of co-ordinates associated with it. These are necessary to support cost calculations as well as for display purpose.
13. Properties can be associated with each network location. Thus, for example, we may record a location's status as a switch site.
14. Also, we usually think of and physically represent the data associated with network location as fields within a record.
15. Thus, it is important to make these decisions in network location selection to avoid the confusion in network design.

1.13.2 Traffic Requirements

1. Traffic requirements must be collected by user which is a part of database.
2. Traffic requirement is dependent upon the choice of location set.
3. Generally, traffic requirements start with raw data which can be as detailed as records of separate sessions (sessions like telephonic voice call sessions). Such records may include source, destination, starting date, starting time, length of session, route, number of packets, number of characters, etc.

4. Data can be viewed in terms of traffic matrix.
5. Matrix can have many dimensions-source, destination, time of day, and application, etc.
6. Also the number of terminals at a location may be known and from this and an estimate of activity per terminal, an estimate of traffic can be obtained.

1.13.3 Link Cost (Tariffs)
1. This is a part of database.
2. This is the published rate for communication services field by the common carriers.
3. Cost includes both monthly and one time charges.
4. It includes installation charges (may be via wired medium or wireless i.e. microwave link, etc.).
5. Some communication costs are usage sensitive such as direct dial telephone cost or packet switched common carrier costs. (either cost per minute or cost per bit) is included.
6. Types of tariffs may be
   (a) Cost dependent.
   (b) Structure dependent.
   (c) Usage sensitive.
   (d) Time of day sensitive.
7. There should be services which provide current tariff information in machine readable form.

1.13.4 Device Characteristics
1. A device must be associated with capacity.
2. If device is modular, it can have both fixed capacity and add-on capacities.
3. Capacity is measured as bits/sec, packets/sec, sessions/sec.
4. The different capacity limitations are a function of the architecture of the device are based on a model of its performance.

1.13.5 Performance Objectives
1. In performance objectives, following points are considered:
   (a) Minimizing cost while satisfying output requirements.
   (b) Limit on the tolerable delay in system that queue.

(c) Losses in system.
(d) Reliability constraints.
(e) Other constraints on delay, loss, etc.
(f) Traffic requirements and related algorithms.

2. Other useful way of looking at a delay objective is as a simple constraint on utilization.

$$D = \frac{D_o}{1 - u_x} \quad \ldots (1.1)$$

where,

D = Delay

D_o = Constant called the service time (transmission time for message)

u_x = Utilization

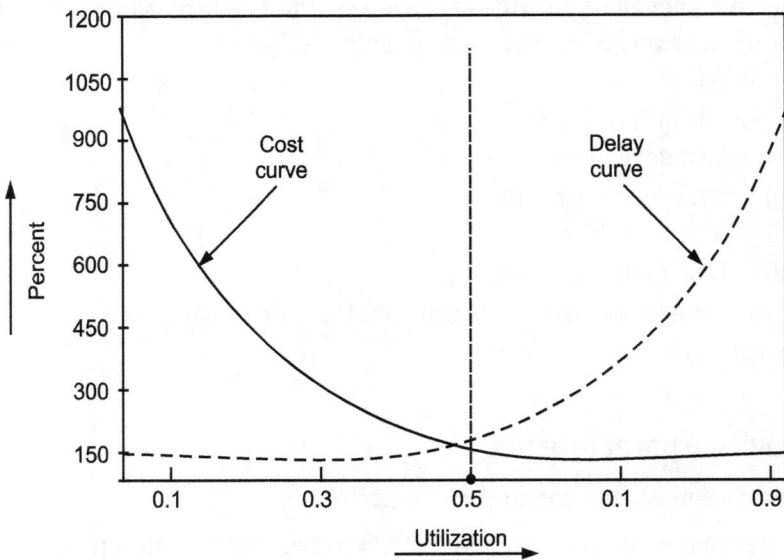

Fig. 1.29

3. Also relationship between utilization and cost 'C_o' is usually given by

$$C_o = \frac{C_1}{u_x} \quad \ldots (1.2)$$

where, C_1 = Cost when utilization is 100% permitted.

4. Combining these relationships from equations (1.1) and (1.2).

$$C_o = \frac{C_1 D}{D - D_o}$$ ... (1.3)

where, C_o = Cost

C_1 = Cost when utilization is 100% permitted

D = Delay

5. Thus, from curve drawn, delay rises sharply but cost decreases slightly. And other region shows where cost rises sharply and delay decreases only slightly.

1.13.6 Design Techniques

The Model:

1. The design process starts with a model of the system, often mathematical.
2. The model involves variables, and two kinds of relations among them, constraints, and the objective.
3. The designer attempts to choose values for the variables so that the constraints are satisfied and the objective optimized.
4. We generally assume that an architecture is given, and that it is only the sizes, numbers, and locations of its elements as well as their interconnections which remain to be determined.
5. The model of the entire communications system is made up of models of traffic and demand, models of communication facilities, and models of terminal and switching devices.
6. There may be many variables but they can be divided into a few categories. There are variables which (i) measure cost and return, (ii) performance and reliability, and (iii) traffic.
7. In most design models, the costs are divided into initial costs, and recurring costs.
8. There are many variables characterizing performance. Delay, blocking, percent packet loss, throughput capacity, mean-time-between failures, and availability are examples; there are many others.
9. These variables define quality of service.
10. Characterizing traffic is often the most time consuming and expensive part of the design process.
11. The first difficulty is that, at best, you only know what traffic there was in the past and not over the future lifetime of the proposed system. But, especially in today's environment of rapid technological change, you often are designing a system for applications which did not previously exist, or if they did exist, were handled previously in such a radically different way from the proposed approach that past data is of little use.

12. Internet systems to support Web traffic, multimedia, and/or electronic commerce are common examples.
13. The next difficulty is that traffic requirements must be specified for each sender of information to each receiver or group of receivers.
14. This gives rise to a combinatorial explosion in required data. For example, if we have 100 users, there are 9,900 potential to-from pairs of users; with 1,000 users there are 999,000 possible pairs.
15. Obviously, for major systems the users must be consolidated into groups. But doing this in an appropriate manner is not trivial. The third difficulty is dealing with the dynamics of traffic.
16. Traffic levels vary in random ways in the short term; often have daily, weekly, monthly, and yearly patterns; and generally, long term trends.
17. The appropriate way to deal with traffic dynamics depends on the applications of the communication system.
18. The selection of relations as constraints or the objective is somewhat arbitrary. Quite often one is interested in the tradeoffs between these relations.
19. For example, in one context you might be interested in minimizing average delay of messages, constrained by the requirement of a given capacity. In other contexts you might wish to maximize the capacity given an upper bound on the average delay as a constraint.

Table 1.3: Summarizes some of the major categories of network design problems

Given	Determine	Objective
Traffic requirements, network topology, routing of traffic.	Capacity of network transmission channels.	Optimize tradeoff between channel costs and network performance.
Traffic requirements, network topology, capacity of network transmission channels.	Routing of traffic in network.	Minimize traffic delay.
Traffic requirements, network topology.	Capacity of network transmission channels, routing of network traffic.	Optimize tradeoff between channel costs and network performance.
Traffic requirements	Network topology, routing of traffic, capacity of network transmission channels.	Optimize tradeoff between channel costs and network performance.
Terminal locations, traffic requirements.	Location of multiplexers, concentrators, and/or routers.	Minimize channel costs.
Terminal locations, traffic requirements, location of multiplexers, concentrators, and/or routers.	Assignment of terminals to multiplexers, concentrators, and/or routers.	Minimize channel costs.

20. Computerized network design tools are often used to select the values of the variables given the relations between them, the constraints, and the objective.
21. We may categorize these tools by the problems they solve and/or by the techniques they used to solve the problems. Table 1.3 summarizes some of the major categories of network design problems.
22. Typically, network design tools provide suites of algorithms solving a variety of these problems.

1.14 Network Design Tools and Algorithms

1. Network design tools are systems built around suites of design algorithms.
2. The tools support the algorithms with user-friendly graphical user interfaces.
3. They also provide network editing facilities so that networks can be easily modified to produce multiple "what if" scenarios.
4. Quite often the tools also add some sort of version control to keep track of all these scenarios.
5. Databases for data such as traffic, device, and tariff information are also provided.
6. Most importantly, the tools provide integration between the various algorithms in the suite.

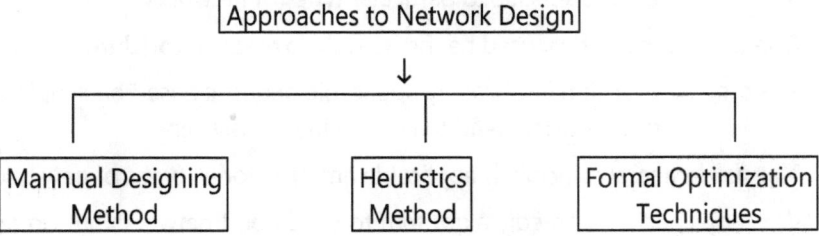

1.14.1 Manual Design Method

Advantages:

1. Here networks designed by hands, even no use of 'rules' at all.
2. The most important aspect of this method is its flexibility.
3. Database need not be required to be assembled.
4. Network designer can be responsive to changes in goals and requirements of network because there is no requirement of initial set up time, etc.
5. Here, in this method, incremental as well as total designs can be done.

Disadvantages:
1. It is rarely quantitative.
2. Decisions can be taken subjectively, inconsistently and unconsciously.
3. It is difficult to repeat a successful design when similar circumstances arise.
4. Also it is difficult to learn from previous mistakes.
5. This method is also usually too labour intensive to allow for the proper consideration of all alternatives.
6. Design mistakes can be possible due to mannual notations.
7. Thus, these problems can be overcome by automating the design process.

1.14.2 Heuristics Method
1. Heuristics are design principles incorporated into algorithms and thus are automatable.
2. They can be made quantitative and repeatable.
3. Many alternatives can be tried and compared.
4. Results can be transferred from one network designer to another network designer to share their experience.
5. Some Heuristics are specific to particular types of networks.
6. One of the most widely used heuristics is the **greedy algorithm.**
7. The greedy algorithm is a broadly applicable heuristic based on simple observation that inexpensive networks tend to contain inexpensive links.
8. This fundamental principle is applicable and true for all types of network.
9. We can expect this greedly algorithm to yield good networks but do not expect it to yield the optimal solution.
10. It is quite possible that least expensive network does not contain some of the least expensive links. It happens that in the case of this simple unconstrained network, the greely algorithm does in fact yield the optimal solution.

1.14.2.1 Introduction to Greedy Algorithm
1. Many of the problems that computer programs are designed to solve have involved optimization or finding a "best" solution. That is, some operation can be performed in a number of different ways, all meeting some basic constraints, and the problem is to find the way that is optimal, in the sense that it maximizes the value of some desirable quantity or minimizes the value of an undesirable one.

2. A *greedy algorithm* is a method for finding an optimal solution to some problem involving a large, homogeneous data structure (such as an array, a tree, or a graph) by starting from an optimal solution to some component or small part of the data structure and extending it, by considering
additional components of the data structure one by one, to an optimal global solution.
3. A greedy algorithm assumes that a local optimum is part of the global optimum.
4. The principle advantage of greedy algorithm is that they are usually straightforward, easy to understand and easy to code.
5. Their principle disadvantage is that for many problems, there is no greedy algorithm. More precisely, in many cases there is no guarantee that making locally optimal improvements in a locally optimal solution yields the optimal global solution.

1.14.2.2 Greedy Algorithm

A **greedy algorithm** is an algorithm that follows the problem solving metaheuristic of making the locally optimum choice at each stage with the hope of finding the global optimum. For instance, applying the greedy strategy to the travelling salesman problem yields the following algorithm: "At each stage visit the unvisited city nearest to the current city".

1. A candidate set, from which a solution is created.
2. A selection function, which chooses the best candidate to be added to the solution.
3. A feasibility function, that is used to determine if a candidate can be used to contribute to a solution.
4. An objective function, which assigns a value to a solution, or a partial solution, and
5. A solution function, which will indicate when we have discovered a complete solution.

There are two ingredients that are exhibited by most problems that lend themselves to a greedy strategy:

(1) **Greedy Choice Property:** We can make whatever choice seems best at the moment and then solve the subproblems arising after the choice is made. The choice made by a greedy algorithm may depend on choices so far. But, it cannot depend on any future choices or all the solutions to the subproblem, it progresses in a fashion making one greedy choice after another iteratively reducing each given problem into a smaller one. In other words, a greedy algorithm never has to go back to change its choices. This is the main difference between it and dynamic programming. Dynamic programming is exhaustive and is guaranteed to find the solution. After every algorithmic stage, dynamic programming makes decisions based on all the decisions made in the previous stage, and may reconsider the previous stage's algorithmic path to solution. A greedy algorithm makes the

decision early and changes the algorithmic path after decision, and will never reconsider the old decisions.

It may not be accurate for some problems.

(2) **Optimal Substructure:** A problem exhibits optimal substructure if an optimal solution to the sub-problem contains within its optimal solution to the problem.

1.14.2.3 Applications of Greedy Algorithm

For most problems, greedy algorithms mostly (but not always) fail to find the globally optimal solution, because they usually do not operate exhaustively on all the data. They can make commitments to certain choices too early which prevent them from finding the best overall solution later.

If a greedy algorithm can be proven to yield the global optimum for a given problem class, it typically becomes the method of choice because it is faster than other optimisation methods like dynamic programming. Examples of such greedy algorithms are **Kruskal's algorithm, Dijkstra's algorithms for finding Single-Source Shortest paths and Prim's algorithm for finding minimum spanning trees and the algorithm for finding optimum Huffman trees.**

1.14.3 Formal Optimization Techniques

1. The set of all possible solutions to a problem is referred to as the **solution space.**
2. The notion of best is expressed in formal optimization techniques by the **objective function.**
3. The best value of the objective function is referred to as the **optimum.**
4. There are also algorithms which always produce optimal solutions like **Simplex method.** This algorithm only works for the class of problems called **linear programming problems.**
5. Linear programs are problems where both the constraints and the objectives are weighted sums of the variables.
   i.e. they are of the form
   $$Z = \sum_{i=1}^{N} a_i x_i$$
   where, x_i are the N variables that we are optimizing over and a_i are the respective coefficient.
6. Another important class of problems is when the solution space and the objective are **convex.**
7. Let us consider we have function of two variables x_j and x_k and we want to find minimum value of this function subject to some constraints.
8. Values of x_j and x_k which satisfy these constraints are said to be **feasible solutions** or simply **solutions.**

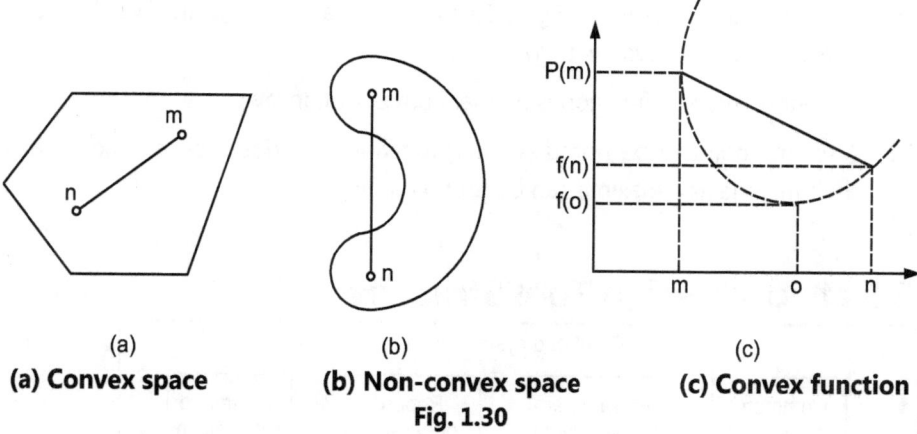

(a)	(b)	(c)
(a) Convex space	(b) Non-convex space	(c) Convex function

Fig. 1.30

9. Assume that the points inside the polygon are all the feasible solutions to the problem.
10. For example, x_j and x_k might be the constraints representing capacity of limitation on the node.
11. This solution space is called as convex in Fig. 1.30 (a) because for any two points 'm' and 'n' inside this region, all the points on the line connecting 'm' and 'n' are also inside the region.
12. Fig. 1.30 (b) is the example of a solution space that is not convex.
13. A convex function is a function with the property that for any point 'o' between 'm' and 'n', f(o) lies below the line connecting f(m) and f(n).
14. Convex functions must be defined on convex sets for this property to hold, since otherwise, f(o) may not even exist.
15. Thus, Fig. 1.30 (c) shows the function called as convex function.
16. Convex functions can be functions of many variables.
17. The minimum of convex function can be found via a local search.
18. If f(o) lies above the line connecting f(m) and f(n) for all 'o' between 'm' and 'n', it is said that 'f' is concave.

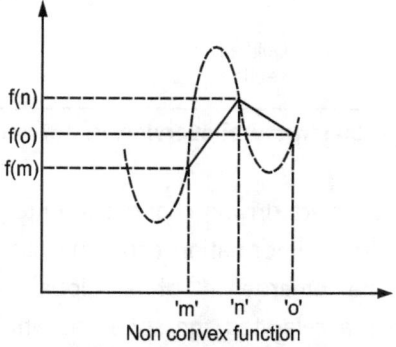

Fig. 1.30: (d) Non-convex function

19. Thus, function shown in Fig. 1.30 (d) is concave on the interval 'm' to 'n' and convex on the interval 'n' to 'o'.

20. For entire interval, function is neither convex or concave.

21. Also one point to be noted is linear functions are both convex and concave and their minima and maxima can be found easily.

1.15 Network Design Tool Structure

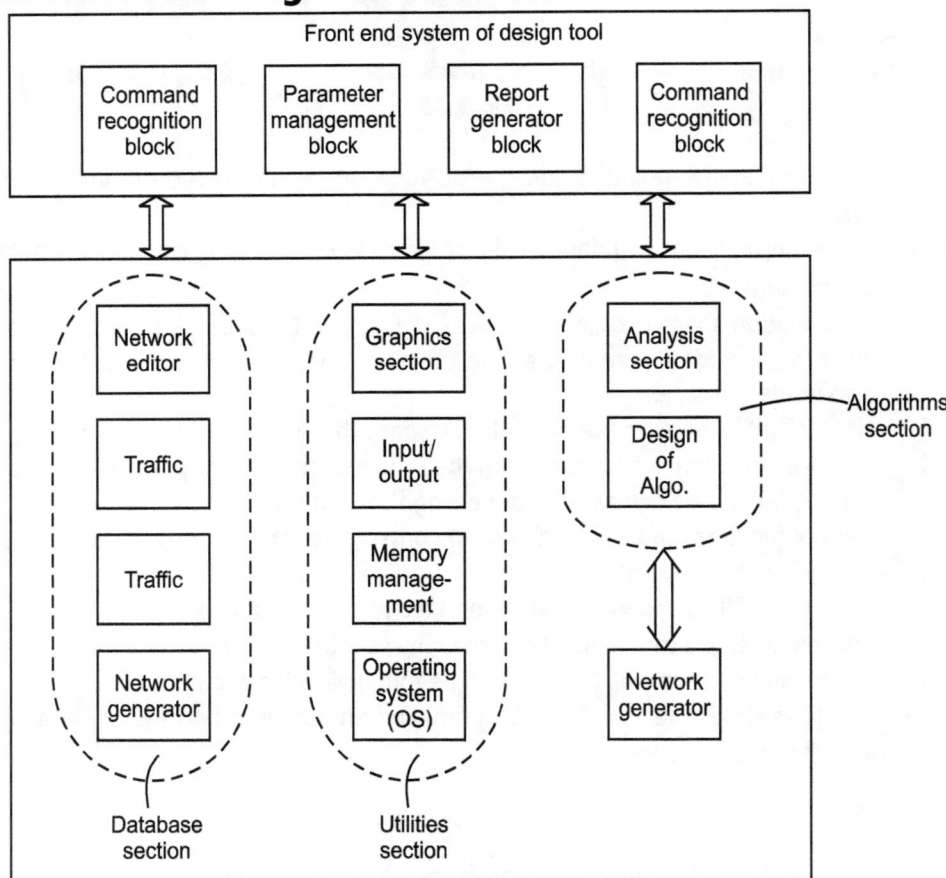

Fig. 1.31: Typical structural overview of network design tool

1. New business practices are driving changes in enterprise networks. The transition from an industrial to an information economy has changed how employees do their jobs, and the emergence of a global economy of unprecedented competitiveness has accelerated the speed at which companies must adapt to technological and financial changes.

2. To reduce the time to develop and market products, companies are empowering employees to make strategic decisions that require access to sales, marketing, financial, and engineering data. Employees at corporate headquarters and in worldwide field offices, as well as telecommuters in home offices, need immediate access to data, regardless of whether the data is on centralized or departmental servers.
3. To develop, sell, and distribute products into domestic and foreign markets, businesses are forming alliances with local and international partners. Businesses are carefully planning their network designs to meet security goals while also offering network access to resellers, vendors, customers, prospective customers, and contract workers located all over the world.
4. To accommodate increasing requirements for remote access, security, bandwidth, scalability, and reliability, vendors and standard bodies introduce new protocols and technologies at a rapid rate. Network designers are challenged to develop state-of-the-art networks even though the state of the art is continually changing.
5. Whether you are a novice network designer or a seasoned network architect, you probably have concerns about how to design a network that can keep pace with the accelerating changes in the internetworking industry.
6. A complete network design tool contains modules that allow the user to use each of the network design techniques as appropriate.
7. The major blocks of network design tools are –
   (a) Front-end section.
   (b) Database section.
   (c) Utilities section.
   (d) Algorithm section.
8. Front end is responsible for both the input and output interface to the user.
9. The main blocks of the front-end sections are
   (a) Report generator section.
   (b) Network display section.
   (c) Parameter management section.
   (d) Command recognizer section.
10. Database section is there to store huge database required for the network designing.
11. To work on realistic problems, the tool must be able to deal with the bulk data needed to support the design process.
12. The database section has the following subsections modules.
    (a) Tariff calculation block.
    (b) Network editor block.
    (c) Network generator block.

13. Utilities module of the network design tool includes the utilities that interface the operating system and are machine specific.
14. The submodules of utilities section are
    (a) Operating system
    (b) Memory management section
    (c) Input/output section.
    (d) Graphics section.
15. Algorithms module includes algorithms for design and analysis.
16. The algorithms section has two submodules.
    (a) Design of algorithms
    (b) Analysis section.

1.16 Telecommunications Network

1. A **telecommunications network** is a network of telecommunications links and nodes arranged so that messages may be passed from one part of the network to another over multiple links and through various nodes.
2. Telecommunications network links (including their endpoints or "nodes") may in turn be built out of hierarchical transmission systems.
4. **Examples of telecommunications networks are:**
   - Computer network.
   - **The Internet Network:** The internet network is a global 'network of networks'. The internet is connected via an Internet Service Provider (ISP) and then becomes part of a network. This network then connects to a larger corporate network that interconnects with several other similar networks through Network Access Points (NAPs).
   - The Public switched telephone network.
   - The global Telex network.
   - The aeronautical ACARS (Aircraft Communications Addressing and Reporting System) network (**Aircraft Communications Addressing and Reporting System (ACARS)**) is a digital datalink system for transmission of short, relatively simple messages between aircraft and ground stations via radio or satellite. The protocol, which was designed by ARINC (**Aeronautical Radio, Incorporated** - established in 1929, is a major provider of transport communications and systems engineering solutions for eight industries: (aviation, airports, defense, government, healthcare, networks, security, and transportation) to replace their VHF voice service and deployed in 1978, uses telex formats. SITA (SITA is a multinational information technology company specializing in providing IT and telecommunication services to the aviation industry. Originally known as the *Société Internationale de Télécommunications Aéronautiques*, the company no longer uses this long name and is now known

simply as SITA.) Later augmented their worldwide ground data network by adding radio stations to provide ACARS service. Over the next 20 years, ACARS will be superseded by the Aeronautical Telecommunications Network (ATN) protocol for Air Traffic Control communications and by the Internet Protocol for airline communications.)

1.17 Telecommunication Network Components

All telecommunication networks are made up of five basic components that are present in each network environment regardless of type or use. **These basic components include terminals, telecommunications processors, telecommunications channels, computers, and telecommunications control software.**

- **Terminals** are the starting and stopping points in any telecommunication network environment. Any input or output device that is used to transmit or receive data can be classified as a terminal component.
- **Telecommunications processors** are support data transmission and reception between terminals and computers by providing a variety of control and support functions. (i.e. convert data from digital to analog and back)
- **Telecommunications channels** are the way by which data is transmitted and received. Telecommunication channels are created through a variety of media of which the most popular include copper wires and coaxial cables. Fiber-optic cables are increasingly used to bring faster and more robust connections to businesses and homes.
- **In a telecommunication environment computers** are connected through media to perform their communication assignments.
- **Telecommunications control software** is present on all networked computers and is responsible for controlling network activities and functionality.

Early networks were built without computers, but late in the 20th century their switching centers were computerized or the networks replaced with computer networks.

1.18 Types of Telecommunication Networks

Types of Telecommunication Networks

- Wide Area Network (WAN)
- Metropolitan Area Network (MAN)
- Campus Area Network (CAN)
- Local Area Network (LAN)
- Personal Area Network (PAN)
- Virtual Private Network (VPN)

- Client/Server Network
- Network Computing
- Peer-to-Peer Network

In its most basic form a network is an interconnected system of things or people. From a technical standpoint a network is a data communication system that interconnects computer systems at different sites, or the connection of two or more computers using a communications system

Most networks can be classified into one of five different types. These include wide area networks (WAN), local area networks, (LAN), virtual private networks (VPN), client/server networks, network computing, and peer-to-peer networks.

Wide Area Network (WAN)
Any network that encompasses a large geographic area is referred to as a WAN or Wide Area Network. Many large businesses and government agencies use WANs to keep their employees and citizens connected as well as provide a quick and effective way to send and receive information.

Metropolitan Area Network (MAN)
A MAN or Metropolitan Area Network is a network that covers a region, often a metropolitan area that is bigger than a Local Area Network and smaller than a Wide Area Network and consists of several interconnected LANs. This network often serves regional businesses that have several locations throughout the region or entire cities. With this configuration, a MAN often is then connected to larger WAN networks.
There are three features that differentiate MANs from LANs or WANs:
1. The area of the network size is between LANs and WANs. The MAN will have a physical area between 5 and 50 km in diameter.
2. MANs do not generally belong to a single organization. The equipment that interconnects the network, the links, and the MAN itself are often owned by an association or a network provider that provides or leases the service to others.
3. A MAN is a means for sharing resources at high speeds within the network. It often provides connections to WAN networks for access to resources outside the scope of the MAN.

Campus Area Network (CAN)
A CAN or Campus Area Network is a network that is restricted to a small geographic area such as a building complex or a college campus. It is smaller than a Metropolitan Area Network but larger than a Local Area Network. The CAN incorporates several LANs and usually has connections to a MAN or WAN.

Local Area Network (LAN)
Similar in many ways to WANs; Local Area Networks or LANs are responsible for connecting computers in a much smaller limited physical area. A good example of a LAN would be a hotel's wireless Internet offering which is self-contained within their own facility.
There are multiple standards for Local Area Networks. Examples include IEEE 802.3 (Ethernet), IEEE 802.11 (Wi-Fi) or ITU-T G.hn (using existing home wires, such as power lines, phone lines and coaxial cables).

Personal Area Network (PAN)
A Personal Area Network (PAN) is a network that is restricted to the area of a person's body. It is much smaller than Local Area Network. It typically incorporates ad hoc connections to other PANs or directly to BlueTooth devices.

Virtual Private Network (VPN)
Virtual Private Networks or VPNs are a type of network that builds on the concept of a WAN however relies upon the internet and an encrypted connection mechanism to establish a secure environment for internal or external employees or customers.

Client/Server Network
The Client-Server network architecture continues to be the main architectural choice for most enterprise network computing. In a client/server environment the client (i.e. PC) relies on a LAN to connect with a back office network server that is responsible for the connection, retrieval, and storage of data and other critical company or personal information.

Network Computing
Network computing is a network architecture that has grown with the Internet and resulting connection speeds. In a network computing architecture a computer uses its web browser to connect to another network computer that actually is running the application. A good example of this architecture in use is Google Docs, or Microsoft Office online. Both services allow users the ability to login to Google or Microsoft servers respectively and work similarly to how it would be performed on their own computing environment.

Peer-to-Peer Network
Peer-to-peer networks are now beginning to be realized for the positive benefits they provide and not as only used for the sharing of copyrighted material. Peer-to-peer networks can be separated into two major types: Central Server and Pure.

In a central server environment one host server maintains all active connections and shared information. When information is requested the central server informs the user where they can receive the file and allows the connection directly to the other PC to download. The best example of this type was the original Napster file sharing service.

A pure peer-to-peer network type has no central server to maintain active users relies instead on the individual computers to seek out all other computers offering the same information being requested. A good example of this type would be BitTorrent software which allows small parts of information to be pulled from many sources which once completed compiles into the one file that is being downloaded.

EXERCISE

1. List the different network components and explain them.
2. Write short notes on:
   (a) Network facilities
   (b) Network devices
3. Explain the use of concentrator in detail by giving suitable examples.
4. Explain the different network functions.
5. Write short notes on:
   (a) Centralized data network
   (b) Integrated data networks
   (c) Distributed data networks.
6. Explain the concept of voice networks and different types of voice networks.
7. Write short notes on:
   (a) LAN
   (b) WAN
   (c) MAN
   (d) Internet
8. Explain in detail the different issues of network designing.
9. Explain the circuit switching, packet switching technique.
10. Compare the different switching technologies.
11. What are the different criterias to select the different routing protocols in data network.
12. Write short notes on:
    (a) Data in support of network design
    (b) Network design tools.
13. Compare Manual design method versus Heuristics design approach method.
14. Explain the formal optimization techniques used for network designing in detail.
15. Draw and explain the structural block diagram of network design tool.

Unit II

BROADBAND TELECOM NETWORKS

2.1 Introduction to Broadband Networks

2.1.1 The Broadband Communication Evolution

1. One primary requirement toward broadband is the increasing demand for information.
2. Another requirement toward broadband is the shifting traffic patterns we are now seeing.
3. This looks at which of the traffic types are becoming dominant on the network and what that means to the network characteristics that they call on.
4. Networks are being used more all the time, and we are experiencing rapid technology advances that present us with different strategies and architectures.
5. It becomes increasingly difficult to make a commitment to a set of technologies today because, after all, tomorrow might introduce a vastly improved architecture.
6. Because products and protocols develop so quickly, it is difficult for a given solution to be widely embraced, and without mass appeal, many products and services never have the opportunity to develop in the market place.
7. Finally, convergence is also driving the move to broadband, as industries, devices, and applications find natural synergies in the digital world and merge platforms with one another.

The following sections examine some of these trends in more detail and explore the ways in which they affect next-generation networks.

2.1.2 Telecommunications Traffic Trends

1. Internet traffic is doubling every 11 months. Along with the increase in the number of users, we are seeing growth of almost 50% per year in the amount of time users are connected; the average connection time is now approaching an hour.
2. Web-enabled devices, both wired and wireless, will view more and more for connectivity to the Web; traffic is growing in a number of different dimensions.
3. Already we have an average of at least five devices (for example, PCs, cell phones, personal digital assistants, MP3 players, pagers, and even clothing).
4. We are looking toward a future of greater numbers of devices communicating with one another, and someday there will be thousands of such devices for each human.

2.1.3 Telecommunications Application Trends

1. Another key trend driving the move to broadband is the changing nature of applications.
2. A whole new generation of business-class services are arising from virtual private networks (VPNs), e-commerce, the capability to handle voice and fax over IP, unified messaging applications, multimedia collaboration, streaming media, the capability to host content or applications, and the capability to cache content on the network edges.
3. All these business-class communications require guaranteed performance, so before they can become fully entrenched as network services, they must provide some level of QoS.
4. We are seeing a transition from portables to wearables, such as watches with medical monitors and pagers, eyeglasses with embedded computer displays, belts and watches with embedded computers, rings with universal product code readers and displays, and badges that have Internet connections and tiny teleconferencing cameras.
5. For this trend to really take off, we need a broadband wireless infrastructure and personal area networks (PANs) to locally connect all these smart devices.
6. We are also evolving to new industry models of information processing and communications. As we move more toward pervasive, or ubiquitous, computing, more and more of our senses—such as smell and taste—will become a part of what we communicate by using a network.
7. Each person will be able to choose the media formats that are conducive to his or her cognitive map and then fully enjoy the realm of sight, sound, smell, and even taste and touch on the network.
8. Visualization will become 3D and life-size, meaning that there will be telepresence.
9. Later this century, we will witness the enhancement and augmentation of our human powers through neural interfaces, bringing about an era, in some 40 years to 50 years, whereby we will be able to engage in virtuality without the constraint of devices that have to be worn, or enclosed cubicles that have to be entered. Reality will be what you make it!
10. For these models of information processing to become a reality requires tremendous bandwidth, extremely low latencies (that is, delays) in the network, guaranteed performance (which means administrated QoS), and broadband wireless access as well as PANs.

2.1.4 The Broadband Infrastructure

1. We are in an era of new, emerging networks that we loosely term *next-generation networks*.
2. Data traffic in these networks is equal to or surpassing voice as the most mission-critical aspect of the network
3. Traffic is growing at an alarming rate. More human users, more machine users, and more broadband access are all contributing to the additional traffic. Established carriers and new startups are deploying huge amounts of fiber-optic cable, introducing new possibilities, and optical technology is revolutionizing the network overall.
4. Next-generation networks will provide competitive rates because of lower construction outlays and operating costs.

2.1.5 Converging Public Infrastructures

1. Public infrastructures are converging on a single set of objectives.
2. The PSTN looks to support high-speed multimedia applications, and therefore it also looks to provide high levels of QoS and the ability to guarantee a granular diversification of QoS.
3. The PSTN has traditionally relied on a connection-oriented networking mode as a means of guaranteeing QoS, initially via circuit switching, and now incorporating ATM as well.
4. The public Internet is also looking to support high-speed multimedia applications, and it must deal with providing QoS guarantees.

2.1.6 Broadband Service Requirements

For next-generation networks to succeed, they must offer a unique set of features, including the following:

- **High speed and capacity:** Higher-bandwidth broadband access (such as 100 Gbps) will drive the need for additional core bandwidth, and discussions are beginning about networks providing exabits per second (that is, 1 billion Gbps).
- **Bandwidth on demand:** Broadband networks must be capable of providing or provisioning bandwidth on demand, as much as is needed, when it is needed—unlike today's static subscription services.
- **Bandwidth reservation:** Broadband networks must be capable of offering reserved bandwidth, so that when you know you will need a high-capacity service for streaming media, you can reserve the network resources so that they are guaranteed at the time and place that you need them.

- **Support of isochronous traffic:** Isochronous traffic is timebounded information that must be transferred within a specific timeframe, and as such has a low tolerance for delay and loss.
- **Agnostic platforms:** Agnostic devices support multiple data protocols (for example, IP, Frame Relay, ATM) and support multiple traffic types, such as voice, data, and video, so that you can aggregate and administer all traffic at a single point.
- **Support for unicasting and multicasting:** In unicasting, streams from a single origination point go directly to a single destination point. In multicasting, streams from a single origination point flow to multiple destination points. This reduces traffic redundancy by limiting the access to a selected group of users.
- **QoS:** As discussed, Broadband networks must provide variable QoS parameters, must ensure that those service levels can be guaranteed, and must ensure that service-level agreements can be honored.

A number of broadband access technologies, both wireline and wireless, have been developed to facilitate next-generation networking. It covers these options, which include the twisted-pair xDSL family; hybrid fiber coax alternatives that make use of cable modems; fiber to the curb; fiber to the home; broadband wireless, including direct broadcast satellite, MMDS (Multichannel multipoint distribution service), LMDS (Local Multipoint Distribution Service), and Free Space Optics; and innovative new uses of powerline to support high-speed communications. "Wireless Communications", 3G wireless promises upto 2 Mbps (but most likely around 384 Kbps).

Intelligent networks, which include programmable networking, are potentially a replacement for the capital-intensive PSTN based on circuit switches. Softswitches, media gateways, Signaling System 7 (SS7) gateways, and service-enabling software developments are critical.

2.2 Present Technologies for Voice, Video and Data Networks

2.2.1 Typical Voice Networks

Type	Data rate	Voice channel	Standard/Proprietary
DS_1	1.544 Mb/s	24	Standard
E_1	2.048 Mb/s	30	Standard
DS_3	44.736 Mb/s	672	Standard

1. The initial system was known as T_1 and carried 24 voice channels over copper wire.

2. Shortly, T_3 became a common carrier system, needed greater capacity than the T_1 offerings.
3. T_3 link support 673 voice calls.
4. These systems were designed originally for voice system, now they can be configured to support data and video applications as well.
5. Thus, for voice communication, a lot of T_3 have to be in operation to support public telephone network.

2.2.2 Typical Data Networks

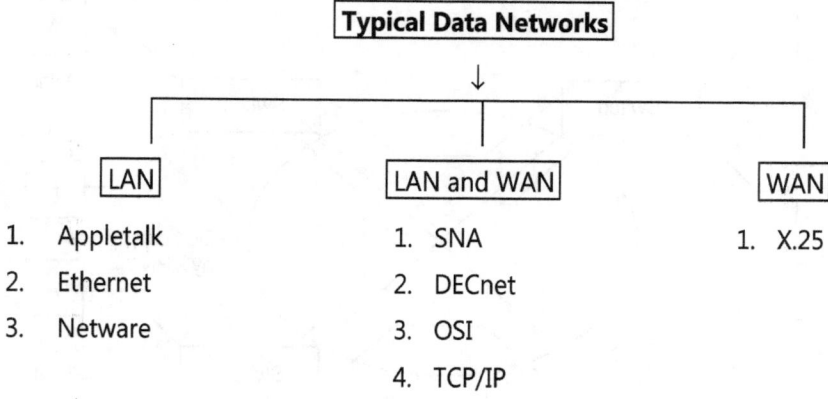

1. Typical data networks for LAN are
    (a) Appletalk from Apple vendor.
    (b) Ethernet by (Xerox, Intel etc.)
    (c) Netware by (Novell corporation).
2. Typical data networks for WAN are
    (a) For example X.25 network by (ITU and ISO).
3. Typical data networks run for LAN/WAN are
    (a) SNA (Simple network architecture) by IBM.
    (b) DECnet by Digital corporation.
    (c) OSI by (ITU and ISO).
    (d) TCP/IP by Internet.
4. So many incomptible systems to do one thing, because data communications and computer industry has had very little regulation imposed upon it.

2.2.3 Need of Virtual Networks

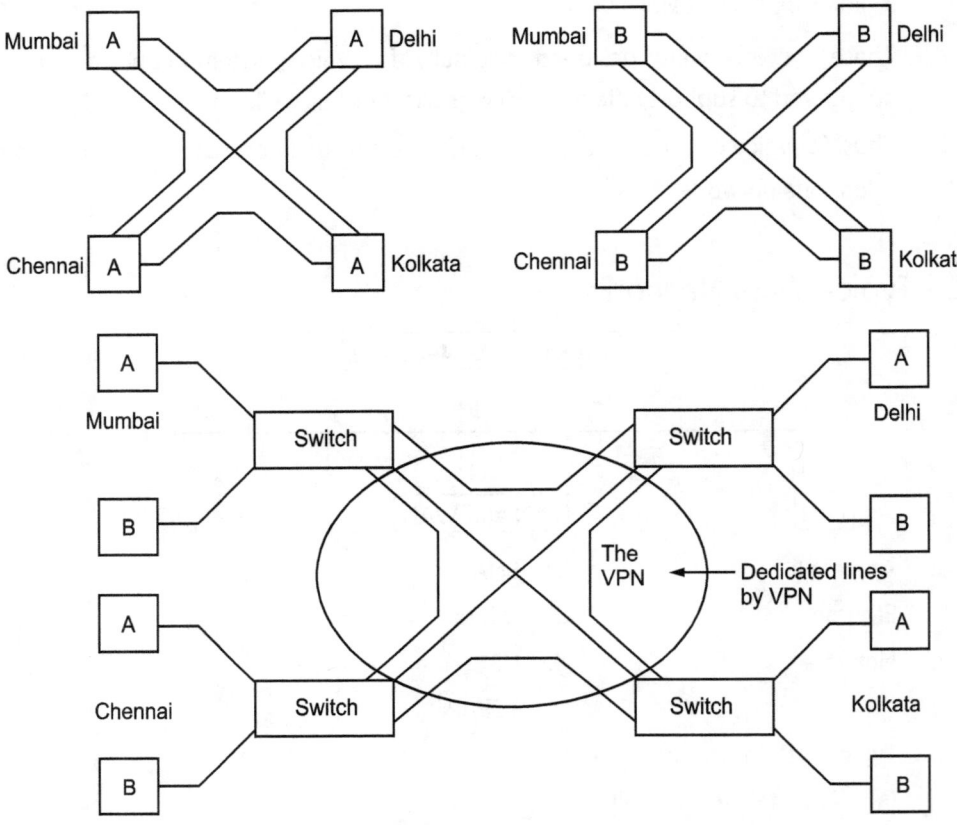

Fig. 2.1: Virtual private network

1. Company 'A' and company 'B' has their dedicated leased lines which are costly.
2. Individually, company 'A' and company 'B' has to pay more for data communication.
3. Fig. 2.1 shows that through use of the VPN, two companies can share the communication facilities.
4. VPN provider provides a network for multiple user.
5. Thus, cost of individual companies reduced by huge amount.
6. VPN services are offered by public X.25 networks, switched T_1 system and ATM networks.
7. Thus, it is proven that ATM offers more powerful VPNs that these older technologies.
8. Also traffic can be voice, video or data make ATM at top priority for implementation.

2.3 ISDN
2.3.1 Introduction
What is ISDN?
1. Integrated Services Digital Network (ISDN) is a state-of-the-art Public Switched Digital Network for provisioning of different services – voice, data and image transmission over the telephone line through the telephone network.
2. ISDN handles all types of information – voice, data, studio-quality sound, static and moving images.
3. They are all digitized, and transmitted at high speed.
4. ISDN can handle many devices and many telephone numbers on the same line.
5. Upto eight separate telephones, fax machines or computers can be linked to a single Basic Rate ISDN connection and have different phone numbers assigned to them.
6. A Basic Rate ISDN line can support upto two calls at the same time.
7. Any combination of voice, fax or PC connections can take place at the same time, through the same ISDN line.
8. From a digital ISDN telephone, you can place a call to an analogue telephone on the PSTN (Public Switched Telephone Network) and vice-versa.
9. Both networks are interconnected by the network carrier in a way similar to the connection between the mobile phone network and the analogue phone network.
10. For the user, it is completely transparent whether he is calling a GSM (Global System for Mobile) telephone, a conventional telephone or an ISDN digital telephone.
11. The single biggest disadvantage is likely to be your physical location. If you are not in an area that is reasonably close to a telephone company's central office (one with the required equipment already installed), ISDN may not be an option for you. If you live in a metro or near a city, ISDN is an ideal choice. But at other remote locations, ISDN is not available.

Availability:
ISDN service is available by and large in all major cities of India. Also ISDN has overseas connectivity with the following countries: Australia, Austria, Belgium, Canada, Denmark, France, Germany, Ireland, Israel, Italy, Japan, Malaysia, Netherlands, Norway, Philippines, Singapore, Switzerland, Thailand, U.A.E., UK, USA.

Services Provided by ISDN:
Due to the large amounts of information that ISDN lines can carry, ISDN applications are revolutionizing the way businesses communicate. ISDN is not restricted to public telephone networks alone; it may be transmitted via packet switched networks, telex, CATV (Community Antenna TV) networks, etc.

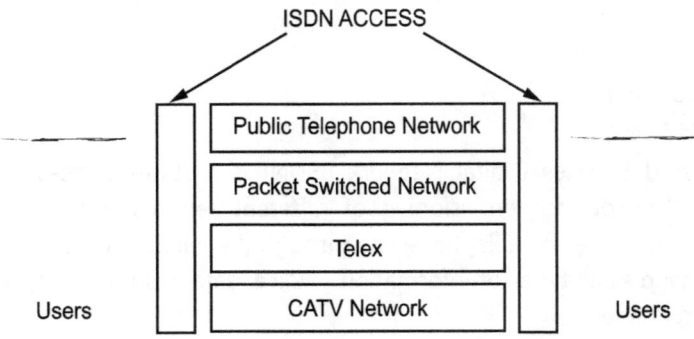

Fig. 2.2: Typical ISDN applications

There are two kinds of services provided by ISDN.

1. **Network Services:**
   - Network services carry the interactions between the user and the network.
   - For example: setting up calls and disconnecting them.

2. **Bearer Services:**
   - Bearer services carry data between two users.
   - For example: voice or fax information encoded as a bit stream.

The following services are offered on a dial-up basis between two ISDN subscribers:
  (i) Desktop Video Conferencing on using three ISDN lines at 64/128 kbps.
  (ii) High quality video conferencing by using three ISDN lines at 384 kbps.
  (iii) Video telephony.
  (iv) Teleconferencing, which facilitates the transmission of pictures, documents and drawings etc. apart from voice and images of the participants.
  (v) High speed data transmission at 64/128 kbps.
  (vi) High speed facsimile at 64/128 kbps with G4 Fax terminal.
  (vii) Access to Internet with a higher bandwidth of 64/128 kbps giving significantly improved response time and quality of service.

Supplementary Services:
ISDN, being a Value Added Service, offers many supplementary features/services:
  (i) Calling Line Identification Presentation
  (ii) Advice of Charge
  (iii) Line Hunting
  (iv) Closed User Group
  (v) User to User Signaling
  (vi) Call Waiting
  (vii) Call forwarding On No Reply, On Busy, Unconditional
  (viii) Multiple Subscriber Number

Bearer Services:
- Circuit switched speech and audio.
- X.25 circuit and packed switched network.
- Frame Relay.
- Circuit switched data.

Teleservices:
- Facsimile – Telephony
- Telex
- Videotext

ISDN Standards:

ISDN is subject to standardization by the ITU-T (International Telecommunication Union-Telecommunication Standard Section) and ETSI (European Telecommunications Standards Institute), which issue recommendations and specifications covering ISDN equipment and interfaces. Standards also exist for types of service, protocols and ISDN numbering.

Operating System Software for ISDN:
- It is of course important to have an operating system, which will support ISDN hardware, allowing your software applications to communicate with and take full advantage of your ISDN terminal adapter.
- First of all, Point-to-Point Protocol (PPP) is the standard Internet access protocol, and it is required for a proper ISDN connection.
- Serial Line Internet Protocol (SLIP) is an older and less efficient protocol, but it is still fairly common.
- SLIP won't work with ISDN, so make sure you have a PPP account. Of course, if your ISP (Internet Service Provider) can provide you with ISDN connectivity, they should know this and it probably won't be an issue.

Different Kinds of ISDN Terminals:

The ISDN telephone line is terminated on a common box called the Network Termination (NT) at the subscriber's premises. The Network Termination unit along with accessories will be provided by the service provider like MTNL or can be procured by the subscriber. The terminal equipment has to be procured by the subscriber himself from the open market.

Types of ISDN Terminal:
(a) ISDN feature phone: This is a simplest type of ISDN phone which has an LCD display and some additional keys.

(b) Terminal adapter (TA).

(c) PC add-on ISDN card.
(d) Video phone.
(e) G4 fax.

Types of Non-ISDN Terminal:
- ISDN terminals such as DTE (Data Terminal Equipment) that predate the ISDN standards are referred to as Terminal Equipment type 2 (TE2).
- Ex. Terminal with physical interface as RS-232 and host computers with X.25 interface.
- This is the old analog telephone.
- Or old-style fax machine.
- Or modem.
- Or whatever we use to hook up to the analog phone line. It can also be other communications equipment that is handled by a TA (Terminal Adapter).

Benefits of ISDN for Network Operators:
1. Avoidance of separate networks for different services.
2. Economical use of the equipment of the digitalized telephone network, especially the copper pair of the subscriber line.
3. Reduction in costs due to simplified operation and maintenance procedures.

How is ISDN line superior to the phone line?
- The signal on the ISDN line – voice or data, is sent in digital mode.
- The signal level at subscriber's terminal equipment is independent of line length.
- An ISDN subscriber can establish two simultaneous independent calls, which could be voice, data, image or combination of any two, whereas only one call is possible on ordinary telephone lines.
- The call set-up time between two ISDN subscribers is extremely short.

2.3.2 ISDN for Voice, Data and Video
- It is the next-generation, digital telephone network that integrates circuit-switched voice and data services over a common access facility.
- There are two types of ISDN lines. Basic Rate ISDN (BRI) is designed for residential customers and small businesses.
- Primary Rate ISDN (PRI) is designed for larger businesses.

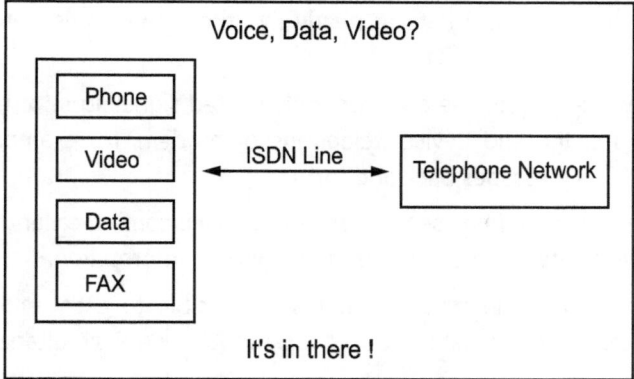

Fig. 2.3: Typical ISDN usage

- ISDN reduces the cost of network administration.
- ISDN simplifies wiring.
- ISDN combines separate voice and data networking requirements.
- ISDN is compatible with BRI/PRI, plus existing analog voice and switched 56 services.
- For residential customers, Basic Rate ISDN (BRI) costs about the equivalent of two phone lines.
- BRI customers can gain high speed Internet access (64 KBPS to 128 KBPS).
- BRI improves the quality of speech in telephone calls. BRI provides an ideal way to keep in touch through personal video conferencing.
- BRI offers improved modem connectivity to non-ISDN systems.
- For business customers, ISDN offers cost savings through the integration of voice and data services.
- PRI provides a great backup solution for leased data lines.
- PRI offers high-quality video conferencing capabilities. PRI costs about the same as standard "channelized T1" services.

2.3.3 Why Digital Communications?

- There are a number of reasons why it is advantageous to carry information, particularly computer data, in a digital format.
- For one, digital lines provide a far cleaner, error-free connection that can ensure reliable transmission worldwide.
- Secondly, digital lines allow equipment that processes data digitally, such as computers or networking routers, to be directly connected, and without the 4 kHz bandwidth limitations imposed by PSTN (voice) telephone lines.

- An ISDN line can carry data at nearly five times the fastest rate achievable using analog modems over PSTN lines.
- Further, while a PSTN line can carry only limited signaling information between the network and the end device (telephone or modem, for example), ISDN lines can carry detailed messages back and forth.
- This information can be used to define multiple incoming callers, to specify the type of incoming data, or to convey useful diagnostic information.
- With digital communications, it is finally possible to carry multiple service types (e.g., voice, computer data, Group 4 fax, motion video) simultaneously on the same network.
- ISDN offers the means to realize a universal in-box integrating voice, voice mail, e-mail, fax and video images from a single application.

2.3.4 ISDN Devices

ISDN Devices:

1. ISDN devices include terminals, terminal adapters (TAs), network-termination devices, line-termination equipment, and exchange-termination equipment.
2. ISDN terminals come in two types. Specialized ISDN terminals are referred to as terminal equipment type 1 (TE1).
3. Non-ISDN terminals, such as DTE, that predates the ISDN standards are referred to as terminal equipment type 2 (TE2).
4. TE1s connect to the ISDN network through a four-wire, twisted-pair digital link. TE2s connect to the ISDN network through a TA.
5. The ISDN TA can be either a standalone device or a board inside the TE2.
6. If the TE2 is implemented as a standalone device, it connects to the TA via a standard physical-layer interface. Examples include RS-232C, V.24, and V.35.
7. Beyond the TE1 and TE2 devices, the next connection point in the ISDN network is the network termination type 1 (NT1) or network termination type 2 (NT2) device.
8. These are network-termination devices that connect the four-wire subscriber wiring to the conventional two-wire local loop.
9. In most other parts of the world, the NT1 is a part of the network provided by the carrier.
10. The NT2 is a more complicated device that typically is found in digital private branch exchanges (PBXs) and that performs layer 2 and 3 protocol functions and concentration services.
11. An NT1/2 device also exists as a single device that combines the functions of an NT1 and an NT2.

ISDN specifies a number of reference points that define logical interfaces between functional groups; such as TAs and NT1s. ISDN reference points include the following:

- **R:** The reference point between non-ISDN equipment and a TA.
- **S:** The reference point between user terminals and the NT2.
- **T:** The reference point between NT1 and NT2 devices.
- **U:** The reference point between NT1 devices and line-termination equipment in the carrier network.

  - Fig. 2.4 illustrates a sample ISDN configuration and shows three devices attached to an ISDN switch at the central office.
  - Two of these devices are ISDN-compatible, so they can be attached through an S reference point to NT2 devices.
  - The third device (a standard, non-ISDN telephone) attaches through the reference point to a TA.
  - Any of these devices also could attach to an NT1/2 device, which would replace both the NT1 and the NT2. In addition, although they are not shown, similar user stations are attached to the far-right ISDN switch.

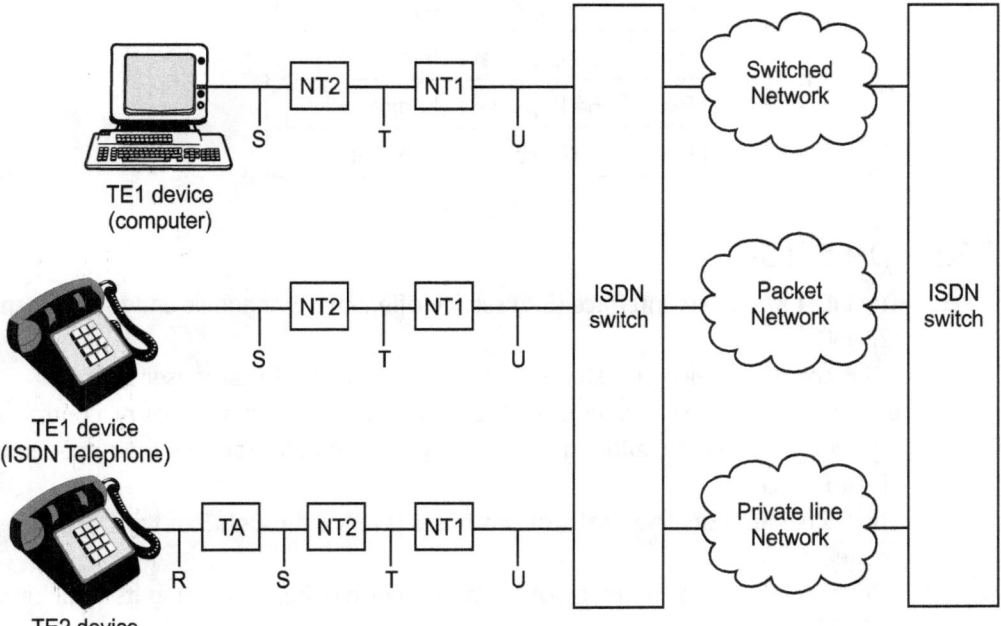

Fig. 2.4: Sample ISDN configuration illustrates relationships between devices and reference points

ISDN Services:

There are two types of services associated with ISDN:
- BRI (Basic Rate Interface) = 2B + 1D
- PRI (Primary Rate Interface) = 23B + 1D
- Hybrid Rate Interface = 1A + 1C

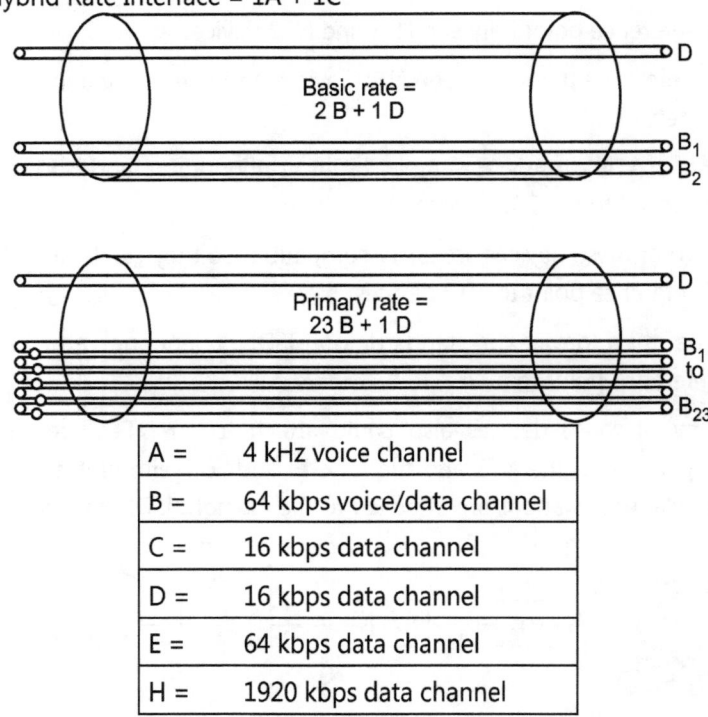

Fig. 2.5

2.3.5 ISDN BRI Service

1. The ISDN Basic Rate Interface (BRI) service offers two B channels and one D channel (2B + D).
2. BRI B-channel service operates at 64 kbps and is meant to carry user data.
3. BRI D-channel service operates at 16 kbps and is meant to carry control and signaling information, although it can support user data transmission under certain circumstances.
4. The D channel signaling protocol comprises layers 1 through 3 of the OSI reference model.
5. BRI also provides for framing control and other overhead, bringing its total bit rate to 192 kbps.
6. The BRI physical layer specification is International Telecommunication Union-Telecommunication Standards Section (ITU-T) (formerly the Consultative Committee for International Telegraph and Telephone [CCITT]).

2.3.6 ISDN PRI Service

1. ISDN Primary Rate Interface (PRI) service offers 23 B channels and 1 D channel in North America and Japan, yielding a total bit rate of 1.544 Mbps (the PRI D channel runs at 64 kbps).
2. ISDN PRI in Europe, Australia, and other parts of the world provides 30 B channels plus one 64 kbps D channel and a total interface rate of 2.048 Mbps.
3. ISDN Primary Rate Service offers you the power to create a seamless communication system that speeds and smoothes the flow of information without the expense of dedicated lines, modems, and special cabling.
4. Primary Rate Service links your PBX to advanced central office systems to provide you with global, digital connectivity and the full functionality of ISDN service.
5. Primary Rate Service is the end-to-end digital network architecture that allows users around the world to transmit voice, data, video, and image – separately or simultaneously – over standard telephone lines or fiber optic circuits via standard interface.
6. A single ISDN channel is a fast and flexible information management tool, but Primary Rate Service is two dozen times more powerful - bundling 24 ISDN channels for delivery to your premises.
7. The Primary Rate Service configuration is known as 23B + D: 23B channels for transport of voice, data, video, and image at 64 kbps, plus a single D channel for call setup and control. The 23 B channels can be used as it is, or rearranged in a wide variety of ways to accommodate highly specific user needs.

Key Applications:
- LAN interconnection
- Video conferencing
- Virtual office
- Backbone LAN access
- Voice and data integration
- Image transfer
- Business continuation and disaster recovery
- PBX

User Benefits:
- Greater access
- Economy with bandwidth available on demand
- Borderless communications
- Exceptional flexibility
- Digital speed and accuracy
- Fast, reliable backup for lines and host computers

What does a B channel do? (UQ - June 2007, Dec. 2007)
- The B channel carries ISDN Bearer Services across the network and so carries the content of call (the voice, fax or data) between users.
- The B channel is a neutral conduit for bits and carries data at 64000 bits per second (56000 bits per second in some North American networks).
- The ISDN does not need to know what the bits represent. The job of the network is to accept a stream of bits supplied by one user at one end of the B channel and to deliver them to the other user at the opposite end of the channel.
- Within an interface, the B channels are numbered. In a Basic Rate Interface they are numbered 1 and 2; in a Primary Rate Interface, they are numbered 1 to 30 (or 23 in North America).
- When two users are connected, there is no relationship between the channel numbers used at each end.
- You might have one user's B channel number 17 connected with the other user's B channel number 2. The ISDN is responsible for managing this relationship.
- Notice that channel number 17 would only be possible on a PRI, while channel number 2 is possible on both a BRI and a PRI.

ISDN does not restrict the interconnection of B channels between the two kinds of interface.

What does the D channel do?
The D channel carries the ISDN Network Services between the user and the network. It maintains the user's relationship with the network.
This includes:
- The requests and responses used when you make or receive a call.
- Call progress messages.
- Messages informing you that the called party has closed the call.
- Error messages telling you why a call has not been established for you.

The D channel operates at 16000 bits per second in a BRI and at 64000 bits per second in a PRI.

B & D Channel Characteristics:
- An ISDN channel has two and only two ends. B channels terminate at a user.
  A B channel can therefore connect two and only two users.
- **B channel** cannot be Y-shaped. B channels are therefore described as **end-to-end**.
- In the case of the D channel, one end is with the user. The other end is in the network.
- **D channel is not end-to-end.**
- You cannot normally notice, how the D channels (the red lines) do not pass through the network.
- Notice also how each user has only one D channel and it is not connected in any way with the D channel of the other user.

- The B channel (the blue line) passes directly across the network.

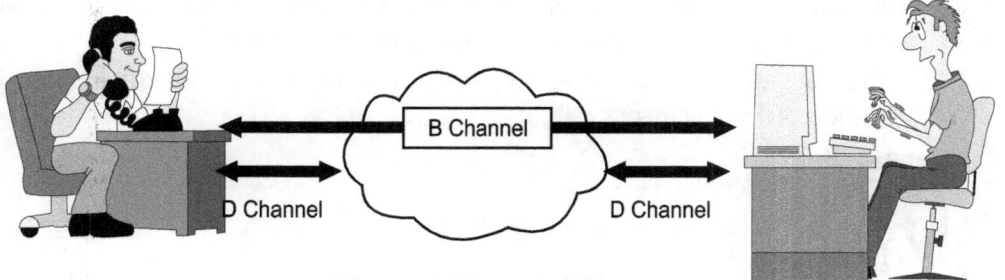

Fig. 2.6: D channel is not end-to-end

How B and D channels share the line: Basic Rate:
- The two B channels and the one D channel that make up a Basic Rate ISDN line are assembled together within the interface using a technique called **Time Division Multiplexing**.

B and D Channel Protocols:
- You must use a protocol to establish meaningful communication across a channel. It is important that both parties to the communication use the same protocol.
- This is particularly important for the D channel. Your signalling requests and responses must be understandable by the network. Even if your ISDN device and ISDN line are both functioning correctly, you might not be able to make successful calls if you are using a D channel protocol that is not the same as the networks.
- ISDN requires that you use a protocol defined by the ITU-T called **Q.931** for signalling in the D channel. However, there are several signalling protocols based on Q.931 in use round the world.
- You have a much greater choice of protocols for the B channel since the B channel is a neutral conduit for data of any type. You can use it to transmit any protocol you wish (e.g. SNA or PPP). However, if the network does not understand the protocol, it cannot give you any assistance if your call has to be delivered to a different type of network (e.g. PSTN), where data conversion is required.

B Channel Characteristics:
- It is important to remember that ISDN channels cannot be divided up into smaller units. Each is provided on an "all or nothing" basis.
- Two users communicating over a B channel have 64000 bits per second available to them. There is nothing they can do to reduce this bandwidth.
- What about the situation where the two users find that 64000 bits per second is not sufficient? The only solution is to add another B channel. This gives them 128000

bits per second. They are **not** using a single B channel of 128000 bits per second. (Don't forget that the speed of a B channel is defined as 64 000 bits per second. Anything which operates at a different speed is not a B channel).

- This means that they will have two parallel calls between them and the phone bill will show two simultaneous calls.

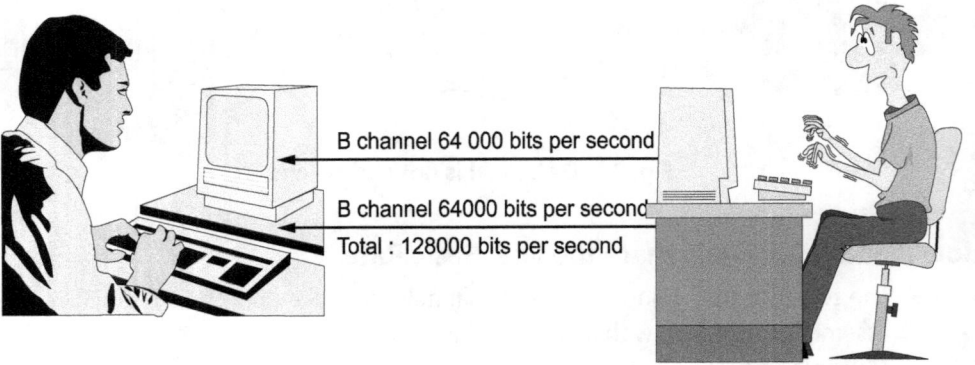

Fig. 2.7: Typical B channel characteristics

Using 2 B Channels:

- Imagine that you are a user communicating with someone else, using two parallel B channels.
- Does the ISDN network care whether these two B channels are connecting the same two users or if they are connecting one user with two others?
- The answer is no. The network treats these as two completely independent calls.

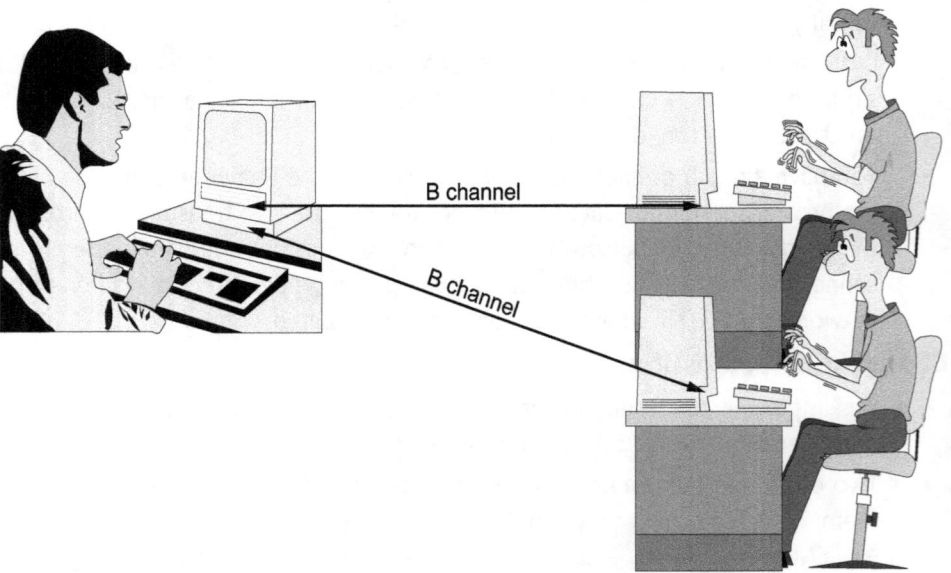

Fig. 2.8: Typical use of 2 B channels

- In Fig. 2.9, the two users are connected using two B channels in parallel. The ISDN is able to route these B channels independently, because it takes no account of the fact that both the channels connect the same pair of users.
- The speed of the two B channels is identical.
- The time it takes for data to travel from one end of the channel to the other is, however, different.
- One user transmits two items of data simultaneously. One is sent in the B channel, which is routed via satellite; the other is sent in the B channel, which takes the direct route. Will both items of data arrive at the same time?

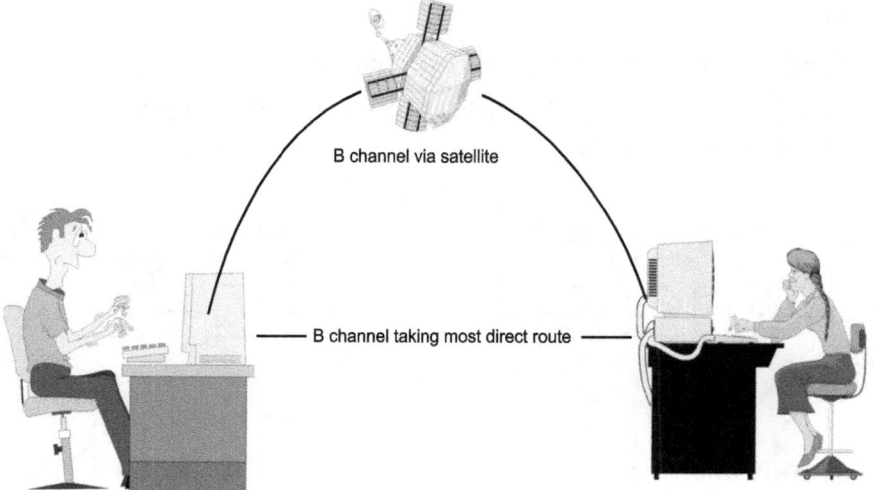

Fig. 2.9: The speed of the two B channels is not identical

- The item of data, which travels down the most direct path, will arrive first. That, which goes via satellite will arrive later because it has further to travel.
- The ISDN makes no attempt to synchronise the data on the two B channels, possibly because it does not understand what the protocol in use. The two B channels are operating independently - the ISDN does not care that they are both connecting the same two users.

Thus, regarding B and D channels, we can summarize the following points:
- The D channel carries Network Services in the form of signalling. This is the way the user maintains his relationship with the network. Each user has one and only one D channel.
- The B channel carries Bearer Services, which are the communication between two users. A single B channel cannot connect more than two users together.
- B channels and D channels share time on the interface.
- B channels cannot be sub-divided to provide less bandwidth.
- More than one B channel can be used together to provide more bandwidth.

2.3.7 ISDN Operation

1. Each B channel can carry a separate telephone call and usually has its own telephone number, called a **Directory Number** (DN).
2. The two B channels can be combined (bonded) to form a single 128 kbps data channel.
3. Fig. 2.10 illustrates a minimal ISDN setup connecting two computers.
4. The incoming twisted pair enters a box provided by the telephone company called the network terminator (NT1), which breaks the 144 kbps channel into the two B and single D sub-channels.
5. The B channels carry customer voice or data signals.
6. The D channel carries signals between your ISDN equipment and the phone company's central office.

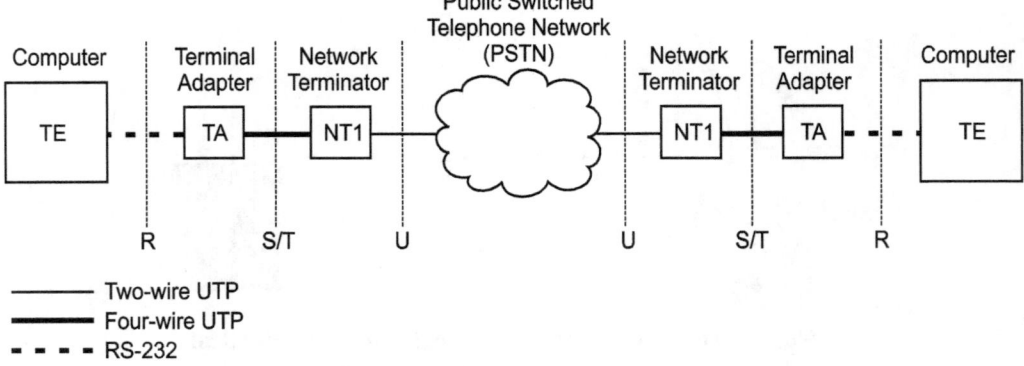

Fig. 2.10: Simple ISDN communication setup between two computers

7. A single four-wire cable carries the 2 B channels and the D channel to a **Terminal Adapter** (TA).
8. The function of this device is to connect any and all **Terminal Equipment** (TE) - computers, fax machines, Local Area Networks, or telephones - to one or both of the **B** channels.
9. In this example, the **TA** is shown as a separate unit, but it could be housed within the computer as an add-in card or integrated feature, or integrated with the **NT1** into a single box as a modem replacement or stand-alone TCP/IP router (network layer device).
10. Also shown are the external ISDN reference points - **R, S/T** and **U**. Each type of reference point represents a different type of interface.
11. The **U** reference point is the incoming unshielded twisted pair (UTP). The **S/T** reference point is a four-wire UTP cable.

12. A typical **TA** for data-only applications might simply emulate a pair of modems, translating standard modem setup and dialing commands into ISDN call-setup commands.
13. Computers are connected to this kind of TA with a normal RS-232 cable. The **TA** provides automatic rate adaptation to match whatever data rate your computer supports with ISDN's 64 kbps channel.
14. An example of a more sophisticated **TA** is the ISDN router, which connects to an ISDN line on one side and a Local Area Network on the other.
15. This type of device is able to support many different kinds of computer without special ISDN software, and contains all the intelligence necessary to move traffic over an ISDN link. Because ISDN is purely digital, the effects of noise are largely eliminated, and because the 64 kbps channel is essentially a pure "bit pipe" with no rate negotiation or handshaking involved, there are no modem speed or protocol differences to cause conflicts.

2.3.8 Analog Calls (Non-ISDN Terminals) and ISDN

Types of Non-ISDN Terminals

- ISDN terminals such as DTE, that predate the ISDN standards, are referred to as terminal equipment type 2 (TE2).
- Ex. Terminal with physical interface as RS-232 and host computers with X.25 interface.
- This is the old analog telephone.
- Or old-style fax machine.
- Or modem.
- Or whatever we use to hook up to the analog phone line. It can also be other communications equipment that is handled by a TA (Terminal Adapter).

1. The key characteristic of ISDN is that it is a digital network. However, many of the devices and networks, with which an ISDN user needs to communicate, are not digital, but analog. In order for these two types of device to communicate, the information which they are exchanging - must be converted from one form to the other.
2. In fact, except for data calls between computers across the ISDN network, almost all other types of calls - voice, fax, modems - will all involve some kind of conversion from digital to analog, or vice versa.
3. Much of this conversion takes place without the user's knowledge or intervention and is handled by the networks and devices involved. However, there are instances where an understanding of what is involved will assist in making successful connections and diagnosing problem areas.

4. You need to pay careful attention to the requirements of the ISDN device in use, particularly when sending and receiving faxes. This section provides the background to the various scenarios involved, and the practical implications for the different types of ISDN devices that are available.

2.3.8.1 Voice over ISDN – 1

- ISDN is a **Digital** network. Everything (including sounds such as voice and modem signals) is carried as a stream of bits.

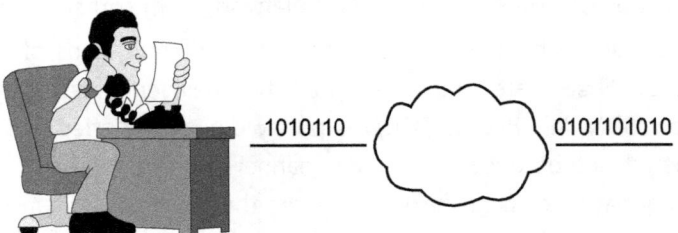

Fig. 2.11: Typical voice over ISDN is represented here

- This means that ISDN telephones need to be able to "digitize" and "un-digitize" sounds.
- This is performed by a device called a **CODEC** (Coder-Decoder), which is located inside the telephone.
- The CODEC translates the sounds into bits in one direction, and translates bits into sounds in the opposite direction.

2.3.8.2 Voice over ISDN – 2

- The analog signal originating in the microphone of the telephone handset is sampled and transformed into a stream of bits (64000 of them every second) that is placed on the B channel.

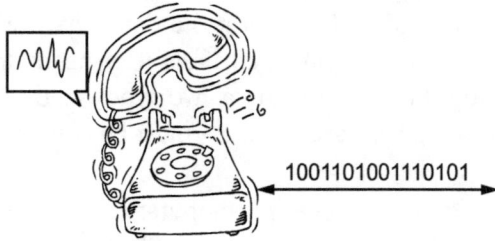

Fig. 2.12: Analog signal sent to the ear-piece of the handset

- Similarly, the incoming bit stream from the B channel is converted back into an analog signal and sent to the ear-piece of the handset.
- B channel is **full duplex**, which means that it can carry data in both directions at once.

2.3.8.3 Voice over ISDN – 3

- The ability to make voice calls from one ISDN telephone to another over a digital B channel is indeed useful. However, the majority of telephones, currently installed worldwide, are analogue devices which are not connected to an ISDN.
- Fortunately, you can make calls between the two networks. For this to work successfully, there has to be a conversion between the bit stream in the B channel and the analog signal required by the PSTN.

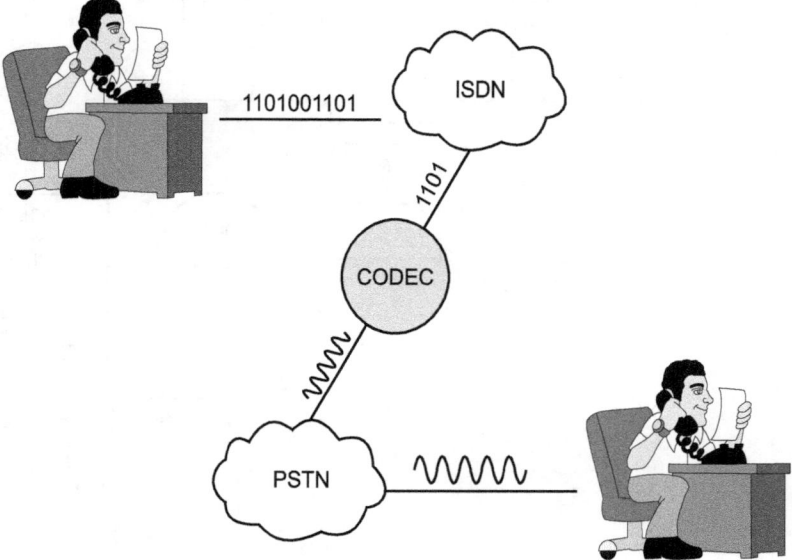

Fig. 2.13: Typical voice over ISDN and PSTN network

- CODECs are located at the boundaries of the digital and analog networks.
- Fortunately, you can make calls between the two networks.
- For this to work, the CODECs inside the network and the telephone **must** use the same rules when formatting the bit stream that represents the users' voices.
- Provided both devices are doing the same processing, then the information can be converted by applying the same rules in reverse.
- Given the presence of the CODEC in the network, and adherence to the correct protocols, any device that can be used on the PSTN, such as a modem or a fax machine, can also pass calls into the ISDN.

2.3.8.4 Analog Fax and Modem over ISDN (Scenario-1)

- Another important idea is introduced here; this is the Terminal Adapter.
- A Terminal Adapter (TA) is always necessary to connect non-ISDN devices (such as a serial port of a PC) to the ISDN. However, a TA can also contain a CODEC if it is intended to support analog phones, fax machines and modems.

- In Fig. 2.14, the modem at the top left can plug into the POTS ports on the TA. The TA will then convert sounds generated by the modem on its POTS port into a bit stream (and vice-versa). This bit stream is identical to that created by an ISDN telephone; that is to say it represents **sounds**.

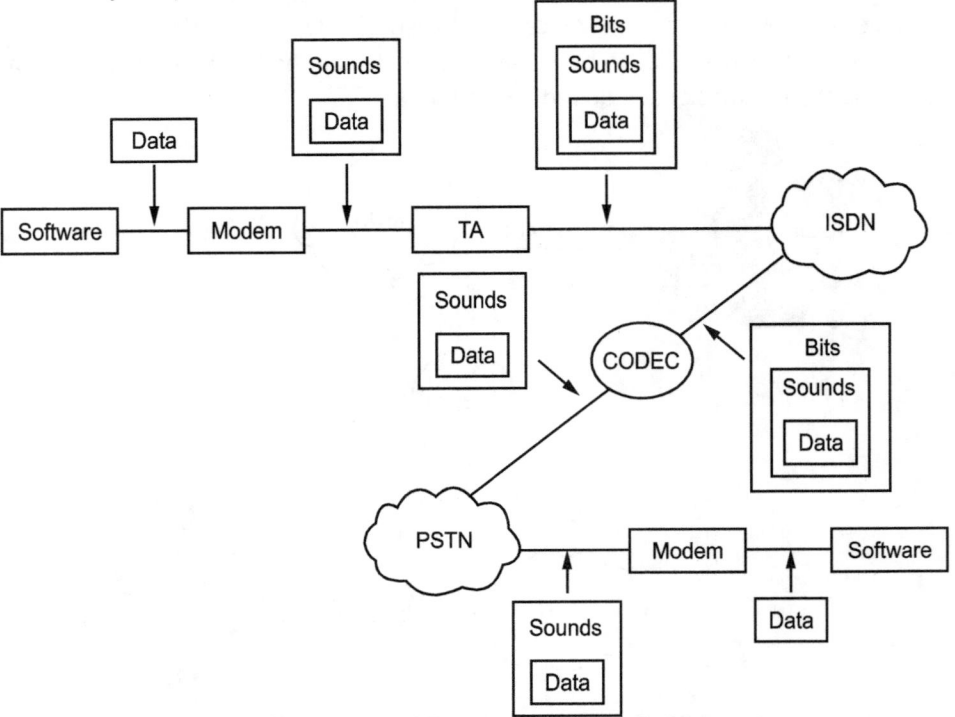

Fig. 2.14: Analog fax and modem over ISDN (Scenario-1)

- Starting in the bottom right-hand corner, data leaves the PC as bits that are converted into sounds by the modem. We now have data encapsulated in sounds.
- These sounds cross the PSTN network until they are encapsulated inside a bit stream by the CODEC at the boundary between the ISDN and the PSTN. This bit stream is then passed from the ISDN network to the Terminal Adapter, which contains a CODEC that converts the bit stream back into sounds. These sounds are sent to the modem at the top left, which converts this back into the original data that entered the modem at the bottom left.
- The process runs in the opposite direction to send the data from the PC in the top left-hand corner to the PC in the bottom right-hand corner. This appears to be a lot of work: the data sent across the ISDN has been encapsulated twice.

2.3.8.5 Analogue Fax and Modem over ISDN (Scenario-2)

- The next step in evolving this configuration is to use an internal modem in the PC.

- Logically this is not different from the previous scenario.

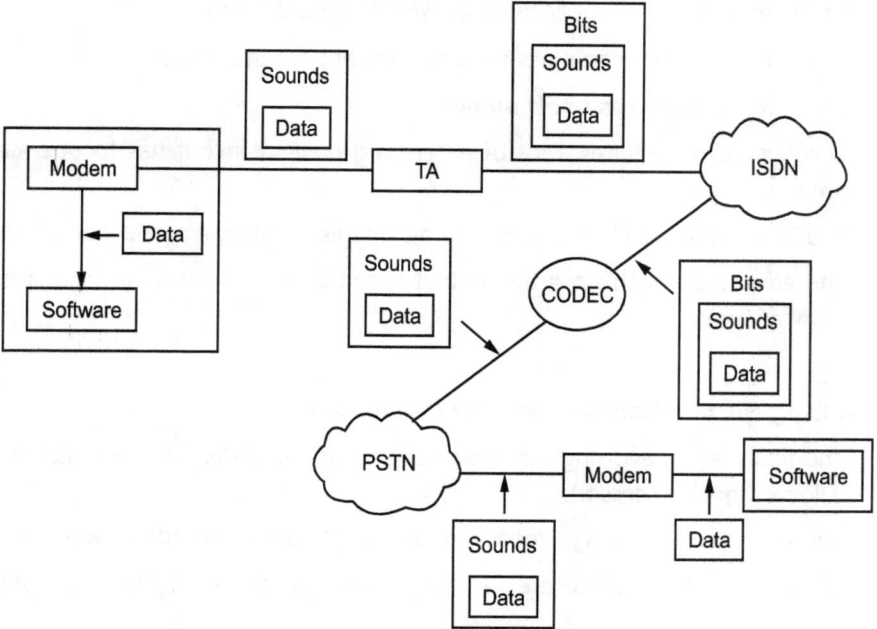

Fig. 2.15: Analog fax and modem over ISDN (Scenario-2)

2.3.8.6 Analog Fax and Modem over ISDN (Scenario-3)

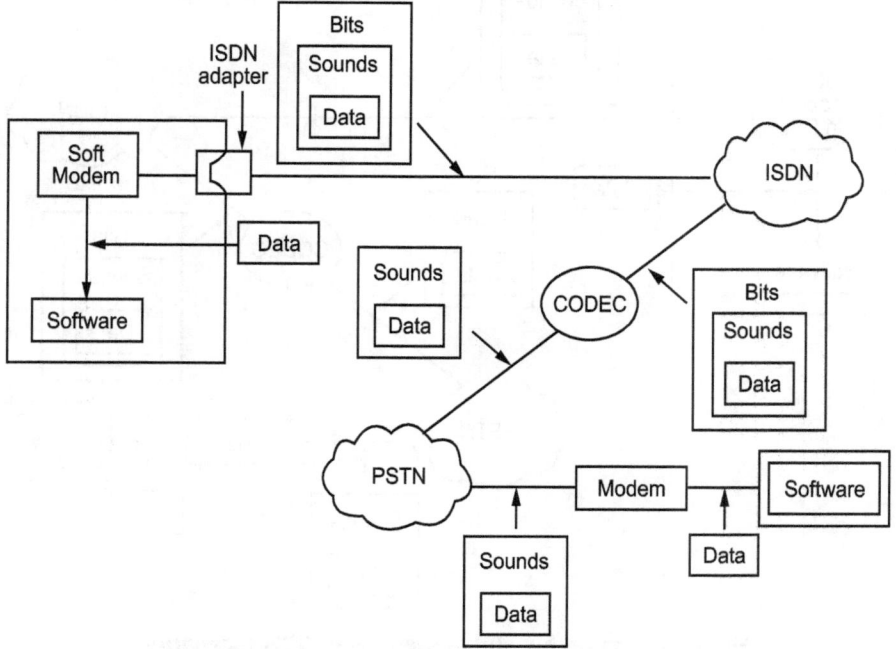

Fig. 2.16: Analog fax and modem over ISDN (Scenario-3)

- We could replace the internal modem with an internal ISDN adapter and a driver, which appears to the application software to be a modem.
- In reality, this driver combines the functions of both the modem and the CODEC.
- This driver is known as a **soft modem**.
- A soft modem requires a lot of processing power, since it has to operate in real time.
- The PC is therefore likely to appear a bit sluggish while the connection is active.
- The advantage of this solution is that it can be used with an inexpensive passive ISDN adapter.

2.3.8.7 Analog Fax and Modem over ISDN (Scenario-4)

- The final step in evolving this scenario is to use an ISDN adapter which has a DSP (Digital Signal Processor).
- This takes the very heavy processing load due to the soft modem away from the PC.
- ISDN adapters with a DSP are generally more expensive than passive adapters.

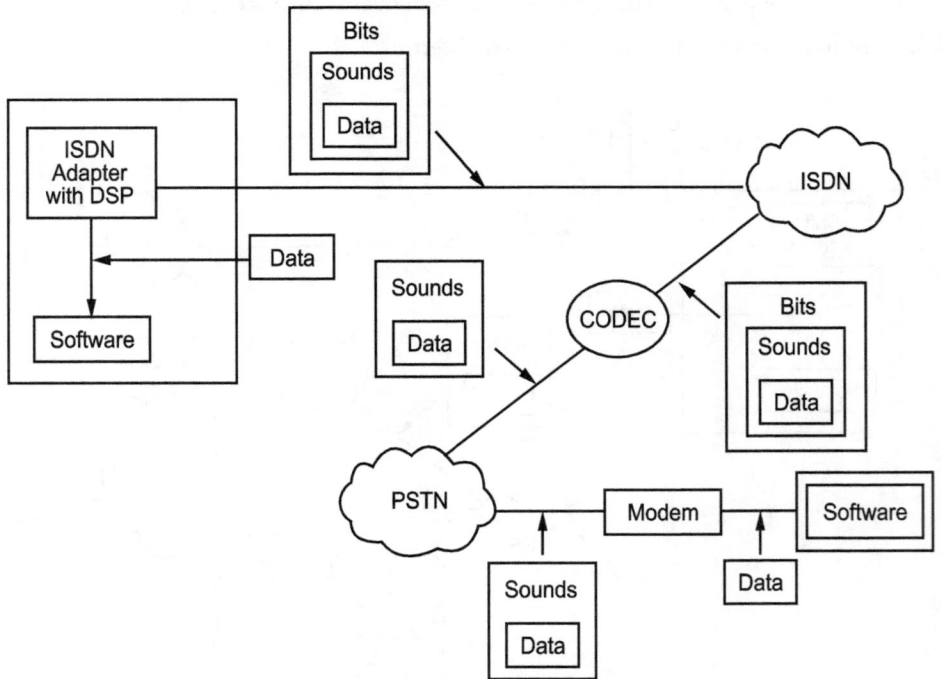

Fig. 2.17: Analog fax and modem over ISDN (Scenario-4)

2.3.8.8 Soft Fax and Soft Modem

- This means that an ISDN adapter with an on-board DSP can also communicate with any device that contains a modem.
- In Fig. 2.18, you can see that we have added a fax machine.

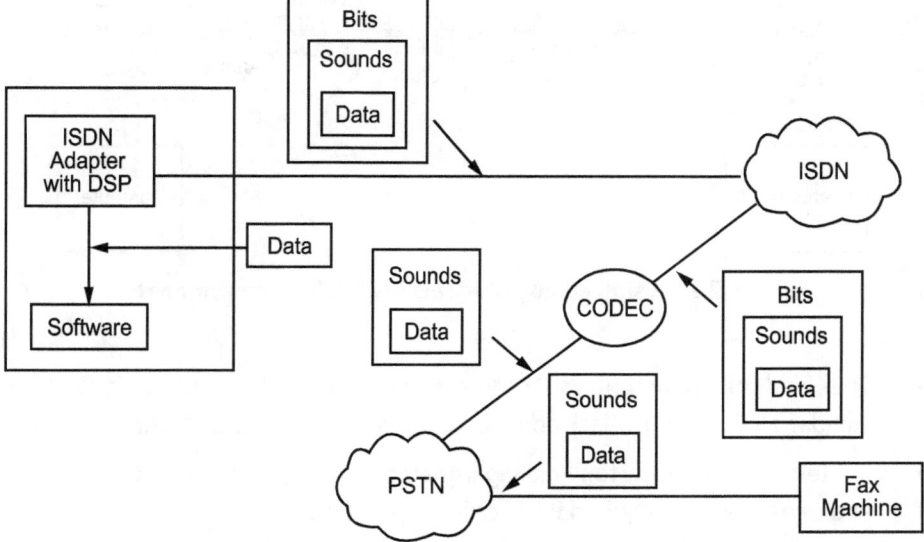

Fig. 2.18: Typical soft fax and soft modem concept implemented

- To perform the job of a modem and a CODEC at the same requires a large amount of processing power.
- DSPs are very powerful processors.
- Nevertheless, you need one DSP for each B channel for which you want to use this technique.
- There is, however, no reason why you could not use an ISDN adapter that has a single DSP and a soft modem driver to handle two modem calls at a time.

2.3.8.9 Analog Modems and ISDN

- So who will you call with your brand new ISDN connectivity? The obvious first answer is your Internet Service Provider (ISP).
- Many ISPs are recognizing the performance and reliability improvements of ISDN over modems and are rolling out ISDN services.
- The data applications of ISDN shown so far, all require that both parties in the connection have ISDN or packet data service.

- What if you need to connect with somebody that isn't ISDN capable? The answer is that you use your analog modem and a TA that supports analog voice connections, or POTS.

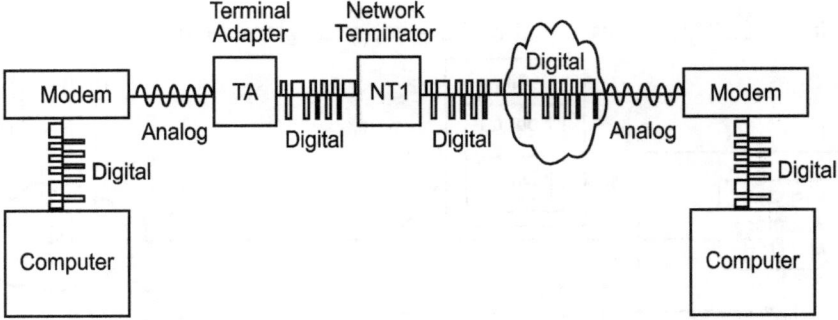

Fig. 2.19: Using analog modems in an ISDN environment

- This kind of TA accepts an ordinary voice or modem audio signal through a standard RJ11 modular jack and digitizes it for transport across the ISDN interface.
- It interprets the touch-tone dialing signals put out by your telephone set or modem and generates the required ISDN call-setup signals.
- If the number you are calling is not an ISDN POP, the telecommunication equipment at the remote end automatically translates the digitized audio back to analog audio, where the destination modem (or human being) hears what it is always heard before ISDN came along.
- In fact, some ISDN TAs include built-in analog modems (sometimes anomalously called "digital modems") just to provide compatibility with existing analog fax and data devices.
- So plan on keeping your modems around at least until the end of the decade; you will still need them occasionally. Fortunately, many TAs provide PSTN's ports without much additional cost, so this is a painless necessity.

Thus we can summarize this ISDN and communication of software, modem and fax machine as follows:
- In ISDN networks everything is carried as a stream of bits.
- Converting digital telephone signals into voice, and vice versa, is done by CODECs.
- Converting data into analog telephone signals, and vice versa, is done by modems.
- A CODEC is the device that allows telephony between an ISDN and the analog network.

- This same CODEC can be used to allow modem and fax calls to cross the same boundary.
- Modems and CODECs always work in pairs - they can be nested together but each must have a partner.
- A Terminal Adapter is an interface between the ISDN and any non-ISDN device, such as a computer or an analog phone.
- If analog devices need to be connected to the ISDN, then the Terminal Adapter will need to perform the function of a CODEC, and have analog (POTS) ports available for modems and fax machines to plug into.
- Internal ISDN adapters can use dedicated chips on the card, or software running on the PC, to implement the digital and analog conversions, thereby removing the requirement for any physical analog devices like fax machines and modems.
- There are three kinds of devices used in data communications with ISDN:
    1. Conventional Modems - These require Terminal Adapter to connect to the ISDN.
    2. ISDN Modems - These combine the functionality of CODEC and modem.
    3. Terminal Adapter - It allows analog devices to connect to the ISDN and contain a CODEC for this purpose.
    4. ISDN Adapters - These merely pass a stream of bits between a protocol driver and the ISDN.

2.3.9 ISDN Equipment and Interface Terminology

U-INTERFACE	U-interface is a 2-wire **digital telephone line** that runs from the telephone company's central office (CO) to an NT1 device. The customer is responsible for supplying all the equipments from the U-interface forward.
NT-1 **Network Termination Type 1**	The **NT1** acts as the boundary between the customer premise and the phone company's network. **NT1** is a Basic Rate **ISDN-only device** that converts a service provider's U-interface to a customer's S/T-interface. It can be stand-alone or integrated into a terminal adapter. The **NT1** interface combines the two B channels and the D channel into a single bit stream at the physical level and is also capable of supporting more than one device attached to an ISDN line, sometimes referred to as a multi-drop configuration.

S/T -INTERFACE	S/T-interface is a common way of referring to either an S- or T-interface. The S/T-interface breaks the signal into two paths- **one transmit, one receive**. In an ISDN PBX, the **NT1** connects using the **T**-interface, and the PBX connects using the S-interface. This intermediate track is called **NT2**.
TE1 **Terminal Equipment Type 1**	**TE1** (Terminal Equipment Type 1) is **ISDN-ready** equipment that can directly connect to the ISDN line (often using an **S/ T**-interface). Examples are ISDN phones, ISDN routers, ISDN computers, etc. They are manufactured from the outset to be completely ISDN compatible.
R-INTERFACE	**R**-interface is a **non-ISDN** interface such as an EIA-232 or a V.35 interface. **R**-interface provides a non-ISDN interface between equipment that is not ISDN compatible with the rest of the ISDN network.
TA **Terminal Adapter**	**TA** is a device that allows non-ISDN-ready equipment, such as PCs, to connect to an ISDN line.
TE2 **Terminal Equipment Type 2**	**TE2** is an equipment that **cannot directly connect** to an ISDN line. A common example of this device is a PC, or a non-ISDN-ready router. **TA** must be used to connect to the ISDN line. Examples of TE2 are RS-232 or [X.25] interface based devices, such as personal computers.
SPID **Service Profile ID**	The **SPID** is a number assigned to an ISDN line by the ISDN service provider that identifies certain characteristics of the line. Usually this number is the telephone number **PLUS** 0101 as an identifier.

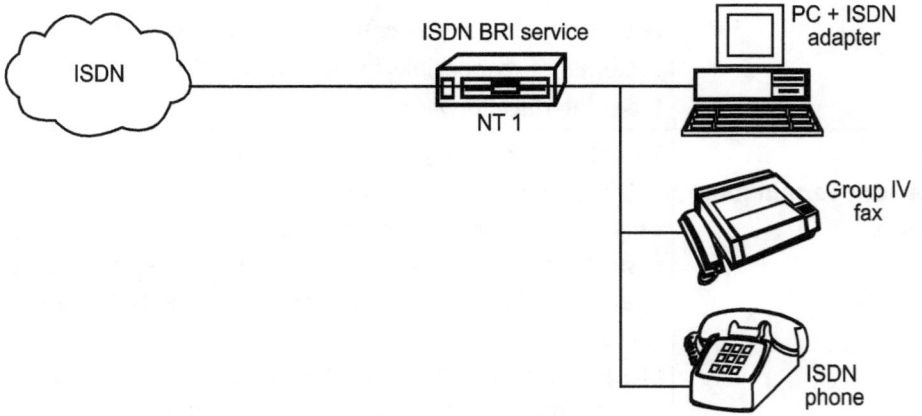

Fig. 2.20: Typical use of NT1 Interface

2.3.9.1 Interfaces

- Generally, the **telephone company** provides its BRI customers with a **U-interface**.
- The U-interface is a two-wire (single pair) interface from the phone switch.
- It supports full-duplex data transfer over a single pair of wires, therefore only a single device can be connected to a U-interface.
- This device is called a **Network Termination-1 (NT-1)**.
- The NT-1 is a relatively simple device that converts the 2-wire U-interfaces into the 4-wire **S/T-interface**.
- The S/T-interface supports multiple devices (upto 7 devices can be placed on the S/T bus) because, while it is still a full-duplex interface, there is now a pair of wires for receiving data, and another for transmitting data.
- Today, many devices have NT-1s built into their design.
- Technically, ISDN devices must go through a **Network Termination-2 (NT-2)** device, which converts the T-interface into the S-interface (Note: the S and T-interfaces are electrically equivalent).
- Virtually all ISDN devices include an NT-2 in their design.
- The NT-2 communicates with terminal equipment, and handles the Layer 2 and 3 ISDN protocols.
- Devices most commonly expect either a U-interface connection (these have a built-in NT-1), or an S/T-interface connection.
- Devices, that connect to the S/T (or S) interface, include ISDN capable telephones and FAX machines, video teleconferencing equipment, bridge/ routers, and terminal adapters. All devices, that are designed for ISDN, are designated **Terminal Equipment 1 (TE1)**.
- All other communication devices that are *not* ISDN capable, but have a POTS telephone interface (also called the **R interface**), including ordinary analog telephones, FAX machines, and modems, are designated **Terminal Equipment 2 (TE2)**.
- A **Terminal Adapter (TA)** connects a TE2 to an ISDN S/T bus.
- Going one step in the opposite direction takes us inside the telephone switch.
- Remember that the U-interface connects the switch to the customer premises equipment.
- This local loop connection is called *Line Termination* (LT function).

- The connection to other switches within the phone network is called *Exchange Termination* (ET function).
- The LT function and the ET function communicate via. the **V-interface**.

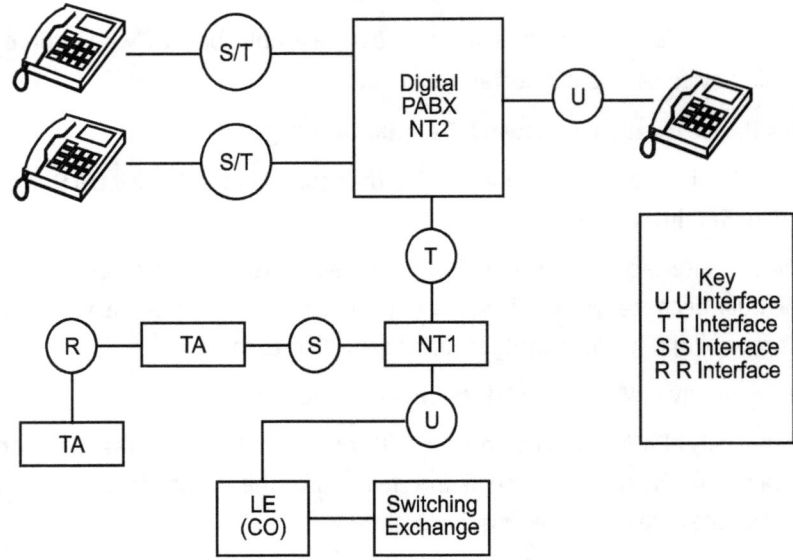

Fig. 2.21: An interface ('reference point') is said to exist between each piece of equipment on the ISDN

2.3.9.2 Examples

NETWORK INTERFACE	RJ-45 for ISDN Basic Rate U-interface (built-in NT1) 128 kbps
DTE INTERFACE	EIA-232 (DB-25) Modem pass through port (3000 only)
DTE DATA RATES	1.2 to 230.4 kbps asynchronous 2400 to 128 kbps synchronous (3010 only)
COMPRESSION	According to standards
PROTOCOLS	Multilink PPP, ITU-T V.120, Clear Channel, Async. BONDING etc.
DIALING SELECTIONS	AT commands, DTR assertion, V.25 bis.
DIAGNOSTICS AND TESTING	Network loopback Remote configuration
ANALOG PORTS	Two standard RJ-11 Each port rings upto three phones within 500 feet

CUSTOM CALLING FEATURES	• Stutter dial tone • Three- and six-way • Conferencing • Call forwarding • Reminder ring • Auto call back • Distinctive ring • Caller ID • Implicit transfer • Visual message waiting indication (Custom calling features must be provided by telephone company.)
ENVIRONMENT	Operating Temperature: 0° to 50°C, (32° to 122°F) Storage Temperature: –20° to 70°C, (–4° to 158°F) Relative Humidity: Upto 95%, non-condensing
PRODUCT INCLUDES	110 V wallmount power supply, CD ROM, one cable to connect ISDN line

2.3.10 ISDN and OSI Architecture

From the point of view of the OSI architecture, an ISDN line has a stack of three protocols –

- Physical layer.
- Data link layer.
- Network layer (the ISDN protocol, properly).

Network layer (the ISDN protocol, properly)
(Layer 3)
Data link layer
(Layer 2)
Physical layer
(Layer 1)

Fig. 2.22: ISDN line has a stack of three protocols

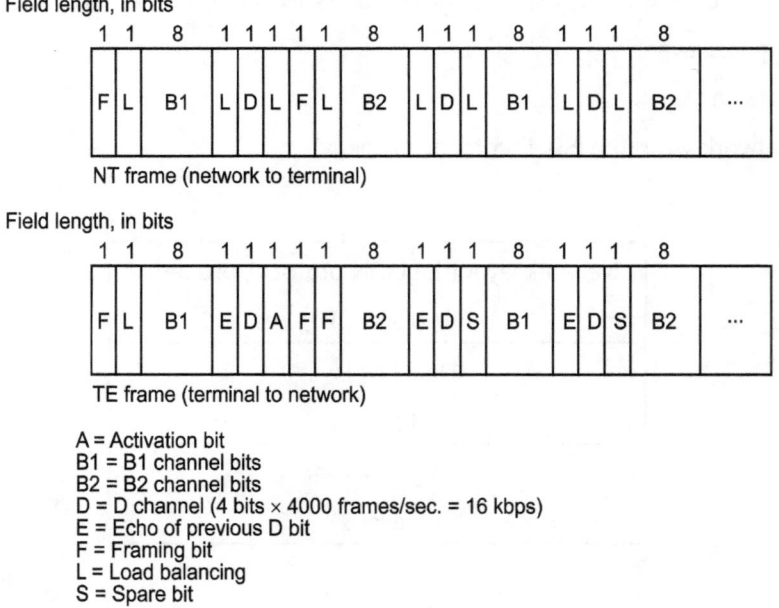

Fig. 2.23: The ISDN is illustrated here in relation to the OSI model

Layer 1 (Physical Layer):

1. ISDN physical layer (Layer 1) frame formats differ depending on whether the frame is outbound (from terminal to network) or inbound (from network to terminal).
2. Both physical layer interfaces are shown in Fig. 2.24.

Field length, in bits

| 1 1 | 8 | 1 1 1 1 1 | 8 | 1 1 1 | 8 | 1 1 1 | 8 |

| F L | B1 | L D L F L | B2 | L D L | B1 | L D L | B2 | ... |

NT frame (network to terminal)

Field length, in bits

| 1 1 | 8 | 1 1 1 1 1 | 8 | 1 1 1 | 8 | 1 1 1 | 8 |

| F L | B1 | E D A F F | B2 | E D S | B1 | E D S | B2 | ... |

TE frame (terminal to network)

A = Activation bit
B1 = B1 channel bits
B2 = B2 channel bits
D = D channel (4 bits × 4000 frames/sec. = 16 kbps)
E = Echo of previous D bit
F = Framing bit
L = Load balancing
S = Spare bit

Fig. 2.24: ISDN Physical layer frame formats

3. The frames are 48 bits long, of which 36 bits represent data. The bits of an ISDN physical layer frame are used as follows:
   - *F* – Provides synchronization.
   - *L* – Adjusts the average bit value.
   - *E* – Used for contention resolution when several terminals on a passive bus contend for a channel.
   - *A* – Activates devices.
   - *S* – Unassigned.
   - B1, B2, and D – Used for user data (B1 for B1 channel bits and B2 for B2 channel bits).
4. Multiple ISDN user devices can be physically attached to one circuit.
5. In this configuration, collisions can result if two terminals transmit simultaneously.
6. ISDN therefore provides features to determine link contention.
7. When an NT receives a D bit from the TE, it echoes back the bit in the next E bit position.
8. The TE expects the next E bit to be the same as its last transmitted D bit.
9. Terminals cannot transmit into the D channel unless they first detect a specific number of ones (indicating "no signal") corresponding to a pre-established priority.
10. If the TE detects a bit in the echo (E) channel that is different from its D bits, it must stop transmitting immediately.
11. This simple technique ensures that only one terminal can transmit its D message at one time.
12. After successful D message transmission, the terminal has its priority reduced by requiring it to detect more continuous ones before transmitting.
13. Terminals cannot raise their priority until all other devices on the same line have had an opportunity to send a D message.
14. Telephone connections have higher priority than all other services, and signaling information has a higher priority than non-signaling information.

Layer 2 (Data Link Layer):

1. Layer 2 of the ISDN signaling protocol is *Link Access Procedure, D channel*, also known as *LAPD*.
2. As LAPD's acronym indicates, it is used across the **D channel** to ensure that control and signaling information flows and has been received properly.

3. LAPD is similar to *High-Level Data Link Control* (HDLC) [HDLC supports a variety of link types and topologies. It can be used with point-to-point and multipoint links, bounded and unbounded media, half-duplex and full-duplex transmission facilities, and circuit-switched and packet-switched networks].
4. LAPD is similar to *Link Access Procedure, Balanced* (LAPB). [LAPB is best known for its presence in the X.25 (WAN service) protocol stack].
5. As the expansion of the LAPD acronym indicates, it is used across the D channel to ensure that control and signaling information flows and is received properly.
6. The LAPD frame format (see Fig. 2.25) uses *supervisory, information,* and *unnumbered* frames.

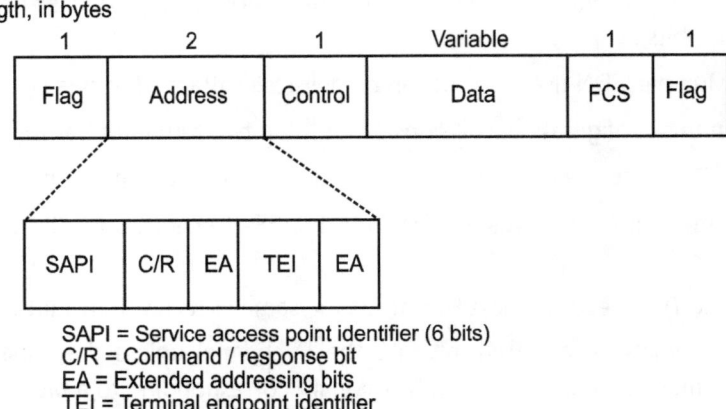

Fig. 2.25: LAPD Frame Format

7. The LAPD *address* field can be either one or two bytes long.

8. If the extended address bit of the first byte is set, the address is one byte; if it is not set, the address is two bytes.

9. The first address field byte contains the *service access point identifier* (SAPI), which identifies the portal at which LAPD services are provided to Layer 3.

10. The C/R bit indicates whether the frame contains a command or a response.

11. The *terminal end-point identifier* (TEI) field identifies either a single terminal or multiple terminals. A TEI of all ones indicates a broadcast.

12. **FCS:** The Frame Check Sequence (FCS) enables a high level of physical error control by allowing the integrity of the transmitted frame data to be checked. The sequence is first calculated by the transmitter using an algorithm based on the values of all the bits in the frame. The receiver then performs the same calculation on the received frame and compares its value to the CRC.

13. **Window size:** LAPD supports an extended window size (modulo 128) where the number of possible outstanding frames for acknowledgement is raised from 8 to

128. This extension is generally used for satellite transmissions where the acknowledgement delay is significantly greater than the frame transmission times. The type of the link initialization frame determines the modulo of the session and an "E" is added to the basic frame type name (e.g., SABM becomes SABME).

14. Frame types:

The following are the Supervisory Frame Types in LAPD:

RR	Information frame acknowledgement and indication to receive more.
REJ	Request for retransmission of all frames after a given sequence number.
RNR	Indicates a state of temporary occupation of station (e.g., window full).

15. The following are the Unnumbered Frame Types in LAPD:

DISC	Request disconnection
UA	Acknowledgement frame
DM	Response to DISC indicating disconnected mode.
FRMR	Frame reject
SABM	Initiator for asynchronous balanced mode. No master/slave relationship
SABME	SABM in extended mode
UI	Unnumbered Information
XID	Exchange Information

Layer 3 (Network Layer):

1. Two Layer-3 specifications are used for ISDN signaling.
2. Together, these protocols support user-to-user, circuit-switched, and packet-switched connections.
3. A variety of call establishment, call termination, information, and miscellaneous messages are specified, including SETUP, CONNECT, RELEASE, USER INFORMATION, CANCEL, STATUS, and DISCONNECT.
4. Fig. 2.26 shows the typical stages of an ISDN circuit-switched call.

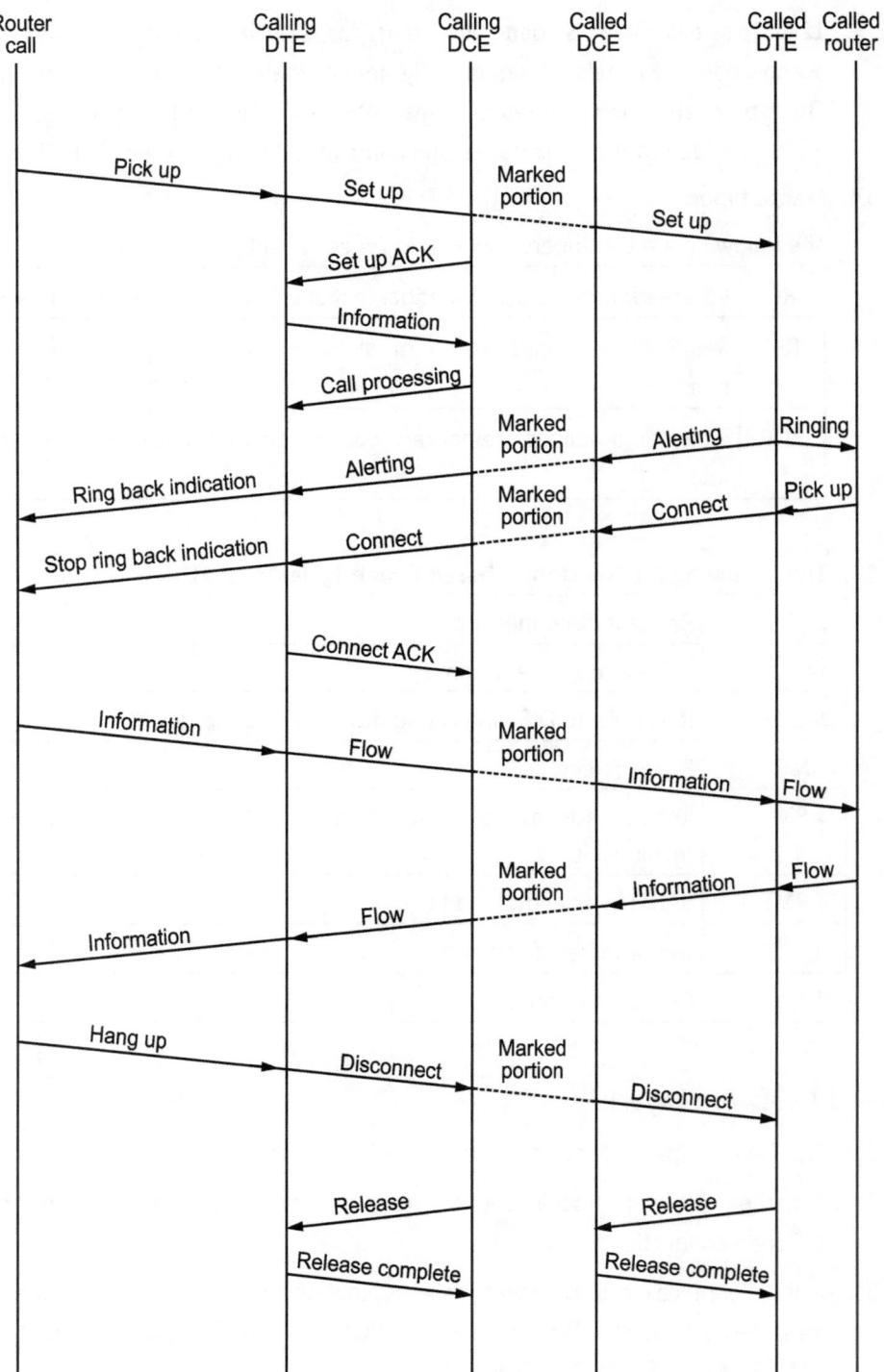

Fig. 2.26: ISDN circuit-switched call stages

2.4 SS7 Protocol

2.4.1 Introduction

Common Channel Signaling is a signaling method in which a signaling channel conveys, by means of labeled messages, signaling information relating to call setup, control, network management, and network maintenance. Examples of Common Channel Signaling systems are CCITT Signaling System No. 7 and various national versions such as ANSI SS7 as originated by the original Bell Communications Research (now named Telcordia Technologies) and AT&Ts original SS6 and SS7 standards.

2.4.2 The Need for SS7

Worldwide telephone networks are undergoing significant changes as methods of call processing and network management are altered to provide new services and to streamline operations. These changes are driven by user demand for enhanced services and the corresponding efforts of telephone operating companies to satisfy current and future needs. Enhanced services require bi-directional signaling capabilities, flexibility of call setup, and remote database access. Earlier signaling systems lacked the sophistication required to deliver much more than plain old telephone service (POTS). These traditional systems use dial pulses and multi-frequency (MF) tones to transmit call and circuit related information such as dialed digits and circuit busy/idle states.

The complexity of adding new functionality to traditional signaling systems meant that a new network signaling architecture was needed. SS7 was developed to satisfy the telephone operating companies' requirements for an improvement to existing signaling systems.

2.4.3 Basic SS7 Network Architecture

A telecommunications network consists of a number of switches and application processors interconnected by transmission circuits. The SS7 network exists within the telecommunications network and controls it. SS7 achieves this control by creating and transferring call processing, network management, and maintenance messages to the network's various components. Fig. 2.28 shows that a SS7 network has three distinct components: Service Switching Points (SSP), Signal Transfer Points (STP), and Service Control Points (SCP). These components may be generically referred to as "nodes" or "signaling points."

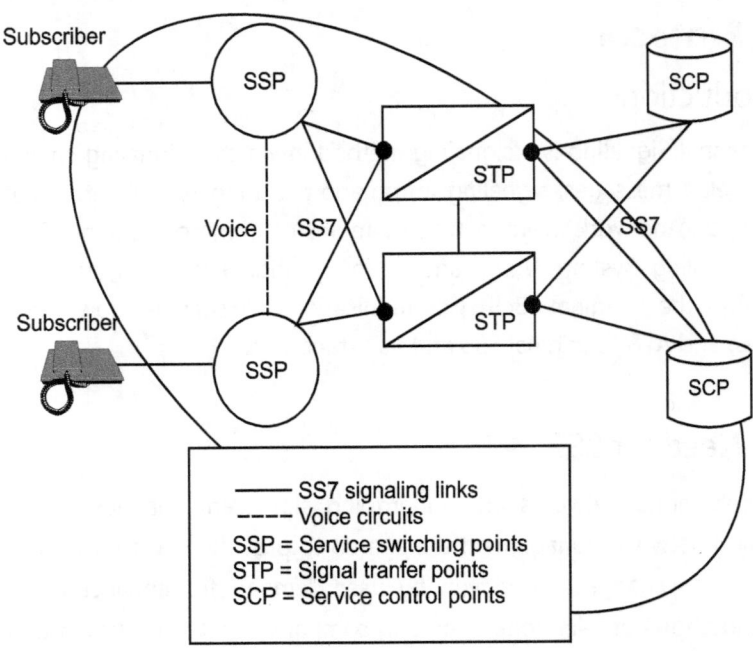

Fig. 2.27: SS7 Signaling Network Architecture

2.4.4 SS7 Signaling Link Types

The lines that transfer messages in the SS7 system are called signaling links. Signaling links are logically organized by link type ("A" through "F") according to their use within the SS7 signaling network. Figure 1.2 shows the relationship between the link names and the link location (type). Signaling links are logically organized by link type ("A" through "F") according to their use in the SS7 signaling network. The "A" (access) links connect the signaling end points (e.g., an SCP or SSP) to the STPs. Only messages originating from or destined to the signaling end point are transmitted on an "A" link. The "B" (bridge) links connect the STP to another STP.

The "C" (cross) link connects STPs performing identical functions into a mated pair. "D" (diagonal) links connect the secondary (e.g., local or regional) STP pair to a primary (e.g., inter-network gateway) STP pair in a quad-link configuration. "E" (extended) links connect the SSP to an alternate STP. An "F" (fully associated) link is connected between two signaling end points (i.e., SSPs and SCPs).

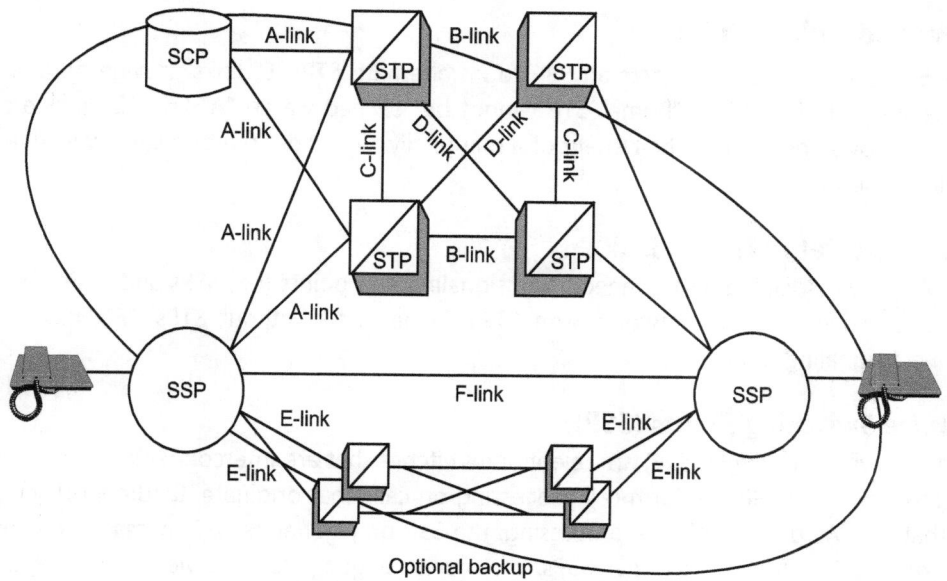

Fig. 2.28: SS7 Signaling Link Types

Access Link (A Link):

An "A" (access) link connects a signaling end point (e.g., an SCP or SSP) to an STP. Only messages originating from or destined to the signaling end point are transmitted on an "A" link.

Bridge Link (B Link):

A "B" (bridge) link connects an STP to another STP. Typically, a quad of "B" links interconnect peer (or primary) STPs (e.g., the STPs from one network to the STPs of another network). The distinction between a "B" link and a "D" link is rather arbitrary. For this reason, such links may be referred to as "B/D" links.

Cross Link (C Link):

A "C" (cross) link connects STPs performing identical functions into a mated pair. A "C" link is used only when an STP has no other route available to a destination signaling point due to link failure(s). Note that SCPs may also be deployed in pairs to improve reliability; unlike STPs, however, mated SCPs are not interconnected by signaling links.

Diagonal Link (D Link):

A "D" (diagonal) link connects a secondary (e.g., local or regional) STP pair to a primary (e.g., inter-network gateway) STP pair in a quad-link configuration. Secondary STPs within the same network are connected via a quad of "D" links. The distinction between a "B" link and a "D" link is rather arbitrary. For this reason, such links may be referred to as "B/D" links.

Extended Link (E Link):
An "E" (extended) link connects an SSP to an alternate STP. "E" links provide an alternate signaling path if an SSP's "home" STP cannot be reached via an "A" link. "E" links are not usually provisioned unless the benefit of a marginally higher degree of reliability justifies the added expense.

Fully Associated Link (F Link):
An "F" (fully associated) link connects two signaling end points (i.e., SSPs and SCPs). "F" links are not usually used in networks with STPs. In networks without STPs, "F" links directly connect signaling points.

Service Switching Points (SSP):
Service Switching Points (SSP) are telephone switches that are interconnected to each other by SS7 links. The SSPs perform call processing on calls that originate, tandem, or terminate at that site. As part of this call processing, the SSP may generate SS7 messages to transfer call-related information to other SSPs, or to send a query to a Service Control Point for instructions on how to route a call.

Signal Transfer Points (STP):
Signal Transfer Points (STP) are switches that relay messages between network switches and databases. Their main function is to route SS7 messages to the correct outgoing signaling link, based on information contained in the SS7 message address fields.

Service Control Points (SCP):
Service Control Points (SCP) contain centralized network databases for providing enhanced services. The SCP accepts queries from an SSP and returns the requested information to the originator of the query. For example, enhanced 800 service uses an SCP database to determine the routing on 800 calls. When an 800 call is initiated by the user, the originating SSP sends a query to an 800 database requesting information to the SSP originating the query and the call proceeds.

2.4.5 SS7 Reliability
To meet the stringent reliability requirements of public telecommunications networks, a number of safeguards are built into the SS7 protocol:
- STPs and SCPs are normally provisioned in mated pairs. On the failure of individual components, this duplication allows signaling traffic to be automatically diverted to an alternate resource, minimizing the impact on service.
- Signaling links are provisioned with some level of redundancy. Signaling traffic is automatically diverted to alternate links in the case of link failures.
- The SS7 protocol has built-in error recovery mechanisms to ensure reliable transfer of signaling messages in the event of a network failure.

2.4.6 ISDN Access Protocol

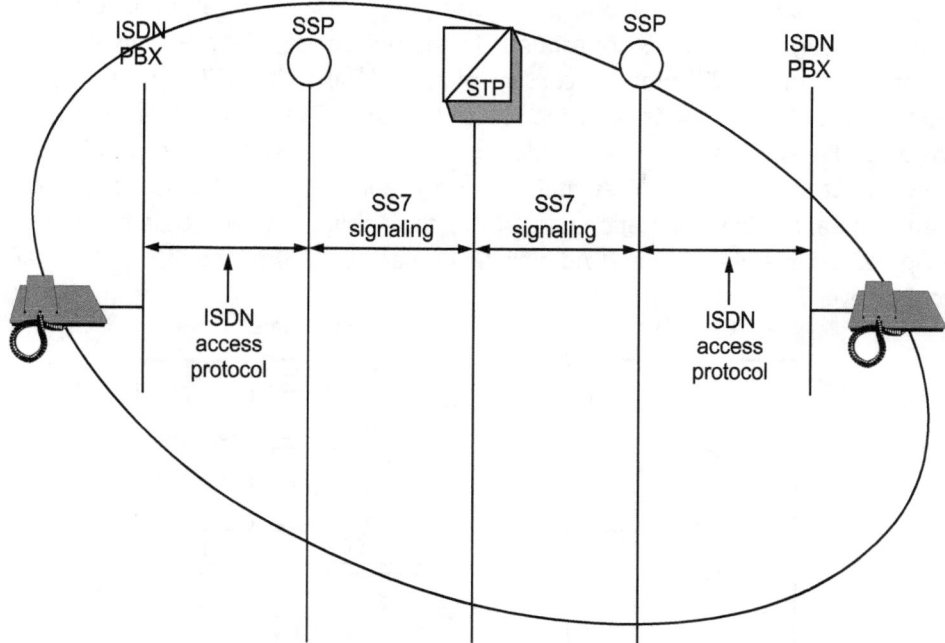

Fig. 2.29: ISDN-AP and SS7 Interface

The Integrated Services Digital Network (ISDN) protocol was designed to provide advanced control messages for the end users. While the SS7 system was designed to provide an internationally standardized, general-purpose signaling system; it was not intended to be used as the signaling standard for access to the telephone network from PBXs or from telephone sets. To satisfy this latter need, the ISDN-AP (Integrated Services Digital Network – Access Protocol) has been developed. Fig. 2.30 shows how the ISDN access protocol can be interconnected with the SS7 system at the telephone switch (SSP) through the user of an ISDNAP/ SS7 Interface. When working together, SS7 and the ISDN-AP provide the end-to-end signaling required to deliver enhanced features to users. As an interim step, some telephone exchange carriers use proprietary access signaling to provide enhanced services.

2.4.7 SS7 Mapped Onto the OSI Layer Model

The Open Systems Interconnection (OSI) standard layer model was developed by the International Standards Organization (ISO) and the CCITT. The OSI model helps to standardize the inter-connection of computers and data terminals to their applications, regardless of their type or manufacturer. The protocols specify seven layers: physical, link, network, transport, session, presentation, and application. Each layer performs specific functions for data exchange and is independent of the other layers. Fig. 2.30 shows how the SS7 layers compare to the OSI 7-Layer Reference Model. The bottom half of the SS7 protocol consists of the Message Transfer Part (MTP). There are three levels to the MTP: Level 1 corresponds to the OSI Layer 1 (Physical Layer); Level 2 corresponds to OSI Layer 2 (Data Link Layer); and, Level 3 corresponds to the bottom of OSI Layer 3 (Network Layer). The upper half of the SS7 protocol consists of several parts. The SS7 Signaling Connection Control Part (SCCP) corresponds to the top of OSI Layer 3. The ISDN-User Part (ISDN-UP) maps onto OSI layer 3 as well, and, in addition, it maps onto Layer 4 (Transport Layer), Layer 5 (Session Layer), Layer 6 (Presentation Layer), and Layer 7 (Application Layer). The Transaction Capabilities Application Part (TCAP), the Application Service Elements (ASE), and the Operations, Maintenance and Administration Part (OMAP) of the SS7 protocol all map onto OSI Layer 7 as well.

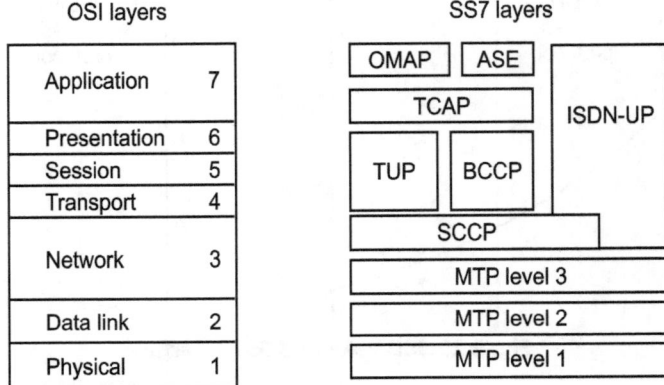

Fig. 2.30: Comparison of the SS7 Protocol Layers and the OSI Model Layers

2.4.8 SS7 Protocol Stack in Detail

This chapter describes the components of the SS7 protocol stack. A stack is a set of data storage locations that are accessed in a fixed sequence. The SS7 stack is compared against the Open Systems Interconnection (OSI) model for communication between different systems made by different vendors.

Fig. 2.32 shows the components of the SS7 protocol stack.

2.4.8.1 SS7 Level 1: Physical Connection

This is the physical level of connectivity, virtually the same as Layer 1 of the OSI model. SS7 specifies what interfaces will be used, for example DS0A or V.35 interface.

Because central offices are already using DS1 and DS3 facilities to link one another, the DS0A interface is readily available in all central offices, and is preferred in the SS7 network. As the demands on the SS7 network increase (local number portability), and as the industry migrates toward ATM networks, the DS1 interface will become the link interface.

2.4.8.2 SS7 Level 2: Data Link

The data link level provides the network with sequenced delivery of all SS7 message packets. Like the OSI data link layer, it is only concerned with the transmission of data from one node to the next, not to its final destination in the network.

Sequential numbering is used to determine if any messages have been lost during transmission. Each link uses its own message numbering series independent of other links.

SS7 uses CRC-16 error checking of data and requests retransmission of lost or corrupted messages. Length indicators allow Level 2 to determine what type of signal unit it is receiving, and how to process it.

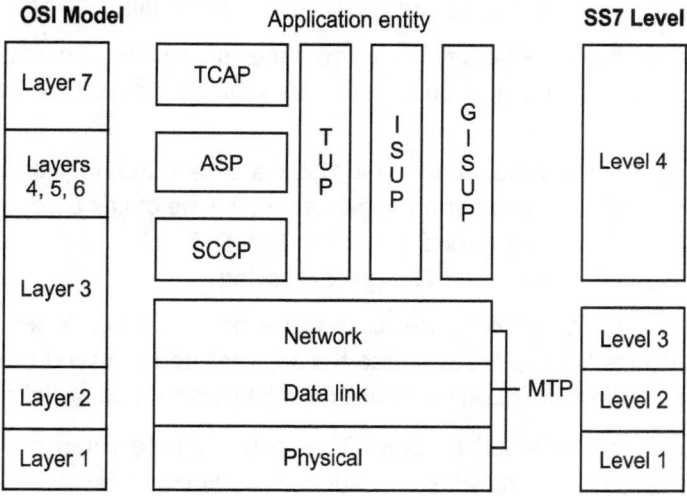

TCAP: Transaction Capabilities Application Part
ASP: Application Service Part
SCCP: Signaling Connection Control Part
TUP: Telephone User Part
ISUP: ISDN User Part
BISUP: Broadband ISDN User Part
MTP: Message Transfer Part

Fig. 2.31: SS7 Protocol Stack

2.4.8.3 SS7 Level 3: Network Level

The network level depends on the services of Level 2 to provide routing, message discrimination and message distribution functions.
- Message Discrimination determines to whom the message is addressed.
- Message Distribution is passed here if it is a local message.
- Message Routing is passed here if it is not a local message.

1 Message Discrimination:

This function determines whether a message is local or remote using the point code and data contained in a lookup table. Messages to remote destinations are passed to the message routing function for additional processing.

2 Message Distribution:

Message distribution provides link, route and traffic management functions.

(a) Link Management: This function uses the Link Status Signal Unit (LSSU) to notify adjacent nodes of link problems. Level 3 will send LSSUs via Level 2 to the adjacent node, notifying it of the problems with the link and its status.

Diagnostics consist of realigning and resynchronizing the link.

- **Realignment:** All traffic is removed from the link, counters are reset to zero, timers are reset and Fill-In Signal Units (FISUs) are sent in the meantime (called the proving period).

- **Proving Period:** Amount of time FISUs are sent during link realignment. The duration of the proving period depends on the type of link used. Specific Company specifies the proving period for a 56 Kbps DS0 link is 2.3 seconds for normal proving and 0.6 seconds for emergency proving.

Another form of link management uses changeover and changeback messages sent using Message Signal Units (MSUs). MSUs advise the adjacent node to send traffic over another link within the same linkset. The alternate link must be within the same linkset.

The bad link is being realigned by Level 3 while traffic is rerouted over alternate links. Changeback message is sent to advise the adjacent node that it can use the newly restored link again. Changeback messages are typically followed by a changeback acknowledgement message.

(b) Route Management: This function provides a means for rerouting traffic around failed or congested nodes. Route management is a function of Level 3 and works together with link management.

Route management informs other nodes of the status of the affected node. It uses Message Signal Units (MSUs) generated by adjacent nodes and is not usually generated by the affected nodes. (Link management only informs adjacent nodes.)

(c) Traffic Management: This function provides flow control if a node has become congested. It allows the network to control the flow of certain messages based on protocol. Traffic management deals with a specific user part within an affected node.

For example, if ISUP is not available at a particular node, a traffic management message can be sent to adjacent nodes informing them that ISUP is not available, without affecting TCAP messages on the same node.

3 Message Routing:

Message discrimination in Level 3 will pass messages to message routing if it determines the message is not local. Message routing reads the called and calling party addresses to determine the physical address in the form of a point code.

Every SS7 node must have its own unique point code. Message routing determines the point code from an address contained in the routing table.

Message Transfer Part:

Protocols are used within the layers (levels) of the SS7 protocol to accomplish functions called for at each level. Levels 1, 2 and 3 are combined into one part, the Message Transfer Part (MTP). (See Fig. 2.32).

MTP provides the rest of the levels with node-to-node transmission, including basic error detection and correction schemes and message sequencing. It provides routing, message discrimination and distribution functions within a node.

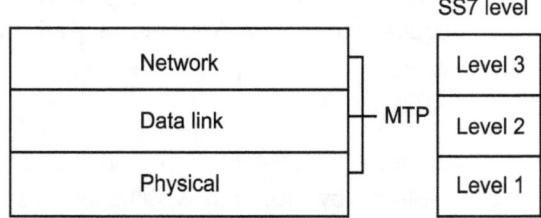

Fig. 2.32: Message Transfer Part Components

2.4.8.4 SS7 Level 4: Protocols, User and Application Parts

Level 4 consists of several protocols, user parts and application parts. (See Fig. 2.33)

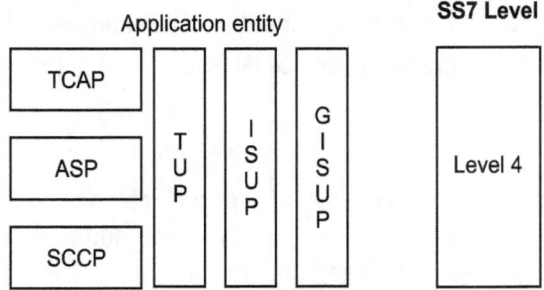

Fig. 2.33: SS7 Level 4 Protocols, User and Application Parts

TCAP:

Transactional Capabilities Application Part (TCAP) facilitates connection to an external database. Information/data received is sent back in the form of a TCAP message. TCAP also supports remote control—ability to invoke features in another remote network switch.

OMAP (Operations, Maintenance and Administrative Part) is an applications entity that uses TCAP services for communications and control functions through the network via a remote terminal. MAP (Mobile Application Part) is used to share cellular subscriber information among different networks. It includes information such as the mobile identification number (MIN), and the serial number of the cellular handset. This information is used by the IS-41 protocol during cellular roaming.

ASP:
Application Service Part (ASP) provides the functions of Layers 4 through 6 of the OSI model. These functions are not presently required in the SS7 network, and are under further study. However, the ITU-T and ANSI standards do reference ASP as viable.

SCCP:
Signaling Connection Control Part (SCCP) is a higher level protocol than MTP that provides end-to-end routing. SCCP is required for routing TCAP messages to their proper database.

TUP:
Telephone User Part (TUP) is an analog protocol that performs basic telephone call connect and disconnect. It has been replaced by ISUP, but is still used in some parts of the world (China).

ISUP:
ISDN User Part (ISUP) supports basic telephone call connect/disconnect between end offices. Used primarily in North America, ISUP was derived from TUP, but supports ISDN and intelligent networking functions. ISUP also links the cellular and PCS network to the PSTN. BISUP (Broadband ISUP) will gradually replace ISUP as ATM is deployed.

BISUP:
Broadband ISDN User Part (BISUP) is an ATM protocol intended to support services such as high-definition television (HDTV), multilingual TV, voice and image storage and retrieval, video conferencing, high-speed LANs and multimedia.

2.5 B-ISDN and ATM
2.5.1 Introduction
1. B-ISDN is an effort by the telephone companies to develop a single integrated digital network that can be used for voice, video, and data communications.

2. Much of the existing telephone system consists of the old circuit-switching equipment that is based on Alexander Graham Bell's original operator-controlled switching system, although far more automatic.
3. In addition, the phone companies have call management systems and newer data services in place such as frame relay.
4. B-ISDN can provide all these services in an integrated framework that scales upto very high data rates.
5. B-ISDN is a CCITT (now referred to as the ITU) recommendation that defines data, voice, and video transmission operating in the megabit-to-gigabit range.
6. As shown in Fig. 2.34, the underlying transfer mode for implementing B-ISDN is cell switching. Refer to "ATM (Asynchronous Transfer Mode)" and "Cell Relay" for more information.
7. In the carrier networks, ATM cells are delivered across a physical network called SONET (Synchronous Optical Network), which now makes up the trunk topology for most of the phone systems.
8. A similar standard used elsewhere in the world is called SDH (Synchronous Digital Hierarchy). SDH is a CCITT recommendation.

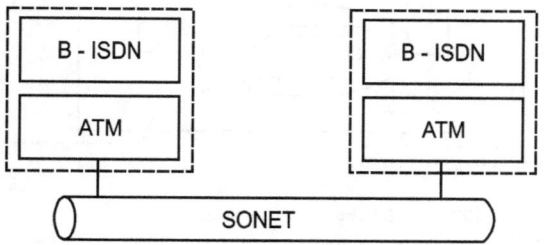

Fig. 2.34: B-ISDN network

9. SONET is the physical transport backbone of B-ISDN.
10. It is a fiber-optic–based networking standard that defines a hierarchy of transmission rates and data framing formats.
11. It is used as a transmission medium to interconnect carrier-switching offices worldwide, and so forms the structure of current and future global communications.
12. B-ISDN, FDDI (Fiber Distributed Data Interface), and SMDS can be transported on SONET networks.
13. SONET is now used as the medium between carrier-switching offices and many customer premises sites.
14. SONET transmission rates start at 51.4 Mbits/sec and increase in 52 Mbits/sec building blocks. Speeds upto 50 Gbits/sec are possible.
15. ATM is the switching technology for B-ISDN and provides B-ISDN users access to the SONET fiber-optic network.

16. Information received at the ATM layer is placed in fixed-length cells, addressed, and transmitted over the SONET network.

17. ATM provides very high-speed switching of these packets between the links attached to the SONET network. ATM takes full advantage of the transmission speeds available on fiber-optic cable.

2.5.2 B-ISDN Architecture

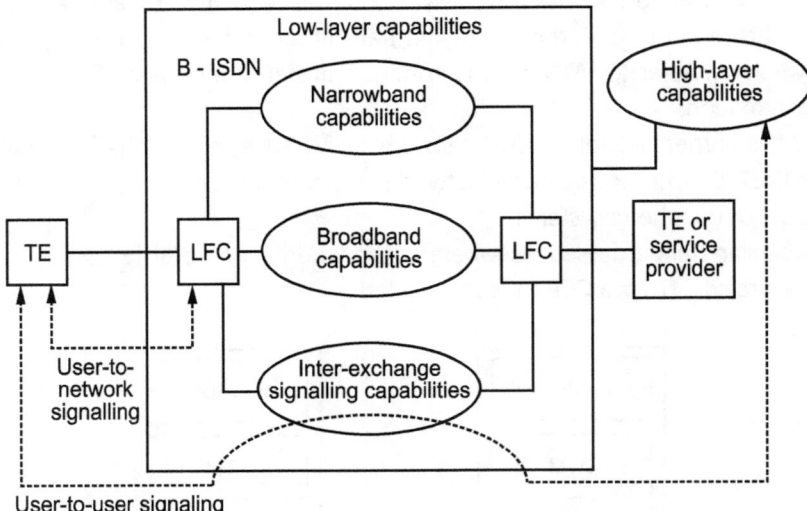

LFC = Local Function Capabilities
TE = Terminal Equipment

Fig. 2.35: B-ISDN architecture

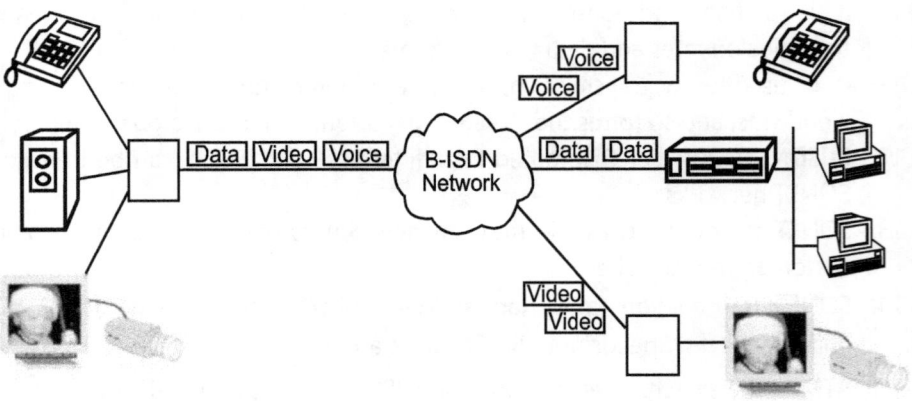

Fig. 2.36: Voice, Video and Data with B-ISDN network

Table 2.1: Typical Broadband Services

Service Categories		Example Services
Interactive Services	Conversational Services	TV Conference
	Messaging Services	Video Mail
	Retrieval Services	Videotex
Distribution Services	Without User Presentation Control	TV Broadcast
	With User Presentation Control	Videography

1. ISDN is a switched service and is designed around intelligent switching components in the carrier network.
2. It allows users to dial any other ISDN point on the network and create a high-speed digital link that can mimic point-to-point T1 lines.
3. However, T1 lines are usually permanently established between two points, while ISDN allows the switching of the line between many different points by the customer.
4. This is due to the intelligent network components. The intelligent network also supports a variety of other services, including call forwarding, caller ID and channel bonding.

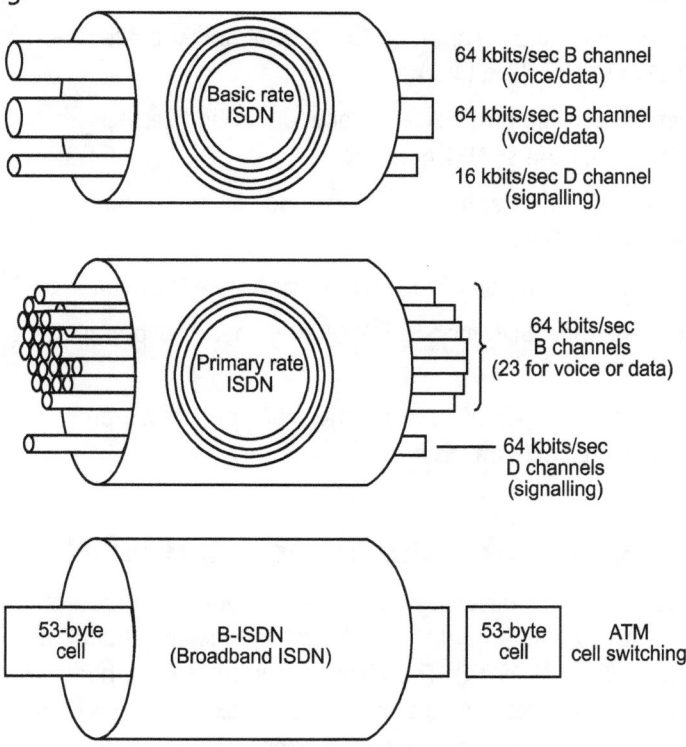

Fig. 2.37: ISDN Implementation

5. B-ISDN provides the intelligent telecommunications services above ATM.
6. It manages the establishment of point-to-point and point-to-multipoint connections through the switched network.
7. It supports on-demand, reserved, and permanent services, as well as connection-oriented and connectionless services.
8. The carriers had big plans to use B-ISDN for services like videotelephony, videoconferencing, electronic newspapers, and TV distribution.
9. Now, B-ISDN is rarely discussed. All you hear about is ATM.
10. SONET is the physical transport backbone of B-ISDN. It is a fiber-optic-based networking standard that defines a hierarchy of transmission rates and data-framing formats.
11. It is used as a transmission medium to interconnect carrier-switching offices worldwide, and so forms the structure of the communications network.
12. SONET is now used as the medium between carrier-switching offices and customers.
13. SONET transmission rates start at 51.4 Mbits/sec and increase in 52 Mbits/sec building blocks.
14. ATM is the switching technology for B-ISDN and provides B-ISDN users access to the SONET fiber-optic network.
15. Information received at the ATM layer is placed in fixed-length cells, addressed, and transmitted over the SONET network.
16. ATM provides very high-speed switching of these packets between the links attached to the SONET network.
17. ATM takes full advantage of the transmission speeds available on fiber-optic cable.
18. Note that neither ISDN nor B-ISDN has gained the popularity envisioned by the carriers.
19. IP networking has gained in popularity and the latest trend is to build converged networks where voice travels in packets.

2.6 Narrow Band-ISDN and Broad Band ISDN

1. The most important development in the computer communications industry in the 1990's is the evolution of the integrated services digital network (ISDN) and broadband ISDN (B-ISDN). The ISDN and B-ISDN have had a dramatic impact on the planning and deployment of intelligent digital networks providing integrated services for voice, data and video. Further, the work on the ISDN and B-ISDN

standards has led to the development of two major new networking technologies; frame relay and asynchronous transfer mode (ATM). Frame relay and ATM have become the essential ingredients in developing high-speed networks for local, metropolitan and wider area applications.

2. The ISDN is intended to be a worldwide public telecommunications network to replace existing public telecommunication networks and deliver a wide variety of services. The ISDN is defined by the standardization of user interfaces and implemented as a set of digital switches and paths supporting a broad range of traffic types and providing value added processing services. In practice, there are multiple networks, implemented within national boundaries but from the user's point of view, the eventual widespread deployment of ISDN will lead to a single, uniformly accessible, worldwide network.

3. The narrowband ISDN is based on the use of a 64 kbps channel as the basic unit of switching and has a circuit switching orientation. The major technical contribution of the narrowband ISDN effort has been frame relay. The B-ISDN supports very high data rates (100's of Mbps) and has a packet switching orientation. The major technical contribution of the B-ISDN effort has been asynchronous transfer mode, also known as cell relay.

4. **N-ISDN services are:**
    - buttons for instant call setup to arbitrary telephones anywhere in the world,
    - displaying the caller's telephone number, name and address while ringing,
    - connecting the telephone to a computer enabling the caller's database record to be displayed on the screen as the call comes in,
    - call forwarding,
    - conference calls worldwide,
    - on line medical, burglar, and smoke alarms giving the address to speed up response.

5. **The new wide area service is called B-ISDN (Broadband Integrated Services Digital Networks). It will offer:**
    - video on demand,
    - live television from many sources,
    - multimedia electronic mail,
    - CD-quality music,
    - LAN interconnection,
    - high-speed data transport for science and industry,
    - many other services, all over the telephone line.

The underlying technology that makes B-ISDN possible is called ATM (Asynchronous Transfer Mode) because it is not synchronous (tied to a master clock).

EXERCISE

1. What are the different broadband service requirements?
2. Briefly explain the present technologies for voice, video and data networks.
3. What are the needs of virtual networks?
4. What are the different problems existing in data and voice integration?
5. What are the different economic advantages of data and voice integration?
6. Write a short note on "Mixed solutions of voice/data communication".
7. Explain in detail QoS factor in Data-voice communication.
8. Write advantages of integrated voice and data network technology.
9. What are the different applications of integrated voice and data network?
10. How "Integrated voice and data network" is beneficial for a business?
11. Write notes on services provided by ISDN.
12. What are the different types of ISDN terminals?
13. List out different non-ISDN terminals.
14. Write detail note on ISDN devices.
15. Explain ISDN PRI service in detail.
16. Write short note on characteristics of B and D channels.
17. Write a short note on "ISDN equipment and interface terminology".
18. Explain "ISDN protocol stack" in detail.
19. Draw and explain "LAPD" format in detail.
20. Explain B-ISDN architecture in detail.
21. What is need of SS7 protocol?
22. Draw and explain basic SS7 Network Architecture.
23. What are the different SS7 signaling link types?
24. Draw the mapping of SS7 with OSI layer mode.
25. Draw and explain the SS7 protocol stack in detail.

Unit III

FRAME RELAY AND ATM

3.1 Frame Relay Technology

Network Services Available for MAN and WAN
- **Dialed Circuit Services**
  - Direct Dialing (DD) and Wide Area Telephone Services (WATS)
- **Dedicated Circuit Services**
  - Voice-grade circuits
  - Wideband Analog Services (40 kHz BW.)
  - T-Carrier Circuits
  - Synchronous Optical Network (SONET)
- **Circuit-Switched Services**
  - Integrated Services Digital Network (Narrowband and Broadband)
- **Packet-Switched Services**
  - X.25, Frame Relay, ATM, SMDS, and Ethernet/IP

Dedicated Circuit Services
There are two main problems with dialed circuits.
- Each connection goes through the regular telephone network on a different circuit, which may vary in quality.
- The data transmission rates on these circuits are usually low 28.8 to 56 Kbps.

One alternative is to establish a private dedicated circuit, which the user leases from the common carrier for their exclusive use, 24 hrs/day, 7 days/week. Dedicate circuits are billed at a flat fee per month and the user has unlimited use of the circuit.

There are six types of dedicated circuits:

1. Voice Grade Circuits:
Voice grade circuits are analog circuits that work in exactly the same manner as traditional telephone lines, except that you do not dial them.

Dedicated voice grade channels often have conditioning (or equalization) done on them to improve data transmission quality by reducing noise and distortion.

2. Wideband Analog Services:
- Wideband analog services are similar to voice grade circuits but they provide much greater bandwidth.

- Typically wideband analog services provide one 48,000 hertz bandwidth channel for use with frequency division multiplexing or as 12 individual voice grade channels (4000 Hz each).

3. T Carrier Circuits:
- T carrier circuits are dedicated digital circuits and are the most commonly used form of dedicated circuit services in North America today.
- Instead of a modem, a channel service unit (CSU) or data service unit (DSU) are used to connect the circuit into the network.
- T-1 circuit provides a data rate of 1.544 Mbps. T-1's allow 24 simultaneous 64 Kbps channels (with TDM) which transport data, or voice messages using pulse code modulation. (64 Kbps ∞ 24 = 1.536 Mbps)
- T-2 circuit (6.312 Mbps) is basically a multiplexed bundle of four T-1 circuits.
- T-3 circuit (44.376 Mbps) is equal to the capacity of 28 T-1 circuits (672 64Kbps channels).
- T-4 circuit (274.176 Mbps) is equal to the capacity of 178 T-1s.

4. SONET Circuits:
- An Optical Network for Dedicated Connection Services.
- SONET has been accepted by the U.S. Standards Agency (ANSI) as a standard for optical (fiber) transmission at gigabits per second speed.
- The International Telecommunications Standards Agency (ITU-T) also standardized a version of SONET under the name of synchronous digital hierarchy (SDH). The two are very similar and can be easily interconnected.
- SONET transmission speeds begin at the OC-1 level (optical carrier level 1) of 51.84 Mbps. Each succeeding rate in the SONET fiber hierarchy is defined as a multiple of OC-1. Several common carriers (e.g. MCI) now use OC-12 circuits at 622.08 Mbps to carry digitized voice traffic. Table 3.1 gives the sonnet specifications.

Table 3.1

SONET Designation	SDH Designation	Speed
OC-1		51.84 Mbps
OC-3	STM-1	155.52 Mbps
OC-9	STM-3	466.56 Mbps
OC-12	STM-4	622.08 Mbps
OC-18	STM-6	933.12 Mbps
OC-24	STM-8	1.244 Gbps
OC-36	STM-12	1.866 Gbps
OC-48	STM-16	2.488 Gbps
OC-192		9.952 Gbps

5. **Digital Subscriber Line Circuits:**
   - A term for the series of standard digital transmission rates or levels based on DS0, a transmission rate of 64 Kbps, the bandwidth normally used for one telephone voice channel.
   - Both the North American T-carrier system and the European E-carrier systems of transmission operate using the DS series as a base multiple. The digital signal is what is carried inside the carrier system.

3.1.1 Switching Network Classification

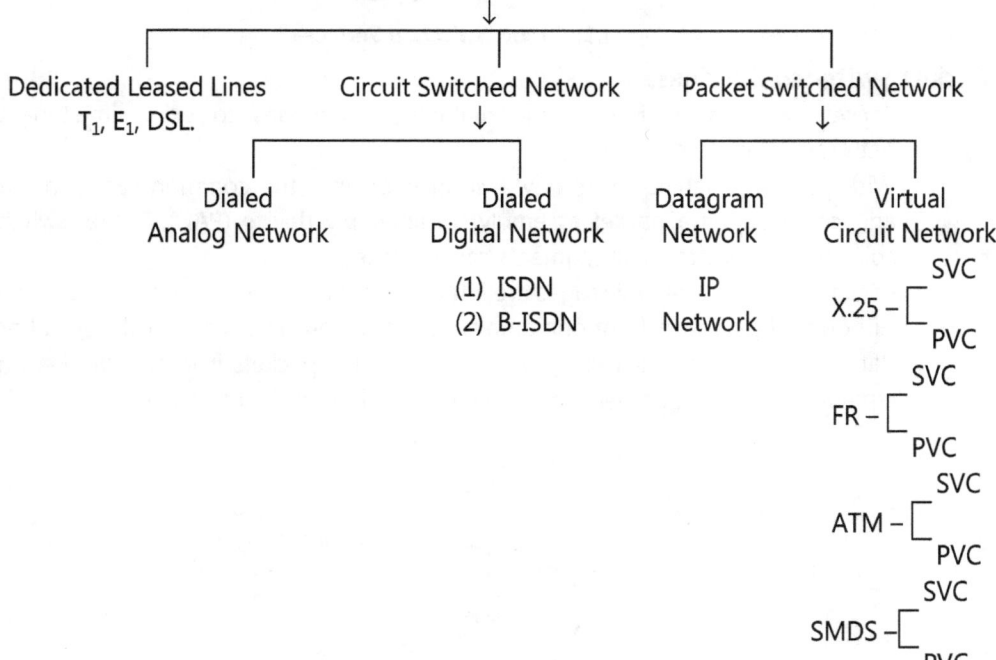

Circuit Switched Services:
- The major problem with dedicated circuit services it that the user must carefully plan all circuits needed.
- In contrast, switched circuits work much like dialed circuits. The user buys a connection into the common carrier's network from the end points of the WAN, without specifying all the interconnecting circuits needed.
- The primary differences from dialed circuits is that the circuits are entirely digital and that they offer higher data transmission rates.

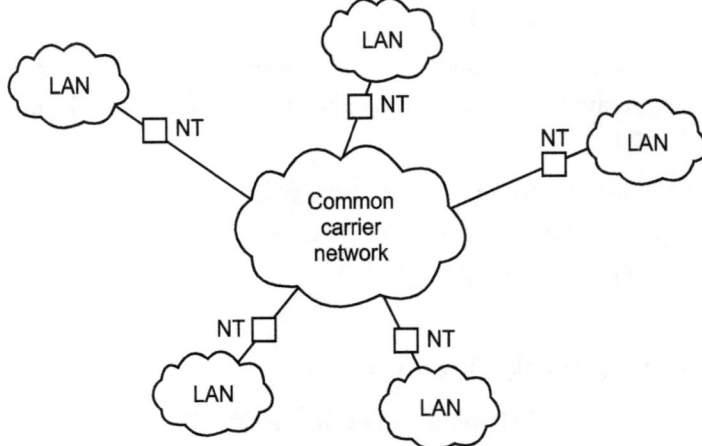

Fig. 3.1: Circuit Switched Services

Packet Switched Services:
- Packet switched services enable multiple connections to exist simultaneously between computers.
- With packet switching users buy a connection into the common carrier network, and connects via a packet assembly/ disassembly device (PAD). Packet switching splits messages into small segments called packets.
- Packets from separate messages are interleaved with other packets for transmission.
- Although the packets from one data stream may mix (interleave) with several other data streams during their journey, it is unlikely that packets from two different data streams will travel together during the entire length of their transmission.

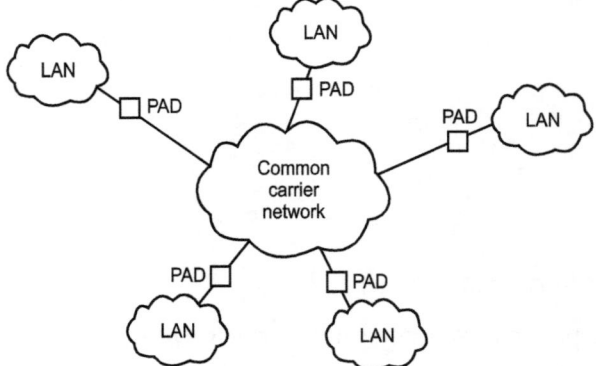

Fig. 3.2: Packet Switched Services

There are two methods used to route packets:
- A **Datagram** is a connectionless service, which adds a destination and sequence number to each packet, in addition to information about the data stream to which the packet belongs. Packets may follow a different route, and are reassembled at the destination.

- In a **Virtual circuit,** the packet switched network establishes an end-to-end circuit between the sender and receiver. All packets for that transmission take the same route over the virtual circuit that has been set up for that transmission.
- Packet switched services are often provided by different common carriers than the one from which organizations get their usual telephone and data services.
- Therefore, organizations often lease dedicated circuits from their offices to the packet switched network. (Like LEASED LINE 64 Kbps, Broadband)

DATAGRAM PACKET NETWORKS

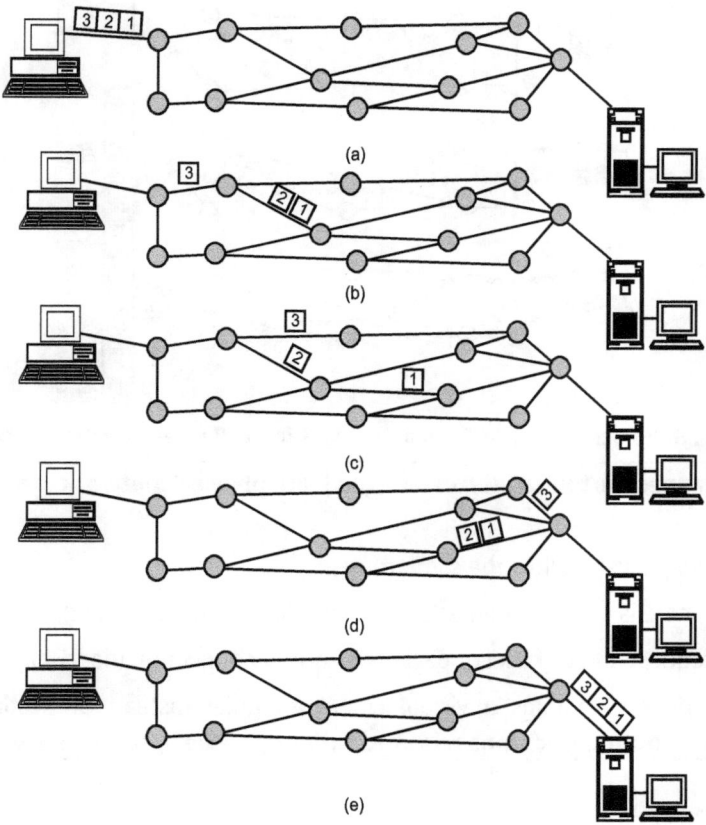

Fig. 3.3: Packet flow in Typical Datagram Packet switched network

- Each packet treated independently.
- Packets can take any practical route.
- Packets may arrive out of order.
- Packets may go missing.
- Receiver is responsible to re-order packets and recover from missing packets.

VIRTUAL CIRCUIT PACKET NETWORK

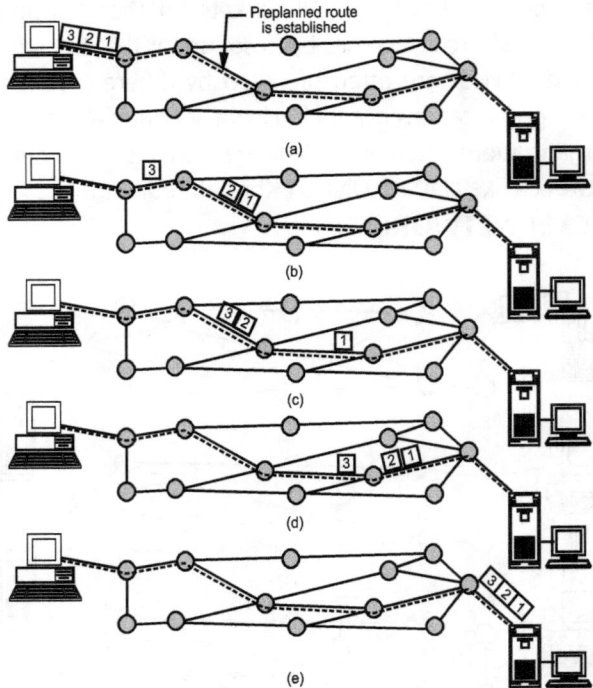

Fig. 3.4: Packet flow in Typical Virtual Circuit Packet switched network

1. Preplanned **virtual route established on physical network** before any packets sent.
   - All packets follow the same route.
   - There is a connection establishment (like Circuit Switching).
2. Call request and call accept packets establish connection (handshake).
3. Each packet contains a virtual circuit identifier instead of destination address. **(i.e. no routing decisions required for each packet), so fast speed is achieved.**

3.1.2 What is a WAN?

- A *WAN* is a data communications network that covers a relatively broad geographic area and that often uses transmission facilities provided by common carriers, such as telephone companies.
- WAN technologies generally function at the lower three layers of the OSI reference model: the physical layer, the data link layer, and the network layer. Fig. 3.5 illustrates the relationship between the common WAN technologies and the OSI model.

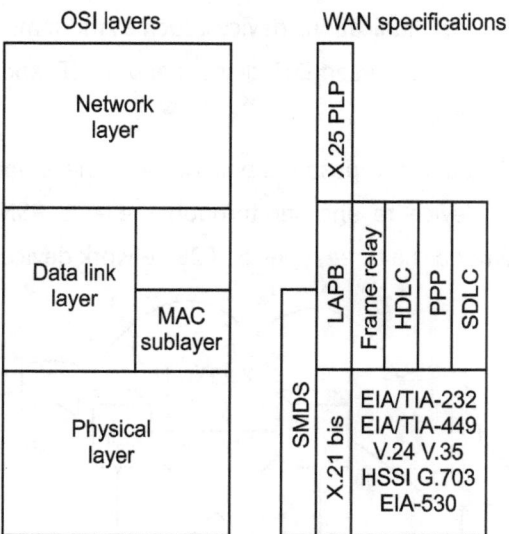

Fig. 3.5: WAN Technologies operate at the Lowest Levels of the OSI Model

3.1.3 Basic X.25 Network

- *X.25* is an International Telecommunication Union-Telecommunication Standardization Sector (ITU-T) protocol standard for WAN communications that defines how connections between user devices and network devices are established and maintained.
- X.25 is designed to operate effectively regardless of the type of systems connected to the network.
- It is typically used in the packet-switched networks (PSNs) of common carriers, such as the telephone companies.
- Subscribers are charged based on their use of the network.
- The development of the X.25 standard was initiated by the common carriers in the 1970s. At that time, there was a need for WAN protocols capable of providing connectivity across public data networks (PDNs).
- X.25 is now administered as an international standard by the ITU-T.

X.25 Devices and Protocol Operation:

- X.25 network devices fall into three general categories: data terminal equipment (DTE), data circuit-terminating equipment (DCE), and packet-switching exchange (PSE).
- Data terminal equipment devices are end systems that communicate across the X.25 network. They are usually terminals, personal computers, or network hosts, and are located on the premises of individual subscribers.

- DCE devices are communications devices, such as modems and packet switches that provide the interface between DTE devices and a PSE, and are generally located in the carrier's facilities.
- PSEs are switches that compose the bulk of the carrier's network. They transfer data from one DTE device to another through the X.25 PSN. Fig. 3.6 illustrates the relationships among the three types of X.25 network devices.

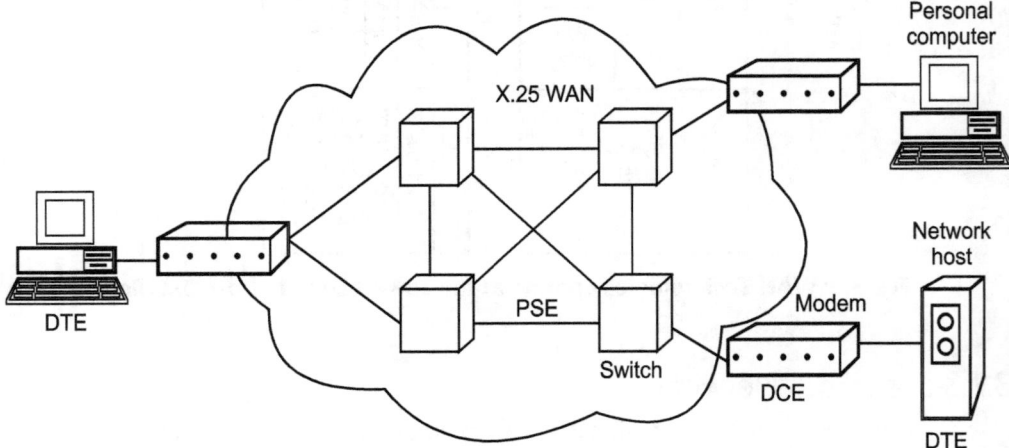

Fig. 3.6: DTEs, DCEs, and PSEs Make Up an X.25 Network

Packet Assembler/Disassembler:

- The *packet assembler/disassembler (PAD)* is a device commonly found in X.25 networks. PADs are used when a DTE device, such as a character-mode terminal, is too simple to implement the full X.25 functionality.
- The PAD is located between a DTE device and a DCE device, and it performs three primary functions: buffering (storing data until a device is ready to process it), packet assembly, and packet disassembly.
- The **PAD buffers data** sent to or from the DTE device.
- It also **assembles outgoing data** into packets and forwards them to the DCE device. (**This includes adding an X.25 header**.)
- Finally, the PAD disassembles incoming packets before forwarding the data to the DTE. (This includes removing the X.25 header.) Fig. 3.7 illustrates the basic operation of the PAD when receiving packets from the X.25 WAN.

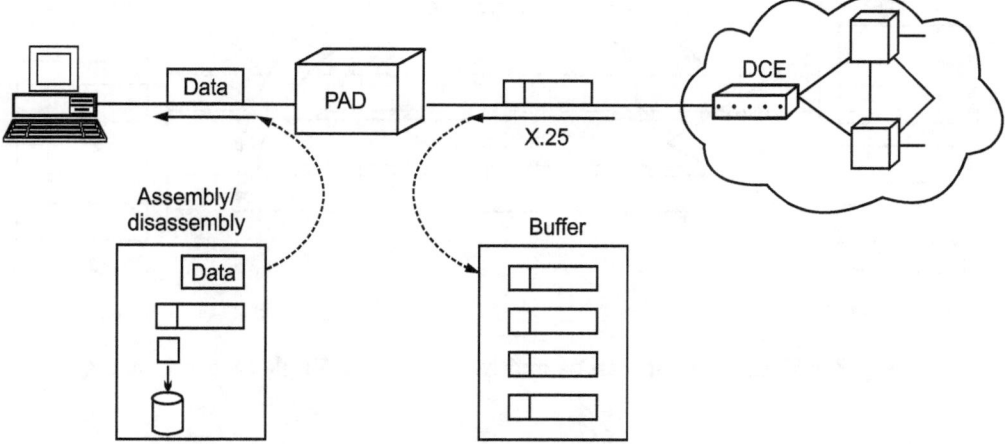

Fig. 3.7: The PAD Buffers, Assembler, and Disassembler Data Packets

X.25 Session Establishment:

- X.25 sessions are established when one DTE device contacts another to request a communication session.

- The DTE device that receives the request can either accept or refuse the connection. If the request is accepted, the two systems begin full-duplex information transfer.

- Either DTE device can terminate the connection. After the session is terminated, any further communication requires the establishment of a new session.

X.25 Virtual Circuits:

- A *virtual circuit* is a logical connection created to ensure reliable communication between two network devices.

- A virtual circuit denotes the existence of a logical, bidirectional path from one DTE device to another across an X.25 network.

- Physically, the connection can pass through any number of intermediate nodes, such as DCE devices and PSEs.

- Multiple virtual circuits (logical connections) can be multiplexed onto a single physical circuit (a physical connection).

- Virtual circuits are demultiplexed at the remote end, and data is sent to the appropriate destinations. Fig. 3.8 illustrates four separate virtual circuits being multiplexed onto a single physical circuit.

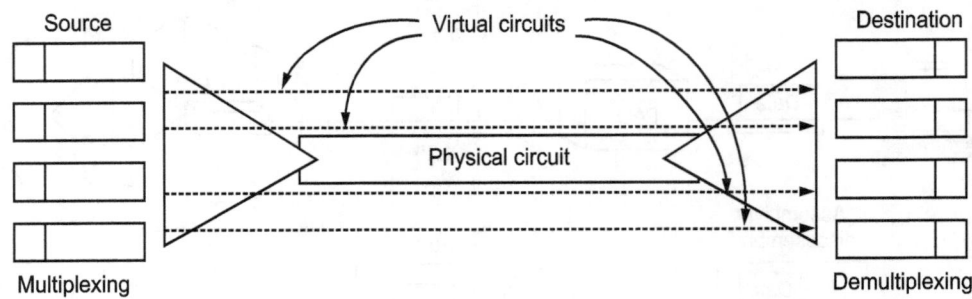

Fig. 3.8: Virtual Circuits can be multiplexed onto a Single Physical Circuit

TYPES OF VIRTUAL CIRCUITS:

Switched Virtual Circuits (Physical connection is always present and temporary logical connection is to be established every time for the data transfer.) *Switched virtual circuits (SVCs)* are temporary connections used in situations requiring only **sporadic** data transfer between DTE devices across the Frame Relay network.

Permanent Virtual Circuits (Physical connection is always present and permanent logical connection is already established so that any time data can be transferred.) *Permanent virtual circuits (PVCs)* are permanently established connections that are used for frequent and consistent data transfers between DTE devices across the network. Communication across a PVC does not require the call setup and termination states that are used with SVCs. PVCs do not require that sessions be established and terminated. Therefore, DTEs can begin transferring data whenever necessary because the session is always active.

- The basic operation of an X.25 virtual circuit begins when the source DTE device specifies the virtual circuit to be used (in the packet headers) and then sends the packets to a locally connected DCE device.
- At this point, the local DCE device examines the packet headers to determine which virtual circuit to use and then sends the packets to the closest PSE in the path of that virtual circuit.
- PSEs (switches) pass the traffic to the next intermediate node in the path, which may be another switch or the remote DCE device.
- When the traffic arrives at the remote DCE device, the packet headers are examined and the destination address is determined. The packets are then sent to the destination DTE device. If communication occurs over an SVC and neither device has additional data to transfer, the virtual circuit is terminated.

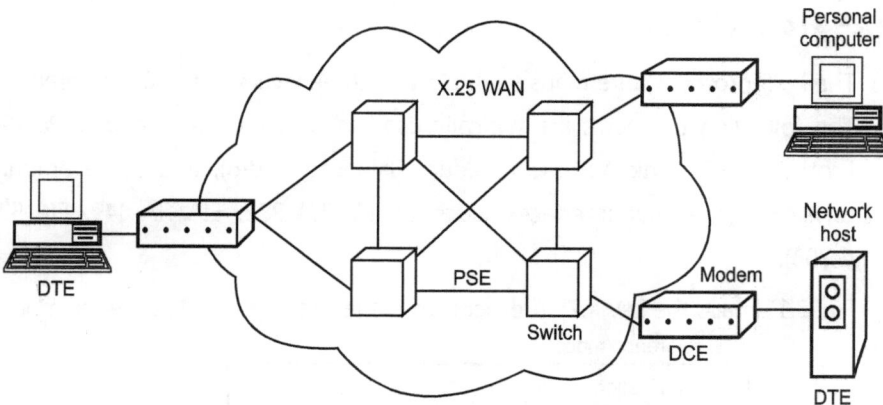

Fig. 3.9: DTEs, DCEs, and PSEs make up an X.25 Network

VC CALL SETUP:

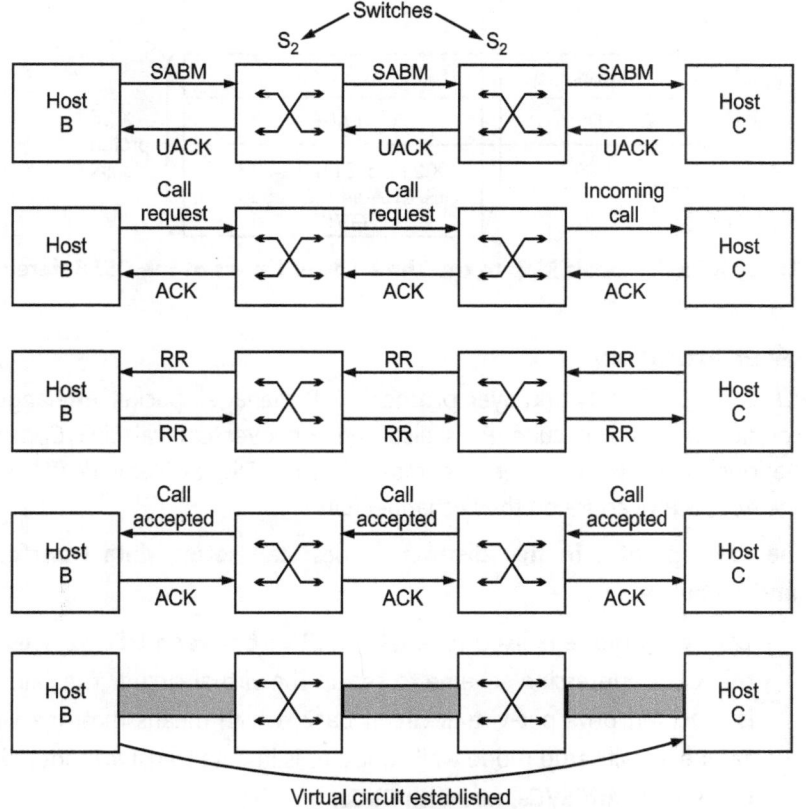

SABM – Sending Set Asynchronous Balanced Mode
UACK – Unnumbered Acknowledge
RR – Ready Receiver

Fig. 3.10: VC Call Setup in Detail

The X.25 Protocol Suite:

- The X.25 protocol suite maps to the lowest three layers of the OSI reference model. The following protocols are typically used in X.25 implementations: Packet-Layer Protocol (PLP), Link Access Procedure Balanced (LAPB), and those among other physical-layer serial interfaces (such as EIA/TIA-232, EIA/TIA-449, EIA-530, and G.703).

- Fig. 3.11 maps the key X.25 protocols to the layers of the OSI reference model.

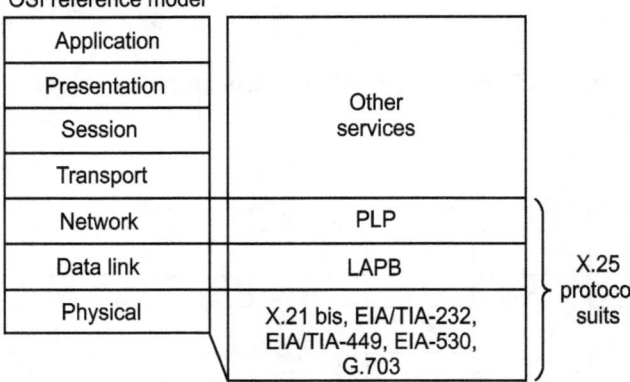

Fig. 3.11: Key X.25 Protocols Map to the Three Lower Layers of the OSI Reference Model

Packet-Layer Protocol:

1. *PLP* is the X.25 network layer protocol. PLP manages packet exchanges between DTE devices across virtual circuits. PLPs also can run over Logical Link Control 2 (LLC2) implementations on LANs and over Integrated Services Digital Network (ISDN) interfaces running Link Access Procedure on the D channel (LAPD).

2. **The PLP operates in five distinct modes: call setup, data transfer, idle, call clearing, and restarting.**

    - **Call setup mode is used to establish SVCs between DTE devices**. A PLP uses the X.121 addressing scheme to set up the virtual circuit. The call setup mode is executed on a per-virtual-circuit basis, which means that one virtual circuit can be in call setup mode while another is in data transfer mode. **This mode is used only with SVCs, not with PVCs.**

    - **Data transfer mode is used** for transferring data between two DTE devices across a virtual circuit. In this mode, PLP handles segmentation and reassembly, bit padding, and error and flow control. This mode is executed on a per-virtual-circuit basis and is **used with both PVCs and SVCs.**

- **Idle mode is used** when a virtual circuit is established but data transfer is not occurring. It is executed on a per-virtual-circuit basis and **is used only with SVCs.**
- **Call clearing mode** is used to end communication sessions between DTE devices and to terminate SVCs. This mode is executed on a per-virtual-circuit basis **and is used only with SVCs.**
- **Restarting mode** is used to synchronize transmission between a DTE device and a locally connected DCE device; this is used only in SVCs.

Four types of PLP packet fields exist:

- **General Format Identifier (GFI):** Identifies packet parameters, such as whether the packet carries user data or control information, what kind of windowing is being used, and whether delivery confirmation is required.
- **Logical Channel Identifier (LCI):** Identifies the virtual circuit across the local DTE/DCE interface.
- **Packet Type Identifier (PTI):** Identifies the packet as one of 17 different PLP packet types.
- **User Data:** Contains encapsulated upper-layer information. This field is present only in data packets. Otherwise, additional fields containing control information are added.

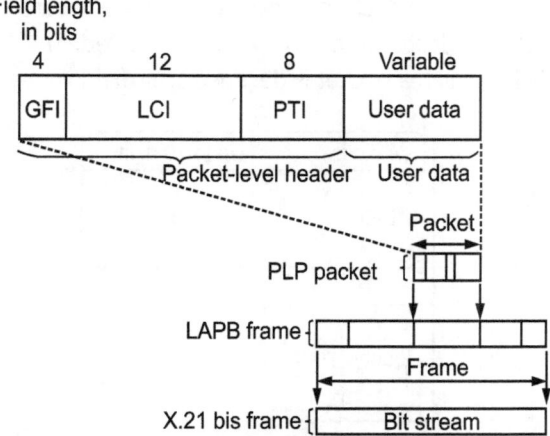

Fig. 3.12: The PLP Packet is encapsulated within the LAPB Frame and the X.21bis Frame

LAPB Frame Format:

LAPB frames include a header, encapsulated data, and a trailer. Fig. 3.13 illustrates the format of the LAPB frame and its relationship to the PLP packet and the X.21bis frame.

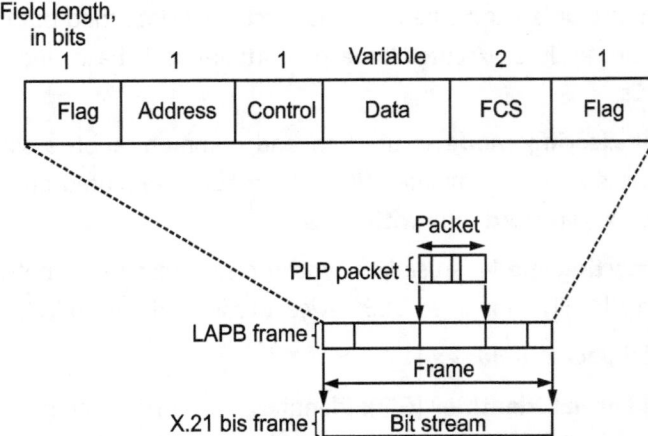

Fig. 3.13: An LAPB Frame includes a Header, a Trailer, and Encapsulated Data

X.121 Address Format:

X.121 addresses are used by the X.25 PLP in call setup mode to establish SVCs. Fig. 3.14 illustrates the format of an X.121 address. The X.121 Address field includes the International Data Number (IDN), which consists of two fields: the Data Network Identification Code (DNIC) and the National Terminal Number (NTN). DNIC is an optional field that identifies the exact PSN in which the destination DTE device is located. This field is sometimes omitted in calls within the same PSN. The DNIC has two subfields: Country and PSN. The Country subfield specifies the country in which the destination PSN is located. The PSN field specifies the exact PSN in which the destination DTE device is located. The NTN identifies the exact DTE device in the PSN for which a packet is destined. This field varies in length.

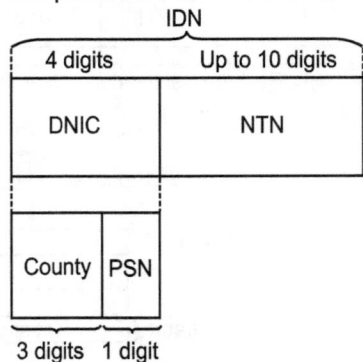

Fig. 3.14: The X.121 Address includes an IDN Field

The X.21bis Protocol:

X.21bis is a physical layer protocol used in X.25 that defines the electrical and mechanical procedures for using the physical medium. X.21bis handles the activation and deactivation of the physical medium connecting DTE and DCE devices. It supports point-to-point connections, speeds up to 19.2 kbps, and synchronous, full-duplex transmission over four-wire media.

Advantages of X.25:

X.25 has been around since the mid 1970's and so is pretty well **debugged and stable**. There are literally no data errors on modern X.25 networks.

Disadvantages of X.25:

1. X.25 does have some drawbacks. There is an **inherent delay** caused by the store-and-forward mechanism. On most single networks, the turn-around delay is about 0.6 seconds. This has no effect on large block transfers, but in flip-flop types of transmissions, the delay can be very noticeable
2. Frame Relay (also called **Fast Packet Switching**) does not store and forward, but simply switches to the destination part way through the frame, reducing the transmission delay considerably.
3. Another problem for the networks is a large requirement for buffering to support the store-and-forward data transfer. One of the reasons that Frame Relay is so cost effective is that storage requirements are minimal.
4. The biggest difference between Frame Relay and X.25 is that **X.25 guarantees data integrity and network managed flow control at the cost of some network delays**. Frame Relay switches packets end to end much faster, but **there is no guarantee of data integrity at all**.

3.1.4 Frame Relay Packet Switching Network

Frame relay is a newer packet switching technology that transmits data faster than X.25. Different common carriers offer frame relay networks with different transmission speeds: 56 Kbps to 45 Mbps.

At present, frame relay suffers from the same problems as ISDN - a lack of standards. Fig. 3.15 indicates the communication between source/destination.

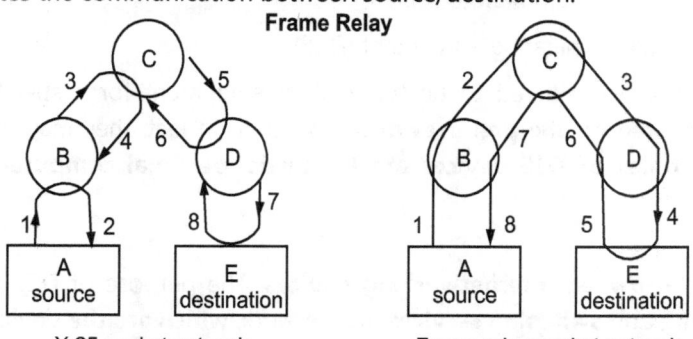

Fig. 3.15: Frame Relay

Table 3.2

Network Characteristic	X.25	Frame Relay (introduced in 1992)
Propagation Delay	High	Low
Error detection and Correction	Done by each X.25 network Node to Node	FR only does error detection (discarding damaged frames); flow and error control are responsibility of higher layer
Protocol family	HDLC	HDLC
Good for interactive use?	Barely acceptable. Rather slow with one second or more round trip delay.	Yes
Good for LAN file transfer	Slow	Yes
Good for voice?	No	Good, standards developing
Ease of implementation	Difficult	Easy
Data Rate	Upto 64 Kbps	56 Kbps to 45 Mbps.
Pacet size	(128 to 512 bytes)	(1610 to 4096 bytes)
Layers defined	**1, 2, 3** of the ISO model	**1, 2** of the ISO model
Packets/frames	X.25 prepares and **sends packets**	Frame relay prepares and **sends frames**
BW allocation	Dynamic	Dynamic
Design aspects	Both are designed primarily for data; variable length frames, delay-tolerant, bursty traffic	Both are designed primarily for data; variable length frames, delay-tolerant, bursty traffic

Frame Relay Devices:

Devices attached to a Frame Relay WAN fall into the following two general categories:

- Data terminal equipment (DTE).
- Data circuit-terminating equipment (DCE).

DTEs generally are considered to be terminating equipment for a specific network and typically **are located on the premises of a customer**. In fact, they may be owned by the customer. **Examples of DTE devices are terminals, personal computers, routers, and bridges.**

DCEs are carrier-owned internetworking devices. The purpose of DCE equipment is to provide **clocking and switching services** in a network, **which are the devices that actually transmit data through the WAN**. In most cases, these are packet switches. Fig. 3.16 shows the relationship between the two categories of devices.

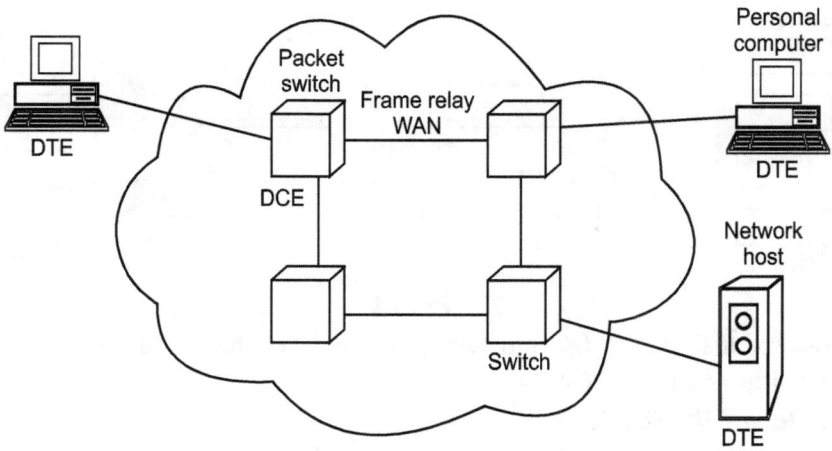

Fig. 3.16: DCEs Generally Reside within Carrier-Operated WANs

- The connection between a DTE device and a DCE device consists of both a physical layer component and a link layer component. The physical component defines the mechanical, electrical, functional, and procedural specifications for the connection between the devices.
- One of the most commonly used **physical layer** interface specifications is the recommended standard **(RS)-232** specification.
- The link layer component defines the protocol that establishes the connection between the DTE device, such as a router, and the DCE device, such as a switch.

Frame Relay Virtual Circuits:

- Frame Relay provides connection-oriented data link layer communication.
- This means that a defined communication exists between each pair of devices and that these connections are associated with a connection identifier.
- This service is implemented by using a Frame Relay virtual circuit, which is a logical connection created between two data terminal equipment (DTE) devices across a Frame Relay packet-switched network (PSN).
- Virtual circuits provide a bidirectional communication path from one DTE device to another and are uniquely identified by a data-link connection identifier (DLCI).
- A number of virtual circuits can be multiplexed into a single physical circuit for transmission across the network. This capability often can reduce the equipment and network complexity required to connect multiple DTE devices.

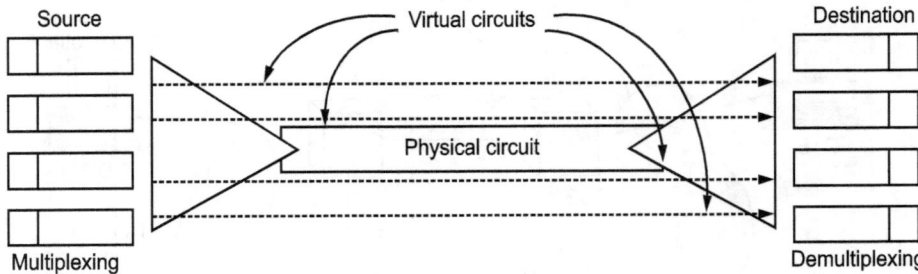

Fig. 3.17

Frame Relay virtual circuits fall into two categories: switched virtual circuits (SVCs) and permanent virtual circuits (PVCs).

FRAME RELAY VC SETUP

Switched Virtual Circuits (Physical connection is always present and temporary logical connection is to be established every time for the data transfer.) Switched virtual circuits (SVCs) are temporary connections used in situations requiring only sporadic data transfer between DTE devices across the Frame Relay network. A communication session across an SVC consists of the following four operational states:

- **Call setup:** The virtual circuit between two Frame Relay DTE devices is established.
- **Data transfer:** Data is transmitted between the DTE devices over the virtual circuit.
- **Idle:** The connection between DTE devices is still active, but no data is transferred. If an SVC remains in an idle state for a defined period of time, the call can be terminated.
- **Call termination:** The virtual circuit between DTE devices is terminated.

After the virtual circuit is terminated, the DTE devices must establish a new SVC if there is additional data to be exchanged. It is expected that SVCs will be established, maintained, and terminated using the same signaling protocols used in ISDN.

Few manufacturers of Frame Relay DCE equipment support switched virtual circuit connections. Therefore, their actual deployment is minimal in today's Frame Relay networks.

Previously not widely supported by Frame Relay equipment, SVCs are now the norm. Companies have found that SVCs save money in the end because the circuit is not open all the time.

Permanent Virtual Circuits (Physical connection is always present and permanent logical connection is already established so that any time data can be transferred.) Permanent virtual circuits (PVCs) are permanently established connections that are used for frequent and consistent data transfers between DTE devices across the Frame Relay network. Communication across a PVC does not require the call setup and termination states that are used with SVCs. PVCs always operate in one of the following two operational states:

- **Data transfer:** Data is transmitted between the DTE devices over the virtual circuit.
- **Idle:** The connection between DTE devices is active, but no data is transferred. Unlike SVCs, PVCs will not be terminated under any circumstances when in an idle state.

DTE devices can begin transferring data whenever they are ready because the circuit is permanently established.

Data-Link Connection Identifier:

Frame Relay virtual circuits are identified by *data-link connection identifiers (DLCIs)*. DLCI values typically are assigned by the Frame Relay service provider (for example, the telephone company). Frame Relay DLCIs have local significance, which means that their values are unique in the LAN, but not necessarily in the Frame Relay WAN. **Fig. 3.18 illustrates how two different DTE devices can be assigned the same DLCI value within one Frame Relay WAN. A Single Frame Relay Virtual Circuit Can Be Assigned Different DLCIs on Each End of a VC.**

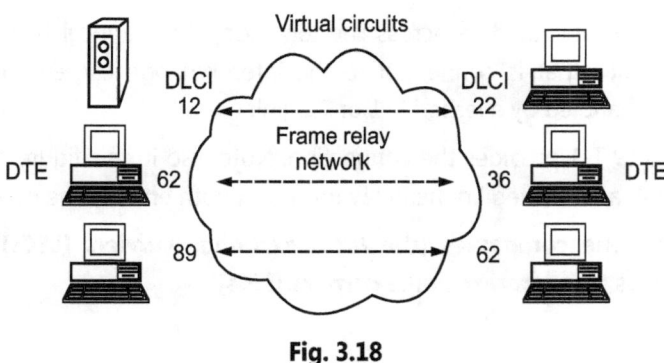

Fig. 3.18

Congestion-Control Mechanisms:

Frame Relay implements two congestion-notification mechanisms:

- Forward-explicit congestion notification (FECN)
- Backward-explicit congestion notification (BECN)

Public Carrier-Provided Networks:

- In public carrier-provided Frame Relay networks, the Frame Relay switching equipment is located in the central offices of a telecommunications carrier.
- Subscribers are charged based on their network use but are relieved from administering and maintaining the Frame Relay network equipment and service. Generally, the DCE equipment also is owned by the tele-communications provider.
- DTE equipment either will be customer-owned or perhaps will be owned by the telecommunications provider as a service to the customer. The majority of today's Frame Relay networks are public carrier-provided networks.

Private Enterprise Networks:

- More frequently, organizations worldwide are deploying private Frame Relay networks.
- In private Frame Relay networks, the administration and maintenance of the network are the responsibilities of the enterprise (a private company).
- All the equipment, including the switching equipment, is owned by the customer.

Where People Use Frame Relay

- Frame Relay is designed as a WAN technology primarily for data.
- More specifically, Frame Relay was developed to carry data traffic across the WAN and link *Local Area Networks* (LANs) to other LANs, as shown in Fig. 3.19.
- The transmission of data across the local loop to the local telephone company's central office that is connected to the interexchange carriers' network switching system is handled by a leased T-1 or T-3 link.
- In Fig. 3.19 T-1 provides the connection. Note also in this figure, the access device is through a dedicated Frame Relay router on both ends of the connection.
- **As telephone companies (the *local exchange carriers* [LECs]), long distance companies (the *interexchange carriers* [IECs]).**

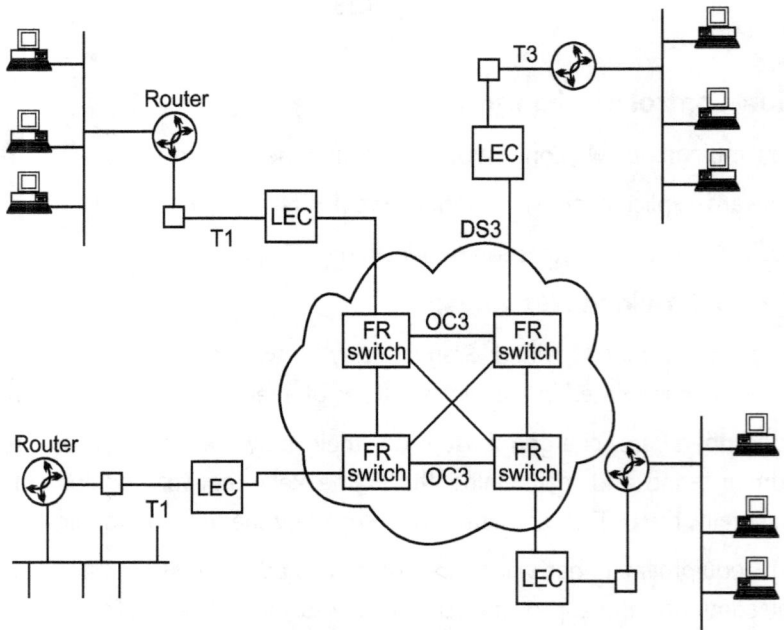

Fig. 3.19: A higher speed Frame Relay Connection

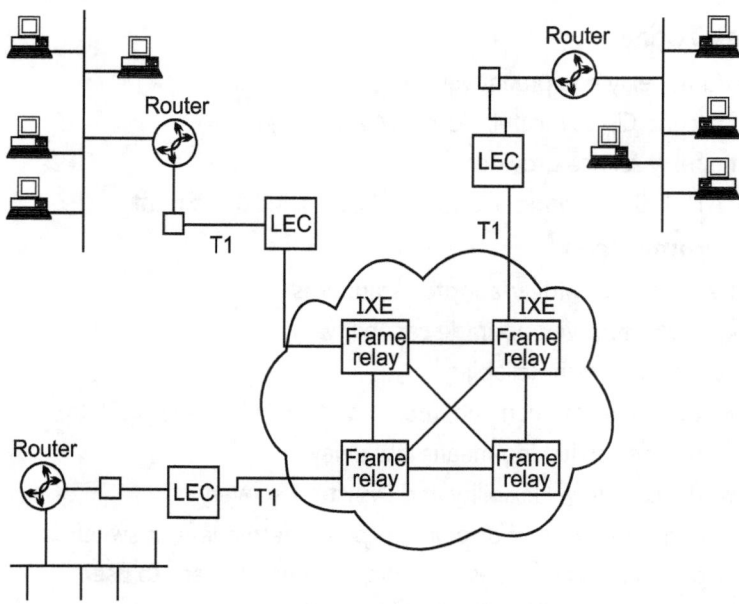

Fig. 3.20: A typical Frame Relay Connection

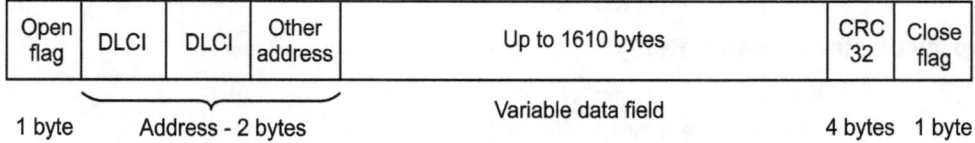

Fig. 3.21: A Frame Relay Frame

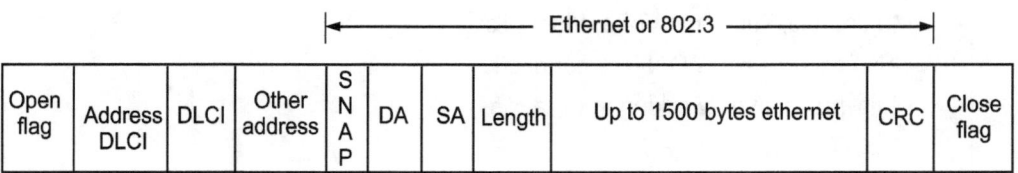

Fig. 3.22: Ethernet and IEEE 802.3 frames fit into the Frame Relay frame

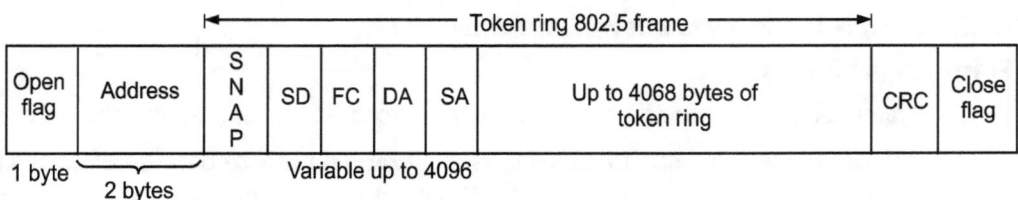

Fig. 3.23: Modified frame size of the Frame Relay information field

Frame Relay Today:
- Key frame relay equipment vendors
  - Lucent, Cisco, Alcatel, Nortel, Motorola
- Frame relay service providers
  - AT&T, Bell Atlantic, Worldcom, SBC Pacific Bell, Sprint

Benefits of Frame Relay:
- Well-established, widely-adopted standards
  - Allows improved upgrade capability
- Low Overhead, High Reliability
  - 2 to 5 bytes of overhead, more bandwidth for sending data
  - Simplified switching means less delay
- Network Scalability, Flexibility and Disaster Recovery
  - VC may be meshed or point-to-point, permanent or switched
  - Additions and changes in network are transparent to user
- Interoperability with New Applications and Services
  - Allows consolidation of LAN, SNA, voice and packetized video
  - Smooth migration to ATM

Applications of Frame Relay:
- File Transfer
  - Character-interactive traffic (e.g. text editing)
  - High Resolution graphics
- Access to Internet and Intranet
- Multimedia, Real Time Voice, Video, Fax
- LAN Peer-to-Peer, WAN Interconnection
- Multi-protocol networking applications
  - ATM, SNA, TCP/IP
- Private backbone networks.

3.1.5 Voice Over Frame Relay

3.1.5.1 Using Frame Relay to Integrate the Enterprise

Frame Relay Basics:
1. Frame relay is defined as a communication protocol as well as a packet data service.
2. This section will describe frame relay as a packet data service because of its ability to create a Wide Area Network (WAN) that can integrate an enterprise infrastructure.

3. The frame relay service is a high speed packetized data service that consists of physical and logical components.
4. **The physical components include Frame Relay Assemblers Disassemblers (FRADs), access circuits, and frame relay ports.**
5. **The logical components consist of permanent virtual circuits (PVCs).**
6. Frame Relay Assemblers Disassemblers (FRADs) are devices, such as routers, that assemble data into frame relay packets and that transmit the packets through the local access circuits to which they are connected.
7. The local access circuits, whose bandwidths can range from 56 kbps to 1544 kbps, are digital circuits that connect the FRADs to the frame relay network provider's site.
8. A frame relay port, whose bandwidth equals that of the local access circuit, physically connects the local access circuit to the frame relay network.
9. Frame Relay's logical component differentiates it from the traditional high speed data services that are physical in nature.
10. The logical component of frame relay consists of Permanent Virtual Circuits (PVCs).
11. PVCs are the logical connections that allow the various sites, having physical network access, to communicate among one and other.
12. Each logical connection is defined in the frame relay provider's network and in the FRAD equipment.
13. **Logical connections in the frame relay providers network are software-defined connections that can create many types of network topologies (i.e., hub- and-spoke, full mesh, partial mesh).**
14. Because the connections are defined using software, companies may provide logical connections in a few hours as opposed to the few weeks that are necessary with traditional high speed data services like private lines.
15. In addition to providing the logical connections within the frame relay provider's network, the FRADs must be programmed to send the data to the correct permanent virtual circuit.
16. Every PVC provided in the frame relay network must also be programmed into the FRAD.
17. FRADs are programmed using data link connection identifiers (DLCIs) that associate an identification number to each PVC.
18. Each PVC has a Committed Information Rate (CIR), that is the bandwidth associated to the logical connection.
19. Frame relay networks have the ability to transmit data at a rate higher than that of the CIR. This allows a "bandwidth-on-demand" feature that improves the performance of bandwidth intensive applications.

Frame Relay History:
1. Frame relay is a Data Link Layer protocol that is built on the existing CCITT (Committee Consultative of International Telephone and Telegraphy) X.25 and ISDN standards.
2. Frame relay is often thought of as the next generation packet network succeeding X.25.
3. X.25 was developed about 20 years ago and was designed for use with "noisy" analog lines.
4. To compensate for the errors caused by these "noisy" data links, X.25 checks and corrects the data traversing every data path.
5. This extensive error checking adversely effects the network throughput as compared to frame relay.
6. Sometimes, depending on the packet size, 50% of the X.25 packets, that traverse a data link, are associated with the X.25's error checking rather than with the application's data.
7. Frame relay, on the other hand, realizes its efficiencies by only making error calculations at the source and destination devices rather than making them at each switching node, as does X.25.
8. Error corrections at each switching node are not necessary because today's digital networks have very few errors compared to those on analog networks. (Digital error rates are less than one error in every 1,000,000 bits transmitted.)
9. Since the error verification and correction burden is removed from the network, network response times are greatly improved.
10. These improved network response times improve the response times of applications that traverse the wide area network.

Frame Relay State-of-the-Art:
1. We believe that frame relay's state-of-the-art incorporates the use of multiprotocol routing, Integrated Services Digital Networks (ISDN), dial access, and/or voice networking within the frame relay network.
2. The incorporation of these additional technologies improves the reliability, performance, and flexibility of the frame relay infrastructure.
3. Multiprotocol routing necessitates that the FRAD equipment, which allows multiple protocols to traverse a single PVC.
4. Multiprotocol routing also makes it easier to increase the capacity utilization of the frame relay links (PVCs: Permanent Virtual Circuits) by allowing many different devices, that communicate using different protocols, to use the same PVC.
5. Companies are also using ISDN to enhance the performance and reliability of their wide area network.

6. ISDN is a high speed data network that allows devices to dial one or more 56 kbps data channels.
7. It operates similarly to the standard telephone service, but multiple connections can be made and those connections are at a data rate of 56 kbps or 64 kbps.
8. Wide area network reliability can be increased by having an alternate network (ISDN) on standby in the event that the frame relay network or access circuits fail.
9. Today's FRAD equipment will automatically switch the connections from the frame relay to ISDN in the event of a frame relay failure.
10. Additionally, improved performance can also be realized by increasing the bandwidth on the physical components of the network.
11. FRADs can dial-up additional bandwidth when pre-programmed thresholds are met. For example, FRAD's can enable additional data channels when line utilization exceeds a pre-defined percentage utilization.
12. Today's frame relay networks are also accessible by remote users with "dial-up to frame relay" data connections.
13. "Dial-up to frame relay" capability is usually cost effective because companies neither have to purchase expensive equipment such as terminal servers and authentication servers nor supply administrative support for user IDs, passwords, or security administration.
14. Frame relay is designed as a data only service, but many companies are using specially designed FRADs to deploy voice applications.
15. The specially designed FRADs packetize voice into frame relay packets and transmit them across the network.
16. This allows companies to use their existing data infrastructure to transport voice calls.
17. Voice applications over the frame relay network are not very popular because today's voice networks are very robust from a price, feature and performance standpoint.
18. However, there are some companies that are transmitting voice over frame relay networks in order to reduce telephone expenditures.

Frame Relay Applications:

1. The most popular frame relay application provides companies with Local Area Network (LAN) to LAN communication.
2. This allows companies to integrate their information systems in order to have employees throughout the enterprise to access specific information residing on a LAN somewhere in the enterprise.
3. The devices on the LANs can communicate over the frame relay network regardless of their native protocol.

4. For example, native protocols that can traverse frame relay networks include SNA, DECnet, IPX, TCP/IP, and AppleTalk.
5. Therefore, frame relay has the ability to make the users perceive that the entire company is on one large LAN.
6. Application software such as groupware, e-mail, document sharing, database and many other LAN applications can utilize frame relay technology.
7. Companies are also integrating communication for legacy systems, such as SNA, onto frame relay networks.
8. This allows companies to connect devices such as cluster controllers and front-end processors directly to FRADs in order to use the frame relay network for communications.
9. Frame relay's ability to support both the legacy applications and LAN applications provides an excellent backbone for those companies that are in the process of migrating their information systems from centralized mainframe processing to distributed client/server systems.
10. Companies can turn up legacy applications on the frame relay network and slowly migrate the LAN applications as they are developed.

3.1.5.2 Frame Relay Technology

1. Today's LANs and computing equipments have the potential to run at much higher speeds and transfer very large quantities of data.
2. With the diversity and complexity of today's networks, management can be a mammoth task if you don't have the proper tools.
3. Each environment is a unique combination of equipment from different vendors.
4. Frame relay, which is a relatively new wide area networking method, is gaining in popularity.
5. It uses a packet-switching technology, similar to X.25, but is more efficient. As a result, it can make your networking quicker, simpler and less costly.

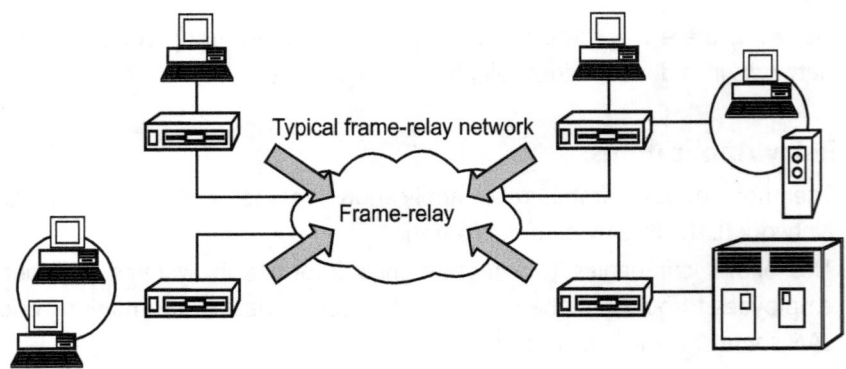

Fig. 3.24: Typical frame relay network connects the different LANs

6. Frame relay was developed to solve communication problems that other protocols could not: the increased need for higher speeds, an increased need for large bandwidth efficiency, particularly for clumping ("bursty" traffic), an increase in intelligent network devices that lower protocol processing, and the need to connect LANs and WANs.
7. Like X.25, frame relay is a packet-switched protocol. But the frame-relay process is streamlined. There are significant differences that make frame relay a faster, more efficient form of networking.
8. A frame-relay network does not perform error detection, which results in a considerably smaller amount of overhead and faster processing than X.25.
9. Frame relay is also protocol independent - it accepts data from many different protocols.
10. This data is encapsulated by the frame-relay equipment, not the network.
11. The intelligent network devices connected to a frame-relay network are responsible for the error correction and frame formatting.
12. Processing time is minimized, so the transmission of data is much faster and more efficient.
13. In addition, frame relay is entirely digital, which reduces the chance of error and offers excellent transmission rates. Frame relay typically operates at 56 kbps to 1.544 mbps.

What does Frame Relay do?
1. Frame relay sends information in packets called frames through a shared frame-relay network.
2. Each frame contains all the information necessary to route it to the correct destination.
3. So in effect, each endpoint can communicate with many destinations over one access link to the network.
4. And instead of being allocated a fixed amount of bandwidth, frame-relay services offer a CIR (committed information rate) at which data is transmitted.
5. But if traffic and your service agreement allow, data can burst above your committed rate.

Why Choose Frame Relay?
1. Since frame relay has a low overhead, it's a perfect fit for today's complex networks.
2. You get several clear benefits: First, multiple logical connections can be sent over a single physical connection, reducing your internetworking costs.
3. By reducing the amount of processing required, you get improved performance and response time.

4. And because frame relay uses a simple link layer protocol, your equipment usually requires only software changes or simple hardware modifications, so you don't have to invest a lot of money to upgrade your system.
5. Since frame relay is protocol independent, it can process traffic from different networking protocols like IP, IPX, and SNA.
6. Frame relay is an ideal choice for connecting Wide Area Networks (WANs) that have unpredictable, high-volume, and bursty traffic.
7. Typically, these applications include data transfer, CAD/CAM, and client-server applications.
8. Frame relay also offers advantages for interconnecting WANs. In the past, setting up WANs required the use of private lines or circuit switching over a leased line.
9. Single, dedicated lines are not needed to make each WAN-to-WAN connection with frame relay, reducing costs.

Permanent Virtual Circuits:
1. Essentially, a permanent virtual circuit (PVC) is your dedicated connection through the shared frame-relay network replacing a dedicated end-to-end line.
2. A PVC is needed for each site in the network, just as a private line is. But in a frame relay network, the bandwidth is shared among multiple users.
3. So any single site can communicate with any other single site without the need for multiple dedicated lines.
4. PVCs function via a Local Management Interface (LMI), which provides control procedures.
5. The control procedures function in three ways: link integrity verification initiated by the user device, network status report giving details of all PVCs, and network notification of whether a PVC's status changes from active to inactive or vice versa.
6. Data-Link Connections (DLCs) are PVCs pre-configured by both sides of the connection.
7. The DLC identifier (DLCI) is used as the logical address for frame-layer multiplexing.

Benefits:
- Virtual circuits can exist simultaneously across a given transmission line. In addition, each device can use more of the bandwidth as necessary, and thus operate at higher speeds.
- High reliability.
- Provides a cost-effective way of providing a secure private IP-based network.
- Used as a low cost carrier to replace networks of leased lines.

These factors make frame relay a desirable choice for data transmission. However, they also necessitate testing to determine that the system works properly and that data is not lost. While frame relay does not guarantee data integrity, the protocols transported over it today mainly have their own error correction mechanisms. Thus frames travel very fast and arrive at its destination with very little delay, to the extent that use of frame relay is almost like that of a direct leased line connections, only cheaper.

Advantages of Frame Relay:

Frame relay offers an attractive alternative to both dedicated lines and X.25 networks for connecting LANs to bridges and routers. The success of the frame relay protocol is based on the following two underlying factors:

- Because virtual circuits consume bandwidth only when they transport data, many virtual circuits can exist simultaneously across a given transmission line. In addition, each device can use more of the bandwidth as necessary, and thus operate at higher speeds.
- The improved reliability of communication lines and increased error-handling sophistication at end stations allows the frame relay protocol to discard erroneous frames and thus eliminate time-consuming error-handling processing.

These two factors make frame relay a desirable choice for data transmission. However, they also necessitate testing to determine that the system works properly and that data is not lost.

3.1.5.3 Frame Relay Structure

1. Standards for the frame relay protocol have been developed by ANSI and CCITT simultaneously.
2. The following discussion of the protocol structure includes the major points from these specifications.
3. The frame relay structure is based on the LAPD (Link Access **Protocol** - Channel D) protocol.
4. In the frame relay structure, the frame header is altered slightly to contain the Data Link Connection Identifier (DLCI) and congestion bits, in place of the normal address and control fields.
5. This new frame relay header is 2 bytes in length and has the following format:

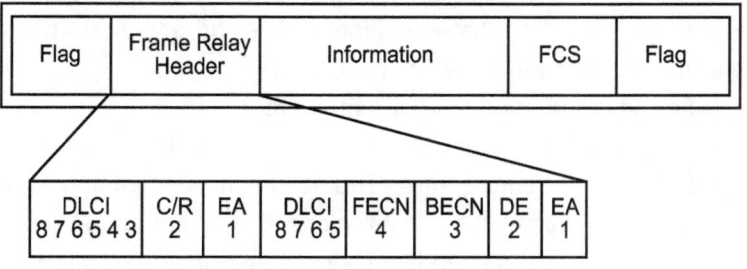

Fig. 3.25: Frame relay header structure

DLCI:
   10-bit DLCI field represents the address of the frame and corresponds to a PVC.
C/R:
   Designates whether the frame is a command or response.
EA:
   Extended Address field signifies upto two additional bytes in the frame relay header, thus greatly expanding the number of possible addresses.
FECN:
   Forward Explicit Congestion Notification (see ECN below).
BECN:
   Backward Explicit Congestion Notification (see ECN below).
DE:
   Discard Eligibility (see DE below).
Information:
   The Information field may include other protocols within it, such as an X.25, IP or SDLC (SNA) packet.

3.1.5.4 Frame Relay Topologies

Frame relay implementations have been deployed in a number of differing manners. Overall, the ideas behind these implementations are similar. Frame relay supports full mesh, partial mesh, and hub and spoke topologies, as follows:

- **Full Mesh**: The full mesh topology is an "all-to-all" implementation and tends to be the most robust. This topology can be considered to have a form of redundancy built into it because each router has connections to every other router (true redundancy involves multiple paths between each router). Should one connection fail, connectivity to remote networks can still be achieved via another router (as long as it was the link that failed, not the router). This topology also results in the least delay for traffic moving across the network. One disadvantage to the full mesh, however, is that it is the most expensive topology to run.
- **Partial Mesh:** The partial mesh topology is a less expensive cousin of the full mesh. Partial mesh involves redundant (multiple path redundancy, not parallel link redundancy) connections between high volume and/or critical sites co-existing with single connections from lower volume and/or
  non-critical sites converging into a central site.
- **Hub and Spoke:** The hub and spoke topology consists of a central site router with connections to all remote sites. This is the most common type of topology implemented in frame relay installations. There are usually very few, if any, redundant connections. Redundant connections are typically provided by ISDN dial backup circuits.

3.1.5.5 The Future of Frame Relay: Interoperability with Asynchronous Transfer Mode (ATM)

1. The future of frame relay is its interoperability with the next generation of high speed packetized data service - Asynchronous Transfer Mode (ATM).
2. ATM is a cell-based high speed network designed to transport voice, data, image, and video information.
3. Rather than variable length frames like frame relay, ATM has fixed 53 byte cells.
4. Because the "packets" have a fixed size, their delay time through a network is fixed.
5. This predictable time delay is ideal for isochronous traffic such as voice and video.
6. Many users prefer to connect their systems to ATM networks from frame relay networks rather than from native ATM networks (ATM equipment on location) because of the bandwidth constraints on low speed native ATM connections.
7. Since ATM uses a 53 byte cell with 5 bytes of header information, the native ATM packets contain about 10% overhead due to the protocol.
8. Frame relay, on the other hand, has a packet size ranging from 500 bytes to 4000 bytes and is less susceptible to protocol overhead from consuming bandwidth.
9. Frame relay access to ATM networks will not append ATM's protocol overhead until the data is in the provider's network making the added overhead invisible to the users.

Thus, we can summarize the frame relay technique as follows:

- Frame relay is a technology that can create a robust wide area networking fabric that integrates information systems together to form an enterprise network.
- It is an affordable and capable service for supporting today's bandwidth intensive applications as well as those residing on legacy systems.
- Because logical connections are defined in software, it is easy to manage moves, changes, additions, and deletions of logical connections.
- Systems analysts should consider the use of frame relay for corporate applications that incorporate information systems at more than one
location because of the technologies many technical, financial, logistical advantages.

3.1.5.6 Additional Possibilities and Benefits Associated with Frame Relay

1. Network managers are constantly seeking new ways to make their company networks more efficient through the use of new and innovative services that are continually being introduced into the market.
2. Often, they are faced with the need to connect remote offices to the corporate backbone to enable access to corporate e-mail, local area networks, mainframe computers, and other corporate services. Frame relay is frequently the technology of choice used to meet these needs.

3. Initially, frame relay gained acceptance as a means to provide end-users with a solution for LAN-to-LAN connections and other data connectivity requirements.
4. Besides providing a flexible and efficient data transport mechanism, frame relay lowered the cost of bandwidth for tying together multi-protocol networks and devices.
5. Over the past few years there has been a migration of legacy traffic such as bisync and SNA from low-speed leased lines onto frame relay.
6. The integration of this so-called legacy traffic with today's LAN-to-LAN connectivity needs provided network managers with a more efficient, flexible, and very cost-effective network.
7. More recently, non-traditional uses are beginning to emerge. Due to advances in areas such as digital signal processing, end-users are beginning to see viable methods, being developed, that incorporate non-data traffic such as voice and video over frame relay.
8. Voice over frame relay (VoFR) technology offers telecommunication and network managers the possibility of consolidating voice and voice-band data (i.e. fax and analog modems) with data services over frame relay.
9. The Frame Relay Forum Technical Committee has developed an Implementation Agreement [FRF.11] in order to allow vendors to interconnect their VoFR-capable equipment.
10. It is anticipated that this work will lay the groundwork for future deployment of VoFR capabilities in multi-vendor and public network environments.
11. Prior to the development of this Implementation Agreement, many equipment vendors developed proprietary methods for implementing voice over frame relay, thus enabling end-users to successfully deploy voice over their frame relay networks.
12. Frame relay will continue to see explosive growth. The acceptance and use of ATM (Asynchronous Transfer Mode, a technology designed with the intent to transport voice, data, and video) will also increase.
13. Both end-users and network service providers will increasingly find that frame relay and ATM do not only coexist, but are complementary; both frame relay and ATM access is offered to, and used by end-users.
14. In addition, service providers have begun to migrate their frame-based networks to ATM-based backbones.
15. The continued use and increased acceptance of frame relay and ATM technologies will bring greater bandwidth and high performance networking to a wider variety of user applications.

16. In addition to giving the reader some insight into how VoFR works, this section will provide an overview of a few of the potential applications of VoFR, some of the considerations faced by end-users, and an overview of the Voice over Frame Relay Implementation Agreement [FRF.11].
17. The intent of this discussion is not to promote or dissuade frame relay users from incorporating voice into their frame relay networks.
18. Instead, it is meant to provide a balanced perspective and information so that readers/users may have more information to decide for themselves as to whether they may benefit from voice over frame relay technology.

3.1.5.7 Voice Over Frame Relay

Theory of Operation:

1. Over the years communication networks have become more reliable. Older, low speed, analog connections, which are often susceptible to network-induced errors, are being replaced with higher speed digital links offering relatively error-free performance.
2. In addition, devices communicating between sites have become more intelligent, allowing them to more readily accommodate network delay, and recover from and re-transmit lost data.
3. Unlike most data communications, which can tolerate delay, voice communications must be performed in near real-time.
4. This means that transmission and network delays must be kept small enough to remain imperceptible to the user.
5. Until recently, packetized voice transmission was not possible due to the requirements of voice bandwidth, and the transmission delays associated with packet-based networks.
6. Packetized voice is now possible; low bit rates are attained by analyzing and processing only the essential components of a voice sample, rather than attempting to digitize the entire voice sample (with all the associates, pauses and repetitive patterns).
7. Current speech processing technology takes the voice digitizing process several steps further than conventional encoding methods.

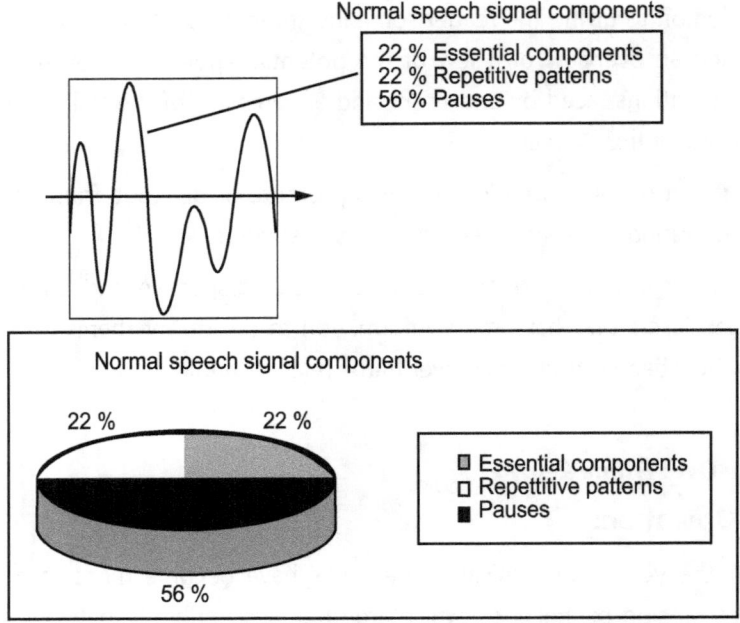

Fig. 3.26: Only 22% of normal speech needs to be sent for high-quality voice communications

8. Human speech is burdened with a tremendous amount of redundant information that is necessary for communications to occur in a natural environment, but which is not needed for a conversation to occur over a communication network.
9. Analysis of a representative voice sample shows that only 22 percent of a typical conversation consists of essential speech components that need to be transmitted for complete voice clarity (Fig. 3.26).
10. The balance is made up of pauses, background noise, and repetitive patterns.

Removal of Repetitive Speech Sounds:

1. Repetitive sounds are inherent in human speech, and are caused by vibrations of the vocal cords.
2. These repetitive sounds (like the 's' in the word *snake* or long 'o' in the word *loan*), are easily compressible.
3. While traveling through the natural environment, perhaps only half of what is spoken will reach the listener's ear.
4. However, in a typical communication network, all of the speech content is transmitted.
5. Transmission of these identical sounds is not necessary; their removal can increase bandwidth efficiency.

Removal of Pauses (Silence Suppression):
1. A person speaking does not provide a continuous stream of information (regardless of how fast he speak).
2. Pauses between words and sentences, and the gaps that occur at the end of one person talking but before the other begins, can also be removed.
3. The pauses may be represented in compressed form and can be recreated at the destination side of the call in order to maintain the natural quality of the spoken communication.
4. The suppression and removal of silent periods can also significantly improve bandwidth utilization.

Voice Frame Formation:
1. The removal of silent periods and redundant information through advanced techniques enables voice to be efficiently "compressed".
2. After the removal of repetitive patterns and silent periods, the remaining speech information may then be digitized and placed into voice packets suitable for transmission over a frame relay network.
3. These packets or frames (both terms are often used interchangeably) also tend to be smaller than the average data frame.
4. The use of smaller packets helps to reduce transmission delay across a frame relay network.
5. The concepts introduced above, provide the basis for efficiently using the smallest amount of bandwidth possible for voice transmission over a frame relay network.

3.1.5.8 Using Voice Over Frame Relay

Potential End User Applications:
1. Telecommunication managers continue to explore alternatives for obtaining the most efficient use of their corporate network resources.
2. Many network managers have migrated their point-to-point leased communication networks [built in the 1980's with TDM (Time Division Multiplexers) equipment] to public and private frame relay networks.
3. Since many of these point-to-point leased line networks carried both voice and data, these network managers are interested in meeting not only their data communication needs, but also their voice communication needs.
4. VoFR (voice over frame relay) offers a potential alternative for carrying voice communications over a frame relay network in order to meet intra-company communication needs.

5. Current users of frame relay may find that they have "excess" bandwidth available even with the tremendous expansion of applications and increase in data traffic.
6. And, even when existing bandwidth is efficiently utilized, some network managers might find that the incremental cost for the additional frame relay network bandwidth needed for voice transport is more cost-effective than some of the standard voice services offered by local and long distance carriers.
7. In other cases, some end-users might find that VoFR is a viable option to be used in place of Off-Premises Extension (OPX) and Private Line Auto Ringdown (PLAR) lines.
8. Of course, the motivation behind the interest in VoFR will vary.
9. VoFR has the potential to provide end-users with greater efficiencies in the use of access bandwidth by functionally integrating voice, data, and fax over a single access link.
10. In addition, VoFR has the potential to provide end-users with a cost-effective option for the transport needs of voice traffic between their company locations.
11. As an example, a network manager may choose to integrate a few voice channels and serial data over the frame relay connection between a branch office and corporate headquarters.
12. By transmitting the voice traffic over the frame relay connection, which is already carrying data traffic (Fig. 3.27), the user has the potential to obtain cost-effective intra-company calling and efficient use of network bandwidth.

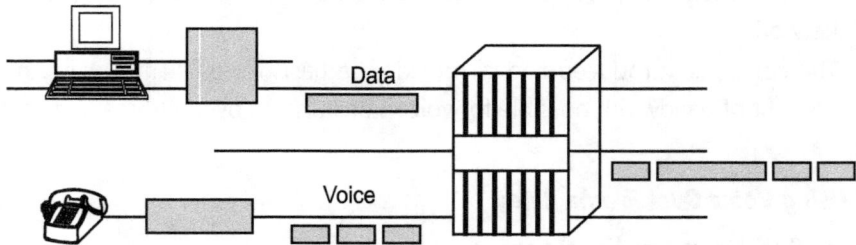

Fig. 3.27: Voice and data being integrated by customer premises equipment

13. The examples provided do not necessarily reflect all the potential possibilities of VoFR.
14. An exploration of the full possibilities and potential for the implementation of VoFR is outside the scope of this chapter.
15. There are many reasons used, and possibilities explored by network managers in their attempt to justify more efficient, flexible, and cost-effective networking capabilities.
16. VoFR represents one of many possible methods that enable users to increase the flexibility and efficiency of their company's network resources.

17. There might, however, be potential trade-offs that the network manager may face when implementing VoFR.
18. Some of the potential trade-offs may include some loss of the quality commonly associated with toll traffic due to VoFR's use of voice compression; the loss of management and administrative benefits associated with carrier voice services (i.e. the loss of consolidated voice billing and invoice itemization, end-user charge back capabilities, and other advanced features such as Caller ID and accounting codes); and the lack of standards defining the acceptable levels of quality for voice transport over a carrier's frame relay network.
19. In addition, carriers offering public frame relay service cannot always guarantee the quality or performance of voice transported over their frame relay networks.
20. In the absence of standards, there are no any specifications, which define the quality of a voice conversation (i.e. delay, tonal and pitch qualities) occurring over the carrier's frame relay service.
21. Since the quality of VoFR is subjective, it is troublesome for the carrier to guarantee complete user satisfaction.
22. The lack of specific voice over frame relay service guarantees and full carrier troubleshooting capabilities is a result of the fact that in today's environment, the implementation of voice over frame relay occurs in equipment on the end-user's premises and outside of the carrier's frame relay network.
23. The potential trade-offs do not necessarily negate the value and promise of VoFR.
24. Significant advances in digital signal processors and compression algorithms often provide voice approaching toll quality.
25. VoFR vendors continue to add advanced capabilities in management and administration capabilities. Future industry work will seek to define standards which define acceptable levels of quality and performance metrics for voice transport through data networks.
26. Some end-users might not be concerned with the potential trade-offs noted; some may find the trade-offs unacceptable in particular situations; others may find that if trade-offs exist, they are outweighed by the potential for costs savings and efficiencies gained by integrating voice and data over frame relay.
27. In the end, it will be upto the customer to decide.

3.1.5.9 *Voice Over Frame Relay Equipment*
Common Considerations Faced By Equipment Vendors:
1. **Vendors offering equipment capable of integrating voice and data traffic over frame relay must consider how they will address issues such as compression, echo cancellation, delay and delay variation, frame loss, and traffic prioritization.**

2. Each of these, and other considerations, can affect voice quality.
3. While vendors offering voice over frame relay-capable equipment may have similar objectives regarding quality and performance, each vendor may choose to pursue these objectives through different hardware and software implementations.
4. Common considerations and a few of the many potential methods used to provide voice over frame relay are presented below.

Voice Compression:

1. Compression of voice is a result of the removal of the silent periods and redundant information found in human speech.
2. Voice compression is used to reduce the amount of information needed to recreate the voice at the destination end.
3. Uncompressed digitized voice and fax require a large amount of bandwidth.
4. This often makes it impractical to transmit these signals over low-speed access links. The use of low bit rate voice compression algorithms can make it possible to provide high quality speech while using bandwidth efficiently.
5. Various algorithms are used to sample speech patterns and reduce the information sent - all while retaining the highest possible level of voice quality.
6. A relatively simple ADPCM (Adaptive Delta Pulse Code Modulation) algorithm can reduce the speech data rate to half that of PCM (Pulse Code Modulation), an ITU standard for digital voice coding, which consumes 64 kbps and is optimized for speech quality.
7. PCM is the voice algorithm that is commonly used in telephone networks today.
8. ADPCM may be used in place of PCM, while maintaining about the same voice quality.
9. In addition to ADPCM, there are a number of standard low bit rate voice compression algorithms (e.g., ITU G.729) as well as proprietary algorithms implemented by various vendors, which provide more significant reductions (i.e. upto 10% or less than that of PCM) in the amount of information required to recreate speech at the receiver.
10. Other voice compression algorithms model speech more efficiently (i.e., with fewer bits) by using advanced predictive techniques.
11. These algorithms further reduce the bandwidth required to maintain good voice quality.
12. Implementation of these advanced compression techniques, and meeting their processing demands, is made possible by the use of Digital Signal Processors (DSPs).

13. A DSP is a microprocessor that is designed specifically to process digitized signals such as those found in voice and video applications.
14. In the last ten years, significant advances in the design of DSPs have occurred.
15. This development has allowed manufacturers to bring to market even higher quality digitization algorithms that consume very little bandwidth.
16. The general function of these strategies is to scrutinize the speech signal more carefully in order to eliminate the redundancies in the signal more completely, and to use the available bits to code the non-redundant parts of the signal in an efficient manner.
17. As the available bit rate is reduced from 64 kbps to 32, 16, 8, and 4 kbps or below, the strategies for redundancy removal and bit allocation need to be ever more sophisticated.
18. Low cost general purpose DSP processors and other advanced compression algorithms allow the possibility of accomplishing voice compression within VoFR-capable devices at lower and lower bit rates.

Echo Cancellation:

1. Echo is a phenomenon found in voice networks. Echo occurs when the transmitted voice is reflected back to the point from which it was transmitted.
2. In voice networks, echo cancellation devices are used within a carrier's network when the propagation delay increases to the point where echo results.
3. The longer the distance, the more the delay, and the more likely that echo will result.
4. Voice transmitted over a frame relay network will also face propagation delays.
5. As the end-to-end delay increases, the echo will become noticeable to the end-user if it is not canceled.

Delay and Delay Variation:

1. The bursty nature and variable frame sizes of frame relay may result in variable delays between consecutive packets.
2. The variation in the time difference between each arriving packet is called "jitter".
3. Jitter can impede the ability of the receiving end CPE to smoothly regenerate voice.
4. Since voice is inherently a continuous waveform, a large gap between the regenerated voice packets will result in distorted sound.
5. Equipment vendors can contribute to the mitigation of jitter across the network by employing fragmentation of data packets in order to transmit uniform packet sizes into the network.

6. To avoid dropping speech samples, data can be buffered sufficiently at the speech decoder to account for the worst-case delay jitter through the network.
7. Equipment vendors look to incorporate this capability within their equipment.

Frame Loss:

1. Compressed voice can usually withstand infrequent packet loss better than data can.
2. If a voice packet is lost, most likely the user will not notice.
3. If excessive frame loss occurs, it is equally unacceptable for VoFR and for data traffic.

Traffic Integration - Fax and Modem Support:

1. Vendors implementing VoFR technology appear to be mimicking switched public voice services.
2. Since VoFR supports fax and data modem services as well, end-users, who have high fax traffic volumes between branches and headquarters, will find this ability beneficial.
3. Voice band fax signals are demodulated at the locally connected equipment and transmitted over the network as digital data in a standard packet format.
4. In effect, the local Voice FRAD tricks the fax machine into thinking it is connected to a remote fax machine across an analog network.
5. However, it is difficult to reliably compress fax and data modem signals to achieve the low bandwidth utilization often necessary for the most efficient integration over frame relay.
6. Some vendors have implemented schemes where voice is compressed to a low bit rate, but upon detection of a fax tone, the bandwidth is reallocated to a higher bit rate to allow for faster fax transmission.

Prioritization:

1. Voice, fax and some data types are delay-sensitive.
2. This means that if the end-to-end delay or the delay variation exceeds a specified limit, the service level will get degraded.
3. To minimize the potential for service degradation, vendors can employ a variety of mechanisms and techniques.
4. To minimize voice traffic delay, a prioritization mechanism that provides service to the delay-sensitive traffic can first be employed.

5. Vendors offering equipment capable of integrating voice and data over frame relay may choose to use a variety of proprietary mechanisms to ensure a balance between voice and data transmission needs.
6. Although they may differ, the concept remains essentially the same.
7. For example, each input traffic type may be configured into one of several priority queues.
8. Voice and fax traffic can be placed in the highest-priority queue, for expeditious delivery to the network.
9. Lower-priority data traffic can be buffered until the higher-priority voice and fax packets are sent (Fig. 3.28 below).

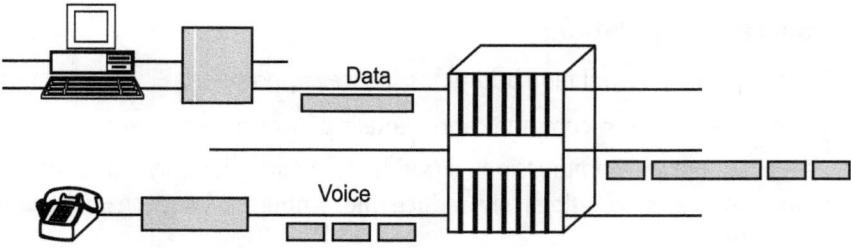

Fig. 3.28: Prioritization places delay-sensitive traffic, such as voice, ahead of lower priority data transmissions

Fragmentation:

1. Fragmentation is used to break up large blocks of data into smaller, less delay-creating frames.
2. This is another means used to ensure the highest level of voice quality possible.
3. Fragmentation attempts to ensure an even flow of voice frames into the network, thus minimizing delay jitter across circuits that carry both, packet-voice and data.

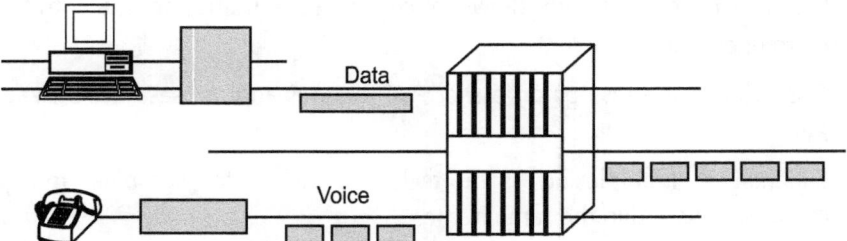

Fig. 3.29: Fragmentation ensures that high priority traffic, such as voice, does not have to wait to be sent. Long data packets can be interrupted to send a voice packet

4. Fragmentation often involves all of the data in the network, to retain consistent voice quality.

5. This is because even if the voice information is fragmented, delay will still occur if a voice frame is held up in the "middle" of the network, behind a large data frame.
6. This fragmentation of data packets (as shown in Fig. 3.63) ensures that voice and fax packets are not unacceptably delayed behind large data packets.
7. Additionally, fragmentation reduces jitter because voice packets can be sent and received more regularly.
8. Fragmentation, especially when used with prioritization techniques, is used to ensure a consistent flow of voice information.
9. The objective of this and other techniques is to enable VoFR technology to provide service approaching toll quality voice.
10. The Frame Relay Forum recommends the use of the Fragmentation Implementation Agreement [FRF.12] when employing fragmentation for VoFR.

Digital Speech Interpolation:

1. Digital speech interpolation addresses silence suppression.
2. The nature of speech communication entails pauses between words and sentences.
3. Advanced voice compression algorithms, which identify and remove these redundant patterns, effectively reduce the amount of speech information to be transmitted.
4. DSI uses advanced voice processing techniques to detect silence periods and suppress transmission of this information.
5. By taking advantage of this technique, bandwidth consumption may be reduced.

Multiplexing Techniques:

1. Some equipment vendors offering voice FRADs (Frame Relay Access Devices) use different bandwidth optimization multiplexing techniques such as Logical Link Multiplexing and Subchannel Multiplexing.
2. Logical Link Multiplexing allows voice and data frames to share the same PVC (Permanent Virtual Circuit).
3. This can provide savings on carrier PVC charges and increase the utilization of the PVC.
4. Subchannel Multiplexing is a technique used to combine multiple voice conversations within the same frame.
5. By allowing multiple voice payloads to be sent in a single frame, packet overhead is reduced.
6. This may offer increased performance on low speed links.
7. This technique can allow slow speed connections to transport small voice packets efficiently across the frame relay network.

Other Considerations:

1. In addition to providing basic services such as encapsulation of data traffic for transport over the frame relay network, voice capable FRADs may sometimes provide connectivity between PBXs and other voice equipment.
2. As a result, the voice FRAD would have to manage different traffic types and accommodate their different needs.
3. When voice is carried over a frame relay network that employs ATM in the backbone, there is no impact due to the use of the ATM backbone since ATM functions purely as a transport medium.

3.1.5.10 Voice Over Frame Relay Implementation Agreement (frf.11)
Overview:

1. Frame Relay Forum Implementation Agreements provide an agreed upon basis for vendors and service providers to develop equipment and services that inter-operate.
2. In the case of VoFR, as with many emerging technologies, vendors are often able to develop and deploy capabilities before the various industry and user organizations achieve consensus on uniform standards and implementations.
3. FRF.11 provides an outline for an agreed-upon basis for VoFR so that companies may build equipment and offer services that will be capable of functionally inter-operating with each other.
4. The IA addresses the following:
   - Transport of compressed voice within the payload of a frame relay frame, via the support of a diverse set of voice compression algorithms such as CS-ACELP, LD CELP, MP-MLQ, PCM, etc.
   - Effective utilization of low bit rate frame relay connections.
   - Multiplexing of upto 255 sub-channels on a single frame relay DLCI, such that a single DLCI may contain both voice and data payloads.
   - Support of multiple voice payloads on the same or different sub-channel(s) within a single frame.

3.1.5.11 Reference Model

1. The reference model for VoFR is shown in Fig. 3.30. Using the VoFR feature, it is possible for any type of VFRAD on the left-hand side of Fig. 3.64 to exchange voice and signaling information with any type of VFRAD on the right-hand side of Fig. 3.30.

2. Three types of devices are shown in Fig. 3.30. The top layer shows end-system devices similar to telephones or fax machines; the middle layer shows transparent multiplexing devices similar to channel banks; the bottom layer shows switching system devices similar to PBX's.
3. A VFRAD connects to a frame relay UNI via physical interfaces as defined in [FRF.1.1].

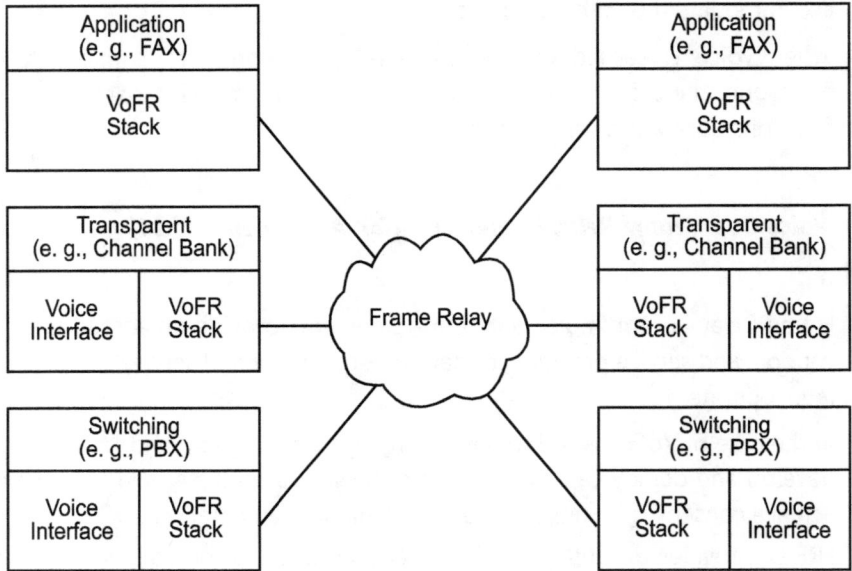

Fig. 3.30 (a): Voice over frame relay network reference model

Thus, we can summarize the frame relay technology as follows:

- Frame relay is beginning to evolve from a single, data-only application technology to one with a broad spectrum of uses.

- Integration of voice and data over frame relay represents one of many promising areas of development that could not only benefit end users, but one that could continue to fuel the continued growth of frame relay services and applications.

- Voice over frame relay (VoFR) technology consolidates voice and voice-band data (i.e. fax and analog modems) with data services over the frame relay network.

- It has the potential to provide end-users with greater efficiencies in the use of access bandwidth and to provide end-users with cost-effective transport of voice traffic for intra-company communications.

3.1.5.12 Congestion-Control Mechanisms In Frame Relay

Frame Relay reduces network overhead by implementing simple congestion-notification mechanisms rather than explicit, per-virtual-circuit flow control. Frame Relay typically is implemented on reliable network media, so data integrity is not sacrificed because flow control can be left to higher-layer protocols. Frame Relay implements two congestion-notification mechanisms:

- Forward-explicit congestion notification (FECN)
- Backward-explicit congestion notification (BECN)

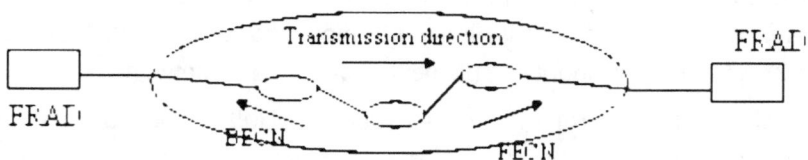

Fig. 3.30 (b)

FECN and BECN each are controlled by a single bit contained in the Frame Relay frame header. The Frame Relay frame header also contains a Discard Eligibility (DE) bit, which is used to identify less important traffic that can be dropped during periods of congestion.

The FECN bit is part of the Address field in the Frame Relay frame header. The FECN mechanism is initiated when a DTE device sends Frame Relay frames into the network. If the network is congested, DCE devices (switches) set the value of the frames' FECN bit to 1. When the frames reach the destination DTE device, the Address field (with the FECN bit set) indicates that the frame experienced congestion in the path from source to destination. The DTE device can relay this information to a higher-layer protocol for processing. Depending on the implementation, flow-control may be initiated, or the indication may be ignored.

The BECN bit is part of the Address field in the Frame Relay frame header. DCE devices set the value of the BECN bit to 1 in frames traveling in the opposite direction of frames with their FECN bit set. This informs the receiving DTE device that a particular path through the network is congested. The DTE device then can relay this information to a higher-layer protocol for processing. Depending on the implementation, flow-control may be initiated, or the indication may be ignored.

Frame Relay Discard Eligibility (DE):

The Discard Eligibility (DE) bit is used to indicate that a frame has lower importance than other frames. The DE bit is part of the Address field in the Frame Relay frame header.

DTE devices can set the value of the DE bit of a frame to 1 to indicate that the frame has lower importance than other frames. When the network becomes congested, DCE devices will discard frames with the DE bit set before discarding those that do not. This reduces the likelihood of critical data being dropped by Frame Relay DCE devices during periods of congestion.

Two methods of handling congestions with in the FR are:

1. Explicit congestion notification (ECN ie FECN and BECN)
2. Consolidated Link layer Management (CLLM)

- CLLM's major function is to augment the BECN mechanism for reporting congestion by allowing the network to report in the "backward" direction in the absence of PVC traffic to carry explicit congestion notification. Both LMI and CLLM operate on DLCI 1023, so the two cannot be implemented on the same network.

- CLLM reports congestion in more detail than LMI, noting both the congestion's cause and its expected duration along with a list of DLCIs that should reduce traffic. To date, few Frame Relay vendors have implemented CLLM. The optional Status Update feature of LMI performs a similar function, and its implementation in the richer set of LMI functions makes LMI seem more attractive.

- It may occur that there are no frames traveling back to the source node which is causing the congestion. In this case, the network will want to send its own message to the problematic source node.

- The standard, however, does not allow the network to send its own frames with the DLCI of the desired virtual circuit.

- To address this problem, ANSI defined the Consolidated Link Layer Management (CLLM).

- The ANSI standard (T1.618) defines the format of the CLLM message. It contains a code for the cause of the congestion and a listing of all DLCIs that should act to reduce their data transmission to lower congestion.

- CLLM messages issues are

    Network congestion, excessive traffic, short term
    Network congestion, excessive traffic, long term
    Facility or equipment failure, short term
    Facility or equipment failure, long term
    Maintenance action, short term
    Maintenance action, long term
    Unknown, short term
    Unknown, long term

ANSI T1.618

Reference Standard: ANSI T1.618.

T1.618 frame structure: fields

bits 8 _ _ _ _ _ _ 1	field
octets 1-i	Address (2, 3 or 4 octets)
octet i+1	Control
octets (i+2)-n	Information

CLLM (Consolidated Link Layer Management) message.

bits 8 _ _ _ _ _ _ 1	field
octets 1-i	Address (2, 3 or 4 octets)
octet i+1	AFh = XID control field
octet i+2	82h = Format identifier
octet i+3	0Fh = Group identifier
octet i+4	Group length octet 1
octet i+5	Group length octet 2
octet i+6	00h = Parameter identifier
octet i+7	04h = Parameter length
octet i+8	105d =Parameter value (IA5 character 'I')
octet i+9	49d =Parameter value (IA5 character '1')
octet i+10	50d =Parameter value (IA5 character '2')
octet i+11	50d =Parameter value (IA5 character '2')
octet i+12	02h = Parameter identifier
octet i+13	01h = Parameter length
octet i+14	Cause value
octet i+15	03h =Parameter value (DLCI identifier)
octet i+16	Parameter length
octets i+17-n	DLCI value octets (1rst DLCI)
	DLCI value octets (ntht DLCI)

T1.618 frame structure: address field

They are 3 possible formats for the address field:

- 2 octets
- 3 octets
- 4 octets

Address field 2 octets

- Octet 1:	
bits 8-3	upper DLCI: Data Link Connection Identifier
bit 2	C/R: Command/Response
bit 1	Address field extension (0)
- Octet 2:	

bits 8-5	lower DLCI: Data Link Connection Identifier
bit 4	FECN: forward explicit congestion notification
bit 3	BECN: backward explicit congestion notification
bit 2	DE: discard eligibility indicator
bit 1	Address field extension (1)

Address field 3 octets

- Octet 1:	
bits 8-3	upper DLCI: Data Link Connection Identifier
bit 2	C/R: Command/Response
bit 1	Address field extension (0)
- Octet 2:	
bits 8-5	DLCI: Data Link Connection Identifier
bit 4	FECN: forward explicit congestion notification
bit 3	BECN: backward explicit congestion notification
bit 2	DE: discard eligibility indicator
bit 1	Address field extension (0)
- Octet 3:	
bits 8-3	lower DLCI or DL-CORE control
bit 2	D/C: DLCI (0) /DL-CORE (1) control indicator
bit 1	Address field extension (1)

Address field 4 octets

- Octet 1:	
bits 8-3	upper DLCI: Data Link Connection Identifier
bit 2	C/R: Command/Response
bit 1	Address field extension (0)
- Octet 2:	
bits 8-5	DLCI: Data Link Connection Identifier
bit 4	FECN: forward explicit congestion notification
bit 3	BECN: backward explicit congestion notification
bit 2	DE: discard eligibility indicator
bit 1	Address field extension (0)
- Octet 3:	
bits 8-2	DLCI: Data Link Connection Identifier
bit 1	Address field extension (0)
- Octet 4:	
bits 8-3	lower DLCI or DL-CORE control
bit 2	D/C: DLCI (0) /DL-CORE (1) control indicator
bit 1	Address field extension (1)

T1.618 frame structure: control field

- octet:		
bits 8-6	M M M	M: modifier function bit
bit 5	P/F	Poll bit when issued as a command
		Final bit when issued as a response
bits 4-3	M M	M: modifier function bit
bits 2-1	1 1	

bits M: 876 - 43	Command	Response	Frame designation
0 0 0 - 0 0	UI		Unnumbered Information
1 0 1 - 1 1		XID	Exchange Identification

The encoding values of the five M bits included in the first octet of the control field can also be listed and ordered according to their hexadecimal code.

P=0	P=1	Type	C/R	Frame designation
03	13	UI	C/R	Unnumbered Information
AF	BF	XID	R	Exchange Identification

Note: Hexadecimal code corresponds to b8-b1 with P/F bit=0 or P/F bit=1.

3.2 ATM Networks

Introduction:

1. Asynchronous transfer mode (ATM) is an advanced implementation of packet switching that provides high-speed data transmission rates to send fixed-size packets over broadband and baseband LANs or WANs.

2. ATM can accommodate:
   - Voice
   - Data
   - Fax
   - Real-time video
   - CD-quality audio
   - Imaging.
   - Multimegabit data transmission.

3. The CCITT defined ATM in 1988 as part of the broadband Integrated Services Digital Network (BISDN), discussed later in this lesson.

4. Because of ATM's power and versatility, it is influencing the development of network communications.

5. It is equally adaptable to LAN and WAN environments, and it can transmit data at very high speeds (155 Mbps to 622 Mbps or more).

ATM Technology:

1. ATM is a broadband cell relay method that transmits data in 53-byte cells rather than in variable-length frames.
2. Fig. 3.31 illustrates an ATM cell. These cells consist of 48 bytes of application information with five additional bytes of ATM header data.
3. For example, ATM would divide a 1000-byte packet into 21 data frames and put each data frame into a cell.
4. The result is a technology that transmits a consistent, uniform packet.

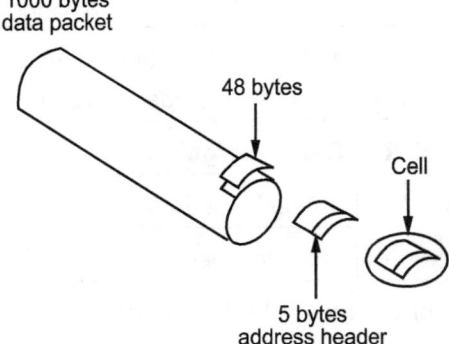

Fig. 3.31: ATM cells have 48 bytes of data and a 5-byte header

5. Network equipment can switch, route, and move uniform-sized frames much more quickly than it can move random-sized frames.
6. The consistent, standard-sized cell uses buffers efficiently and reduces the work required to process incoming data. The uniform cell size also helps in planning application bandwidth.
7. Theoretically, ATM can offer throughput rates of upto 1.2 gigabits per second.
8. Currently, however, ATM measures its speed against fiber-optic speeds that can reach as high as 622 Mbps, most commercial ATM boards will transmit data at about 155 Mbps.
9. As a reference point, at 622 Mbps ATM could transmit the entire contents of the latest edition of the *Encyclopedia Britannica*, including graphics, in less than one second. If the same transfer were tried using a 2400-baud modem, the operation would take more than two days.
10. ATM can be used in LANs and WANs at approximately the same speed in each.
11. ATM relies on carriers such as AT&T and Sprint for implementation over a wide area.
12. This creates a consistent environment that does away with the concept of the slow WAN and the differing technologies used in the LAN and WAN environments.

ATM Components:
1. ATM components are currently available through only a limited number of vendors.
2. All hardware in an ATM network must be ATM-compatible.
3. Implementing ATM in an existing facility will require extensive equipment replacement.
4. This is one reason why ATM has not been adopted more quickly.

However, as the ATM market matures, various vendors will be able to provide:
- Routers and switches to connect carrier services on a global basis.
- Backbone devices to connect all the LANs within a large organization.
- Switches and adapters that link desktop computers to high-speed ATM connections for running multimedia applications.

5. **ATM Media:** ATM does not restrict itself to any particular media type. It can be used with existing media designed for other communication systems including:
   - Coaxial cable.
   - Twisted-pair cable.
   - Fiber-optic cable.
6. However, these traditional network media, in their present forms, do not support all of ATM's capabilities. An organization called the ATM Forum recommends the following physical interfaces for ATM:
   - FDDI (100 Mbps)
   - Fiber Channel (155 Mbps)
   - OC3 SONET (155 Mbps)
   - T3 (45 Mbps)
7. **ATM Switches:** ATM switches are multiport devices that can act as either of the following:
   - Hubs to forward data from one computer to another within a network.
   - Router-like devices to forward data at high speeds to remote networks.
8. In some network architectures, such as Ethernet and Token Ring, only one computer at a time can transmit. In Fig. 3.32, three routers are feeding data into the ATM switch and onto the ATM network at the same time.

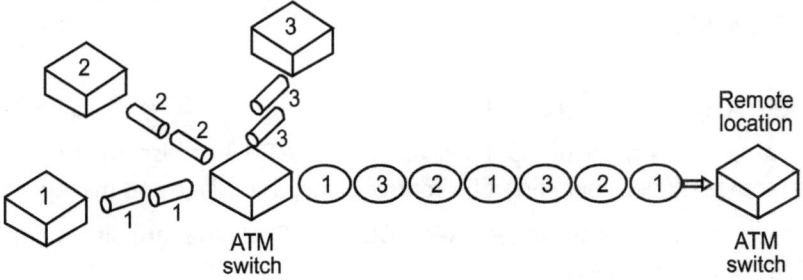

Fig. 3.32: ATM switches act as multiplexers allowing multiple data input

3.2.1 Why ATM?
1. ATM stands for Asynchronous Transfer Mode.
2. ATM is a connection-oriented technique that requires information to be buffered and then placed in a cell.
3. When there is enough data to fill the cell, the cell is then transported across the network to the destination specified within the cell.
4. We can see that ATM is very similar to packet-switched networks, but there are several important differences:
   - ATM provides cell sequence integrity. i.e. cells arrive at the destination in the same order as they left the source. This may not be the case with other packet-switched networks.
   - Cells are much smaller than standard packet-switched networks. This reduces the value of delay variance, making ATM acceptable for timing sensitive information like voice.
   - The quality of transmission links has lead to the omission of overheads, such as error correction, in order to maximize efficiency.
   - There is no space between cells. At times when the network is idle, unassigned cells are transported.
5. These are the techniques that allow ATM to be more flexible than Narrow-band ISDN (N-ISDN), and hence ATM was chosen as the broadband access to ISDN by the CCITT (now ITU - International Telecommunication Union).
6. The broadband nature of ATM allows for a multitude of different types of services to be transported using the same format.
7. This makes ATM ideal for true integration of voice, data and video facilities on one network. By consolidation of services, network management and operation is simplified.
8. However, new terms of network administration must be considered, such as billing rates and quality of service agreements.
9. The flexibility inherent in the cell structure of ATM allows it to match the rate at which it transmits to that generated by the source.
10. Many new high bit-rate services, such as video, are variable bit rate (VBR). Compression techniques create bursty data which is well suited for transmission using ATM cells.

3.2.2 The Protocol Reference Model
1. In a similar way to the OSI 7-layer model, ATM has also developed a protocol reference model, consisting of a control plane, user plane and management plane.
2. The model also incorporates SAPs, SDUs and PDUs that are also mentioned in the OSI layered approach.

3. As the diagram below shows, the User plane (for information transfer) and Control plane (for call control) are structured in layers.
4. Above the Physical Layer rests the ATM Layer and the ATM Adaptation Layer (AAL). Management provides network supervision. **The ATM reference model relates to the lowest two layers of the OSI reference model.**

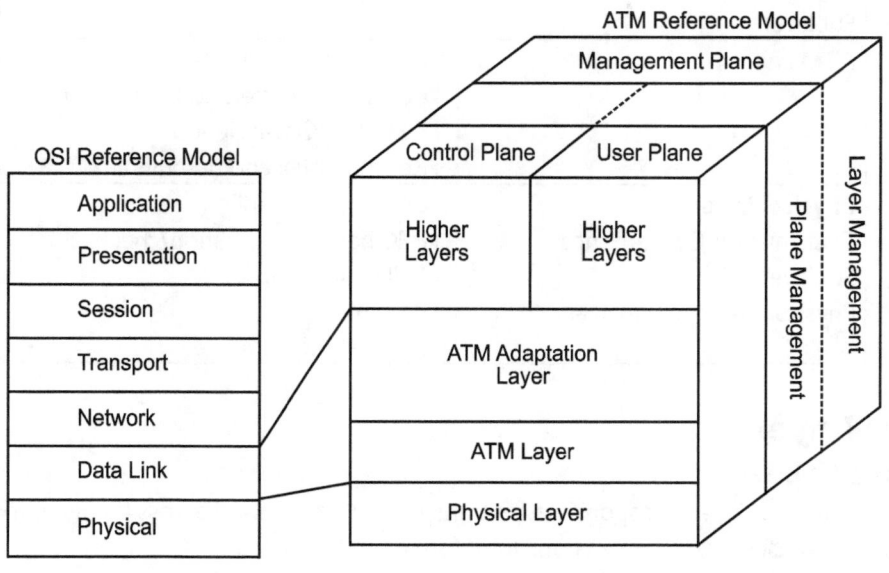

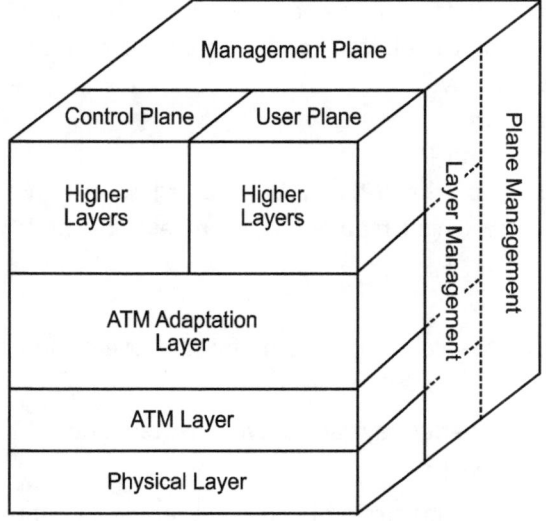

Fig. 3.33: ATM has also developed a protocol reference model, consisting of a control plane, user plane and management plane

The AAL and Physical layers are further divided into sublayers, and the functions of these layers are shown below.

Layer/Sublayer	Function
ATM Adaptation Layer Convergence Sublayer Segmentation and Reassembly Sublayer	Convergence Segmentation and Reassembly
ATM Layer	Generic Flow Control Cell header generation/extraction Cell VPI/VCI translation Cell multiplex and demultiplex
Physical Layer Transmission Convergence Sublayer Physical Medium Sublayer	Cell-rate decoupling HEC header generation/check Cell delineation Bit timing Physical medium

ATM Layer

Responsibilities:
1. The ATM layer is responsible for transporting information across the network.
2. ATM uses virtual connections for information transport.
3. The connections are deemed virtual because although the users can connect end-to-end, connection is only made when a cell needs to be sent.
4. The connection is not dedicated to the use of one conversation. The connections are divided into two levels:
   - The Virtual Path
   - The Virtual Channel

These are the properties of the VP and VC that allow cell multiplexing. There is a complication in that cell switching requires only the value of the VP identifier, VPI to be known.

Cell Structure:
1. The structure of the cell is important for the overall functionality of the ATM network.
2. A large cell gives a better payload to overhead ratio, but at the expense of longer, more variable delays.
3. Shorter packets overcome this problem, however the amount of information carried per packet is reduced.
4. A compromise between these two conflicting requirements was reached, and a standard cell format chosen.

5. The ATM cell consists of a 5-octet header and a 48-octet information field after the header. This is shown below.

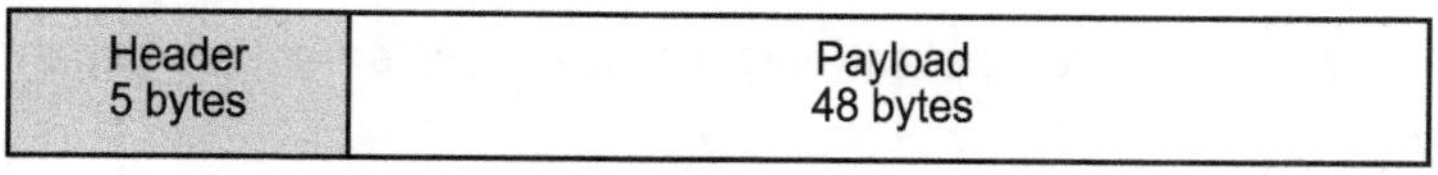

| Header 5 bytes | Payload 48 bytes |

Fig. 3.34: ATM cell

6. The information contained in the header is dependent on whether the cell is carrying information from the user network to the first ATM public exchange (User-Network Interface - UNI), or between ATM exchanges in the trunk network (Network-Node Interface - NNI).
7. The formats of the two types of header are shown below.
8. Notice the similarity between the two, with only the UNI having a Generic Flow Control, GFC, field.

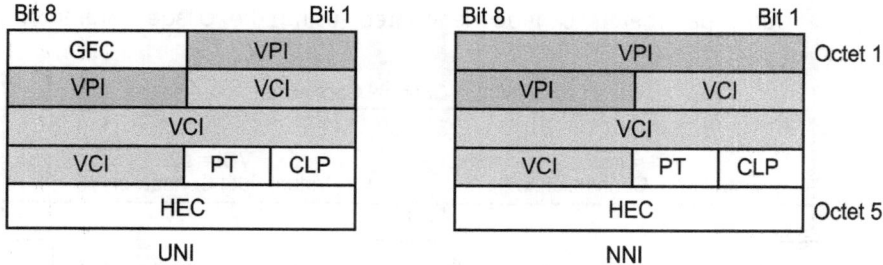

Fig. 3.35: Descriptions of all the fields contained in the ATM cell headers, GFC, VPI, VCI, PT, CLP, HEC, are found in the ATM Dictionary

(CLP – Cell Loss Priority, PT – Payload Type, HEC – Header Error Control)

Virtual Channels:

1. The connection between two endpoints is called a Virtual Channel Connection, VCC.
2. It is made up of a series of virtual channel links that extend between VC switches.
3. The VC is identified by a Virtual Channel Identifier, VCI.
4. The value of the VCI will change as it enters a VC switch, due to routing translation tables.
5. Within a virtual channel link the value of the VCI remains constant.
6. The VCI (and VPI) are used in the switching environment to ensure that channels and paths are routed correctly.
7. They provide a means for the switch to distinguish between different types of connection.
8. There are many types of virtual channel connections, these include:

- User-to-user applications: Between customer equipment at each end of the connection.
- User-to-network applications: Between customer equipment and network node.
- Network-to-network applications: Between two network nodes and includes traffic management and routing.

9. Virtual channel connections have the following properties:
   - A VCC user is provided with a quality of service, QoS, specifying parameters such as cell-loss ratio, (CLR), and cell-delay variation, (CDV).
   - VCCs can be switched or semi-permanent.
   - Cell sequence integrity is maintained within a VCC.
   - Traffic parameters can be negotiated, using the Usage Parameter Control, (UPC).

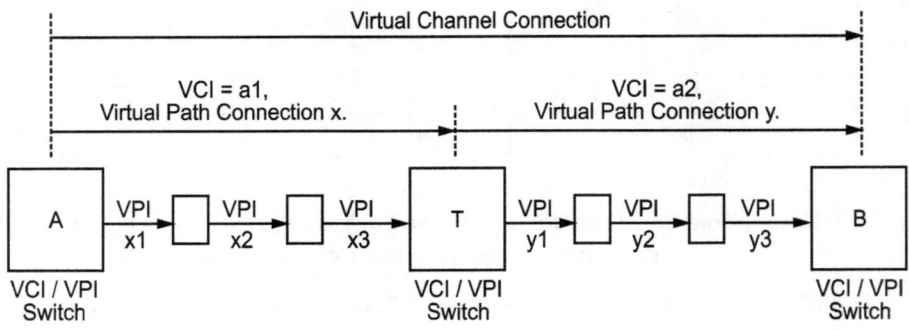

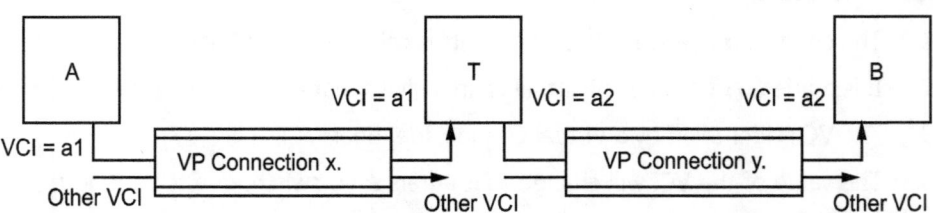

Fig. 3.36: A detailed diagram showing the relationship between virtual channels and paths is shown

Virtual Paths:

1. A virtual path (VP) is a term for a bundle of virtual channel links that all have the same endpoints.
2. As with VCs, virtual path links can be strung together to form a virtual path connection (VPC).

3. A VPC endpoint is where its related VPIs are originated, terminated or translated.
4. Virtual paths are used to simplify the ATM addressing structure.
5. VPs provide logical direct routes between switching nodes via intermediate cross-connect nodes.
6. A virtual path provides the logical equivalent of a link between two switching nodes that are not necessarily directly connected on a physical link.
7. It therefore allows a distinction between logical and physical network structure and provides the flexibility to rearrange the logical structure according to traffic requirements. This is best shown in Fig. 3.70.
8. As with VCs, virtual paths are identified in the cell header with the Virtual Path Identifier (VPI).
9. Within an ATM cross-connect, information about individual virtual channels within a virtual path is not required, as all VCs within one path follow the same route as that path.

ATM Adaptation Layer:

Responsibilities:

1. The ATM Adaptation Layer (AAL) performs the necessary mapping between the ATM layer and the higher layers.
2. This task is usually performed in terminal equipment, or terminal adaptors (TA) at the edge of the ATM network.
3. The ATM network is independent of the services it carries.
4. Thus, the user payload is carried transparently by the ATM network.
5. The ATM network does not process, or know the structure of the payload.
6. This is known as semantic independence.
7. The ATM network is also time independent, as their is no relationship between the timing of the source application and the network clock.
8. All of this independence must be built into the boundary of the ATM network, and falls into the realm of the AAL. The AAL must also cope with:
   - Data flow to application
   - Cell delay variation, CDV
   - Loss of cells
   - Misdelivery of cells
9. It would have been possible to develop separate AALs for each type of telecommunication service offered, however, the many common factors between services has meant that a small set of AAL protocols is sufficient to cover the envisaged possibilities.

10. A telecommunication service is defined on the following parameters:
    - Timing relationship between source and destination.
    - Bit-rate.
    - Connection mode.
11. Parameters such as communication assurance are treated as quality of service parameters. As a result, four classes of service have been defined.

Class:	A	B	C	D
Timing relationship between source and destination	Required	Required	Not Required	Not Required
Bit rate	Constant	Variable	Variable	Variable
Connection mode	Connection-oriented	Connection-oriented	Connection-oriented	Connectionless

Fig. 3.37: There are four classes of service

12. The classes of service are general concepts, but these they are mapped onto different specific AAL types.
    - Class A: AAL 1.
    - Class B: AAL 2.
    - Class C & D: AAL 3/4.
    - Class C & D: AAL 5.
13. The AAL is organised on two sublayers:
    - The Convergence Sublayer.
    - The Segmentation and Reassembly Sublayer.
14. Information pertaining to the CS and SAR is found in the ATM dictionary.
15. The CS, which performs the tasks of processing cell delay variation, synchronisation and handling cell loss, is broken up into two parts:
    - The Service Specific CS (SSCS)
    - The Common Part CS (CPCS)
16. Again, information about these two sublayers is found in the dictionary.
17. A diagram below shows the relationship between the layers and sublayers of the AAL.

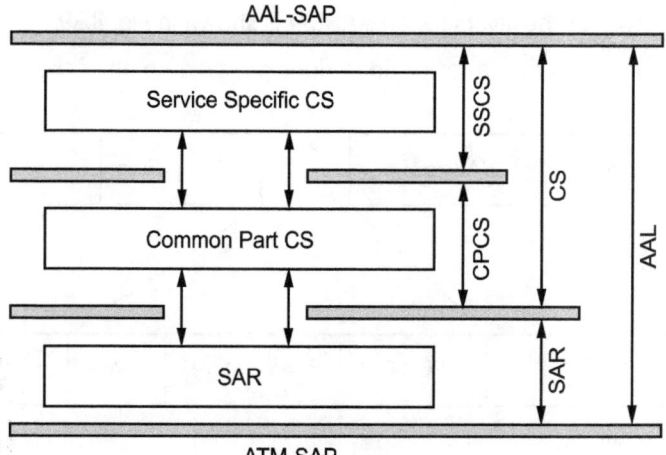

Fig. 3.38: Relationship between the layers and sublayers of the AAL

18. Information that moves between layers of the AAL follows a naming convention.
19. Protocol Data Units (PDUs) contain the information between peer layers, while Service Data Units (SDUs) pass data across Service Access Points (SAPs).
20. This is shown clearly in a diagram in the ATM dictionary.
21. Below is a list of the defined AAL types. Contained with each type is a list of applications suited to that particular AAL.

AAL Type 1:

- Circuit transport to support synchronous (e.g. 64 kBit/s) and asynchronous (e.g. 1.5, 2 MBit/s) circuits.
- Video signal transport for interactive and distributive services.
- Voice band signal transport.
- High quality audio transport.

AAL Type 2:

AAL 2 has not currently been defined, but services for this type may include:
- Transfer of service data units with a variable source bit-rate.
- Transfer of timing information between source and destination.

AAL Types 3/4:

- AAL 3 was designed for connection-oriented data, while AAL 4 for connectionless-oriented data.
- They have now been merged to form AAL 3/4.

- The structure of the layers for an AAL 3/4 is shown in Fig. 3.39.
- Note how the user data for payload does not take up all of the payload area of the cell.

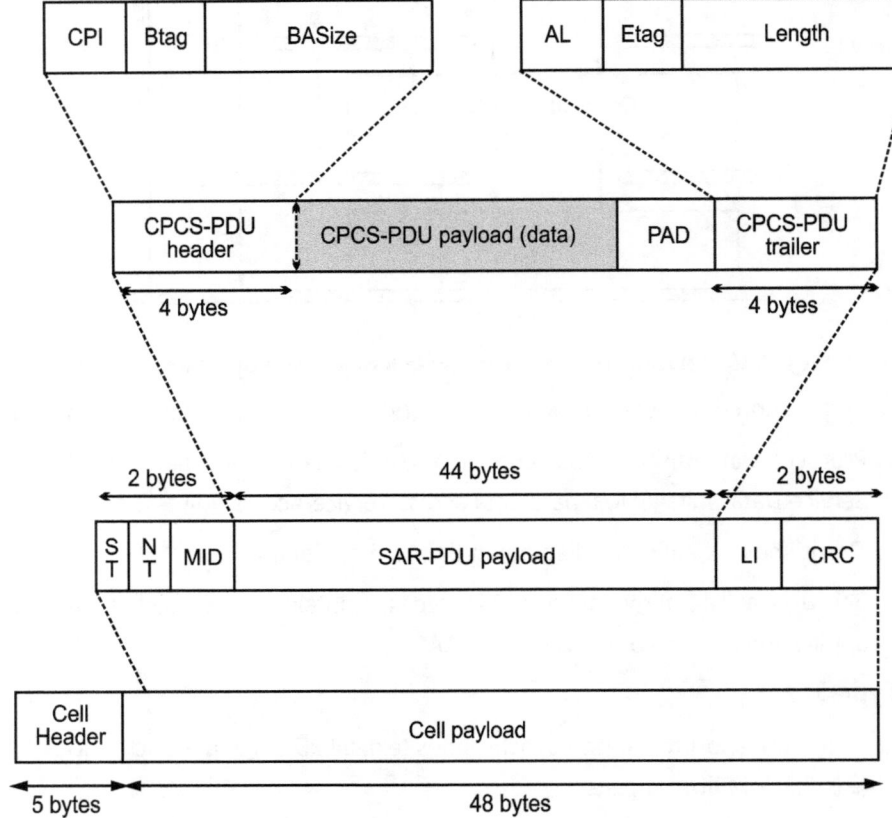

Fig. 3.39: The structure of the layers for an AAL 3/4 is shown in the diagram

- (ST) Segment Type (2 bits): Indicates whether segment is beginning, continuation, end or single segment message.
- (SN) Sequence Number (4 bits): Allows sequence of SAR-PDUs to be numbered modulo 16.
- (MID) Multiplexing Identification (10 bits): Allows for more than one connection over a single ATM-layer connection. The value of the MID must be unique over the current VP only.
- (LI) Length Indicator (6 bits): Indicates the number of bytes of CS-PDU information in the SAR-PDU, as the amount of information may not fill the 44 bytes available.
- (CRC) Cyclic Redundancy Check Code (10 bits): Used to detect errors in the SAR-PDU. This includes the CS_PDU and user data.

- (CPI) Common part indicator (1 octet).
- (Btag) Beginning tag (1 octet).
- (BASize) Buffer Size allocation (2 octets).
- (PAD) Padding (0 to 3 octets).
- (AL) Alignment (1 octet).
- (Etag) End tag (1 octet).
- (length) Length of CPSU-PDU payload (2 octets).

AAL Type 5:
- AAL 5 is designed for the same class of service as AAL 3/4, but contains less overheads.
- It allows the full 48 bytes of payload to be used for transportation of CS-PDU segments, not just SAR-PDU segments.
- There is a CRC field incorporated into the CS-PDU field, as indicated below.

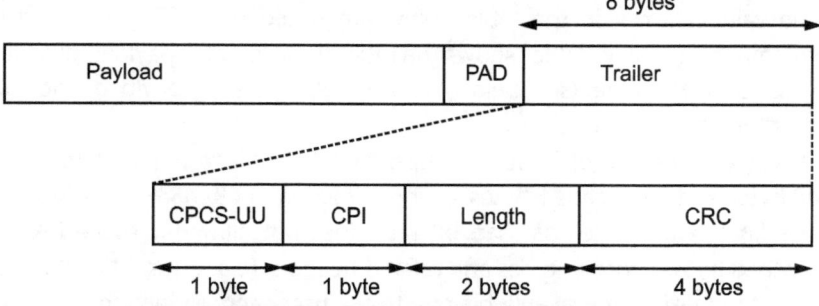

Fig. 3.40: CRC field incorporated into the CS-PDU field

Physical Layer:

Responsibilities:
The physical layer has two sublayers:
- Physical Medium sublayer.
- Transmission Convergence sublayer.

The physical layer is responsible for the transmission of the data across a physical link, in much the same way as the physical layer of the OSI reference model. Fig. 3.41 shows the role of the interface between the ATM layer and the physical layer.

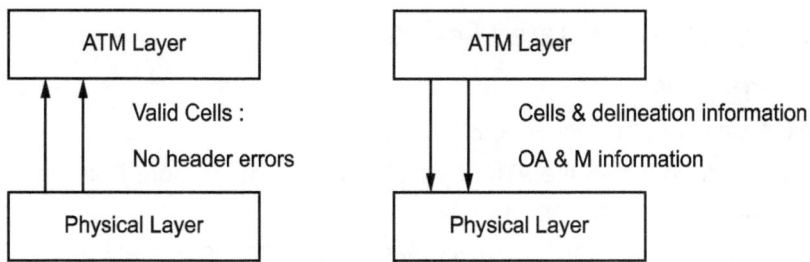

Fig. 3.41: The role of the interface between the ATM layer and the physical layer

Transfer Capacity:

1. The CCITT Recommendation I.432 defines two bit-rates for the physical layer:
   - 155 520 kBit/s.
   - 622 080 kBit/s.
2. The transportation medium may either be electrical or optical, and can use SDH-based or cell-based framing.
3. Different countries are currently introducing SDH (Synchronous Digital Hierarchy) into their network and so this chapter will concentrate on this framing for ATM.
4. The bit rates mentioned above are the gross bit rates of the physical layer and hence contain transportation overheads of the carrier, and also of the layers above the physical layer (ATM Adaptation Layer and ATM Layer).
5. This causes the actual user data bit rate to be less than the gross rate by a significant amount.
6. The values shown in the table below are based on a SDH frame structure. The column "fraction available" shows the ratio of payload to (payload plus header).
7. Thus, a SDH frame (see below) allows 260 bytes of payload and 10 bytes of overhead and pointers.
8. This gives a fraction of 260/270. Similarly for ATM cell formats, payload is 48 bytes and overheads 5 bytes, giving a fraction of 48/(48 + 5) = 48/53.
9. The final value of cell-payload bit rate does not allow for space taken up in the payload by AAL format types and related headers, (e.g. CRCs, MIDs, CPIs, etc).
10. Thus the maximum available bit-rate to the user cannot reach that of the maximum available for cell-payload and is dependent on the AAL type used.

	Fraction available	STM-1 (kBit/s)	STM-4 (kBit/s)
Gross Physical Layer bit-rate	1.0	155 520	622 080
Maximum bit-rate for ATM cells	260/270	149 760	599 040
Maximum bit-rate for ATM payload	48/53	135 631	542 526

Fig. 3.42: Different bit rates

3.2.3 Connection-Orientated Service

Signalling Principles:

1. ATM is a connection-orientated technique.
2. A connection within the ATM layer consists of one or more links, each of which is assigned an identifier.
3. A lot of applications, such as Constant Bit Rate (CBR) Services and X.25 data service are best handled by connection-orientated communications.

4. With ATM and other connection-orientated techniques, a connection has to be established before information transfer takes place.

5. ATM uses an out of band signaling system in dedicated Signaling Virtual Channels (SVCs).

6. There are different types of SVCs for different requirements:

    - The Meta-Signalling Virtual Channel (MSVC) is bi-directional and permanent. It is used to establish, check and release point-to-point and selective broadcast SVCs.

    - The point-to-point signalling channel is bidirectional and is used to establish, control and release VCCs and VPCs that carry user data.

    - Broadcast SVCs are unidirectional and can send signalling messages to all, or select endpoints.

    - General SVCs are like Broadcast SVCs, but do not allow selected groups.

Traffic Control:

In order for a broadband network based on ATM to achieve a high level of performance, traffic control capabilities have to be introduced. The CCITT Recommendations are as follows:

- Connection admission control.
- Usage parameter control.
- Priority control.
- Congestion control.

These control mechanisms are outlined below.

Connection Admission Control:

Connection admission control is the set of actions taken by the network at the call setup phase in order to establish whether a VC/VP connection can be established. A connection can only be established if the network resources are available to provide the required quality of service. The introduction of a new connection should not affect the QoS of other established connections. Source traffic can be identified by parameters such as,

- Peak duration
- Average bit rate
- Burstiness
- Peak bit rate

Usage Parameter Control:

Usage parameter control is the set of actions taken by the network to monitor and control user traffic volume and cell routing validity. Its main purpose is to protect network resources from malicious as well as unintentional misbehaviour, which can affect the QoS parameters of existing connections by detecting violations of negotiated parameters. **UPC** includes monitoring the following functions:

- Validity of VPI/VCI values.
- Monitoring VP/VC traffic volumes to check for violations.
- Monitoring total traffic volumes on links.

Priority Control:

Priority Control is determined using the cell loss priority bit in the cell header. Information can be broken into more and less important parts. Thus different components of the same signal will be treated differently by the network control mechanisms.

Congestion Control:

1. Congestion is defined as a state of network elements in which, due to traffic overload, the network is not able to guarantee a QoS to already established connections and to new connection requests.
2. Congestion control tries to minimise congestion effects and avoid the problem spreading. Congestion control could, for example, reduce the peak bit rate available to a user.

Cell Delay Variation and Queues:

1. As explained above, the small sized cells allow for small delay variation, CDV.
2. This is useful for the transportation of isochronous media, which requires data (especially voice) to be sent at fixed intervals.
3. Small delay variation allows for "virtual" isochronous transmission.
4. Traffic shaping schemes try to shape traffic into isochronous flow, with regular time intervals at the output.
5. The leaky bucket is an example of a traffic shaping scheme.
6. The leaky bucket algorithm uses a buffer of finite size that incoming traffic is placed into.
7. Traffic is allowed to drain out of the bucket and sent on the network at a rate, p. Excess data that cannot fit into the buffer is discarded.
8. The leaky bucket algorithm has the effect of shaping bursty traffic into a flow of equally spaced cells, each being emitted 1/p units of time after the previous cell.
9. The size of the buffer limits the cell delay. Hence to limit CDV, a small buffer is required.

3.2.4 Connectionless Service

1. ATM is connection-orientated communication.
2. However, there are many applications, such as mail services and other data services that are characterized by small amounts of data, sent sporadically.
3. To save time and expense, no connection is established - i.e. a connectionless service. User information is sent in a message containing all necessary addressing and routing information.
4. This is used in local area networks that employ Carrier Sense Multiple Access with Collision Detection (CSMA/CD) network structures (e.g. ethernet).
5. It is possible for ATM to be used in a connectionless configuration.
6. An ATM connectionless data service allows the transfer of information among service subscribers without the need for end-to-end call establishment.
7. A connectionless data service will require the introduction of connectionless servers.
8. The connectionless servers route cells to their destination according to the routing information contained in the cells.
9. The connectionless service sits on top of ATM, i.e. it is not integrated into the functionality of the ATM switch.
10. This requires a direct connection between each user and the connectionless server.
11. These connections can be semi-permanent or switched.
12. The use of direct connection means that only n connections are required for n users.
13. Fig. 3.43 indicates the provision of a connectionless service on ATM.

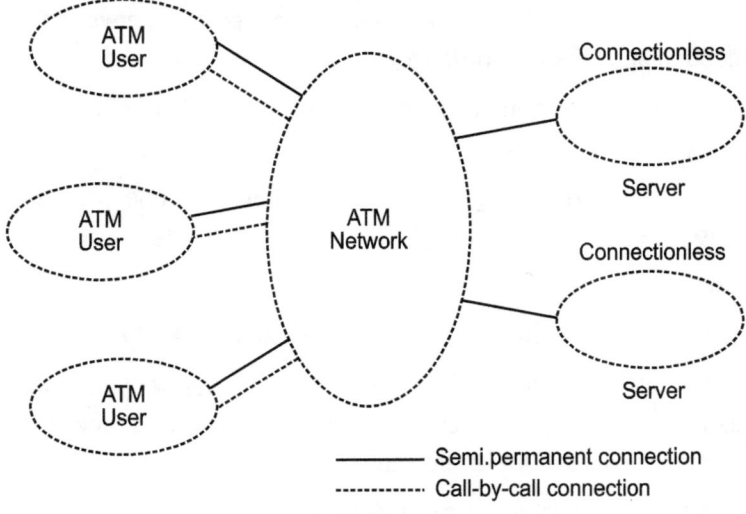

Fig. 3.43

3.2.5 LAN Traffic over ATM

1. The first ATM networks are likely to be installed by companies that have a specific high bandwidth need.
2. These could include single locations, between buildings (across a campus), or across a high speed (E3) link.
3. Other solutions to the joining of LANs exist, such as FDDI. However, these solutions are not suitable for the Wide Area Networks (WANs), and the data must be transformed into something else for transmission.
4. ATM, on the other hand, if used throughout the LAN, then the transition to a MAN or WAN would be "seamless", as the same language and technologies would be used throughout.
5. This is an example of the **scalability** of ATM - the ability to handle different bit rates for different situations, and being able to upgrade to higher rates as technology progresses.

3.2.6 ATM LAN Network Configurations

1. This section of the chapter covers topologies of different ATM network configurations.
2. This includes some migrations towards ATM-based solutions, as well as highlighting problems of other non ATM-based solutions.
3. As LANs increasingly require communication with each other, due to multimedia and other bandwidth hungry services, the connections between the LANs become overloaded and create a bottleneck.
4. Although there are alternative solutions to this problem, ATM is the most "future-proof".
5. Note that in the examples given below, ethernet is just one of the services that ATM can interface.

Current Situation:

1. Fig. 3.44 shows the current situation in a typical office environment.
2. The Ethernet backbone, that joins together the Ethernet subnetworks, becomes a bottleneck, as only one user can access the backbone at a time, even if they do not require the services of the entire line.
3. A solution to this bottleneck must be found.

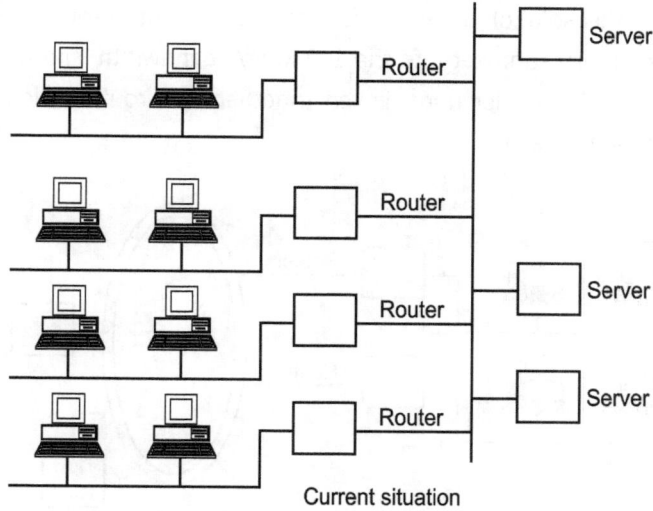

Fig. 3.44: Current situation in a typical office environment

FDDI (Fiber Distributed Data Interface) Solution:

FDDI provides a solution to the bottleneck problem, by increasing the speed of the backbone from 10 MBit/s (in the Ethernet case), to 100 MBit/s (FDDI).

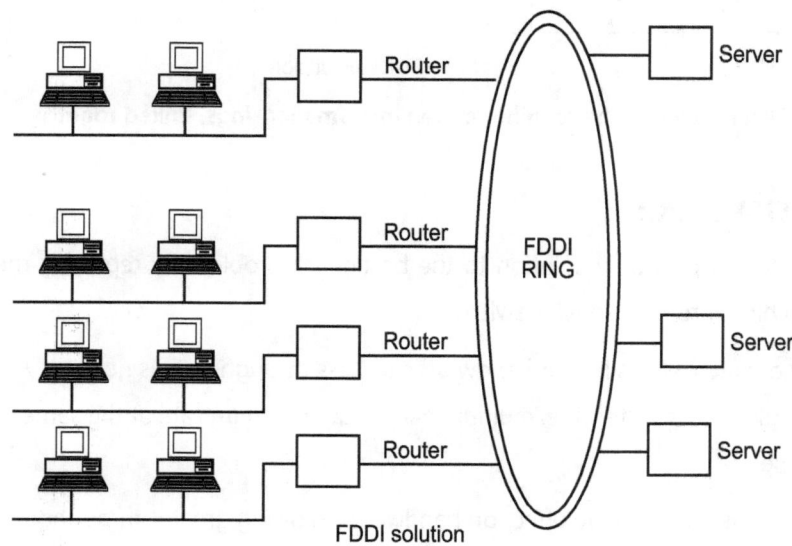

Fig. 3.45: FDDI provides a solution to the bottleneck problem

The problem with this solution, however, is that it is not "future-proof". Future bandwidth hungry applications may soon eat into the 100 MBit/s bandwidth, and the FDDI ring would have to be broken into smaller rings, linked together with routers. Hence the bottleneck returns at the router interface.

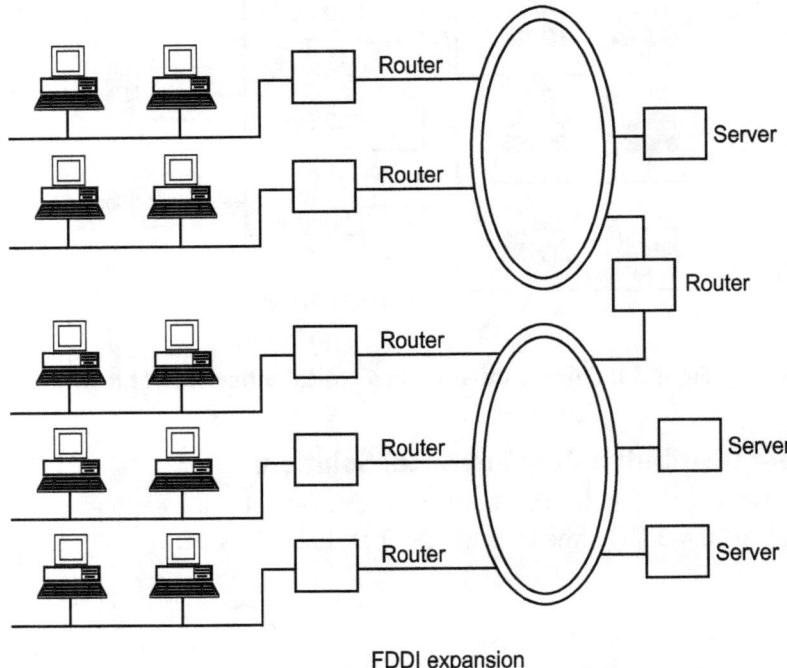

FDDI expansion

Fig. 3.46: FDDI ring would have to be broken into smaller rings, linked together with routers

Interim ATM Solution:

1. ATM can provide a solution to the bottleneck problem by replacing the backbone architecture with an ATM switch.

2. The switch allows higher bandwidths to pass through, as it is not a single access system. i.e. multiple parties can communicate at the same time.

3. This has a cumulative effect on bandwidth, allowing greater throughput.

4. The ATM solution also allows different protocols between the routers and ATM switches (e.g. SDH, E1, E3), so that these connections are upgradable as the demand on that connection increases.

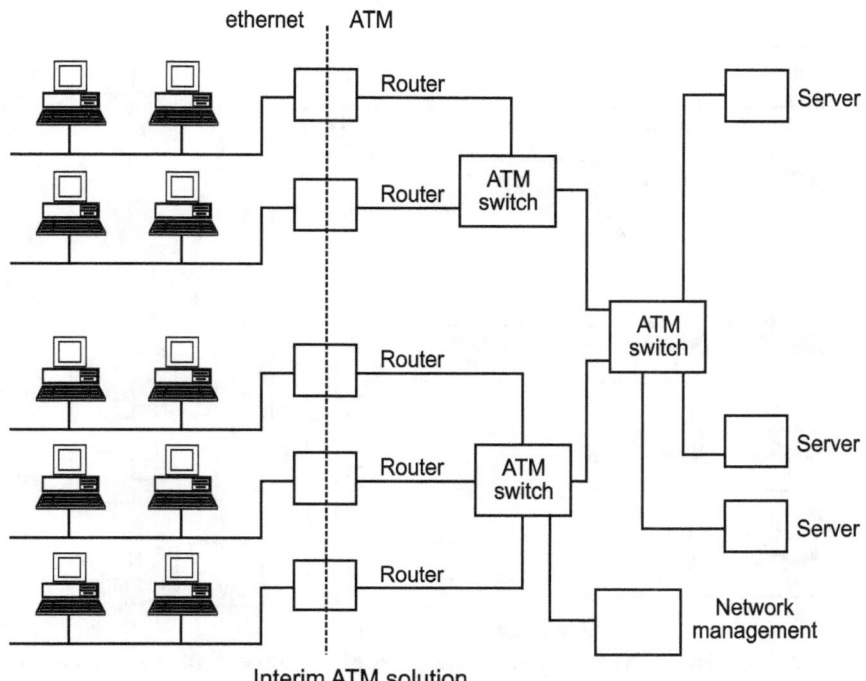

Interim ATM solution

Fig. 3.47: ATM can provide a solution to the bottleneck problem by replacing the backbone architecture with an ATM switch

"Virtual LAN" ATM Solution:

1. With the installation of adaptor cards in the ATM switch, (in this example Ethernet), virtual LANs can be created.

2. This means that workstations may be grouped to form a LAN, even though they are separated by physical links.

3. The ATM switch provides the logical connections for the LANs.

4. This allows workstations to be able to move in physical location without the need to change LAN.

5. The functionality of this system is provided by network management, that allows the administrator easy access to the entire ATM network through a remote terminal.

Thus, ATM is a scalable, flexible and "future-proof" technology that allows for transportation of various forms of information, including data, voice, video or multiples of them. Global standards are being introduced to ensure compatibility. It is primarily for these reasons that ATM was chosen as the method for the implementation of broadband services.

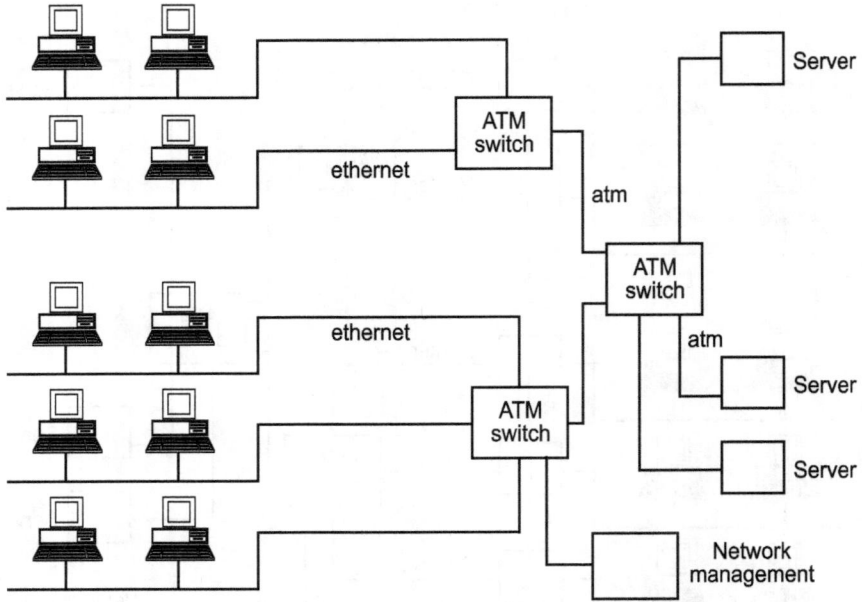

"Virtual Lan" ATM solution

Fig. 3.48: The ATM switch provides the logical connections for the LANs

3.2.7 ATM Devices and ATM Interfaces

1. An ATM network consists of an ATM switch and ATM end systems.
2. The ATM switch handles transmission of cells through the ATM network.
3. Its functions are: accepting the incoming cell from an ATM end station or another ATM switch; reading and updating the cell-header information and switching the cell towards its destination.
4. The ATM end system contains an ATM network interface adapter.
5. Examples of such end systems are workstations, routers, and LAN switches.

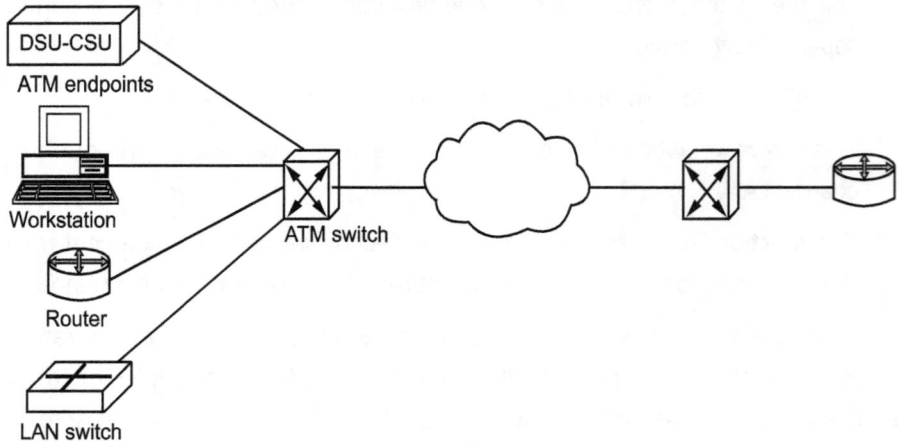

Fig. 3.49: An ATM network

ATM Network Interfaces:

1. An ATM network consists of a set of ATM switches interconnected by point-to-point ATM links or interfaces.
2. ATM switches support two primary types of interfaces: *UNI* and *NNI*.
3. The UNI connects ATM end systems (such as hosts and routers) to an ATM switch. The NNI connects two ATM switches.
4. Depending on whether the switch is owned and located at the customer's premises or publicly owned and operated by the telephone company, UNI and NNI can be further subdivided into public and private UNIs and NNIs.
5. A private UNI connects an ATM endpoint and a private ATM switch.
6. Its public counterpart connects an ATM endpoint or private switch to a public switch.
7. A private NNI connects two ATM switches within the same private organization.
8. A public one connects two ATM switches within the same public organization.
9. An additional specification, the *Broadband Interexchange Carrier Interconnect* (B-ICI), connects two public switches from different service providers.
10. Fig. 3.50 illustrates the ATM interface specifications for private and public networks.

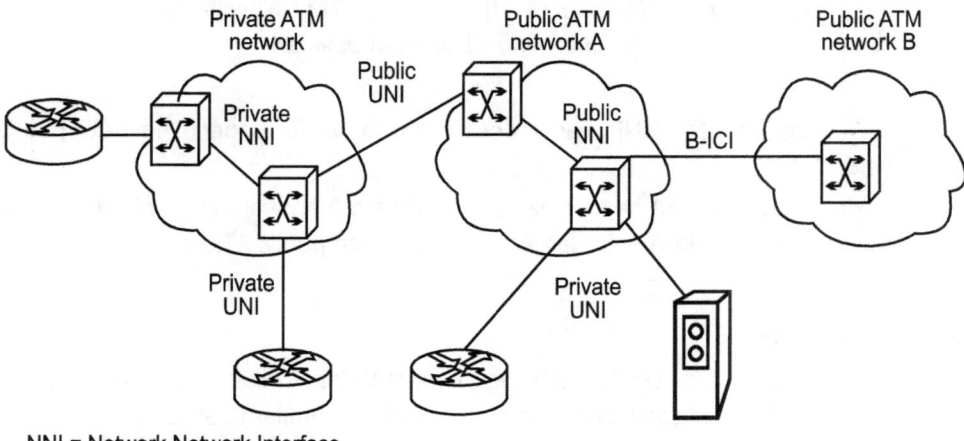

NNI = Network Network Interface
UNI = User Network Interface

Fig. 3.50: ATM interface specifications differ for private and public networks

3.2.8 ATM Cell-Header Format

- An ATM cell-header can be one of the two formats: *UNI* or *NNI*.
- The UNI header is used for communication between ATM endpoints and ATM switches in private ATM networks.

- The NNI header is used for communication between ATM switches. Fig. 3.50 depicts the basic ATM cell format, the ATM UNI cell-header format, and the ATM NNI cell-header format.

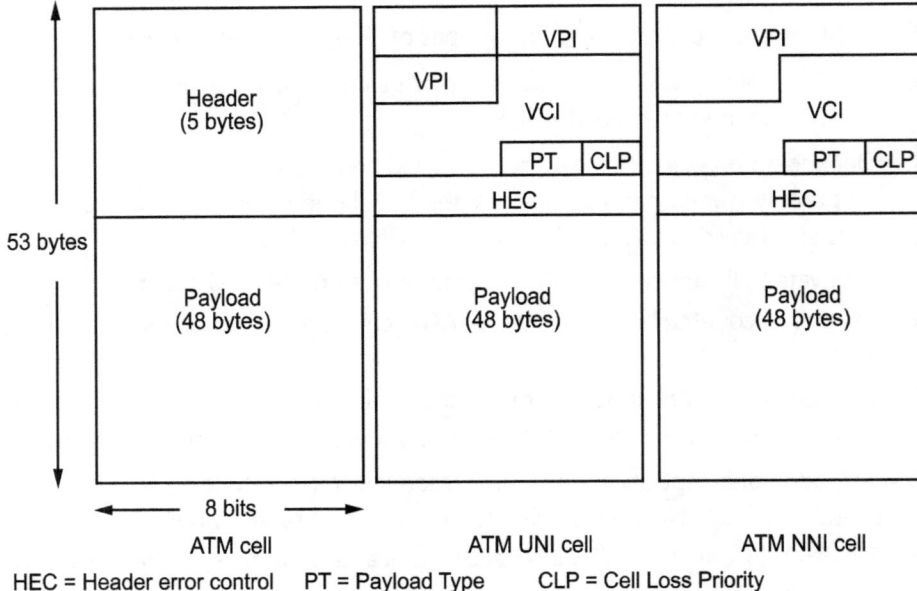

Fig. 3.51: An ATM cell, ATM UNI cell, and ATM NNI cell-header each containing 48 bytes of payload

1. Unlike the UNI, the NNI header does not include the Generic Flow Control (GFC) field.
2. Additionally, the NNI header has a Virtual Path Identifier (VPI) field that occupies the first 12 bits, allowing for larger trunks between public ATM switches.

3.2.9 ATM Services

1. Three types of ATM services exist: *Permanent Virtual* Circuits (PVC), *Switched Virtual* Circuits (SVC), and connectionless service (which is similar to SMDS).
2. A PVC allows direct connectivity between sites.
3. In this way, a PVC is similar to a leased line. Among its advantages, a PVC guarantees availability of a connection and does not require call setup procedures between switches. Disadvantages of PVCs include static connectivity and manual setup.
4. An SVC is created and released dynamically and remains in use only as long as data is being transferred. In this sense, it is similar to a telephone call.

5. Dynamic call control requires a signalling protocol between the ATM endpoint and the ATM switch.

6. The advantages of SVCs include connection flexibility and call setup that can be handled automatically by a networking device. Disadvantages include the extra time and overhead required to set up the connection.

Table 3.3: Differences between PVCs and SVCs

PVCs	SVCs
Connected on a permanent basis. Users are charged a flat rate.	Dynamically connected as needed. Users are charged only for time and resources used.
Manually configured, permanent connections. Each PVC must be configured at both end systems and on all ATM switches in the network.	Dynamically signalled. SVCs are configured only on the end systems; they do not require configuration on all ATM switches in the network.
Provisioned when the connection is set up. Bandwidth and services allocated to the PVC are not available to other applications even when not in use.	Can request bandwidth and ATM service quality information needed for a particular connection. Once the connection is released, network resources are made available to other users or applications.
Cannot take alternate routes in the event of a failure in the network.	Can take alternate routes in the event of a failure in the network.

3.2.10 ATM Virtual Connections

1. ATM networks are fundamentally connection-oriented, which means that a *Virtual Channel* (VC) must be set up across the ATM network prior to any data transfer. (A virtual channel is roughly equivalent to a virtual circuit.)

2. Two types of ATM connections exist: *Virtual Paths*, which are identified by Virtual Path Identifiers, and *Virtual Channels*, which are identified by the combination of a VPI and a *Virtual Channel Identifier* (VCI).

3. A virtual path is a bundle of virtual channels, all of which are switched transparently across the ATM network on the basis of the common VPI. All VCIs and VPIs, however, have only local significance across a particular link and are remapped, as appropriate, at each switch.

4. A transmission path is a bundle of VPs. Fig. 3.52 illustrates how VCs concatenate to create VPs, which, in turn, concatenate to create a transmission path.

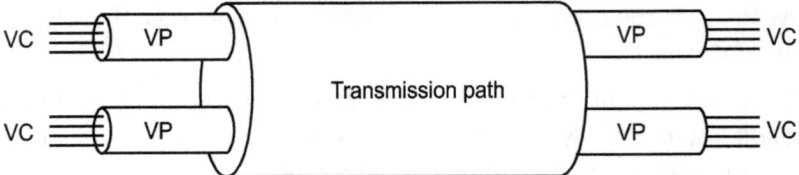

Fig. 3.52: VC concatenate to create VPs

3.2.11 ATM Switching Operations

1. The basic operation of an ATM switch is straightforward: The cell is received across a link on a known VCI or VPI value.
2. The switch looks up the connection value in a local translation table to determine the outgoing port (or ports) of the connection and the new VPI/VCI value of the connection on that link.
3. The switch then retransmits the cell on that outgoing link with the appropriate connection identifiers.
4. Because all VCIs and VPIs have only local significance across a particular link, these values are remapped, as necessary, at each switch.

3.2.12 ATM Quality of Service (QoS)

1. ATM supports QoS guarantees composed of *traffic contract, traffic shaping*, and *traffic policing*.
2. A traffic contract specifies an envelope that describes the intended data flow.
3. This envelope specifies values for peak bandwidth, average sustained bandwidth, and burst size, among others.
4. When an ATM end system connects to an ATM network, it enters a contract with the network, based on QoS parameters.
5. Traffic shaping is the use of queues to constrain data bursts, limit peak data rate, and smooth jitters so that traffic will fit within the promised envelope.
6. ATM devices are responsible for adhering to the contract by means of *traffic shaping*.
7. ATM switches can use *traffic policing* to enforce the contract. The switch can measure the actual traffic flow and compare it against the agreed-upon traffic envelope.
8. If the switch finds that traffic is outside of the agreed-upon parameters, it can set the *cell-loss priority* (CLP) bit of the offending cells.
9. Setting the CLP bit makes the cell discard eligible, which means that any switch handling the cell is allowed to drop the cell during periods of congestion.

3.3 Voice Over ATM

1. VoATM enables a router to carry voice traffic (for example, telephone calls and faxes) over an ATM network.
2. An ATM network is a cell-switching and multiplexing technology designed to combine the benefits of circuit switching (constant transmission delay and guaranteed capacity) and packet switching (flexibility and efficiency for intermittent traffic).
3. All traffic to or from an ATM network is prefaced with a Virtual Path Identifier (VPI) and Virtual Channel Identifier (VCI).
4. A VPI-VCI pair is considered a single virtual circuit.
5. Each virtual circuit is a private connection to another node on the ATM network.
6. Each virtual circuit is treated as a point-to-point mechanism to another router or host and is capable of supporting bi-directional traffic.
7. Each ATM node establishes a separate connection to every other node in the ATM network with which it must communicate.
8. All such connections are established by means of a Permanent Virtual Circuit (PVC) or a Switched Virtual Circuit (SVC) with an ATM signalling mechanism.
9. This signaling is based on the ATM Forum User-Network Interface (UNI) Specification V3.0.
10. Each virtual circuit is considered as a complete and separate link to a destination node.
11. Data can be encapsulated as needed across the connection, and the ATM network disregards the contents of the data.
12. The only requirement is that data be sent to the ATM processor card of the router in a manner that follows the specific ATM adaptation layer (AAL) format.
13. An ATM connection transfers raw bits of information to a destination router or host.
14. The ATM router takes the Common Part Convergence Sublayer (CPCS) frame, carves it up into 53 byte cells, and sends the cells to the destination router or host for reassembly.
15. In AAL5 format, 48 bytes of each cell are used for the CPCS data and the remaining 5 bytes are used for cell routing.
16. The 5 byte cell header contains the destination VPI-VCI pair, payload type, Cell Loss Priority (CLP), and Header Error Control (HEC) information.

3.3.1 AAL Technology

1. AAL defines the conversion of user information into the ATM cells.
2. AAL protocols perform a convergence function; that is, they take whatever traffic is to be sent across the ATM network, establish the appropriate connections, and then package the traffic received from the higher layers into the 48 byte information payload that is passed down to the ATM layer for transmission.
3. At the receiving level, the AAL layer must receive the information payloads passed up from the ATM layer and put the payloads into the form expected by the higher layer.
4. The AAL layers provide a service to the higher layers that correspond to the four classes of traffic. AAL1 and AAL2 handle isochronous traffic, such as voice and video, but are not relevant to the router. AAL3/4 and AAL5 support data communications by segmenting and reassembling packets.
5. AAL2 is a bandwidth-efficient, standards-based trunking method for transporting compressed voice, voice-band data, circuit-mode data, and frame-mode data.
6. VoATM with AAL2 trunking provides the following functionality :
    - Increased quality of service (QoS) capabilities
    - Robust architecture
    - Signalling transparency
    - CAS and CCS support

AAL5 is designed to support only message-mode, non-assured operation. AAL5 packets contain 48 bytes of data and a 5 byte header.

3.3.2 Variable Bit Rate Real-Time Options for Traffic Shaping

1. Variable Bit Rate (VBR) is a QoS class defined by the ATM Forum for ATM networks.
2. VBR is subdivided into a Real-Time (RT) class and Non-Real Time (NRT) class.
3. RT VBR is used for connections in which there is a fixed timing relationship between samples, as in the case of traffic shaping.
4. NRT VBR is used for connections in which there is no fixed timing relationship between samples, but which still need a guaranteed QoS.
5. Traffic shaping prevents a carrier from discarding incoming calls from a router.
6. Traffic shaping is performed by configuring the peak, average, and burst options for voice traffic.
7. Burst is required if the PVC is carrying bursty traffic. Peak, average, and burst are required, so the PVC can effectively handle the bandwidth for the number of voice calls.

3.3.3 Voice Over ATM System

1. As real-time voice services have been traditionally supported in the WAN via circuit-based techniques (e.g., via T1 multiplexers or circuit switching), it is natural to map these circuits to ATM CBR PVCs (CBR is constant bit rate) using circuit emulation and ATM adaptation Layer 1 (AAL1).
2. However, there are significant disadvantages in using circuit emulation in that the bandwidth must be dedicated for this type of traffic (whether there is useful information being transmitted or not), providing a disincentive for corporate users to implement circuit emulation as a long-term strategy.
3. For example, a T1 1.544 Mbps circuit requires 1.74 Mbps of ATM bandwidth when transmitted in circuit-emulation mode.
4. This does not downplay its importance as a transitional strategy to address the installed base.
5. As technology has evolved, the inherent burstiness of voice and many real-time applications can be exploited (along with sophisticated compression schemes) to decrease the cost of transmission significantly through the use of VBR–RT connections over ATM.
6. VBR techniques for voice exploit the inherently bursty nature of voice communication, as there are silence periods that can result in increased efficiency.
7. The following silence periods (in decreasing levels of importance) arise :
   - When no call is up on a particular trunk; that is, the trunk is idle during off-peak hours (trunks are typically engineered for a certain call-blocking probability : at night, all the trunks could be idle).
   - When the call is up, but only one person is talking at a given time.
   - When the call is up, and no one is talking.
8. Work is just starting in the ATM Forum on ATM adaptation for VBR voice.
9. The addition of more bandwidth-effective voice coding (e.g., standard voice is coded using 64 kbps PCM) is economically attractive, particularly over long-haul circuits and T1 ATM interfaces.
10. Various compression schemes have been standardized in the industry (e.g., G720 series of standards).
11. Making these coding schemes dynamic, provides the network operator the opportunity to free up bandwidth under network-congestion conditions.
12. For example, with the onset of congestion, increased levels of voice compression could be dynamically invoked, thus freeing up bandwidth and potentially alleviating the congestion while diminishing the quality of the voice during these periods.
13. A further enhancement to the support of voice over ATM is to support voice switching over SVCs.

14. This entails interpreting PBX signalling and routing voice calls to the appropriate destination PBX (see Fig. 3.53).
15. The advantage from a traffic management perspective is that connection admission controls can be applied to new voice calls; under network congestion conditions, these calls could be rerouted over the public network and therefore not cause additional levels of congestion.

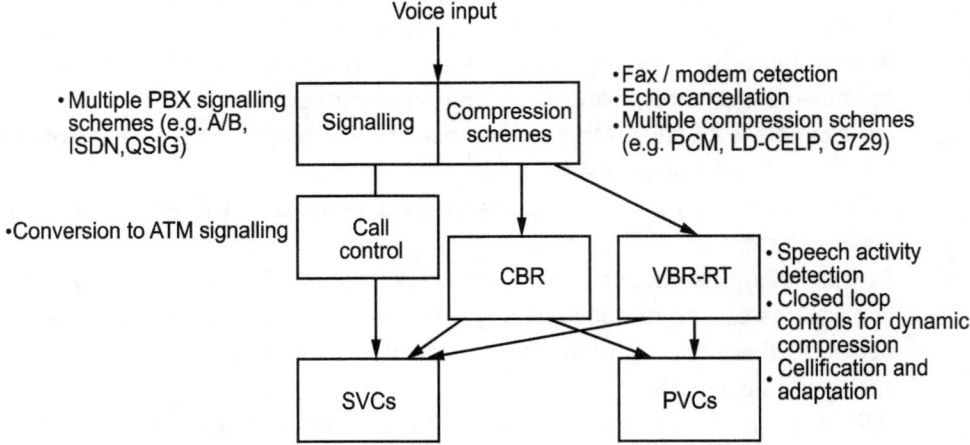

Fig. 3.53: Voice Switching over SVCs

The ATM Forum is currently focusing its efforts on voice handled on CBR SVCs. VBR–RT voice is a future standards activity.

3.3.4 Fragmentation

- It is built into ATM, with its small, fixed-size, 53 byte cells.
- Very fast ATM switches speed data through the ATM network.
- The high bandwidth associated with ATM reduces congestion problems, providing extremely reliable service.
- Carriers can therefore promise customers Quality of Service (QoS), stipulated in Service Level Agreements (SLAs).

3.3.5 ATM Prioritization

- It is implemented through QoS parameters.
- ATM was designed from the outset to carry voice as well as all types of data.
- ATM Adaptation Layer 1 (AAL1) protocol in ATM's Constant Bit Rate (CBR) service was the de facto standard for VoATM.
- However, this protocol proved inefficient for voice applications.

- CBR, the highest quality class of ATM service, provides Circuit Emulation Service (CES), which transmits a continuous bit stream of information.
- This allocates a constant amount of bandwidth to a connection for the duration of a transmission.
- Although it guarantees high quality voice, CES monopolizes bandwidth that could be used for other applications.
- In addition, in the interest of reducing delay, CES might send the fixed-size ATM cells half empty rather than waiting 6 milliseconds for 47 bytes of voice to fill the cell.
- This wastes over 20 bytes of bandwidth per ATM cell.

3.3.6 Voice Compression

- It is not necessary in pure-ATM networks, which enjoy ample bandwidth.
- However, in hybrid ATM-frame relay networks (for example, with ATM headquarters and frame relay branches), voice compression is required since frame relay uses voice compression.
- ATM must therefore be equipped to support voice compression that will work with VoFR equipment at the remote site.

3.3.7 ATM Traffic Management

A number of issues related to congestion control can be included under the general category of traffic management. But congestion control is not the only issue. There re many other issues involved in the ATM traffic management. We will discuss these issues in the following discussion.

(A) Fairness:

Due to congestion the flows of packets between the source and destination are delayed and packets will be lost. It is necessary to assure that various flows suffer equally due to congestion. So imply discarding the packet, on some basis like last in last discarded. This type of practice is not fair. In order to bring fairness in the congestion control, a node can maintain a separate queue for each logical connection or for the same source destination pair. If all of the queue buffers are of equal length, then the queues with highest traffic load will have to discard packets more often. This will allow the connections with lower traffic to a fair share of the traffic.

(B) Quality of Service:

All the types of traffic flows cannot be treated equally because they have different characteristics. For example, the voice and video traffic is sensitive to delays but insensitive to the loss of data. However, the other traffic such as file transfer and electronic mail are not sensitive to delays but they are sensitive to the loss of data. Moreover, different traffic flows have different priorities and at the time of congestion the flows having higher priority should be given more importance.

(C) Reservation:

One can avoid congestion and also provide assured service by using a reservation scheme. Such a scheme is an integral part of ATM networks. For a traffic flow, the QoS decides certain values of parameters. As long as the traffic flow is within limits, the agreed QoS is provided. One aspect of a reservation scheme is traffic policing.

3.4 ATM Traffic Management

3.4.1 ATM Traffic Management Basics

1. Broadly speaking, the objectives of ATM traffic management are to deliver quality-of-service (QoS) guarantees for the multimedia applications and provide overall optimization of network resources. Meeting these objectives enables enhanced classes of service and offers the potential for service differentiation and increased revenues, while simplifying network operations and reducing network cost.

2. ATM traffic management and its various functions can be categorized into three distinct elements based on timing requirements.

3. First, are nodal-level controls that operate in real time. These are implemented in hardware and include queues supporting different loss and delay priorities, fairly weighted queue-servicing algorithms, and rate controls that provide policing and traffic shaping. Well-designed switch-buffer architectures and capacity are critical to effective network operation. Actual network experience and simulation has indicated that large, dynamically allocated output buffers provide the flexibility to offer the best price performance for supporting various traffic types with guaranteed QoS. Dynamically managing buffer space means that all shared buffer space is flexibly allocated to VCs on an as-needed basis. Additionally, per virtual connection (VC) queuing enables traffic shaping, and early and partial packet-level discard have been shown to improve network performance significantly.

4. Second, network-level controls operate in near real time. These are typically, but not exclusively, implemented in software including connection admission control (CAC) for new connections, network routing and rerouting systems, and flow-control-rate adaptation schemes. Network-level controls are the heart of any traffic-management system. Connection admission controls support sophisticated equivalent-bandwidth algorithms with a high degree of configuration flexibility, based on the cell rate for CBR VCs, average cell rate plus a configurable increment for VBR VCs, and minimum cell rate for ABR VCs. Dynamic class-of-service routing standards define support for fully distributed link-state routing protocols, auto-reconfiguration on failure and on congestion, and dynamic load spreading on trunk groups.

5. Flow control involves adjusting the cell rate of the source in response to congestion conditions and requires the implementation of closed loop congestion mechanisms. This does not apply to CBR traffic. For VBR and UBR traffic, flow control is left as a CPE function. With ABR, resource management (RM) cells are defined, which allow signaling of the explicit rate to be used by traffic sources. This is termed rate-based flow control. ABR is targeted at those applications that do not have fixed or predictable bandwidth requirements and require access to any spare bandwidth as quickly as possible while experiencing very low cell loss. This allows network operators to maximize the bandwidth utilization of their network and sell spare capacity to users at a substantial discount while still providing QoS guarantees. To enhance the effectiveness of network-resource utilization, the ABR standard provides for end-to-end, segment-by-segment, and hop-by-hop service adaptation.

6. Third, network engineering capabilities operating in non-real time support data collection, configuration management, and planning tools (see Figure 3.54).

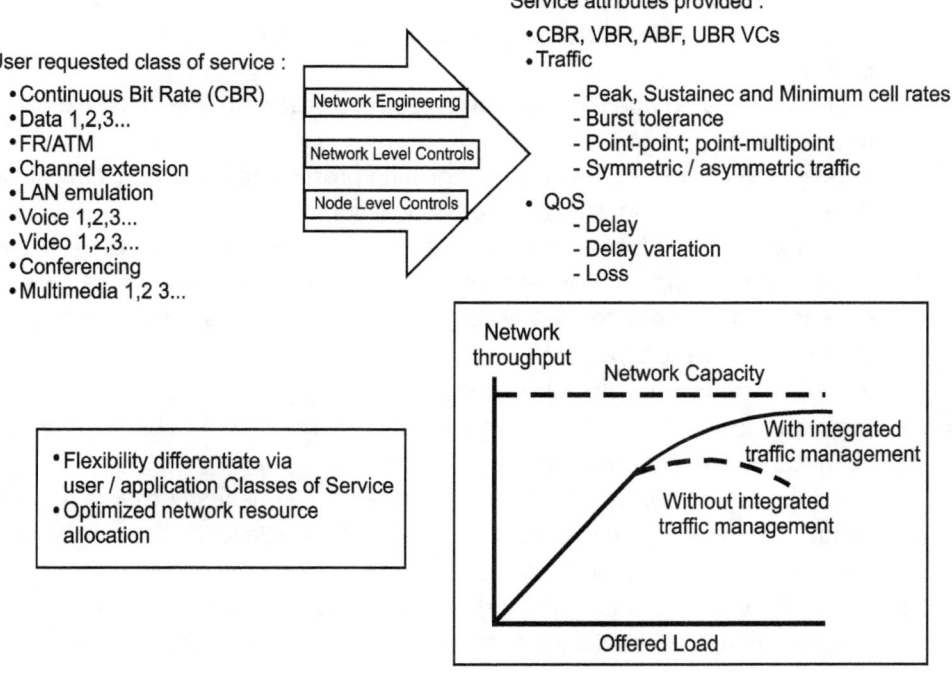

Fig. 3.54: Network Engineering Capabilities

3.5 ATM Traffic management in Detail

1. Quality of Service is one of the most important issues of ATM networks, in part because of the variety of services supported. As it was mentioned earlier, the user and the carrier must agree on a traffic contract.

2. The exact user requirements are coded with the help of traffic parameters and QoS parameters. According to the agreed contract, the network must be able to deliver requested service with adequate QoS provided the user offers a traffic which doesn't break the rules set in the contract.
3. On the other hand, carriers desire to maximize the efficiency of their network resources and fill the trunks to the highest capacity possible while still trying to fulfill the traffic contract requirements.
4. The traffic load in ATM networks changes randomly.
5. As ATM cells traverse the network, they can enter the congested area.
6. Some network elements my slow down the transmission that can bring some amount of delay as a result of congestion.
7. What's more due to occasional network failures some cell may become lost.
8. Cells representing traffic from different users and of different classes are switched, multiplexed, and buffered. Therefore, there is a need for traffic management mechanisms capable of delivering desired QoS for the users that signed a traffic contract.
9. Their work starts when the customer communicates to the network his traffic requirements.
10. In case of SVCs, it is the task for the signaling protocol to inform the network about the requested characteristics of a new connection.
11. The application software at the customer device that uses its ATM API to communicate with the ATM network initiates this process. Then all the parameters, depending on the service class, are automatically sent with a signaling protocol (e.g. UNI) to the nearest ATM switch.
12. In PVC environment traffic characteristics are configured manually at the user and the network side. Finally the network decides whether it is feasible to accept a new connection with requested QoS.
13. Once the connection is established, the network permanently checks if the traffic contract is not broken by the user equipment and ensures that the connection does not interfere with other services.
14. As can be easily noticed, traffic management in ATM is not restricted to only one function. In fact several different mechanisms are needed to provide QoS.

3.5.1 Connection Admission Control

1. In high-speed networks such as ATM it is not reasonable to wait for congestion to occur and then take necessary measures, for instance telling the source to slow down the transmission.
2. This is due to the fact that in the interval between sending the notification and having it arrived at the source, thousands of additional packets may arrive and the situation may deteriorate further.

3. What is even more important, the nature of traffic (realtime services) implies that for some sources it is not possible to slow down their traffic.
4. Consequently, ATM network work according to which it is better to prevent congestion rather than recover from congestion.
5. A tool for preventing congestion in ATM network is called the Connection Admission Control (CAC).
6. This process uses traffic descriptors to determine the characteristics of the new connection, the knowledge of the current network capacity and committed load to other users.
7. When a customer device wants a new virtual circuit, it must describe the traffic to be offered and the service expected (e.g. AAL type, QoS parameters, conformance definition).
8. The network (in fact the ATM switch) checks to see if it is possible to handle this connection without adversely affecting existing connections and decreasing the QoS they observe.
9. Then multiple potential routes may have to be examined to find the one that would satisfy user requirements.
10. If no route can be located the call is rejected.
11. However, the customer may lower his requirements with regards to service requested and try to establish the connection again.
12. The implementation of the CAC mechanism is not subject to standardization as it is internal to a switch and dependent on the carrier policies.

3.5.2 Resource Reservation and Management

1. Resource reservation as well as resource management is the techniques of reserving resources in advance, usually at setup time. Once the CAC process has accepted a new call, network management support systems are used to provision adequate resources in each network element along the route.
2. Information included in a traffic descriptor is used to reserve bandwidth in network elements.
3. This reservation must account for the user requirements but at the same time it should maximize the utilization of network capacity and avoid congestion.
4. The common approach to simplify the network traffic engineering problems by segregating the different types of traffic, which has similar characteristics and QoS needs onto separate connections.
5. For example, all the CBR connections can be grouped within one Virtual Path.

6. This approach works fine as long as reservations are made for a connection that request only the peak rate.
7. Such connections are typically of long term duration, so the reservation can be performed manually.
8. The traffic descriptor can contain not only the peak bandwidth, but also the average bandwidth (example, SCR).
9. The trouble is that VBR services generate traffic of bursty nature, thus taking the advantage of statistical multiplexing.
10. For such a service category manual reservation of resources is not efficient and may lead to overprovisioning of network resources.
11. Hence, more automated mechanisms such as CAC accompanied by signaling and dynamic routing capabilities based on traffic management and link state information are needed.
12. The primary objective for the network is to reserve the resources in a way that resources should be available for traffic of any QoS category at any time.

3.5.3 Usage Parameter Control

1. Usage Parameter Control (UPC), sometimes referred to as traffic policing, is the term used to describe the techniques that the node employs at the UNI to ensure that the user conforms to the traffic contract.
2. The primary task of the UPC function is to make sure that the traffic generated at specific sources does not deteriorate the QoS observed by the customers who offered traffic according to their traffic contracts.
3. The mechanism for using and enforcing the quality of service parameters is based on a specific algorithm called the Generic Cell Rate Algorithm (GCRA).
4. The objective for the GCRA is to check every cell to see if conforms to the parameters for its virtual connection.
5. The ATM Forum documents propose the two possible implementations of the GCRA : virtual scheduling algorithm and a leaky bucket algorithm.
6. The latter algorithm is presented in the Fig. 3.55.
7. GCRA has two parameters : an incrementing factor, which is the maximum allowed arrival rate (PCR in case of CBR) and a limiting factor, which is the amount of variation herein that is tolerable (CDVT in case of CBR).

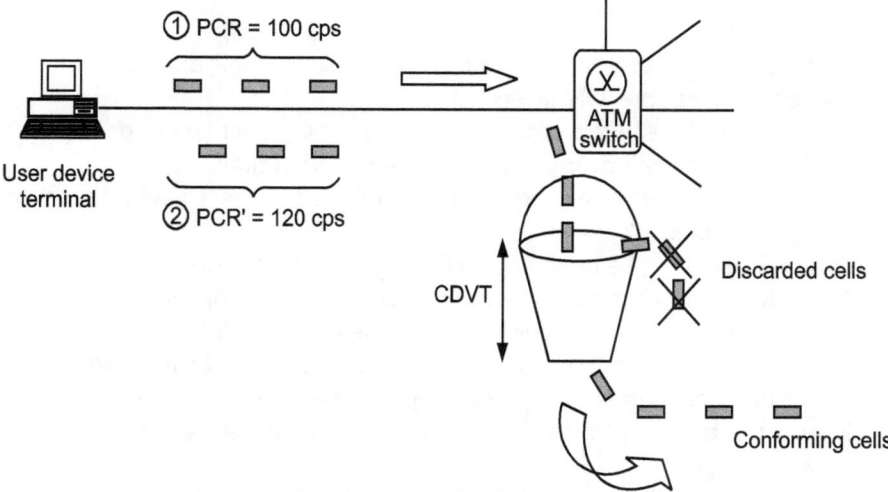

Fig. 3.55: The Leaky Bucket Algorithm

8. In normal conditions, all the cells transmitted at PCR enter the leaky bucket algorithm.
9. As long as the minimum cell arrival time (the reciprocal of PCR, T = 1/PCR) is equal to the value set in a traffic contract, cells drains out through the hole at the bottom of the bucket and they are considered as conforming cells.
10. Assuming that PCR is equal to 100 cps (see case no 1), this means that every 10 ms a new cell should arrive to the switch.
11. The problem arises with a sender who tends to generate cells more frequently, thus violating the agreed contract.
12. If the cells are inserted to the leaky bucket with too short time interval, the liquid level gradually increases.
13. This is caused by the fact that cells can leak at the bottom not quicker than with the PCR but they enter the bucket with PCR' which is slightly bigger (seen case no 2) than PCR.
14. Once the level of 'liquid' in the bucket is equal to CDVT value, cell start leaking out.
15. The cell that leaks out can be marked (CLP = 1) or must be immediately discarded (in case of CBR QoS category).
16. The GCRA is also used to make sure the mean rate does not exceed SCR for any substantial period.
17. In fact for VBR-RT service category there is a request to deploy two instance of CGRA.
18. One of them will test the traffic with incrementing factor of 1/PCR and limiting and CDVT, and the second will use accordingly 1/SCR and BT parameters.
19. In addition to providing a tool for conformance testing the GCRA can also shape the traffic and remove some of the burstiness.

3.5.4 Traffic Shaping
1. Workstations typically produce bursts of cells, so that it is difficult to multiplex such cells efficiently at the ATM layer.
2. In order to cope with this problem a traffic shaping function can be implemented to spread out such cells over a slightly longer period of time.
3. In most cases traffic shaping is performed before the traffic policing operation (UPC) is executed.
4. This may decrease the number of cells tagged and discarded.
5. The ATM cell traffic is monitored to smooth the stream of cells and avoid clumping of cells that might result in cell loss due to delay variation.
6. The traffic shaping operation can be performed either at the egress of the user device or at the ingress of the switching device at then network side.
7. In practice, by using traffic shaping, much more efficient use can be made of the network capacity.
8. The penalty for this is reduced performance for users of bursty data, since their bursts of data are spread out over a longer time that can be difficult to cope with for some applications.
9. There is no standardized mechanism for traffic shaping.
10. In practice shaping needs only to take place once, and that is at the customer premises equipment (CPE).

3.5.5 Cell Loss Priority Control
1. Every ATM cell contains the CLP field in the header.
2. This field is used to implement a very rudimentary control mechanism.
3. If the CLP bit is set to 1 (CLP = 1), the cell can be discarded depending on the actual network conditions and carrier policy.
4. The cell with the CLP field not set (CLP = 0) represents higher priority.
5. The CLP control mechanism may discard low priority cells during time of congestion.
6. In result the degradation of network service to all users whose cells are of higher priority is minimized.
7. The cells that have CLP field not set can be subject of tagging procedure if they violate the traffic contract.
8. In fact all the cells that are considered by the GCRA as non-conforming can have their CLP changed from 0 to 1 or can be immediately discarded.
9. The earlier alternative is more attractive to a customer as his traffic is likely to be delivered to the destination unless congestion conditions occur along the route.

3.5.6 Explicit Forward Congestion Indication
1. The Explicit Forward Congestion Notification (EFCI) is the traffic management mechanism that makes the use of the EFCI bit in the PTI field of an ATM cell header.
2. It is based on the idea that a node which experiences a congestion state may notify its adjacent node (with regards to the virtual circuit route) about the congestion.

3. The EFCI bit is set when, for example, a buffer threshold has been exceeded. The basic assumption behind this concept is based on the conclusion that a receiver can notify the transmitter that in turn slows down the transmission.
4. Provided that the EFCI is implemented at a large scale, the congestion should decrease or disappear.
5. This approach has a number of constraints such dependence on the round trip delay and customer behaviour.
6. However, when combined with other traffic management mechanisms it may come out as the sufficient solution.

3.5.7 Rate-based Congestion Control in ABR Service

1. Both CBR and VBR traffic sources are of real-time or semi-real time nature.
2. For these traffic types it is generally not possible for the sender to adjust to the actual network condition and slow down the transmission.
3. However, there is a group of services like the transport of network layer packets which have dynamic and unpredictable nature on one hand, and can consume as much bandwidth as possible while being the 'best effort' service at the same time.
4. Needless to say, due to the requirements of higher layers (including application layer) they request for a minimum amount of bandwidth to operate efficiently.
5. For this reason, the standard bodies defined ABRQoS category.
6. ABR service has been primarily designed for delay-tolerant and cell loss-intolerant data applications.
7. This category, as opposed to others, introduces a dynamic cell rate-based network feedback mechanism and supports a minimum cell rate.
8. The basic model is that after every k data cells, each source transmits a special RM (Resource Management) cell.
9. The RM cell is distinguished with the combination of bits in the PTI field of a cell header.
10. RM cells travel along the same path as the data cells, but it is treated in a special way along the route.
11. When it reaches the destination, it is examined, updated, and sent back to the source. The path for RM cells is presented in the Fig. 3.56.

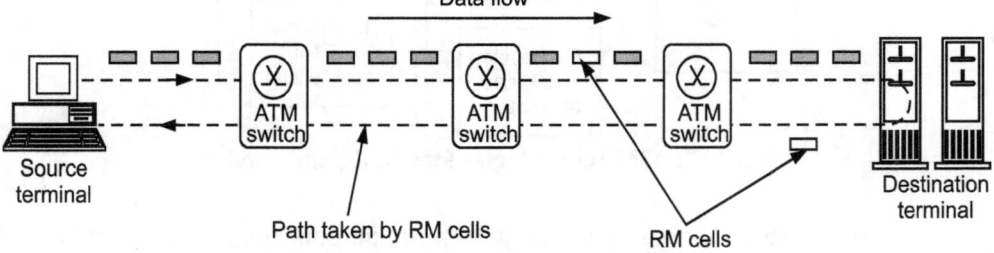

Fig. 3.56: The path taken by RM cells in ABR operation

12. The congestion control is based on the idea that each sender has a current rate ACR (Actual Cell Rate) that is greater than MCR but lower than PCR.
13. When congestion is absent, ACR is increased up to PCR.
14. If congestion occurs, ACR is decreased.
15. Each RM cell sent contains the rate at which the sender would like to transmit.
16. This value is called ER (Explicit Rate).
17. The RM cells passes along the path and the switches that are congested can reduce the value of ER.
18. Reduction can be imposed either in the forward or in the reverse direction.
19. Since no switch may increase it, the sender gets the knowledge of what the current maximum acceptable rate is.
20. Then it can adjust ACR to transmit cells at the rate that the slowest switch in the path can handle.
21. This short description does not cover the ABR related information completely so some further reading is advised.

3.6 ATM Applications

ATM technologies, standards, and services are being applied in a wide range of networking environments, as described briefly below (see Figure 3.57).

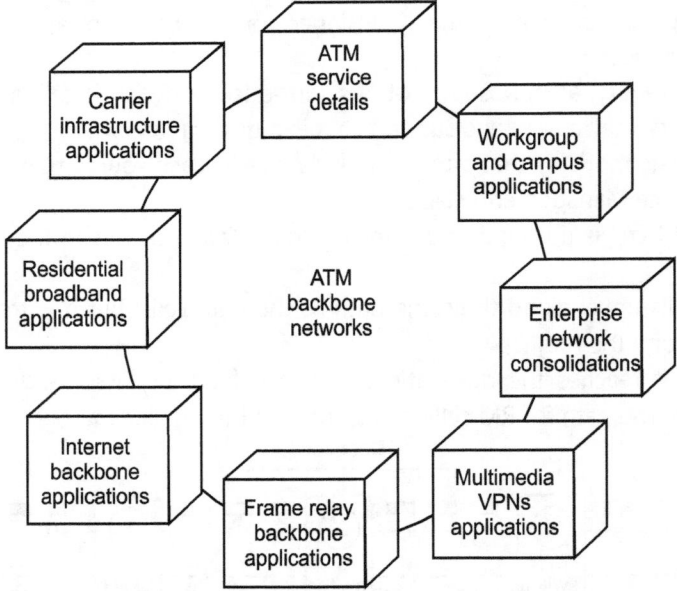

Fig. 3.57: ATM Technologies Standards, and Services

- **ATM services :** Service providers globally are introducing or already offering ATM services to their business users.

- **ATM workgroup and campus networks :** Enterprise users are deploying ATM campus networks based on the ATM LANE standards. Workgroup ATM is more of a niche market with the wide acceptance of switched-Ethernet desktop technologies.
- **ATM enterprise network consolidation :** A new class of product has evolved as an ATM multimedia network-consolidation vehicle. It is called an ATM enterprise network switch. A full-featured ATM ENS offers a broad range of in-building (e.g., voice, video, LAN, and ATM) and wide-area interfaces (e.g., leased line, circuit switched, frame relay, and ATM at narrowband and broadband speeds) and supports ATM switching, voice networking, frame-relay SVCs, and integrated multiprotocol routing.
- **Multimedia virtual private networks and managed services :** Service providers are building on their ATM networks to offer a broad range of services. Examples include managed ATM, LAN, voice and video services (these being provided on a per-application basis, typically including customer-located equipment and offered on an end-to-end basis), and full-service virtual private-networking capabilities (these including integrated multimedia access and network management).
- **Frame-relay backbones :** Frame-relay service providers are deploying ATM backbones to meet the rapid growth of their frame-relay services to use as a networking infrastructure for a range of data services and to enable frame relay to ATM service interworking services.
- **Internet backbones :** Internet service providers are likewise deploying ATM backbones to meet the rapid growth of their frame-relay services, to use as a networking infrastructure for a range of data services, and to enable Internet class-of-service offerings and virtual private intranet services.
- **Residential broadband networks :** ATM is the networking infrastructure of choice for carriers establishing residential broadband services, driven by the need for highly scalable solutions.
- **Carrier infrastructures for the telephone and private-line networks :** Some carriers have identified opportunities to make more-effective use of their SONET/SDH fiber infrastructures by building an ATM infrastructure to carry their telephony and

3.7 ATM VS Frame Relay

Sr. No	Frame Relay	ATM
1	Frame relay uses variable packet sizes. The packet size varies, depending on the amount of data that is being sent.	ATM uses a fixed packet size, which is the 53 byte cell that was depicted earlier.
2	Frame relay, while although is useful to	ATM cannot only work within a local area

Sr. No	Frame Relay	ATM
	connect different local area networks, it cannot actually work within one.	network, but they can also work within a wide area network.
3	Frame relay is easy and inexpensive to install, and is readily supported in software. For a lot of users, it simply means a software upgrade on existing equipment, which minimizes network investment.	ATM more often requires a more complex installation, and is not readily supported in some software.
4	Frame relay does have a varied packet size, it is the variance that can often mean a low overhead within the packet, which makes it a more efficient method for transmitting data.	ATM's fixed packet size, while optimized for handling multimedia traffic at high speeds, can sometimes leave a lot of overhead within the packet, especially in short transactions, where cells are often not full.
5	Frame relay is found to be more efficient with lower speed connections (T1 and below), because with lower speeds, the concern with the overhead for data application. First, at speeds of 2 Mbps and below, Frame Relay is more bandwidth efficient than ATM.	ATM is normally utilized for high bandwidths of 34 Mbps and upwards. ATM didn't do well initially because it was only offered as a service on T-3 connections, whose 45 Mbps capacity was more than most businesses needed or wanted to pay for. Frame relay, on the other hand, was less expensive than the common alternative - dedicated circuits - - and was cost-effective at 56 Kbps.
6	Frame relay is not cell based.	While ATM is cell based.
7	Frame relay is not isochronous.	While ATM is isochronous.
8	Frame relay has not a LANE deployment.	While ATM has the sort.
9	Frame relay LMI is completely different then ATM ILMI.	ATM ILMI is totally different than FR LMI.

You can find these similarities between the frame relay and ATM :

They are virtual circuit based.

They are NBMA technologies.

They have burst rate features.

They have congestions avoidance techniques.

Sr. No	Frame Relay	ATM
	They have traffic shaping or management techniques. FECN of frame relay is equivalent to the EFCI of ATM. BECN of frame relay is equivalent to the RRM of the ATM. Frame relay won in the WAN. ATM lived on, though in carrier core networks, where it is slowly being decommissioned. Ultimately, both frame relay and ATM are losing as they are being pushed out by MPLS.	

Frame relay versus ATM

	Frame relay	ATM
Dynamic bandwidth allocation	●	●
Frame size	Variable	Fixed
Scalable to high speeds	◐	●
Suiable for WANs, MANs	●	●
Suitable for LANs and campus networks	○	●
Carries data	●	●
Carries voice and/for video	◐	●
Supports quantifiable QoS	◐	●
Cost-effective medium-speed data-only requirements	●	◐

● Highly suitable   ◐ Somewhat suitable   ○ Not suitable

EXERCISE

1. Draw and explain "LAPD" format in detail.
2. Write short note on "Voice over frame relay".
3. What are the different applications of frame relay?
4. What are the different advantages of frame relay?
5. Write about different topologies of frame relay.
6. Draw and explain voice over frame relay network reference model.
7. Draw and explain ATM reference model.
8. Write short note on cell structure of ATM network.
9. Write concept of virtual channels in ATM.
10. What are the responsibilities of ATM adaptation layer?

11. Draw and explain "ATM cell-header format".
12. Write short notes on "ATM QoS".
13. Write detail note on "Voice over ATM".
14. Explain the basic X.25 network system.
15. What are the different advantages and disadvantages of X.25 network?
16. Compare X.25 and frame relay network.
17. What are the different frame relay devices?
18. Explain frame relay VC setup.
19. What is the concept of DLCI in frame relay?
20. What are the different benefits of frame relay?
21. What are the different applications of frame relay?
22. Explain the different frame relay topologies.
23. Write short notes on voice over frame relay.

Unit IV

BROADBAND ACCESS AND ROUTING TECHNOLOGIES

4.1 Introduction to broadband Access

4.1.1 Broadband Access Solutions

1. Broadband access options are very important—they very well may determine how well you are able to grow professionally and personally.

2. The main drivers toward broadband are user's desires to find information that is valuable to them, to be connected, and to experience the multimedia spectacle of the Internet.

3. In general, the view is that households and small- and medium-size enterprises—rather than the traditional corporate customers—will account for most of that market.

4. What drives a telecommunication company to consider deploying broadband access in the first place?

5. One reason is that it may be experiencing slower rates of growth or even a decline in its core business of providing fixed-link telephone services.

6. Also, there is a great deal of competition going on among many alternative networks, and there is an ongoing growth in the demand for non-voice services.

7. After a telecommunication company decides to deploy broadband access, it has to decide which of the available broadband media options to deploy: twisted-pair (that is, xDSL), coax, fiber, wireless, or one of the emerging options (see Table 4.1).

8. The important factor is the cost of installing the new distribution system, given the physical footprint realities such as the terrain and environmental conditions.

9. Finally, the telecommunication company needs to consider the performance level of the distribution system in terms of the requirements to implement the services strategy.

10. This also deals with the physical footprint realities (for example, broadband wireless may work very well in one area but provide poor performance in another because there are many trees whose leaves act as obstacles to the microwave). This chapter talks about the issues with regard to each of the broadband media.

Table 4.1: Broadband Media Options

Medium	Deployment Examples
Twisted-pair	HDSL, IDSL, SDSL, M/SDSL, ADSL, RADSL, VDSL
Coax	HFC
Fiber	FTTC, FTTH, PONs
Wireless	DBS/DTH, MMDS, LMDS, Free Space Optics, unlicensed bands
Emerging	Powerline, Ethernet-in-the-loop, HomePNA

Table 4.2: Transmission Media Characteristics

Media Type	Frequency Spectrum	Performance Error Rate	Distance Between Repeaters	Security	Cost
Twisted-pair	1 MHz	Poor to fair (10^{-5})	Short (1.2 miles / 2 km)	Poor	Low
Coaxial	1 GHz	Good (10^{-7} to 10^{-9})	Short (1.5 miles / 2.5 km)	Good	Moderate
Microwave	100 GHz	Good (10^{-9})	Medium (upto 45 miles / 72 km)	Poor	Moderate
Satellite	100 GHz	Good (10^{-9})	Long (upto 22,3000 miles / 36,000 km)	Poor	Moderate to high
Fiber	75 THz	Great (10^{-11} to 10^{-13})	Long (upto 4,000 miles / 6,400 km)	Good	Moderate to high

As discussed, broadband network services are predominantly planned as separate overlay networks. When incremental deployment occurs via intelligent edge switches, the result is separate networks for separate services. Integrated access is the key to the cost savings of the converged network architecture.

4.2 Cable Modem

1. In order for the user to be able to connect to Internet through the aforementioned cable architecture, the user will have to have a special **Cable Modem**, which will enable high-speed data connection.
2. The Cable Modem will have two connectors. One of the connectors will be used for the TV set outlet, the other will be used for the computer (Fig. 4.1).
3. It is true, though, that Cable Modem Modulates and Demodulates signals.
   In reality, Cable Modems are a lot more complex than telephone modems.
4. They have properties of a modem, radio, bridge, router, coder and other elements.
5. Presently, there are not many Cable Modems offered on the market. Most of them are still in the testing phase; however, some of the producers like Hybrid, IBM, Intel, Hewlett Packard, LANCity, Motorola and others are already announcing their newest products in the market.

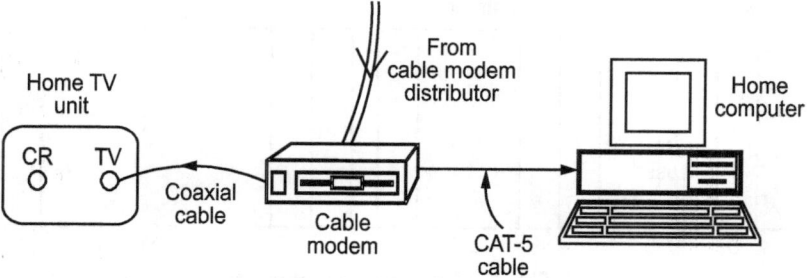

Fig. 4.1: Connecting a Cable Modem

4.2.1 What is a Cable Modem?

1. Traditional dial-up modems provide online access through the public telephone network at upto 56,000 bits per second (kbps).
2. A cable modem, on the other hand, provides high-speed Internet access through a cable television network at more than 1 million bits per second (mbps).
3. Cable modems are typically external devices placed next to your computer.

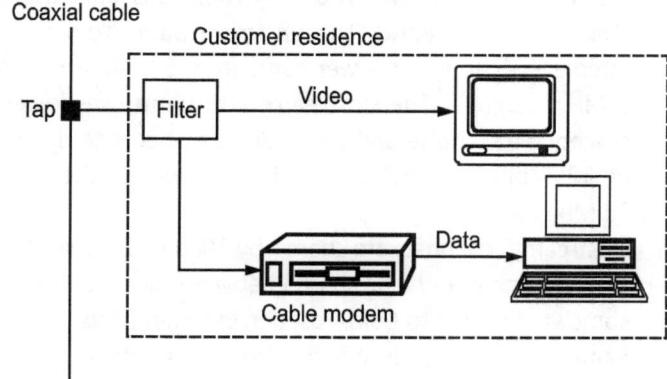

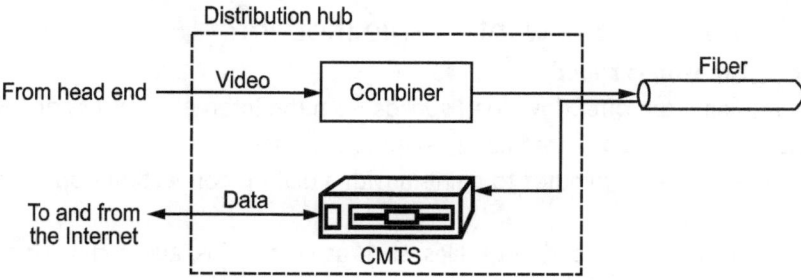

Fig. 4.2 (a): Cable modem configurations

- Co-axial cable has a bandwidth of 5 to 750 MHz approximately.
- This BW is divided into three bands:
  (a) Video   (b) Downstream data   (c) Upstream data

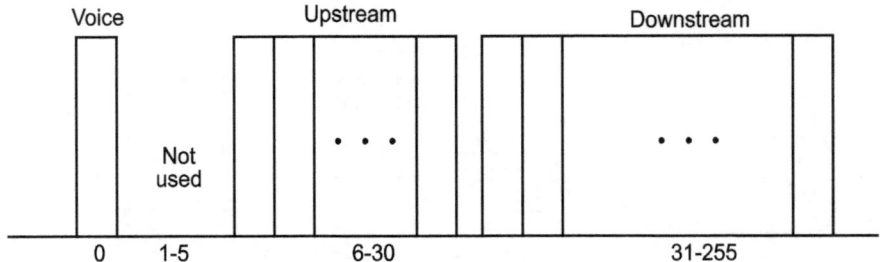

Fig. 4.2 (b): Cable bandwidth

- **Video Band:** The downstream-only **video band** occupies frequencies from 54 to 550 MHz. Since each TV channel occupies 6 MHz, this can accommodate more than 80 channels.
- **Downstream Data Band:** The downstream data (from the Internet to the subscriber premises) occupies the upper band, from 550 to 750 MHz. This band is also divided into 6-MHz channels. The downstream data can be received at 30 Mbps. The standard specifies only 27 Mbps. However, since the cable modem is connected to the computer through a 10BASE-T cable, this limits the data rate to 10 Mbps.
- **Upstream Data Band:** The upstream data (from the subscriber premises to the Internet) occupies the lower band, from 5 to 42 MHz. This band is also divided into 6 MHz channels. The **upstream data band** uses lower frequencies that are more susceptible to noise and intereference. Theoretically, downstream data can be sent at 12 Mbps (2 bits/Hz $\times$ 6 MHz). However, the data rate is usually less than 12 Mbps.
- Upstream 6 channels are shared by 1000 to 2000 subscribers in time-sharing mode. These channels must be shared between subscribers in same neighbourhood. This is somewhat similar to CSMA used in Ethernet LANs.
- Same concept is applicable for downstream data.

4.2.2 Why would someone want a cable modem?
1. **The No. 1 reason is speed.**
2. Cable modems can offer download speeds from the Internet in excess of 1 Mbps at least 20 times as fast as a traditional telephone modem.
3. Web pages that take minutes to paint in with a dial-up connection pop up instantly with a cable modem.
4. If you frequently download large files, such as video clips, audio clips or software, cable modems will make life much easier.
5. **The second reason is "always-on" connectivity.**
6. With a cable modem, there's no need to dial into an Internet service provider (ISP).
7. Simply click on your browser and you are on the Internet. No more waiting, no more busy signals.

4.2.3 How does a cable modem work?
1. A cable television system typically has 60 or more channels, and most of them are used for programming services like CNN, BBC, ESPN, DISCOVERY, SPORTS and HBO.
2. These channels also can be used to offer high-speed Internet access service.
3. Cable modems connect to the cable network with a standard coaxial cable, just like the wiring that is plugged into your television set to receive cable TV service.
4. The cable modem then connects to your PC through a standard Ethernet interface.

4.2.4 How fast are cable modem connections?
1. Many cable companies and Internet providers cable modems as 100 times faster than a dial-up Internet connection, or the equivalent of more than 5 Mbps.
2. That, however, is a slight exaggeration.
3. Theoretically, it can be done. But realistically, it rarely happens for a number of technological reasons.
4. A more accurate figure would be 1 Mbps about 20 times faster than a 56 kbps dial-up connection.
5. Another note: Cable modems are typically asymmetric, meaning that download speeds are faster than upload speeds.
6. When calculating Internet-access speeds, it is important to recognize the difference between bits and bytes.
7. Web browsers, such as Netscape Navigator, often report download speeds in kilobytes per second (KB/s).
8. Modems report speeds in kilobits per second (kbps).
9. There are eight bits in each byte. So, if your browser is downloading a file at 100 KB/s over a cable modem connection, that is equal to 800 Kbps.

4.2.5 What does "always on" mean?
1. It means that the cable modem is continuously connected to the Internet whenever your computer is turned on.
2. When you want surf the Web, all you need to do is type in a site's address.
3. There is no need to "dial up" an Internet service provider, as you must do with traditional telephone modems.

4.2.6 Who manufactures cable modems?
More than 20 companies, including 3 Com, Cisco Systems, Com21, Motorola, Nortel Networks, Philips, Terayon, Thomson, Toshiba, Samsung and Sony.

Network (Ethernet):

An Ethernet (LAN) connection is 10 Mbits/s or 100 Mbits/s, and is used to connect many computers that can all "talk" directly to each other. Normally they will all talk with a few servers and printers, but the network is all-to-all. The distance is normally limited to below 1 km.

4.2.7 Cable Modem System

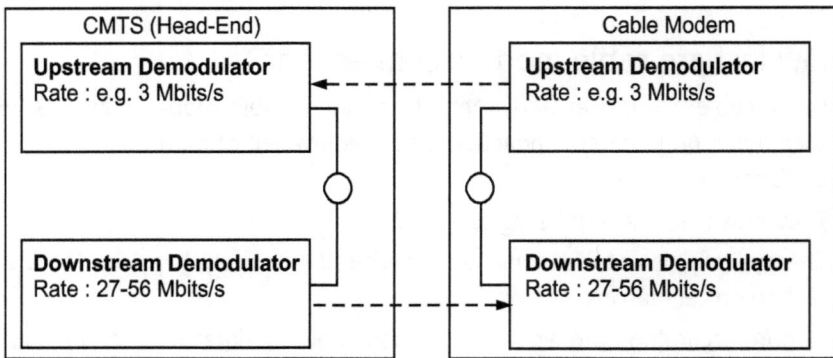

Fig. 4.3: Cable modem structure

1. The term "Cable Modem" is quite new and refers to a modem that operates over the ordinary cable TV network cables.
2. Basically you just connect the Cable Modem to the TV outlet for your cable TV, and the cable TV operator connects a Cable Modem Termination System (CMTS) in his end (the Head-End) as shown in Fig. 4.3.
3. Actually the term "Cable Modem" is a bit misleading, as a Cable Modem works more like a Local Area Network (LAN) interface than as a modem.
4. A Cable Modem connection is something in-between.
5. The speed is typically 3-50 Mbits/s and the distance can be 100 km or even more.
6. The Cable Modem Termination System (CMTS) can talk to all the Cable Modems (CM's), but the Cable Modems can only talk to the CMTS.
7. If two Cable Modems need to talk to each other, the CMTS will have to relay the messages.
8. For millions of people, television brings news, entertainment and educational programs into their homes. Many people get their TV signal from cable television (CATV) because cable TV provides a clearer picture and more channels.
9. Many people, who have cable TV, can now get a high-speed connection to the Internet from their cable provider.

10. Cable modems compete with technologies like asymmetrical digital subscriber lines (ADSL).

11. In this article, we will look at how a cable modem works and see how 100 cable television channels and any Web site out there can flow over a single coaxial cable into your home.

4.2.8 Inside the Cable Modem

Cable modems can be either internal or external to the computer. In some cases, the cable modem can be a part of a set-top cable box, requiring that only a keyboard and mouse be added for Internet access. In fact, if your cable system has upgraded to digital cable, the new set-top box the cable company provides will be capable of connecting to the Internet, whether or not you receive Internet access through your CATV connection. Regardless of their outward appearance, all cable modems contain certain key components:

- **A tuner**
- **A demodulator**
- **A modulator**
- **A media access control (MAC) device**
- **A microprocessor**

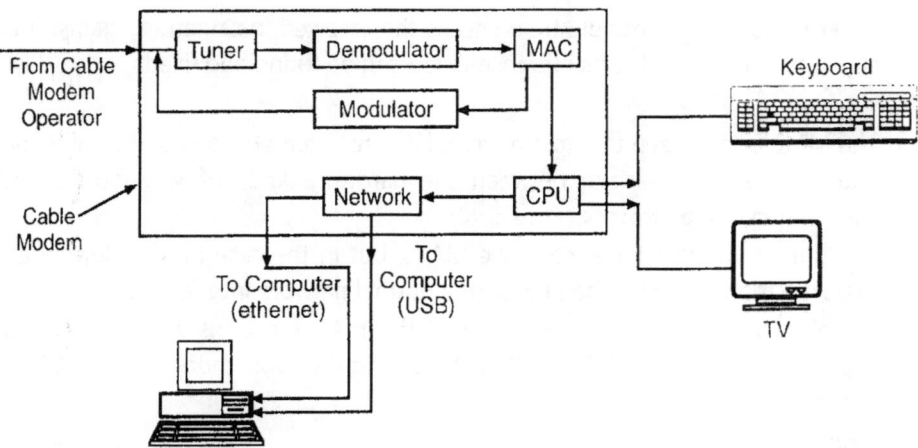

Fig. 4.4: The internals of cable modem

Tuner:

1. The tuner connects to the cable outlet, sometimes with the addition of a **splitter** that separates the Internet data channel from normal CATV programming.

2. Since the Internet data comes through an otherwise unused cable channel, the tuner simply receives the modulated digital signal and passes it to the demodulator.
3. Other systems, most often those with more limited capacity for channels, will use the cable modem tuner for downstream data and a dial-up telephone modem for upstream traffic.
4. In either case, after the tuner receives a signal, it is passed to the demodulator.

Modulator:

In cable modems that use the cable system for upstream traffic, a modulator is used to convert the digital computer network data into radio frequency signals for transmission. This component is sometimes called a **burst modulator,** because of the irregular nature of most traffic between a user and the Internet, and consists of three parts:
- A section to insert information used for error correction on the receiving end,
- A QAM modulator and
- A digital-to-analog (D/A) converter.

Demodulator:

1. The most common demodulators have four functions.
2. A quadrature amplitude modulation (QAM) demodulator takes a radio frequency signal that has information encoded in it by varying both the amplitude and phase of the wave, and turns it into a simple signal that can be processed by the analog-to-digital (A/D) converter.
3. The A/D converter takes the signal, which varies in voltage, and turns it into a series of digital 1's and 0's.
4. An error correction module then checks the received information against a known standard, so that problems in transmission can be found and fixed.

MAC:

1. The MAC sits between the upstream and downstream portions of the cable modem, and acts as the interface between the hardware and software portions of the various network **protocols**.
2. All computer network devices have MACs, but in the case of a cable modem, the tasks are more complex than those of a normal network interface card.
3. For this reason, in most cases, some of the MAC functions will be assigned to a central processing unit (CPU), either the CPU in the cable modem or the CPU of the user's system.

Microprocessor:

1. The microprocessor's job depends somewhat on whether the cable modem is designed to be part of a larger computer system or to provide Internet access with no additional computer support.
2. In situations calling for an attached computer, the internal microprocessor still picks up much of the MAC function from the dedicated MAC module.

3. Thus, if you are one of the first users to connect to the Internet through a particular cable channel, then you may have nearly the entire bandwidth of the channel available for your use.
4. As new users, especially heavy-access users, are connected to the channel, you will have to share that bandwidth, and may see your performance degrade as a result.
5. It is possible that, in times of heavy usage with many connected users, performance will be far below the theoretical maximums.

4.2.9 Speed/Standards/Connection

Table 4.3 gives a comparison of a file download of 500 KB using different techniques.

Table 4.3: Comparison of a file download of 500 KB using different techniques

Time to transmit a single 500 KB image		
Telephone Modem	28.8 Kbps	6-8 minutes
ISDN	64 Kbps	1-1.5 minutes
Cable Modem	10 Mbps	Approximately 1 second

A representative sample of the way data speeds are provided on cable modems is shown in Table 4.4.

Table 4.4: Representative asymmetrical data cable modem speeds

Sample Cable Modem Speeds	Upstream	Downstream
General Instrument	1.5 Mbps	30 Mbps
Hybrid/Intel	96 Kbps	30 Mbps
LANcity	10 Kbps	10 Mbps
Motorola	768 Kbps	30 Mbps
Zenith	4 Mbps	4 Mbps

Standards:
1. Modems are available today from a variety of vendors, all with their own unique technical approach.
2. These modems are making it possible for cable companies to enter the data communications market now.
3. In the longer term, modem costs must drop and greater interoperability is desirable.
4. Customers who buy modems that work in their current cable system need assurance that the modem will work if they move to a different geographic location served by a different cable company.
5. Furthermore, agreement on a standard set of specifications will allow the market to enjoy economies of scale and drive down the price of each individual modem.

6. Ultimately, those modems will be available as standard peripheral devices offered as an option to customers buying new personal computers at retail stores.
7. Specifications were to be developed in three phases, and then be presented to standards setting bodies for approval as standards.
8. Individual vendors were free to offer their own implementations with a variety of additional competitive features and future improvements.
9. A data interoperability specification will comprise a number of interfaces. The resultant specification is called *Data Over Cable Service Interface Specification* (DOCSIS), which architecturally is shown in Fig. 4.5 as it relates to the TCP/IP protocol stack. Note that there are several sublayers added into the DOCSIS specification at the bottom layers (for example, layer 1 and 2) of the protocol stack.
10. This is to simplify the connection and add the dimension of security into the DOCSIS specifications.

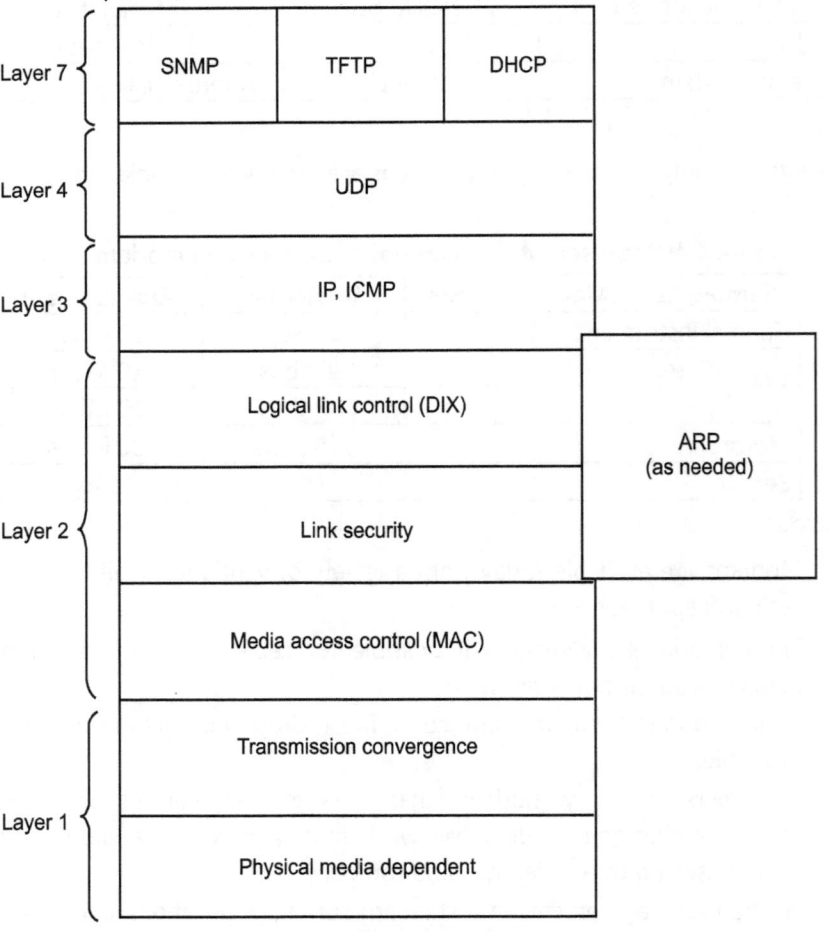

Fig. 4.5: The DOCSIS Model

11. Some interfaces reside within the cable network. Several of these system-level interfaces also will be specified in order to ensure interoperability of such important functions as authentication for login/logout, ease of installation of cable modems for reliable customer activation, and spectrum management over the cable network's hybrid fiber/coaxial plant.

Applications:

Cable modems open the door for customers to enjoy a range of high-speed data services, all at speeds hundreds of times faster than telephone modem calls. Subscribers can be fully connected, 24 hours a day, to services without interfering with cable television service or phone service. Among these services are

- **Information services:** Access to shopping, weather maps, household bill paying, and so on, Internet access E-mail, discussion groups, and the World Wide Web.
- **Business applications:** Interconnecting LANs or supporting collaborative work.
- **Cablecommuting:** Enabling the already popular notion of working from home.
- **Education:** Allowing students to continue to access educational resources from home.

The promises of advanced telecommunication networks, once more hype than fact, are now within reach. Cable modems and other technology are being deployed to make it happen. Regardless of the technology selected, the main goal is to get the high-speed data communications on the cable adjacent to the TV and entertainment. This gives the CATV companies the leverage to act in an arbitrage situation, competing with the local telephone companies who have dragged their feet in moving high-speed services to the consumer's door.

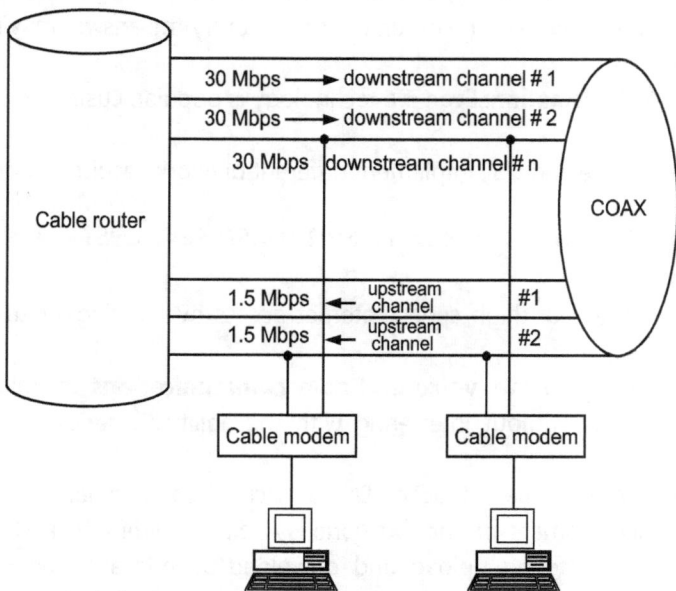

Fig. 4.6: Different speeds on the up-and-down stream flows

As shown in Fig. 4.6, there are several up-and-down speed capabilities that can be shared to deliver asymmetrical speeds to the consumer's door. In the particular figure, the download speed is upto 30 Mbps, whereas the upstream operates at 1.5 Mbps. For many, this is sufficient based on their applications.

4.3 DSL Technology

4.3.1 Cable Modem or DSL (Digital Subscriber Line)?

1. Two of the most popular technologies that offer speedy access to the World Wide Web are DSL broadband and the cable modem.
2. There are several reasons why this is the case and the first one is that both of these Internet connections are considerably faster than the standard dialup connections.
3. However, when you compare the speed of data transfer between DSL and a cable modem there is a bit of variance depending on various technical aspects.
4. Because of these variances, DSL and the cable modem might have the advantage at different times.
5. An overview of both technologies will clearly show the advantages and disadvantages of both.

4.3.2 Points of Evaluation

When evaluating cable and DSL services, consider the following:

- **Speed:** One of these technologies has faster speed than the other in theory. However, that technology may not deliver on the promise in everyday use.
- **Popularity:** In one country, one of these services enjoys significantly greater popularity than the other. In other country the answer may be different.
- **Customer Satisfaction:** Even if a technology is popular, customers may be unhappy with it.
- **Security:** Cable and DSL implement different network security models.

4.3.3 What is the difference between these services?

DSL Service:
1. Provides always-on high speed Internet access over a single dedicated telephone line.
2. This technology allows **voice and data communications** to utilize the same line simultaneously without interfering with the ability to send or receive telephone calls.
3. The most predominant type of DSL service in commercial use for business and residential customers around the world is ADSL or asymmetrical DSL.
4. ADSL offers differing upload and download speeds and can be configured to deliver speeds from the network to the customer upto 120 times faster than dialup service and 100 times faster than ISDN (Integrated Service Digital Network).

5. Typically, the delivered download speed for most networks is in the range of 50 times faster than ordinary 28.8 kbps dial-up.
6. In striving to provide more speed, Typical Network download speed for residential service is from 768 kbps to 1.5 mbps.
7. **DSL download speed is excellent for general Internet access and for applications where downstream speed is most important, such as video-on-demand.**
8. The upload speed, which presently is not as fast as cable, is more than adequate for sending files and documents to other people or pages to a web site.

4.3.4 ADSL

- ADSL is an asymmetric communication technology designed for residential customers, it is not suitable for business users.
- Business users require large bandwidth in both directions.

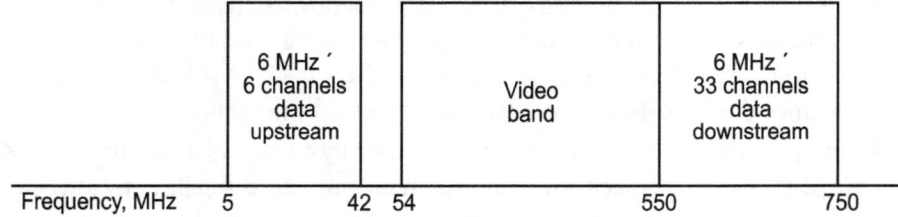

Fig. 4.7 (a): Bandwidth division

- **Channel 0** is reversed for voice communication.
- **Channel 1 to 5** are not used to allow a gap between voice and data communication.
- Channel 6 to 30 (25 channels) are used for upstream data transfer and control. One channel is for control and 24 channels are for data transfer.

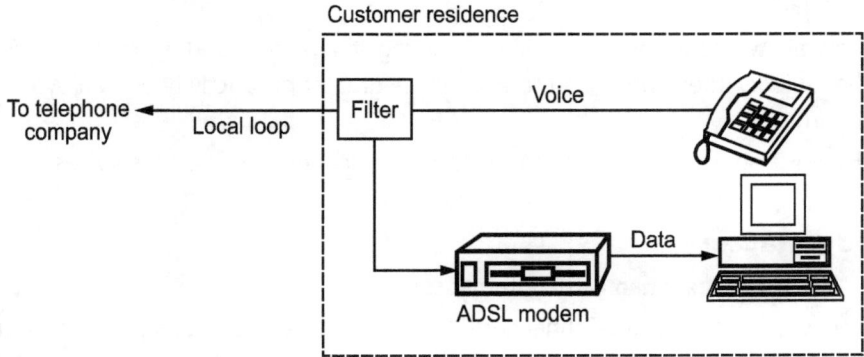

Fig. 4.7 (b): ADSL communication

- Channels 31 to 255 (225 channels) are used for downstream data transfer and control. One channel for control and 224 channels are for data transfer.
- Upstream data speed = 24 channels × 4 kHz × 15 bits/Hz
  = 1.44 Mbps
- Downstream data speed = 224 channels × 4 kHz × 15 bits/Hz
  = 13.4 Mbps
- Because of high S/N ratio the actual bit rate is much lower than mentioned rates i.e. upstream = 64 Kbps to 1 Mbps and downstream = 500 Kbps to 8 Mbps.

Cable Broadband Service,

1. On the other hand, also offers an always-on high speed Internet connection.
2. Internet access is delivered over cable television line utilizing "shared technology" - that is all subscribers on the system share a single connection to the Internet.
3. While cable modems may have greater potential downloading capabilities (upto 200 times faster than a 28.8 kbps modem from the Internet to home), that bandwidth is "shared" among users on the system, and connection speed will therefore vary, sometimes dramatically, as more users are online at the same time.
4. Although many cable systems have the capability to deliver from 10 to 20 Mbps of download speed, most actually limit system downloads to significantly lower levels.
5. Typical download speeds for the majority of residential cable services range from 300 Kbps to 600 Kbps with speed sometimes exceeding 1.2 Mbps, but not on a consistent basis.
6. Too many people trying to send or receive data on a cable network at the same time **causes congestion** and **slows the cable connection speed** (Upload and Download) considerably.
7. In many instances, this will cause cable to be slower than DSL.
8. However, DSL and cable broadband downloads are still significantly faster than ordinary dial-up.
9. This allows consumers to enjoy streaming videos and audio presentations without herky-jerky interruption and to experience greater productivity and enjoyment on the Internet.
10. Here is a summary of the advantages and disadvantages of both services.

DSL Advantages:

- DSL is **cheaper than cable** Internet service.
- Always-On Internet Connection 24 hours/7days. No dial up. There is no busy signals.

- Connection is unique and speed is not affected by the number of users on-line at the same time. DSL speed stays consistent.
- Upload speed is comparable to cable.
- Customers can dial up services remotely when travelling.
- Optional Static IP address supports server hosting for gaming, home office users, and telecommuters.
- Surf the Internet and talk on the phone at the same time.

Cable Advantages:

- Always-On Internet Connection 24 hours/7days. No dial up. No busy signals.
- **You can browse the Net, watch cable TV, and be on the phone at the same time.**
- Downloads upto 100 times faster than a 28.8 K modem; however, typical speeds tend to be much lower than the maximum. Speed potential is greater.
- Cable provides bundled discounts for TV, Internet, and telephone services.
- Cable offers a much wider service area.

DSL Disadvantages:

- Only as reliable as your phone line. Service may be subject to interruption by severe weather.
- Service is currently limited to an area within close proximity of local telephone facilities (18,000 feet or a little over 3 miles).

Cable Disadvantages:

- Service can be affected by the weather and reliability can be an issue.
- Shared bandwidth causes speed slowdowns especially during periods of peak demand. The more users on the system at the same time, the slower the speed.
- Shared bandwidth technology exposes users to privacy concerns.
- Dynamic IP address does not support server hosting for web site, e-mail or gaming.

Keep in mind that no service is perfect. Cable offers greater speed potential; DSL offers an individual Internet connection with more consistent high speed and a greater measure of privacy and security.

Additional features, such as firewall protection, spam blocking software and anti-virus software make DSL a popular choice for new subscribers.

4.3.5 Cable Modem Vs DSL

Table 4.5 compares general characteristics between cable modem service and DSL service. Again, your choice of service may depend on what is available in your area. Providers often offer special pricing for new subscribers, which may include free installation, discounts on monthly rates for the first few months of service, or free modems.

Table 4.5

Parameters	Cable Modem	DSL
Installation Fee	Same for both	Same for both
Monthly Rates	Cheap	Cheaper than Cable Modem
Pricing Specials	May get price break when combined with cable TV and phone service	May get price break when combined with cable TV and phone service
Connection Speed: Upload	128 kbps to 500 kbps	128 kbps to 1.5 Mbps
Connection Speed: Download	1 Mbps to 3 Mbps	144 kbps to 9 Mbps
Hardware Requirement	Ethernet card Cable modem (usually obtained from provider)	Ethernet card DSL modem (usually obtained from provider)
Set Up	Relatively easy set up	Set up can be difficult
Availability	More widespread than DSL	Sometimes difficult to determine if service is available
Performance	Line shared with others; speeds vary accordingly	Dedicated line, so speed is guaranteed; performance may depend on location

4.3.6 xDSL TECHNOLOGY

Overview:

1. One of the major problems facing Internet service providers (*ISP-telephone companies*) is the ability to maintain and preserve their installed base.
2. Ever since the Telecommunications Act of 1996, there has been mounting pressure on the ISPs to provide faster and more correct Internet access.
3. In order to provide the higher-speed communications abilities, these carriers have continually looked for new means of providing the service.
4. However, the ISPs have an installed base of unshielded twisted pair in the local loop that cannot be ignored or abandoned.
5. Therefore, a new form of communications was needed to work over the existing copper cable plant.
6. One of the technologies selected was the use of xDSL. The DSL family includes several variations of what is known as digital subscriber line.

7. The lower case x in front of the DSL stands for the many variations. These will include –
    - Asymmetrical digital subscriber line (ADSL)
    - ISDN (like) digital subscriber line (IDSL)
    - High bit-rate Digital Subscriber Line (HDSL)
    - Consumer Digital Subscriber Line (CDSL)
    - Single High Speed DSL (SHDSL)
    - Rate-adaptive digital subscriber line (RADSL)
    - Very high-bit rate digital subscriber line (VDSL)
    - Single or symmetric digital subscriber line (SDSL)
8. One can see that the variations are many. Each DSL capability carries with it differences in speed, throughput, and facilities used.
9. The most popular of this family under today's technology is the use of ADSL.
10. ADSL is a technology being provided primarily by the ISPs because the existing cable plant can be supported, and the speed throughput can vary, depending on the quality of the copper.
11. However, the most important and critical factor in dealing with ADSL technology is the capability to support speeds between 1.5 Mbps upto 8.192 Mbps.
12. At the same time, the ISP can also support *Plain Old Telephone Service* (POTS) for voice or fax communications on the same line. What this means is that the ISP does not have to install all new cabling to support high-speed communications access to the Internet.

IDSL:

1. DSL refers to a pair of modems that are installed on the local loop (also called *the last mile*) to facilitate higher speeds for data transmission.
2. Network providers do not provide a line; they use the existing lines in place and add the DSL modems to increase the throughput.
3. DSL modems offer duplex operations transmission in both directions at the same time.
4. The speed of a DSL modem may be 160 Kbps on copper at distances up to 18K using the twisted pair wires.
5. The bandwidth used is from 0 to 80 kHz, as opposed to the arbitrarily limited 0 to 3300 Hz on a voice line.
6. This is the IDSL using the 144 Kbps full duplex, which gives us what is known as the *Basic Rate Interface* (BRI).
7. The IDSL technique is all digital operating at two channels of 64 Kbps for voice or nonvoice operation and a 16 Kbps data channel for signaling, control, and data packets.

8. ISDN was very slow to catch on, but the movement to the Internet created a whole new set of demands for the carriers to deal with. The term IDSL is new, but the gist is the same. DSL is used to deliver ISDN services.

9. As the deployment of IDSL was speeding up on the local loop, the providers developed a new twist, called "*always on, ISDN*" mimicking a leased set of channels that are always connected. By bonding the channels together, Internet users can surf the Net at speeds of 128 Kbps in each direction. Note this is asymmetrical DSL.

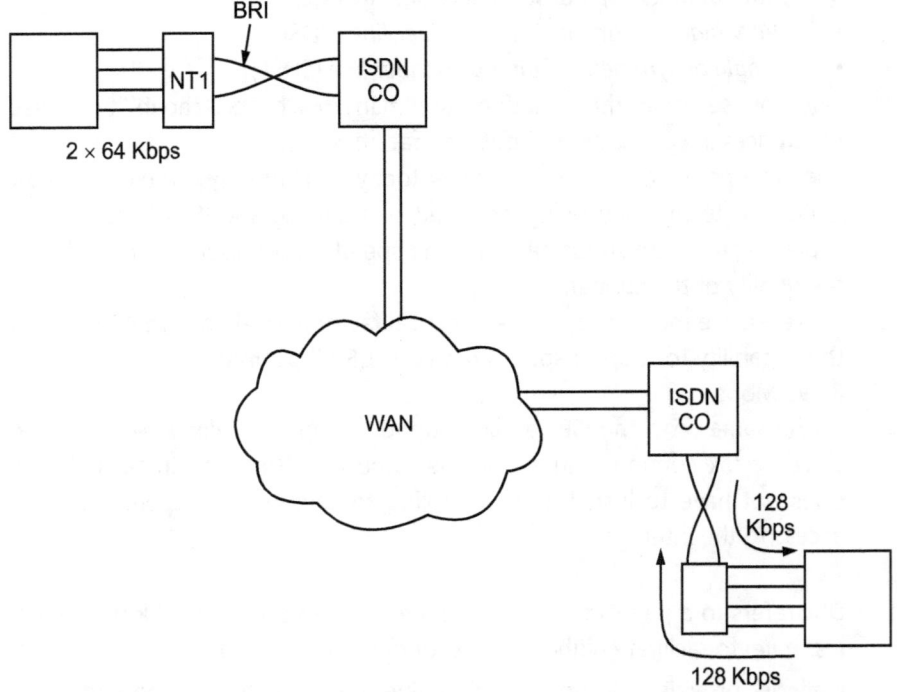

Fig. 4.8: The ISDL line connection enables 128 kbps in total simultaneously

HDSL:

1. These two high-data-rate DSLs are symmetric services capable of 1.5 Mbps and 2.048 Mbps speeds, respectively. HDSL requires two or three-wire pairs.
2. In 1958, the Bell Laboratories developed a voice multiplexing system that used a 64 Kbps voice modulation technique called *pulse coded modulation* (PCM).
3. This produces a data rate of 1.544 Mbps or what we know as a T1. We now refer to this as a *Digital Signal Level 1* (DS-1) at the framed data rate. This rate of data transfer is used in the United States, Canada, and Japan.
4. T1 (and E1) uses Alternate Mark Inversion (AMI), which demands all of the bandwidth and corrupts the cable spectrum quickly. As a result, the providers can only use a single T1 in a 50-pair cable and could not install another in adjacent cables because of the corruption.

5. Further limitations required the providers to remove bridge taps, clean up splices, and remove load coils from the wires to get the T1 to work.
6. To circumvent these cabling problems, HDSL was developed as a more efficient way of transmitting T1 (and E1) over the existing copper wires. HDSL does not require the repeaters on a local loop of upto 12 K. Bridge taps will not bother the service, and the splices are left in place.
7. This means that the provider can offer HDSL as a more efficient delivery of 1.544 Mbps. The modulation rate on the HDSL service is more advanced. Sending 768 Kbps on one pair and another 768 Kbps on the second pair of wires splits the T1. Nearly all the providers today deliver T1 capabilities on some form of HDSL.

SDSL:

1. Symmetric Digital Subscriber Line. This indicates a subscriber line service that utilizes the same data rate for upstream and downstream. This term is applicable to HDSL Technology also.
2. The goal of the DSL family was to continue to support and use the local copper cable plant.
3. SDSL was developed to provide high-speed communications on that single cable pair but at distances no greater than 10 K.
4. Despite this distance limitation, SDSL was designed to deliver 1.544 Mbps on the single cable pair.
5. Typically, however, the providers offer SDSL at 768 Kbps. This creates a dilemma for the carriers because HDSL can do the same things as SDSL.

ADSL:

1. SDSL uses only one pair of wires, but is limited in its distance to provide duplex, high-speed communications.
2. Not all users require symmetrical speeds at the same time.
3. ADSL was, therefore, designed to support differing speeds in both directions over a single cable pair at distances of upto 18 K.
4. Because the speeds requested are typically for access to the Internet (or intranet), most users look for higher speeds in a download direction and the lower speed for an upward direction.
5. Therefore, the asymmetrical nature of this service meets those needs.

RADSL:

1. An asymmetric service, rate-adaptive DSL promises to provide speeds of 8 Mbps–600 Kbps downstream and 1 Mbps–128 Kbps upstream, while offering simultaneous voice service.
2. RADSL can dynamically adjust to line conditions.

3. Typically with equipment, installed assumptions are made based on minimum performance characteristics and speeds.
4. In some cases, special equipment is used to condition the circuit to achieve those speeds.
5. However, if the line conditions vary, the speed will be dependent on the sensitivity of the equipment.
6. In order to achieve variations in the throughput and be sensitive to the line conditions, RADSL was developed.
7. This gives the flexibility to adapt to the changing conditions and adjust the speeds in each direction to potentially maximize the throughput on each line.
8. Additionally, as line conditions change, you can see the speeds changing in each direction during the transmission.
9. Many of the ISPs have installed RADSL as their choice, given the local loop conditions. Speeds of upto 768 Kbps are the preferred rates offered by the incumbent providers.

CDSL:

1. Consumers are not all looking for symmetrical high-speed communication in order to achieve access to the Internet.
2. Furthermore, the speeds of ADSL technology are more than the average consumer may be looking for.
3. As a result, the lower-speed communications capability was developed by using CDSL as the model.
4. With other forms of DSL (such as ADSL and RADSL), splitters are used on the line to separate the voice and the data communications.
5. CDSL does not use, nor need, a splitter on the line. Moreover, speeds of upto 1 Mbps in the download direction and 160 Kbps in the upward direction are provided.
6. It is expected that the speeds and DSL will meet the needs of the average consumer for some time to come.
7. As a result, a universal ADSL working group developed what is called *ADSL-lite*. This was ratified in late 1998, using the specifications from this working group for delivery to the average consumer.
8. Because of the changes in speeds with this technique, the telephone companies are in a position to support a lower-speed DSL strictly through the use of the modems without the concern for local loop.
9. An example of this DSL-lite (G.Lite) service is provided with the Nortel 1 Mb modem.

SHDSL:

1. It is a Symmetric High Bit Rate Digital Subscriber Loop.
2. SHDSL conforms to the International Telecommunications Union G.991.2 recommendations, leveraging capabilities of older DSL and other transport technologies, such as SDSL, HDSL and HDSL2, IDSL, ISDN, T-1, and E-1.
3. One of the most significant improvements SHDSL brings to the business market is increased reach — at least 30 percent greater than any earlier symmetric DSL technology.
4. Furthermore, SHDSL supports repeaters, which further increase the reach capability of this technology.
5. Another critical advantage of SHDSL is its increase in symmetric bandwidth. In a typical installation, upto 2.3 Mbps will be available on a single copper pair.
6. For greater bandwidth needs in the future, a 4-wire model that can provide up to 4.6 Mbps is also supported by the new standard.
7. SHDSL is also rate adaptive, enabling flexible revenue-generation models and enabling service providers to offer service-level agreements that ensure businesses get the service they want, when they want it.
8. G.SHDSL stands for *Symmetric High Bit Rate Digital Subscriber Loop* defined by the new ITU Global Standard G991.2 as of February 2001.
9. This service delivers voice and data services based on highly innovative communication technologies and will thus be able to replace older communication technologies such as T1, E1, HDSL, HDSL2, SDSL, ISDN, and IDSL in the future.
10. SHDSL provides high symmetric data rates with guaranteed bandwidth and low interference with other services. By supporting equal upstream and downstream data rates, G.SHDSL better fits the needs of
    - Remote LAN access
    - Web-hosting
    - Application sharing
    - Video conferencing
11. G.SHDSL targets the small business market. Multiple telephone and data channels, video conferencing, remote LAN access, and leased lines with customer-specific data rates are among its many exciting characteristics.
12. Spectrally friendly with other DSLs, it supports symmetric data rates varying from 192 Kbps to 2.320 Mbps across greater distances than other technologies.
13. In an ATM-based network on the customer side, an *Integrated Access Device* (IAD) is installed to convert voice and data into ATM cells.

14. An IAD can also contain some routing functionality.
15. Data is converted using AAL5 (ATM Adaptation Layer), while voice requires AAL1 (without compression) or AAL2 (with compression and micro cells).
16. These cells are mapped together in the SHDSL frame and recovered later on in the DSLAM.
17. An ATM switch routes the cells either to an *Internet service provider* (ISP) or to a voice gateway that translates the voice cells back into the TDM world.
18. The voice part of the SHDSL frame will be treated in a similar fashion to normal ISDN or POTS services.
19. However, the data needs to be converted into ATM.
20. This can be done either in an IAD, resulting in a mix of TDM and ATM on the SHDSL line, or at the central office side.
21. In the second case, it is necessary to protect the data on the line.
22. This can be easily done by an HDLC protocol.
23. The division between voice and data should be done in the loop carrier so that the ATM cells can be sent directly to the ATM backbone in order not to congest the PSTN network.
24. This approach has the advantage of being more bandwidth efficient because the HDLC overhead is smaller than the ATM overhead.
25. Additionally, the Segmentation And Reassembly (SAR) functionality can be centralized in the DLC.
26. However, because an IAD normally uses Ethernet to connect to a LAN, some intelligence is required at the subscriber side to process the Ethernet MAC and also have SAR functionality.

VDSL:

1. The fastest and newest DSL on the block, very high-speed DSL is an asymmetric service, offering speeds of 12.9–52.8 Mbps.
2. Clearly, changes will always occur as we demand faster and more reliable communications capabilities.
3. It was only a matter of time until some users demanded higher-speed communications than was offered by the current DSL technologies.
4. As a result, VDSL was introduced to achieve the higher speeds.
5. If, in fact, speeds of upto 50 Mbps are demanded, then the distance limitations of the local cable plant will be a factor.
6. In order to achieve the speeds, you can expect that a fiber feed will be used to deliver VDSL.
7. This technique will most likely carry ATM traffic (cells) as its primary payload.

Table 4.6 summarizes the speeds and characteristics of the DSL technologies discussed. These are the typical installation and operational characteristics; others will certainly exist in variations of installation and implementation.

Table 4.6: Summary of DSL speeds and operations using current methods

Service	Explanation	Download	Upload	Mode of Operation
ADSL	Asymmetric DSL	1.5 to 8.192 Mbps	16 to 640 Kbps	Different up and down speeds, one pair wire
RADSL	Rate Adaptive DSL	64 Kbps to 8.192 Mbps	16 to 768 Kbps speeds	Different up and down. Many common operations use 768 Kbps. One pair wire.
CDSL	Consumer DSL	1 Mbps	16 to 160 Kbps	Now ratified as DSL-lite (G.lite). No splitters. One pair wire.
HDSL	High-data rate DSL	1.544 Mbps in North America	1.544 Mbps	Symmetrical services. Two pairs of wire.
	2.048 Mbps	2.048 Mbps in rest of world		
IDSL	ISDN DSL	1.44 Kbps (64 + 64 + 16) as BRI	144 Kbps (64 + 64 + 16) as BRI	Symmetrical operation. One pair of wire. ISDN BRI
SDSL	Single DSL	1.544 Mbps, 2.048 Mbps	1.544 Mbps, 2.048 Mbps	Uses only 1 pair but typically provisioned at 768 Kbps. One pair wire.
VDSL	Very high data rate DSL	13 to 53 ± Mbps	1.5 to 6.0 Mbps	Fiber needed and ATM probably used.
SHDSL (G.SHDSL)	Single high-speed DSL or 384 Kbps	192 Kbps to 2.360 Mbps or 384 Kbps to 4.720 Mbps	192 Kbps to 2.360 Mbps. Using 2 pair to 4.720 Mbps	Using 1 pair.

xDSL Coding Techniques:

1. Many approaches were developed as a means of encoding the data onto the xDSL circuits.
2. The most common are Carrierless Amplitude Phase Modulation (CAP) and discret multitone (DMT) modulation.
3. Quadrature with Phase Modulation (QAM) has also been used, but the important part is the standardization.
4. The industry, as a rule, selected DMT, but several developers and providers have used CAP.
5. It is, therefore, appropriate to summarize both of these techniques. The SHDSL technology uses a trellis-coded pulse amplitude modulation (TCPAM) technique to gain the benefits of the single-pair services or two-pair service.

4.4 Wireless Local Loop (WLL)

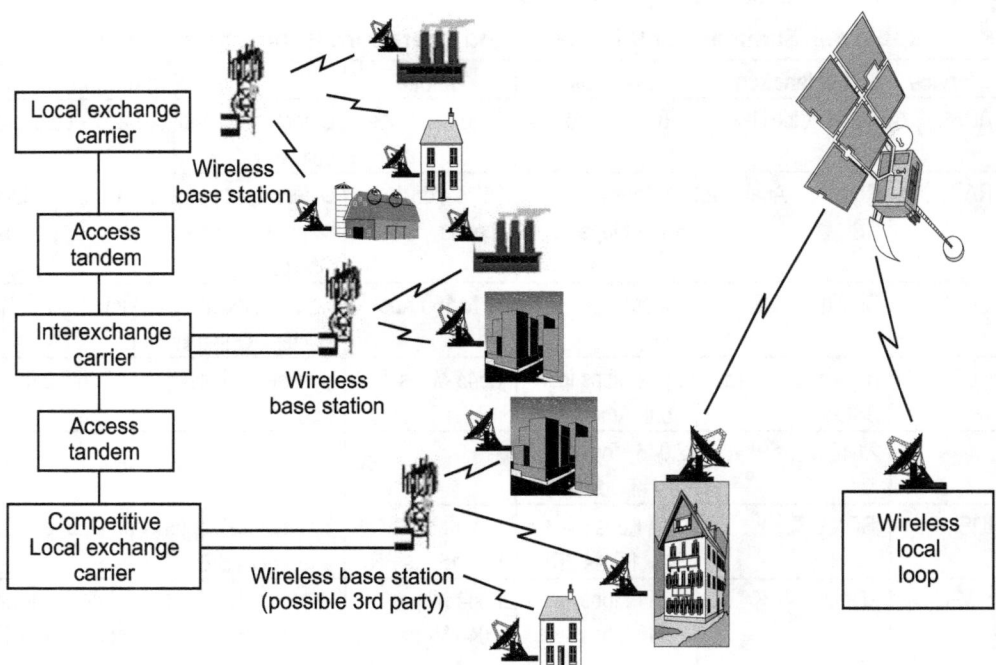

Fig. 4.9: WLL Conceptual Model

1. Sometimes called radio in the loop (RITL) or fixed-radio access (FRA), WLL is a system that connects subscribers to the public switched telephone network (PSTN) and providing Broadband Internet connection using radio signals as a substitute for copper for all or part of the connection between the subscriber and the switch.

2. This includes cordless access systems, proprietary fixed radio access, and fixed cellular systems.

3. In many developing countries, there is tremendous demand for new business and residential telephone service. More and more operators are looking to wireless technologies to rapidly provide thousands of new subscribers with high-quality telephone service at a reasonable price.

   - Existing landline operators can extend their network with WLL.
   - Cellular operators can capitalize on their current network to deliver residential service with WLL.
   - New service providers can quickly deploy non-traditional WLL solutions to rapidly meet a community's telephony needs.

4. Old Wireless Local Loop is an ideal application to provide telephone service to a remote rural area.
5. This system is based on a full-duplex radio network that provides local telephone-like service among a group of users in remote areas.
6. These areas could be connected via radio links to the national telephone network, though allowing the WLL subscriber to call or be reached by any telephone in the world.
7. This WLL unit consists of a radio transceiver and the WLL interface assembled in one metal box.
8. Two cables and a telephone connector are the only outlets from the box; one cable connects to a Yagi directional antenna and a phone receptacle to connect to a common telephone set.
9. A fax or modem could also be connected for fax or computer communication.
10. These WLL solutions are particularly popular in remote or sparsely populated areas of developing countries, where cabled infrastructure is either too expensive to deploy or where speed of deployment is an issue.

4.4.1 WLL can provide the following services

- Voice Data Low
- Speed
- Point to
- Point Data
- CATV Video
- Conferencing
- Internet
- Access (High Speed)
- Multimedia Services

4.4.2 Wireless Local Loop (WLL) Standards

- Mobile:
    - CDMA (USA).
    - TDMA (USA).
    - GSM (ITU - Worldwide).
    - UMTS 3rd Generation (World).
    - Personal Handy-phone System (PHS in Japan, PAS/Xiaolingtong in China).
- Fixed Wireless or local area network:
    - DECT, for local loop (ITU-Worldwide, except the USA)
    - corDECT (variant of DECT originates from India)
    - LMDS

4.4.3 Fixed Wireless Technology

1. Fixed wireless technologies, especially point-to-point microwave connections have a long history in the backhaul networks of phone companies, cable TV companies, utilities and government agencies.

2. More recently though, technology has advanced to enable higher frequencies and smaller antennas, resulting in lower cost systems that could be sold by carriers for last mile of communications.

4.4.4 Fixed WLL Options

1. Microwave - Microwaves are very short waves in the upper range of the radio spectrum used mostly for point-to-point communication systems. Initially these systems used radio spectrum in the 1 GHz range, but improvements in technology has enabled commercial systems to transmit in the 40 GHz region.

2. **LMDS (Local multipoint distribution service) - This band (27.5 GHz to 28.35 GHz, 29.1 GHz to 29.25 GHz and 31 GHz to 31.3 GHz) is being used for point-to-multipoint applications similar to the 39 GHz band - Internet access and telephony. LMDS, though, only has a 3-mile coverage radius and uses TDMA (Time-Division Multiple Access) so that multiple customers can share the same radio channel.**

3. MMDS (Multichannel multipoint distribution service) - This band, located at 2.5 GHz, was initially used to distribute cable television service. Currently MMDS is being developed for residential Internet service - but installations have not been profitable and service delays have been widespread.

4. UNII (Unlicensed National Information Infrastructure) - Bands between 5.15 GHz and 5.35 GHz and from 5.725 GHz to 5.825 GHz have been reserved for unlicensed use. For instance, power requirements are set in order to minimize interference between providers. Devices are also limited to wide-bandwidth, high-data-rate digital operations to ensure equipment manufacturers have the flexibility to design and manufacture a variety of broadband devices using different technologies and modulation techniques.

4.4.5 Advantages of using the Fixed wireless technology for LAN

Some of the various advantages of adopting a fixed wireless paradigm are:

1. The entry and setup costs are very small, i.e. setup cost is very low and expansion can always be opted on demand.

2. Systems can be setup with great ease and speed. All equipment can be carried and installed with great ease.
3. Equipment can be setup only after a customer signs up. This is different from wired systems because for wired LANS, a complete infrastructure has to be built even before the customers show up.
4. Thus, the build out becomes "Demand Based" which is a major advantage when compared to wired architectures.
5. Cost of upgrading can be substantially less, as there is no other infrastructure other than the end equipment, once the equipment is designed to be upgradable, upgrading becomes very easy.
6. There is less overhead of changing the transmission equipment and many problems of wired LANS such as tracing of damage in transmission equipment, do not exist at all.
7. Once the basic infrastructure is handled, quality of service can be achieved.
8. Bandwidth reuse is very high because of the cell structure used.
9. Network management, maintenance and operation costs can be very less.

The recent wireless networks have the ability to offer a wide range of one way and two way, voice data and video service transmission capabilities with a capacity many times larger than any current wireless or non-wireless service.

4.4.6 Different Methods Available for Fixed Wireless Communication

1. In order to achieve fixed wireless communication, various physical media equipment can be used ranging from infrared, microwave to radio wave.
2. A major problem with using Infrared signal is that they can be obstructed by physical objects, thus there should be an unobstructed path between the communicating equipment, which is not always possible.
3. Microwave systems operate at less than 500 milli watts power.
4. For the fixed service, Broadband wireless access systems are of particular interest.
5. Few reasons for this are, they are very quick to install, and are economical and cost effective.
6. And also interconnection of the base station to fixed PSTN is possible and easy.
7. For using the broadband signal there are various issues that need discussion, one important issue being the spectrum that can be used.

4.4.7 Typical WLL Phones

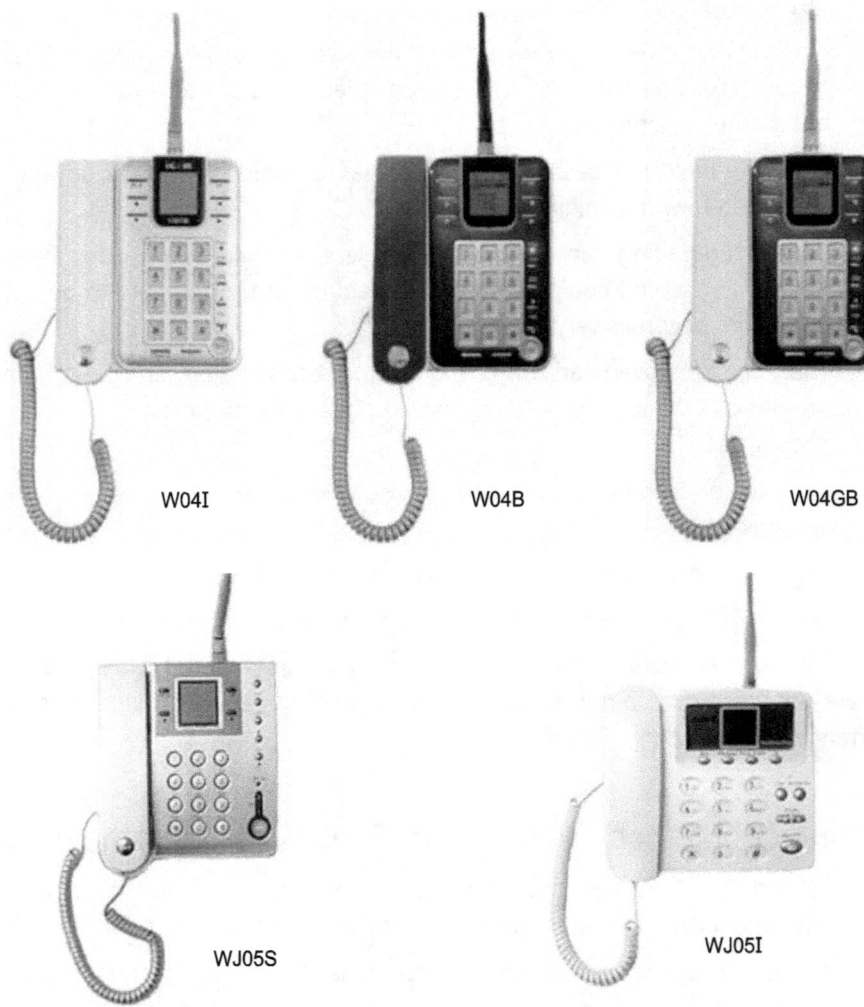

Fig. 4.10

4.4.8 Specifications of Typical WLL Phone

Specifications	CDMA 800 MHz WLL Phones
Air Interface	CDMA 2000 1xRTT
TX Frequency	824.64~849.37 MHz
PX Frequency	869.64~893.37 MHz
Channel Space	1.25 MHz
Vocoder	8K/13K QCELP, 8K EVRC

Specifications	CDMA 800 MHz WLL Phones
Main Chipset	Qualcomm Processor MSM 5000/5100
Date Rate	Up to (Max) 153 Kbps High Speed Data
Data Access	RS-232 Interface
Operation Temperature	−10 to +50
Operation Storage	−20 to +70
LCD Type & Size	8/6 lines 4 Gray Wide LCD display (128 ∞ 128 pixel)
Internal Back-up Battery	Talk Time over 3 hours, Standby Time over 72 hours
Internal BatteryType	Li-Ion Capacity 3.6 V 1800 mA
Weight	1200 g (with back battery and full packing condition)
Dimension	160 (L) ∞ 170 (W) ∞ 60 (H) mm
Power AC Adapter	Input AC 110~240 V, 50/60 Hz, Output DC 4.2V 700~1,000 mAh
Antenna	Dipole Antenna type
Features	
A-Key	Supporting A-Key Function
SMS & VMS	Two-way Short Messaging service & Voice Service
Lighting	Keypad and LCD back lighting
Audible Call Log Alerts	Incoming & Outgoing, SMS Incoming and Outgoing, Missed Calls
Phone Book	2400 phone memories
Tones	Dial Tones, Ring Tones
Melody	Single Music Sound, or 16 poly Music Sound (option)
Dialing	3 Way Speed Dialing (One/Two/Three Touch Dialing)
PIM	Alarm Clock, Notepad, Scheduler
Retry	Automatic Sending (Auto Redial and Retry) by holding last digit
Others	Calendar, Calculator, World Time, Power supply LED
Language	English (standard), Spanish (option)

4.5 Leased lines

4.5.1 What is a leased line?

A leased line is a **high-performance and permanently available Internet connection carrying voice, data and Internet traffic;** which is rented from telecommunication providers. Unlike normal dial-up connections, a leased line is always active. Leased lines deliver dedicated, guaranteed bandwidth and are supported by comprehensive Service-Level Agreements (SLA) and are also referred to as a private line, E1, T1, E3, T3, Dedicated Access, Point to point or Frame Relay.

Leased lines utilise two components:
- the **actual physical cabling** (fiber or copper) that links you to the ISP's network, and
- the **routing equipment** (router converts the leased line (X21) protocol to Ethernet for use on your office network) on each end which determines the speed at which the line runs.

Bandwidth can be tailored to a company's requirements, **ranging from 64 Kbps to 155 Mbps or more**. The required speed depends on the number of employees who will be allowed access to the Internet and the types of Internet applications that will be used frequently. The company can also upgrade the bandwidth of the leased line to provide the appropriate speed of Internet connection for the business. You should be careful when choosing the bandwidth, because the bandwidth determines:
- the number of network users who will be able to access the Internet at any time;
- the kind of Internet services they are able to access at high speed
- the number of hits or visits your web site can receive at any time
- the type of information your web site can serve.

4.5.2 Typical Users of Leased Lines

Leased Lines are normally used by businesses:
- Who require high quality 24/7 access to the Internet.
- Who are running mission critical applications, cannot afford downtime and require Service Level Agreements.
- With multiple offices that need connecting.
- Workers needing to remotely access office-based applications.

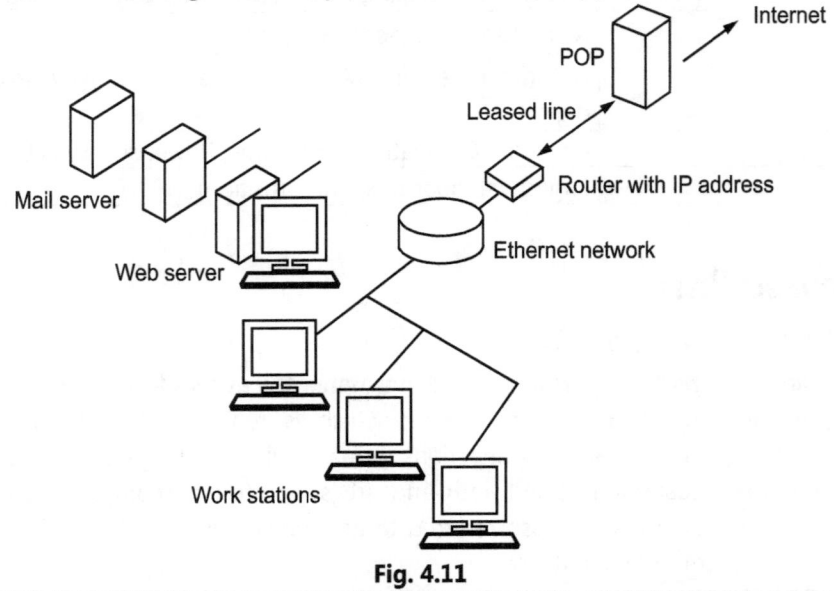

Fig. 4.11

4.5.3 Types of Leased Lines

E1 – An E1 is the European format for digital transmission, a dedicated telecommunications connection supporting data rates of 2.048 Mbits per second, similar to the T1 system used in the United States. The E1 carries signals at 2 Mbps
(32 channels at 64 Kbps, with 2 channels reserved for signalling and controlling). Providers can divide the connection into different lines for data and voice communication or use the channel for one high speed data circuit. Most service providers allow you to buy just some of these individual channels, known as fractional E1 access. Dividing the connection is called multiplexing.

There are also other types of hosting:

E3 – E3 is the European designation for T3, a long-distance, point-to-point communications circuit service that operates at 44 Mbps and can carry 672 channels of 64 kbps.

T1 – A T1 is the US format for digital transmission; a dedicated connection supporting data rates of 1.544 Mbits per second. A T-1 line actually consists of
24 individual channels, each of which supports 64 Kbits per second. Each
64 Kbits/second channel can be configured to carry voice or data traffic. Most telephone companies allow you to buy just some of these individual channels, known as fractional T1 access.

E1 and *T1* *lines may be interconnected for international use.*

T3 – Supports data rates of about 45 Mbps. It actually consists of 672 individual channels, each of which supports 64 Kbps. T-3 lines are used mainly by Internet Service Providers (ISPs) connecting to the Internet backbone and for the backbone itself.
T-3 lines are sometimes referred to as DS3 lines.

OC – OC or Optical Carrier is used to specify the speed of fiber optic networks conforming to the SONET standard. Common OC levels are OC-1 (51.84 Mbps), OC-3 (155.52 Mbps), OC-12 (622.08 Mbps), OC-24 (1.244 Gbps), OC-48 (2.488 Gbps) and OC-192 (9.952 Gbps).

FRAME RELAY – It is a packet-switching protocol for connecting devices on a Wide Area Network (WAN). Frame Relay networks in the U.S. support data transfer rates at T1 and T3 speeds. In fact, you can think of Frame Relay as a way of utilising existing
T1 and T3 lines owned by a service provider. In Europe, Frame Relay speeds vary from 64 Kbps to 2 Mbps.

LES CIRCUIT – LES Circuit or LAN Extension Service Circuit is a permanent connection between two customer's premises, which is wholly dedicated for that customer's use and can be used to transport data between LAN, within each building.

A LAN Extension circuit literally extends the coverage of a LAN outside the confines of a single building. It is usually available in speeds of 10, 100 and 1000 Mbps. If a company needs a secure, reliable circuit that is "always on" and has no usage charges, LAN Extension circuits are ideal.

PRIVATE CIRCUITS - Private Circuits are one of the most well established digital data circuits. They are point-to-point circuits between two sites providing dedicated capacity and may be used for voice, video or data traffic or a combination of all of these. The actual traffic that is carried between the A and B ends depends on the type of customer premise equipment (CPE) installed.

MPLS – MPLS or Multiprotocol Label Switching is a standards-approved technology for speeding up network traffic flow and making it easier to manage. It is called multiprotocol because it works with the Internet Protocol (IP), Asynchronous Transport Mode (ATM), and frame relay network protocols.

4.5.4 Advantages

Leased line has a number of advantages:

- **Secure and private** - Leased Line is dedicated entirely to you, which means it is yours to use exclusively.
- **High throughput** - Because no one else ever uses it you have total access to it (24 hours a day), which means there is never a delay in sending information.
- **Reliable** – Leased line is delivered on copper or fiber optic transmission network and is monitored around the clock to provide you with a highly reliable service.
- Resilience can be developed as part of the solution.
- **Cost Control and Savings** - The fee for the connection is a fixed monthly, quarterly or annual rate.
- Upload and download speeds are the same.
- **Wide choice of bandwidths**.
- Readily available **SLAs**.
- **Guaranteed bandwidth** for critical business usage.
- Leased lines are **suitable for web hosting**.
- Always-on connection.
- Leased line can serve hundreds of users simultaneously.
- Your business will become more efficient and react faster to crucial information.

4.5.5 Disadvantages
- Relatively expensive to install and rent.
- Not suitable for single or home workers.
- Lead times can be long, upto 45 working days.
- Distance - Cost is often dependent on customer's distance to nearest POP of service provider.

Leased lines have traditionally been the most expensive broadband option. However, service providers will normally provide a Service Level Agreement (SLA) to confirm their contractual requirement in ensuring the service is maintained. *This is often lacking in cheaper alternatives.*

4.5.6 Leased Line Uses
Leased lines will allow you:
- **To connect your network to the Internet** – To give your network users outgoing access to the Internet. One of the most common uses of an E1 line is an "Internet E1". This connection is used to provide Internet access to businesses of all sizes. Internet E1's have become one of the most popular ways for multiple users in one location to connect to the Internet.
- **To connect your internal or external server to the Internet** – Leased line is the only solution, if you want to publish information either externally through a Web or FTP server, or internally through an intranet or extranet server.
- **To connect offices together (LAN to LAN connection)** – E1 lines have multiple uses; they can connect a location to a carrier's Frame Relay network, Internet backbone and voice network. They can also connect the local area networks of two of your remote offices through a dedicated leased line. This will allow you to access file servers at your second office, use other applications and generally to create fast and effective communication between the two locations. You can link as many sites you wish with the leased line. However, you must be aware that these leased lines do not automatically provide you with a connection to the Internet. You will require one more leased line to connect your offices to the Internet, after they are already connected. **This is often referred to as private line or point-to-point service. While still available today, private line (point-to-point) E1's are traditionally more expensive than Frame Relay and VPN connections.** Therefore, in case you have offices in different countries or remote locations, you can use the Internet as a Virtual Private Network.

4.5.7 Alternative Solutions
- **VPNs** – A VPN connection is a point-to-point connection between the user's computer and the company's server that allows private data by mobile employees, telecommuters, business partners and remote sites to be sent securely over a shared or public network, such as the Internet. This eliminates the need for costly

point-to-point leased lines, but reliable and fast Internet connections are still required from the client's premises to the ISP's POP. This may be a leased line, ADSL or SDSL, or wireless connection. Leased lines will offer the best resilience and will be more expensive than other connectivity options but will be cheaper that a point-to-point leased line that was necessary before VPNs became available.

- **ADSL** – ADSL or Asymmetric Digital Subscriber is a technology that allows more data to be sent over existing copper telephone lines. It supports data rates from 512 Kbps to 2Mbps when receiving data (the downstream rate) and
256 Kbps when sending data (the upstream rate). The latter can cause problems as most businesses requiring Internet connectivity for remote users, VPNs and web hosting will need the greater upstream. Also ADSL is distant dependent from an enabled exchange and service level agreements are invariably lacking.
- **SDSL** – SDSL or symmetric digital subscriber line is a technology that allows more data to be sent over existing copper telephone lines. SDSL supports data rates upto 4 Mbps. It works by sending digital pulses in the high-frequency area of telephone wires and cannot operate simultaneously with voice connections over the same wires and is called symmetric because it supports the same data rates for upstream and downstream traffic and hence solves one of the issues with ADSL. Providing good Service Level Agreements can be obtained and contention ratios of < 5: 1 are available, SDSL can be a viable alternative to leased lines. However, like ADSL, the service is distance dependant. *Also if you require 1: 1 contention ratios then the cost differential between SDSL and leased lines will reduce dramatically.*
- **HDSL** – HDSL or High speed Digital Subscriber Line is form of Digital Subscriber Line, providing T1 or E1 connections over two or three twisted-pair copper lines. Voice telephone services cannot operate on the same lines. It is not intended for home users, but instead is intended for the telephone company's own feeder lines, Interexchange connections, Internet servers, and private data networks.

4.5.8 Costs of Leased Lines

The fee for the leased line connection is a fixed monthly, quarterly or annual rate. The primary factors affecting the fee are: distance between end points (customer's distance to nearest POP of service provider), and the speed of the circuit.

In the annual rental, the following is usually included (you need to check):
- Pre-configured router, static IP addresses.
- All circuit charges.
- All bandwidth charges.
- SMTP mail transferor POP3 accounts, DNS.
- Domain name hosting (if you require it).
- 24 hour network monitoring and fault detection.
- Access to experienced technical staff.

4.5.9 Selecting a Leased Line Provider

- First of all **decide on which *type* of leased line** best suits your company's needs.
- Next, **select 3-5 providers who are *qualified* to provide the services you require and ask them to quote**.
- The initial vendor analysis incorporates a number of business, technical, service level and pricing factors. This will ensure that the leased line providers that quote you are qualified to meet your *exact* needs. For example, this will take into account **which ISPs have POPs near to the offices** that you need leased line connections.
- **Compare service offerings, pricing, support levels and service level agreements**.
- **Talk with the sales and technical staff**. See if you are comfortable with them. This is important as they will be part of your team.

Other important criteria: Can you trust your ISP to be around tomorrow? Are they a strong robust, stable provider? To make sure you have selected the right service provider, who will meet your needs, ask them following questions:

- How long have they been *strategically* serving your type of company
- Do they proactively monitor your connection? – Make sure that your ISP proactively monitors all routers on the network.
- Are they a backbone provider? – Most ISPs resell Internet connectivity from a Tier 1 network provider. There are pros and cons to an ISP owning and operating its own network and it is worth checking what your ISPs position is regarding this.
- What do their clients say about them? (Past and present)
- Who takes full responsibility for the efficiency of your service provider's services?
- Will their technical support meet your needs?
- How quickly can they provision your services?
- Do they provide a single point of contact?
- Do they have a dedicated account manager? ISDN Emergency Back-up Service – Is it available / included?
- Service guarantees and unlimited customer support via telephone and e-mail SLA – What exactly is being offered in the Service Level Guarantee? - Money back or compensation?

4.5.10 Question and Answers on Leased Lines

Q. 1 What is a leased line?
Ans. A leased line is a high-performance and permanently available Internet connection carrying voice, data and Internet traffic; which is rented from telecommunications providers.

Q. 2 Can everyone have a leased line?
Ans. Leased lines work in conjunction with the existing telephone network infrastructure, so offer a very wide geographical coverage. This is not like other

connectivity solutions such as broadband, which are only available in certain parts of the country. However, cost will depend on location of your company.

Q. 3 What is the lead time for a leased line?
Ans. Lead time depends on service provider, but it can be long (even upto 45 working days).

Q. 4 How fast is a leased line?
Ans. Bandwidth can range from 64 k through to 155 Mb.

Q. 5 Is a leased line suitable for heavy bandwidth use?
Ans. Yes, leased lines are a permanently available Internet connection and offer the most resilient method of access. They offer high-speed connections and guaranteed symmetric bandwidth, which means you are not competing with other users for the bandwidth.

Q. 6 Is there an SLA?
Ans. It depends on service provider, but most of them offer a 99.5% service level agreement on leased lines. This means that they guarantee uptime of your line of 99.5% of the time.

Q. 7 What can I use a leased line for?
Ans. Leased lines are suitable for various applications. There are no restrictions on leased line use, you will need to make sure you get the correct size line to support your business. You can use it for Internet access, to connect your internal or external server to the Internet, to connect offices together etc.

Q. 8 What size leased line would suit my business?
Ans. That depends on how many users you have and how heavily your users will use this line. It is also possible to upgrade your leased line as your business grows.

Q. 9 What is the difference between copper and fiber?
Ans. The difference is that fiber-optics use light pulses to transmit information down fiber lines instead of using electronic pulses to transmit information down copper lines. Therefore, fiber optic networks are usually operating at high speeds (up into the gigabits), they have large carrying capacity, and greater resistance to electromagnetic noise such as radios, motors or other nearby cables. In addition, fiber optic cables cost much less to maintain.

4.5.11 Glossary

ATM – Asynchronous Transfer Mode is an International Telecommunication Union-Telecommunications Standards Section (ITU-T) standard for cell relay wherein information for multiple service types, such as voice, video, or data, is conveyed in small, fixed-size cells.

CPE – Customer Premise Equipment is the telecommunications equipment owned by an organization and located on its premises. CPE equipment includes PBXs (private branch exchanges), telephones, key systems, facsimile products, modems, voice-processing equipment, and video communication equipment.

ETHERNET - Ethernet is the most widely-installed local area network (LAN) technology. It is a local-area network (LAN) architecture developed by Xerox Corporation in cooperation with DEC and Intel in 1976. Ethernet uses a bus or star topology and supports data transfer rates of 10 Mbps.

FRAME RELAY – It is a packet-switching protocol for connecting devices on a Wide Area Network (WAN). Frame Relay networks in the U.S. support data transfer rates at T1 and T3 speeds. In fact, you can think of Frame Relay as a way of utilising existing T1 and T3 lines owned by a service provider. In Europe, Frame Relay speeds vary from 64 Kbps to 2 Mbps.

IP – The Internet Protocol (IP) is the method or protocol by which data is sent from one computer to another on the Internet. It specifies the format of packets, also called datagrams, and the addressing scheme. Most networks combine IP with a higher-level protocol called Transmission Control Protocol (TCP), which establishes a virtual connection between a destination and a source. IP by itself is something like the postal system. It allows you to address a package and drop it in the system, but there is no direct link between you and the recipient.

ISP – Internet Service Provider is a company that provides access to the Internet.

LAN – Local Area Network is a group of computers and associated devices that share a common communications line or wireless link and typically share the resources of a single processor or server within a small geographic area (for example, within an office building). Usually, the server has applications and data storage that are shared in common by multiple computer users. A local area network may serve as few as two or three users (for example, in a home network) or as many as thousands of users (for example, in an FDDI network).

MWI – Market Watch Intelligence is index that OneStopClick uses to evaluate and select vendor partners most suited to client's specific project. The initial vendor analysis incorporates a number of business, technical, service level and pricing factors. The MWI Indexes are used to filter and select those vendors who can meet client's exact needs.

POP – Point of Presence is an access point to the Internet. ISPs have typically multiple POPs. A point of presence is either a physical location, part of the facilities of a telecommunications provider that the ISP rents or a separate location from the telecommunications provider that houses servers, routers, ATM switches and digital/analog call aggregators.

ROUTER - On the Internet, a router is a device or, in some cases, software in a computer, that determines the next network point to which a packet should be forwarded toward its destination. The router is connected to at least two networks and decides which way to send each information packet based on its current understanding of the state of the networks it is connected to.

SLA – Service Level Agreement is a contract between a network service provider and a customer that specifies, usually in measurable terms, what services the network service provider will furnish. Many Internet service providers ISPs provide their customers with an SLA.

VPN – Virtual Private Network connection is a point-to-point connection between the user's computer and the company's server that allows private data by mobile employees, telecommuters, business partners and remote sites to be sent securely over a shared or public network, such as the Internet.

WAN – Wide area network (WAN) is a computer network that spans a relatively large geographical area. Typically, a WAN consists of two or more local-area networks (LANs).

4.6 Wireless Broadband via MMDS

1. Multichannel Multipoint Distribution System (MMDS) is a wireless technology for delivering video and high-speed internet access.
2. Operating on the 2.1 GHz and 2.5-2.7 GHz frequencies, MMDS is ideally suited for the delivery of broadband access to voice and data, and is often referred to as "wireless cable".
3. Similar to broadcast television, wireless high-speed data via MMDS is transmitted from a tower, usually located on a mountain or tall building, to special antennas affixed to residential or commercial buildings. Line-of-sight is required for MMDS.

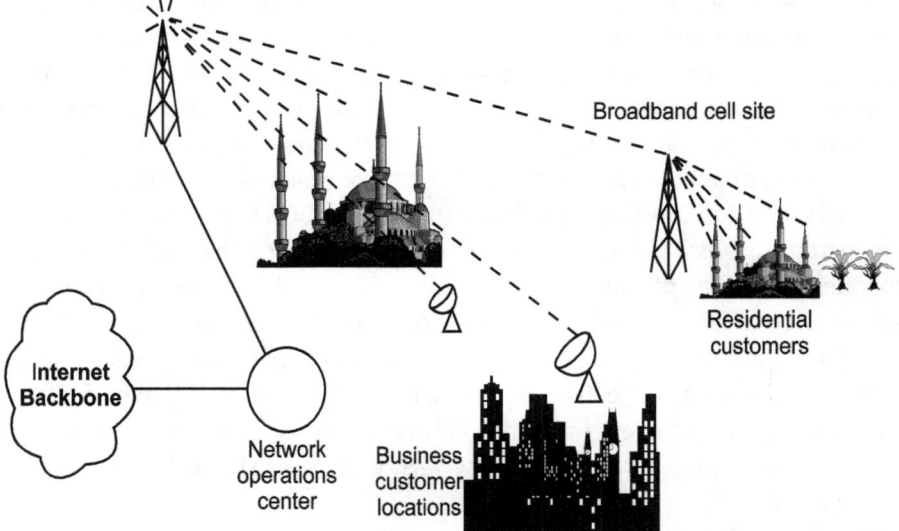

Fig. 4.12: Two-way MMDS Architecture

4. MMDS systems can be rapidly deployed and are an extremely cost-effective solution for high-speed internet access when compared to cable or DSL networks.
5. While cable or DSL networks involve capital-intensive network deployment and maintenance costs, wireless solutions such as MMDS provide a huge savings advantage as the primary investment lies only in subscriber equipment.
6. The transmission radius coverage for MMDS is up to 50 km (35 miles).

7. MMDS has proven to be a low cost and effective solution as the "last-mile" alternative to cable and DSL in both rural and metropolitan areas around the world.

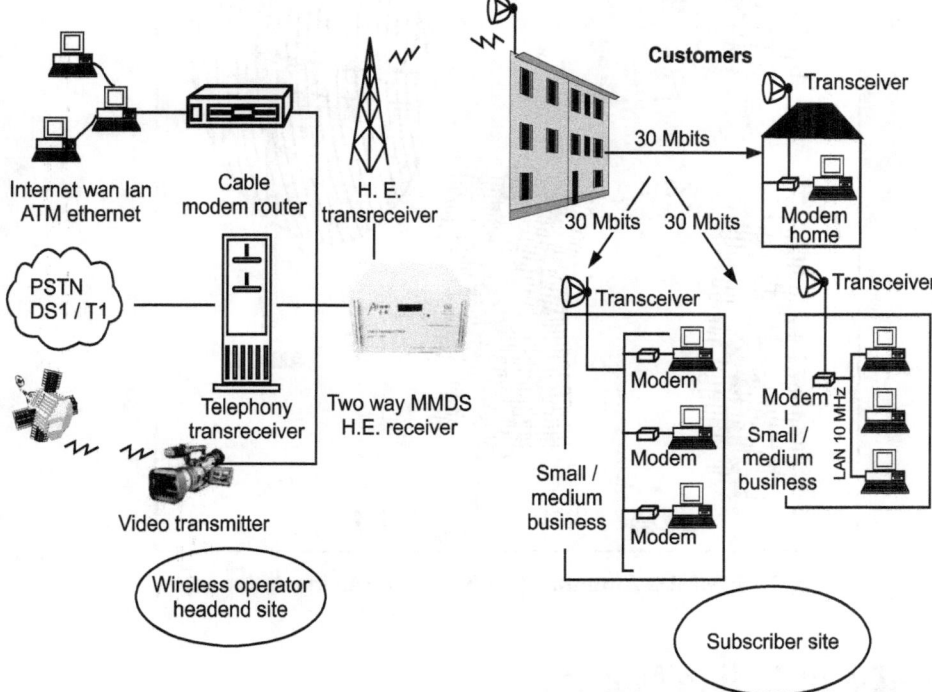

Fig. 4.13: Two-way MMDS Configuration

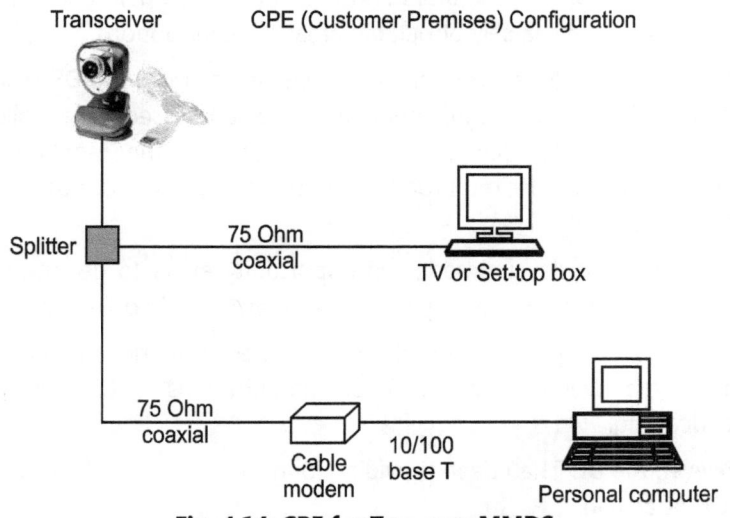

Fig. 4.14: CPE for Two-way MMDS

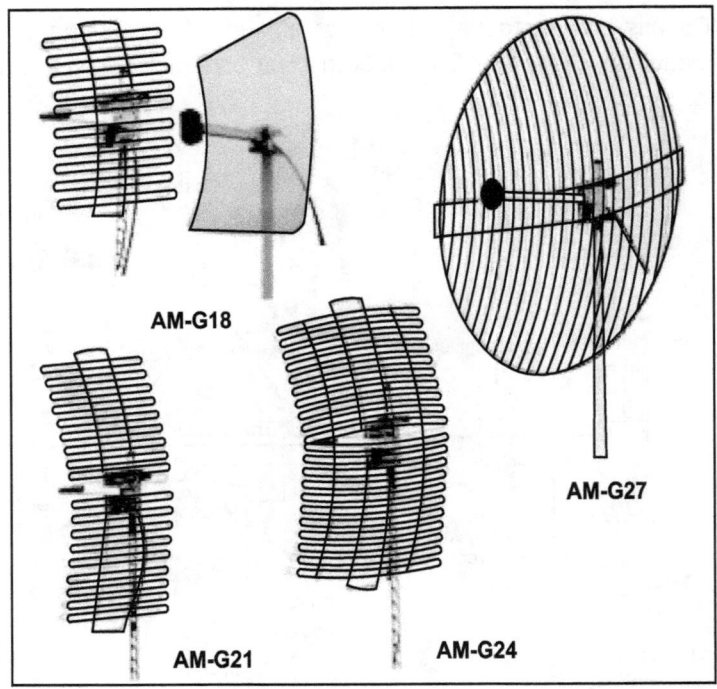

Fig. 4.15: MMDS Antennas (High Gain Receiving Antenna)

4.7 MMDS in Indian Market

4.7.1 Advantages and Disadvantages of MMDS

1. The existing cable TV operators find it profitable to operate in densely populated areas, leaving the sparsely populated areas to other options.

2. Either direct-to-home (DTH) satellite systems or LMDS/MMDS systems can fill in this void. The possible regulatory issues to be addressed are as follows: First, both cable and MMDS/LMDS systems would provide the regulatory authority to preview/censor un desired broadcasts/retransmissions as opposed to DTH systems using satellites.

3. At this stage of development, the opportunity exists to get the option for DTH foreclosed, as already done by some countries in the Middle East.

4. Second, for example, the current business rules of the government of India do not permit the Department of Telecommunications (DOT) to do TV signal broadcasting.

5. However, the DOT had been providing long-distance links as well as local end links to Doordarshan.

6. Therefore, the provisioning of the medium would still fall into the domain of the public telecommunications operators, and they should lobby for change in the existing regulations.

7. This is important because there would be stiff competition between cable and public telecommunications operators for this market if and when the same is opened up.

8. Third, the most promising frequency band for LMDS is 27.5 to 29.5 GHz, which is presently sparsely used the world over. Of course, satellite operators are eyeing this band for mobile and fixed satellite services.

9. The FCC (in the United States) is likely to allocate 1 GHz of bandwidth each to LMDS and satellite services.

10. The review done in the Test and Experimentation Center (TEC) on the frequencies beyond 1 GHz also has recommended shared usage. An early resolution of this issue would be beneficial for long-term growth.

11. Advantages of using MMDS include:
    - It has chunks of underutilized spectrum that will, once completely digital, become increasingly valuable and flexible.
    - System implementation, which is little more than putting an installed transmitter on a high tower and a small receiving antenna on the customer's balcony or roof, is quick and inexpensive.
    - Moreover, since MMDS services have been around for 20 years, there is a wealth of experience—at least with respect to the one-way distribution technology

4.7.2 Expected Deployment Profile

Currently, there are 4.5 million subscribers in 70 nations all using analogue MMDS technology. For example, the TV market in India is projected to grow rapidly by the end of the year 2002 fueled by the following factors:

- TV advertisement to grow fivefold.
- Number of TV channels expected in the range 70 to 85.
- Number of TV households to increase by 10.4 percent.
- Number of cabled households to increase by 6.9 percent.
- Cable penetration to increase to 59 percent.

In contrast, it is important to note that the projected growth of demand for telecommunications in India falls far short of the preceding figures. There is therefore an anomaly in this because a telephone is still an inexpensive proposition for most households.

4.8 Digital Loop Carrier (DLC)

1. A **Digital Loop Carrier** (DLC) is a system which uses digital transmission to extend the range of the local loop farther than would be possible using only twisted pair copper wires. A DLC digitizes and multiplexes the individual signals carried by the local loops onto a single datastream on the DLC segment.
2. DIGITAL LOOP CARRIER (DLC) is equipment that bundles a number of individual phone line signals into a single multiplexed digital signal for local traffic between a telephone company central office and a business complex or other outlying service area. Typically, up to 24 analog voice calls are combined into a single signal and transmitted over a single copper T-carrier system or E-carrier line, an optical fiber cable, or a wireless connection. In a home, business, or other installation using digital loop carrier, the analog phone lines of individual users are connected to a local DLC box which then converts the analog signals into digital and combines (multiplexes) them into one signal that it sent to the phone company's central office on the single line. At the central office, the combined signal is separated back into the original signals. An estimated 20% of today's telephone users are being served by digital loop carriers.
3. Digital loop carrier can carry traffic for regular phone calls (plain old telephone service) and Integrated Services Digital Network (ISDN) service. More recently, approaches have been developed for using DLC to handle the higher bandwidth of Digital Subscriber Line (DSL) service.
4. Digital loop carrier is typically used as an efficient way to provide service to an office building or complex and to extend service to new areas outside the current local loop. DLC is also used to set up telephone service in emergency situations. Customers can easily migrate from a T-1 or E-1 line to fiber optic when it becomes needed and is available.

Reasons for using DLCs

1. Subscriber Loop Carrier systems were ordained to solve two problems: to reduce copper cable pair requirements; and to overcome electrical constraints on long loops. A number of pressing issues supplied motivation for technology that would reduce cable pair deployments.
2. Those issues include the following:
   - Imminent cable supply shortages (minimal unused pairs in existing route).
   - Cable route congestion (inability to add cable due to lack of space, particularly in urban street, bridge, and building conduit).
   - Construction challenges (in areas of difficult terrain) when limited cable pairs are already available.
   - Expense due to cable cost and the associated labour-intensive installation work (especially to solve the specific problems listed above).
3. Long loops, such as those terminating at more than 18,000 feet from the central office, pose electrical challenges.

4. When the subscriber goes off-hook, a cable pair behaves like a single loop inductance coil with a −48 V dc potential and an Electric current of between 20–50 mA dc. Electrical current values vary with cable length and gauge.
5. A minimum current of around 20 mA dc is required to convey terminal signaling information to the network. There is also a minimum power level required to provide adequate volume for the voice signal.
6. A variety of schemes were implemented before DLC technology to offset the impedance long loops offered to signaling and volume levels. They included the following:
    1. Use heavy-gauge conductors – Up to 19 gauge (approximately the gauge of pencil lead), which is costly and bulky. The heavy-gauge cables yielded far fewer pairs per cable and led to early congestion in cable routes, especially in bridge crossings and other areas of limited space.
    2. Increase battery voltage – This violation of operating standards could pose a safety hazard.
    3. Add amplifiers to power the voice signal on long loops. This however, requires volumes of auxiliary equipment, a myriad number of cross wiring points, and extensive record-keeping.
    4. Add signal regeneration and signal extension equipment – The comments regarding amplifiers apply here as well.
    5. Add loading coils to reduce the attenuation of voice signals over long loops. These have detrimental effect to new transmission technologies using the local loop, like DSL, and must be removed.
7. DLC eliminates the need for these remedies by extending out closer to the customer the line card which digitizes the voice signal for use by the PSTN. Once the voice signal is digitized, it is easily manipulated and is no longer subject to the vagaries of the analog loop caused by distance, impedance, attenuation and noise.
8. The DLC solution was dubbed "pair gain" (from the days when DLC was deployed to recover copper pairs in the loop plant environment).

Configuration

1. In a typical configuration, DLC remote terminals are installed in new neighborhoods or buildings as a means of reducing the labour and complexity of installing individual local loops from the customer to the central office (CO).
2. A fiber optic cable or several copper pairs for the whole system from the CO to the DLC remote terminal replace the individual pair previously needed for each loop. DLC remote terminals are typically stored in Serving Area Interfaces–metal cabinets alongside or near roadways that overlie communications rights-of-ways.
3. With the growth in popularity of digital subscriber line (DSL) and the benefits provided by shorter metallic loops used with DLC systems, digital loop carriers are sometimes integrated with digital subscriber line access multiplexers (DSLAM), both systems then taking advantage of the digital transmission link from the DLC to the CO.

4. Fiber-in-the-loop (FITL) systems are functionally equivalent to DLC. FITL accomplishes the same two primary functions DLC was intended for: pair gain and the elimination of electrical constraints due to long metallic loops. FITL architectures vary from simply deploying fiber feeder plants (between central office and remote terminal site) to "fiber to the curb" and, ultimately "fiber to the home" where an optical network unit (ONU) is located at each home.

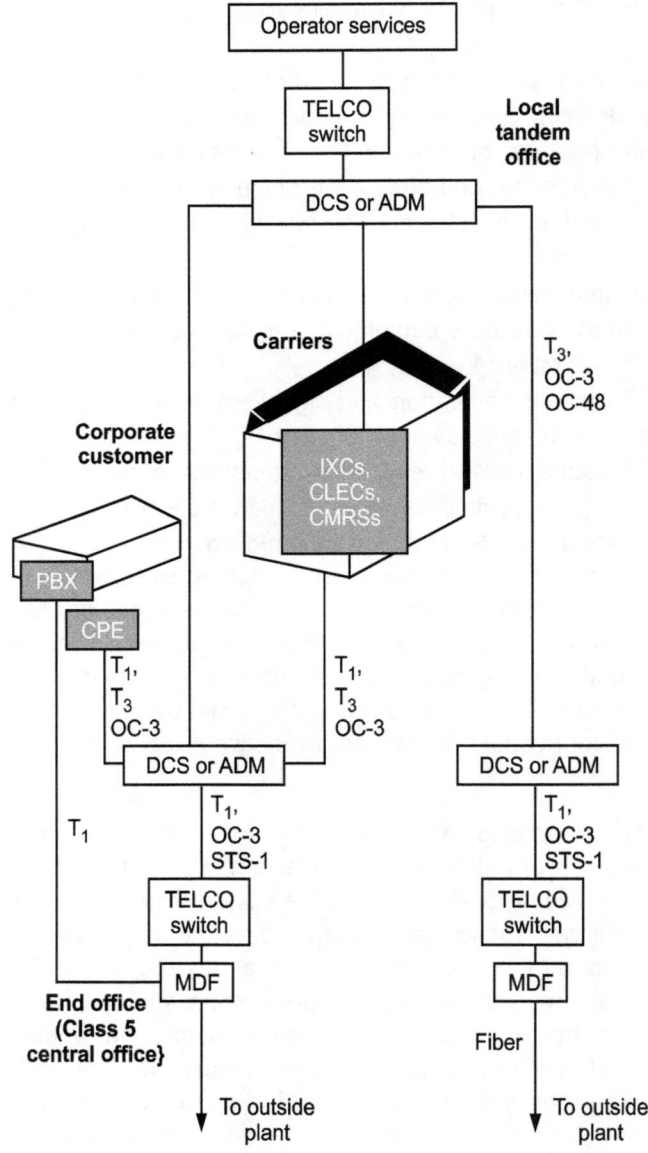

Fig. 4.16: Telephone System Levels

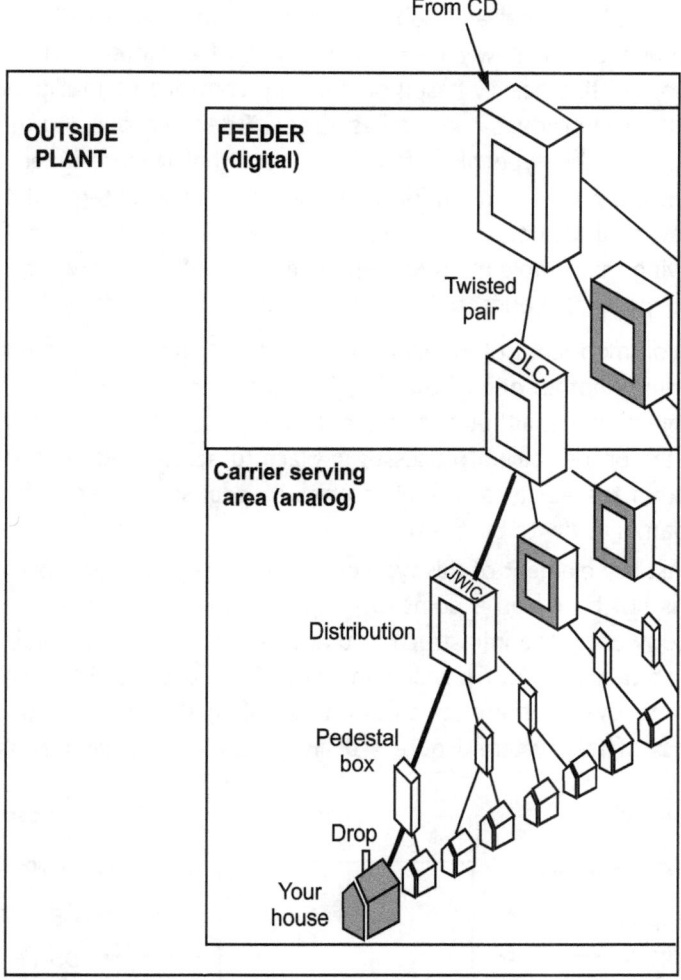

Fig. 4.17: Outside Plant and DLC

4.9 Next-Generation Digital Loop Carriers (NGDLC)

Next-Generation Digital Loop Carriers for Rural and Suburban Applications

1. NGDLC is the market where Advanced Fibre Communications (AFC) entered the local loop access industry. Some of AFC's founders had a rich history in the digital loop carrier business and the next generation loop carrier business. Almost immediately, they realized that fiber was not ubiquitous in the infrastructure. In fact, fiber is rare and inconsistently used from place to place. Sometimes there are T-carriers; sometimes not even that, and other times there is no infrastructure at all. This understanding was the basis for the NGDLC for rural and suburban applications.

2. The NGDLC for rural and suburban applications uses 1990's technology to take advantage of the newly developed power of computing and integrated-circuit technology. It is heavily based on software control and intelligence. A carryover from the last product, it is used as a service-delivery tool, and the most important attribute of this type of system is the fact that it is designed for mixed-media transmission. Media migration is made simple: the system takes advantage of whatever infrastructure is in place, whether T carrier, analog, fiber, or coax. In achieving that simple migration, the network offers a very economic solution for low to moderate concentrations of subscribers.

3. The common control remains low. NGDLC offers low common control and flexibility. Another one of the keys in this type of technology is a dynamic time-slot interchanger, although this is not widely used. As yet, many customers do not have the proper billing processes in place to accommodate it. The fault does not lie within the ability of the electronics to peel subscribers off, but rather in the company's ability to bill them.

4. The last key element of this type of system is its mixed-network architecture. That is, it is not based on a point-to-point or ring architecture but rather on a mesh topology using the infrastructure that is in place. This is helpful, as most housing developments do not develop in rings—they develop in mesh topologies. The ability to overlay the electronics on top of that network topology is key to the success of this system. Figure 4.18 lists the range of services that such systems offer.

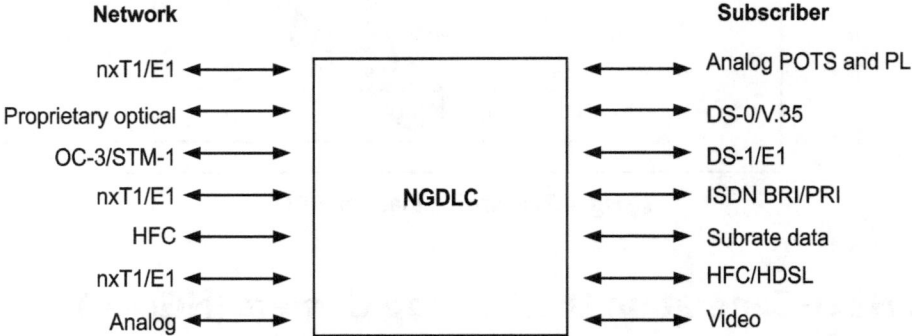

Fig. 4.18: Next Generation Digital Loop Carriers for Rural and Suburban Applications

5. The demand is higher than ever for more services and more bandwidth. Although analog POTS and private line must be covered just as cost-effectively as ever, the infrastructure must be put in place to carry some of the higher bit-rate services: ISDN, subrate data, and more T1 services, along with HDSL/HFC to corporate locations. On the network side, nxT1 or E1 are usually used. What is different from the previous architecture is that NGDLC has the ability to take advantage of any of the network infrastructure that is in place, whether it be HFC, coaxial fiber, OC-3, or proprietary optical.

4.10 WiMAX (Worldwide Interoperability for Microwave Access)

4.10.1 What is WiMAX?

- **WiMAX** is short for Worldwide Interoperability for Microwave Access.
- It is a metropolitan wireless standard created by the companies Intel and Alvarion in 2002 and ratified by the IEEE (Institute of Electrical and Electronics Engineers) under the name IEEE-802.16. More precisely, **WiMAX** is the commercial designation that the WiMAX Forum gives to devices which conform to the IEEE 802.16 standard, in order to ensure a high level of interoperability among them.

4.10.2 Goals of WiMAX

- The goal of WiMAX is to provide high-speed Internet access in a coverage range several kilometres in radius.
- In theory, WiMAX provides for speeds around 70 Mbps with a range of 50 kilometres.
- The WiMAX standard has the advantage of allowing wireless connections between a *Base Transceiver Station* (BTS) and thousands of subscribers without requiring that they be in a direct line of sight (LOS) with that station.
- This technology is called NLOS for non-line-of-sight.
- In reality, WiMAX can only bypass small obstructions like trees or a house and cannot cross hills or large buildings. When obstructions are present, actual throughput might be under 20 Mbps.

4.10.3 Operating Principle of WiMAX

At the heart of WiMAX technology is the **base transceiver station**, a central antenna which communicates with subscribers' antennas. The term *point-multipoint link* is used for WiMAX's method of communication.

4.10.4 Fixed WiMAX and WiMAX Portable

The revisions of the IEEE 802.16 standard fall into two categories:

- **Fixed WiMAX**, also called *IEEE 802.16-2004*, provides for a fixed-line connection with an antenna mounted on a rooftop, like a TV antenna. Fixed WiMAX operates in the 2.5 GHz and 3.5 GHz frequency bands, which require a licence, as well as the licence-free 5.8 GHz band.

- **Mobile WiMAX**, also called *IEEE 802.16e*, allows mobile client machines to be connected to the Internet. Mobile WiMAX opens the doors to mobile phone use over IP, and even high-speed mobile services.

Standard	Frequency	Speed	Range
Fixed WiMAX (802.16-2004)	2-11 GHz (3.5 GHz in Europe)	75 Mbps	10 km
Mobile WiMAX (802.16e)	2-6 GHz	30 Mbps	3.5 km

4.10.5 Applications of WiMAX

- One of WiMAX's potential uses is to cover the so-called "last mile" (or "last kilometre) area, meaning providing high-speed Internet access to areas which normal wired technolgies do not cover (such as DSL, cable, or dedicated T1 lines).
- Another possibility involves using WiMAX as a *backhaul* between two local wireless networks, such as those using the WiFi standard. WiMAX will ultimately enable two different hotspots to be linked to create a mesh network.

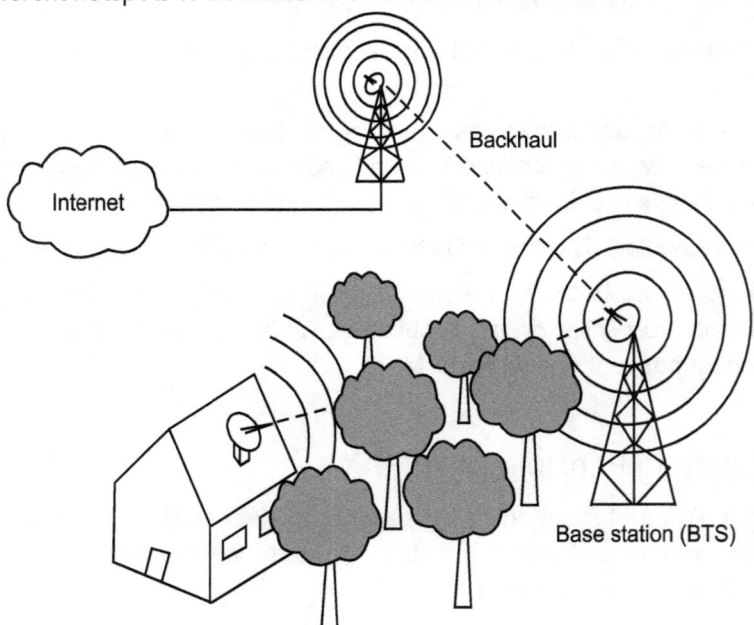

Fig. 4.19: Typical Application if WiMAX

4.10.6 WiMAX and Quality of Service

- The WiMAX standard natively supports **Quality of Service** (often called *QoS* for short), the ability to ensure that a service works when used. In practice, WiMAX lets bandwidth be reserved for a given purpose.

- Some applications cannot work properly when bottlenecks occur. This is the case for Voice over IP (*VOIP*), as spoken communication is ineffective when gaps a second long are introduced.

4.10.7 WiMAX Standards

Standard	Frequency	Status	Range
IEEE std 802.16	Defines wireless metropolitan area networks (WMANs) on frequency bands higher than 10 GHz.	October 2002	Obsolete
IEEE std 802.16a	Defines wireless metropolitan area networks on frequency bands from 2 to 11 GHz inclusive.	October 9, 2003	Obsolete
IEEE 802.16b	Defines wireless metropolitan area networks on frequency bands from 10 to 60 GHz inclusive.		Merged with 802.16a (Obsolete)
IEEE std 802.16c	Defines options (profiles) for wireless metropolitan area networks in unlicensed frequency bands.		July 2003
IEEE 802.16d (IEEE std 802.16-2004)	Revision incorporating the 802.16, 802.16a, and 802.16c standards.	October 1st, 2004	Active
IEEE std 802.16e	Allows wireless metropolitan area networks to be used by mobile clients.		not ratified
IEEE std 802.16f	Allows wireless mesh networks to be used.		not ratified

4.11 Uses of WiMAX

The bandwidth and range of WiMAX make it suitable for the following potential applications:
- Connecting Wi-Fi hotspots to the Internet.
- Providing a wireless alternative to cable and DSL for "last mile" broadband access.
- Providing data and telecommunications services.
- Providing a source of Internet connectivity as part of a business continuity plan. That is, if a business has both a fixed and a wireless Internet connection, especially from unrelated providers, they are unlikely to be affected by the same service outage.
- Providing portable connectivity.

4.11.1 Broadband Access

- Companies are evaluating WiMAX for last mile connectivity. The resulting competition may bring lower pricing for both home and business customers or bring broadband access to places where it has been economically unavailable.
- WiMAX access was used to assist with communications in Aceh, Indonesia, after the tsunami in December 2004. All communication infrastructure in the area, other than amateur radio, was destroyed, making the survivors unable to communicate with people outside the disaster area and vice versa. WiMAX provided broadband access that helped regenerate communication to and from Aceh.
- In addition, WiMAX was donated by Intel Corporation to assist the FCC and FEMA (**Federal Emergency Management Agency**) in their communications efforts in the areas affected by Hurricane Katrina. In practice, volunteers used mainly self-healing mesh, VoIP, and a satellite uplink combined with Wi-Fi on the local link.

4.11.2 Subscriber Units (Client Units)

- WiMAX subscriber units are available in both indoor and outdoor versions from several manufacturers. Self-install indoor units are convenient, but radio losses mean that the subscriber must be significantly closer to the WiMAX base station than with professionally-installed external units. As such, indoor-installed units require a much higher infrastructure investment as well as operational cost (site lease, backhaul, maintenance) due to the high number of base stations required to cover a given area. Indoor units are comparable in size to a cable modem or DSL modem. Outdoor units are roughly the size of a laptop PC, and their installation is comparable to the installation of a residential satellite dish.
- With the potential of mobile WiMAX, there is an increasing focus on portable units. This includes handsets (similar to cellular smartphones), PC peripherals (PC Cards or USB dongles), and embedded devices in laptops, which are now available for Wi-Fi services. In addition, there is much emphasis from operators on consumer electronics devices such as Gaming consoles, MP3 players and similar devices. It is notable that WiMAX is more similar to Wi-Fi than to 3G cellular technologies.
- Current certified devices can be found at the WiMAX Forum web site. This is not a complete list of devices available as certified modules are embedded into laptops, MIDs (Mobile internet devices), and private labelled devices.

4.11.3 Mobile Handset Applications

- On May 7, 2008, Sprint, Imagine, Google, Intel, Comcast, Bright House, and Time Warner announced a pooling of an average of 120 MHz of spectrum and merged with Clearwire to form a company which will take the name Clear. The new company hopes to benefit from combined services offerings and network resources as a springboard past its competitors. The cable companies will provide media services to other partners while gaining access to the wireless network as a Mobile virtual network operator. Google will contribute Android handset device development and applications and will receive revenue share for advertising and other services they provide. Sprint and Clearwire gain a majority stock ownership in the new venture and ability to access between the new Clear and Sprint 3G networks. Some details remain unclear including how soon and in what form announced multi-mode WiMAX and 3G EV-DO devices will be available. This raises questions that arise for availability of competitive chips that require licensing of Qualcomm's IPR.

- Some analysts have questioned how the deal will work out: Although fixed-mobile convergence has been a recognized factor in the industry, prior attempts to form partnerships among wireless and cable companies have generally failed to lead to significant benefits to the participants. Other analysts point out that as wireless progresses to higher bandwidth, it inevitably competes more directly with cable and DSL, thrusting competitors into bed together. Also, as wireless broadband networks grow denser and usage habits shift, the need for increased backhaul and media service will accelerate, therefore the opportunity to leverage cable assets is expected to increase.

4.11.4 Backhaul/Access Network Applications

- WiMAX is a possible replacement candidate for cellular phone technologies such as GSM and CDMA, or can be used as an overlay to increase capacity. It has also been considered as a wireless backhaul technology for 2G, 3G, and 4G networks in both developed and poor nations.
- In North America, backhaul for urban cellular operations is typically provided via one or more copper wire line T1 connections, whereas remote cellular operations are sometimes backhauled via satellite. In most other regions, urban and rural backhaul is usually provided by microwave links. (The exception to this is where the network is operated by an incumbent with ready access to the copper network, in which case T1 lines may be used). WiMAX is a broadband platform and as such has much more substantial backhaul bandwidth requirements than legacy cellular applications. Therefore traditional copper wire line backhaul solutions are not appropriate. Consequently the use of wireless microwave backhaul is on the rise in North America and existing microwave backhaul links in all regions are being upgraded. Capacities of between 34 Mbit/s and 1 Gbit/s are routinely being deployed with latencies in the order of 1 ms. In many cases, operators are

aggregating sites using wireless technology and then presenting traffic on to fiber networks where convenient.
- Deploying WiMAX in rural areas with limited or no internet backbone will be challenging as additional methods and hardware will be required to procure sufficient bandwidth from the nearest sources — the difficulty being in proportion to the distance between the end-user and the nearest sufficient internet backbone.

4.12 Integration with an IP based Network

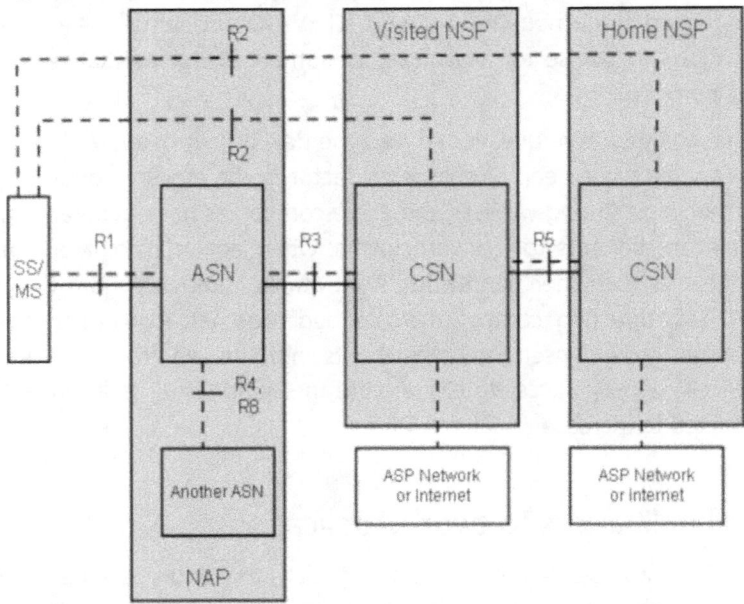

Fig. 4.20: The WiMAX Forum WiMAX Architecture

1. The WiMAX Forum has proposed an architecture that defines how a WiMAX network can be connected with an IP based core network, which is typically chosen by operators that serve as Internet Service Providers (ISP); Nevertheless the WiMAX BS provide seamless integration capabilities with other types of architectures as with packet switched Mobile Networks.

2. The WiMAX forum proposal defines a number of components, plus some of the interconnections (or reference points) between these, labeled R1 to R5 and R8:
    - SS/MS: the Subscriber Station/Mobile Station
    - ASN: the Access Service Network
    - BS: Base station, part of the ASN
    - ASN-GW: the ASN Gateway, part of the ASN

- CSN: the Connectivity Service Network
- HA: Home Agent, part of the CSN
- AAA: Authentication, Authorization and Accounting Server, part of the CSN
- NAP: a Network Access Provider
- NSP: a Network Service Provider

3. It is important to note that the functional architecture can be designed into various hardware configurations rather than fixed configurations.
4. For example, the architecture is flexible enough to allow remote/mobile stations of varying scale and functionality and Base Stations of varying size - e.g. femto, pico, and mini BS as well as macros.

4.13 Comparison with Wi-Fi (Wi-Fi vs. Wi-Max)

Comparisons and confusion between WiMAX and Wi-Fi are frequent because both are related to wireless connectivity and Internet access.

- WiMAX is a long range system, covering many kilometers, that uses licensed or unlicensed spectrum to deliver a point-to-point connection to the Internet.
- Different 802.16 standards provide different types of access, from portable (similar to a cordless phone) to fixed (an alternative to wired access, where the end user's wireless termination point is fixed in location.)
- Wi-Fi uses unlicensed spectrum to provide access to a network.
- Wi-Fi is more popular in end user devices.
- WiMAX and Wi-Fi have quite different quality of service (QoS) mechanisms.
- WiMAX uses a mechanism based on connections between the base station and the user device. Each connection is based on specific scheduling algorithms.
- Wi-Fi has a QoS mechanism similar to fixed Ethernet, where packets can receive different priorities based on their tags. For example, VoIP traffic may be given priority over web browsing.
- Wi-Fi runs on the Media Access Control's CSMA/CA protocol, which is connectionless and contention based, whereas WiMAX runs a connection-oriented MAC.
- Both 802.11 and 802.16 define Peer-to-Peer (P2P) and ad hoc networks, where an end user communicates to users or servers on another Local Area Network (LAN) using its access point or base station.

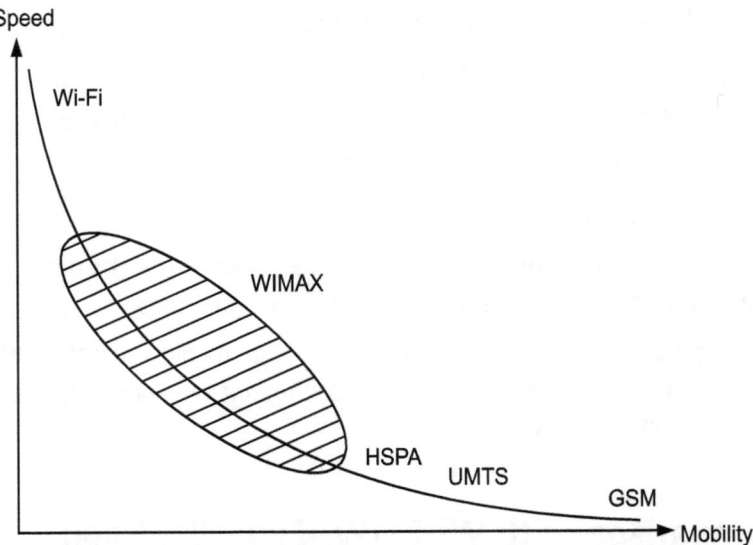

Fig. 4.21: Competating technologies (Speed vs. Mobility of wireless systems: Wi-Fi, HSPA, UMTS, GSM)

4.14 Routing Basics - What Is Routing?

Routing is the act of moving information across an internetwork from a source to a destination. Along the way, at least one intermediate node typically is encountered. Routing is often contrasted with bridging, which might seem to accomplish precisely the same thing to the casual observer. The primary difference between the two is that bridging occurs at Layer 2 (the link layer) of the OSI reference model, whereas routing occurs at Layer 3 (the network layer). This distinction provides routing and bridging with different information to use in the process of moving information from source to destination, so the two functions accomplish their tasks in different ways.

The topic of routing has been covered in computer science literature for more than two decades, but routing achieved commercial popularity as late as the mid-1980s. The primary reason for this time lag is that networks in the 1970s were simple, homogeneous environments. Only relatively recently has large-scale internetworking become popular.

4.15 Routing Components

Routing involves two basic activities : determining optimal routing paths and transporting information groups (typically called packets) through an internetwork. In the context of the routing process, the latter of these is referred to as packet switching. Although packet switching is relatively straightforward, path determination can be very complex.

4.16 Path Determination

Routing protocols use metrics to evaluate what path will be the best for a packet to travel. A metric is a standard of measurement, such as path bandwidth, that is used by routing algorithms to determine the optimal path to a destination. To aid the process of path determination, routing algorithms initialize and maintain routing tables, which contain route information. Route information varies depending on the routing algorithm used.

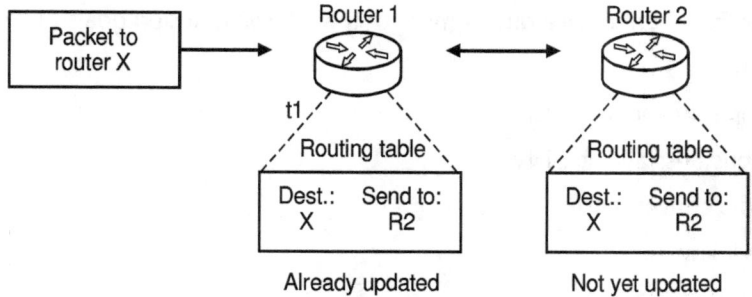

Fig. 4.22: Destination/Next Hop Associations determine the Data's Optimal Path

Routing algorithms fill routing tables with a variety of information. Destination/next hop associations tell a router that a particular destination can be reached optimally by sending the packet to a particular router representing the "next hop" on the way to the final destination. When a router receives an incoming packet, it checks the destination address and attempts to associate this address with a next hop. Fig. 4.1 depicts a sample destination/next hop routing table.

Routing tables can also contain other information, such as data about the desirability of a path. Routers compare metrics to determine optimal routes, and these metrics differ depending on the design of the routing algorithm used.

Routers communicate with one another and maintain their routing tables through the transmission of a variety of messages. The routing update message is one such message that generally consists of all or a portion of a routing table. By analyzing routing updates from all other routers, a router can build a detailed picture of network topology. A link-state advertisement, another example of a message sent between routers, informs other routers of the state of the sender's links. Link information can also be used to build a complete picture of network topology to enable routers to determine optimal routes to network destinations.

4.17 Routing Algorithms

Routing algorithms can be differentiated based on several key characteristics. First, the particular goals of the algorithm designer affect the operation of the resulting routing protocol. Second, various types of routing algorithms exist, and each algorithm has a different impact on network and router resources. Finally, routing algorithms use a variety of metrics that affect calculation of optimal routes. The following sections analyze these routing algorithm attributes.

4.18 Routing Design Goals

Routing algorithms often have one or more of the following design goals:
- Optimality
- Simplicity and low overhead
- Robustness and stability
- Rapid convergence
- Flexibility

4.18.1 Optimality

Refers to the capability of the routing algorithm to select the best route, which depends on the metrics and metric weightings used to make the calculation. For example, one routing algorithm may use a number of hops and delays, but it may weigh delay more heavily in the calculation. Naturally, routing protocols must define their metric calculation algorithms strictly.

4.18.2 Simplicity

Routing algorithms also are designed to be as simple as possible. In other words, the routing algorithm must offer its functionality efficiently, with a minimum of software and utilization overhead. Efficiency is particularly important when the software implementing the routing algorithm must run on a computer with limited physical resources.

4.18.3 Robustness and Stability

Routing algorithms must be robust, which means that they should perform correctly in the face of unusual or unforeseen circumstances, such as hardware failures, high load conditions, and incorrect implementations. Because routers are located at network junction points, they can cause considerable problems when they fail. The best routing algorithms are often those that have withstood the test of time and that have proven stable under a variety of network conditions.

4.18.4 Rapid Convergence

In addition, routing algorithms must converge rapidly. Convergence is the process of agreement, by all routers, on optimal routes. When a network event causes routes to either go down or become available, routers distribute routing update messages that permeate networks, stimulating recalculation of optimal routes and eventually causing all routers to agree on these routes. Routing algorithms that converge slowly can cause routing loops or network outages.

4.18.5 Flexibility

Routing algorithms should also be flexible, which means that they should quickly and accurately adapt to a variety of network circumstances. Assume, for example, that a network segment has gone down. As many routing algorithms become aware of the problem, they will quickly select the next-best path for all routes normally using that segment. Routing algorithms can be programmed to adapt to changes in network bandwidth, router queue size, and network delay, among other variables.

4.19 Routing Metrics

Routing tables contain information used by switching software to select the best route. But how, specifically, are routing tables built? What is the specific nature of the information that they contain? How do routing algorithms determine that one route is preferable to others?

Routing algorithms have used many different metrics to determine the best route. Sophisticated routing algorithms can base route selection on multiple metrics, combining them in a single (hybrid) metric. All the following metrics have been used:

- Path length
- Reliability
- Delay
- Bandwidth
- Load
- Communication cost

Path Length

Path length is the most common routing metric. Some routing protocols allow network administrators to assign arbitrary costs to each network link. In this case, path length is the sum of the costs associated with each link traversed. Other routing protocols define hop count, a metric that specifies the number of passes through internetworking products, such as routers, that a packet must taken route from a source to a destination.

Reliability

Reliability in the context of routing algorithms, refers to the dependability (usually described in terms of the bit-error rate) of each network link. Some network links might go down more often than others. After a network fails, certain network links might be repaired more easily or more quickly than other links. Any reliability factors can be taken into account in the assignment of the reliability ratings, which are arbitrary numeric values usually assigned to network links by network administrators.

Routing Delay

Routing delay refers to the length of time required to move a packet from source to destination through the internetwork. Delay depends on many factors, including the bandwidth of intermediate network links, the port queues at each router along the way, network congestion on all intermediate network links, and the physical distance to be travelled. Because delay is a conglomeration of several important variables, it is a common and useful metric.

Bandwidth

Bandwidth refers to the available traffic capacity of a link. All other things being equal, a 10-Mbps Ethernet link would be preferable to a 64 kbps leased line. Although bandwidth is a rating of the maximum attainable throughput on a link, routes through links with greater bandwidth do not necessarily provide better routes than routes through slower links. For example, if a faster link is busier, the actual time required to send a packet to the destination could be greater.

Load

Load refers to the degree to which a network resource, such as a router, is busy. Load can be calculated in a variety of ways, including CPU utilization and packets processed per second. Monitoring these parameters on a continual basis can be resource-intensive itself.

Communication Cost

Communication cost is another important metric, especially because some companies may not care about performance as much as they care about operating expenditures. Although line delay may be longer, they will send packets over their own lines rather than through the public lines that cost money for usage time.

4.20 Routing Algorithm Types

There are several ways in which we can classify routing algorithm.
- A. Based on responsiveness:
    1. Static Routing
    2. Dynamic Routing

B. Based on Topology:
1. Centralized Routing
2. Distributed Routing.

4.20.1 Static Vs Dynamic

Static routing algorithms are hardly algorithms at all, but are table mappings established by the network administrator before the beginning of routing. These mappings do not change unless the network administrator alters them. Algorithms that use static routes are simple to design and work well in environments where network traffic is relatively predictable and where network design is relatively simple.

Because static routing systems cannot react to network changes, they generally are considered unsuitable for today's large, constantly changing networks. Most of the dominant routing algorithms today are *dynamic routing algorithms*, which adjust to changing network circumstances by analyzing incoming routing update messages. If the message indicates that a network change has occurred, the routing software recalculates routes and sends out new routing update messages. These messages permeate the network, stimulating routers to rerun their algorithms and change their routing tables accordingly.

Dynamic routing algorithms can be supplemented with static routes where appropriate. A router of last resort (a router to which all unroutable packets are sent), for example, can be designated to act as a repository for all unroutable packets, ensuring that all messages are at least handled in some way.

4.20.2 Distributed Routing Vs Centralized Routing

The routing function is calculated in routers or nodes as packets travel across the network. Headers contain only *destination* address, used by routers to select output channel(s). Each router knows only its neighbourhood, since the designer has encoded the whole topology distributively into individual routers. Distributed routing is especially favorable in symmetric or regular topologies, since all routers use the same routing algorithm.

In Centralized routing, the routing function is determined by a *centralized controller*.

At that time there were two basic models for building communication networks: centralized and decentralized. In a centralized network, all nodes are connected directly and only to a centralized hub or switch. All data is sent from an individual node to the center and then routed to its destination. If the center is destroyed or not functioning all communication is effectively cut off. If the route between a node and the center is destroyed or not functioning, that node is effectively cut off. A decentralized network uses several centralized hubs. It is almost like several small-centralized networks joined together. Each individual node is still dependent upon the proper functioning of its hub and the route to it.

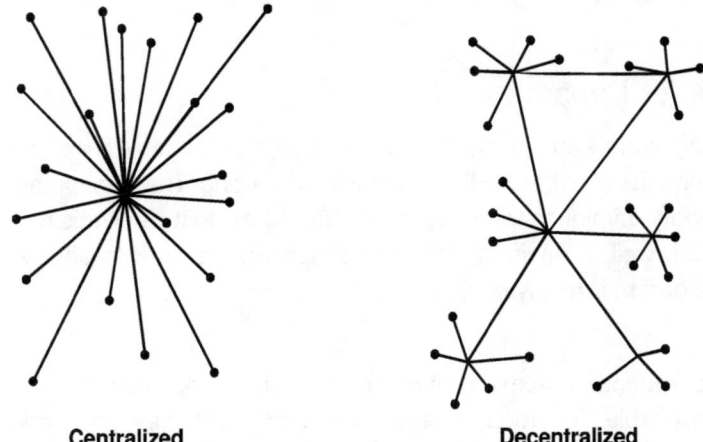

Centralized   **Decentralized**

Fig. 4.23: Indicates the Centralized and Decentralized network Scenario

Engineers suggested a third alternative — a distributed network — "a communication network which will allow several hundred major communication stations to talk with one another though after an enemy attack. A distributed network would have no centralized switch. Each node would be connected to several of its neighbouring nodes in a sort of lattice-like configuration. Therefore, each node would have several possible routes to send data. If one route or neighbouring node was destroyed, another path would be available.

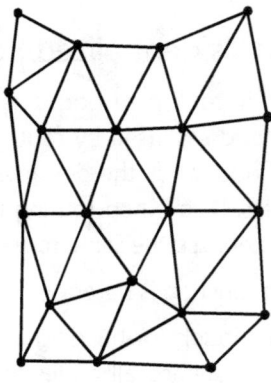

Distributed

Fig. 4.24: Indicates the Distributed network Scenario

In centralized routing algorithms, all route choices are made at the Routing Control Center (RCC). In distributed algorithms, the computation of routes is shared among the network nodes with information exchanged between them as necessary. Because computation is distributed evenly across the whole network, the network is not vulnerable to the breakdown of the RCC. The applicability of reconfigurable computing in routing varies according to the routing method. In static routing, reconfigurable computing methods help in accelerating the computations to fill the lookup tables. In adaptive routing, reconfigurable computing allows the routing algorithm to run in hardware where parallelism is exploited to the fullest, and when network conditions change, a different routing algorithm is swapped in to run in the same hardware. Traditionally, adaptive routing algorithms have been run in software, but running these algorithms in reconfigurable hardware brings speed advantages. Whether the routing method is centralized or distributed is not essential to the applicability of reconfigurable computing, since both central and distributed algorithms can be adaptive. The pros and cons of routing methods and the applicability of reconfigurable computing are presented in Table 4.7.

Table 4.7: Characteristics of routing methods

Routing method	Advantages	Disadvantages	Applicability of reconfigurable computing
Static	Simple, fast	Inflexible	Precomputation of the routing tables
Adaptive	Adapts to network changes	Complex, requires careful planning	Good
Centralized	Relieves nodes from computation	Vulnerability of the RCC	Depends on the routing algorithm
Distributed	Large tolerance to link failures	Vulnerability to oscillations	Depends on the routing algorithm

4.20.3 Distributed Vs Centralized Implementation

Route computation and management can be performed either (1) at a centralized route server or (2) in a distributed fashion at each router/switch.

Step 1 : Request received by R_1.

Step 2 : Request forwarded to route server.

Step 3 : Route server computes route (R_1, R_2, R_3, R_5) and returns the route.

Step 4 : The route is signaled.

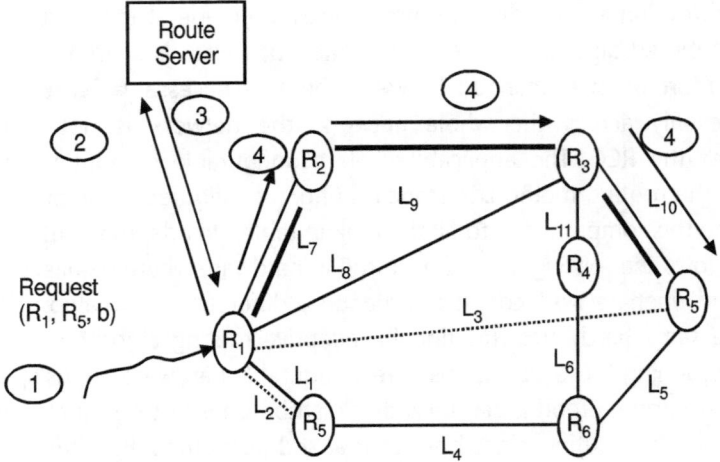

Fig. 4.25 (a): Centralized routing implementation using route server

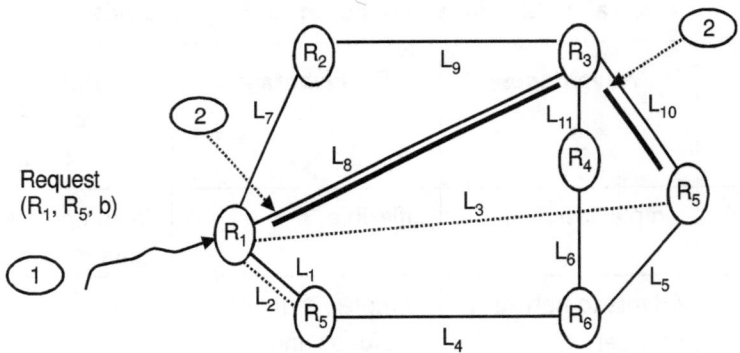

Fig. 4.25 (b): Distributed routing implementation

Step 1 : Request received by R_1.

Step 2 : Router R_1 computes route (R_1, R_3, R_5) and signals the path.

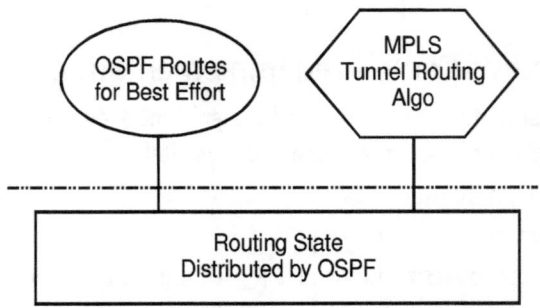

Fig. 4.26: Distributed routing algorithm

1. A Network Service Provider (NSP) operating label-switched networks such as ATM or Multi-Protocol Label Switching (MPLS) networks, sets up end-to-end bandwidth-guaranteed Label-Switched Paths (LSPs) to satisfy the connectivity requirements of its client networks.

2. In the centralized approach (Fig. 4.25 (a)), each router forwards the incoming request for a new LSP to a well-known route server, which then computes and returns the route.

3. In this approach, the route server has full information on the network state at its disposal for the route computation.

4. In the distributed implementation model (Fig. 4.25 (b)), a router computes routes for a LSP request based on its "local" view of the network state constructed from link-state updates sent by network nodes.

5. In this case, the overhead of distributing per-path information whenever new paths are established or old ones removed can be prohibitively high.

6. Therefore, distributed route computations are often limited to link-specific state instead of path-specific state, resulting in sub-optimal performance compared to their centralized counterpart.

7. For the ease of deployment, it is necessary that any new state information be collected and disseminated using existing routing protocols such as OSPF (Fig. 4.26).

8. The existing OSPF protocol disseminates topology and link state such as *up, down* status.

9. The OSPF path-computation algorithm uses this information to construct the route table for forwarding the best-effort traffic.

10. New extensions to OSPF have been proposed to distribute additional link state such as residual link bandwidth, delay etc. required for QoS routing.

11. The LSP routing algorithms will use such additional state information to construct MPLS paths and corresponding per-port label-swapping table.

12. Thus Centralized is simpler, but prone to failure and congestion, Centralized preferred in traffic engineering scenarios where complex optimization problems need to be solved and where routes chosen are long-lived.

13. The source-based route be signaled to fix the path and to minimize packet header information, for example, ATM, Frame-relay network etc.

14. The route is condensed and placed in each header in the network like IP routing network.

Summary: Distributed Routing Techniques	
Link State	**Vectoring**
1. Topology information is *flooded* within the routing domain.	1. Each router knows little about network topology.
2. Best end-to-end paths are computed locally at each router.	2. Only best next-hops are chosen by each router for each destination network.
3. Best end-to-end paths determine next-hops.	3. Best end-to-end paths result from composition of all next-hop choices.
4. Based on minimizing some notion of distance.	4. Does not require any notion of distance.
5. Works only if policy is *shared* and *uniform*.	5. Does not require uniform policies at all routers.
6. Examples: OSPF, IS-IS	6. Examples: RIP, BGP

4.21 Other Routing Techniques and Algorithms

4.21.1 Dijkstra's Algorithm for Finding the Shortest Path

Dijkstra's algorithm is an example of a **labelling algorithm**. It finds the shortest route from the initial vertex to any other vertex in the network. At each stage (iteration), a new vertex is assigned a **final label**. This label is the shortest distance from the start vertex to this vertex. Also, the **working values** of vertices are improved at each stage (the working value is the shortest distance found so far).

When recording the final and working values by hand, it is useful to use the following table:

Order of labelling	Final Value
Working Values	

The algorithm works as follows :
1. Label the start vertex's final value as 0 (as it is the origin), and label it 1.
2. Update the working values (if they have no working value yet, or if the new working value is lower) of all the vertices that can be reached directly from the last vertex labelled.
3. Choose the unlabelled vertex with the smallest working value, and record its working value as its final value and record its order of labellling.
4. Repeat steps 2 and 3 until the destination vertex is labelled.

The working value for the destination vertex is its best working value. The shortest route can now be found by tracking back :

If vertex **a** lies on the route, then vertex **b** is the previous vertex if the

label at a - label at b = weight of edge ab

Example of using Dijkstra's algorithm to get from A to C:

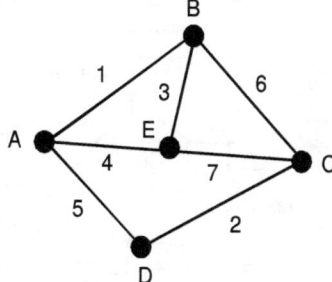

1. Label the start vertex's final value as 0 (as it is the origin), and label it 1.

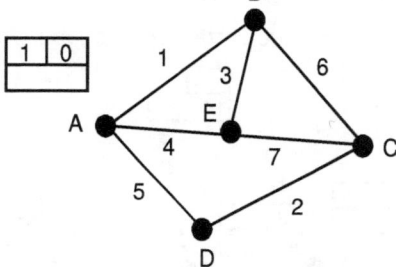

2. Update the working values of B, E and D.

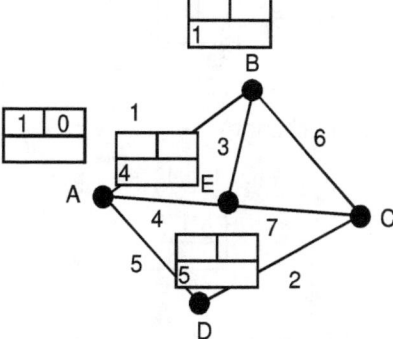

3. Choose the vertex with the lowest working value (B), and record its working value as its final value and the order in which it was labelled.

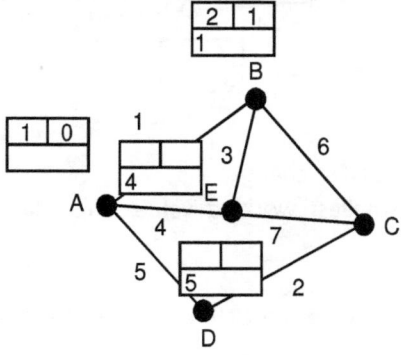

4. Update all working values.

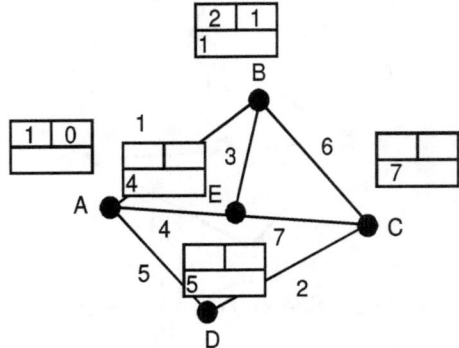

5. Label the smallest working value vertex with no label (E), final value=working value.

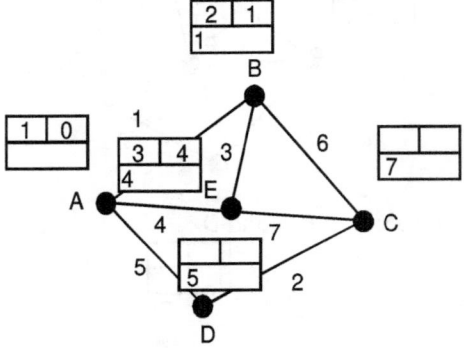

6. Update working values (no change).
7. Choose smallest working value (D), label.

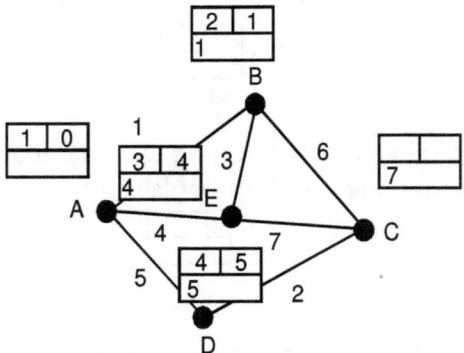

8. Update working values (No change).
9. Choose and label smallest working value, unlabelled, vertex. It is C, so C's final working value is 7.
   To find the path:
   $7 - 5 = 2$ and $7 - 1 = 6$ so the path can either be ADC or ABC (it does not matter which we choose).

4.21.2 Flooding Algorithm

- Flooding is a technique to update topology databases.
- In *simple flooding*, each incoming packet is sent out on every outgoing link or interface except for the interface it entered.
- The flooding process thus generates a vast number of duplications and what is worse, the process does not stop unless some measures are taken to damp the generation of duplicates.
- For instance, the flooding process can be stopped when the time to live (TTL) of the initial packet, which is decremented at each hop, attains the value 0.
- In that case, the flooding process only reaches routers TTL hops away from the initial router.
- Another technique is to compare sequence numbers of received flooded packets and discard the older ones.
- As shown in Fig. 4.6, the propagation times are obviously not all the same on all links. But this implies that the routing tables may grow large since an identification of each new flooded packet needs be stored the first time in order to determine and discard later revisits.
- The more refined updating technique is *selective flooding* which is based on multicast. Only via a minimum spanning tree, topology update information is distributed to all nodes.
- In case the graph does not change, selective flooding may have benefits when the loading of the network is high. Indeed, selective flooding consumes minimal network capacity provided the network topology does not change and the multicast tree entries are already computed.
- Just in heavy traffic when more updates may be necessary, the more robust flooding may cause too high an overhead due to duplicate packets.
- In addition to its simplicity, flooding is very robust as long as the network is connected, because flooding distributes information over all possible paths and, hence, assures that the information is received in the shortest time.
- In fact, no other algorithm such as selective flooding can be faster if we make abstraction from the flooding overhead of duplicates that consumes network resources and causes additional delay.

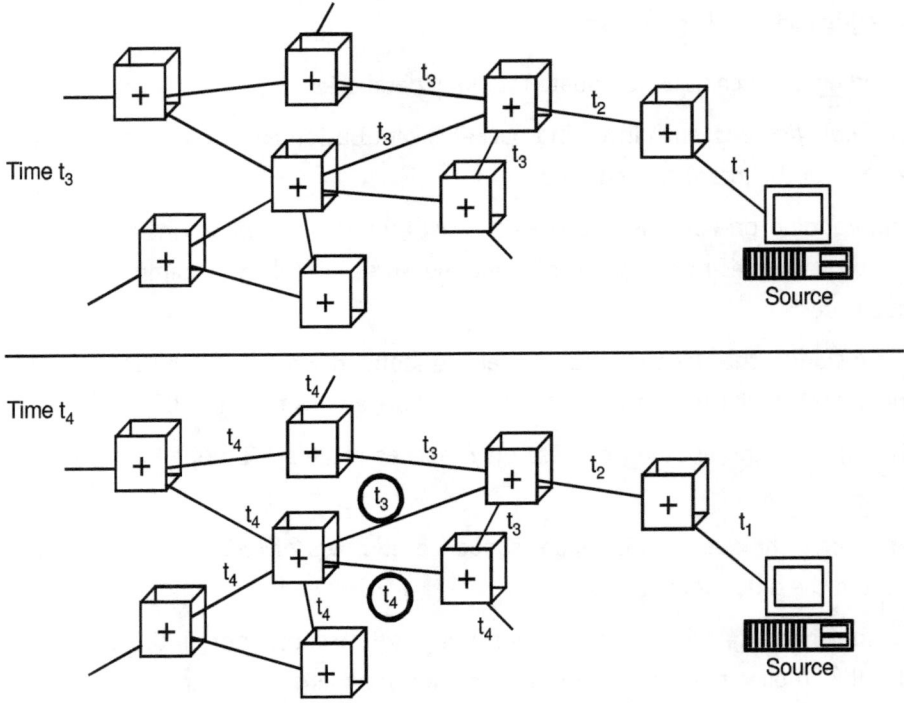

Fig. 4.27: The Flooding of a packet as a function of time

- In multi-hop wireless networks and ad hoc networks, routing based on flooding has been proposed.
- Another application of flooding, though a rather naive one, is QoS routing.
- The source node floods a test packet with the desired QoS fields, for example, minimum capacity, jitter and delay.
- Each intermediate router first modifies the QoS fields and appends his IP address to the path list before flooding that modified test packet to all outgoing interfaces.
- There are various ways to update the QoS field, but the simplest one consists for *min-max metrics* such as the capacity of computing the minimum of the previous capacity and the available capacity of the link corresponding to the outgoing interface and for *additive metrics* such as the delay of adding the delay of that outgoing link to the previous value.
- The destination receives the many duplicate packets in the order of increasing end-to-end transfer delay since flooding proceeds over all paths including the shortest path from A to B, the second shortest, etc.
- Hence, when the end-to-end delay bound of a duplicate packet dp is exceeded, all duplicates arriving later than dp are discarded.

- The best QoS path is then found by comparing and/or computing the best of the other QoS fields, in this example, available capacity and jitter.
- Perhaps in small networks, this way of QoS routing may work satisfactorily, but in large networks with N nodes it is questionable because an order of O ((N − 2)!) different paths between A and B are possible.
- Hence, an excessive number of duplicate packets is generated per source-destination pair and per QoS flow.

4.21.3 Distance - Vector Routing Algorithm

- Distance-vector routing protocols base their routing decisions on the number of hops or some predefined cost to a destination.

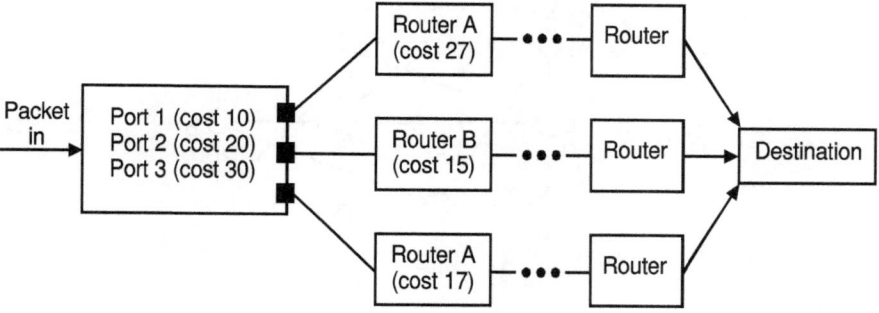

Fig. 4.28: Distance-vector routing

- This information is provided by neighbouring routers. The technique generally follows the Bellman-Ford algorithm.
- A common distance-vector routing protocol is RIP (Routing Information Protocol).
- A router with a number of ports such as that pictured in Fig. 4.28 has a cost assigned to each of its ports.
- These costs are assigned by the network administrator as a value that can show preference for one router over another.
- Routers inform other routers of their cost assignments, and these neighbouring routers add up the costs to come up with a figure that is used to determine the most efficient route through a network. For example :

    Port 1 cost 10 + neighbour cost 27 = 37

    Port 2 cost 20 + neighbour cost 15 = 35

    Port 3 cost 30 + neighbour cost 17 = 47

- In this case, the router would send the packet through port 2 because it represents the least cost to the destination.

- The neighbouring router attached to port 2 will then calculate additional pathways through other routers, if necessary. Note that other routes are used during heavy traffic or for prioritized traffic.
- Routing information is exchanged among routers approximately every 30 seconds. From this information, routers rebuild their tables by adding new routes or deleting old routes.
- Routing tables include network numbers, port numbers, cost metrics, and the address of the next hop.
- Note that distance-vector routing is not suitable for large networks that have hundreds of routers or networks that are constantly updated.
- On large networks, the table update process can take so long that tables in the farthest routers may fall out of synchronization with other tables.

Example of Distance - Vector Routing Algorithm

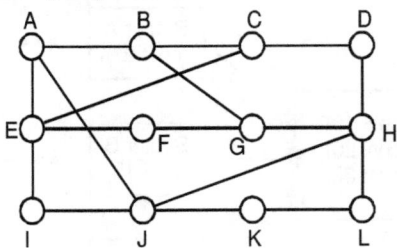

Destination	Weight	Line
A	8	A
B	20	A
C	28	I
D	20	H
E	17	I
F	30	I
G	18	H
H	12	H
I	10	I
J	0	---
K	6	K
L	15	K

Fig. 4.29: A typical network graph and routing table for router J

DV algorithms are also known as Bellman-Ford routing algorithms and Ford-Fulkerson routing algorithms. In these algorithms, every router has a routing table that shows it the best route for any destination. A typical graph and routing table for router J is shown in Fig. 4.29.

As the table shows, if router J wants to get packets to router D, it should send them to router H. When packets arrive at router H, it checks its own table and decides how to send the packets to D.

In DV algorithms, each router has to follow these steps:

1. It counts the weight of the links directly connected to it and saves the information to its table.
2. In a specific period of time, it sends its table to its neighbour routers (not to all routers) and receive the routing table of each of its neighbours.
3. Based on the information in its neighbours' routing tables, it updates its own.

One of the most important problems with Distance Vector algorithms is called "**count to infinity**." Let us examine this problem with an example:

Imagine a network with a graph as shown below. As you see in this graph, there is only one link between A and the other parts of the network. Here, you can see the graph and routing table of all nodes:

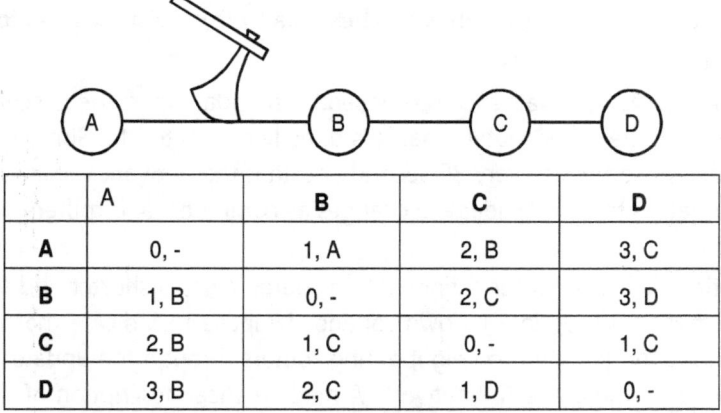

	A	B	C	D
A	0, -	1, A	2, B	3, C
B	1, B	0, -	2, C	3, D
C	2, B	1, C	0, -	1, C
D	3, B	2, C	1, D	0, -

Fig. 4.30: Network graph and routing tables

Now imagine that the link between A and B is cut. At this time, B corrects its table. After a specific amount of time, routers exchange their tables, and so B receives C's routing table. Since C does not know what has happened to the link between A and B, it says that it has a link to A with the weight of 2 (1 for C to B, and 1 for B to A -- it does not know B has no link to A). B receives this table and thinks there is a separate link between C and A, so it corrects its table and changes infinity to 3 (1 for B to C, and 2 for C to A, as C said). Once again routers exchange their tables. When C receives B's routing table, it sees that B has changed the weight of its link to A from 1 to 3, so C updates its table and changes the weight of the link to A to 4 (1 for C to B, and 3 for B to A, as B said).

This process loops until all nodes find out that the weight of link to A is infinity. This situation is shown in the table below. In this way, experts say Distance-Vector algorithms have a **slow convergence rate**.

Table 4.8: The "count to infinity" problem

	B	C	D
Sum of weight to A after link cut	∞,A	2,B	3,C
Sum of weight to B after 1st updating	3,C	2,B	3,C
Sum of weight to A after 2nd updating	3,C	4,B	3,C
Sum of weight to A after 3rd updating	5,C	4,B	5,C
Sum of weight to A after 4th updating	5,C	6,B	5,C
Sum of weight to A after 5th updating	7,C	6,B	7,C
Sum of weight to A after n^{th} updating	...	...	...
∞	∞	∞	∞

One way to solve this problem is for routers to send information only to the neighbours that are not exclusive links to the destination. For example, in this case, C should not send any information to B about A, because B is the only way to A.

RIP (Routing information protocol) is the best example of Distance-Vector Routing.

The RIP algorithm works like this:

1. **Update:** At regular intervals each router sends an update message describing its routing database to all the other routers that it is directly connected to. Some routers will send this message as often as every 30 seconds, so that the network will always have up-to-date information to quickly adapt to changes as computers and routers come on and off the network.

2. **Propagation:** When a router X finds that a router Y has a shorter and faster path to a router Z, then it will update its own routing database to indicate that fact. Any faster path is quickly propagated to neighbouring routers through the update process, until it is spread across the entire RIP network. A mathematical description of this algorithm is shown below:
   - Let $D(i,j)$ be the metric for the best route from router i to router j.
   - Let $d(i,j)$ represent the distance from router i to router j, set to infinite if i and j are the same or if i and j are not immediate neighbours.
   - The best distance is then

     $D(i, i) = 0$, for all i

     $D(i, j) = \min(d(i, k) + D(k, j))$, for $i <> j$, over all k

estimates of distance to each destination address. The RIP routing protocol uses UDP because it is particularly efficient, and there are no problems if a message gets, which is fine for router updates where another update will be coming along shortly anyway.

4.21.4 Link-State Routing Algorithm

In LS algorithms, every router has to follow these steps:
1. Identify the routers that are physically connected to them and get their IP addresses. When a router starts working, it first sends a "HELLO" packet over network. Each router that receives this packet replies with a message that contains its IP address.
2. Measure the delay time (or any other important parameters of the network, such as average traffic) for neighbour routers.
3. In order to do that, routers send **echo packets** over the network. Every router that receives these packets replies with an echo reply packet. By dividing round trip time by 2, routers can count the delay time. (Round trip time is a measure of the current delay on a network, found by timing a packet bounced off some remote host.) Note that this time includes both transmission and processing times -- the time it takes the packets to reach the destination and the time it takes the receiver to process it and reply.
4. Broadcast its information over the network for other routers and receive the other routers' information.
5. In this step, all routers share their knowledge and broadcast their information to each other. In this way, every router can know the structure and status of the network.
6. Using an appropriate algorithm, identify the best route between two nodes of the network. In this step, routers choose the best route to every node. They do this using an algorithm, such as the **Dijkstra's shortest path algorithm**.
7. In this algorithm, a router, based on information that has been collected from other routers, builds a graph of the network. This graph shows the location of routers in the network and their links to each other. Every link is labeled with a number called the **weight** or **cost**. This number is a function of delay time, average traffic, and sometimes simply the number of hops between nodes. For example, if there are two links between a node and a destination, the router chooses the link with the lowest weight.

OSPF (Open Shortest Path First) protocol is the Best Example of Link-State Routing.
- *Open Shortest Path First* (OSPF) is an interier *link-state* routing protocol developed for IP networks, and is based on the *shortest path first* (SPF) algorithm.
- Routers within the same hierarchical area send each other *link-state advertisements* (LSAs) containing information about their attached interfaces, and the metrics used.
- They use this information together with the SPF algorithm to calculate the shortest path to each node. OSPF can operate within a *hierarchy*, usually an internetwork with a single administration and a common routing strategy.
- This *routing domain* (or *autonomous system*) can be split into a number of *areas*. Routers with a connection to two or more areas are called *area border routers*, and maintain a separate *topological database* for each area.

- The database holds the information extracted from link-state advertisements received from other routers in the same area. Because the routers share the same information, they have identical databases.
- OSPF uses either *intra-area routing* (if the source and destination are in the same area), or *inter-area routing* (if they are in different areas).
- Routing information is distributed through the OSPF backbone, which consists of all area border routers and any other routers to which they are connected that do not reside within a specific area. In the diagram below, the backbone consists of routers 4-6, and 10-12.

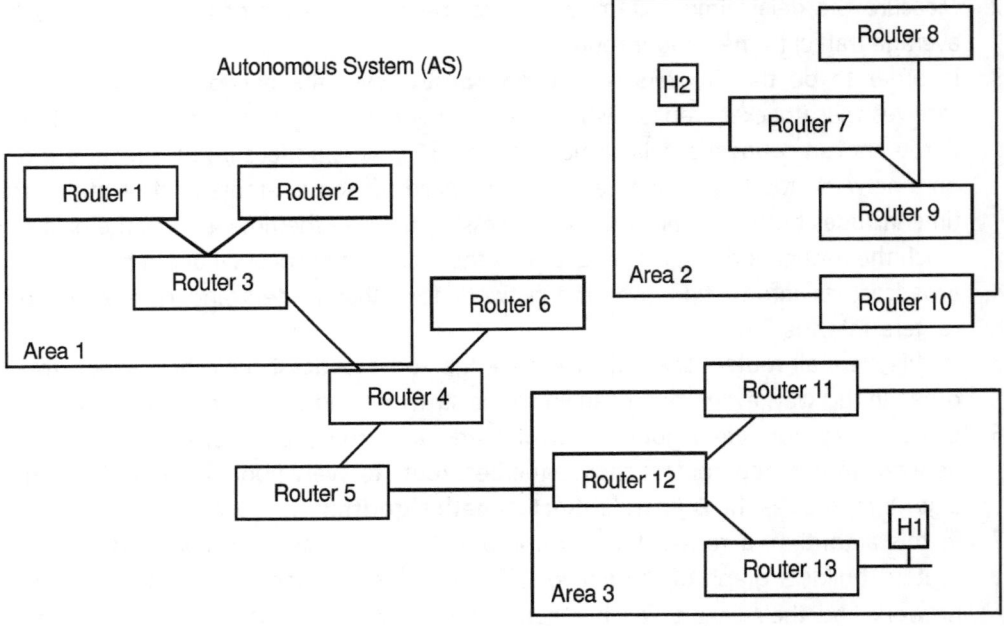

Routing areas

Fig. 4.31: Link-State routing example

- If host H1 wants to send a packet to H2, the packet is sent to router 12 via intra-area router 13, then along the backbone to area border router 10 via router 11.
- Router 10 forwards the packet to H2 via intra-area routers 9 and 7.
- Border routers running OSPF learn about external routes using an *exterior* routing protocol such as *Border Gateway Protocol* (BGP).
- When a router is powered up, it "acquires" neighbors (routers to which it has a connection) by exchanging Hello messages with them.
- Neighbouring routers continue to exchange these messages to let each other know that they are still functional. On networks supporting more than two routers, a *designated router* is elected, and takes responsibility for generating link-state advertisements, which are exchanged only between adjacent (neighbouring) routers.

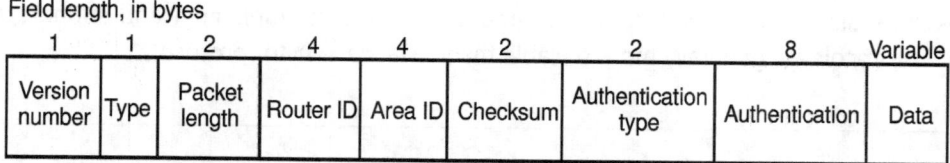

Fig. 4.32: OSPF packet format

All OSPF packets employ a 24-byte header (see above). The header fields are described below:

- *Version number* - identifies the OSPF version used.
- *Type* - identifies the OSPF packet type as one of the following :
  - *Hello* - establishes and maintains neighbour relationships.
  - *Database description* - describes the contents of the topological database.
  - *Link-state request* - requests updated link-state information from a neighbour router.
  - *Link-state update* - contains one or more link state advertisements.
  - *Link-state acknowledgement* - acknowledges a link-state update.
- *Packet length* - specifies the packet length, including the header, in bytes.
- *Router ID* - identifies the source of the packet.
- *Area ID* - identifies the area to which the packet belongs.
- *Checksum* - checks the contents of the packet for errors.
- *Authentication type* - contains the authentication type.
- *Authentication* - contains the authentication information.
- *Data* - contains encapsulated upper-layer information.

Link-State Versus Distance Vector

Link-state algorithms (also known as shortest path first algorithms) flood routing information to all nodes in the internetwork. Each router, however, sends only the portion of the routing table that describes the state of its own links. In link-state algorithms, each router builds a picture of the entire network in its routing tables. Distance - vector algorithms (also known as Bellman-Ford algorithms) call for each router to send all or some portion of its routing table, but only to its neighbours. In essence, link-state algorithms send small updates everywhere, while distance - vector algorithms send larger updates only to neighbouring routers. Distance - vector algorithms know only about their neighbours.

Because they converge more quickly, link-state algorithms are somewhat less prone to routing loops than distance - vector algorithms. On the other hand, link-state algorithms require more CPU power and memory than distance - vector algorithms.

Link-state algorithms, therefore, can be more expensive to implement and support. Link-state protocols are generally more scalable than distance - vector protocols.

EXERCISE

1. Write a short note on broadband access solutions.
2. What are the different broadband media options with different media characteristics?
3. Explain process of distribution of CATV in detail.
4. What are the requirements to transmit cable TV channels and Internet data over same cable?
5. Explain cable modem technology in detail.
6. What is DOCSIS model?
7. Explain Adsl technology in detail.
8. What are different advantages and disadvantages of ADSL and cable modem technology?
9. Distinguish Cable modem versus DSL.
10. Explain what is xDSL and its variants.
11. Compare xDSL variants with their upload and download speed of data transfer.
12. What is WLL?
13. Explain the services provided by WLL. Also explain the standards used for WLL.
14. What is fixed WLL technology?
15. Write the typical specifications of WLL phone.
16. What is leased line?
17. What are types and typical users of leased line?
18. What are the advantages and disadvantages of leased lines?
19. Explain the concept of routing used in telecommunication network.
20. Explain the different design goals of typical routing algorithm.
21. Classify the routing algorithms and explain the concept of static routing.
22. Compare link state versus distance vector routing.

Unit V

QoS AND RELIABILITY ISSUES OF TELECOM NETWORKS

5.1 The Reliability in Telecommunication Networks

In today's highly competitive communications industry landscape, service providers are intensely focused on both their top and bottom lines. The costs of maintaining and extending their existing portfolio of telecom network assets are already too high, and without implementing an industry standards-based horizontal service delivery platform (SDP), there is no room for service providers to differentiate themselves and remain competitive.

The modern era of performance engineering has little overt similarity to the classical studies done 30 years ago. At present, there are perhaps four areas of particular interest.

Traffic characterization

The first area is that of traffic and applications behavior and categorization.

Network control

The second area is that of network control. With the varied use of networks today, a whole range of mechanisms must be deployed in order to ensure that they run smoothly; and that neither general overloads, focused events, nor any fault conditions can result in uncontrollable degradation.

Reliable Data services

The third area is the whole arena of data services. ATM is now so well understood, and so well performing in comparison to much that runs over it, that its performance importance is diminishing (exactly as that of LAP-D diminished as attention moved to the higher layers). IP on the other hand provides a whole range of control facilities and traffic interactions that are little understood, and a vast array of parameters that need to be set by operator or customer.

Quality of Service
In addition, it is becoming ever more important; its performance in absolute terms is (by classical carrier standards) very poor, and it is being re-engineered to provide separation, QoS, and security. There can be little surprise that this is a prime focus of much performance effort today.

Management systems

Finally, there is an increasing emphasis upon management systems, the backoffice processes which are at least as important to a profitable business as the network QoS itself. These range in scope from traffic and network monitoring and fault reporting, to billing and customer service systems, and their remit is more typically the huge distributed database or computer system than the communications network itself. Where once the fault-lines within teletraffic were between switches and networks, circuit-switched and packet, or old technology and new, now those of performance lie more between networks and systems, or prediction and reporting.

The increasing realization within the industry that an integrated approach is necessary, covering not only the whole hardware platform life cycle, but also the entire range of related process issues, which determine every customer's experience, has resulted in a huge broadening of the scope of performance work. There has never before been such diversity or vitality in the field.

5.2 QoS

5.2.1 QoS Introduction

Quality of Service (QoS) for networks is an industry-wide set of standards and mechanisms for ensuring high-quality performance for critical applications.

By using QoS mechanisms, network administrators can use existing resources efficiently and ensure the required level of service without reactively expanding or over-provisioning their networks.

Traditionally, the concept of quality in networks meant that all network traffic was treated equally.

The result was that all network traffic received the network's best effort, with no guarantees for reliability, delay, variation in delay, or other performance characteristics.

With best-effort delivery service, however, a single bandwidth-intensive application can result in poor or unacceptable performance for all applications.

The QoS concept of quality is one in which the requirements of some applications and users are more critical than others, which means that some traffic needs preferential treatment.

5.2.2 Network Characteristics Managed by QoS

The goal of QoS is to provide preferential delivery service for the applications that need it by ensuring sufficient bandwidth, controlling latency and jitter, and reducing data loss. Table 5.1 describes these network characteristics.

Table 5.1: Network Characteristics Managed by QoS

Network Characteristic	Description
Bandwidth	The rate at which traffic is carried by the network.
Latency	The delay in data transmission from source to destination.
Jitter	The variation in latency.
Reliability	The percentage of packets discarded by a router.

The Internet Engineering Task Force (IETF) defines two major models for QoS on IP-based networks: Integrated Services (Intserv) and Differentiated Services (Diffserv). These models encompass several categories of mechanisms that provide preferential treatment to specified traffic. The QoS mechanisms have been discussed later.

5.2.3 Uses and Benefits of QoS

Network administrators can use QoS to guarantee throughput for mission-critical applications so that their transactions can be processed in an acceptable amount of time.

Network administrators can also use QoS to manage User Data Protocol (UDP) traffic.

Unlike Transmission Control Protocol (TCP), UDP is an inherently unreliable protocol that does not receive feedback from the network and, therefore, cannot detect network congestion.

Network administrators can use QoS to manage the priority of applications that rely on UDP, such as multimedia applications, so that they have the required bandwidth even in times of network congestion, but do not overwhelm the network.

QoS provides the following benefits:

1.	Gives administrators control over network resources and allows them to manage the network from a business, rather than a technical, perspective.
2.	Ensures that time-sensitive and mission-critical applications have the resources they require, while allowing other applications access to the network.
3.	Improves user experience.
4.	Reduces costs by using existing resources efficiently, thereby delaying or reducing the need for expansion or upgrades.

5.2.4 Network Technologies and Support for QoS

QoS depends on support throughout the network.

To achieve QoS from sender to receiver, all of the network elements through which a traffic flow passes such as network interface cards, switches, routers, and bridges must support QoS.

If a network device along this path does not support QoS, the traffic flow receives the standard first-come, first-served treatment on that network segment.

Network technologies such as Frame Relay, asynchronous transfer mode (ATM), and the more traditional local area network (LAN) technologies (including Ethernet, Token Ring, and 802.11 wireless LAN) support QoS mechanisms.

ATM, in particular, offers a high degree of support for QoS. Because ATM is a connection-oriented networking technology, it can establish a service contract that guarantees a specific quality of service and can allocate network resources. ATM enforces the service contract and allocates bandwidth at the hardware level.

Service level guarantees and resource allocations such as those provided by ATM are not supported by the more traditional IEEE 802 LAN technologies.

These LAN technologies do not support QoS mechanisms at the hardware level, but at higher levels of the Open Systems Interconnection (OSI) reference model only.

For these types of technologies, QoS is primarily based on the concept of priority, in which one data transmission receives delivery preference over other transmissions.

Traditional IEEE 802 LAN technologies are connectionless, so a host that sends a transmission cannot detect the state of the network or the state of the destination host prior to the transmission.

Traffic on these network technologies, therefore, is subject to delay at points along the way, making bandwidth availability and delivery time difficult to predict.

Although high-priority traffic typically arrives at its destination before lower-priority traffic, high-priority traffic cannot be guaranteed to arrive within a specified time.

Although QoS is more difficult to implement on connectionless networks, there is growing interest in developing QoS for IP-based networks.

5.2.5 Quality of Service in Networks

In the fields of packet-switched networks and computer networking, the traffic engineering term **Quality of Service (QoS)** refers to control mechanisms that can provide different priority to different users or data flows, or guarantee a certain level of performance to a data flow in accordance with requests from the application program.

Quality of Service guarantees are important if the network capacity is limited, especially for real-time streaming multimedia applications, for example voice over IP and IP-TV, since these often require fixed bit rate and may be delay sensitive.

The Quality of Service can be defined as, "The degree of measure of satisfaction of the user of the system".

A network or protocol that supports Quality of Service may agree on a traffic contract with the application software and reserve capacity in the network nodes during a session establishment phase.

During the session it may monitor the achieved level of performance, for example the data rate and delay, and dynamically control scheduling priorities in the network nodes. It may release the reserved capacity during a tear down phase. A best-effort network does not support Quality of Service.

The term **Quality of Service** is sometimes used as a quality measure with many alternative definitions, rather than referring to the control mechanisms.

In computer networking, a good QoS may mean advanced QoS mechanisms, or high probability that the network is able to provide the requested level of performance.

High QoS is often confused with a high **level of performance**, for example high bit rate, low latency and low bit error probability.

In the field of telephony, telephony quality of service QoS was defined in the ITU standard X.902 as "A set of quality requirements on the collective behavior of one or more objects".

Another widespread definition used especially in telephony and streaming video is "user perceived performance". In this context, QoS is the cumulative effect on subscriber satisfaction of all imperfections affecting the service.

This definition includes the human in the assessment and demands an appropriate subjective weighting of diverse defects such as response time, interrupts, noise, cross-talk, loudness levels, frequency response, noticeable echos, etc., and also includes grade of service.

With the advent of digital telephone networks, new types of impairments, such as the effects of bit errors in codecs, arose together with a tendency to express QoS in terms of engineering parameters that can be measured objectively, eliminating the uncertainty of human subjectivity.

This definition resembles to the Mean Opinion Score (MOS) value, which is a subjective quality measure that can be predicted based on objective performance measures.

5.2.6 Problems

When the Internet was first deployed many years ago, it lacked the ability to provide Quality of Service guarantees due to limits in router computing power.

It therefore ran at default QoS level, or "best effort". There were four "Type of Service" bits and three "Precedence" bits provided in each message, but they were ignored. These bits were later re-defined as DiffServ Code Points (DSCP) and are largely honored in peered links on the modern Internet.

Many things can happen to packets as they travel from origin to destination, resulting in the following problems as seen from the point of view of the sender and receiver:

Dropped packets

The routers might fail to deliver (*drop*) some packets if they arrive when their buffers are already full. Some, none, or all of the packets might be dropped, depending on the state of the network, and it is impossible to determine what will happen in advance. The receiving application must ask for this information to be retransmitted, possibly causing severe delays in the overall transmission.

Delay

It might take a long time for a packet to reach its destination, because it gets held up in long queues, or takes a less direct route to avoid congestion. Alternatively, it might follow a fast, direct route. Thus, delay is very unpredictable.

Jitter

Packets from source will reach the destination with different delays. This variation in delay is known as jitter and can seriously affect the quality of streaming audio and/or video.

Out-of-order delivery

When a collection of related packets is routed through the Internet, different packets may take different routes, each resulting in a different delay. The result is that the packets arrive in a different order to the one with which they were sent. This problem necessitates special additional protocols responsible for rearranging out-of-order packets to an isochronous state once they reach their destination. This is especially important for video and VoIP streams where quality is dramatically impacted by both latency or lack of isochronicity.

Error

Sometimes packets are misdirected, or combined together, or corrupted, while *en route*. The receiver has to detect this and, just as if the packet was dropped, ask the sender to repeat itself.

5.2.7 Applications Requiring QoS

A defined Quality of Service may be required for certain types of network traffic, for example:
- Streaming multimedia may require guaranteed throughput
- IP telephony or Voice over IP (VOIP) may require strict limits on jitter and delay
- Video Teleconferencing (VTC) requires low jitter
- Alarm signalling (e.g. Burglar alarm)
- Dedicated link emulation requires both guaranteed throughput and imposes limits on maximum delay and jitter
- A safety-critical application, such as remote surgery may require a guaranteed level of availability (this is also called *hard QoS*).

These types of service are called **inelastic**, meaning that they require a certain level of bandwidth to function - any more than required is unused, and any less will render the service non-functioning.

By contrast, *elastic* applications can take advantage of however much or little bandwidth is available. For example, a remote system administrator may want to prioritize variable, and usually small, amounts of SSH(Secure Shell) traffic to ensure a responsive session even over a heavily-laden link.

5.2.8 Obtaining QoS

- **Per call**
- **In call**
- **In advance:** When the expense of mechanisms to provide QoS is justified, network customers and providers typically enter into a contractual agreement termed an **SLA (Service Level Agreement)** which specifies guarantees for the ability of a network/protocol to give guaranteed performance/throughput/ latency bounds based on mutually agreed measures, usually by prioritising traffic.
- **Reserving resources:** Resources are being reserved at each step on the network for the call as it is set up. An example is RSVP, Resource Reservation Protocol.

5.2.9 QoS Mechanisms

1. Quality of Service can be provided by generously over-provisioning a network so that interior links are considerably faster than access links.
2. This approach is relatively simple, and may be economically feasible for broadband networks with predictable and light traffic loads.
3. The performance is reasonable for many applications, particularly those capable of tolerating high jitter, such as deeply-buffered video downloads.
4. The Internet Engineering **Task Force (IETF) defines two major models for QoS on IP-based networks: Integrated Services (Intserv) and Differentiated Services (Diffserv).**
5. These models encompass several categories of mechanisms that provide preferential treatment to specified traffic.
6. The following Table 5.2 describes th three general categories of QoS mechanisms.

Table 5.2

Category of QoS Mechanisms	Description
Admission control	Determine which applications and users are entitled to network resources. These mechanisms specify how, when, and by whom network resources on a network segment (subnet) can be used.
Traffic control	Regulate data flows by classifying, scheduling, and marking packets based on priority and by shaping traffic (smoothing bursts of traffic by limiting the rate of flow). Traffic control mechanisms segregate traffic into service classes and control delivery to the network. The service class assigned to a traffic flow determines the QoS treatment the traffic receives.

7. The **Intserv** model integrates resource reservation and traffic control mechanisms to support special handling of individual traffic flows.
8. The **Diffserv** model uses traffic control to support special handling of aggregated traffic flows.
9. Commercial VoIP services are often competitive with traditional telephone service in terms of call quality even though QoS mechanisms are usually not in use on the user's connection to his ISP and the VoIP provider's connection to a different ISP.
10. Under high load conditions, however, VoIP quality degrades to cell-phone quality or worse.
11. The mathematics of packet traffic indicate that a network with QoS can handle four times as many calls with tight jitter requirements as one without QoS.
12. The amount of over-provisioning in interior links required to replace QoS depends on the number of users and their traffic demands.
13. As the Internet now services close to a billion users, there is little possibility that over-provisioning can eliminate the need for QoS when VoIP becomes more commonplace.
14. For narrowband networks more typical of enterprises and local governments, however, the costs of bandwidth can be substantial and over provisioning is hard to justify. In these situations, two distinctly different philosophies were developed to engineer preferential treatment for packets which require it.
15. Early work used the **"IntServ"** philosophy of reserving network resources. In this model, applications used the Resource Reservation Protocol (RSVP) to request and reserve resources through a network.
16. While **IntServ** mechanisms do work, it was realized that in a broadband network typical of a larger service provider, Core routers would be required to accept, maintain, and tear down thousands or possibly tens of thousands of reservations.

17. It was believed that this approach would not scale with the growth of the Internet, and in any event was antithetical to the notion of designing networks so that Core routers do little more than simply switch packets at the highest possible rates.
18. The second and currently accepted approach is "DiffServ" or differentiated services. In the DiffServ model, packets are marked according to the type of service they need.
19. In response to these markings, routers and switches, use various queuing strategies to tailor performance to requirements. (At the IP layer, differentiated services code point (DSCP) markings use the 6 bits in the IP packet header).
20. At the MAC layer, VLAN IEEE 802.1Q and IEEE 802.1D can be used to carry essentially the same information.
21. Routers supporting **DiffServ** use multiple queues for packets awaiting transmission from bandwidth constrained (e.g., wide area) interfaces.
22. Router vendors provide different capabilities for configuring this behavior, to include the number of queues supported, the relative priorities of queues, and bandwidth reserved for each queue.
23. In practice, when a packet must be forwarded from an interface with queuing, packets requiring low jitter (e.g., VoIP or VTC-**Video Teleconferencing**) are given priority over packets in other queues.
24. Typically, some bandwidth is allocated by default to network control packets (e.g., ICMP and routing protocols), while best effort traffic might simply be given whatever bandwidth is left over.
25. Additional bandwidth management mechanisms may be used to further engineer performance, to include:
    - Traffic shaping (rate limiting):
        - token bucket
        - leaky bucket
    - Scheduling algorithms:
        - weighted fair queuing (WFQ)
        - class-based weighted fair queuing
        - weighted round robin (WRR)
        - deficit weighted round robin (DWRR)
    - congestion avoidance:
        - RED, WRED - Lessens the possibility of port queue buffer tail-drops and this lowers the likelihood of TCP global synchronization
        - Policing (marking/dropping the packet in excess of the committed traffic rate and burst size)
        - Explicit congestion notification
        - Buffer tuning

26. As mentioned, while **DiffServ** is used in many sophisticated enterprise networks, it has not been widely deployed in the Internet. Internet peering arrangements are already complex, and there appears to be no enthusiasm among providers for supporting QoS across peering connections, or agreement about what policies should be supported in order to do so.
27. QoS skeptics further point out that if you are dropping many packets on elastic low-QoS connections, you are already dangerously close to the point of congestion collapse on your inelastic high-QoS applications, without any way of further dropping traffic without violating traffic contracts.
28. One compelling example of the need for QoS on the Internet relates to this issue of congestion collapse.
29. The Internet relies on congestion avoidance protocols, as built in to TCP, to reduce traffic load under conditions that would otherwise lead to Internet Meltdown. QoS applications such as VoIP and IPTV, because they require largely constant bitrates cannot use TCP, and cannot otherwise reduce their traffic rate to help prevent meltdown either.
30. QoS contracts limit traffic that can be offered to the Internet and thereby enforce traffic shaping that can prevent it from becoming overloaded, hence they are an indispensable part of the Internet's ability to handle a mix of real-time and non-real-time traffic without meltdown.
31. Asynchronous Transfer Mode (ATM) network protocol has an elaborate framework to plug in QoS mechanisms of choice.
32. Shorter data units and built-in QoS were some of the unique selling points of ATM in the telecommunications applications such as video on demand, voice over IP.

5.2.10 QoS Priority Levels

Priority Level	Traffic Type
0	Best Effort
1	Background
2	Standard (Spare)
3	Excellent Load (Business Critical)
4	Controlled Load (Streaming Multimedia)
5	Video (Interactive Media) (Less than 100 ms latency and jitter)
6	Voice (Interactive Voice) (Less than 10 ms latency and jitter)
7	Network Control Reserved Traffic (Lowest latency and jitter)

5.2.11 QoS-Enabled Solutions

In brief, QoS addresses latency, jitter, and packet-drop issues by supporting the following components and features on typical network devices:

- Classifying and marking traffic such that network devices can differentiate traffic flows.
- Traffic conditioning to tailor traffic flows to specific traffic behavior and throughput.
- Marking traffic rates above specific thresholds as lower priority.
- Dropping packets when rates reach specific thresholds.
- Scheduling packets such that higher-priority packets transmit from output queues before lower-priority packets.
- Managing output queues such that lower-priority packets awaiting transmit do not monopolize buffer space.

Applying QoS components and features to an enterprise or service provider network provides for deterministic traffic behavior. In other words, QoS-enabled infrastructures allow you to do the following:

- Predict response times for end-to-end packet flows, I/O operations, data operations, transactions, etc.
- Correctly manage and determine abilities of jitter-sensitive applications such as audio and video applications.
- Streamline delay-sensitive applications such as VoIP.
- Control packet loss during times of inevitable congestion.
- Configure traffic priorities across the entire network.
- Support applications or network requirements that entail dedicated bandwidth.
- Monitor and avoid network congestion.
- The next section discusses the two QoS service models that are the building blocks of any QoS implementation.

5.2.12 QoS Service Models

1. The two QoS architectures used in IP networks when designing a QoS solution are the IntServ and DiffServ models.

2. The QoS service models differ by two characteristics: how the models enable applications to send data, and the way in which networks attempt to deliver the respective data with a specified level of service.

3. A third method of service is best-effort service, which is essentially the default behavior of the network device without any QoS. In summary, the following list restates these three basic levels of service for QoS:

- **Best-effort service:** The standard form of connectivity without any guarantees. This type of service, in reference to Catalyst switches, uses first-in, first-out (FIFO) queues, which simply transmit packets as they arrive in a queue with no preferential treatment.
- **Integrated services:** IntServ, also known as hard QoS, is an absolute reservation of services. In other words, the IntServ model implies that traffic flows are reserved explicitly by all intermediate systems and resources.
- **Differentiated services:** DiffServ, also known as soft QoS, is class-based, where some classes of traffic receive preferential handling over other traffic classes. Differentiated services use statistical preferences, not a hard guarantee like integrated services. In other words, DiffServ categorizes traffic and then sorts it into queues of various efficiencies.

Choosing the type of service to use in a multilayer-switched network depends on the following factors:
- Application support
- Technology upgrade speed and path
- Cost

5.2.13 WAN QoS

The QoS configuration and application differs between high-speed interfaces on switches and low-speed WAN on routers or WAN modules of switches. This section highlights a few QoS configurations and features that are applicable to low-speed serial interfaces. Specifically, this section introduces weighted fair queueing (WFQ) and low-latency queuing (LLQ).

5.2.13.1 Weighted Fair Queueing

Flow-based and class-based WFQ applies priority (or weights) to identified traffic to classify traffic into conversations and to determine how much bandwidth each conversation is allowed relative to other conversations. WFQ classifies traffic into different flows based on such characteristics as source and destination address, protocol, and port and socket of the session. WFQ is the default queueing mechanism for E1 and slower links.

Class-based WFQ (CBWFQ) extends the standard WFQ functionality to provide support for user-defined traffic classes. This enables you to specify the exact amount of bandwidth to be allocated for a specific class of traffic. Taking into account available bandwidth on the interface, you can configure up to 64 classes and control distribution among them.

5.2.13.2 Low-Latency Queueing

The distributed LLQ feature brings the ability to specify low-latency behavior for a traffic class. LLQ allows delay-sensitive data to be dequeued and sent first, before packets in other queues are dequeued, giving delay-sensitive data preferential treatment over other traffic.

The **priority** command is used to allow delay-sensitive data to be dequeued and sent first. LLQ enables use of a single priority queue within which individual classes of traffic are placed.

LLQ offers these features:

- LLQ supports multiple traffic types over various Layer 2 technologies, including High-Level Data Link Control (HDLC), Point-to-Point Protocol (PPP), ATM, and Frame Relay.
- All classes are policed to bandwidth to ensure that other traffic is serviced.
- The rate limit is per class, even if multiple classes point traffic to a priority queue.
- Over subscription of bandwidth is not allowed for the priority class.
- No WRED support is provided on priority classes. WRED is allowed only on bandwidth classes.
- Bandwidth and priority are mutually exclusive.

5.3 Delay in Telecom Networks

Understanding Delay in Packet Voice Networks

- When you design networks that transport voice over packet, frame, or cell infrastructures, it is important to understand and account for the delay components in the network.
- If you account correctly for all potential delays, it ensures that overall network performance is acceptable.
- Overall voice quality is a function of many factors that include the compression algorithm, errors and frame loss, echo cancellation, and delay.
- This section explains the sources of delay when you use router/gateways over packet networks.
- Though the examples are geared to Frame Relay, the concepts are applicable to Voice over IP (VoIP) and Voice over ATM (VoATM) networks as well.

5.3.1 Basic Voice Flow
The flow of a compressed voice circuit is shown in Fig. 5.1.

- The analog signal from the telephone is digitized into pulse code modulation (PCM) signals by the voice coder-decoder (codec).
- The PCM samples are then passed to the compression algorithm, which compresses the voice into a packet format for transmission across the WAN.
- On the far side of the cloud, the exact same functions are performed in reverse order. The entire flow is shown in Fig. 5.1.

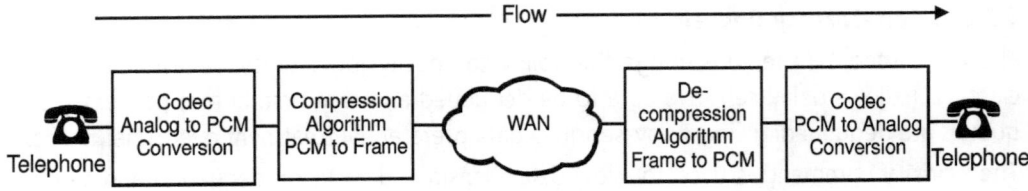

Fig. 5.1: End-to-End Voice Flow

- Based on how the network is configured, the router/gateway can perform both the codec and compression functions or only one of them.
- For example, if an analog voice system is used, then the router/gateway performs the codec function and the compression function as shown in Fig. 5.2.

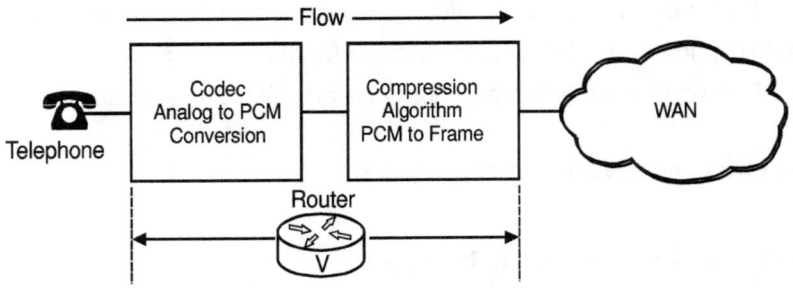

Fig. 5.2: Codec Function in Router/Gateway

If a digital PBX is used, the PBX performs the codec function and the Router processes the PCM samples passed to it by the PBX. An example is shown in Fig. 5.3.

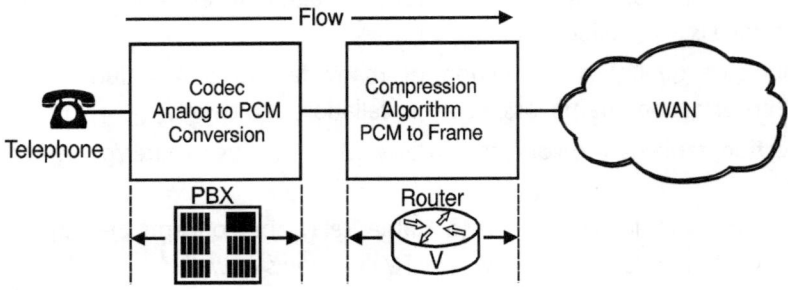

Fig. 5.3: Codec Function in PBX

5.3.2 How Voice Compression Works

- The high complexity compression algorithms used in router/gateways analyze a block of PCM samples delivered by the Voice codec.
- These blocks vary in length based on the coder. For example, the basic block size used by a G.729 algorithm is 10 ms whereas the basic block size used by the G.723.1 algorithm is 30 ms. An example of how a G.729 compression system works is shown in Fig. 5.4.

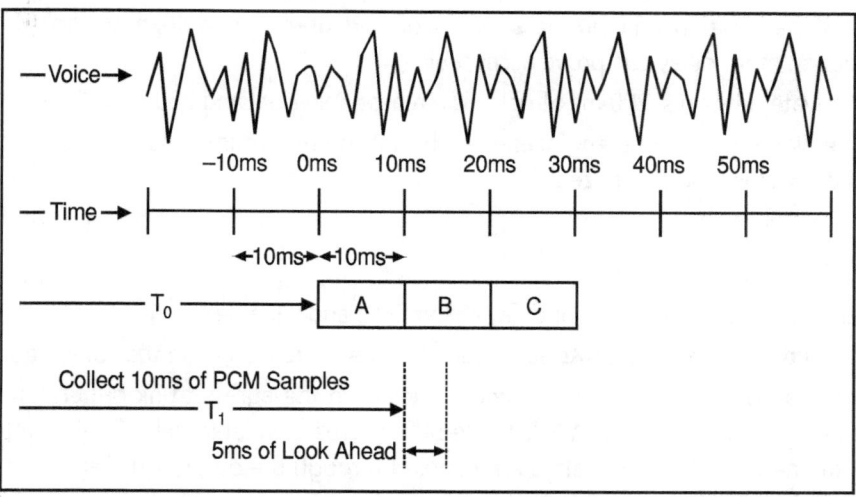

Fig. 5.4: Voice Compression

- The analog voice stream is digitized into PCM samples and delivered to the compression algorithm in 10 ms increments. The look ahead is discussed in Algorithmic Delay.

5.3.3 Standards for Delay Limits

The International Telecommunication Union (ITU) considers network delay for voice applications in Recommendation G.114. This recommendation defines three bands of one-way delay as shown in Table 5.3.

Table 5.3: Delay Specifications

Range in Milliseconds	Description
0-150	Acceptable for most user applications.
150-400	Acceptable provided that administrators are aware of the transmission time and the impact it has on the transmission quality of user applications.
Above 400	Unacceptable for general network planning purposes. However, it is recognized that in some exceptional cases this limit is exceeded.

- **Note:** These recommendations are for connections with echo adequately controlled. This implies that echo cancellers are used. Echo cancellers are required when one-way delay exceeds 25 ms (G.131).
- These recommendations are oriented for national telecom administrations.
- Therefore, these are more stringent than when normally applied in private voice networks.

- When the location and business needs of end users are well-known to the network designer, more delay can prove acceptable.
- For private networks, 200 ms of delay is a reasonable goal and 250 ms a limit.
- All networks need to be engineered such that the maximum expected voice connection delay is known and minimized.

5.3.4 Sources of Delay

There are two distinct types of delay called fixed and variable.
- **Fixed delay components** add directly to the overall delay on the connection.
- **Variable delays arise** from queuing delays in the egress trunk buffers on the serial port connected to the WAN. These buffers create variable delays, called jitter, across the network. Variable delays are handled through the de-jitter buffer at the receiving router/gateway.

Fig. 5.5 identifies all the fixed and variable delay sources in the network. Each source is described in detail in this section.

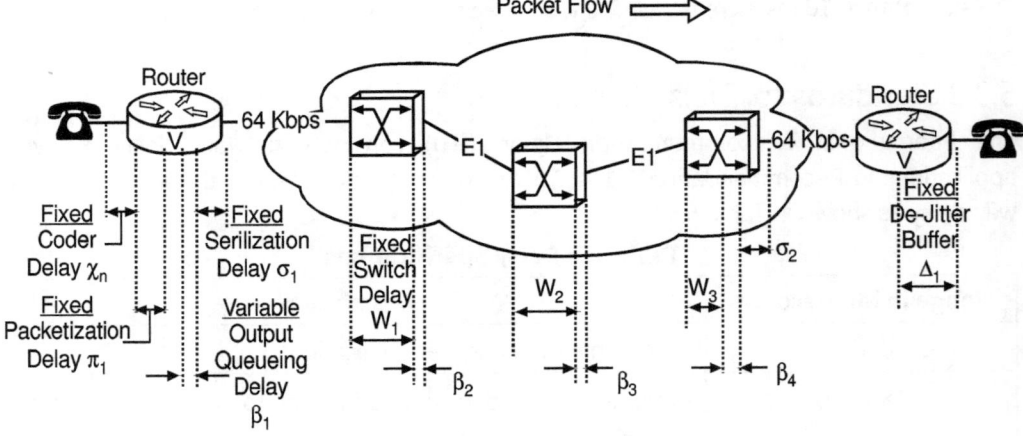

Fig. 5.5: Delay Sources

Different Delays are

1. Coder (Processing) Delay
2. Algorithmic Delay
3. Packetization Delay
4. Serialization Delay
5. Queueing/Buffering Delay
6. Network Switching Delay
7. De-Jitter Delay

5.3.4.1 Coder (Processing) Delay

- Coder delay is the time taken by the digital signal processor (DSP) to compress a block of PCM samples.
- This is also called processing delay (χ_n). This delay varies with the voice coder used and processor speed. For example, algebraic code excited linear prediction (ACELP) algorithms analyze a 10 ms block of PCM samples, and then compress them.
- The compression time for a Conjugate Structure Algebraic Code Excited Linear Prediction (CS-ACELP) process ranges from 2.5 ms to 10 ms based on the loading of the DSP processor.
- If the DSP is fully loaded with four voice channels, the Coder delay is 10 ms. If the DSP is loaded with only one voice channel, the Coder delay is 2.5 ms. For design purposes, use the worst case time of 10 ms.
- Decompression time is roughly ten percent of the compression time for each block. However, the decompression time is proportional to the number of samples per frame because of the presence of multiple samples.
- Consequently, the worst-case decompression time for a frame with three samples is 3×1 ms or 3 ms. Usually, two or three blocks of compressed G.729 output are put in one frame while one sample of compressed G.723.1 output is sent in a single frame.

Best and worst case coder delays are shown in Table 5.4.

Table 5.4: Best and Worst Case Processing Delay

Coder	Rate	Required Sample Block	Best Case Coder Delay	Worst Case Coder Delay
ADPCM, G.726	32 Kbps	10 ms	2.5 ms	10 ms
CS-ACELP, G.729A	8.0 Kbps	10 ms	2.5 ms	10 ms
MP-MLQ, G.723.1	6.3 Kbps	30 ms	5 ms	20 ms
MP-ACELP, G.723.1	5.3 Kbps	30 ms	5 ms	20 ms

5.3.4.2 Algorithmic Delay

- The compression algorithm relies on known voice characteristics to correctly process sample block N.
- The algorithm must have some knowledge of what is in block N+1 in order to accurately reproduce sample block N.
- This look ahead, which is really an additional delay, is called algorithmic delay. This effectively increases the length of the compression block.
- This happens repeatedly, such that block N+1 looks into block N+2, and so forth and so on. The net effect is a 5 ms addition to the overall delay on the link.

- This means that the total time required to process a block of information is 10 m with a 5 ms constant overhead factor. See Fig. 5.4: Voice Compression.
  1. Algorithmic Delay for G.726 coders is 0 ms.
  2. Algorithmic Delay for G.729 coders is 5 ms.
  3. Algorithmic Delay for G.723.1 coders is 7.5 ms
- For the examples in the remainder of this section, assume G.729 compression with a 30 ms/30 byte payload. In order to facilitate design, and take a conservative approach, the tables given in the remainder of this document assume the worst case coder delay.
- The coder delay, decompression delay, and algorithmic delay is lumped into one factor which is called the coder delay.
- The equation used to generate the lumped Coder Delay Parameter is:

Equation 1: Lumped Coder Delay Parameter

```
(Worst Case Compression Time Per Block)
                +
(De-Compression Time Per Block)
  × (Number of Blocks in Frame)
                +
        (Algorithmic Delay)

= "Lumped" Coder Delay Parameter
```

The lumped Coder delay for G.729 that is used for the remainder of this document is:

Worst Case Compression Time Per Block: 10 ms

Decompression Time Per Block × 3 Blocks 3 ms

Algorithmic Delay 5 ms --------------------------

Total (χ) 18 ms

5.3.4.3 Packetization Delay

- Packetization delay (π_n) is the time taken to fill a packet payload with encoded/compressed speech.
- This delay is a function of the sample block size required by the vocoder and the number of blocks placed in a single frame.
- Packetization delay can also be called Accumulation delay, as the voice samples accumulate in a buffer before they are released.
- As a general rule, you need to strive for a packetization delay of no more than 30 ms.
- In the router/gateways, you need to use these figures from Table 5.5 based on configured payload size.

Table 5.5: Common Packetization

Coder	Speed	Payload Size (Bytes)	Packetization Delay (ms)	Payload Size (Bytes)	Packetization Delay (ms)
PCM, G.711	64 Kbps	160	20	240	30
ADPCM, G.726	32 Kbps	80	20	120	30
CS-ACELP, G.729	8.0 Kbps	20	20	30	30
MP-MLQ, G.723.1	6.3 Kbps	24	24	60	48
MP-ACELP, G.723.1	5.3 Kbps	20	30	60	60

You have to balance the Packetization delay against the CPU load. The lower the delay, the higher the frame rate, and the higher the load on the CPU. On some older platforms, 20 ms payloads can potentially strain the main CPU.

Pipeline Delay in the Packetization Process

Though each voice sample experiences both algorithmic delay and packetization delay, in reality, the processes overlap and there is a net benefit effect from this pipelining. Consider the example shown in Fig. 5.6.

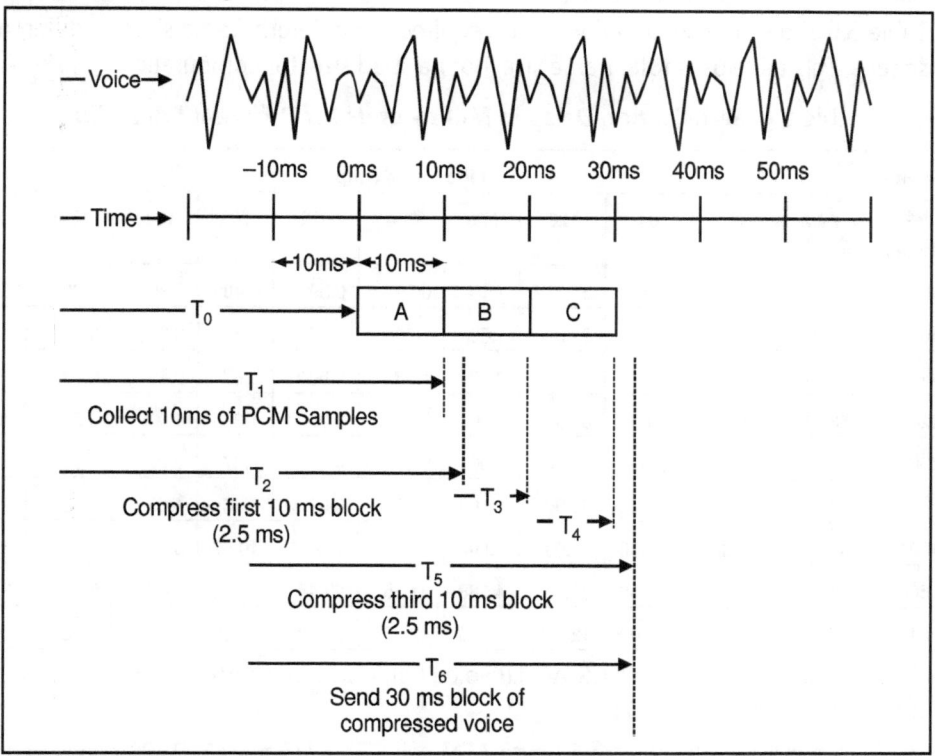

Fig. 5.6: Pipelining and Packetization

The top line of the figure depicts a sample voice wave form. The second line is a time scale in 10 ms increments. At T_0, the CS-ACELP algorithm begins to collect PCM samples from the codec. At T_1, the algorithm has collected its first 10 ms block of samples and begins to compress it. At T_2, the first block of samples has been compressed. In this example, the compression time is 2.5 ms, as indicated by $T_2 - T_1$.

The second and third blocks are collected at T_3 and T_4. The third block is compressed at T_5. The packet is assembled and sent (assumed to be instantaneous) at T_6. Due to the pipelined nature of the Compression and Packetization processes, the delay from when the process begins to when the voice frame is sent is $T_6 - T_0$, or approximately 32.5 ms.

For illustration, this example is based on best case delay. If the worst case delay is used, the figure is 40 ms, 10 ms for Coder delay and 30 ms for Packetization delay.

Note that these examples neglect to include algorithmic delay.

5.3.4.4 Serialization Delay

- Serialization delay (σ_n) is the fixed delay required to clock a voice or data frame onto the network interface.
- It is directly related to the clock rate on the trunk. At low clock speeds and small frame sizes, the extra flag needed to separate frames is significant.
- Table 5.6 shows the serialization delay required for different frame sizes at different line speeds. This table uses total frame size, not payload size, for computation.

Table 5.6: Serialization Delay in Milliseconds for Different Frame Sizes

Frame Size (bytes)	Line Speed (Kbps)									
	19.2	56	64	128	256	384	512	768	1024	1544	2048
38	15.83	5.43	4.75	2.38	1.19	0.79	0.59	0.40	0.30	0.20	0.15
48	20.00	6.86	6.00	3.00	1.50	1.00	0.75	0.50	0.38	0.25	0.19
64	26.67	9.14	8.00	4.00	2.00	1.33	1.00	0.67	0.50	0.33	0.25
128	53.33	18.29	16.00	8.00	4.00	2.67	2.00	1.33	1.00	0.66	0.50
256	106.67	36.57	32.00	16.00	8.00	5.33	4.00	2.67	2.00	1.33	1.00
512	213.33	73.14	64.00	32.00	16.00	10.67	8.00	5.33	4.00	2.65	2.00
1024	426.67	149.29	128.00	64.00	32.00	21.33	16.00	10.67	8.00	5.31	4.00
1500	625.00	214.29	187.50	93.75	46.88	31.25	23.44	15.63	11.72	7.77	5.86
2048	853.33	292.57	256.00	128.00	64.00	42.67	32.00	21.33	16.00	10.61	8.00

In the table, on a 64 Kbps line, a CS-ACELP voice frame with a length of 38 bytes (37 + 1 flag) has a serialization delay of 4.75 ms.

Note: The serialization delay for a 53 byte ATM cell (T1: 0.275 ms, E1: 0.207 ms) is negligible due to the high line speed and small cell size.

5.3.4.5 Queueing/Buffering Delay

- After the compressed voice payload is built, a header is added and the frame is queued for transmission on the network connection.
- Voice needs to have absolute priority in the router/gateway. Therefore, a voice frame must only wait for either a data frame that already plays out, or for other voice frames ahead of it.
- Essentially the voice frame waits for the serialization delay of any preceding frames in the output queue.
- Queueing delay (β_n) is a variable delay and is dependent on the trunk speed and the state of the queue. There are random elements associated with the queueing delay.
- For example, assume that you are on a 64 Kbps line, and that you are queued behind one data frame (48 bytes) and one voice frame (42 bytes).
- Because there is a random nature as to how much of the 48 byte frame has played out, you can safely assume, on average, that half the data frame has been played out.
- Based on the data from the serialization table, your data frame component is 6 ms * 0.5 = 3 ms. When you add the time for another voice frame ahead in the queue (5.25 ms), it gives a total time of 8.25 ms queuing delay.
- How one characterizes the queueing delay is up to the network engineer. Generally, one needs to design for the worst case scenario and then tune performance after the network is installed.
- The more voice lines available to the users, the higher the probability that the average voice packet waits in the queue. The voice frame, because of the priority structure, never waits behind more than one data frame.

5.3.4.6 Network Switching Delay

- The public frame relay or ATM network that interconnects the endpoint locations is the source of the largest delays for voice connections. Network Switching Delays (ω_n) are also the most difficult to quantify.
- If wide-area connectivity is provided by typical company equipment, or some other private network, it is possible to identify the individual components of delay.
- In general, the fixed components are from propagation delays on the trunks within the network, and variable delays are from queueing delays clocking frames into and out of intermediate switches.
- In order to estimate propagation delay, a popular estimate of 10 microseconds/mile or 6 microseconds/km (G.114) is widely used.
- However, intermediate multiplexing equipment, backhauling, microwave links, and other factors found in carrier networks create many exceptions.

- The other significant component of delay is from queueing within the wide-area network. In a private network, it can be possible to measure existing queueing delays or to estimate a per-hop budget within the wide-area network.
- Typical carrier delays for US frame relay connections are 40 ms fixed and 25 ms variable for a total worst case delay of 65 ms. For simplicity, in examples 6-1, 6-2, and 6-3, any low speed serialization delays in the 40 ms fixed delay are included.
- These are figures published by US frame relay carriers, in order to cover anywhere to anywhere coverage within the United States. It is to be expected that two locations which are geographically closer than the worst case have better delay performance, but carriers normally document just the worst case.
- Frame relay carriers sometimes offer premium services. These services are usually for voice or Systems Network Architecture (SNA) traffic, where the network delay is guaranteed and less than the standard service level.
- For instance, a US carrier recently announced such a service with an overall delay limit of 50 ms, rather than the standard service's 65 ms.

5.3.4.7 De-Jitter Delay
- Because speech is a constant bit-rate service, the jitter from all the variable delays must be removed before the signal leaves the network.
- In typical router/gateways this is accomplished with a de-jitter (Δ_n) buffer at the far-end (receiving) router/gateway.
- **The de-jitter buffer transforms the variable delay into a fixed delay.**
- It holds the first sample received for a period of time before it plays it out. This holding period is known as the initial play out delay.

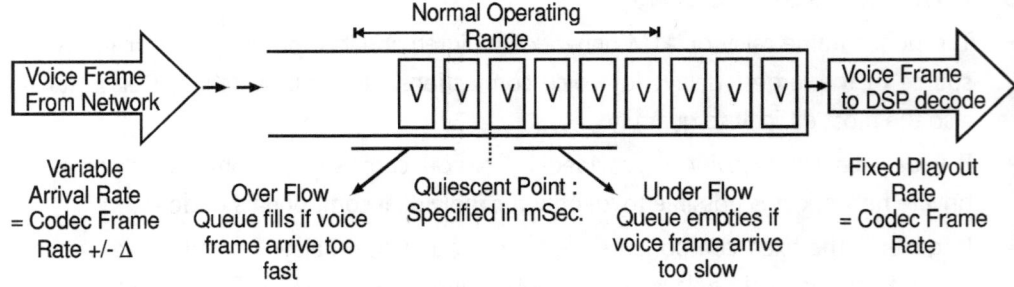

Fig. 5.7: De-Jitter Buffer Operation

- It is essential to handle properly the de-jitter buffer.
- If samples are held for too short a time, variations in delay can potentially cause the buffer to under-run and cause gaps in the speech.

- If the sample is held for too long a time, the buffer can overrun, and the dropped packets again cause gaps in the speech.
- Lastly, if packets are held for too long a time, the overall delay on the connection can rise to unacceptable levels.
- The optimum initial play out delay for the de-jitter buffer is equal to the total variable delay along the connection. This is shown in Fig. 5.8.

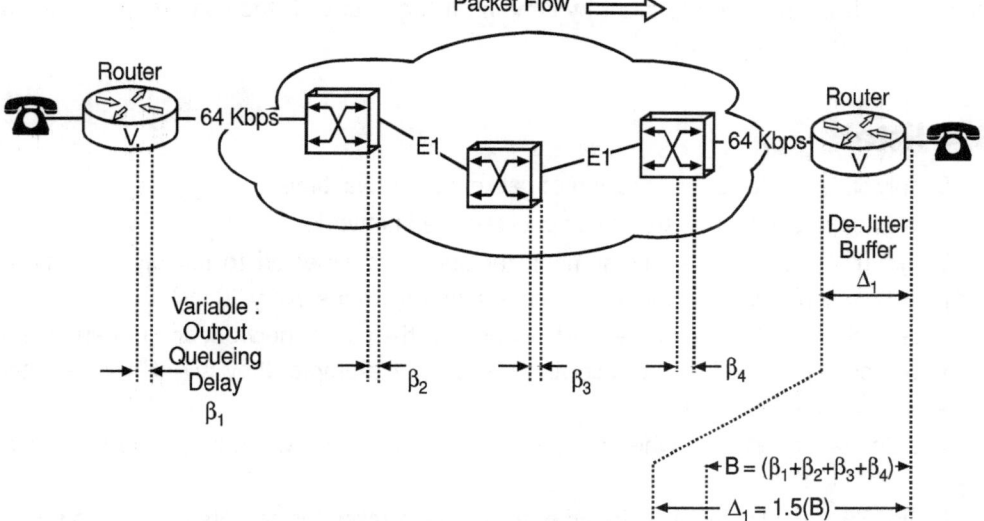

Fig. 5.8: Variable Delay and the De-Jitter Buffer

Note: The de-jitter buffers can be adaptive, but the maximum delay is fixed. When adaptive buffers are configured, the delay becomes a variable figure. However, the maximum delay can be used as a worst case for design purposes.
- The initial playout delay is configurable. The maximum depth of the buffer before it overflows is normally set to 1.5 or 2.0 times this value.
- If the 40 ms nominal delay setting is used, the first voice sample received when the de-jitter buffer is empty is held for 40 ms before it is played out.
- This implies that a subsequent packet received from the network can be as much as 40 ms delayed (with respect to the first packet) without any loss of voice continuity.
- If it is delayed more than 40 ms, the de-jitter buffer empties and the next packet received is held for 40 ms before play out to reset the buffer. This results in a gap in the voice played out for about 40 ms.
- The actual contribution of de-jitter buffer to delay is the initial play out delay of the de-jitter buffer plus the actual amount the first packet was buffered in the network.
- The worst case is twice the de-jitter buffer initial delay (assumption is that the first packet through the network experienced only minimum buffering delay).

- In practice, over a number of network switch hops, it is probably not necessary to assume the worst case.
- The calculations in the examples in the remainder of this document increase the initial play out delay by a factor of 1.5 to allow for this effect.
- The concept is applicable for all Telecom Networks.

Note: In the receiving router/gateway, there is delay through the decompression function. However, this is taken into account by lumping it together with the compression processing delay as discussed previously.

5.4 Jitter

- Simply stated, *jitter* is the variation of packet interarrival time.
- Jitter is one issue that exists only in packet-based networks.
- While in a packet voice environment, the sender is expected to reliably transmit voice packets at a regular interval (for example, send one frame every 20 ms).
- These voice packets can be delayed throughout the packet network and not arrive at that same regular interval at the receiving station (for example, they might not be received every 20 ms; see Fig. 5.9).
- The difference between when the packet is expected and when it is actually received is *jitter*.
- In Fig. 5.9, you can see that the amount of time it takes for packets A and B to send and receive is equal (D1=D2).
- Packet C encounters delay in the network, however, and is received *after* it is expected.

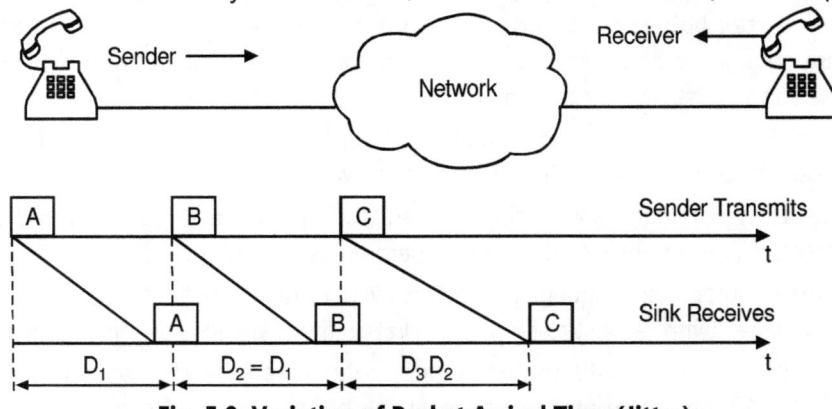

Fig. 5.9: Variation of Packet Arrival Time (Jitter)

- This is why a *jitter buffer*, which conceals interarrival packet delay variation, is necessary.
- Voice packets in IP networks have highly variable packet-interarrival intervals.
- Recommended practice is to count the number of packets that arrive late and create a ratio of these packets to the number of packets that are successfully processed.

- You can then use this ratio to adjust the jitter buffer to target a predetermined, allowable late-packet ratio. This adaptation of jitter buffer sizing is effective in compensating for delays.
- Note that jitter and total delay are *not* the same thing, although having plenty of jitter in a packet network can increase the amount of total delay in the network.
- This is because the more jitter you have, the larger your jitter buffer needs to be to compensate for the unpredictable nature of the packet network.
- Most DSPs do not have infinite jitter buffers to handle excessive network delays.
- Sometimes it is better to just drop packets or have fixed-length buffers instead of creating unwanted delays in the jitter buffers.
- If your data network is engineered well and you take the proper precautions, jitter is usually not a major problem and the jitter buffer does not significantly contribute to the total end-to-end delay.

5.4.1 Handling of Jitter in Packet Voice Networks

- Jitter is defined as a variation in the delay of received packets.
- At the sending side, packets are sent in a continuous stream with the packets spaced evenly apart.
- Due to network congestion, improper queuing, or configuration errors, this steady stream can become lumpy, or the delay between each packet can vary instead of remaining constant.
- The concept is applicable for all Telecom Networks.
- Fig. 5.10 illustrates how a steady stream of packets is handled.

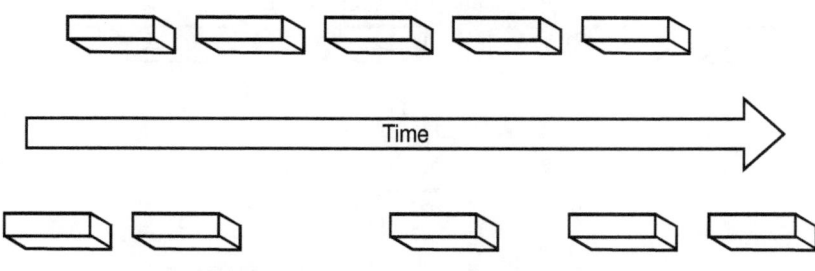

Fig. 5.10

- When a router receives a Real-Time Protocol (RTP) audio stream for Voice over IP (VoIP), it must compensate for the jitter that is encountered.
- The mechanism that handles this function is the playout delay buffer.
- The playout delay buffer must buffer these packets and then play them out in a steady stream to the digital signal processors (DSPs) to be converted back to an analog audio stream.

- The playout delay buffer is also sometimes referred to as the de-jitter buffer.

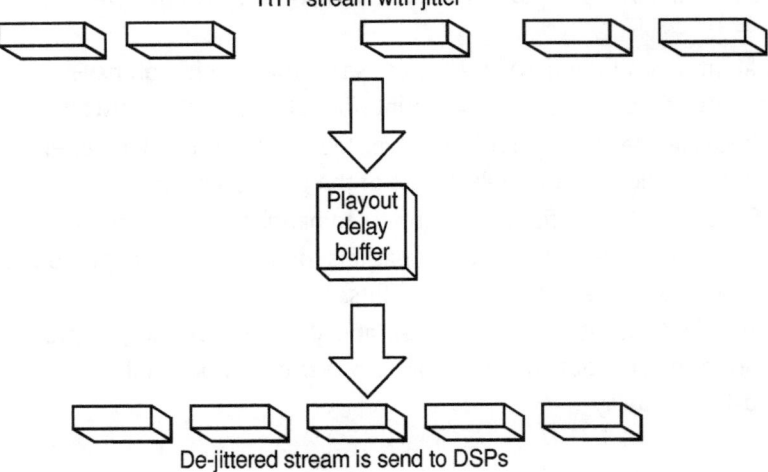

- **Fig. 5.11: Illustrates how jitter is handled**.
- If the jitter is so large that it causes packets to be received out of the range of this buffer, the out-of-range packets are discarded and dropouts are heard in the audio.
- For losses as small as one packet, the DSP interpolates what it thinks the audio should be and no problem is audible.
- When jitter exceeds what the DSP can do to make up for the missing packets, audio problems are heard.
- The concept is applicable for all Telecom Networks.

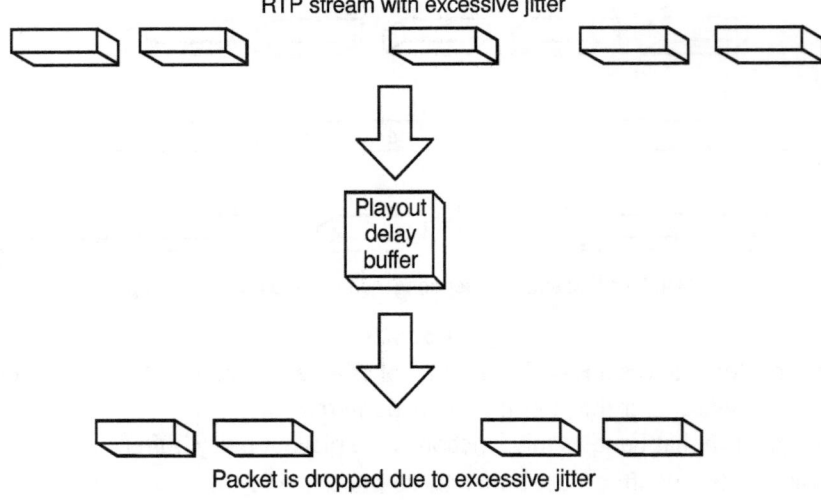

Fig. 5.12: Illustrates how excessive jitter is handled

5.4.2 Jitter in a Frame Relay Environment
Three parameters need to be addressed to find the jitter in a Frame Relay environment:
- Traffic Shaping
- Fragmentation
- Queueing

5.4.2.1 Traffic Shaping
- You need to ensure that you are shaping the traffic that leaves the router to the actual Committed Information Rate (CIR) that the carrier provides.
- Verify this by looking at the Frame Relay statistics and check with the carrier. The first place to look is at the Frame Relay statistics.
- What you should be concerned with in the command output are the values that show if there has been congestion in the frame network.
- These values are the forward explicit congestion notification (FECN), backward explicit congestion notification (BECN) and discard eligible (DE) parameters.
- You should be concerned with only input packets since Cisco does not send any of these.
- You may see one or more of these values incrementing. This depends on the type and configuration of the frame switches that the provider uses.
- In general terms, if you have Frame Relay traffic shaping, and are configured for the same CIR as the circuit, you should never see these values increment. If you do see these values increment, and you match the true CIR of the circuit, something in the frame provider's network is not configured properly.
- One good example of this is if you purchase a zero CIR circuit, but have a burst value. Some providers sell the zero CIR permanent virtual circuit (PVC).
- This is fine for data, but causes problems with voice quality. If you look at the command output from a zero CIR circuit, the number of DE or FECN packets equals the number of input packets.
- To take this a step further, if you have a PVC that is provisioned by the carrier to be 128 kbs and the CIR of the router is set to 512 kbs, you see these counters increment (at a slower rate).
- Remember that you are only looking at packets that come into the router interface and that this rate is controlled by the traffic-shaping parameters configured on the router at the opposite end of the PVC.
- Conversely, you control what is input to the other router by which traffic-shaping parameters are configured on the local end.
- It is very important that you not exceed the CIR for the PVC that is provisioned by the carrier. You can be below this CIR without having problems. However, if you exceed it, you will see congestion.

- The reason you are able to see the congestion in this fashion is because the CIR that is configured for a specific PVC on a frame switch dictates the rate that traffic is passed by that switch (for that PVC).
- When the configured CIR on the frame switch is exceeded by the actual data rate it receives, it must buffer the frames that exceed the CIR until the capacity is available to forward the buffered packets.
- Any packet that is buffered gets either the DE bit set or the FECN bit set by the frame switch.
- As always, you also want to closely examine the interface statistics, and look for drops or errors to be sure that everything functions correctly at the physical layer.
- How this relates to jitter is if this occurs, and some packets need to be buffered in the frame network, they have a longer latency in getting to the remote router.
- However, when there is no congestion, they get through in the latency time that you normally expect.
- This causes a variation in the delta time between packets received at the remote router. Hence, jitter.
- The concept is applicable for all Telecom Networks.

5.4.2.2 Fragmentation
- Fragmentation associates more with serialization delay than with jitter.
- However, under certain conditions, it can be the cause of jitter.
- Fragmentation should always be configured in the Frame Relay map class when doing packetized voice.
- The configuration of this parameter has two effects on the interface.
- The first effect is that all packets larger than the size specified are fragmented.
- The second effect is less apparent, but is just as important.
- Without fragmentation, the queuing strategy shown in the output of the **show interface x** command shows that first in first out (FIFO) queueing is in use.
- Once fragmentation is applied to the Frame Relay map class, the output of this command shows the queueing strategy as dual-FIFO.
- This creates the priority queue that is used for voice traffic on the interface.
- If you still experience jitter problems at the recommended value, lower the fragmentation value one step at a time until voice quality becomes acceptable.
- The concept is applicable for all Telecom Networks.

5.4.2.3 Queueing
1. There are two generally accepted queueing methods used for VoIP traffic in this type of environment:
   - IP RTP Priority Queueing
   - Low Latency Queueing

2. One method or the other should be used, they should not both be configured.
3. If the queueing operation looks correct according to the documentation, then you can conclude that queueing works properly and the problem lies elsewhere.
4. Queueing is generally not a cause of jitter since the variations in delay created by it are relatively small.
5. However, if VoIP packets do not get queued properly and there is data on the same circuit, jitter can result.
6. The concept is applicable for all Telecom Networks.

Conclusion
1. Jitter is a variation in packet latency for voice packets.
2. Jitter is generally caused by congestion in the IP network.
3. The congestion can occur either at the router interfaces or in a provider or carrier network if the circuit has not been provisioned correctly.
4. The DSPs inside the router can make up for some jitter, but can be overcome by excessive jitter.
5. This results in poor voice quality.
6. The cause of jitter is that a packet gets queued or delayed somewhere in the circuit, where there was no delay or queueing for other packets.
7. This causes a variation in latency.
8. Jitter can be caused both by router misconfiguration and by PVC misconfiguration by the carrier or provider.

5.5 Bandwidth in Telecom Networks

Bandwidth is a central concept in many fields, including information theory, radio communications, signal processing, and Telecom Networks.

Definition 1: Bandwidth
Is a measure of frequency range, measured in hertz.

Example: The range of frequencies within which the performance of the antenna, with respect to some characteristics, conforms to a specified standard. (2.4-2.5 GHz antenna has 100 MHz bandwidth).

Definition 2: Bandwidth
The amount of data that can be transmitted in a fixed amount of time, expressed in bits per second (bps) or bytes per second.

Example: A V.90 modem supports a maximum theoretical bandwidth of 56 Kbps. Fast Ethernet supports a theoretical maximum bandwidth of 100 Mbps.

Network bandwidth is not the only factor that determines the "speed" of a network as perceived by the end user. The other key element of network performance, **latency**, also affects network applications in important ways. Manufacturers of network hardware have done a great job of promoting the concept of bandwidth. Virtually everyone knows the bandwidth rating of their modem or their broadband Internet service. Essentially, bandwidth represents the capacity of the connection, and it is obvious that the greater the capacity, the more likely that greater performance will follow.

Bandwidth can refer to both actual and theoretical throughput, and it is important to distinguish between the two. For example, a V.90 modem supports 56 Kbps of **peak bandwidth**, but due to limitations of the telephone lines and other factors, it is impossible for a home dial-up network to actually achieve this level. Likewise a Fast Ethernet network theoretically supports 100 Mbps of bandwidth but this level can never be achieved in practical use thanks to overhead in the hardware and in the computer's operating system.

Analog Systems

- For analog signals, which can be mathematically viewed as a function of time, bandwidth is the width, measured in hertz, of a frequency range in which the signal's Fourier transform is nonzero.
- This definition can be relaxed wherein bandwidth would be the range of frequencies that the signal's Fourier transform has a power above a certain threshold, say 3 dB within the maximum value, in the frequency domain.
- Bandwidth of a signal is a measure of how rapidly it fluctuates with respect to time.
- Hence, the greater the bandwidth, the faster the variation in the signal.
- The word bandwidth applies to signals as described above, but it could also apply to systems.
- In the latter case, to say that a system has a certain bandwidth is a short-hand for saying that the transfer function of the system has a certain bandwidth.
- As an example, the 3 dB bandwidth of the function depicted in Fig. 5.13 is $f_2 - f_1$, whereas other definitions of bandwidth would yield a different answer.
- The fact that real baseband systems have both negative and positive frequencies can lead to confusion about bandwidth, since they are sometimes referred to only by the positive half, and one will occasionally see expressions such as $B = 2W$, where B is the total bandwidth, and W is the positive bandwidth.

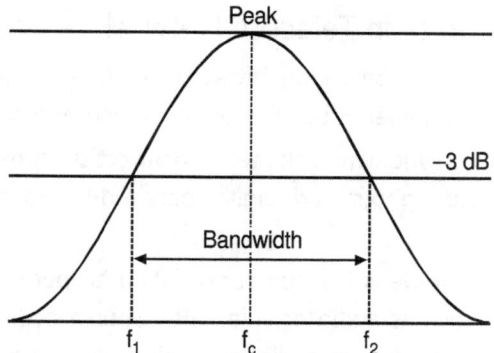

Fig. 5.13: 3dB bandwidth

- For instance, this signal would require a lowpass filter with cutoff frequency of at least W to stay intact. The bandwidth of an electronic filter is the part of the filter's frequency response that lies within 3 dB of the response at the center frequency of its peak.
- In signal processing and control theory, the bandwidth is the frequency at which the closed-loop system gain drops to −3 dB. In basic electric circuit theory when studying Band-pass and Band-reject filters, the bandwidth represents the distance between the two points in the frequency domain where the signal is $\frac{1}{\sqrt{2}}$ of the maximum signal strength.
- In photonics, the term bandwidth occurs in a variety of meanings.

Digital Systems

- In a digital communication system, bandwidth has a dual meaning.
- In the technical sense, it is a synonym for baud rate, the rate at which symbols may be transmitted through the system.
- It is also used in the colloquial sense to describe channel capacity, the rate at which bits may be transmitted through the system.
- Hence, a 66 MHz digital data bus with 32 separate data lines may properly be said to have a bandwidth of 66 MHz and a capacity of 2.1 Gbit/s but it would not be surprising to hear such a bus described as having a "bandwidth of 2.1 Gbit/s."
- Similar confusion exists for analog modems, where each symbol carries multiple bits of information so that a modem may transmit 56 kbit/s of information over a phone line with a bandwidth of only 12 kHz.
- In discrete time systems and digital signal processing, bandwidth is related to sampling rate according to the Nyquist-Shannon sampling theorem.
- Bandwidth is also used in the sense of commodity, referring to something limited or something costing money. Thus, communication costs bandwidth, and improper use of someone else's bandwidth may be called bandwidth theft.

5.5.1 Bandwidth/Bit rate in Telecom Network

- In telecommunications and computing, **bitrate** (sometimes written **bit rate**, **data rate** or as a variable R_{bit}) is the number of bits that are conveyed or processed per unit of time.
- Bit rate is often used as synonym to the terms **connection speed**, **transfer rate**, channel capacity, maximum throughput and digital bandwidth capacity of a communication system.
- In digital multimedia, *bitrate* is the number of bits used per unit of time to represent a continuous medium such as audio or video after source coding (data compression). In this sense, it corresponds to the term digital **bandwidth consumption**, or goodput.
- The concept is applicable for all Telecom Networks.
- The bit rate is quantified using the 'bit per second' (**bit/s** or **bps**) unit, often in conjunction with a SI prefix such as kilo (kbit/s or kbps), Mega (Mbit/s or Mbps), Giga (Gbit/s or Gbps) or Tera (Tbit/s or Tbps).

Progress

Looking at the development of transmission speeds, Moore's Law may be applied not only to transistor densities, but as well as to transmission speeds: bitrates doubled about every 18 months.

Improvement in Applied Bitrates:

year	WAN	LAN	WLAN
2005	16 M	1 G	100 M
2000	2 M	100 M	10 M
1995	128 k	10 M	1 M

5.5.2 Bitrates in Multimedia Communications

1. In digital multimedia communications, bitrate represents the amount of information, or detail, that is stored per unit of time of a recording. The bitrate depends on several factors:
    - the original material may be sampled at different frequencies.
    - the samples may use different numbers of bits.
    - the data may be encoded by different schemes.
    - the information may be digitally compressed by different algorithms or to different degrees.

2. Generally, choices are made about the above factors in order to achieve the desired trade-off between minimizing the bitrate and maximizing the quality of the material when it is played.
3. If lossy data compression is used on audio or visual data, differences from the original signal will be introduced; if the compression is substantial, or lossy data is decompressed and recompressed, this may become noticeable in the form of compression artifacts.
4. Whether these affect the perceived quality, and if so how much, depends on the compression scheme, encoder power, the characteristics of the input data, the listener's perceptions, the listener's familiarity with artifacts, and the listening or viewing environment.
5. Experts and audiophiles may detect artifacts in many cases in which the average listener would not. Some musicians enjoy the distinct artifacts of low bitrate (sub-FM quality) encoding and there is a growing scene of net labels distributing stylized low bitrate music.
6. The bitrates in this section are approximately the *minimum* that the *average* listener in a typical listening or viewing environment, when using the best available compression, would perceive as not significantly worse than the reference standard:

Audio (MP3)
- 32 kbit/s — MW (AM) quality
- 96 kbit/s — FM quality
- 128 - 160 kbit/s - Decent quality, difference can sometimes be obvious
- 192 kbit/s — Good quality, difference can only be heard by a few
- 224 - 320 kbit/s — High quality, nearly lossless quality

Other audio
- 4 kbit/s — minimum necessary for recognizable speech (using special-purpose speech codecs)
- 8 kbit/s — telephone quality (using speech codecs)
- 500 kbit/s–1 Mbit/s — lossless audio as used in formats such as FLAC (free lossless audio codec), WavPack or Monkey's Audio
- 1411 kbit/s — PCM (WAV) sound format of Compact Disc Digital Audio

Video (MPEG2)
- 16 kbit/s — videophone quality (minimum necessary for a consumer-acceptable "talking head" picture)
- 128 – 384 kbit/s — business-oriented videoconferencing system quality
- 1 Mbit/s — VHS quality
- 5 Mbit/s — DVD quality
- 15 Mbit/s — HDTV quality

5.5.3 Bandwidth in Broadband Networks

- A term that you hear often when discussing telecommunications is *bandwidth*. Bandwidth is a critical commodity.
- Historically, bandwidth has been very expensive, as it was based on the sharing of limited physical resources, such as twisted-pair copper cables and coax.
- *Bandwidth* is largely used today to refer to the capacity of a network or a telecom link, and it is generally measured in bits per second (bps).
- *Bandwidth* actually refers to the range of frequencies involved—that is, the difference between the lowest and highest frequencies supported—and the greater the range of frequencies, the greater the bandwidth, and hence the greater the number of bits per second, or information carried.
- The concept is applicable for all Telecom Networks.

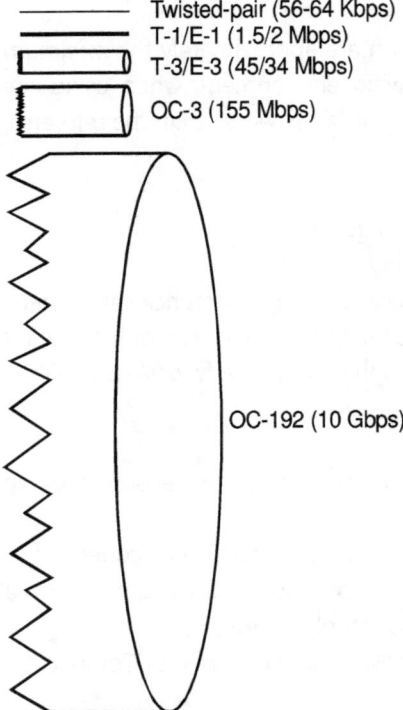

Fig. 5.14: Typical BW in Broadband Networks

5.6 Throughput

1. In communication networks, **throughput** is the amount of digital data per time unit that is delivered to a certain terminal in a network, from a network node, or from one node to another, for example via a communication link.

2. The throughput is usually measured in bit per second (bit/s or bps).
3. The **system throughput** or **aggregate throughput** is the sum of the data rates that are delivered to all terminals in a network.
4. Often **maximum throughput** is implied by the term **throughput**. The **maximum throughput** of a node or communication link is synonym to its **capacity**.
5. The maximum throughput is defined as the asymptotic throughput when the load (the amount of incoming data) is very large.
6. In packet switched systems where the load and the throughput are equal (where there are no packet drops), the maximum throughput may be defined as the load in bit/s when the delivery time (the latency) asymptotically reaches infinity.
7. The concept is applicable for all Telecom Networks.

5.6.1 Channel Utilization

1. The **channel utilization** in percentage is the achieved throughput related to the physical data rate in bit/s of a digital communication channel (also known as the network access connection speed, the digital bandwidth or the channel capacity).
2. For example, if the throughput is 70 Mbit/s in a 100 Mbit/s Ethernet connection, the channel utilization is 70%.
3. In a point-to-point or point-to-multipoint communication link, where only one terminal is transmitting, the maximum throughput is often equivalent to or very near the physical data rate (the channel capacity), since the channel utilization can be almost 100% in such a network, except for a small inter-frame gap.
4. For example in Ethernet, the interframe gap is 12 bytes, and the maximum frame size 1538 bytes (1500 byte payload + 12 byte interframe gap + 8 byte preamble + 14 byte header + 4 byte trailer). This corresponds to a maximum channel utilization of (1538-12)/1538•100% = 99.2%, or a maximum throughput of 99.2 Mbit/s in a 100 Mbit/s Ethernet connection.
5. In a Telecom network, the throughput that is achieved from one computer to another may be lower than the maximum throughput, and than the network access channel capacity, for several reasons, for example:
   - The channel capacity may be shared by other users. If a bottle neck communication link physical data rate R is shared by N, every user typically achieves a throughput of approximately N/R if fair queueing best-effort communication is assumed.
   - Flow control, for example in the TCP protocol, affects the throughput if the bandwidth delay product is larger than the TCP window, i.e. the buffer size. In that case the sending computer must wait for acknowledgement of the data packets before it can send more packets.

- Packet loss due to Network congestion. Packets may be dropped in switches and routers when the packet queues are full due to congestion.
- Packet loss due to bit errors.
- TCP congestion avoidance controls the data rate. So called "slow start" occurs in the beginning of a file, and after packet drops caused by router congestion or bit errors in for example wireless links.
- Scheduling algorithms in routers and switches. If fair queueing is not provided, users that send large packet will get higher bandwidth. Some users may be prioritized in a weighted fair queueing (WFQ) algorithm if differentiated or guaranteed quality of service (QoS) is provided.
- Ethernet "backoff" waiting time after collisions.
- The concept is applicable for all Telecom Networks.

5.6.2 Throughput, Goodput and Overhead

1. The maximum throughput is often an unreliable measurement of perceived speed, for example the file transmission speed in bits per second.
2. As pointed out above, the achieved throughput is often lower than the maximum throughput. Also, the protocol overhead affects the perceived speed.
3. The throughput is not a well-defined measure when it comes to how to deal with protocol overhead.
4. The most simple definition is the number of bits per second that are physically delivered.
5. A typical example where this definition is practised is an Ethernet network. In this case, the maximum throughput is the gross bitrate or raw bitrate.
6. However, in schemes that include forward error correction codes (channel coding), the redundant error code is normally excluded from the throughput.
7. An example in modem communication, where the throughput typically is measured in the interface between the PPP protocol and the circuit switched modem connection. In this case, the maximum throughput is often called net bitrate or useful bitrate.
8. To determine the actual speed of a network or connection, the goodput measurement definition may be used. For example in file transmission, the goodput corresponds to the file size (in bits) divided by the file transmission time.
9. The goodput is the amount of useful information that is delivered per second to the application layer protocol. Dropped packets, packet retransmissions and protocol overhead are not counted. **Because of that, the goodput is lower than the throughput.**
10. The concept is applicable for all Telecom Networks.

5.6.3 Goodput

1. In computer networks and wireless networks, **goodput** is the application level throughput, i.e. the number of useful bits per unit of time forwarded by the network from a certain source address to a certain destination, excluding protocol overhead, and excluding retransmitted data packets.
2. For example, if a file is transferred, the goodput that the user experiences corresponds to the file size in bits divided by the file transfer time.
3. The goodput is generally lower than the throughput (the gross bit rate that is transferred physically), which generally is lower than network access connection speed (the channel capacity or digital bandwidth).
4. Examples of factors that may cause lower goodput than throughput are:
   - Protocol overhead.
   - Retransmission of lost or corrupt packets, caused by bit errors or packet dropping in congested switches and routers. Automatic repeat request (ARQ), i.e. retransmission of lost or corrupt data packets, is supported by the TCP protocol, some UDP based application layer protocols, and by reliable data link layer protocol used for example in wireless networks.
   - Collision detection in the Ethernet CSMA/CD protocol, and collision avoidance in for example wireless local area networks using the CSMA/CA protocol, may cause "backoff" waiting time (i.e. increased interframe gap) and retransmission.
   - The concept is applicable for all Telecom Networks.

Example

Imagine that a file is being transferred using HTTP over a switched ethernet connection with a total channel capacity of 100 megabits per second. The file cannot be transferred over ethernet as a single contiguous stream, instead it must be broken down into individual segments, called packets. These packets must be no larger than the maximum transmission unit of ethernet, which is 1500 bytes. Each packet requires 20 bytes of IP header information and 20 bytes of TCP header information, so only 1460 bytes are available per packet for the file transfer data itself. Furthermore, the packets are transmitted over ethernet in a frame which imposes a 38 byte overhead per packet. Given these overheads, the maximum *goodput* is $\frac{1460}{1538} \cdot 100$ Mbit/s which is 94.92 megabits per second or 11.866 megabytes per second. The concept is applicable for all Telecom Networks.

5.6.4 Throughput over Analog Channels

1. The maximum throughput of a point-to-point or point-to-multipoint physical transmission medium, is equal to or near the channel capacity.

2. This is affected by modulation method and physical layer protocol overhead such as error correction coding, bit synchronization and equalizer training sequences.
3. The maximum throughput may be related to the analog bandwidth of a physical transmission medium, measured in hertz.
4. The link spectral efficiency in bit/s/Hz is the maximum throughput divided by the analog bandwidth. It is a measure of the efficiency of the digital transmission scheme.
5. In wireless networks or cellular systems, the system spectral efficiency in bit/s/Hz/area unit, bit/s/Hz/site or bit/s/Hz/cell, is the maximum system throughput (aggregate throughput) divided by the analog bandwidth and some measure of the system coverage area.
6. The concept is applicable for all Telecom Networks.

5.6.5 Throughput and Latency

1. Normally, throughput and latency are opposed goals.
2. The concept is applicable for all Telecom Networks.
3. To improve latency you typically want to increase how much the computer checks to see if you are trying to interact.
4. This checking overhead slows you down. However, there is one very common exception to this rule. Network protocols and programs tend to synchronize both ends regularly.
5. If these synchronizations are slow, then throughput can suffer tremendously.
6. The perceived speed is mostly based on the speed of requests made or responsiveness.
7. As such, responsiveness has far less to do with throughput than latency.
8. To illustrate this, consider a truck full of magnetic tape en route from Kashmir to Kanyakumari.
9. The time or latency it takes to deliver the data may be several days, but the amount or throughput of data delivered will exceed the throughput of a broadband connection.
10. In contrast, the broadband connection, which has a throughput many times less than that of the truck, has a relatively low latency and can deliver smaller amounts of data much faster.
11. For a user, surfing the Internet for instance, the latter which has a lower latency is perceived as "faster".
12. Latency is measured from the time a request (e.g. a single packet) leaves the client to the time the response (e.g. An Acknowledgment) arrives back at the client from the serving entity.
13. The unit of latency is time. Throughput on the other hand is the amount of data that is transferred over a period of time.
14. For example if over ten seconds, twenty packets are transferred then the throughput would be 20/10=2 packets per second.

15. Throughput can have many units (for example: "bits/second," "bytes/second," or "packets/second"), but it is always measured in a volume-per-time ratio.

5.7 Crosstalk and Interference
Telecom Network Cables
1. You might be tempted to think that a cable is a cable, but then you look around and notice that there are lots of different types on sale, and that data rates seem to be much greater than they used to be.
2. Why only a few years ago everyone had 10 M Ethernet and now that's old had and everybody has at least 100 M and increasingly 1000Base T (Gigabit) Ethernet. Something must be different.
3. Well the reality is that all cables are not equal, and increasing the data rate brings a lot of new factors into play.
4. A cable that operates happily at 10 M is a different beast at 1000 M and as you start to use all four pairs in the cabling (as you have to do to get the faster rates) you introduce a whole raft of new problems that need to be considered when testing the cabling.

What Slows the Data Down in Telecom Networks?
1. An electrical signal is composed of electrons moving along the wire.
2. As the frequency increases (and hence the potential amount of data you can send), a number of new phenomena appear, and these need to be taken into account when installing and testing the cabling.
3. As a consequence the standards have had to change to take these effects into account.
4. There are three main classes of problem that cause data to be weakened, lost, or corrupted beyond acceptable limits.
   (A) Attenuation (signal loss/degradation)
   (B) Noise (Internal, External, Crosstalk)
   (C) Delays (Skew)

(A) Attenuation (Signal Loss/Degradation)
1. We are all used to the fact that in nature as a signal travels further from its source it weakens.
2. The same is true of electrical signals in wires. Beyond a limit (different for each type of cable), the signal is too weak or distorted to be recognisable. Cable length is the major factor for attenuation measurement.
3. Attenuation is also dependent on frequency, becoming greater as frequency increases.
4. Higher Temperatures increase attenuation too, about 0.4% per degree Celsius for Cat5e cabling.

5. Attenuation is measured in decibels (dB). Confusingly signal loss is measured in negative numbers, e.g. −3dB and the negative sign is usually ignored, so the example would read as 3db of loss.
6. Consequently, lower numbers are better. So 2 dB is better than 4 dB.
7. Just about all the electrical properties of the cabling have an effect on attenuation too.

Resistance

Resistance is a function of the cross-sectional area of the conductor. Resistance in the wire limits the signal and dissipates the energy as (a small amount of) increased heat. The longer or thinner the wires, the greater the resistance.

Mutual Capacitance

The insulation covering the individual wires in the cable inevitably absorbs some of the signal. Since many wires are placed very close together, they store this energy, acting in electrical terms, like a capacitor. High Density Polyethylene (HDPE) is commonly used because its electrical properties at high frequencies help to minimise the losses. Cables that are designed for lower frequency applications may perform poorly at higher frequencies.

Impedance

Electrically, impedance is a combination of resistance, capacitance, and inductance expressed in Ohms. Typical cables are rated at around 100 Ohms. A so called Return Loss occurs when a signal hits a high impedance, for example an incorrect connector or a cable fault, and is bounced back. Potential bounced signals can cause problems on high speed networks, the higher the network speed the more pronounced the problem. Poorly fitted or wrongly specified connectors are a major cause. Infinite impedance indicates a cut in the cable. Zero impedance indicates a short circuit.

(B) Noise

1. Any electrical signal on the wire not part of the sender's original signal is classed as noise.
2. Noise is generated both internally and externally.
3. Twisted pair cables produce no interference, the twists cancel each other out, in theory that is. In real life any variation in the thickness of the wire, in the cable insulation, and in the capacitance of wires or insulation will cause a mismatch and consequently noise. Good quality cables minimise the noise but cannot remove it altogether.

External Noise

Electrical interference can come from many sources. Cables should always be installed in separate conduits away from mains cables. In industrial applications electric motors (in lifts/elevators), fluorescent lights and air conditioners, are major sources of interference.

In areas of electrical noise, it is common to shield cables or to use other technologies, such as optical fibre to avoid interference.

Crosstalk

Crosstalk is likely to be much greater than any other noise effect. When a signal travels down a conductor, an electric field is created, which interferes with any wires close by. This is Crosstalk and gets larger at higher frequencies and the more parallel the wires. The twists in the pairs should (in theory) cancel this effect. For good signal cancellation, it is important that the twists are symmetrical and that adjacent pairs have different twists.

Crosstalk is measured in decibels (dB).

(C) Delays

Electrical signals travel very fast, but not infinitely fast. Typical twisted pair cables run at 60% to 90% of the velocity of light. The time taken for a signal to travel down the pair is the Propagation Delay. The propagation delay in itself is not normally an issue, the recommended cable lengths will already have taken this into account. However, Delay Skew, described below is a significant factor.

Skew

Think back to the fact that the wires are twisted and therefore the length of the pairs that make up the cable are not equal. Signals sent at the same time will therefore arrive at slightly different times. This difference in arrival times is the Delay Skew, and must be within 50 nanoseconds for Cat5, Cat5e and Cat6 cables.

If Delay Skew is excessive then network devices will have trouble communicating, resulting in very slow or totally non-functioning networks.

5.7.1 Cross Talk and Interference in Telecom Networks

1. In electronics, the term **crosstalk** (**XT**) has the following meanings:
   - Undesired capacitive, inductive, or conductive coupling from one circuit, part of a circuit, or channel, to another.
   - Any phenomenon by which a signal transmitted on one circuit or channel of a transmission system creates an undesired effect in another circuit or channel.
   - In a recording setting, the term "crosstalk" can refer to the leakage (or "bleeding") cf sound from one instrument into a microphone placed in front of another musical instrument or singer. A common example is the leakage of the high-pitched, heavily-amplified sound of the lead guitar into the microphones for other instruments.

2. In telecommunication or telephony, crosstalk is often distinguishable as pieces of speech or signaling tones leaking from other people's connections.
3. If the connection is analog, twisted pair cabling can often be used to reduce the effects of crosstalk.
4. Alternatively, the signals can be converted to digital form, which is much less susceptible to crosstalk.
5. In integrated circuit design, crosstalk normally refers to a signal affecting another nearby signal.
6. Usually the coupling is capacitive, and to the nearest neighbor, but other forms of coupling and effects on signal further away are sometimes important, especially in analog designs.
7. See signal integrity for tools used to measure and prevent this problem, and substrate coupling for a discussion of crosstalk conveyed through the IC substrate.
8. There are a wide variety of possible fixes, with increased spacing, wire re-ordering, and shielding being the most common.
9. There are two types of crosstalk:
    - NEXT - **N**ear **E**nd **cross**Talk, where a transmitter induces noise onto the nearby receiver on the same end of the cable, causing noise between signals travelling in opposite directions.

      Possible solution: separated upstream and downstream channels, as DMT (discrete multitone) does.

    - FEXT - **F**ar **E**nd **cross**Talk, where a transmitter induces noise onto the receiver on the other side of the cable, causing noise between signals travelling in the same direction.

      Possible solution: reduce transmission power wisely, in regard to the length of the cable.

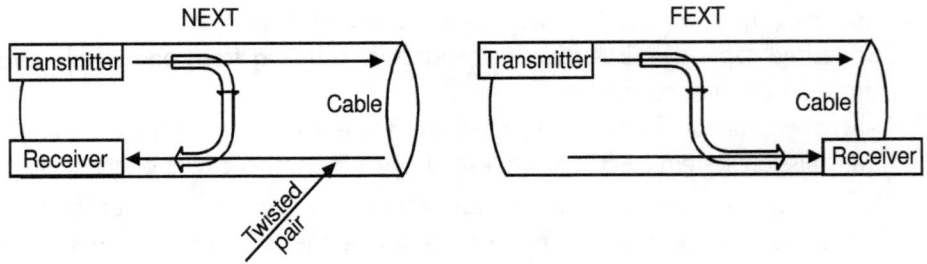

Fig. 5.15: Crosstalk showing FEXT and NEXT in cable

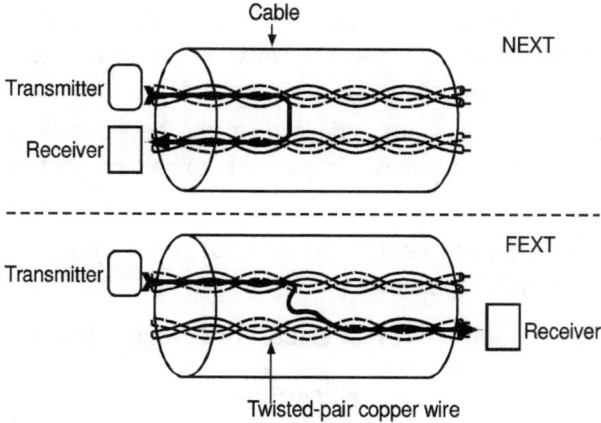

Fig. 5.16: Crosstalk showing FEXT and NEXT in twisted pair cable

5.7.2 Near End Crosstalk (NEXT)

1. This stands for Near End cross Talk, and it occurs because alternating current flow produces an electromagnetic field around the cable, this field then induces a current flow in adjacent cables.
2. The strength of this field increases with the frequency of the signal, and because the speed of data transmissions is ever increasing, NEXT is a big problem.
3. The name 'Cross Talk' comes from the telecommunications industry, you may have heard a faint conversation in the background while on the phone yourself, this is caused by the electromagnetic effect between adjacent telephone wires.
4. In the transmission of data, cross talk is at its highest level in the RJ45 connection as it enters the cable, or at the 'Near End'.
5. The term 'Near End' is slightly confusing because data can travel in both directions, and the NEXT test is carried out in both directions automatically by the tester, so the NEXT result is relative to the end of the cable that it was carried out on.

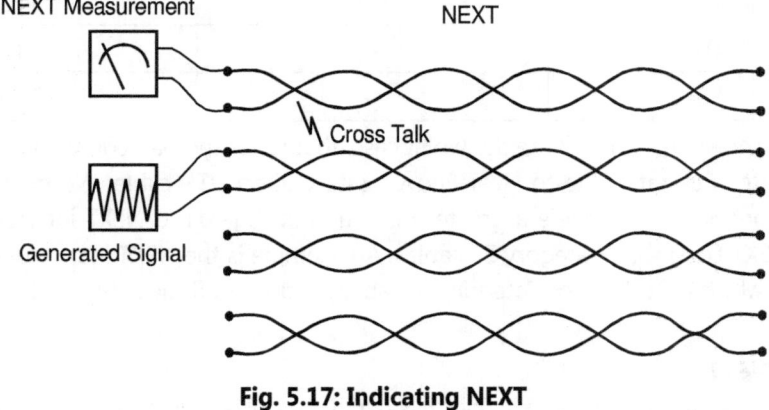

Fig. 5.17: Indicating NEXT

6. The twists in a cable help to cancel out the effects of NEXT and the more twists there are, the better the cancellation, however, the twists also increase attenuation, so there is a trade off between NEXT cancellation and attenuation.
7. The twist rates in data cables are optimized for the best overall performance, the twist rates are also varied for each pair within the cable to help combat crosstalk.

Table 5.7 shows the pair-to-pair Near End Crosstalk loss values as a function of the frequency for Category 5e and 6 solid UTP cables.

Table 5.7: Pair-to-pair NEXT loss values for Category 5e and 6 UTP cables

Frequency (MHz)	Pair-to-Pair NEXT Loss (dB) Category 5e Cable, solid	Pair-to-Pair NEXT Loss (dB) Category 6 Cable, solid
0.150	–	86.7
0.772	67.0	76.0
1.0	65.3	74.3
4.0	56.3	65.3
8.0	51.8	60.8
10.0	50.3	59.3
16.0	47.2	56.2
20.0	45.8	54.8
25.0	44.3	53.3
31.25	42.9	51.9
62.5	38.4	47.4
100.0	35.3	44.3
200.0	–	39.8
250	–	38.3

The values shown in Table 5.7 are the worst case, that is, for the pair combination causing the worse interference ratio due to Near End Crosstalk of an UTP cable. We may notice, then, that Category 6 cables provide a greater insulation in regards to NEXT interference (higher value of NEXT Loss) than Category 5e cables. An example is the NEXT loss values at 100 MHz frequency, which is 35.3 dB for Category 5e cables, and 44.3 dB for Category 6 cables.

5.7.2.1 PSNEXT
1. This stands for Power Sum Near End Cross Talk and is actually just a calculation.

2. When a tester carries out the NEXT test, it measures the cross talk on each pair as affected by each of the other three pairs individually, PSNEXT is simply the addition of the three NEXT results for each pair.
3. So this is the combined effect that a pair would be subject to when used in a network that supports a four pair transmissions method, e.g.. Gigabit Ethernet.

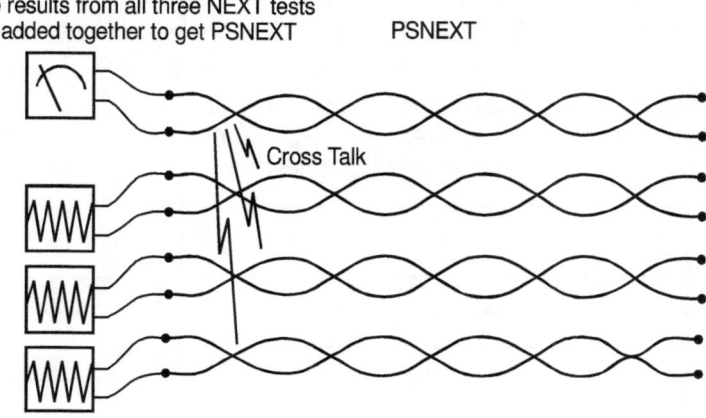

Fig. 5.18

Table 5.8 shows the same interference ratios for powersum NEXT Loss (PS-NEXT Loss).

Table 5.8: Powersum NEXT loss values for Category 5e and 6 UTP cables

Frequency (MHz)	Powersum NEXT (dB) Loss Category 5e Cable, solid	Powersum NEXT (dB) Loss Category 6 Cable, solid
0.150	74.7	84.7
0.772	64.0	74.0
1.0	62.3	72.3
4.0	53.3	63.3
8.0	48.8	58.8
10.0	47.3	57.3
16.0	44.2	54.2
20.0	42.8	52.8
25.0	41.3	51.3
31.25	39.9	49.9
62.5	35.4	45.4
100.0	32.3	42.3
200.0	–	37.8
250.0	–	36.3

The electrical insulation between the pairs for the powersum NEXT loss condition is smaller, as expected, that is, in such a condition the Near End Crosstalk interference is greater, and therefore the safe limits for ensuring certain more demanding applications (full-duplex applications for instance) may be determined taking as a reference this Near End Crosstalk loss test method.

It is also clear here that Category 5e cables are more susceptible to Near End Crosstalk interference than Category 6 cables. For instance, we may take the values for both at a frequency of 100 MHz. For Category 6 cables, the PS-NEXT loss is 42.3 dB (greater insulation) and for Category 5e cables 32.3 dB (smaller insulation).

Fig. 5.19 shows, graphically, the PS-NEXT responses for Cat. 5e and Cat. 6 channels.

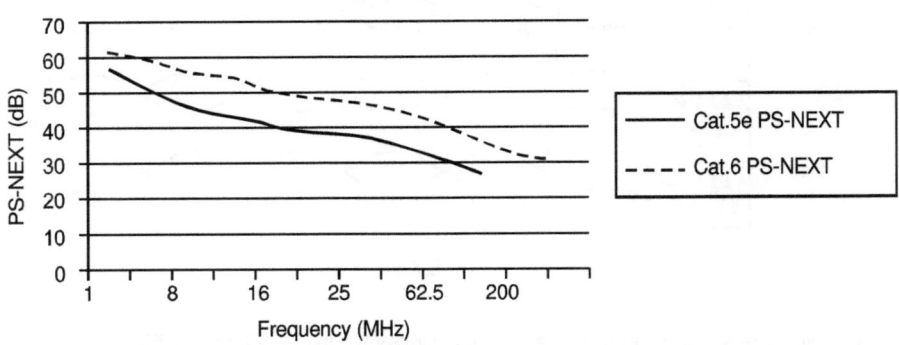

Fig. 5.19: PS-NEXT Loss responses for Category 5e and 6 channels

5.7.3 FEXT, ELFEXT and PSELFEXT

1. Basically, Far End Cross Talk (FEXT) is like NEXT but it is measured at the far end (well that seems logical!). However, on its own FEXT does not mean much because the length of the cable determines how much the signal is attenuated before it can affect the pairs at the far end.
2. To compensate for this, and to provide a more meaningful result, the attenuation is subtracted from the FEXT test and the result is then called **Equal Level Far End Cross Talk (ELFEXT)**.

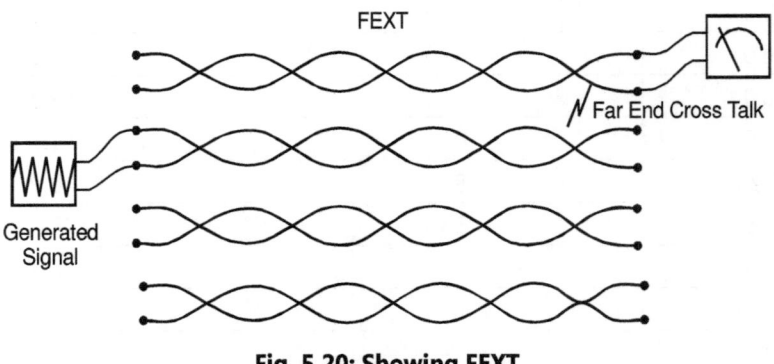

Fig. 5.20: Showing FEXT

3. It takes into account the amount of signal loss. ELFEXT is calculated for each pair of cables and will be slightly different for each pair. Very high values indicate excessive attenuation or high far end crosstalk.
4. And of course, no test parameter these days would be complete without adding the results together for each pair and calling it a Power Sum measurement, so now we have **Power Sum Equal Level Far End Cross Talk or PSELFEXT** for short.

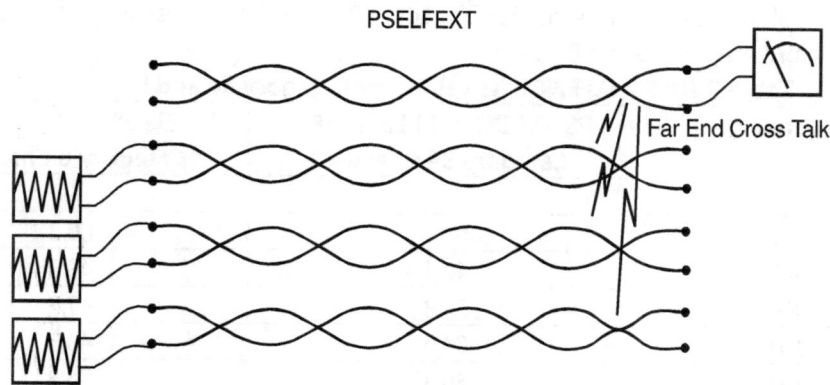

Fig. 5.21: Showing PSEFEXT

Table 5.9 shows the pair-to-pair ELFEXT values as a function of the frequency for Category 5e and 6 UTP cables.

Table 5.9: Pair-to-pair ELFEXT values for Category 5e and 6 UTP cables with 100 metre in length

Frequency (MHz)	Pair-to-Pair ELFEXT (dB) Category 5e Cable, solid	Pair-to-Pair ELFEXT (dB) Category 6 Cable, solid
0.772	–	70.0
1.0	63.8	67.8
4.0	51.8	55.8
8.0	45.7	49.7
10.0	43.8	47.8
16.0	39.7	43.7
20.0	37.8	41.8
25.0	35.8	39.8
31.25	33.9	37.9
62.5	27.9	31.9
100.0	23.8	27.8
200.0	–	21.8
250.0	–	19.8

Once again one can see that the insulation between the pairs of UTP cables reduces as the frequency increases, proving that, for high frequencies, the Far End Crosstalk interference ratios are more important. Likewise we may notice that Category 6 cables offer a greater insulation for Far End Crosstalk than Category 5e cables. In any frequency within the range of interest, the ELFEXT value for Category 6 cables is numerically higher than that for Category 5e cables at the same frequency.

Table 5.10 shows the powersum ELFEXT Loss (PS-ELFEXT) values as a function of the frequency for Category 5e and 6 channels.

Table 5.10: PS-ELFEXT Loss values for Category 5e and 6 channels

Frequency (MHz)	PS-ELFEXT (dB) Loss (dB) Category 5e Channel	PS-ELFEXT (dB) Loss (dB) Category 6 Channel
0.772	–	–
1.0	54.4	60.3
4.0	42.4	48.2
8.0	36.3	42.2
10.0	34.4	40.3
16.0	30.3	36.2
20.0	28.4	34.2
25.0	26.4	–
31.25	24.5	30.4
62.5	18.5	24.3
100.0	14.4	20.3
200.0	–	14.2
250.0	–	12.3

The PS-ELFEXT behavior is similar to the ELFEXT, however, with lower numerical values. This was already expected, since upon the evaluation of the PS-ELFEXT all pairs are contributing to the FEXT interference ratios, therefore, the interference levels increase, and the insulation between the pairs decreases.

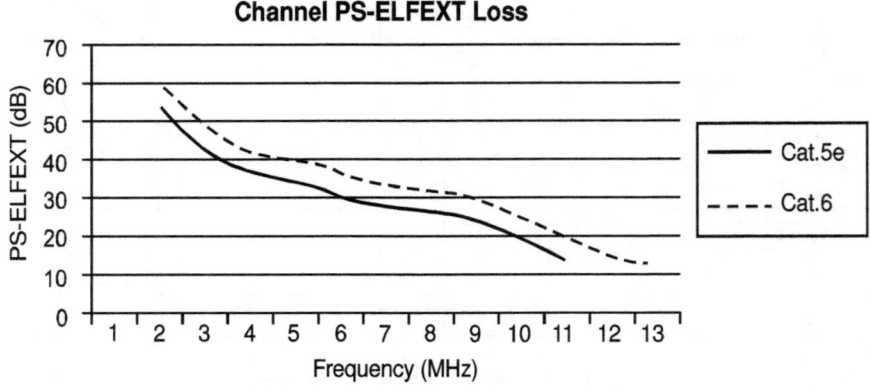

Fig. 5.22: PS-ELFEXT Loss for Cat. a5e and Cat. 6 channels

Fig. 5.22 shows graphically, the responses for PS-ELFEXT Loss for Categories 5e and 6 channels.

5.7.4 Measurement of Next and Fext

Crosstalk is measured in two ways.

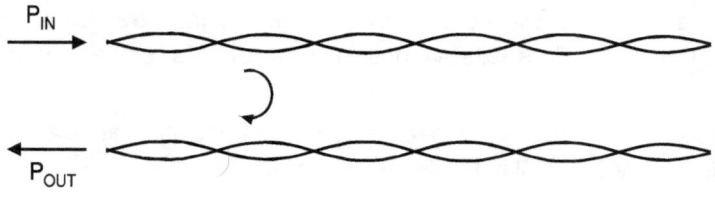

Fig. 5.23

Near End Crosstalk (NEXT) is measured at one end only of a cable, by transmitting a signal into one pair and measuring the resulting signal power on an adjacent pair at the same end.

$$\text{NEXT} = P_{OUT} / P_{IN}$$
$$= 10 \,(\log_{10} P_{OUT} / P_{IN}) \text{ dB}$$

To be sure that the measured signal is really due to crosstalk, and not to some other source of interference, the receiver is tuned to the same frequency as the transmitter. This can be a single frequency or it can be swept across the frequency spectrum.

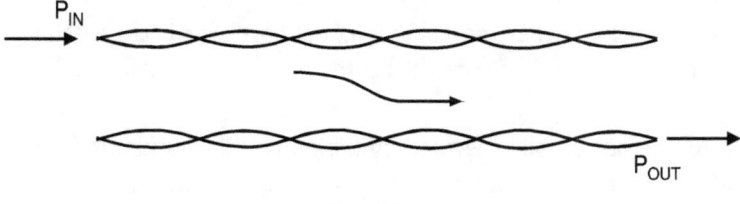

Fig. 5.24

Far End Crosstalk (FEXT) is measured at both ends of a cable, by transmitting a signal into one pair at one end and measuring the resulting signal power on an adjacent pair at the other end.

The Far End Crosstalk is given by:

$$\text{FEXT} = P_{OUT} / P_{IN}$$
$$= 10 \,(\log_{10} P_{OUT} / P_{IN}) \text{ dB}$$

By measuring both NEXT and FEXT, and noting the difference between the two measurements, we can determine whether the crosstalk is caused by a fault near to one end of the line or whether it is caused by evenly distributed coupling along the length.

5.7.5 Signal to Noise Ratio (SNR)

1. As the name implies this compares the signal strength to the amount of noise on the pair.
2. A more accurate term for a similar thing is Attenuation to Crosstalk Ratio (ACR).
3. Both terms are also slightly misleading.
4. ACR is not a ratio, it is just the difference between signal strength and NEXT, and SNR includes internal as well as external noise (which for most practical purposes makes no difference).
5. You will hear both terms used to mean the same thing. Only in areas of extreme electrical interference will ACR and SNR be significantly different.
6. Obviously the difference between the level of noise and the level of signal is important.
7. You are aiming to get a good signal much stronger than any noise.
8. Attenuation greater as frequency increases and NEXT gets lower.
9. The difference for any cable is the ACR. Theoretical bandwidth limits are always higher than the rates used in practical cabling.

5.7.6 Attenuation to Crosstalk (NEXT) Ratio - ACR

1. Attenuation to Crosstalk Ratio is not exactly a transmission parameter, but a mathematical relation between two parameters - Attenuation and Crosstalk, specifically the Near End Crosstalk (NEXT) in this case.
2. We can also anticipate that the ELFEXT (Equal Level Far End Crosstalk) is virtually the same parameter relation but considering the Far End Crosstalk (FEXT) in place of NEXT now.
3. Although ACR is not usually specified by the applicable standards, it may be very useful to evaluate the level of performance of a given cabling system.
4. It can also be used to classify as well as qualify cabling system's performance from different vendors by comparing their ACR responses. The better the ACR (higher number), the better the system performance.
5. We can also refer (roughly) to ACR as the SNR (Signal to Noise Ratio) of a given cabling system.
6. To be more precise in this definition, we should say that ACR is a good SNR indicator when the interference considered is the one from NEXT couplings.
7. Likewise ELFEXT should be considered as the SNR of a given cabling system when the interference of most concern is the one from the FEXT coupling. Both parameter ratios are important in terms of interference response of telecommunications cabling systems.
8. Fig. 5.25 shows that ACR is the difference between the values of Attenuation and NEXT for a given frequency within a frequency range.

9. Graphically, ACR can be interpreted as the separation between the parameters Attenuation and NEXT within a frequency range. Higher the separation, better the system performance of a given channel or more "noise-free" the channel will be.
10. For ACR positive (ACR>0), the communication can be guaranteed. When the ACR is equal to zero (ACR=0), we can say, theoretically, there is a state of uncertainty, i.e., the communication can not be either guaranteed or not. In practice, the communication is not possible under this condition.
11. For a negative ACR (ACR<0), the communication cannot be established at all.

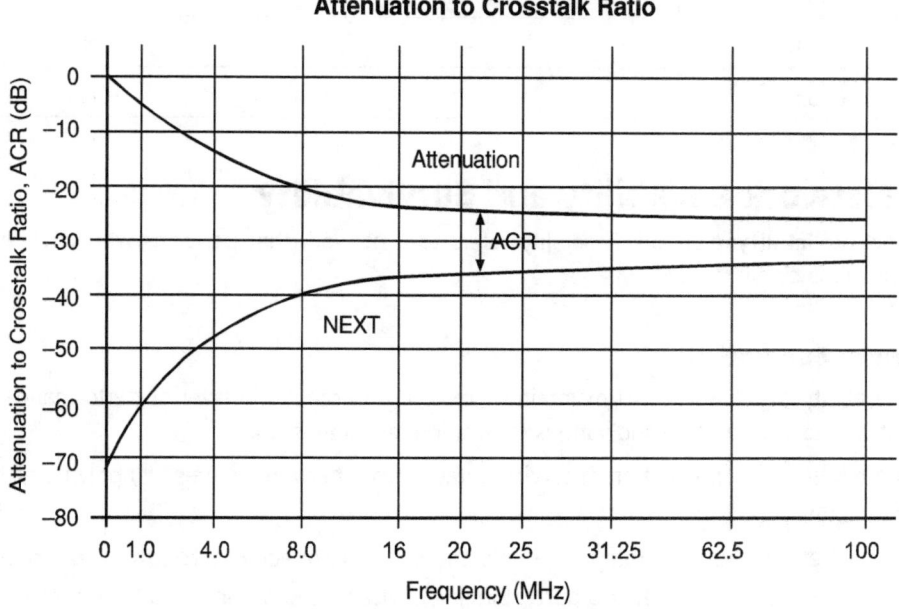

Fig. 5.25: Attenuation to Crosstalk Ratio

Table 5.11 shows the PS-ACR response for Category 5e and 6 channels.

Table 5.11: PS-ACR response for Category 5e and 6 channels

Frequency (MHz)	Category 5e Channel PS-ACR (dB)	Category 6 Channel PS-ACR (dB)
1.0	54.8	59.9
4.0	46.0	56.5
8.0	39.3	49.9
10.0	36.9	47.7
16.0	31.5	42.6

Frequency (MHz)	Category 5e Channel PS-ACR (dB)	Category 6 Channel PS-ACR (dB)
20.0	28.8	40.0
25.0	25.9	37.2
31.25	22.8	34.3
62.5	12.0	24.1
100.0	3.1	15.8
200.0	–	0.4
250.0	–	–5.7

5.8 Network Reliability and Survivability

Network Reliability: Network Reliability refers to a network that performs when needed even under adverse circumstances.

Network Survivability:
(a) The ability of a network to maintain or restore an acceptable level of performance during network failures by applying various restoration techniques, and
(b) The mitigation or prevention of service outages from network failures by applying preventive techniques.
   (1) When we make a telephone call, the call is connected through a communication network to the receiving party. Similarly, when we send an e-mail using the Internet, the message is sent through a communication network to the recipient.
   (2) Such communication networks are made up of nodes and links that connect the nodes by hardware as well as the software components that allow for the functionality to communicate through such networks.
   (3) Network reliability refers to the reliability of the overall network to provide communication in the event of failure of a component or components in the network.
   (4) Communication network reliability depends on the sustainability of both hardware and software.
   (5) A variety of network failures, lasting from a few seconds to days depending on the failure, is possible.
   (6) Traditionally, such failures were primarily from hardware malfunctions that result in downtime (or "outage period") of a network element (a node or a link).

(7) Thus, the emphasis was on the element-level network availability and, in turn, the determination of overall network availability. However, other types of major outages have received much attention in recent years. Such incidents include accidental fiber cable cut, natural disasters, and malicious attack (both hardware and software).

(8) These major failures need more than what is traditionally addressed through network availability.

(9) For one, these types of failures cannot be addressed by congestion control schemes alone because of their drastic impact on the network.

(10) Such failures can, for example, drop a significant number of existing network connections; thus, the network is required to have the ability to detect a fault and isolate it, and then either the network must reconnect the affected connections or the user may try to reconnect it (if the network does not have reconnect capability).

(11) At the same time, the network may not have enough capacity and capability to handle such a major simultaneous "reconnect" phase. Likewise, because of a software and/or protocol error, the network may appear very congested to the user. Thus, network reliability nowadays encompasses more than what was traditionally addressed through network availability.

5.8.1 Consider the example of Network Reliability and Survivability for Local Exchanges in Telecom Networks

(1) To reduce the likelihood of disruption to large numbers of lines and circuits, local carriers should increase the redundancy of network elements through such efforts as the use of fiber optic rings in the local loop or alternative switching network rather than concentration of more customers on fewer, larger switches should also be considered.

(2) Finally, local carriers should identify and eliminate where reasonable single points of potential failure in the network, especially in critical servcies provided to consumers.

(3) To that end, the Commission could require local exchange carriers to provide route diversity for each end office where reasonable.

(4) Local carriers should mechanize outside plant records and implement supporting databses to provide real time information on the physical location of outside plant facilities so as to ensure the existence of geographic diversity for the individual carrier and other users of the carrier's facilities (e.g. other carriers and end users).

(5) Improved information as to the physical path of facilities serving the customer will also facilitate emergency preparedness and speed recovery efforts during a major outage.

(6) The Commission should require local carriers to routinely certify that they comply with the recommendations of the Network Reliability and Interoperability Council.

(7) To maintain diversity on all critical links of the Signal System 7 (SS7) network, carriers should ensure that their SS7 vendors connect to SS7 switching nodes and databases in a geographically diverse manner.

(8) Network survivability refers to the inherent design of the network or specific elements of the network to provide a high level of assurance than it will continue to operate during a natural or manmade event affecting some portion of the network. Generally, speaking, it is applied to individual segments of the network or a composite of such segments rather than the network as a whole. The level of assurance given to any segment of the network is defined by specifying the range of conditions over which it will continue to operate during an event. For example, each central office switch in the network is designed to operate for a limited period of time without commercial power through the use of a standby power generator and battery reserve power.

5.8.2 How to Implement Network Reliability and Survivability?

1. Competition within the telecommunications companies is growing fiercer by the day.
2. Therefore, it is vital to ensure a high level of quality and reliability within all telecommunications systems in order to guard against faults and the failure of components and network services.
3. Within large-scale systems, such quality and reliability problems are ever higher.
4. The metrics of Quality and Reliability have to date only been available in journals and technical reports of companies, which have designed or produced major parts of systems used in large applications.
5. In a medium-sized home two nodes that need to communicate may be beyond direct communication range.
6. The home control system therefore needs to support a mesh network structure enabling the two nodes to use other nodes as routing nodes.
7. Fig. 5.26 shows a typical mesh network with a solid line illustrating the communications path between two nodes, which are beyond direct communication range.
8. The mesh network also serves as the basis for the self-healing functionalities.
9. RF communications links vary over time due to their strong correlation to the physical environment.
10. For example, when a door open/closes, furniture is/are moved, or there are simply many people moving about, RF links may fail because the environment is changing.
11. In these situations, the self-healing mechanisms in the technology will automatically reroute the message through other nodes until the message reaches the destination node.

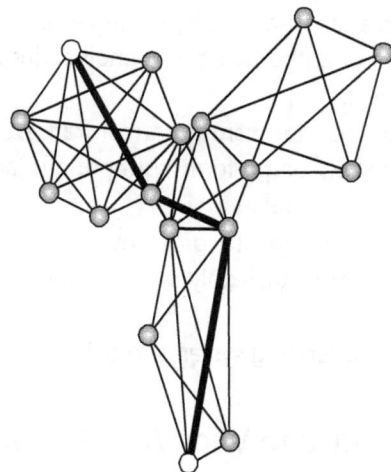

Fig. 5.26: Typical mesh network with a solid line illustrating the communications path between two nodes, which are beyond direct communication range

5.9 Network Attacks/Protection

5.9.1 Data Risks for Wide Area Telecom Networks

Wide area network data is vulnerable to attack in a variety of ways, including those listed below. The most important defenses against these attacks is the encryption of highly sensitive data in storage and in transit across networks, and the use of strong authentication (e.g. one-time passwords) to control access to stored data such as critical systems and business processes. Strong authentication and encryption provide additional layers of security to institutions' most valuable assets.

- Intercepting authentication or other sensitive information, often using software or hardware devices is known as "sniffers." "Sniffers," originally designed to diagnose network-related problems, are specialized software or hardware tools that intercept information in transit over networks.
- Guessing passwords that protect accounts or system services, particularly default passwords that have not been changed.
- Retrieving and decoding password files.
- Sequentially or randomly dialing every number on a telephone exchange (known as "war dialing") to detect unprotected modems at desktop systems, servers or routers to gain access to, or control over, networks.
- Deceiving the network so that it recognizes an unauthorized, possibly external, desktop system as an authorized, internal desktop system ("spoofing") to gain unauthorized access to networks and/or sensitive data.

- Attempting to gain information or access by posing as a help desk or repair person, or as an individual in a position of authority ("social engineering") to gain access to networks, desktop systems and servers.
- Inserting software, which does not disrupt normal transactions, into desktop systems or servers to gather information or perform surreptitious acts ("Trojan horses") to gain control of the desktop system or server.
- Intercepting authenticated sessions to preempt access by a desktop system to gain control of a session with access to highly sensitive information or business procedures ("hijacking").
- Exploiting vulnerabilities in operating systems to gain control of computers.

5.9.2 Other Attacks Relative to Wide Area Network Communications

5.9.2.1 The Passive Attack

1. In a passive attack, information is intercepted without modification (e.g. a wiretap).
2. Information obtained during a passive attack can be used successfully to perpetrate an active attack.
3. All means of communications can be intercepted and monitored.
4. Some types of passive attacks require direct access to the communications line.
5. Once an intruder identifies a communications line, attaching a passive wire tap is relatively easy.
6. Contrary to popular belief, it is economically and technically feasible to tap fiber optic lines.

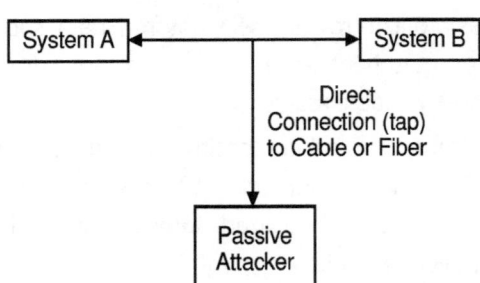

Fig. 5.27: Direct Passive Attack on a Physical Network Line

7. A passive attack on a physical line (e.g. fiber or cable) is illustrated in Fig. 5.27.
8. Other passive attacks are independent of communications and do not require a direct wire tap.
9. The monitoring of microwave, satellite, cellular phone and laser link transmissions is technically simple.
10. In these instances, it is less likely that the source of the attack will be located.
11. A passive attack on an RF channel (microwave, satellite or cellular phone) is illustrated in Fig. 5.28.

12. Some communications circuits actually radiate information which can be received and interpreted by an unauthorized party. Electrical and electronic circuits emanate transmissions when they operate, causing this radiation.

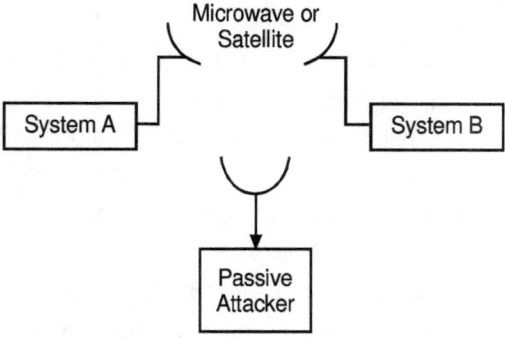

Fig. 5.28: Passive Attack on a Wireless Link

5.9.2.2 The Active Attack

1. Active attacks involve intercepting information and its modification.
2. Data fields can be changed, inserted, deleted or duplicated during transmission.
3. Today's expanded use of electronic payment mechanisms has increased the active attack exposure.
4. Microwave transmissions etc., and radiated information are less of a concern for data modification, however, they can easily be intercepted.
5. An active attack will have an increased chance of succeeding if the audit trail can be manipulated or broken.
6. Direct modification or suppression of the audit trail will reduce the chances of detection and tracing of that attack.
7. However, any theft of electronic money (e.g. illegally modified account balances) must allow for the withdrawal of real money and its conversion into something more portable.
8. For instance, conversion of the money into diamonds will effectively break the audit trail.

5.9.2.3 Denial of Service Attack

1. The use of a communication facility may be interfered with using a "denial-of-service attack".
2. A familiar form of this attack is "SPAMing" a network address or SPAMing a network service provider.
3. The sending of multiple messages which may or may not have any meaning or discernable purpose across a network (such as advertising a product to all subscribers of a major service provider) overwhelms network and router bandwidth.

4. The effect on a business using that service provider is that service is denied until the undesired traffic is cleared.

5.9.2.4 System Penetration
1. Penetration of a host computer is an increasing risk to stored data.
2. With the increased use of Personal Computers (PCs) and modems, and the need to provide expanded services to more sophisticated users, unauthorized system penetration is a real risk. Such attacks are reported frequently.
3. During a successful system penetration, stored data can be accessed and modified and computer operations can be disrupted.
4. Similarly, transactions can be added, deleted, or changed.
5. Clearly, the protection of security information itself (e.g. access codes and passwords) is of vital concern.
6. Such information can be intercepted during transmission and used to penetrate a system, through impersonation of an authorized user.
7. A more subtle form of system penetration is exploiting proprietary networks to obtain free telecommunications or to intentionally exceed the network capacity.
8. Such occurrences may have the direct impact of overloading the network and disrupting customer service.
9. This may lead to a decision to deactivate security controls or use a back-up method of operation with lesser protection to overcome the operating problem.
10. This reaction may be the intended result of the penetrators in order to attempt an active attack.

5.9.2.5 Insiders
1. Fraud and occurrence statistics identify trusted insiders as the usual perpetrators of abuse.
2. Insiders include such groups as employees and trusted officers.
3. Suppliers of service employed to support and operate systems should also be viewed as insiders since they have inside information or access.
4. In technically complex areas, this expertise may be more extensive than that within the financial institution or its customer.
5. Thus, groups such as suppliers of software, telecommunications and engineering service personnel, as well as employees, should be considered as potential risks.
6. The contractual responsibilities and awareness of specific security requirements of the financial institution should therefore be carefully defined for each group of trusted servants.

5.9.2.6 Public and Private Network Vulnerabilities

1. The confidentiality of data transmitted over public networks poses additional risks to those identified for internal networks.
2. "Dedicated" or "leased" lines may provide an inappropriate sense of security.
3. These lines use the infrastructure of public networks and therefore are vulnerable to the same attacks as the public networks themselves.
4. Although the security of public networks are upgraded constantly, they have many of the same characteristics as local and wide area networks and are regularly subjected to the same types of attacks that were previously described.
5. In addition, lines may be tapped, and at some point in traversing the network, data may be transmitted via microwave, wireless or satellite links that are susceptible to being intercepted.
6. Finally, key public network operations and support personnel may be able to access highly sensitive data being transmitted over the networks.
7. Confidential data transmitted via public networks may be intercepted or compromised by individuals for whom the data is not intended.
8. Therefore, it is prudent to encrypt sensitive and highly sensitive data transmitted via public networks.

5.9.3 ATM Network Security: Vulnerabilities and Risks

1. Asynchronous Transfer Mode (ATM) network usually has less security exposures than TCP/IP network because it is often used in the backbone for a private or semi-private network with fiber cables as the media.
2. The cost to break into an ATM network is higher than to a TCP/IP network.
3. However, there are still many vulnerabilities in the ATM network, as listed below.
4. **Information Sniffing:** The attacker connects or taps into the transmission media and gain unauthorized access to the data.
5. **ATM Based Spoofing:** IP spoofing is possible in 'Classical IP over ATM' (CLIP) networks. Whenever the ATM address of a server is known, an attacker can establish a direct ATM connection to that host. The attacker can now register with the IP address of a trusted host by sending a carefully crafted 'InATMARP-Reply' message over this connection. After successful registration, spoofed IP packets can be sent over this connection. Moreover, due to the "ATMARP-Cache poisoning", the attacked server will send reply packets back to the attacker on the same ATM connection.
6. **Denial of Service:** ATM is a connection-oriented technique. A connection, which is called Virtual Circuit (VC) in ATM, is managed by a set of signals. VC is established by SETUP signals and can be disconnected by RELEASE or DROP PARTY signals. If an attacker sends RELEASE or DROP PARTY signal to any intermediate switch on the way of a VC, then the VC will be disconnected. By sending these signals frequently, the attacker can greatly disturb the communication between one user to another,

therefore will damage the Quality of Service (QoS) in ATM communication. There are other methods causing Denial of Service in an ATM network, which are not discussed in details here.

7. **Virtual Circuits (VC) Hijacking:** If two end switches between a communication of an ATM network compromise, the attacker can steal a VC from another user. For example, VC1 and VC2 are two virtual channels owned by two different users U1 and U2, which is from switch A to switch B. If A and B have compromised, then A can switch VC1's cells going from A to B through VC2 and B will switch back those cells to VC1. Since switches will forward cells based on the VCI (Virtual Channel Identifier) or VPI (Virtual Path Identifier) in the cell header, A and B can just alter these fields back and forth. Switches between A and B won't notice these changes and will switch the assumed VC2's cells just like the authentic VC2's cells. In ATM network, if quality of service is guaranteed, then user 1 can gain a lot by stealing a higher quality channel which user 1 is not entitled to use.

8. **ATM Switch Attack:** An attacker might use the P-NNI (Private Network-Network Interface) protocol in order to manipulate a switch. He could inject incorrect information in the peer group database or even try to configure routing loops into the hierarchic structure. He might block the communication of whole peer groups or even redirect communication over his workstation. The blocking of a peer group is very similar to the manipulation of routers with incorrect 'ICMP-Host/Net-unreachable' messages. Attacks based on the P-NNI protocol can use replies to 'HELLO' messages of a peer group leader to inject malicious information about 'link states'. The peer group leader in turn will broadcast these changes to its group members. Peer group members that have updated their link state information with faked information are likely to make the wrong routing decision.

9. **ILMI Attack:** The 'Integrated Local Management Interface' (ILMI) is used at the interface between switch and workstation. The protocol is based on the 'Simple Network Management Protocol' (SNMP). ILMI does not provide a mechanism for the authentication. An attacker who does not need to authenticate himself can use the ILMI to register additional ATM addresses for his workstation. By using the additional registered address the attacker can bypass address filters which have been configured at the switch. The attacker could also try to register himself with the ATM address of an offline workstation. ILMI can also be used to automatically configure the interface type of an ATM switch-port. An attacker may use ILMI to pretend that he is a switch by setting the interface type to "ONNI" (Network to Network Interface).

10. **Traffic Analysis:** the hacker can get information by collecting and analyzing the ATM network traffic information such as the volume, timing and the communication parties of a VC, even the content of the information is encrypted. The source and destination parties can be obtained from the cell header (normally is in clear text) as well as information in the routing table.

5.9.3.1 ATM Security Issues at Each ATM Plane

1. Each layer in the ATM reference model has its own weaknesses and must play its own role in terms of addressing security concerns.
2. The **ATM User plane** must provide security services like access control, authentication, data confidentiality and integrity. Other services like key exchange, certification infrastructure and negotiation of security options might be useful to meet the variety of the customers' requirements. Therefore, they also should be supported by user plane.
3. The **ATM Control plane** can interact with the switching table, or to manage the virtual channel. Several attacks mentioned above are relative to the control plane. The key point to secure control plane is to provide authentication of signal. If the message recipient or even the third party can verify the source of this message, then denial of service attack can not happen. And Control plane authentication could also be used to provide the auditing information for accurate billing which should be immune to repudiation.
4. **The ATM Management plane** security scheme should consider the following areas: Bootstrapping security, authenticated neighbor discovery, the Interim Local Management Interface security and permanent virtual circuit security. The security recovery and security management features are mainly implemented in the management plane.
5. Since all data passing through the ATM layer, authentication, confidentiality and integrity are also required in the ATM layer. ATM layer security has to be implemented on ATM endpoint to ATM endpoint, border ATM switch to border ATM switch and ATM end point to switches basis.
6. Table 5.12 summarizes the main issues at each ATM layer:

Table 5.12

Parameter	User data flows	Signaling	Management flows
Data and traffic flow confidentiality	disclosure of data (exchanged over one VPI/VCI connection)	disclosure of the communicating parties identities and VPI/VCI associated to the connection	disclosure of the amount of user data exchanged
Integrity	tampered cells processing	connection release	connection release
Overloading	useful cells processing prevent	multiple connection set ups	useful cells processing prevent

7. The ATM Forum, an organization define ATM standards, has issued a few documents defining the security framework, requirements and implementation specifications.
8. Vendors are mostly following the ATM Forum specifications in their product development and deployment.

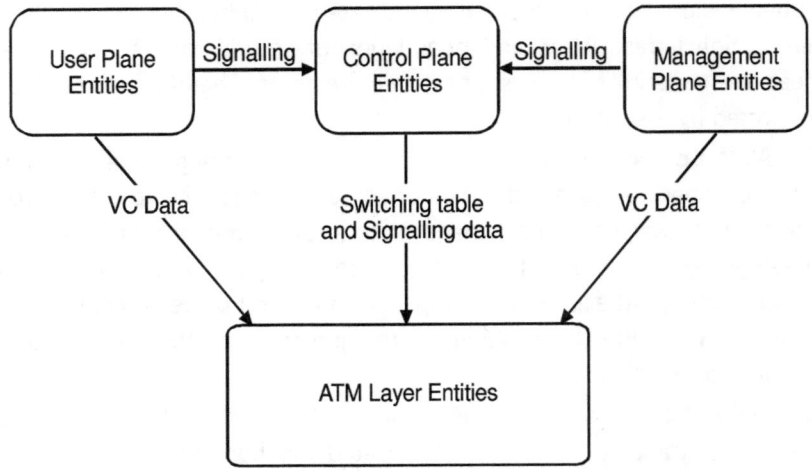

Fig. 5.29: Different Planes in ATM network

5.9.4 Frame Relay Network Security: Vulnerabilities and Mitigations

1. Frame Relay, an OSI layer 2 technology, offers virtual private connection between network devices.
2. The frame relay network consists of a group of interconnected nodes (switches), which relay the frame relay data across the network on the appropriate permanent virtual circuit (PVC).
3. Frame Relay, used a classic Virtual Private Network (VPN) technology, has much less security risks than TCP/IP network.
4. For this reason, Frame Relay is used by industries such as financial and government organizations to transmit high sensitivity data.
5. However, there are still many vulnerabilities in the Frame Relay network, as listed below:
    - **Sniffing:** Intercepting authentication or other sensitive information, often using sniffing devices (software or hardware).
    - **Passwords:** Guessing passwords that protect accounts or system services, particularly default passwords, retrieving and decoding password files.
    - **War Dialing**: Sequentially or randomly dialing every number on a telephone exchange to detect unprotected modems at desktop systems, servers or routers to gain access to, or control over, networks.

- **Spoofing:** Deceiving the network so that it recognizes an unauthorized, possibly external, desktop system as an authorized, internal desktop system to gain unauthorized access to networks and/or sensitive data.
- **Hijacking:** Intercepting authenticated sessions to preempt access by a desktop system to gain control of a session with access to highly sensitive information or business procedures.

5.9.4.1 Frame Relay Security Risk Mitigation

1. The most important defenses against these attacks are the encryption of highly sensitive data in storage and in transit across networks, and the use of strong authentication to control access to stored data such as critical systems and business processes.
2. A frame relay encryption device offers secure communications on an end-to-end basis, establishing a virtual private network within the public frame relay network.
3. To ensure that no modification has occurred to the data during its transmission, and to verify the source of the frame, a frame relay encryption system should have a cryptographic authentication field attached to the frame relay packet.
4. All packets sent to a DLCI designated as cipher should have a crypto authentication code at the beginning of the user data field.
5. If the crypto authentication header is missing or incorrect, the packet is rejected, thereby forming a firewall between the WAN and the router or FRAD on the receiving end of the transmission.
6. As a result, this provides assurance that only authorized incoming and outgoing messages are permitted.

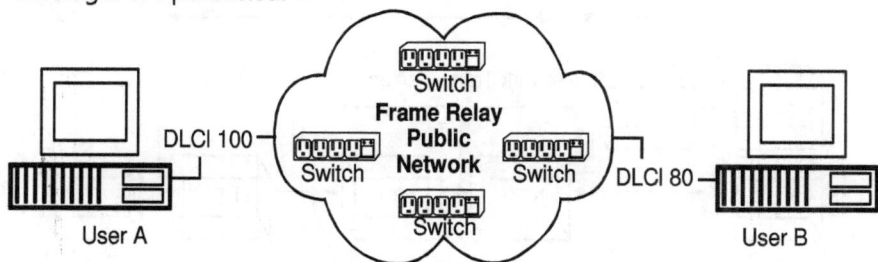

Fig. 5.30: Typical Frame Relay Network ready for protection

5.9.5 ISDN Protection

1. Analog and digital plain old telephony service (POTS) is increasingly replaced by technologies that integrate voice, data, and video communication services.
2. The integrated services digital network (ISDN) offers the embedding of this advanced multimedia communication into the subscriber loop.
3. Nowadays widely available, ISDN builds a promising approach to improve company's, public authority's, or individual's telecommunication facilities.

4. However, a secure means of transferring sensitive information in any publicly accessible communication infrastructure is a major concern.
5. In particular, authenticated and confidential communication is of paramount importance.
6. In this Section, we describe the implementation of a paradigm where advanced security services are offered by the ISDN infrastructure as an additional service.
7. The encryption model is based on transparently integrating the security devices into the ISDN network termination (NT).
8. This makes the approach independent from both the terminal equipment (TE), and the service used, as well as independent from the ISDN switches and exchanges installed by the service provider.
9. This section shows integration of the security device into the ISDN architecture, as well as the design of a data encryption standard (DES). TripleDES encryption unit being the buttress of the ISDN security solution.
10. The ISDN security concept is illustrated in Fig. 5.31. The security unit has been integrated into the ISDN NT between the S reference point and the U reference point.
11. The B-channels B1 and B2 respectively the D-channel are intercepted at the interface between the S/T bus interface terminating the subscriber premises side and the U tranceiver terminating the subscriber loop.
12. That ensures that the approach is independent from both the ISDN exchange that interfaces to a standard line termination (LT) unit, and the end-user equipment that interfaces to a standard S/T component.

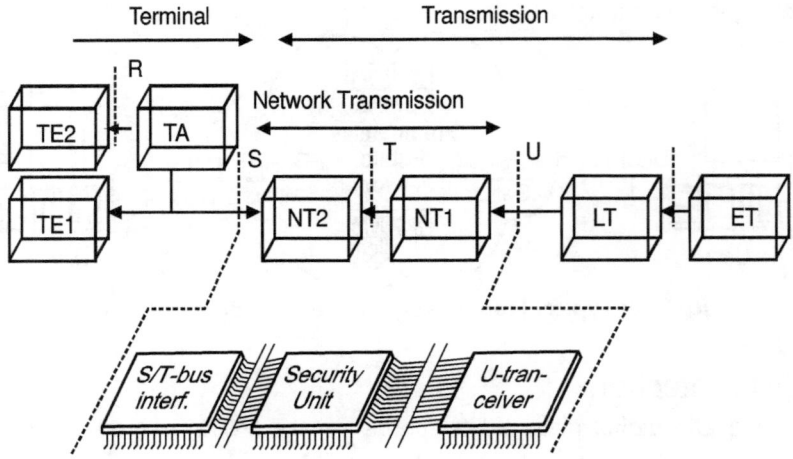

Fig. 5.31: Typical ISDN network Protection Mechanism

13. We now take a closer look to what has been termed "security unit" in the figure above.

14. The interface the security unit is applied to is the standardized IOM-2. (**ISDN**-Oriented Modular-interface).
15. Thus, we call the approach IOM-interception: A field programmable gate array (FPGA) called IOM interceptor extracts the B-channel and D-channel information from the IOM data stream.
16. A microprocessor monitors the signaling information, performs the sequencing of the user channels to the encryption unit, as well as is employed to perform authentication.
17. Finally, the very large scaled integrated (VLSI) encryption circuit performs user data encryption and decryption.
18. In addition, photo couplers decouple the security unit from the ISDN NT and a monitoring interface is provided. This scenario is illustrated in Fig. 5.32.

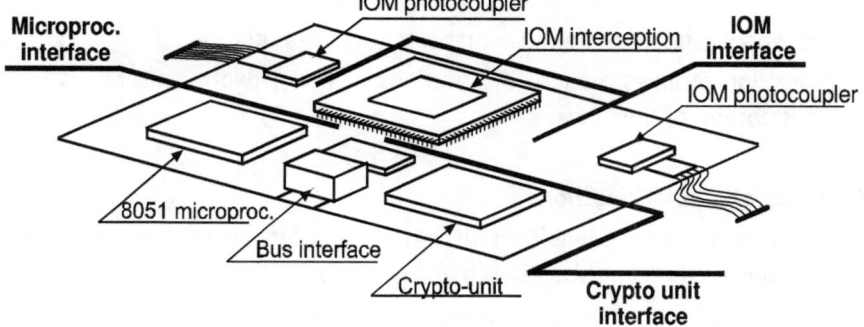

Fig. 5.32: Typical Implemented ISDN security

19. Exploiting the synergies between ISDN and asynchronous transfer mode (ATM) security requirements, a similar approach is followed in the ATM security area.
20. Actually, the crypto unit used is the high speed ATM DES or tripleDES encryptor.
21. It features DES and 3DES in cipher block chaining (CBC) and electronic code book (ECB) operational mode at transfer coverage of up to 155 Mbps.
22. Although such high rates are not required in ISDN, it is a key agile encryptor with on-chip content addressable memory (CAM) and key storage that enables switching between keys assigned to different connections.
23. This fits the ISDN requirements where the two B channels need to be assigned unique keys. What came out of the project is shown in Fig. 5.32 i.e. the comprehensive solution to ISDN security in action.

5.9.6 SONET/SDH Protection

1. Due to the large amount of information being transferred over the network there is a large financial stake in ensuring that the transport services are as readily available as possible.

2. Synchronous Optical Network/Synchronous Digital Hierarchy (SONET/SDH) has been the workhorse of network protection for the past two decades employed in a number of configurations that provide redundant transmission paths.
3. Should a fault occur in any of the transmission paths, the network can rapidly perform what is called a protection switching.
4. The services provided in the area of protection switching are typically referred to as automatic protection switching (APS).
5. When protection switching occurs, communication services are generally restored within 50 ms.
6. In its simplest form, SONET/SDH protection is based on the fielding and implementation of alternate paths for traffic divided between the working portion of the network and the protection portion of the network.
7. The working facilities are those that carry the live traffic.
8. Protection facilities refer to the portions of the network available for traffic if the work portion of the network fails.

5.9.6.1 Network Failure Conditions

1. Even if the network is engineered with a significant margin to ensure high-quality data transfer, there are situations that can cause SONET/SDH facilities to fail.
2. These can be "hard failures" which means complete loss of service or "soft failures" which means degraded modes where the signals being received have an unacceptably high bit-error rate (BER).
3. SONET/SDH protection schemes are designed to react and recover from several conditions, which can include:

1. **Backhoes**
   - Construction
2. **Equipment Failures**
   - Networks are not 100% protected
3. **Mechanical Failures**
   - Vibration, bending of fiber
4. **Natural Disasters**
   - Bad Weather, Earth Quake
5. **Procedural Error (Human)**
   - Pushing the wrong button?

Equipment failures: SONET/SDH equipment is designed to meet some minimum reliability and availability requirements. However, these requirements are statistical in nature, and problems and faults can occur. Critical path components such as lasers and the associated electronics can fail, either in hard modes or in soft modes.

Backhoe fade: Many telecommunications outages are caused each year when heavy construction machines called "backhoes" dig-up underground fibers, cutting them and causing massive service disruptions.

Mechanical failures: Vibration resulting from any number of environmental factors (such as trains on adjacent railroad beds) can affect optical connections over time. Small bends in fiber, sometimes referred to as micro-bending, can lead to degraded signal levels, resulting in lower signal-to-noise ratios (SNRs) that lead to unacceptable BERs.

Natural Disasters: Network failures resulting from weather related incidents, earth quakes, fire could be very destructive to the communication services.

Procedural error: Human error is a significant contributor to the total number of outages in the network.

5.9.6.2 Solution Over Network Failure Conditions

1. There are many solutions to the problems that can affect SONET/SDH equipment.
2. While all of the solutions involve some use of redundant transmission systems, they can be found in a number of network configurations.
3. These physical configurations include: Table 5.13 provides a comparison of various facility restoration techniques.

Table 5.13: Comparison of Restoration Techniques

Restoration Technique	System Complexity Protection	Restoration Time	Major Concern	Best Network Topology	Impacted Area
Diverse Protection	Simple	50 ms	cost	Point to point or hubbed	2 points
Linear	Simple	seconds-minutes	cost	Point to point or hubbed	3 points
Ring	Medium	50 ms	capacity exhaust	Ring	Small Network
Mesh	Complex	seconds-minutes	complex and slow	Mesh	Large Network

4. Linear protection: Between any two points, there can be a number of transmission lines (or fibers in this case).
5. If the primary path fails, then the system can automatically switch to an alternate line.
6. Automatic Protection Switching (APS) architectures and services can trace their ancestry to T-carrier networks.

7. This heritage came in the form of **"1 : N"** forms of protection switching, where N referred to the number of working links protected by a single protection link.

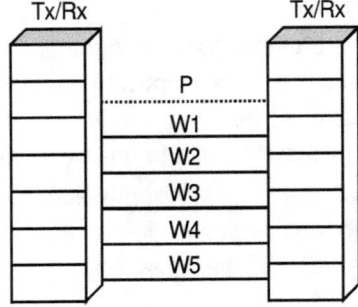

Fig. 5.33: 1 : N Linear Protection System

8. Fig. 5.33 shows an example of 1:5 systems where there is one protection system for 5 working systems, W1-W5. N usually has an upper limit of 14 for availability reasons.
   - Linear Systems with 1 : N Protection provides faster restoration (<50 ms).
   - N is from 1 to 14.
   - Economical solution since it shares protection sources among several working systems.
   - Can not handle simultaneous failures.
9. The 1 : N protection architectures provide only a single protection service for a number of working channels.
10. This works reasonably well in scenarios where the failures are distributed widely enough that the single protect resources are sufficient to provide the desired network availability.
11. If, for example, a network provider wants to be sure that their network is protected against a single fault or event causing a significant outage, then the N working channels should be fielded in a diverse routing scenario.
12. One of the more significant network problems is associated with the backhoe fade, so the 1 : N architectures should only be fielded when the various work spans are run on independent physical routes.
13. Pulling the collection of N spans into a bundled distribution would be an example of a poor 1 : N system architecture.
14. Additionally, the protection span would need to be directed along a separate route.
15. Ring-based protection: There are several flavors of ring architectures, and the manner in which they protect the SONET/SDH payload varies.
16. The general concept is that the collection of SONET/SDH equipment is arranged into a closed loop (where the physical paths through the ring eventually find their way back to the same start and end points).

17. When fiber breaks occur, signals can be redirected over diverse routes, taking paths through alternate network elements.
18. The selection of the preferred architecture is largely up to the network architect's discretion.
19. The network architect will need to consider a number of criteria, including the size, scope, cost, and availability constraints on their network.
20. There are several forms of ring protection employed in SONET/SDHs, and a number of options can be considered in the deployment of SONET/SDH architectures.
    - The UPSR is the fastest protection-switching method.
    - Traffic is redundantly presented to the recipient device all the time.
    - The protection switching is relegated to a local switch that is extremely fast.
    - More processing is required for path switching and the receiver must have split copies and the intelligence to accomplish the task.
    - 50% of the fiber in each ring is generally not used with UPSR.
    - Supports two or four fiber.

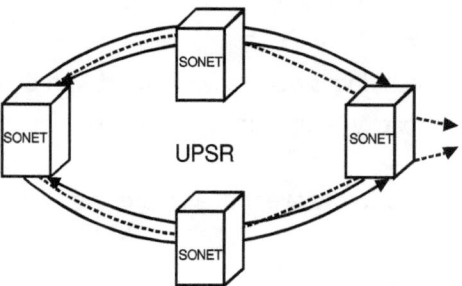

Fig. 5.34: UPSCR (Unidirectional Path Switching Architecture)

21. SONET/SDH has mechanisms to protect at either the line or path level. Which direction the signals flow in a ring?
22. Signals can all route in the same direction (unidirectional) or in opposite directions (bidirectional).
23. How many fibers are being used in each link? Either one- or two-pair (two- or four-fiber) configurations are selected.
24. The number of combinations in which these options can be employed leads to an alphabet soup of SONET/SDH protection schemes.
25. In unidirectional ring architectures, the information flows in a single direction through the ring.
26. All traffic can usually be sent simultaneously in both directions.
27. If some event occurs that degrades one of the paths through the network, it is up to the receiving network element to select the incoming traffic to be processed.

28. Given the differences in propagation lengths between the two directions, unidirectional rings are most frequently found in tightly-constrained geographical applications.
29. If the default route takes a longer path, it can introduce undesirable timing characteristics as the distances and number of network elements grow.
30. Each of these configurations can be realized in either two- or four-wire configurations.
31. Recent dense wavelength division multiplexing (DWDM) ring implementations have also provided what amount to sub-line oriented protection architectures, but leverage on the basic concepts applied in the earlier SONET/SDH ring protection schemes.
32. Like unidirectional rings, bidirectional rings (BLSR) are arranged as closed-loop network elements connected by two or four fibers between each neighbouring element.
33. The major difference between the two implementations is the selection of the route taken by the working traffic.
34. In bidirectional rings, the work traffic is selected from the shorter of the two routes.
35. Bidirectional rings provide the advantage of minimizing network delays. Fig. 5.35 shows the schematic of the four-fiber and two-fiber bi-directional ring architecture.
    - In the event of a link failure, traffic is looped back in the SONET/SDH element adjacent to the failure.
    - 50% of the fiber in each ring is generally not used with BLSR.
    - 50% of the fiber capacity is in standby mode waiting for a "protection event" to occur.
    - Line switching is simple. In the event of a failure, the NE locally switches the traffic.

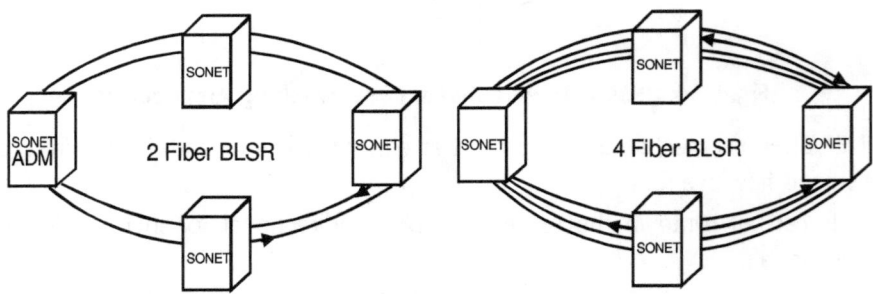

Fig. 5.35: Bidirectional Ring Architecture

36. Both two and four-fiber architectures can be employed in either the uni- or bidirectional architectures.
37. Because of the smaller geographical applications employed by unidirectional rings, the four-fiber case is reserved for the case of the bidirectional rings.
38. The primary distinction between the two- and four-fiber case is that when two fibers are used in a ring architecture, 50% of each fiber can be used for working traffic, with the remaining 50% reserved for protection traffic.

39. Only half of the fiber's capacity can be consumed for traffic.
40. When the fiber count is increased to four fibers, the full capacity of each link can be employed.
41. Where half of each link had been reserved for protection traffic in the two-fiber case, the four-fiber rings are arranged so that each fiber is carrying either working traffic or protection traffic, never both.
42. When a fault occurs, the receiving station immediately redirects its attention to the better of the two inputs.
43. The final distinguishing characteristic of SONET/SDH APS services is the selection of path or line switching architectures.
44. The key characteristic distinguishing the two approaches is that where line switching selects between one of two OC-N lines switching all channels being carried, path switching can only affect a subset of the payload channels carried by an OC-N bundle.
45. Line switching has been the preferred method of protection because it can be handled by any line-terminating equipment, and occurs closer to the location of the fault.
46. Path switching requires considerably more processing overhead, and greatly adds to the complexity (and cost) of the SONET/SDH path-terminating equipment.
47. However, path switching provides the advantage of ensuring the quality of the received payload traffic that, in some cases, may have traversed several interconnected rings.

5.9.7 DSL Network Risk and Protection

The discussion here is limited to the security issues involved in the DSL connection itself as well as the different network topologies used to hook up a DSL connection.

ADSL Benefits

The main advantages of ADSL are:
- Always on, no "connection setup" waiting.
- Shared Internet connection possible between several hosts
- Faster than ISDN or analog modem access
- May be the cheapest alternative for frequent users.

Risks

The principle risk of an unsecured ADSL connection is unauthorized access from the Internet to your host(s) on the local network (on the LAN side of the ADSL router/modem).

Such unauthorized access is made more probable since the connection is "always on" and hence attackers can quietly try to crack your machines as you sleep. With "normal" dial-up connections, it's easier to notice unusual activity as one works on the machine when connected to the Internet. Possible impact of such unauthorized access:

1. Your computer could be misused to publish porn images, warez (pirated software archive), or as a hub for hacker forums.
2. Your computer could be misused to attack other machines (hundreds of so called 'attack (ro)bots' or 'zombies' can be used to cause major disruption to other Internet sites or users.). Your machine is then used to hide the identity of the real attackers, and you seem to be the person who is carrying out the attacks.
3. Your computer could be misused for mass mailing (i.e. spam).
4. Theft of information (loss of privacy/confidentiality), and possible misuse for financial gain (credit card numbers, misuse of banking software, blackmail).
5. Destruction of information or programs.
6. Changing of information (loss of integrity).
7. Lost time trying to get hackers out, reinstall or clean up after them.
8. If your computer is misused, it could generate massive amounts of traffic which will cost you money unless you have a flat-rate Internet access. In addition sites which have been 'attacked by you' may block your address from their sites.

5.9.7.1 Security Risks
1. Let us look at some traditional security risks to see how DSL is susceptible to them.
2. Later in this section, we will discuss how to mitigate these risks through proper engineering of DSL network connections.

5.9.7.2 Eavesdropping
1. Eavesdropping risks arise when an outsider is able to listen in on your local network traffic.
2. This information-gathering may range from spying on file transfers around your network to gathering information about the network configuration itself, such as the names of users, computers and other system resources.
3. Eavesdropping may directly compromise your network (e.g., spying on network file transfers), or may be the source of information that could aid further intrusion attempts (e.g., knowing the system resources to attack).
4. In the most pathological extreme, it is possible to build a DSL connection that forces all traffic, even intra-LAN local traffic, over the DSL connection.
5. With the higher speeds offered by DSL connections, the casual user might not even notice this happening. More sophisticated DSL connection techniques can dramatically reduce the eavesdropping threat.

5.9.7.3 Probing
1. Probing is a term that refers to the practice of examining a host and testing its response to various probes.

2. A typical probe attack involves an automated program that scans a host's TCP/UDP ports, looking for running services that respond to queries.
3. The attacker can then attempt to exploit weaknesses in any responding services. For example, the infamous Internet Worm, developed by Robert Morris and unleashed Nov. 2, 1988, used a number of techniques to breach system security.
4. One mechanism it used was to probe hosts, looking for running instances of the "finger" program; once found, the worm would try to exploit an unknown buffer overrun bug in many versions of the finger program, causing the worm's code to be executed on the target host.
5. A DSL-connected LAN, with its permanent connection, is an attractive target for a probing attack. Porous DSL connections can leak a constant stream of information to outside probers, giving them the first to hold on your LAN security walls.

5.9.7.4 Impersonation

1. Impersonation can take a number of different forms, but one example is IP address stealing.
2. For example, depending on your network configuration, it may be possible for another DSL subscriber to "steal" your IP address, causing all information addressed to your computer (including, say, the results of your online banking statement request), to pass instead to the attacker's host.
3. In reality, IP address stealing is usually an impractical attack, but it highlights two fundamental principles for security on the Internet: (1) Any security mechanism based on IP addresses is flawed; (2) Assume that any plaintext sent over the Internet is open to prying eyes.
4. Unlike a PPP dialup connection, or a routed T1 connection, a bridged DSL connection is susceptible to IP address stealing.

5.9.7.5 Denial-of-Service

1. DoS attacks do not attempt to obtain private information or to delete or corrupt files on attacked hosts.
2. Rather, they attempt to make a host unusable by keeping it too busy performing useless functions.
3. Many simple DoS attacks do not work well over a dialup connection, because it is just not possible to send enough traffic over an analog modem to have a serious negative impact on a modern PC.
4. However, with a high-speed DSL connection, it becomes possible to generate serious DoS attacks.

5.9.7.6 Viruses
1. Virus attacks are familiar to many: they occur when a file, placed on a host and executed, performs harmful actions, including attempting to spread itself to other hosts on the network.
2. DSL connections, even with a secure network topology, do not innately protect against virus attacks, and ISPs have started to recognize this opportunity.
3. Good virus protection should be a primary concern for any network, especially one with a DSL connection.

5.9.7.7 Connection Types
1. The first factor influencing the security of a DSL connection is the type of connection used by the provisioning ISP.
2. For this discussion, the underlying DSL physical layer technology—SDSL, ADSL, RADSL, etc.—is immaterial. Regardless of the xDSL technology used, ISPs need to build a network topology on top of the DSL bit pipe.
3. Options include a bridged connection; a routed connection; or a Point-to-Point Protocol (PPP) connection, either PPPoA (PPP over ATM) or PPPoE (PPP over Ethernet).

5.9.7.8 Bridged Connection
1. The connection type with the least inherent security is a bridged connection.
2. A bridged connection is a DSL modem with an Ethernet interface that logically acts as an Ethernet bridge between the client device and the ISP's network.
3. As such, the DSL modem in the bridged case acts exactly like a standard Ethernet bridge between two Ethernet segments: the clients and the ISPs.
4. Bridged connections of this type are infamous for their susceptibility to eavesdropping.
5. A bridged connection is also more susceptible to IP address stealing than other DSL connection types.

5.9.7.9 Routed Connections
1. A routed connection is a DSL connection in which Layer 3 IP routing is used to connect the customer to the ISP.
2. In other words, the DSL modem functions as an IP router.
3. The DSL modem has its own IP address in this scenario, one of a subnet of addresses assigned to the customer. For this reason, routed connection types are rare for residential customers.

4. The security characteristics of a routed connection are similar to those of the Internet at large.
5. Local traffic, even LAN broadcasts, is not passed over the router to the ISP.
6. It is also difficult for others to steal an IP address, since the ISP generally knows which IP subnet ranges are assigned to which customers, and has its routers configured accordingly.

5.9.7.10 PPP Connections
1. PPPoA and PPPoE are mechanisms to build a Point-to-Point Protocol logical link over ATM and Ethernet, respectively.
2. The PPP was originally conceived for building an endpoint-to-endpoint data link layer over a simple construct like a serial line.
3. The security characteristics of PPPoA and PPPoE are similar. Typically, as part of the PPP link establishment, some sort of ID/password is required.
4. The ISP can use this credential set for authorization and billing purposes.
5. As with routed connections, a Windows network will not show up on external Network Neighbourhood lists unless special efforts are made to advertise its existence.
6. The IP address is typically assigned as part of the link establishment in such a way that the ISP knows which IP addresses are where.
7. This makes IP address stealing a difficult task.

5.9.7.11 Implementing Protection Techniques
1. There are three basic ways to hook up a LAN to a DSL connection: a direct connection, a multihomed gateway host or a turnkey firewall solution.
2. These connections also apply to a single PC hookup. The detail discussion of these techniques is beyond the scope of this book.
3. Also following topologies must be used to make the DSL connection secured.
4. If you are starting out with new hardware, I'd recommend one of the following setups when integrating your Firewall.
5. The modem topology is better than with routers, since the configuration is easier and it's cheaper to buy a modem than an ADSL router.
6. Note that the modem must be external and not a internal card in a PC.
7. Recommended Topology of ADSL connection

Assuming one single PC is being protected:

Phone----ADSL ---- Firewall --------------- Internal PC
line   modem

Assuming a small network of up to 4 PCs are being protected:

Phone----ADSL ---- Firewall -------- Hub -- Internal PCs
line   modem   Incl.router

Phone----ADSL ---- Firewall --------------- Internal PCs
line   modem   Incl.router+hub

Assuming more than 4 PCs are being protected, or a hub/switch is already available:

Phone----ADSL ---- Firewall -------- Hub -- Internal PCs
line   modem   Incl.router

8. **Disabling remote access to routers***

   You should **disable remote access** (or Remote Administration) on your router. Some routers have remote access enabled by default. Consult the manual that came with your device for further information on how to do this.

9. **Changing router usernames and passwords***

   The factory default setting for a router's username and password is usually "admin" or "administrator". To make your router more secure, change these default usernames and passwords to something only you will know. Please keep a record of your chosen username and password in a safe place.

10. **Protecting wireless access to routers***

    Some ADSL routers can also function as wireless (Wi-Fi) access points. Anyone with Wi-Fi enabled hardware and who comes within the broadcast range of your wireless access point may be able to use your Internet connection without your knowledge. In order to prevent this, most wireless routers will allow you to set up security measures such as:

    Disable broadcasting the name of the access point
    Enabling WEP (**Wired Equivalent Privacy**) or even WPA (Wi-Fi Protected Access) encryption
    Allow access to computers with specific MAC addresses
    Disable the wireless capability of the router completely

Note that instructions for setting any of the above restrictions will vary from one router to the next, and you should consult the manual that came with your router for further information.

11. **Use of firewalls**

A hardware or software firewall protects a computer from Internet intrusion attempts. Many routers have built-in firewalls, but if you access the Internet using a normal ADSL modem you should seriously consider installing a firewall. Some software-based firewall packages are free.

12. Use of antivirus software

This security measure is not limited to ADSL users. Antivirus software is not a luxury; it is essential. It will protect our members from viruses that are hidden within e-mails (on domains that we manage and administer on our own mail platforms). But, malicious code can be hidden inside Web pages, software, instant messages, pictures, text files, hard drives, removable storage devices as well as e-mails. Purchasing a reputable, commercial antivirus package, preferably with anti-spyware and anti-trojan functionality built in, is highly recommended.

13. Changing your Internet password

ADSL users are advised to change their passwords regularly, especially if they suspect that someone may be trying to use their account details. Users can easily change their passwords online.

14. Updating Operating System regularly

OS developers release new security patches for OS frequently accordingly one should update all patches regularly.

5.10 Wireless Network attacks and Protection

1. **Wireless security** is the prevention of unauthorized access or damage to computers using wireless networks.
2. Wireless networks are very common, both for organizations and individuals. Many laptop computers have wireless cards pre-installed. The ability to enter a network while mobile has great benefits. However, wireless networking has many security issues. Hackers have found wireless networks relatively easy to break into, and even use wireless technology to crack into wired networks.
3. As a result, it's very important that enterprises define effective wireless security policies that guard against unauthorized access to important resources. Wireless Intrusion Prevention Systems are commonly used to enforce wireless security policies.
4. The risks to users of wireless technology have increased as the service has become more popular. There were relatively few dangers when wireless technology was first introduced. Crackers had not yet had time to latch on to the new technology and wireless was not commonly found in the work place.
5. However, there are a great number of security risks associated with the current wireless protocols and encryption methods, and in the carelessness and ignorance that exists at the user and corporate IT level. Cracking methods have become much more sophisticated and innovative with wireless. Cracking has also become much easier and more accessible with easy-to-use Windows or Linux-based tools being made available on the web at no charge.

6. Some organizations that have no wireless access points installed do not feel that they need to address wireless security concerns. In-Stat various company Group have estimated that 95% of all corporate laptop computers that were planned to be purchased in 2005 were equipped with wireless.

7. Issues can arise in a supposedly non-wireless organization when a wireless laptop is plugged into the corporate network. A cracker could sit out in the parking lot and gather info from it through laptops and/or other devices as handhelds, or even break in through this wireless card-equipped laptop and gain access to the wired network.

5.11 Types of unauthorized access

Accidental Association

- Unauthorized access to company wireless and wired networks can come from a number of different methods and intents.
- One of these methods is referred to as "accidental association".
- When a user turns on a computer and it latches on to a wireless access point from a neighbouring company's overlapping network, the user may not even know that this has occurred.
- However, it is a security breach in that proprietary company information is exposed and now there could exist a link from one company to the other. This is especially true if the laptop is also hooked to a wired network.

Malicious Association

- "Malicious associations" are when wireless devices can be actively made by crackers to connect to a company network through their cracking laptop instead of a company access point (AP).
- These types of laptops are known as "soft APs" and are created when a cracker runs some software that makes his/her wireless network card look like a legitimate access point. Once the cracker has gained access, he/she can steal passwords, launch attacks on the wired network, or plant trojans.
- Since, wireless networks operate at the Layer 2 level, Layer 3 protections such as network authentication and virtual private networks (VPNs) offer no barrier. Wireless 802.1x authentications do help with protection but are still vulnerable to cracking.
- The idea behind this type of attack may not be to break into a VPN or other security measures. Most likely the cracker is just trying to take over the client at the Layer 2 level.

Ad-hoc Networks

- Ad-hoc networks can pose a security threat. Ad-hoc networks are defined as peer-to-peer networks between wireless computers that do not have an access point in between them. While these types of networks usually have little protection, encryption methods can be used to provide security.
- The security hole provided by Ad-hoc networking is not the Ad-hoc network itself but the bridge it provides into other networks, usually in the corporate environment, and the unfortunate default settings in most versions of Microsoft Windows to have this feature turned on unless explicitly disabled.
- Thus the user may not even know they have an unsecured Ad-hoc network in operation on their computer. If they are also using a wired or wireless infrastructure network at the same time, they are providing a bridge to the secured organizational network through the unsecured Ad-hoc connection.
- Bridging is in two forms. A direct bridge, which requires the user actually configure a bridge between the two connections and is thus unlikely to be initiated unless explicitly desired, and an indirect bridge which is the shared resources on the user computer.
- The indirect bridge provides two security hazards. The first is that critical organizational data obtained via the secured network may be on the user's end node computer drive and thus exposed to discovery via the unsecured Ad-hoc network.
- The second is that a computer virus or otherwise undesirable code may be placed on the user's computer via the unsecured Ad-hoc connection and thus has a route to the organizational secured network.
- In this case, the person placing the malicious code need not "crack" the passwords to the organizational network, the legitimate user has provided access via a normal and routine log-in.
- The malfactor simply needs to place the malicious code on the unsuspecting user's end node system via the open (unsecured) Ad-hoc connection.

Non-traditional Networks

- Non-traditional networks such as personal network Bluetooth devices are not safe from cracking and should be regarded as a security risk.
- Even barcode readers, handheld PDAs (Personal Digital Assistants), and wireless printers and copiers should be secured.
- These non-traditional networks can be easily overlooked by IT personnel who have narrowly focused on laptops and access points.

Identity Theft (MAC Spoofing)

- Identity theft (or MAC spoofing) occurs when a cracker is able to listen in on network traffic and identify the MAC address of a computer with network privileges.
- Most wireless systems allow some kind of MAC filtering to only allow authorized computers with specific MAC IDs to gain access and utilize the network.
- However, a number of programs exist that have network "sniffing" capabilities. Combine these programs with other software that allow a computer to pretend it has any MAC address that the cracker desires, and the cracker can easily get around that hurdle.
- MAC filtering is only effective for small residential (SOHO) networks, since it only provides protection when the wireless device is "off the air". Any 802.11 device "on the air" freely transmits it unencrypted MAC address in its 802.11 headers, and it requires no special equipment or software to detect it.
- Anyone with an 802.11 receiver (laptop and wireless adapter) and a freeware wireless packet analyzer can obtain the MAC address of any transmitting 802.11 within range.
- In an organizational environment, where most wireless devices are "on the air" throughout the active working shift, MAC filtering only provides a false sense of security since it only prevents "causal" or unintended connections to the organizational infrastructure and does nothing to prevent a directed attack.

Man-in-the-middle Attacks

- A man-in-the-middle attacker entices computers to log into a computer which is set up as a soft AP (Access Point).
- Once this is done, the hacker connects to a real access point through another wireless card offering a steady flow of traffic through the transparent hacking computer to the real network. The hacker can then sniff the traffic.
- One type of man-in-the-middle attack relies on security faults in challenge and handshake protocols to execute a "de-authentication attack".
- This attack forces AP-connected computers to drop their connections and reconnect with the cracker's soft AP.
- Man-in-the-middle attacks are enhanced by software such as LANjack and AirJack, which automate multiple steps of the process.
- What once required some skill can now be done by script kiddies. Hotspots are particularly vulnerable to any attack since there is little to no security on these networks.

Denial of Service

- A Denial-of-Service attack (DoS) occurs when an attacker continually bombards a targeted AP (Access Point) or network with bogus requests, premature successful connection messages, failure messages, and/or other commands.

- These cause legitimate users to not be able to get on the network and may even cause the network to crash. These attacks rely on the abuse of protocols such as the Extensible Authentication Protocol (EAP).
- The DoS attack in itself does little to expose organizational data to a malicious attacker, since the interruption of the network prevents the flow of data and actually indirectly protects data by preventing it from being transmitted.
- The usual reason for performing a DoS attack is to observe the recovery of the wireless network, during which all of the initial handshake codes are re-transmitted by all devices, providing an opportunity for the malicious attacker to record these codes and use various "cracking" tools to analyze security weaknesses and exploit them to gain unauthorized access to the system.
- This works best on weakly encrypted systems such as WEP, where there are a number of tools available which can launch a dictionary style attack of "possibly accepted" security keys based on the "model" security key captured during the network recovery.

Network Injection

- In a network injection attack, a cracker can make use of access points that are exposed to non-filtered network traffic, specifically broadcasting network traffic such as "Spanning Tree" (802.1D), OSPF (Open Shortest Path First), RIP (Routing Information Protocol), and HSRP (**Hot Standby Router Protocol**).
- The cracker injects bogus networking re-configuration commands that affect routers, switches, and intelligent hubs.
- A whole network can be brought down in this manner and require rebooting or even reprogramming of all intelligent networking devices.

Caffe Latte Attack

- The Caffe Latte attack is another way to defeat WEP. It is not necessary for the attacker to be in the area of the network using this exploit.
- By using a process that targets the Windows wireless stack, it is possible to obtain the WEP key from a remote client.
- By sending a flood of encrypted ARP (*address resolution protocol*) (requests, the assailant takes advantage of the shared key authentication and the message modification flaws in 802.11 WEP.
- The attacker uses the ARP responses to obtain the WEP key in less than 6 minutes.

5.12 Wireless Intrusion Prevention Systems

1. A Wireless Intrusion Prevention System (WIPS) is the most robust way to counteract wireless security risks.

2. A WIPS is typically implemented as an overlay to an existing Wireless LAN infrastructure, although it may be deployed standalone to enforce no-wireless policies within an organization.
3. Large organizations with many employees are particularly vulnerable to security breaches caused by rogue access points.
4. If an employee (trusted entity) in a location brings in an easily available wireless router, the entire network can be exposed to anyone within range of the signals.
5. WIPS is considered so important to wireless security that in July 2009, the PCI Security Standards Council published wireless guidelines for PCI DSS (Payment Card Industry Data Security Standard) recommending the use of WIPS to automate wireless scanning and protection for large organizations.

5.13 Security Options

There are three principal ways to secure a wireless network.
- For closed networks (like home users and organizations) the most common way is to configure access restrictions in the access points. Those restrictions may include encryption and checks on MAC address. Another option is to disable ESSID (Extended Service Set Identification) broadcasting, making the access point difficult for outsiders to detect. Wireless Intrusion Prevention Systems can be used to provide wireless LAN security in this network model.
- For commercial providers, hotspots, and large organizations, the preferred solution is often to have an open and unencrypted, but completely isolated wireless network. The users will at first have no access to the Internet nor to any local network resources. Commercial providers usually forward all web traffic to a captive portal which provides for payment and/or authorization. Another solution is to require the users to connect securely to a privileged network using VPN.
- Wireless networks are less secure than wired ones; in many offices intruders can easily visit and hook up their own computer to the wired network without problems, gaining access to the network, and it's also often possible for remote intruders to gain access to the network through backdoors like Back Orifice. One general solution may be end-to-end encryption, with independent authentication on all resources that shouldn't be available to the public.

5.13.1 Wireless Security Best Practices

Many folks setting up wireless home networks rush through the job to get their Internet connectivity working as quickly as possible. That's totally understandable. It's also quite risky as numerous security problems can result. Today's Wi-Fi networking products don't always help the situation as configuring their security features can be time-consuming and non-intuitive. The recommendations below summarize the steps you should take to improve the security of your home wireless network.

1. **Change Default Administrator Passwords (and Usernames)**

At the core of most Wi-Fi home networks is an access point or router. To set up these pieces of equipment, manufacturers provide Web pages that allow owners to enter their network address and account information. These Web tools are protected with a login screen (username and password) so that only the rightful owner can do this. However, for any given piece of equipment, the logins provided are simple and very well-known to hackers on the Internet. Change these settings immediately.

2. **Turn on (Compatible) WPA/WEP Encryption**

All Wi-Fi equipment supports some form of *encryption*. Encryption technology scrambles messages sent over wireless networks so that they cannot be easily read by humans. Several encryption technologies exist for Wi-Fi today. Naturally you will want to pick the strongest form of encryption that works with your wireless network. However, the way these technologies work, all Wi-Fi devices on your network must share the identical encryption settings. Therefore, you may need to find a "lowest common demoninator" setting.

3. **Change the Default SSID**

Access points and routers all use a network name called the SSID. Manufacturers normally ship their products with the same SSID set.

For example: The SSID for Linksys devices is normally "linksys." True, knowing the SSID does not by itself allow your neighbours to break into your network, but it is a start. More importantly, when someone finds a default SSID, they see it is a poorly configured network and are much more likely to attack it. Change the default SSID immediately when configuring wireless security on your network.

4. **Enable MAC Address Filtering**

Each piece of Wi-Fi gear possesses a unique identifier called the *physical address* or *MAC address*. Access points and routers keep track of the MAC addresses of all devices that connect to them. Many such products offer the owner an option to key in the MAC addresses of their home equipment, that restricts the network to only allow connections from those devices. Do this, but also know that the feature is not so powerful as it may seem. Hackers and their software programs can fake MAC addresses easily.

5. **Disable SSID Broadcast**

In Wi-Fi networking, the wireless access point or router typically broadcasts the network name (SSID) over the air at regular intervals. This feature was designed for businesses and mobile hotspots where Wi-Fi clients may roam in and out of range. In the home, this roaming feature is unnecessary, and it increases the likelihood someone will try to log in to your home network. Fortunately, most Wi-Fi access points allow the SSID broadcast feature to be disabled by the network administrator.

6. **Do Not Auto-Connect to Open Wi-Fi Networks**

Connecting to an open Wi-Fi network such as a free wireless hotspot or your neighbour's router exposes your computer to security risks. Although not normally enabled, most computers have a setting available allowing these connections to happen automatically without notifying you (the user). This setting should not be enabled except in temporary situations.

7. Assign Static IP Addresses to Devices

Most home networkers gravitate toward using *dynamic IP addresses*. DHCP technology is indeed easy to set up. Unfortunately, this convenience also works to the advantage of network attackers, who can easily obtain valid IP addresses from your network's DHCP pool. Turn off DHCP on the router or access point, set a fixed IP address range instead, then configure each connected device to match. Use a private IP *address range* (like 10.0.0.x) to prevent computers from being directly reached from the Internet.

8. Enable Firewalls on each Computer and the Router

Modern network routers contain built-in firewall capability, but the option also exists to disable them. Ensure that your router's firewall is turned on. For extra protection, consider installing and running *personal firewall software* on each computer connected to the router.

9. Position the Router or Access Point Safely

Wi-Fi signals normally reach to the exterior of a home. A small amount of signal leakage outdoors is not a problem, but the further this signal reaches, the easier it is for others to detect and exploit. Wi-Fi signals often reach through neighboring homes and into streets, for example. When installing a wireless home network, the position of the access point or router determines its reach. Try to position these devices near the center of the home rather than near windows to minimize leakage.

10. Turn Off the Network During Extended Periods of Non-Use

The ultimate in wireless security measures, shutting down your network will most certainly prevent outside hackers from breaking in! While impractical to turn off and on the devices frequently, at least consider doing so during travel or extended periods offline. Computer disk drives have been known to suffer from power cycle wear-and-tear, but this is a secondary concern for broadband modems and routers. If you own a wireless router but are only using it wired (Ethernet) connections, you can also sometimes turn off Wi-Fi on a broadband router without powering down the entire network.

5.14 Jitter and Jitter Measurement

1. **Jitter** is the time variation of a periodic signal in electronics and telecommunications, often in relation to a reference clock source. Jitter may be observed in characteristics such as the frequency of successive pulses, the signal amplitude, or phase of periodic signals. Jitter is a significant, and usually undesired, factor in the design of almost all communications links (e.g., USB, PCI-e, SATA, OC-48). In clock recovery applications it is called *timing jitter*.
2. Jitter can be quantified in the same terms as all time-varying signals, e.g., RMS, or peak-to-peak displacement. Also like other time-varying signals, jitter can be expressed in terms of spectral density (frequency content).

3. *Jitter period* is the interval between two times of maximum effect (or minimum effect) of a signal characteristic that varies regularly with time. *Jitter frequency*, the more commonly quoted figure, is its inverse. Generally, very low jitter frequency is not of interest in designing systems, and the low-frequency cut-off for jitter is typically specified at 1 Hz.

5.14.1 Packet Jitter in Computer Networks

1. In the context of computer networks, the term *jitter* is often used as a measure of the variability over time of the packet latency across a network.
2. However, for this use, the term is imprecise. The standards-based term is *packet delay variation* (PDV). PDV is an important quality of service factor in assessment of network performance.
3. A network with constant latency has no variation (or jitter). Packet jitter is expressed as an average of the deviation from the network mean latency.

5.14.2 Compact Disc Seek Jitter

1. In the context of digital audio extraction from Compact Discs, **seek jitter** causes extracted audio samples to be doubled-up or skipped entirely if the Compact Disc drive re-seeks. The problem occurs during seeking because the Red Book (audio CD standard) does not require block-accurate addressing. As a result, the extraction process may restart a few samples early or late, resulting in doubled or omitted samples.
2. These glitches often sound like tiny repeating clicks during playback. A successful approach of correction in software involves performing overlapping reads and fitting the data to find overlaps at the edges. Most extraction programs perform seek jitter correction. CD manufacturers avoid seek jitter by extracting the entire disc in one continuous read operation using special CD drive models at slower speeds so the drive does not re-seek.
3. Due to additional sector level addressing added in the Yellow Book (CD standard), CD-ROM data discs are not subject to seek jitter.
4. A *jitter meter* is a testing instrument for measuring clock jitter values, and is used in manufacturing DVD and CD-ROM discs.

5.14.3 Phase Jitter Metrics

1. For clock jitter, there are three commonly used metrics: *absolute jitter, period jitter,* and *cycle-to-cycle jitter*.
2. Cycle-to-cycle jitter is the difference in length of any two adjacent clock periods. Accordingly, it can be thought of as the discrete-time derivative of period jitter. It can

be important for some types of clock generation circuitry used in microprocessors and RAM interfaces.
3. All of these jitter metrics are really measures of a single time-dependent quantity, and hence are related by derivatives as described above. Since they have different generation mechanisms, different circuit effects, and different measurement methodology, it is still useful to quantify them separately.
4. In the telecommunications world, the unit used for the above types of jitter is usually the *UI* (or *Unit Interval*) which quantifies the jitter in terms of a fraction of the ideal period of the clock. This unit is useful because it scales with clock frequency and thus allows relatively slow interconnects such as T1 to be compared to higher-speed internet backbone links such as OC-192. Absolute units such as *picoseconds* are more common in microprocessor applications. Units of *degrees* and *radians* are also used.
5. If jitter has a Gaussian distribution, it is usually quantified using the standard deviation of this distribution (aka. *RMS*). Often, jitter distribution is significantly non-Gaussian. This can occur if the jitter is caused by external sources such as power supply noise. In these cases, *peak-to-peak* measurements are more useful. Many efforts have been made to meaningfully quantify distributions that are neither Gaussian nor have meaningful peaks (which is the case in all real jitter). All have shortcomings but most tend to be good enough for the purposes of engineering work. Note that typically, the reference point for jitter is defined such that the *mean* jitter is 0.
6. In networking, in particular IP networks such as the Internet, jitter can refer to the variation (statistical dispersion) in the delay of the packets.

5.15 Types of Jitter
There are three types:
1. Random jitter
2. Deterministic jitter

5.15.1 Random Jitter
Random Jitter, also called Gaussian jitter, is unpredictable electronic timing noise. Random jitter typically follows a Gaussian distribution or Normal distribution. It is believed to follow this pattern because most noise or jitter in a electrical circuit is caused by thermal noise, which does have a Gaussian distribution. Another reason for random jitter to have a distribution like this is due to the central limit theorem. The central limit theorem states that composite effect of many uncorrelated noise sources, regardless of the distributions, approaches a Gaussian distribution. One of the main differences between random and deterministic jitter is that deterministic jitter is bounded and random jitter is unbounded.

5.15.2 Deterministic Jitter

Deterministic jitter is a type of clock timing jitter or data signal jitter that is predictable and reproducible. The peak-to-peak value of this jitter is bounded, and the bounds can easily be observed and predicted. Periodic jitter, data-dependent jitter, and duty-cycle dependent jitter are all types of deterministic jitter.

5.15.3 Total Jitter

Total jitter (T) is the combination of random jitter (R) and deterministic jitter (D):

$$T = D_{\text{peak-to-peak}} + n \times R_{rms},$$

in which the value of n is based on the bit error rate (BER) required of the link.
A common bit error rate used in communication standards such as Ethernet is 10^{-12}.

5.16 Testing and Measurement of Jitter

1. Testing for jitter and its measurement is of growing importance to electronics engineers because of increased clock frequencies in digital electronic circuitry to achieve higher device performance. Higher clock frequencies have commensurately smaller eye openings, and thus impose tighter tolerances on jitter. For example, modern computer motherboards have serial bus architectures with eye openings of 160 picoseconds or less. This is extremely small compared to parallel bus architectures with equivalent performance, which may have eye openings on the order of 1000 picoseconds.
2. Testing of device performance for jitter tolerance often involves the injection of jitter into electronic components with specialized test equipment.
3. Jitter is measured and evaluated in various ways depending on the type of circuitry under test. For example, jitter in serial bus architectures is measured by means of eye diagrams, according to industry accepted standards. A less direct approach—in which analog waveforms are digitized and the resulting data stream analyzed—is employed when measuring pixel jitter in frame grabbers. In all cases, the goal of jitter measurement is to verify that the jitter will not disrupt normal operation of the circuitry.
4. There are standards for jitter measurement in serial bus architectures. The standards cover jitter tolerance, jitter transfer function and jitter generation, with the required values for these attributes varying among different applications. Where applicable, compliant systems are required to conform to these standards.

5.17 Prevention of Jitter

5.17.1 Anti-jitter Circuits

Anti-jitter circuits (AJCs) are a class of electronic circuits designed to reduce the level of jitter in a regular pulse signal. AJCs operate by re-timing the output pulses so they align more closely to an idealised pulse signal. They are widely used in clock and data recovery circuits in digital communications, as well as for data sampling systems such as the analog-to-digital converter and digital-to-analog converter. Examples of anti-jitter circuits include phase-locked loop and delay-locked loop. Inside digital to analog converters jitter causes unwanted high-frequency distortions. In this case it can be suppressed with high fidelity clock signal usage.

5.17.2 Jitter Buffers
1. Jitter buffers or de-jitter buffers are used to counter jitter introduced by queuing in packet switched networks so that a continuous playout of audio (or video) transmitted over the network can be ensured. The maximum jitter that can be countered by a de-jitter buffer is equal to the buffering delay introduced before starting the play-out of the mediastream. In the context of packet-switched networks, the term *packet delay variation* is often preferred over *jitter*.
2. Some systems use sophisticated delay-optimal de-jitter buffers that are capable of adapting the buffering delay to changing network jitter characteristics. These are known as adaptive de-jitter buffers and the adaptation logic is based on the jitter estimates computed from the arrival characteristics of the media packets. Adaptive de-jittering involves introducing discontinuities in the media play-out, which may appear offensive to the listener or viewer. Adaptive de-jittering is usually carried out for audio play-outs that feature a VAD/DTX encoded audio, that allows the lengths of the silence periods to be adjusted, thus minimizing the perceptual impact of the adaptation.

5.17.3 Dejitterizer
A dejitterizer is a device that reduces jitter in a digital signal. A dejitterizer usually consists of an elastic buffer in which the signal is temporarily stored and then retransmitted at a rate based on the average rate of the incoming signal. A dejitterizer is usually ineffective in dealing with low-frequency jitter, such as waiting-time jitter.

5.18 Transport Layer Functions

In computer networking, the **Transport Layer** is a group of methods and protocols within a layered architecture of network components within which it is responsible for encapsulating application data blocks into data units (datagrams, segments) suitable for transfer to the network infrastructure for transmission to the destination host, or managing the reverse transaction by abstracting network datagrams and delivering their payload to an application. Thus the protocols of the Transport Layer establish a direct, virtual host-to-host communications transport medium for applications and therefore also referred to as *transport protocols*.

Transport layers are contained in both the TCP/IP model, which is the foundation of the Internet, and the Open Systems Interconnection (OSI) model of general networking. The definitions of the Transport Layer are slightly different in these two models. This article primarily refers to the TCP/IP model. See also the OSI model definition of the Transport Layer.

The most well-known transport protocol is the Transmission Control Protocol (TCP). It lent its name to the title of the entire Internet Protocol Suite, *TCP/IP*. It is used for connection-oriented transmissions, whereas the connectionless User Datagram Protocol (UDP) is used for simpler messaging transmissions. TCP is the more complex protocol, due to its stateful design incorporating *reliable* transmission. Other prominent protocols in this group are the Datagram Congestion Control Protocol (DCCP) and the Stream Control Transmission Protocol (SCTP).

5.18.1 Detail Transport Layer Functions

The Transport Layer is responsible for delivering data to the appropriate application process on the host computers. This involves statistical multiplexing of data from different application processes, i.e. forming data packets, and adding source and destination port numbers in the header of each Transport Layer data packet. Together with the source and destination IP address, the port numbers constitutes a network socket, i.e. an identification address of the process-to-process communication. In the OSI model, this function is supported by the Session Layer.

Some Transport Layer protocols, for example TCP, but not UDP, support virtual circuits, i.e. provide connection oriented communication over an underlying packet oriented datagram network. A byte-stream is delivered while hiding the packet mode communication for the application processes. This involves connection establishment, dividing of the data stream into packets called segments, segment numbering and reordering of out-of order data.

Finally, some Transport Layer protocols, for example TCP, but not UDP, provide end-to-end reliable communication, i.e. error recovery by means of error detecting code and automatic repeat request (ARQ) protocol. The ARQ protocol also provides flow control, which may be combined with congestion avoidance.

UDP is a very simple protocol, and does not provide virtual circuits, nor reliable communication, delegating these functions to the application program. UDP packets are called datagrams, rather than segments.

TCP is used for many protocols, including HTTP web browsing and email transfer. UDP may be used for multicasting and broadcasting, since retransmissions are not possible to a large amount of hosts. UDP typically gives higher throughput and shorter latency, and is therefore often used for real-time multimedia communication where packet loss occasionally can be accepted. **For example:** IP-TV and IP-telephony, and for online computer games.

In many non-IP-based networks, for example X.25, Frame Relay and ATM, the connection oriented communication is implemented at network layer or data link layer rather than the Transport Layer. In X.25, in telephone network modems and in wireless communication systems, reliable node-to-node communication is implemented at lower protocol layers.

The OSI Model defines five classes of transport protocols, *TP0*, providing the least error recovery, to *TP4*, which is designed for less reliable networks.

5.18.2 Transport Layer Services

There is a long list of services that can be optionally provided by the Transport Layer. None of them are compulsory, because not all applications require all available services.

- **Connection-oriented:** This is normally easier to deal with than connection-less models, so where the Network layer only provides a connection-less service, often a connection-oriented service is built on top of that in the Transport Layer.
- **Same Order Delivery:** The Network layer doesn't generally guarantee that packets of data will arrive in the same order that they were sent, but often this is a desirable feature, so the Transport Layer provides it. The simplest way of doing this is to give each packet a number, and allow the receiver to reorder the packets.
- **Reliable data:** Packets may be lost in routers, switches, bridges and hosts due to network congestion, when the packet queues are filled and the network nodes have to delete packets. Packets may be lost or corrupted in Ethernet due to interference and noise, since Ethernet does not retransmit corrupted packets. Packets may be delivered in the wrong order by an underlying network. Some Transport Layer protocols, for example TCP, can fix this. By means of an error detection code, for example a checksum, the transport protocol may check that the data is not corrupted, and verify that by sending an ACK message to the sender. Automatic repeat request schemes may be used to retransmit lost or corrupted data. By introducing segment numbering in the Transport Layer packet headers, the packets can be sorted in order. Of course, error free is impossible, but it is possible to substantially reduce the numbers of undetected errors.
- **Flow control:** The amount of memory on a computer is limited, and without flow control a larger computer might flood a computer with so much information that it can't hold it all before dealing with it. Now-a-days, this is not a big issue, as memory is cheap while bandwidth is comparatively expensive, but in earlier times it was more important. Flow control allows the receiver to respond before it is overwhelmed. Sometimes this is already provided by the network, but where it is not, the Transport Layer may add it on.
- **Congestion avoidance:** Network congestion occurs when a queue buffer of a network node is full and starts to drop packets. Automatic repeat request may keep the network in a congested state. This situation can be avoided by adding congestion avoidance to the flow control, including slow-start. This keeps the bandwidth

consumption at a low level in the beginning of the transmission, or after packet retransmission.
- **Byte orientation:** Rather than dealing with things on a packet-by-packet basis, the Transport Layer may add the ability to view communication just as a stream of bytes. This is nicer to deal with than random packet sizes, however, it rarely matches the communication model which will normally be a sequence of messages of user defined sizes.
- **Ports:** (Part of the Transport Layer in the TCP/IP model, but of the Session Layer in the OSI model) Ports are essentially ways to address multiple entities in the same location.
  For example: The first line of a postal address is a kind of port, and distinguishes between different occupants of the same house. Computer applications will each listen for information on their own ports, which is why you can use more than one network-based application at the same time.

5.18.3 Comparison of TCP/IP Transport Protocols

	UDP	TCP	DCCP	SCTP
Packet header size	8 Bytes	20-60 Bytes	12 or 16 bytes	12 Bytes + Variable Chunk Header
Transport Layer packet entity	Datagram	Segment	Datagram	Datagram
Port numbering	Yes	Yes	Yes	Yes
Error detection	Optional	Yes	Yes	Yes
Reliability: Error recovery by automatic repeat request (ARQ)	No	Yes	No	Yes
Virtual circuits: Sequence numbering and reordering	No	Yes	Yes	Optional
Flow control	No	Yes	Yes	Yes
Congestion avoidance: Variable congestion window, slow start, time outs	No	Yes	Yes	Yes
Multiple streams	No	No	No	Yes
ECN support	No	Yes	Yes	Yes
NAT friendly	Yes	Yes	Yes	No

5.18.4 Comparison of OSI Transport Protocols

The OSI model defines five classes of connection-mode transport protocols designated class 0 (TP0) to class 4 (TP4). Class 0 contains no error recovery, and was designed for use on network layers that provide error-free connections. Class 4 is closest to TCP, although TCP contains functions, such as the graceful close, which OSI assigns to the Session Layer. All OSI connection-mode protocol classes provide expedited data and preservation of record boundaries. Detailed characteristics of the classes are shown in the following table:

Feature Name	TP0	TP1	TP2	TP3	TP4
Connection oriented network	Yes	Yes	Yes	Yes	Yes
Connectionless network	No	No	No	No	Yes
Concatenation and separation	No	Yes	Yes	Yes	Yes
Segmentation and reassembly	Yes	Yes	Yes	Yes	Yes
Error Recovery	No	Yes	No	Yes	Yes
Reinitiate connection (if an excessive number of PDUs are unacknowledged)	No	Yes	No	Yes	No
multiplexing and demultiplexing over a single virtual circuit	No	No	Yes	Yes	Yes
Explicit flow control	No	No	Yes	Yes	Yes
Retransmission on timeout	No	No	No	No	Yes
Reliable Transport Service	No	Yes	No	Yes	Yes

5.19 QoS Improvement Techniques

There are following techniques to improve the QoS:
1. Scheduling (FIFO Queuing, Priority Queuing, Weighted fair Queuing).
2. Traffic Shaping (Leaky bucket, Token Bucket Algo.)
3. Resource reservation.
4. Admission control.

5.19.1 Packet Scheduling

Queues represent locations where packets may be held (or dropped). Packet scheduling refers to the decision process used to choose which packets should be serviced or dropped. Buffer management refers to any particular discipline used to regulate the occupancy of a particular queue. At present, support is included for drop-tail (FIFO) queueing, RED buffer management, CBQ (including a priority and round-robin scheduler), and variants of Fair Queueing including, Fair Queueing (FQ), Stochastic Fair Queueing (SFQ), and Deficit Round-Robin (DRR). In the common case where a *delay* element is downstream from a queue, the queue may be *blocked* until it is re-enabled by its downstream neighbour. This is the mechanism by which transmission delay is simulated. In addition, queues may be forcibly blocked or unblocked at arbitrary times by their neighbors (which is used to implement multi-queue aggregate queues with inter-queue flow control). Packet drops are implemented in such a way that queues contain a "drop destination"; that is, an object that receives all packets dropped by a queue. This can be useful to (for example) keep statistics on dropped packets.

5.19.2 Traffic Shaping Algorithms

Traffic shaping is used for a number of purposes:
- Time-sensitive data may be given priority over traffic that can be delayed briefly with little-to-no ill effect.
- A large ISP (Internet service provider) may shape the traffic of an independent reseller.
- In a corporate environment, business-related traffic may be given priority over other traffic.
- An ISP may limit bandwidth consumption for certain applications to reduce costs and create the capacity to take on additional subscribers. This practice can effectively limit a subscriber's "unlimited connection" and is often imposed without notification.
- Traffic shaping could be an integral component of the proposed two-tiered Internet, in which certain customers or services would get traffic priority for a premium charge.

Traffic Shaping Algorithms (Leaky Bucket versus Token Bucket)

Two predominant methods for shaping traffic exist: a leaky bucket implementation and a token bucket implementation. Sometimes they are mistakenly lumped together under the same name. Both these schemes have distinct properties and are used for distinct purposes. They differ principally in that the leaky bucket imposes a hard limit on the data transmission rate, whereas the token bucket allows a certain amount of burstiness while imposing a limit on the average data transmission rate.

High Level View

The **token bucket** is a control mechanism that dictates when traffic can be transmitted, based on the presence of tokens in the bucket--an abstract container that holds aggregate network traffic to be transmitted. The bucket contains tokens, each of which can represent a unit of bytes or a single packet of predetermined size. Tokens in the bucket are removed ("cashed in") for the ability to send a packet. The network administrator specifies how many tokens are needed to transmit how many bytes. When tokens are present, a flow is allowed to transmit traffic. If there are no tokens in the bucket, a flow cannot transmit its packets. Therefore, a flow can transmit traffic up to its peak burst rate if there are adequate tokens in the bucket and if the burst threshold is configured appropriately.

The Token Bucket Algorithm

The algorithm can be conceptually understood as follows:
- A token is added to the bucket every $1/r$ seconds.
- The bucket can hold at the most *b* tokens. If a token arrives when the bucket is full, it is discarded.
- When a packet (network layer PDU) of *n* bytes arrives, *n* tokens are removed from the bucket, and the packet is sent to the network.
- If fewer than *n* tokens are available, no tokens are removed from the bucket, and the packet is considered to be *non-conformant*.

The algorithm allows bursts of up to b bytes, but over the long run the output of conformant packets is limited to the constant rate, r. Non-conformant packets can be treated in various ways:
- They may be dropped.
- They may be enqueued for subsequent transmission when sufficient tokens have accumulated in the bucket.
- They may be transmitted, but marked as being non-conformant, possibly to be dropped subsequently if the network is overloaded.

To calculate the time for which the Token Bucket Algorithm allows burst of maximum possible size, assume that the capacity of the Token Bucket is C bytes, the token arrival rate is R bytes/second and the maximum possible transmission rate is M bytes/second and S is the number of seconds for which it is possible to transmit at maximum rate. Then, the following equality holds $C + R * S = M * S$ which gives $S = C / (M - R)$ seconds

Implementers of this algorithm on platforms lacking the clock resolution necessary to add a single token to the bucket every 1/r seconds may want to consider an alternative formulation. Given the ability to update the token bucket every S milliseconds, the number of tokens to add every S milliseconds = $(r * S) / 1000$.

5.19.3 Resource Reservation and its Main Attributes

1. Resource Reservation System requests resources for simplex flows: a traffic stream in only one direction from sender to one or more receivers.
2. Resource Reservation System is not a routing protocol but works with current and future routing protocols.
3. Resource Reservation System is receiver oriented: in that the receiver of a data flow initiates and maintains the resource reservation for that flow.
4. Resource Reservation System maintains *soft state* (the reservation at each node needs a periodic refresh) of the host and routers' resource reservations, hence supporting dynamic automatic adaptation to network changes.
5. Resource Reservation System provides several reservation styles (a set of reservation options) and allows for future styles to be added to protocol revisions to fit varied applications.
6. Resource Reservation System transports and maintains traffic and policy control parameters that are opaque to Resource Reservation System.

5.19.4 Admission Control

1. **Admission control** is a network Quality of Service (QoS) procedure. Admission control determines how bandwidth and latency are allocated to streams with various requirements. Admission control schemes therefore need to be implemented between network edges and core to control the traffic entering the network.

2. An application that wishes to use the network to transport traffic with QoS must first request a connection, which involves informing the network about the characteristics of the traffic and the QoS required by the application. This information is stored in a traffic contract. The network judges whether it has enough resources available to accept the connection, and then either accepts or rejects the connection request. This is known as *Admission Control*. Admission Control in ATM networks is known as Connection Admission Control (CAC). In 802.11 networks it is known as Call Admission Control.
3. Admission control is useful in situations where a certain number of connections (phone conversations, for example) may all share a link, while an even greater number of connections causes significant degradation in all connections to the point of making them all useless such as in Congestive collapse.

5.20 Repeaters

1. As signals travel along a network cable (or any other medium of transmission), they degrade and become distorted in a process that is called attenuation. If a cable is long enough, the attenuation will finally make a signal unrecognizable by the receiver.
2. A Repeater enables signals to travel longer distances over a network. Repeaters work at the OSI's Physical layer. A repeater regenerates the received signals and then retransmits the regenerated (or conditioned) signals on other segments.

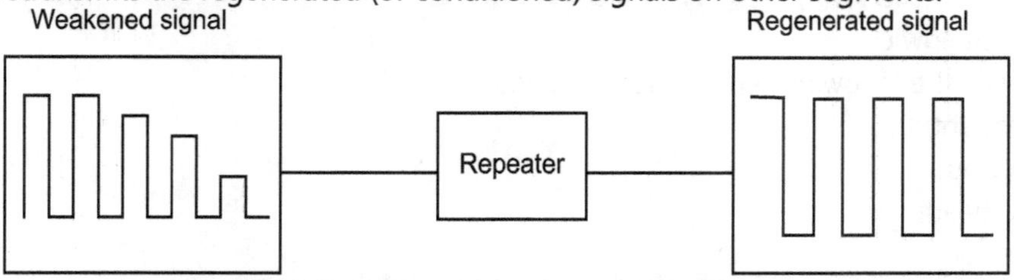

Fig. 5.36: Weakened Signal is Regenerated Using REPEATER

3. To pass data through the repeater in a usable fashion from one segment to the next, the packets and the Logical Link Control (LLC) protocols must be the same on the each segment. This means that a repeater will not enable communication, for example, between an 802.3 segment (Ethernet) and an 802.5 segment (Token Ring). That is, they cannot translate an Ethernet packet into a Token Ring packet. In other words, repeaters do not translate anything.
4. Actual network devices that serve as repeaters usually have some other name. **Active hubs. For example:** are repeaters. Active hubs are sometimes also called "multiport repeaters," but more commonly they are just "hubs." Other types of "passive hubs" are not repeaters. In Wi-Fi, access points function as repeaters only when operating in so-called "repeater mode."

EXERCISE

1. Discuss the Reliability in Telecommunication Networks.
2. List the different Network characteristics managed by QoS.
3. Explain the uses and benefits of QoS.
4. Discuss the different QoS mechanism.
5. Explain QoS Model and discuss priority levels.
6. Explain the role of Delay in packet switched voice networks.
7. Explain how voice compression works.
8. Discuss the different standards for delay limits.
9. Write a detail note on Delay sources in typical telecom network.
10. Write short notes on the following:
    Coder delay
    Algorithmic delay
    Packetization delay
    Seralization delay
    Queueing/Buffering delay
    Network switching delay
    De-jitter delay
11. How to handle jitter in packet voice network?
12. Explain the jitter effect in frame relay network.
13. Explain the following terms in telecom network:
    (a) Bandwidth (b) Bit rate
14. Explain the following terms in telecom network.
    Throughtput
    Goodput
    Overheads
    Latency
15. Write a detail note on "Crosstalk and interference in Telecom networks.
16. What is NEXT and FEXT? Explain with proper examples.
17. Explain the term "Attenuation to crosstalk (NEXT) Ratio-ACR".
18. Discuss network reliability and network survivability.
19. What are the different data risks for wide area telecom networks?
20. Explain the ATM network security aspects.
21. Explain the frame relay network security aspects.
22. Explain ISDN network protection.
23. Explain schemes of SONET/SDH protection.
24. Explain the different solutions over telecom network failure conditions considering network topology as main factor.
25. Explain risk and protection aspects of typical DSL network.

Unit VI

TELECOM NETWORK MANAGEMENT

6.1 Telecommunication Network Management Architecture, Cube and Support Environment

Definition and Overview:

The telecommunications management network (TMN) provides a framework for achieving interconnectivity and communication across heterogeneous operating systems and telecommunications networks. TMN was developed by the International Telecommunications Union (ITU) as an infrastructure to support management and deployment of dynamic telecommunications services.

The telecommunications industry is seeing rapid and ongoing change. With emerging technologies, deregulation, and increased consumer demand, companies are presented with a wide range of opportunities and challenges. As companies unify their networks and systems, they must merge new technologies and legacy systems. This is no small task, as company's networks may encompass analog and digital systems, multiple vendor equipment, different types of subnetworks, and varied management protocols.

6.1.1 TMN Framework (Telecommunication Management Network)

1. TMN provides a framework for networks that is flexible, scalable, reliable, inexpensive to run, and easy to enhance.
2. TMN provides for more capable and efficient networks by defining standard ways of doing network-management tasks and communicating across networks.
3. TMN allows processing to be distributed to appropriate levels for scalability, optimum performance, and communication efficiency.
4. TMN principles are incorporated into a telecommunications network to send and receive information and to manage its resources.
5. A telecommunications network is comprised of switching systems, circuits, terminals, etc.
6. In TMN terminology, these resources are referred to as network elements (NEs).
7. TMN enables communication between operations support systems (OSS) and NEs.
8. The term TMN is introduced by the ITU-T (the former CCITT) as an abbreviation for 'Telecommunications Management Network'.
9. The concept of a TMN is defined by **Recommendation M.3010**.

10. TMN has a strong **relationship with OSI management**, and defines a number of concepts that have **relevance for Internet Management**.
11. According to M.3010, "a TMN is conceptually a separate network that interfaces a telecommunications network at several different points".
12. The relationship between a TMN and the telecommunications network that is managed is shown in Fig. 6.1.
13. According to this figure, the interface points between the TMN and the telecommunications network are formed by **Exchanges and Transmission systems.**
14. For the purpose of management, these Exchanges and Transmission systems are connected via a *Data Communication Network* to one or more *Operations Systems*.
15. The Operations Systems perform most of the management functions; these functions may be carried out not only by human operators but also automatically.
16. It is possible that a single management function will be performed by multiple Operations Systems.
17. In this case, the Data Communication Network is used to exchange management information between the Operations Systems.
18. The Data Communication Network is also used to connect *Work Stations*, which allow operators to interpret management information.
19. Work Stations have man-machine interfaces, the definition of such interfaces fall outside the scope of TMN (Work Stations are therefore drawn at the border of the TMN).

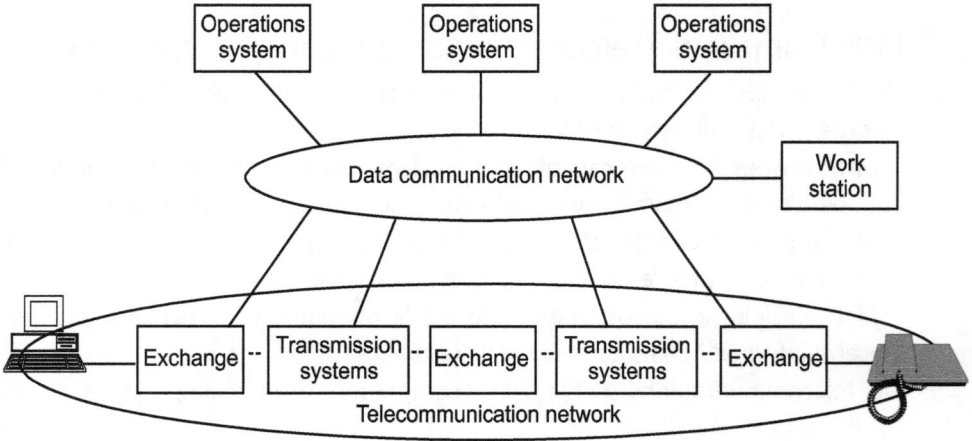

Fig. 6.1: General relationship of a TMN to a telecommunications network

20. TMN uses object-oriented principles and standard interfaces to define communication between management entities in a network. The standard management interface for TMN is called the Q3 interface.

21. TMN architecture and interfaces, defined in the ITU M.3000 recommendation series, build on existing open systems interconnection (OSI) standards. These standards include, but are not limited to:
    - **Common management information protocol (CMIP)** - defines management services exchanged between peer entities.
    - **Guideline for definition of managed objects (GDMO)** - provides templates for classifying and describing managed resources.
    - **Abstract syntax notation one (ASN.1)** - provides syntax rules for data types.
    - **Open systems interconnect reference model** – defines the seven-layer OSI reference model.
22. Since their publication, the TMN standards have been embraced and promulgated by other standards bodies, most notably by the Network Management Forum (NMF), Bellcore, and the European Telecommunications Standards Institute (ETSI). In general, the NMF and Bellcore efforts are directed toward accelerating implementation and providing a generic frame work for establishing detailed requirements. At the same time, technology-centric forums such as the Synchronous Optical Network (SONET) Interoperability Forum (SIF) and the Asynchronous Transfer Mode Forum (ATMF) are specifying TMN-compliant management interfaces.
23. **TMN, OSI, and Management:**
    - TMN is based on the OSI management framework and uses an object-oriented approach, with managed information in network resources modeled as attributes in managed objects. Management functions are performed by operations comprised of common management information service (CMIS) primitives.
    - A network's managed information, as well as the rules by which that information is presented and managed, is referred to as the management information base (MIB). Processes that manage the information are called management entities. A management entity can take on one of two possible roles: manager or agent. Manager and agent processes send and receive requests and notifications using the CMIP.
24. **TMN: Several Viewpoints**
    - The benefits of TMN (multivendor, interoperable, extensible, scalable, and object-oriented) are important because they allow companies to manage complex and dynamic networks and services, and they allow those same companies to continue to expand services, maintain quality, and protect legacy investments. TMN describes telecom network management from several viewpoints: a logical or business model, a functional model, and a set of standard interfaces. Each of these is critically important and interdependent.
25. Recommendation M.3010 defines the general TMN management concepts and introduces several management architectures at different levels of abstraction:

- A **functional architecture**, which describes a number of management functions.
- A **physical architecture**, which defines how these management functions may be implemented into physical equipment.
- An **information architecture**, which describes concepts that have been adopted from OSI management.
- A **Logical Layered Architecture** (LLA), which includes one of the best ideas of TMN: a model that shows how management can be structured according to different responsibilities.

6.1.2 Functional Architecture

1. Five different types of function blocks are defined by TMN's functional architecture.
2. It is not necessary that all of these types are present in each possible TMN configuration. On the other hand, most TMN configurations will support multiple function blocks of the same type.
3. Fig. 6.2 has been copied from the TMN recommendations and shows all five types of function blocks.
4. In this figure, two types (OSF and MF) are completely drawn within the box labelled 'TMN'.
5. This way of drawing indicates that these function blocks are completely specified by the TMN recommendations.
6. The other three types (WSF, NEF and QAF) are drawn at the edge of the box to indicate that only parts of these function blocks are specified by TMN.
7. The following pages provide short descriptions of, plus the relation between these five function blocks.

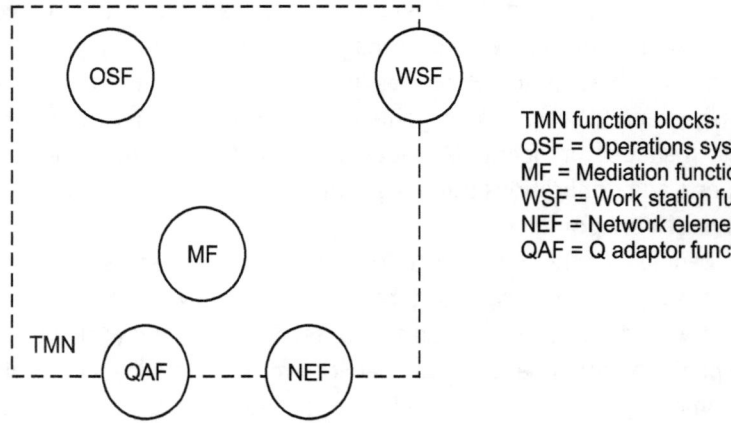

Fig. 6.2: TMN Function blocks

8. The TMN functional architecture introduces the concept of reference point to delineate function blocks.
9. Five different classes of reference points are identified.

10. Three of them (q, f and x) are completely described by the TMN recommendations; the other classes (g and m) are located outside the TMN and only partially described.

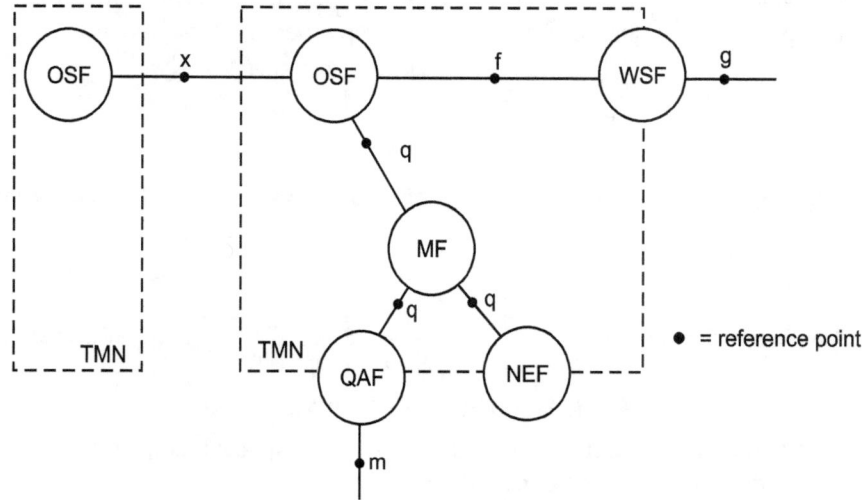

Fig. 6.3: Example of reference points between function blocks

11. Fig. 6.3 provides an example of reference points and function blocks.
12. The picture shows for instance that the Mediation Function (MF) can be reached via q reference points and that the m reference point can be used to reach the Q Adaptor Function (QAF) from outside TMN.

6.1.3 Physical Architecture

1. Next to a functional architecture, TMN also defines a physical architecture.
2. The latter architecture shows how TMN's functions, which were defined by the functional architecture, can be implemented into physical equipment.
3. TMN's physical architecture is thus defined at a lower abstraction level than TMN's functional architecture (Fig. 6.4).

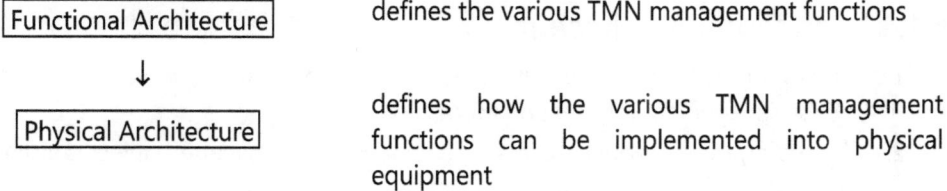

Fig. 6.4: TMN has defined multiple, related architectures

4. The physical architecture shows how function blocks should be mapped upon building blocks (physical equipment) and reference points upon interfaces.

5. In fact, the physical architecture defines how function blocks and reference points can be implemented (Fig. 6.5).
6. It should be noted however that one function block may contain multiple functional components and one building block may implement multiple function blocks.

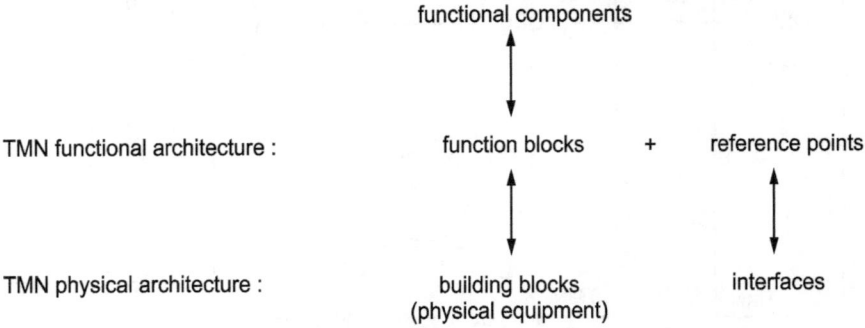

Fig. 6.5: Relation between TMN Architectures

7. To avoid confusion between the functional and physical architecture, it is helpful to understand the following conventions.
8. Names of reference points are written in lower case, names of interfaces in upper case (subscripts may be added). Reference points are drawn as small filled circles (bullets), interfaces as open circles.
9. Function blocks are shown as big circles or ellipses, building blocks are drawn as boxes.

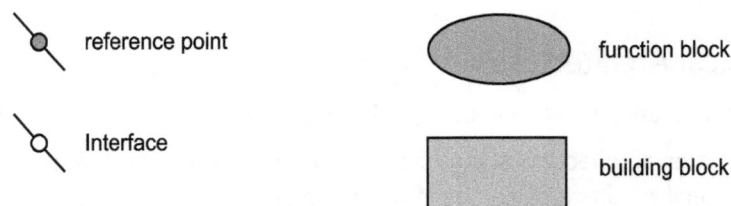

Fig. 6.6: Drawing conventions

6.1.4 Information Architecture

1. TMN's information architecture uses an object-oriented approach and is based on OSI's Management Information Model.
2. According to this model, the management view of a managed object is visible at the managed object boundary.
3. At this boundary, the management view is described in terms of (Fig. 6.7).
   - Attributes, which are the properties or characteristics of the object.
   - Operations, which are performed upon the object.

- Behaviour, which is exhibited in response to operations.
- Notifications, which are emitted by the object.

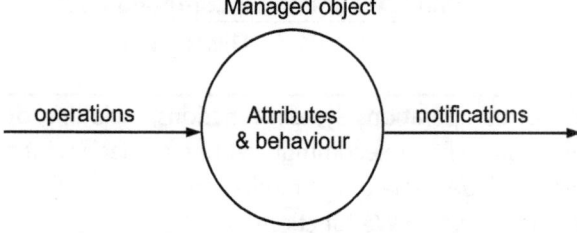

Fig. 6.7

4. The managed objects reside within managed systems, which include agent functions to communicate with the manager.
5. TMN uses the same manager-agent concept as OSI.
6. Because TMN's information architecture is a copy from OSI's information architecture, this tutorial will not discuss the information architecture any further.

6.1.5 The TMN Functional Model

The TMN enables telecommunication service providers to achieve interconnectivity and communication across operating systems and telecommunications networks. Interconnectivity is achieved via standard interfaces that view all managed resources as objects.

6.1.5.1 TMN Building Blocks

The TMN is represented by several building blocks that provide an overall embodiment of the management issues and functions of TMN. Fig. 6.8 illustrates the building blocks in TMN.

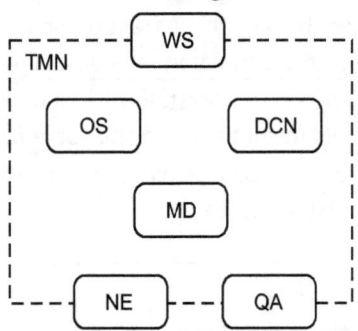

Fig. 6.8: TMN building blocks

Table 6.1 lists and describes each TMN component and the function that it performs. In some cases, functions may be performed within other system components. The mediation device (MD), for instance, may also provide some of the functions defined as operations systems (OSs), Q adapters (QAs), and workstations (WSs). In addition, the OS may also provide some of the MDs, QAs, and WSs.

Table 6.1: Functional Components

System Component	Description
OS	Performs operations system functions, including operations monitoring and controlling telecommunications-management functions; the OS can also provide some of the mediation, q-adaption, and WS functions.
MD	Performs mediation between local TMN interfaces and the OS information model; mediation function may be needed to ensure that the information, scope, and functionality are presented in the exact way that the OS expects. Mediation functions can be implemented across hierarchies of cascaded MDs.
QA	The QA enables the TMN to manage NEs that have non-TMN interfaces. The QA translates between TMN and non-TMN interfaces. A TL1 Q-adapter, for example, translates between a TL1 ASCII message-based protocol and the CMIP, the TMN interface protocol; likewise, simple network management protocol (SNMP) Q-adapter translates between SNMP and CMIP.
NE	In the scope of TMN, an NE contains manageable information that is monitored and controlled by an OS. In order to be managed within the scope of TMN, an NE must have a standard TMN interface. If an NE does not have a standard interface, the NE can still be managed via a Q-adapter. The NE provides the OS with a representation of its manageable information and functionality (i.e., the MIB). Note that the NE contains NE functionality that is, the functions required in order to be managed by an OS. As a building block, the actual NE can also contain its own OS function, as well as QA function, MD function, etc.
WS	The WS performs workstation functions. WSs translate information between TMN format and a displayable format for the user.
Data Communication Network (DCN)	The DCN is the communication network within a TMN. The DCN represents OSI layers 1 to 3.

6.1.5.2 Distribution of TMN Management Functions

One type of management activity can be broken into a series of nested functional domains, each of which can exist in the same or separate logical layers. Each functional domain is under the control of an OS. Because management can be divided among OSs within the TMN environment, distributed management tasks can occur. One user transaction might encompass several management tasks. The logical layers enable that transaction to be processed across several OSs in a tree-like but nested hierarchy. Note that functional domains are nested within one another, and OS functional blocks communicate with each other. The layers may be distributed to recursive subordinate OSs within one TMN environment.

6.1.5.3 OSI Functionality in TMN
Stack Support:
TMN defines a message communication function (MCF). All building blocks with physical interfaces need to have an MCF. An MCF provides the protocol layers necessary to connect a block to a DCN (i.e., layers 4 to 7). An MCF can provide all seven OSI layers, and it can provide protocol convergence functions for interfaces that use some other layer configurations (e.g., a short stack).

Manager and Agent Roles:
TMN function blocks can act in the role of a manager and/or agent. The manager/agent concepts are the same as those used for CMIP and OSI management. In other words, a manager process issues directives and receives notifications, and an agent process carries out directives, sends responses, and emits events and alarms. As shown below, a building block may be viewed as a manager to one peer, even though it is viewed as an agent to another peer.

6.1.6 The Standard Interfaces and Classes of application for TMN
6.1.6.1 The Standard Interfaces of TMN
In the TMN model, specific interfaces between two TMN components communicate with one another. The TMN interfaces are as follows:

Table 6.2: TMN Interfaces

TMN Interfaces	Description
Q	The Q interface exists between two TMN-conformant functional blocks that are within the same TMN domain. The Qx carries information that is shared between the MD and the NEs that it supports. The Qx interface exists between the NE and MD; QA and MD; and MD and MD. The Q3 interface is the OS = interface. Any functional component that interfaces directly to the OS uses the Q3 interface. In other words, the Q3 interface is between the NE and OS; QA and OS; MD and OS; and OS and OS.
F	The F interface exists between a WS and OS, and between a WS and MD.
X	The X interface exists between two TMN-conformant OSs in two separate domains, or between a TMN-conformant OS and another OS in a non-TMN network.

Two other reference points, g and m, are outside the scope of TMN. They are between non-TMN entities and the non-TMN portion of the WSF and QAF, respectively.
In Fig. 6.9, each line represents an interface between two TMN components.

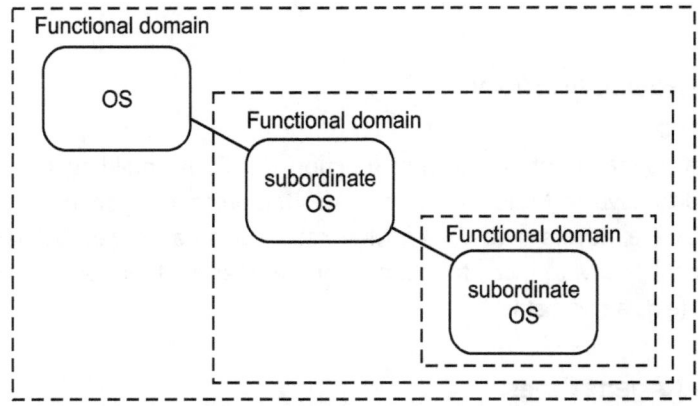

Fig. 6.9: Standard Interfaces Between TMN Components

More About the Q Interfaces:
There are two classes of Q interfaces: Q3 and Qx. Fig. 6.10 illustrates which function blocks can communicate via which Q interface.

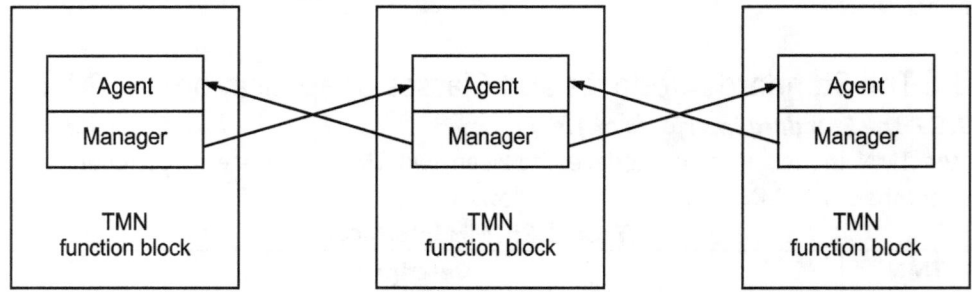

Fig. 6.10: Q Interfaces

Q3 Interface:
The Q3 interface is the lifeline to the operations system-Q3 is the only interface that QAs, MDs, or NEs may use to communicate directly with the OS. If a QA or NE does not use the Q3 interface, it cannot communicate directly with the OS; instead, it must communicate via an MD.

Qx Interface:
The Qx interface always operates with a MD. It never takes the place of a Q3 interface. The MD can interpret between local management information provided by a Qx interface and the OS information provided by a Q3 interface.

6.1.6.2 Classes of Applications in TMN

1. Two classes of applications have been defined to support the various TMN functions: *interactive and file transfer.*
2. The interactive class of applications in most cases exchange information using a request/reply paradigm such as requesting the alarm status, remote inventory of an equipment, and receiving a response.
3. The file transfer application requires remote manipulation of files and bulk transfer of data such as software download.
4. For the interactive class of applications, the content is determined using information models that define the management views of the resource and the application function.
5. For file transfer class, the structure of the file, and information in the records will define the contents.
6. The architecture and principles used in specifying the interactive class of applications within TMN draw heavily upon the foundations laid out by the OSI Systems management series of standards.
7. As a side note, managing the OSI protocols using Systems Management specifications has taken a backseat to their use in TMN.
8. This can be attributed to the fact that the industry has embraced the use of Internet protocols for communications between applications much more than the lower layers of OSI protocols.
9. Some specifications do exist for managing network and transport layer protocols for public-switched network as well as others are evolving to manage upper layers including applications such as directory.
10. Various interfaces within the TMN physical architecture were identified in previous Section.
11. It was also pointed out that only two of the interfaces, Q3 and X, have been well specified to date.
12. Both these interfaces support two classes of applications – *interactive and file transfer.*
13. The communication requirements for Q3 and X interfaces are specified using, for the most part, OSI protocols.
14. The reason for the phrase "the most part" is because lower layer protocols other than those developed as part of OSI suite are also included.
15. Specifically, Internet transport protocol has been included as one of the alternatives.
16. The OSI Systems Management protocol developed as part of the system management application mentioned above is specified as the requirement for exchanging management information belonging to the interactive class.

17. ISO protocol File Transfer and Access Management (FTAM) is required for the file transfer class.

18. Details of these requirements are defined in ITU Recommendations Q.811 and Q.812.17.

19. In order to support directory functions mentioned above, the recommendations also include X.500 Directory protocols.

20. It should be noted that both TMN and OSI architectural standards have been significantly influenced by the concepts in software development methods.

21. As an example, both architectures have subdivided a complex problem by separating concerns and addressing them individually.

22. **The interactive classes of applications** are characterized by bursty, time critical information that may be asynchronous. For example, reporting an alarm from a termination point is time critical in that the alarm must be reported as soon as it occurs instead of waiting for a period of time.

23. **The file-oriented class of applications** as the name suggests applies to applications where information stored as files is remotely managed (accessed, created, and modified). In contrast to the interactive class, these applications are not based on a command/response type of exchange and hence are not bursty or time critical. The duration for performing these applications is much longer compared to the **interactive class. Examples of applications of this class are downloading software (new generic, Patch etc.) accounting data, and memory backup and restoration.**

24. The third type of class of application defined within TMN is called "Directory Services". **This is orthogonal to the previous two in that the interactive and file transfer applications pertain to the exchange of management information.** Directory Services addresses the support environment for the proper functioning of TMN. These services are required to provide the necessary mapping between the application entity and the address to be used for setting up connection.

25. Viewing management information and activities in terms of different levels of abstractions leads to modular and flexible definitions and facilitates building complex applications with relative ease.

6.1.7 The TMN Logical Model

TMN supplies a model of logical layers that define or suggest the management level for specific functionality. The same type of functions can be implemented at many levels, from the highest level, which manages corporate or enterprise goals, to a lower level, which is defined by a network or network resource. Starting with the bottom level, these hierarchy layers include NEs, element-management layer (EML), network-management layer (NML), service-management layer (SML), and business-management layer (BML). Once management is defined at the lower layers, additional management applications can be built on this foundation.

Table 6.3: Logical Layers

Layer	Concerned With
BML	High-level planning, budgeting, goal setting, executive decisions, business-level agreements (BLAs), etc.
SML	Uses information presented by NML to manage contracted service to existing and potential customers; this is the basic point of contact with customers for provisioning, accounts, quality of service, and fault management. The SML is also the key point for interaction with service providers and with other administrative domains. It maintains statistical data to support quality of service, etc. OSs in the SML interface with OSs in the SML of other administrative domains via the X interface. OSs in the SML interface with OSs in the BML via the Q3 interface.
NML	The NML has visibility of the entire network, based on the NE information presented by the EML OSs. The NML manages individual NEs and all NEs as a group. In other words, the NML has the first managed view of the network. The NML coordinates all network activities and supports the demands of the SML. OSs in the NML interface with OSs in the SML via the Q3 interface.
EML	Manages each network element; the EML has element managers, or OSs, each of which are responsible for the TMN-manageable information in certain NEs. In general, an element manager is responsible for a subset of the NEs. An element manager manages network element data, logs, activity, etc. Logically, MDs are in the EML, even when they are physically located in some other logical layer, such as the NML or SML. An MD communicates with an EML OS via the Q3 interface. In addition, an EML OS presents its management information from a subset of the NEs to an OS in the NML through the Q3 interface.
Network-Element Layer (NEL)	The NEL presents the TMN-manageable information in an individual NE. Both the Q-adapter, which adapts between TMN and non-TMN information, and the NE are located in the NEL. In other words, the NEL interfaces between the proprietary manageable information and the TMN infrastructure.

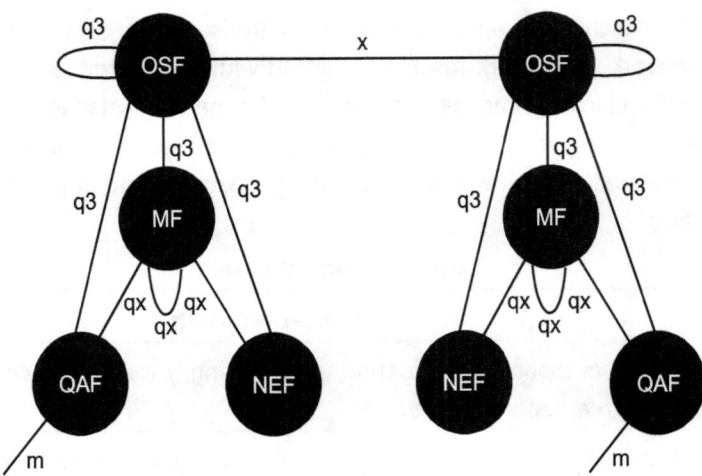

Fig. 6.11: Example: TMN Components across the Logical Layers

6.1.8 TMN Solutions

The key challenge for service providers, original equipment manufacturers (OEMs), software vendors, and integrators is to develop TMN-conformant, robust applications that can perform varied network management operations in a changing, multivendor, multiplatform network. Service providers and independent software vendors need to deploy solutions that:

1. Reduce time to market.
2. Reduce cost.
3. Support increasing demands for higher quality.
4. Incorporate legacy systems and are future-proof.
5. Conform to industry standards for TMN.

Integrating Legacy Equipment:

Legacy network equipment and systems, which are generally not TMN-conformant, understand ASCII messages, not TMN-conformant operations. The ASCII messages are often proprietary to a specific vendor or platform. TMN's standard interfaces provide for a machine-readable, programmatic interface to an NE's ASCII message-based or bitstream, informally-defined information model.

By defining standard interfaces, TMN does not mandate that network elements themselves be replaced with CMIP-conformant hardware or management messages. By allowing for intelligent mediation components, Q-adaptors, and MDs, TMN enables companies to bring all systems and equipment into a distributed, scalable, and interoperable managed solution.

A Q-adaptor can impose a machine-readable, object-oriented structure on a flat proprietary or legacy information model. An example of an NE with an informal, flat information model would be an NE that is managed by ASCII-based TL1 messages. These messages are human-readable, but are formally defined only as hard-copy message definitions.

By using a Q-adaptor to derive information from messages, and then interpreting between that information and an object-oriented, machine-readable form, a systems developer can expose a machine-manageable interface to the OS.

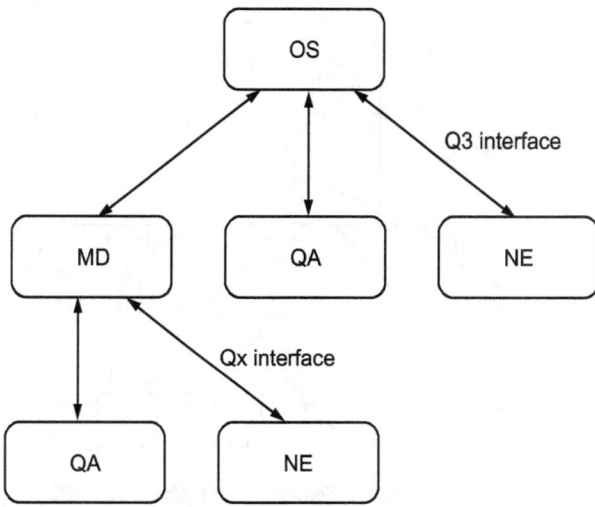

Fig. 6.12: A Q-adaptor Translates Between CMIP/Q3 and Proprietary Interfaces

Another use for a Q-adaptor would be the integration of a legacy enterprise network into the TMN infrastructure. Most enterprise networks manage resources by using the SNMP services. By adapting between SNMP and CMIP, the legacy network can be brought into the TMN realm.

Sometimes Q-adaption is all that is needed to convert an NE's interface to one that an OS can use. Often, however, further refinement is needed. A MD can further reconstitute or impose structure on this interface so that it matches the OS application's expected format.

Standardized, Object-Oriented Programmatic Interface:

The recently introduced TMN/C++ application-programming interface (API) is being promoted by NMF and is referred to as the NMF API. The NMF API offers a standardized, object-oriented API for telecommunications management applications. The architecture comprises three modular, layered APIs.

1. A managed object interface (the GDMO/C++ API) provides a framework for accessing and implementing managed objects in a hierarchical, tree-like model.
2. A service interface (the CMIS/C++ API) provides for the basic management information model services, which include:
    - The sending and receiving of requests and responses that create and delete objects, as well as get and set their attributes.
    - The reporting of events that occur in the network.

3. A data interface (the ASN.1/C++ API) defines a role-independent interface to the data itself and to its encoding.

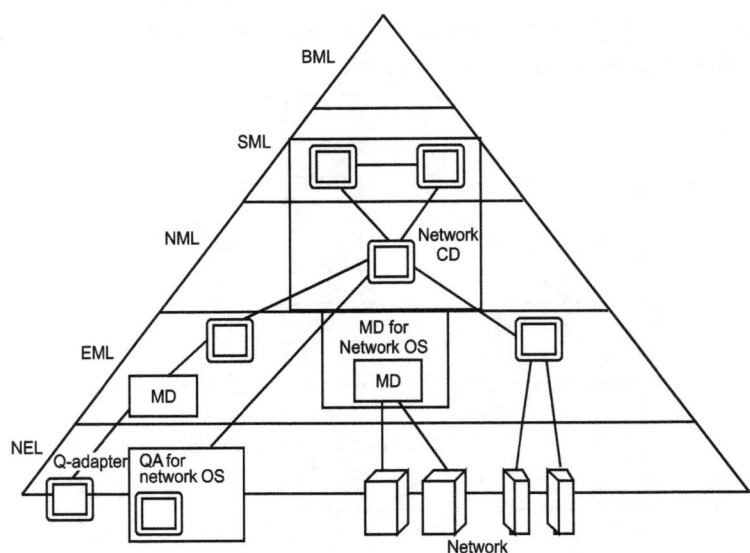

Fig. 6.13: NMF's TMN/C++ High-Level API

4. Prior to the NMF API, there were already some widely accepted standard APIs for TMN applications.
5. The most common was XMP/XOM, which provided a C-language API for managing objects. The utility of XMP/XOM as an API in the TMN domain, however, was hampered by its high degree of abstraction.
6. It was and is generally perceived as difficult to use, and most TMN platforms that boast XMP/XOM compliance also offer more easy-to-use API layers to hide it.
7. The NMF API overcomes the difficulties of this previous API, and provides a more natural development language (C++), straightforward interfaces, and platform-independent exposed interfaces. The NMF API provides the following advantages:

- The NMF API's platform-independent API has reusable C++ classes, so interface codes can be reused across diverse applications from built-in NE agents to large applications for SML platforms. This reduces time to market, lowers development costs, and shortens the learning curve for a development team.

- The NMF API also supports two distinct application types: specific and generic. Specific applications implement a static information model. Generic applications provide for changing management information and dynamically interpret network changes into the information model.

- Ease of use mandates that the programming language be the most natural for expressing the nature of managed resources as objects, so the NMF API uses the C++ language. C++, with its compartmentalized class representation, exposes the network's information model but hides its complexities behind the public methods and data types of specific classes.
- The NMF API provides for complete representation of the TMN model GDMO, common management information service element (CMISE), and ASN.1. Development efforts do not need to restrict functionality or to impose unnecessary limitations based on some subset of the information model.

Tools to Automate TMN-Conformant Application Building:

1. Tools are available that automate the task of building TMN-conformant agent or manager applications.
2. TMN agent and manager toolkits can be implemented and customized to match your company's GDMO/ASN.1 MIB representations.
3. These products should have the following features in order to maximize the advantages of TMN and to most productively support a TMN infrastructure:

    - **Dynamic information modeling:** The ability to add or change the network configuration or functionality without reinstalling or recompiling applications and implementations.
    - **Automated prototyping:** Tools that can compile GDMO/ASN.1 information models and produce model-specific exposed C++ interfaces and other required reports and data formats.
    - **System-management functions (SMFs):** Generate, filter, forward, and log incoming events and alarms.
    - **Platform-independent interfaces and tools:** Testing and simulation tools that focus on the behavior of a manager or agent, not on its implementation; these tools should be able to act in the role of agent, manager, or both. MIB-building tools that help the developer to construct a GDMO/ASN.1-conformant information model for any managed network.
    - **Q-adaption capability or compatibility:** The ability to interface to and thus integrate legacy NEs (such as TL1 message-based equipment types) as well as enterprise network systems (SNMP-based information).
    - **Conformance to all TMN standards:** Implementation of service, data, and managed object layers of the NMF API, and support for specific and generic application types.

4. Thus, Companies need to continue to operate at the cutting edge of today's industry and to gain footholds in emerging technologies.

5. By understanding TMN concepts, implementing TMN management applications, and building a TMN infrastructure, companies can maximize the value of current systems and equipment and be ready for the future.

6.1.9 TMN CUBE

1. A different view is provided in terms of three planes that form the TMN cube (Fig. 6.14).
2. The reason for this perspective is to show that physical architecture is realization of the components required to form the various planes.
3. The logical plane corresponds to functional blocks such as OSF described earlier.
4. The management functional plane includes the information architecture as well as the application functional component.
5. The reason for combining these two concepts is to point out that the information architecture addresses both these areas: Management information is dependent on both the managed resource as well as the Management application function (e.g., performance monitoring of severely errored seconds for a subscriber termination).
6. The third plane defines communications requirements for exchanging the management information in the function plane for the activities described in the logical plane. A physical realization of a TMN requires the three planes.

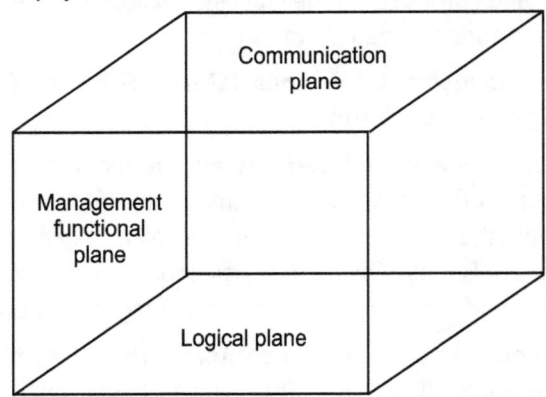

Fig. 6.14: TMN Cube

6.1.9.1 Logical Plane

Activities Distribution:

1. The logical function blocks NEF, OSF, MF, WSF, and QAF described earlier may also be viewed as a distributed set of activities in support of TMN.

2. In some cases, even if the same activity is performed by more than one function block, differences exist in the details of management information. Consider the activity–generation of management information. A network element performing this activity will generate what is specific to itself such as a critical alarm in a circuit pack contained in the network element or collect traffic statistics for the number of blocked calls.

3. A mediation device or a gateway network element that includes mediation capabilities may also support the generation capability.

4. **In recognition of the fact that multiple activities are performed in a TMN, the logical function blocks are further decomposed into various components. These are: Management application function (MAF), Information conversion function (ICF), Message communication function (MCF), Workstation support function (WSSF), User interface support function (UISF), Directory system function (DSF), Directory access function (DAF), and Security function (SF).**

5. Each of the logical function blocks identified earlier may have one or more of these functional components. The activity to generate management information is part of the management application function. Table 6.4 shows how these functional components may be distributed within TMN function blocks.

Table 6.4: Distribution of Management Activities

Logical Function Block	Possible Activities
OSF	MAF, WSSF, ICF, DAF, DSF, SF
NEF	MAF, DSF, DAF, SF
MF	MAF, ICF, WSSF, DSF, DAF, SF
QAF	MAF, ICF, DSF, DAF, SF

Levels of Abstractions:

1. In addition to decomposing the function blocks in terms of the components related to activities, the information managed by an OSF may be further separated into various levels of abstractions.

2. These are sometimes referred to as layers as discussed earlier.

3. In order to support various telecommunication services, a network element is often managed by a management system.

4. The information is managed at the elemental level. The level of abstraction for the element level information processed by the management system is referred to as element management layer (EML).

5. The EML abstraction provides the view relative to each network element. However, to understand network level impact, a higher-level abstraction is required.

6. An example is a fiber cut between NEs which impacts network level.
7. In the above example, loss of signal alarm may be issued relative to various terminations that are associated with the cut fiber in the two network elements.
8. Functions are required to correlate these various alarms and determine the root cause of the alarm, namely fiber cut. The information processing and determination of the root cause for the network failure is a level of abstraction referred to as *network management level* (NML).
9. The network level abstraction makes visible the details of the components of the network.
10. However, consider the case where a customer is only interested in the knowledge of whether the service is protected to guarantee service availability.
11. The customer is not concerned about how this objective for the quality of service (say 99.999% availability) is met by the service provider. Hiding the details of the network level information and projecting a service perspective is referred to as *service management level* (SML).
12. The highest level of abstraction is known as the *business management level* (BML). As the name implies, the information associated with this level of abstraction addresses enterprise objectives.
13. TMN standards and implementations have defined specifications that are relevant to all the layers except the BML. This is to be expected because the management information is driven by market needs, enterprise specific considerations, and goals, which are not subject to standardization.
14. These levels of abstractions are typically shown in presentations using a pyramid-like figure where the highest point of the pyramid is BML.

Fig. 6.15 illustrates these levels.

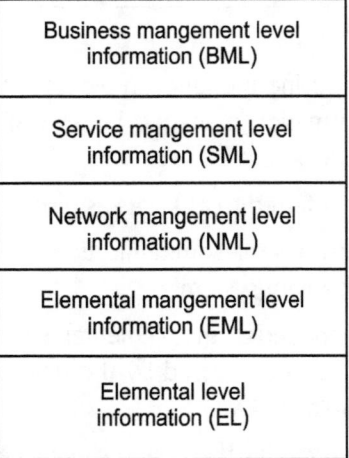

Fig. 6.15: Illustrates the levels

15. Although these five levels of abstractions are defined theoretically, these levels should not be equated to imply that management systems are separated according to these levels.
16. In addition, there are no strict boundaries specifically in the case of EML, NML, and SML abstractions.

6.1.9.2 Management Functions Plane
Functional Components:
1. Given the logical partitioning of functions in terms of NEF, MF, OSF, and WSF, the information required for successful management for all levels of abstractions mentioned earlier are derived from another category of functions referred to as *TMN function sets*.
2. These TMN function sets are grouped into five categories following the five areas of OSI management defined in ISO 7498 Part 4 (X.700).
3. **These are configuration, fault, performance, security, and accounting.**
4. The number of function sets within each area vary. These function sets are further divided into TMN functions that are atomic.
5. Even though many of the standards have been developed using these five categories, it should be noted that to avoid duplication, a set of management functions are defined (and continue to evolve).
6. These are sometimes referred to as "common." An example of such a function is "controlling reporting events (irrespective of the functional area such as an alarm for fault and threshold crossing alert for performance) to specific destination according to a defined schedule."

Levels of Abstractions:
1. It is easy to see that the management functions in the five functional areas can address different levels of abstraction.
2. Consider the function set *Alarm surveillance*. One of the lower level functions in this set is reporting alarms.
3. The alarm is determined by the network element to be at a severity level of major because a switch to the protecting circuit pack took place after the alarm occurred.
4. A report alarm message for this level of abstraction is likely to include the identity of the circuit pack, severity of the alarm, probable cause for the failure, and the identity of the protecting circuit pack.
5. A 5×5 matrix results by combining the levels of abstractions in the logical plane and the five areas of management functions in this plane. However, it is obvious that not all areas of management functions will be applicable in all cases (alarm functions in a business management abstractions are not meaningful).

Table 6.5: TMN Functional Components

Functional Area	Function Sets
Fault	Alarm surveillance, fault isolation, and testing.
Configuration	Provisioning, status and control, and installation.
Performance	Performance monitoring, traffic management, and quality of services.
Security	Security of management and management of security.
Accounting	Usage metering, billing.

6.1.9.3 External Communications Plane

Infrastructure Components:

1. The logical and functional planes together define how responsibilities, to meet the functional aspects of network management as an application, are partitioned among the various function blocks.
2. Management by definition implies that system(s) in the managing role monitors and controls a set of resources in managed system(s).
3. To perform these management activities, it is to be expected that communication between the systems is required via an external interface.
4. The communication aspects may be further divided into two categories.
5. Infrastructure components are required to convey the management information irrespective of resources being managed and the actual application (performance monitoring, alarm surveillance, etc.).
6. These components define functions such as end-to-end integrity, segmenting, and retransmission of messages based on the size of the packets supported by the underlying network along with a well-defined structure for management information.
7. The infrastructure requirements are dependent on the class of application.
8. Two classes of applications have been defined to support the various TMN functions: *interactive and file transfer*.
9. The interactive class of applications in most cases exchange information using a request/reply paradigm such as requesting the alarm status, remote inventory of an equipment, and receiving a response.
10. The file transfer application requires remote manipulation of files and bulk transfer of data such as software download.
11. Different options are provided so that various networking protocols (SS7, ISDN, X.25) available in existing networks may be used.

Contents of Exchange:

1. The infrastructure components define the fundamental communications requirements and are for the most part reusable across applications.
2. Using the structure for exchanging the management information, the content may vary based on the resource being managed and the TMN function.

3. For example, the exchanged information to report an alarm from a synchronous digital hierarchy (SDH), virtual tributary (VT) termination point will differ from the request/response regarding the state information.
4. The levels of abstraction defined earlier also play a role in determining the content by identifying the type of resource being managed.
5. For example, the element management level abstraction may be for the individual terminations in the network element, while the network management level abstraction may be relative to a circuit formed between terminations at two end points.

6.1.9.4 Physical Realization
1. All three planes are essential in completing the picture for TMN.
2. The information and activities in each of these planes when implemented in products results in the physical realization of these concepts.

6.1.10 Support Environment for TMN
The basic building blocks of TMN are captured with the capabilities illustrated with the three planes. However, to facilitate realizations of TMN concepts, two other support services have been identified: **Directory and Security**.

Directory Services:
1. Directory services are present (either implicitly or explicitly) when communication between two systems is required.
2. Consider the case where a network element has an alarm that must be sent to an operation system. The network element must know the address of the OS (network address and the application entity to receive the alarm) so that successful communication can be established.
3. To meet the basic goals of TMN, it is not required that an explicit implementation of directory support services are required. However, the requirements supported by a directory system must be accounted for in some way in order to have an interoperable interface.

Security Services:
1. The security services identified are: authentication, access control, data confidentiality, data integrity, and no repudiation.
2. A high-level definition of these services are: authentication of the communicating entities are verified when establishing an association; access control is used to assure that the entity invoking a request to perform a management operation has the appropriate privileges; data confidentiality services protect the information exchanged; using data integrity services, it is possible to detect that the message has been modified; and data non repudiation assures that the sender cannot later refute that the message has been sent by that sender.

3. Even though security services provide support environment, unlike directory services, in some applications they are required.
4. The requirements for these services are determined by the security policies established by the enterprise, namely the service provider.

6.1.11 Management Application of Systems
1. Systems Management was developed as part of OSI suite of application protocols.
2. The problem being solved here is the management of the communication protocol stacks in the end system.
3. This is very similar to the problem related to managing the Internet protocols using Simple Network Management Protocol (SNMP).
4. The OSI protocols at different layers may be managed in one or three ways: layer operation where the management information is included in the protocol (charging information in X.25); a protocol designed for managing the protocol of a specific layer (known as layer management); and Systems Management where a management application protocol is used to manage the communication stack.
5. The System Management functions address activities that are required to support management applications. Examples are controlling event reports to different destinations according to some specified schedule, different types of scheduling mechanisms to activate and deactivate management capabilities, and retaining historical information on events.
6. The architecture and principles used in specifying the interactive class of applications within TMN draw heavily upon the foundations laid out by the OSI Systems Management series of standards.
7. Some specifications do exist for managing network and transport layer protocols for public-switched network as well as others are evolving to manage upper layers including applications such as directory.

6.2 Detailing Functional Components and Requirements

Telecommunications Management Network (TMN) was introduced by ITU-T Recommendation M.3000 in 1985 as a reference model for the Operation Support System (OSS) of telecommunications service providers. The TMN concept is an architectural framework for the interconnection of different types of OSS components and network elements. TMN also describes the standardized interfaces and protocols used for the exchange of information between OSS components and network elements, and the total functionality needed for network management.

The TMN model compose of the following four layers:
- **Business management layer:** It performs functions related to business aspects, analyzes trends and quality issues, for example, or to provide a basis for billing and other financial reports.

- **Service management layer:** It performs functions for the handling of services in the network: definition, administration and charging of services.
- **Network management layer:** It performs functions for distribution of network resources: configuration, control and supervision of the network.
- **Element management layer:** It contains functions for the handling of individual network elements. This includes alarm management, handling of information, backup, logging, and maintenance of hardware and software.

On the other hand, the TMN model can be viewed from the functional perspective, in which the model is described as the following five functional components:

- **Fault management:** Fault recognition, isolation, reporting and recording.
- **Accounting management:** Collection, buffering and delivery of payment and accounting information.
- **Performance management:** Collection, buffering and delivery of operating statistics for network optimization and capacity planning.
- **Configuration management:** Installation of network equipment, setting of states and parameters, configuration of network capacity.
- **Security management:** Administration of authorization functions; handling of simultaneous use of an OSS, protection against intrusion from un-authorized users.

The above five functional areas form the basis of all network management for both data or telecommunications.

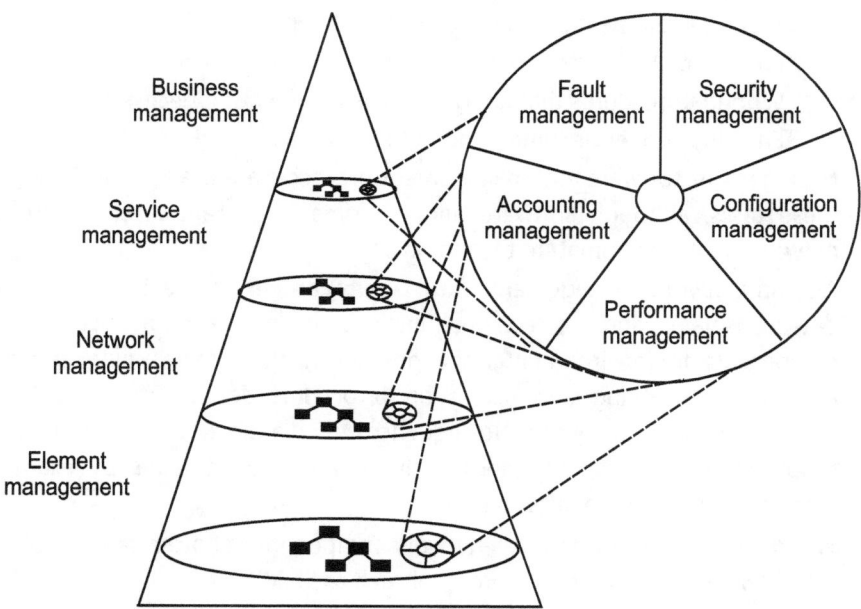

Fig. 6.16: Functional Components of Network Management System

6.2.1 Fault Management

1. Fault management is the ability to locate faults, determine their cause, and make corrections.
2. It also includes implementing fault-tolerant hardware systems and fault-tolerant procedures, as discussed under "Fault Tolerance". Fault management is concerned with keeping systems available for users, and involves the following:
   - Continuous monitoring and the collection of statistics on workstations, traffic conditions, and usage, so that potential faults can be forecast and avoided.
   - Setting threshold conditions that can warn you with alarms of conditions on the network that may cause failures.
   - Setting alarms that warn of performance degradation on servers, routers, and wide area network links.
   - Setting alarms that warn of resource usage problems, such as a server that is almost out of disk space.
   - The ability to remotely control workstations and other devices.
   - The ability to perform some or all of the above tasks from a single management location, which may be extremely remote from some sites.
3. Fault management requires certain procedures, personnel, and equipment to handle alarm conditions, as listed here:
   - Using pager devices to warn staff members who are not at the office
   - Testing equipment such as protocol analyzers
   - Preparing an inventory of spare parts
   - Writing procedures that unskilled users can follow, if necessary
   - Ensuring proper documentation of all systems
4. Management software and management protocols are available to handle some of these tasks, although software and equipment for centralized control of large networks is still an immature technology.
5. Also in network management, **fault management** is the set of functions that detect, isolate, and correct malfunctions in a telecommunications network, compensate for environmental changes, and include maintaining and examining error logs, accepting and acting on error detection notifications, tracing and identifying faults, carrying out sequences of diagnostics tests, correcting faults, reporting error conditions, and localizing and tracing faults by examining and manipulating database information.
6. When a fault or event occurs, a network component will often send a notification to the network operator using a protocol such as SNMP.
7. An alarm is a persistent indication of a fault that clears only when the triggering condition has been resolved.

6.2.1.1 Need for Fault Management

1. No system is infallible.
2. Ability to detect, recover and limit the impact of failures in a system is the most challenging job and is what every mission critical business should put in place.
3. Understanding, monitoring and managing the individual elements of a system may not be a problem, but as the system increases in size and complexity, understanding the relationship between the various elements in the system, monitoring and managing their interrelationship and the problems that arise due to their interrelationship become tedious and challenging.
4. Moreover, an army of personnel cannot be deployed to just administer the system. This is where Web **NMS (Network Management System)** as a Fault Management system comes into play.
5. Web NMS provides room to quickly design and deploy comprehensive fault management services that enhance performance and availability.
6. Web NMS correlates and manages notifications and presents critical information that meets the needs of managers. Notifications are modeled as objects that can be tracked and managed easily.
7. Web NMS is a highly flexible and extensible framework in which domain specific filters and rules can be easily plugged in. It provides secure, scalable, flexible and reliable solution to manage mission-critical environments.

6.2.1.2 Network Notifications and Event Flow

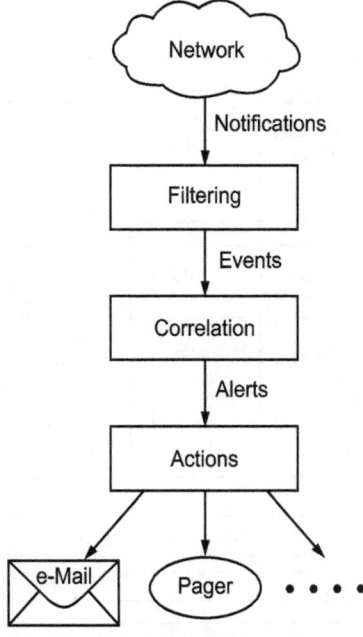

Fig. 6.17: Typical network notification and event flow

1. In Web NMS, Event is the basic unit of management information that is complete in itself and relates to an occurrence like discovery of an element, status update of an element or failure in an element.
2. Events form a repository of information for all the occurrences in the system. Alarm results from correlation of events and represents failure or fault in a network element that may need immediate attention.
3. These Event and Alert objects define the basic attributes and actions needed for effective fault management.
4. Users can also model their own objects by extending the basic units to plug-in their domain specific properties. It is also possible to add additional attributes to these basic units or their derivatives at runtime.

6.2.1.3 Fault Management Architecture

1. Notifications are raw data received from the network.
2. These cryptic data needs to be converted to a format which could be understood by the console operators.
3. Information such as whom to call, whom to page, procedures to fix the problem etc., on receipt of a notification, should to be readily available to effectively crackdown the problem.
4. The non-productive time spent on trying to find out what to do or where to start should be eliminated.

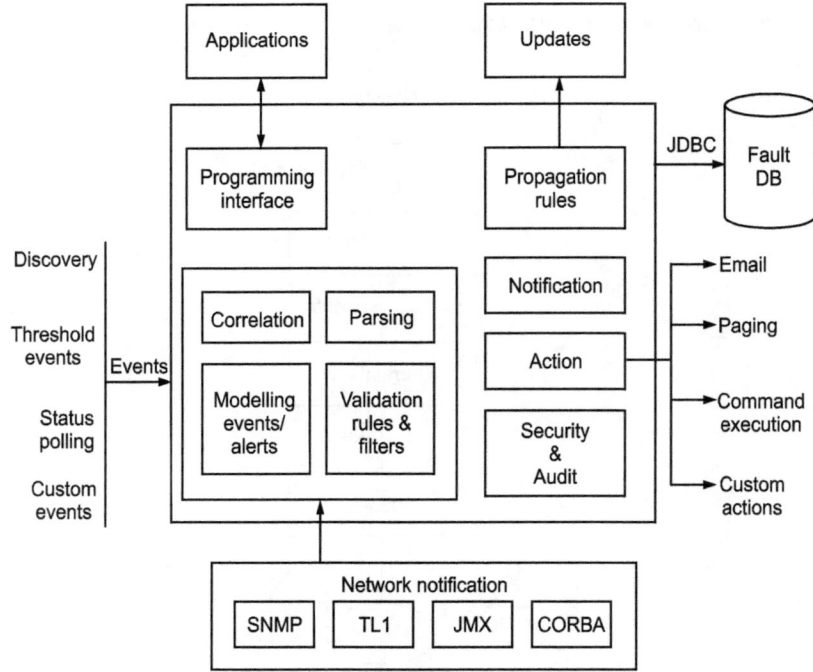

Fig. 6.18: Fault Management Architecture

5. Web NMS addresses these issues effectively and more efficiently.
6. It has a flexible architecture where filters and parsers can be plugged in easily.
7. Filters help in validating the notifications received from the various managed elements and also in applying domain specific rules.
8. Rules can be structured to validate the incoming events based on time, thresholds, or count.
9. For example, transient system failures occur as a normal part of network operation.
10. Rules become quite handy in these circumstances and can be used to filter out transient network failures.
11. This helps in reducing the thousands of events to ten or twenty actual problems that needs to be addressed. Parsers are simple but powerful mechanism that help in disseminating the raw data as fast as possible to the concerned parties in a meaningful manner.
12. Web NMS allows automated action to be taken at various levels of the event flow, some of the actions supported out of box include e-mail, paging, command execution, custom actions etc.
13. Apart from the automated actions, it has a powerful notification mechanism. External applications can register with NMS for notifications. Registered applications are notified during the various stages of event flow.
14. RDBMS (relational database management system) is used as the persistence layer, which facilitates achieving the high level goals of availability, scalability, performance, concurrence and atomicity of all the operations.
15. All the persistent information is stored in the database and these information are used for generating reports and for auditing. An internal caching mechanism helps to speed up transactions.
16. The rich set of services offered by the fault management module are also exposed through a set of well defined and easy to use APIs (Application Programming Interfaces), using which scalable, secure and reliable applications can be developed with ease.

6.2.2 Accounting Management
1. The field of Accounting Management is concerned with the
    - Collection of resource
    - Consumption data for the purposes of capacity and
    - Trend analysis
    - Tariffing/Pricing
    - Cost allocation, auditing, and billing.
    - Collections and Finance
    - Usage measurement
    - Enterprise control

2. Since accounting applications do not have uniform security and reliability requirements, it is not possible to devise a single accounting protocol and set of security services that will meet all needs.
3. Thus, the goal of accounting management is to provide a set of tools that can be used to meet the requirements of each application.
4. The various terms related to the Accounting Management are

Accounting: The collection of resource consumption data for the purposes of capacity and trend analysis, cost allocation, auditing, and billing. Accounting management requires that resource consumption be measured, rated, assigned, and communicated between appropriate parties.

Archival accounting: In archival accounting, the goal is to collect all accounting data, to reconstruct missing entries as best as possible in the event of data loss, and to archive data for a mandated time period. It is "usual and customary" for these systems to be engineered to be very robust against accounting data loss. This may include provisions for transport layer as well as application layer acknowledgements, use of non-volatile storage, interim accounting capabilities (stored or transmitted over the wire), etc. Legal or financial requirements frequently mandate archival accounting practices, and may often dictate that data be kept confidential, regardless of whether it is to be used for billing purposes or not.

Rating: The act of determining the price to be charged for use of a resource.

Billing: The act of preparing an invoice.

Usage sensitive billing: A billing process that depends on usage information to prepare an invoice can be said to be usage-sensitive. In contrast, a process that is independent of usage information is said to be non-usage-sensitive.

Auditing: The act of verifying the correctness of a procedure. In order to be able to conduct an audit, it is necessary to be able to definitively determine what procedures were actually carried out so as to be able to compare this to the recommended process. Accomplishing this may require security services such as authentication and integrity protection.

Cost Allocation: The act of allocating costs between entities. Note that cost allocation and rating are fundamentally different processes. In cost allocation, the objective is typically to allocate a known cost among several entities. In rating the objective is to determine the amount to be charged for use of a resource. In cost allocation, the cost per unit of resource may need to be determined; in rating, this is typically a given. Interim accounting: Interim accounting provides a snapshot of usage during a user's session. This may be useful in the event of a device reboot or other network problem that prevents the reception or generation of a session summary packet or session record. Interim accounting records can always be summarized without the loss of information. Note that interim accounting records may be stored internally on the device (such as in non-volatile storage) so as to survive a reboot and thus may not always be transmitted over the wire.

Session record: A session record represents a summary of the resource consumption of a user over the entire session. Accounting gateways creating the session record may do so by processing interim accounting events or accounting events from several devices serving the same user.

Accounting Protocol: A protocol used to convey data for accounting purposes.

Intra-domain accounting: Intra-domain accounting involves the collection of information on resource usage within an administrative domain, for use within that domain. In intra-domain accounting, accounting packets and session records typically do not cross-administrative boundaries.

Inter-domain accounting: Inter-domain accounting involves the collection of information on resource usage within an administrative domain, for use within another administrative domain. In inter-domain accounting, accounting packets and session records will typically cross-administrative boundaries.

Real-time accounting: Real-time accounting involves the processing of information on resource usage within a defined time window. Time constraints are typically imposed in order to limit financial risk.

Accounting server: The accounting server receives accounting data from devices and translates it into session records. The accounting server may also take the responsibility for the routing of session records to interested parties.

MODEL FOR ACCOUNTING FUNCTION

Information and process flow ⟶

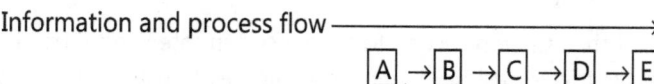

- A - Usage measurement and collection
- B - Create usage records
- C - Apply tariff and create charges associated with usage
- D - Create service transaction record
- E - Generate bills for subscriber

Fig. 6.19: Model for Accounting function

Accounting Management Architecture:

1. The accounting management architecture involves interactions between network devices, accounting servers, and billing servers.
2. The network device collects resource consumption data in the form of accounting metrics.
3. This information is then transferred to an accounting server. Typically this is accomplished via an accounting protocol, although it is also possible for devices to generate their own session records.
4. The accounting server then processes the accounting data received from the network device.
5. This processing may include summarization of interim accounting information, elimination of duplicate data, or generation of session records.

6. The accounting server then processes the accounting data received from the network device. This processing may include summarization of interim accounting information, elimination of duplicate data, or generation of session records.
7. The processed accounting data is then submitted to a billing server, which typically handles rating and invoice generation, but may also carry out auditing, cost allocation, trend analysis or capacity planning functions.
8. Session records may be batched and compressed by the accounting server prior to submission to the billing server in order to reduce the volume of accounting data and the bandwidth required to accomplish the transfer.
9. One of the functions of the accounting server is to distinguish between inter and intra-domain accounting events and to route them appropriately.
10. For session records containing a Network Access Identifier (NAI) is used. The distinction can be made by examining the domain portion of the NAI. If the domain portion is absent or corresponds to the local domain, then the session record is treated as an intra-domain accounting event. Otherwise, it is treated as an inter-domain accounting event.
11. Intra-domain accounting events are typically routed to the local billing server, while inter-domain accounting events will be routed to accounting servers operating within other administrative domains.
12. While it is not required that session record formats used in inter and intra-domain accounting be the same, this is desirable, since it eliminates translations that would otherwise be required.
13. Where a proxy forwarder is employed, domain-based access controls may be employed by the proxy forwarder, rather than by the devices themselves.
14. The network device will typically speak an accounting protocol to the proxy forwarder, which may then either convert the accounting packets to session records, or forward the accounting packets to another domain.
15. In either case, domain separation is typically achieved by having the proxy forwarder sort the session records or accounting messages by destination.
16. Where the accounting proxy is not trusted, it may be difficult to verify that the proxy is issuing correct session records based on the accounting messages it receives, since the original accounting messages typically are not forwarded along with the session records.
17. Therefore where trust is an issue, the proxy typically forwards the accounting packets themselves. Assuming that the accounting protocol supports data object security, this allows the end-points to verify that the proxy has not modified the data in transit or snooped on the packet contents.
18. Fig. 6.20 illustrates the accounting management architecture.

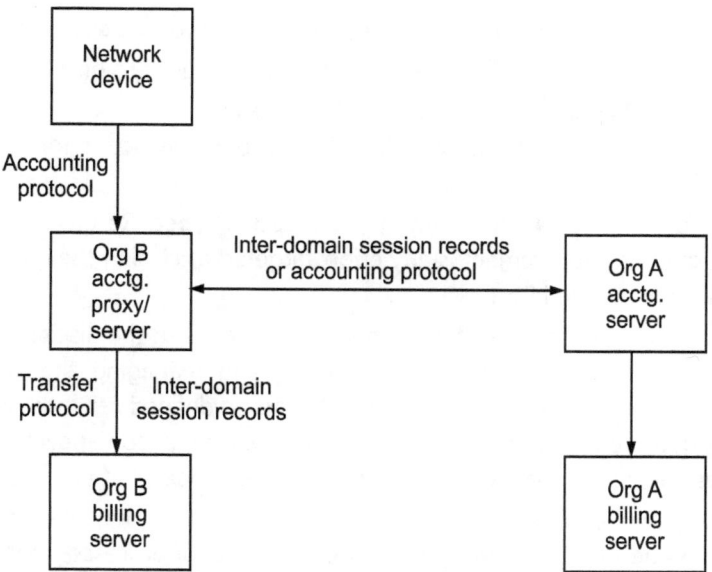

Fig. 6.20: Accounting Management Architecture

6.2.3 Performance Management

6.2.3.1 Introduction

Performance measurement is the process of assessing progress toward achieving predetermined goals, while performance management is building on that process adding the relevant communication and action on the progress achieved against these predetermined goals. The function sets are identified for this field are:

- Performance quality assurance.
- Performance monitoring.
- Performance control.
- Performance analysis.

In network performance management, following things are included:

(a) a set of functions that evaluate and report the behavior of telecommunications equipment and the effectiveness of the network or network element and

(b) a set of various subfunctions, such as gathering statistical information, maintaining and examining historical logs, determining system performance under natural and artificial conditions, and altering system modes of operation.

- In organizational development (OD), **performance** can be thought of as Actual Results vs Desired Results. Any discrepancy, where Actual is less than Desired, could constitute the performance improvement zone. Performance management and improvement can be thought of as a cycle:

1. *Performance planning* where goals and objectives are established.
2. *Performance coaching* where a manager intervenes to give feedback and adjust performance.
3. *Performance appraisal* where individual performance is formally documented and feedback delivered.

A performance problem is any gap between Desired Results and Actual Results. Performance improvement is any effort targeted at closing the gap between Actual Results and Desired Results.

- Application Performance Management (APM) refers to the discipline within systems management that focuses on monitoring and managing the performance and availability of software applications. APM can be defined as workflow and related IT tools deployed to detect, diagnose, remedy and report on application performance issues to ensure that application performance meets or exceeds end-users'-and businesses'-expectations.
- Business performance management (BPM) is a set of processes that help businesses discover efficient use of their business units, financial, human and material resources.
- Operational performance management (OPM) focus is on creating methodical and predictable ways to improve business results, or performance, across organizations.

Simply put, performance management helps organizations achieve their strategic goals. Rather than discarding the data accessibility previous systems fostered, performance management harnesses it to help ensure that an organization's data works in service to organizational goals to provide information that is actually useful in achieving them and focus on the Operational Networking Processes between that performance level.

6.2.3.2 Need for Performance Management

The main task of Network management systems is to monitor and control the network infrastructure. As computer networks increase in size, heterogeneity and complexity, effective management of such networks becomes more important and much difficult. In the present business world, each and every hour counts. An hour of network downtime means an hour of lost business and hence lost opportunities. Pro-actively managing the Network's health and performance is indispensable for any mission critical business and is something, which the administrators of large networks have to put in place.

The main challenges in this area include

- Identifying the data that needs to be collected.
- Interpreting the collected data.
- Disseminating the data and
- Presenting the data...., which helps in network Performance management.

6.2.3.3 Performance Management Architecture

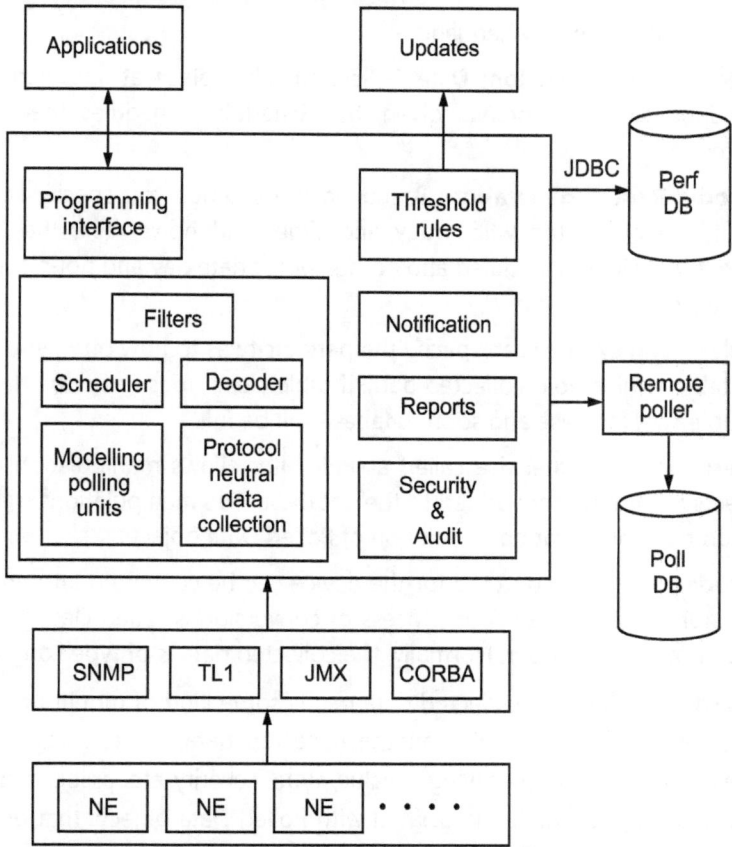

Fig. 6.21: Performance Management Architecture

Typical Web NMS Performance module is made up of the following components:

Data Collection Service (Protocol Neutral Data Collection):
- This provides multi protocol Data collection support. Data can be collected from TL1(Transaction Language 1) devices, CORBA devices etc. Default data collection takes place with respect to SNMP devices.
- User can plug in his own Protocol provider to facilitate data collection for that protocol.
- Data collection process can be customized to suit user requirements.
- Observers can be set to monitor data collection process and get notified.

Data Collection Objects (Modeling Polling units):
Data collection process has been well-studied and modeled using objects that define
- What data to collect (Polling Objects and Polled Data) and
- Where to store the collected data

Scheduler:

This component takes care of scheduling –

- **Periodic data collection:** Data Collection takes place at specified time intervals. Based on the time interval given, the Scheduler schedules the Data Collection process.

- **Periodic Report generation:** Based on the settings you specify i.e. which report should be generated when (day and time) and how often, the time of report generation will be scheduled and at the appropriate day and hour, the report will be produced.

- **Tables clean up:** You can specify the periodicity as to how often you want to delete the tables which hold collected data. If table clean up is not done then the number of tables will increase and soon database will be full.

- **Filter:** The filter otherwise called as Poll Filter allows manipulation of Polled Data objects before they are added to the database. The manipulations will be some kind of addition, modification or deletion of Polled Data objects.

- **Decoder:** The data collected for the device can be converted into any other format and stored in database. This process of conversion is called Decoding and is taken care of by Data decoder. Normally, the collected data is of type Long or String.

- **Threshold Rules:** The collected data needs some kind of monitoring which is done by applying Threshold rules on the collected data. These rules are nothing but Threshold objects each having a value, type, severity etc. associated with it. These threshold objects will be associated with Polled Data objects that define what data to collect and thus monitor constantly whenever data gets collected. Any violation in Threshold rule will result in notifications sent to the administrator.

Notification:

Notification refers to messages sent to the network users for intimating some aspect of network happening. By default Web NMS Performance module supports notifications via three means:

- **Threshold Notification:** Whenever collected data exceeds Threshold value, a Threshold event is generated and sent to Fault module, which handles it.

- **Collected data Observers (Poll observers):** You can set Observers to get intimated when data is collected. You might like to do so when you want to do something with data before it gets stored in database.

- **Poll Unit Observers:** You may wish to receive notifications whenever any change is made in existing Data collection configuration. Poll units are objects, which hold definition of what data to collect and from where.

Reporting:

The collected data can be grouped into meaningful sets and represented in formatted manner called Reports. You can create your own reports and add it to existing set of reports. Reports can be scheduled to be generated periodically. Many types of reports are provided including "On demand" reports.

Security and Audit:

Authorization privileges are available using, which the administrator can create user accounts and associate Performance related operations permitted for him. User Based Views can also be created and coupled with permissions on what the user can do on Performance objects.

Programming Interface:

This refers to a rich set of API methods, which help you in customizing, extending and configuring Performance module to suit your requirements. Javadocs for API methods are also available along with extensive Help documents.

Configuring and Customizing Performance Module:

You may have your own set of requirements for which you would like to customize and configure Web NMS Performance module. Following gives you the list which you can configure and customize:

1. Data collection
2. Data storage
3. Reports
4. Threshold generation
5. Graphs
6. Distributed Polling
7. Performance Client
8. Managed Object inputs to Performance module

You can do the above listed using **API methods** and using **Configuration files**.

6.2.4 Configuration Management (CM)

6.2.4.1 Introduction

Configuration Management (CM) describes a series of processes and procedures developed in the information technology community to establish and maintain system integrity. It provides a holistic approach for effectively controlling system change and is an integral part of the systems engineering process. CM helps to verify that changes to subsystems are considered in terms of the entire system, minimizing adverse effects.

The function set groups in this area pertain to planning the telecom network to meet required measures, installing telecom network equipments, provisioning them in setting up circuits as well as for services offered to subscribers and controlling/ monitoring status of the telecom network. The main functions set groups are –
- Network planning and engineering
- Installations
- Service planning and negotiations
- Provisioning and
- Status and control

Effective CM provides the following essential benefits to a project:
1. Reduces confusion and establishes order.
2. Organizes the activities necessary to maintain product integrity.
3. Ensures correct product configurations.
4. Limits legal liability by providing a record of actions.
5. Reduces life-cycle costs.
6. Enables consistent conformance with requirements.
7. Provides a stable working environment.
8. Enhances compliance with standards.
9. Enhances status accounting.

In short, CM can provide cost effective project insurance when properly planned, organized, and implemented. It must be integral to your overall project execution, and to your charter/customer agreement. If the CM process is unreasonable or unresponsive, people will try to circumvent the process, leading to chaos and a loss of the benefits of true CM.

6.2.4.2 Configuration Management Process

The general CM process, graphically demonstrated below, is made up of the following elements:
- **Configuration Identification:** The process of documenting and labeling the items in the system, by providing a unique identifier to track changes and identify item location.
- **Change Management:** The process of assessing impacts of a possible change to a system, determining the fate of the proposed change, executing the approved changes, and ensuring that the change is properly documented.
- **Configuration Status Accounting:** The process of ensuring that all of the relevant information about an item is up to date and as detailed as necessary.
- **Configuration Audits:** The process of analyzing Configuration Items and their respective documentation to ensure that it reflects the current situation.

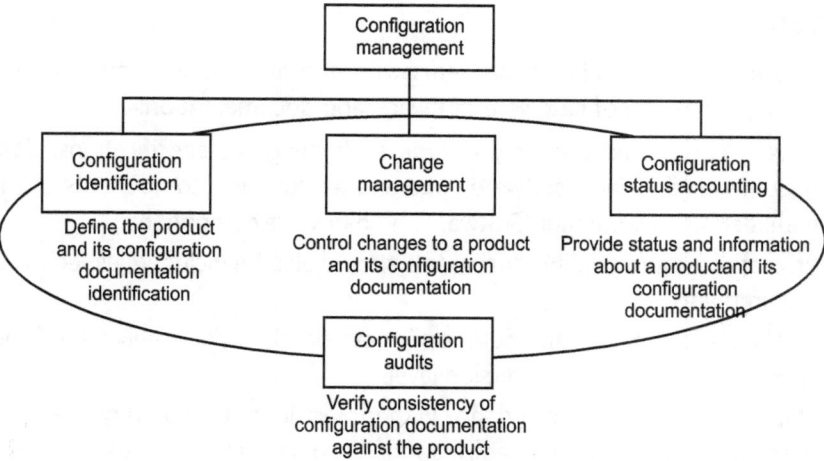

Fig. 6.22

6.2.4.3 Process Description

While CM is a major element of a change control program, it is such a multifaceted discipline that it should be considered not simply as another activity, but as a program in and of itself. Establishing an effective CM program requires an understanding of CM functions and of the overall CM process.

6.2.4.4 Functions of Configuration Management

CM is comprised of four primary functions: identification, change control, status accounting, and auditing. These are shown in Fig. 6.23, along with their sub functions. All CM activity falls within the bounds of these functions.

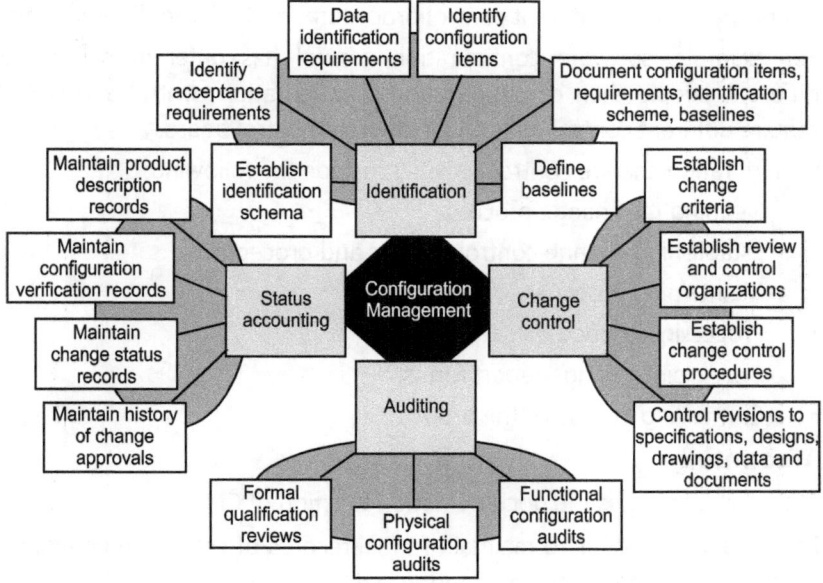

Fig. 6.23: Major functions of Configuration Management

Identification:

1. This function identifies those items whose configuration needs to be controlled, usually consisting of hardware, software, and documentation.
2. These items would probably include such things as specifications, designs, data, documents, drawings, software code and executables, components of the Telecom engineering environment (Software and hardware components).
3. Project plans and guiding documents should also be included, especially the project requirements.
4. A schematic of names and numbers is developed for accurately identifying products and their configuration or version level.
5. This must be done in accordance with project identification requirements. Finally, a baseline configuration is established for all configuration items and systems.
6. Although key components to be managed are requirements and source code, related documentation and data should be identified and placed under CM control.

Change Control:

1. Configuration control establishes procedures for proposing or requesting changes, evaluating those changes for desirability, obtaining authorization for changes, publishing and tracking changes, and implementing changes.
2. This function also identifies the people and organizations who have authority to make changes at various levels (configuration item, assembly, system, project, etc.).
3. Additionally, various change criteria are defined as guidelines for the control organizations. Different types of configuration items or different systems will probably need different control procedures and involve different people.
4. For example, software configuration control has different needs and involves different people than communications configuration control and would probably require different control rules and a different control board.
5. Configuration change control activities include the following:
   - Defining the change process.
   - Establishing change control policies and procedures.
   - Maintaining baselines.
   - Processing changes.
   - Developing change report forms.
   - Controlling release of the product.

Status Accounting:

1. Status accounting is the documentation function of CM.
2. Its primary purpose is to maintain formal records of established configurations and make regular reports of configuration status.

3. These records should accurately describe the product, and are used to verify the configuration of the system for testing, delivery, and other activities.
4. Status accounting also maintains a history of change requests and authorizations, along with status of all approved changes.
5. Key information about the project and configuration items can be communicated to project members through status accounting.
6. Telecom engineers can see what fixes or files were included in which baseline.
7. Project managers can track completion of problem reports and various other maintenance activities.

Auditing:
1. Effective CM requires regular evaluation of the configuration.
2. This is done through the auditing function, where the physical and functional configurations are compared to the documented configuration.
3. The purpose of auditing is to maintain the integrity of the baseline and release configurations for all controlled products.
4. Auditing is accomplished via both informal monitoring and formal reviews.
5. Configuration auditing verifies that the software product is built according to the requirements, standards, or contractual agreement.
6. Test reports and documentation are used to verify that the software meets the stated requirements.
7. The goal of a configuration audit is to verify that all software products have been produced, correctly identified and described, and that all change requests have been resolved according to established CM processes and procedures.
8. Informal audits are conducted at key phases of the software life cycle.
9. There are two types of formal audits that are conducted before the software is delivered to the customer: **Functional Configuration Audit (FCA) and Physical Configuration Audit (PCA).**
10. Configuration audit activities include the following:
    - Defining audit schedule and procedures.
    - Identifying who will perform the audits.
    - Performing audits on established baselines.
    - Generating audit reports.

6.2.4.5 Typical Configuration Management Solutions for Servers
1. Configuration Management Solutions for Servers is policy-based change and configuration management software that enables administrators to efficiently and reliably inventory, provision and maintain software and content across heterogeneous server platforms.

2. Ensuring application availability and reliability on data center and distributed servers, Configuration Management Solutions for Servers manages and secures all software layers–operating systems, patches, applications, middleware and settings– on data center, blade and web servers, resulting in increased server software reliability and stability at reduced costs.

3. Configuration Management Solutions for Servers is proven by enterprise customers around the world to deliver deployment reliability in highly complex and large-scale IT environments.

4. It automates change management, resulting in rapid provisioning and updating of servers, increased application reliability and availability and improved IT operational efficiency.

Features:

Configuration Management Solutions for Servers enables IT professionals to:

- Collect server hardware and software inventory across multiple platforms.
- Monitor software usage patterns.
- Prepare an application package and conduct impact analysis prior to distribution.
- Target individual data center servers, distributed servers or server farms for deployment and maintenance according to business policies.
- Provision and manage operating systems, applications and content on distributed servers from any location in attended or unattended "lights-out" mode.
- Acquire, test, distribute and assure compliance of security patches, hot fixes and service packs.
- Integrate with other system management tools.
- Leverage a common infrastructure for management of software and content on virtually any device, any platform and any network for all enterprise users.
- Scale to meet enterprise needs.

6.2.5 Security Management

6.2.5.1 Overview

1. Security is concerned with ensuring legitimate use, maintaining confidentiality, data integrity, and auditing in the network.

2. Security Management involves identifying the assets, threats, vulnerabilities, and taking protective measures, which if not done may lead to unintended use of computing systems.

3. Network management applications are increasing in size and complexity to address a broad segment of heterogeneous computing environments.

4. The complexity of network infrastructure demands a highly scalable application providing end-to-end solution that goes beyond the basic network management needs.

5. With these, the following are the three important aspects of information security that are to be taken care from the security service point of view:
   - **Security Attack:** Any action that comprises the security information owned by an organization.
   - **Security Mechanism:** A mechanism that is designed to detect, prevent, or recover from a security attack.
   - **Security Service:** A service that enhances the security of the data processing systems and the information transfers in the network.

6. Thus, the services are intended to counter security attacks, and they make use of one or more security mechanisms to provide the service. In general, Security threats can be classified as follows.

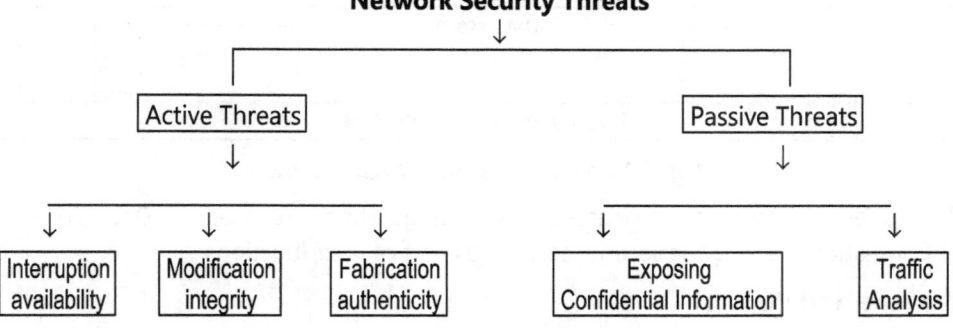

6.2.5.2 What does Security Services Offer?

Typical Web NMS provides Security Management as an out-of-the-box service, designed with the above objectives in mind. Since the security logic is completely separate from the management application's business logic, the Web NMS platform provides an environment where other applications can seamlessly integrate into the platform to utilize the security services.

6.2.5.3 Components of Security Framework

Security Module provides a framework that consists of the following:
- Authentication
- Access Control
- Authorization Admin
- Cryptography
- Audit
- Pluggable Logic
- Security Data Store

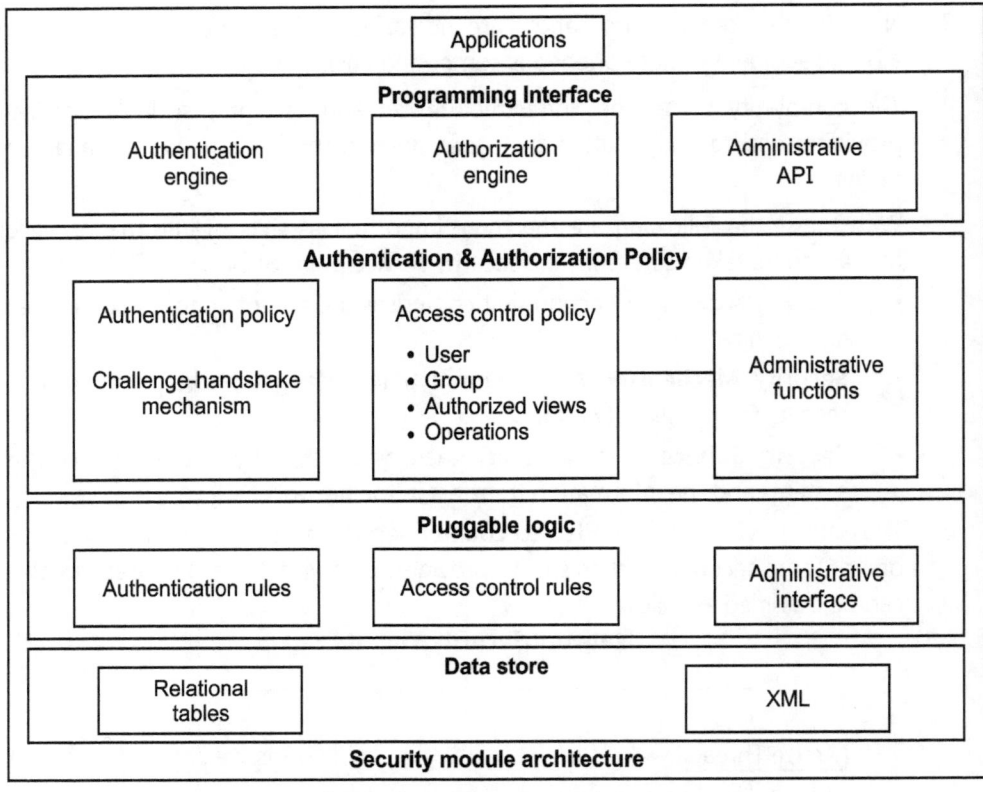

Fig. 6.24: Security Module Architecture

The other management services such as Configuration, Provisioning, Data Collection, Event Correlation, etc. use the security services as part of their functions.

Authentication Policy:

- With the applications built on the Web NMS platform being user centric, the authentication mechanism is used to verify the credentials before allowing access to the platform.
- Authentication Policy provided includes a Challenge-Handshake mechanism where the credentials of the user is verified using a 3-way handshake.
- The passwords are never sent across to the authentication module; rather a one-way-hash (called key) is used.
- This provides protection against playback attack using an incrementally changing identifier and a variable challenge value.

Access Control:

- The applications built with Web NMS platform model their own object based on the entity they deal with.

- Support for user-groups provides a mechanism to collectively associate access rights to a set of users.
- Also, it is not sufficient to just tie up the access rights of a user with the operation performed. Hence, it becomes necessary to have a framework where the permissions are associated with the subsets of objects concerned with the application. This in turn gives a fine-grained access control.
- The Authorization policy is designed with "Fine-Grained Access Control" as the focus. With vast number of users using the application, it becomes necessary that each one works within the allowed space.
- Considering the complexity of applications, the Access Control Policy should have the flexibility to define access rights of a user to operate on subset of objects that the applications work with.
- These Authorized Scopes consist of set of properties associated with the user operations.
- Thus, managed object properties such as network, Ip address, node, type etc. can be used in authorized views to control the access of the users to a specific type of devices within a given Ip range in a specified network alone.

Authorization Admin:

- Once the authorization level is well defined then assigning operations and achieving the respective fine-grained access becomes simple with the available set of security-oriented administrative functions.
- The Authorization Admin module takes care of security administrative operations like maintaining user profile, associating views with groups, setting permissions to perform operations, adding new operations, and thereby defining scopes for custom view.

Cryptography:

- To maintain a secured channel in network communication and to secure the storage of sensitive information like passwords, it becomes necessary to adopt a mechanism, which is secured by itself, and withstand the security attacks.
- Keeping these objectives in mind, Typical Security Management supports cryptogram support to ensure a secured data communication.
- This is achieved with the help of RSA Data Security Algorithm for cryptography.
- Here the original message (plain text) is encrypted with a public key and in the receiver end the encrypted plain text also called, as cipher test is decrypted with the private key that is only known by the receiver alone and thus ensuring a foolproof communication mechanism.

Audit:
- In this world of internetworking where hundreds and thousands of users access the network, it becomes essential to audit the details of network users activities.
- This in turn provides an Intrusion Detection Control mechanism where the user operations need to be logged in as per convenience.
- This aspect of security service is very well taken care by the Audit Service, where the user as well as the network manager can view and have the copy of the audit trails of the NMS users, including the time and status of operation performed by the users.
- This enables the network administrator to take necessary steps when an unauthorized execution is attempted by any user.

Pluggable Logic:
- The rules for authentication and authorization can easily be extended/modified.
- As security requirements of the application can change, it is important that the authorization rules be extendable.
- The rules could be related with the logic used in verifying permissions when multiple groups and scopes are involved.
- The associated permission can be extended to allow or disallow access based on the applications needs.
- Thus, the user can write his own implementation class for the authentication and authorization services and make it pluggable to suit his own environment.

Security Data Store:
- The Web NMS platform can be deployed in various environments.
- It becomes necessary to support different data store for storing the security information, depending on the requirements. Security module provides the ability to plug in the security service with existing/any other data store.
- This adds to the various deployment options available with Web NMS platform. Different data store like Relational Database, XML (Extensible Markup Language), LDAP (Lightweight Directory Access Protocol) etc. can be integrated seamlessly. Security Module provides Administrative interfaces to configure the data store. The administrative functions are based on the authentication and authorization policy.

6.3 Management Services

1. Management services were introduced to bring together requirements functions in the context of a specific technology. A subset of the ones recognized in M.3200 are: Switched telephone network, Mobile communications network, Switched data network, Intelligent network, common channel signaling system no.7 network, N-ISDN, B-ISDN, and dedicated and reconfigurable leased circuits network.

2. We step into a discussion of signaling systems that make wonderful things happen in the convergence world-coupled with that discussion is the idea of computer and telephony integration. We also look at the concept of *Integrated Services Digital Network* (ISDN), which is not as popular in the North American countries as in many international markets.
3. **The requirements for the maintenance aspects of B-ISDN network managed area are specified in ITU recommendation M.3207.**
4. **The maintenance aspect include function sets in fault, performance, security and configuration functional areas.**
5. **The management functions sets alarm surveillance, Testing, fault correction, performance management control, and security management defined in Recommendation M.3400 are augmented to include B-ISDN specific function.**
6. After a few ideas have sunk in, we move on to a higher-speed data networking strategy, with the use of Frame Relay. After Frame Relay, we discuss the use of *Asynchronous Transfer Mode* (ATM) for its merits and benefits.
7. Thus we look at T1, T2, and T3 on copper or coax cable, which is a journey down memory lane for some. We also contrast the international market opportunities with E1, E2, and E3. However, by adding a little fiber to the diet, we provide these digital architectures on *Synchronous Optical Network* (SONET) or *Synchronous Digital Hierarchy* (SDH) services.
8. **In contrast to the previous example, the intersection of the managed area for leased circuit service and customer network management is not technology dependent.**
9. **Depending on the quality of the service requested and the sub networks used in providing the end-to-end connection, different technologies may be used.**
10. **This management service is described in recommendation M.3208.1.**
11. **The two examples above show the variations in the definition of the management service in the terms of the technology being managed and relevant TMN management function.**
12. **Thus to provide an end to end service like a high capacity digital service all these managed areas are very likely required along with the multiple management services identified in recommendation M.3200.**

6.4 Community Definitions

1. The functional area and management functions addressed requirements from the perspective of operating a network in a secure manner and billing for the services provided.

2. For example, for providing supplementary services does not depend on whether the access network is coaxial, fiber or hybrid fiber coaxial.
3. Community definitions provide yet another approach to defining requirements where functionalities are identified such as –
   - alarm management.
   - subnetwork connection management.
   - topology management.
4. The components in defining a community include the role with the
   - carnality information.
   - policies required.
   - policies permitted.
   - prohibited actions and
   - features negotiable

   in a contract.
5. There are no specific algorithms or rules to determine the granularity of a community definition. One approach is to consider the atomic functions identified in Recommendation M.3400 and develop detailed requirements using the community approach "configure, a simple subnetwork connection".

6.5 Requirements Capture

There are basically two types of approach for studying capture requirements.
1. Simple approach.
2. Formal approach.

In the simple **method**, the philosophy is that the requirements must be specified in a user-friendly manner. They should be validated by those who are very knowledgeable in the operation of the network without requiring special training to understand specialized notations.

This approach used the structures for defining a management service and a management function available in Recommendation M.3020.

The simple approach provides a user-friendly method for the presentation of requirements, it lacks rigor. In addition when the requirements are translated into the interface definitions, specifications do not include tractability of the requirements.

Formal approach is a natural way to support tractability, efforts can be made to explicitly define the mapping of interface definitions to requirements even with the simple approach. The simple and formal approaches are illustrated using the customer network management of a leased circuit service in Recommendation M.3208. This is a management service where the management area is the leased circuit service. The scope of this service is restricted to point-to-point leased circuits. In simple approach the management context description poles has two sections: (1) Service Customer (SC), (2) Service Provider (SP). Also management functions in simple approach are:

(1) Leased circuit service configuration function set.
(2) Created leased circuit function.
(3) Information.

6.6 Network Planning Support

1. Simulation helps in the network planning and design.
2. To determine the new or modified network planning and design, simulation can also find the unused capacity in an existing network.
3. It can be used to find design flaws in an existing network that are responsible for recurring performance problems such as bottlenecks.
4. Advantages of a Multiprotocol network simulators provide a rich opportunity for efficient experimentation.
5. Disparate research efforts using a common simulation environment can yield substantial benefits, including improved validation of the behavior of existing protocols –
   - A rich infrastructure for developing new protocols,
   - The opportunity to study large-scale protocol interaction in a controlled environment, and
   - Easier comparison of results across research efforts.
6. Simulation offers significant advantages as a basis for projects in Telecom networks and computer networking.
7. Because many unimportant details can be abstracted away, and also because simulations can be completely repeatable, it is possible to address the same concepts more quickly than is possible with actual networks.

6.7 Telecom Network Management Protocol Requirements

6.7.1 The Standard Interfaces of TMN

In the TMN model, specific interfaces between two TMN components communicate with one another. The TMN interfaces are as follows.

Table 6.6: TMN Interfaces

TMN Interfaces	Description
Q	The Q interface exists between two TMN-conformant functional blocks that are within the same TMN domain. The Qx carries information that is shared between the MD and the NEs that it supports. The Qx interface exists between the NE and MD; QA and MD; and MD and MD. The Q3 interface is the OS = interface. Any functional component that interfaces directly to the OS uses the Q3 interface. In other words, the Q3 interface is between the NE and OS; QA and OS; MD and OS; and OS and OS.
F	The F interface exists between a WS and OS, and between a WS and MD.
X	The X interface exists between two TMN-conformant OSs in two separate domains, or between a TMN-conformant OS and another OS in a non-TMN network.

Two other reference points, g and m, are outside the scope of TMN. They are between non-TMN entities and the non-TMN portion of the WSF and QAF, respectively.

In Fig. 6.25, each line represents an interface between two TMN components.

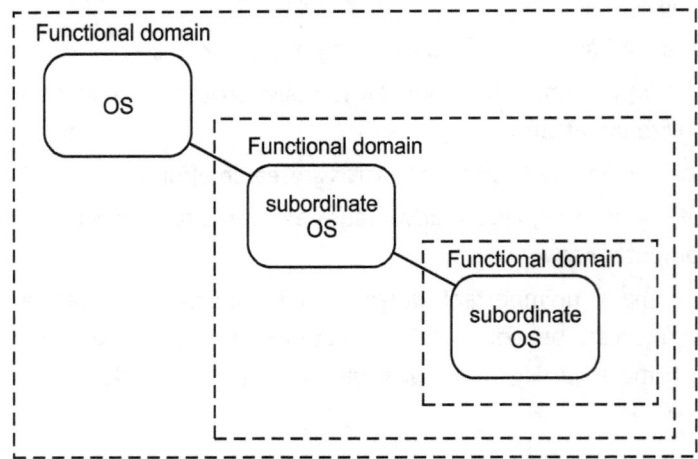

Fig. 6.25: Standard Interfaces between TMN Components

More About the Q Interfaces:

There are two classes of Q interfaces: Q3 and Qx. Fig. 6.26 illustrates which function blocks can communicate via which Q interface.

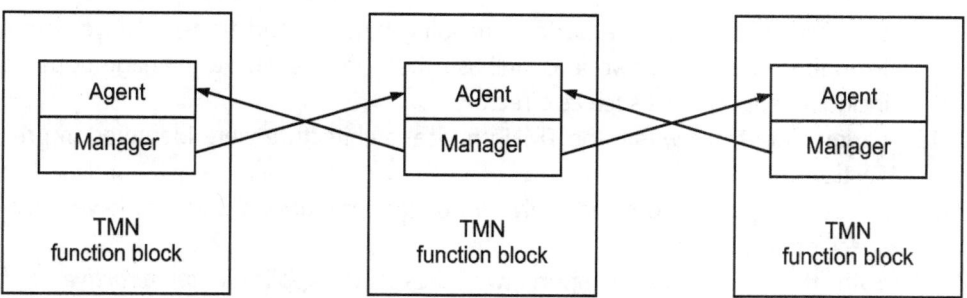

Fig. 6.26: Q Interfaces

Q3 Interface:

The Q3 interface is the lifeline to the operations system-Q3 is the only interface that QAs, MDs, or NEs may use to communicate directly with the OS. If a QA or NE does not use the Q3 interface, it cannot communicate directly with the OS; instead, it must communicate via an MD.

Qx Interface:

The Qx interface always operates with a MD. It never takes the place of a Q3 interface. The MD can interpret between local management information provided by a Qx interface and the OS information provided by a Q3 interface.

6.7.2 Classes of Applications in TMN

1. Two classes of applications have been defined to support the various TMN functions: *interactive and file transfer*.
2. The interactive class of applications in most cases exchange information using a request/reply paradigm such as requesting the alarm status, remote inventory of an equipment, and receiving a response.
3. The file transfer application requires remote manipulation of files and bulk transfer of data such as software download.
4. For the interactive class of applications, the content is determined using information models that define the management views of the resource and the application function.
5. For file transfer class, the structure of the file, and information in the records will define the contents.
6. The architecture and principles used in specifying the interactive class of applications within TMN draw heavily upon the foundations laid out by the OSI Systems management series of standards.
7. As a side note, managing the OSI protocols using Systems Management specifications has taken a backseat to their use in TMN.
8. This can be attributed to the fact that the industry has embraced the use of Internet protocols for communications between applications much more than the lower layers of OSI protocols.

9. Some specifications do exist for managing network and transport layer protocols for public-switched network as well as others are evolving to manage upper layers including applications such as directory.
10. Various interfaces within the TMN physical architecture were identified in previous Section.
11. It was also pointed out that only two of the interfaces, Q3 and X, have been well specified to date.
12. Both these interfaces support two classes of applications-*interactive and file transfer*.
13. The communication requirements for Q3 and X interfaces are specified using, for the most part, OSI protocols.
14. The reason for the phrase "the most part" is because lower layer protocols other than those developed as part of OSI suite are also included.
15. Specifically, Internet transport protocol has been included as one of the alternatives.
16. The OSI Systems Management protocol developed as part of the system management application mentioned above is specified as the requirement for exchanging management information belonging to the interactive class.
17. ISO protocol File Transfer and Access Management (FTAM) is required for the file transfer class.
18. Details of these requirements are defined in ITU Recommendations Q.811 and Q.812.17.
19. In order to support directory functions mentioned above, the recommendations also include X.500 Directory protocols.
20. It should be noted that both TMN and OSI architectural standards have been significantly influenced by the concepts in software development methods.
21. As an example, both architectures have subdivided a complex problem by separating concerns and addressing them individually.
22. **The interactive classes of applications** are characterized by bursty, time critical information that may be asynchronous. For example, reporting an alarm from a termination point is time critical in that the alarm must be reported as soon as it occurs instead of waiting for a period of time.
23. **The file-oriented class of applications** as the name suggests applies to applications where information stored as files is remotely managed (accessed, created, and modified). In contrast to the interactive class, these applications are not based on a command/response type of exchange and hence are not bursty or time critical. The duration for performing these applications is much longer compared to the interactive class. **Examples of applications of this class are downloading software (new generic, Patch etc.) accounting data, and memory backup and restoration.**
24. The third type of class of application defined within TMN is called **"Directory Services". This is orthogonal to the previous two in that the interactive and file transfer applications pertain to the exchange of management information.**

Directory Services addresses the support environment for the proper functioning of TMN. These services are required to provide the necessary mapping between the application entity and the address to be used for setting up connection.
25. Viewing management information and activities in terms of different levels of abstractions leads to modular and flexible definitions and facilitates building complex applications with relative ease.

6.7.3 Lower Layer Protocol Requirements

1. It specifies the following layers of the OSI reference model.
   - Physical
   - Data link
   - Network
   - Transport.
2. These requirements allow an implementation to use many different networking protocols.
3. The names and a brief definition of these profiles are given here.
4. The profiles are further separated into connection mode, connectionless mode and internet mode.

Table 6.7: Lower Layer Protocol Requirement Profiles

Name of Profile	Description
Internet-based	Internet TCP/IP with RFC 1006 which specifies the use of OSI upper layers over TCP/IP by providing OSI Transport Class 0 services.
CLNSI	LAN using CSMA/CD with ISO Connectionless Protocol (CLNP) and OSI Transport Protocol (class 4 only)
CLNS2	CLNP over X.25 and OSI Transport Protocol (class 4 only).
CLNS3	CLNP over ISDN B- or D-channel and OSI Transport Protocol (class 4 only).
CONS1	X.25 LAPB, X.25 packet interface with OSI Transport Protocol (classes 0, 2, 4).
CONS2	X.32 packet mode on ISDN D-channel with OSI Transport Protocol (classes 0, 2, 4); uses the adaptation function for providing OSI connection mode service from ISDN.
CONS3	X.31 packet mode on ISDN B-channel with OSI Transport Protocol (classes 0, 2, 4); uses the adaptation function for providing OSI connection mode service from ISDN.
CONS5	Signaling System No. 7 MTP and SCCP with OSI Transport Protocol (classes 0, 2, 4); adaptation of SS7 MTP/SCCP to provide OSI connection service is not completely specified.
CONS6	LAN with X.25 packet interface and OSI Transport Protocol (classes 0, 2, 4).

5. **Connection mode:** Typical example of connection mode lower layer protocol profile is shown in Fig. 6.27.

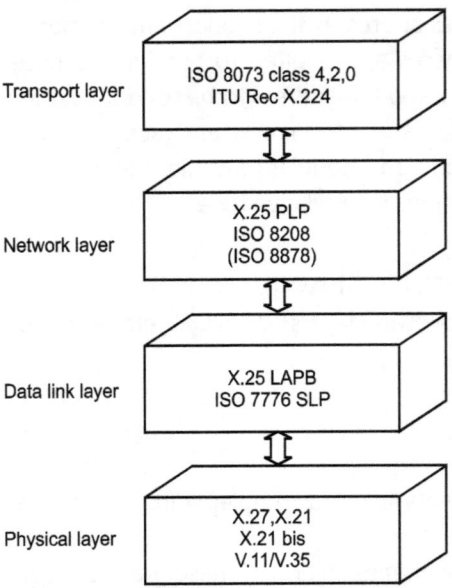

Fig. 6.27: Protocols for CONS1 profile

6. In all cases except with the internet profile, the transport layer requirements are identical assuming class 4 for all the profiles.
7. OSI transport protocol defines five classes with increasing functionality.
8. Class 4 has all features and supports the recovery mechanisms required when an unreliable network is used.
9. CONS1 uses X.25 packet switched protocol for the network layer and LAPB for the data link layer.
10. **Connectionless mode:** Fig. 6.28 shows the protocol requirements for connectionless profile CLNS2.

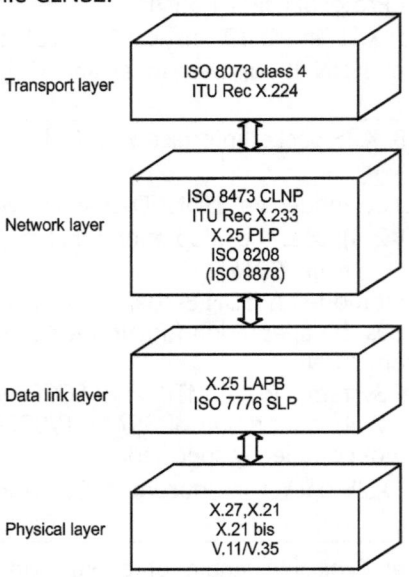

Fig. 6.28: Protocols for CLNS2 profile

11. The difference between this profile and CONS1 is the addition of connectionless network protocol (CLNP) in the network layer.
12. CLNP provides the facilities of internetworking between connection-oriented and connectionless profiles.
13. Only transport class 4 is supported for all the profiles using this mode.
14. **Internet mode:** The protocol profiles for connection-oriented and connection-less mode use the OSI suite of protocols. Protocols for internet profile are shown in Fig. 6.29.

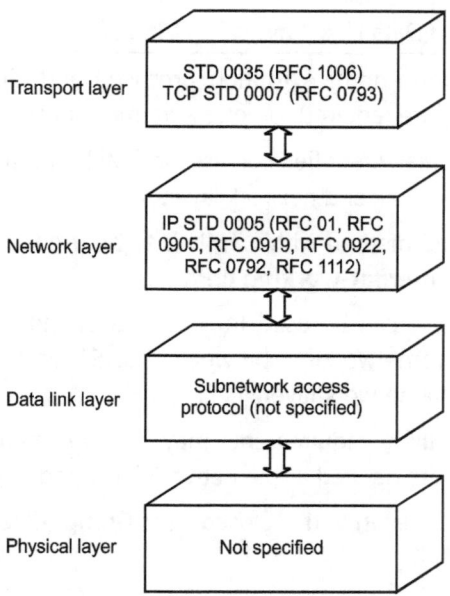

Fig. 6.29: Protocols for Internet profile

15. The internet standard STD0035 defines a method for using OSI upper layers over the existing TCP/IP based networks.
16. This protocol profile is the predominant mode used by implementations, specifically for the Q3 interface.

6.7.3.1 Conformance Requirement

1. The protocol profiles discussed specify the requirements in terms of the base standards to be used for protocol specifications.
2. In any protocol specification, several options are included to address varying enterprise and technology requirements.
3. To improve interoperability between implementations, international standards profiles have been developed for the protocol identified for CONS1, CLNS1 and CLNS2.
4. These profiles specify detailed parameter level support and value ranges required for interoperability.

Table 6.8: International Standard Profiles

Protocol Profile	ISP
CONS 1	Transport ISO/IEC ISP 10609-1
	Network, Data Link and Physical – ISO/IEC ISP 10609-9
CLNS1	Transport, Network ISO/IEC 10608-1
	Data Link, Physical ISO/IEC 10608-2
CLNS2	Transport, Network ISO/IEC 10608-1
	Data Link, Physical ISO/IEC 10608-5

5. ISO/IEC 10589 (Intra-domain routing protocol) and ISO/IEC 10747 (Inter-domain routing protocol) are required for intra and inter domain **routing** respectively.

6. The protocol profiles identified for use on TMN interfaces include different stacks specifically for data link and network layers.

7. The recommended method within TMN is to be use the Network Layer Relay (NLR) function with an **internet-working unit**.

8. Network layer relay can be used for internetworking between CLNS1 and CLNS2. However, for internetworking between CONS1 and CLNS2, internetworking is required above the network layer.

9. Even though **security** requirements may be implemented at multiple layers, the selected options are defined at the network layer and application layer.

10. For Network layer security, the Closed User Group (CUG) defined as part of X.25 is specified for CONS1.

6.7.4 Upper Layer Protocol Requirements

1. The upper layers are treated together for each application class in contrast to the lower layers.

2. The nature of the application defines requirements at the session and presentation layers.

3. The concept of functional units are important for upper layers of OSI reference model.

4. Depending on the functions supported by the layer, multiple services are defined.

5. Functional units are a mechanism whereby the services are grouped together into meaningful collection.

6. The major reason for defining the functional units is to allow for negotiating their use during an association.

7. Depending on the services, the use of the functional units may or may not be negotiable.

8. The requirements for both the interactive and file transfer classes are provided using the functional units defined in session, presentation layers and ACSE (Association Control Service Element).
9. Two classes of applications have been defined to support the various TMS functions: *interactive and file transfer.*
10. The interactive class of applications in most cases exchange information using a request/reply paradigm such as requesting the alarm status, remote inventory of an equipment, and receiving a response.
11. The file transfer application requires remote manipulation of files and bulk transfer of data such as software download.
12. For the interactive class of applications, the content is determined using information models that define the management views of the resource and the application function.
13. For file transfer class, the structure of the file, and information in the records will define the contents.
14. The architecture and principles used in specifying the interactive class of applications within TMN draw heavily upon the foundations laid out by the OSI Systems management series of standards.
15. As a side note, managing the OSI protocols using the System Management specifications has taken a backseat to their use in TMN.
16. This can be attributed to the fact that the industry has embraced the use of Internet protocols for communications between applications much more than the lower layers of OSI protocols.
17. Some specifications do exist for managing network and transport layer protocols for public-switched network as well as others are evolving to manage upper layers including applications such as directory.
18. Various interfaces within the TMN physical architecture were identified in previous section.
19. It was also pointed out that only two of the interfaces, Q3 and X, have been well specified to date.
20. Both these interfaces support two classes of applications – *interactive and file transfer.*
21. The communication requirements for Q3 and X interfaces are specified using, for the most part, OSI protocols.
22. The reason for the phrase "the most part" is because lower layer protocols other than those developed as part of OSI suite are also included.
23. Specifically, Internet transport protocol has been included as one of the alternatives.
24. The OSI Systems Management protocol developed as part of the system management application mentioned above is specified as the requirement for exchanging management information belonging to the interactive class.

25. ISO protocol File Transfer and Access Management (FTAM) is required for the file transfer class.
26. Details of these requirements are defined in ITU Recommendations Q.811 and Q.812.17.
27. In order to support directory functions mentioned above, the recommendations also include X.500 Directory protocols.
28. It should be noted that both TMN and OSI architectural standards have been significantly influenced by the concepts in software development methods.
29. As an example, both architectures have subdivided a complex problem by separating concerns and addressing them individually.
30. **The interactive classes of applications** are characterised by bursty, time critical information that may be asynchronous. For example, reporting an alarm from a termination point is time critical in that the alarm must be reported as soon it occurs instead of waiting for a period of time.
31. **The file-oriented class of applications** as the name suggests applies to applications where information stored as files is remotely managed (accessed, created, and modified). In contrast to the interactive class, these applications are not based on a command/response type of exchange and hence are not bursty or time critical. The duration of performing these applications is much longer compared to the **interactive class. Examples of applications of this class are downloading software (new generic, Patch etc.) accounting data, and memory backup and restoration.**
32. The third type of class of application defined within TMN is called **"Directory Services". This is orthogonal to the previous two in that the interactive and file transfer applications pertain to the exchange of management information.** Directory Services addresses the support environment for the proper functioning of TMN. These services are required to provide the necessary mapping between the application entity and the address to be used for setting up connection.
33. Viewing management information and activities in terms of different levels of abstractions leads to modular and flexible definitions and facilities building complex applications with relative ease.

6.7.5 Security Requirements

1. The security requirements specified in Recommendation Q.812 for both interactive and file-oriented class of applications vary between 'Q3' and 'X' interface.
2. Because 'X' interface is between different TMNs, the support for the authentication functional unit is mandatory.
3. A generic standard exists for providing security for any applications. This is known as Generic Upper Layer Security (GULS) and is defined in X.830 series.
4. GULS defines an approach where the presentation layer performs functions such as encryption and decryption.

5. In case of interactive class of applications, a new Recommendation Q.813 is being developed and planned to be available as an approved Recommendation.
6. This standard defines a generic approach for remote operations-based applications to support a method for protecting protocol data units.

6.7.6 What is SNMP?

Executive Summary:
- **SNMP is the most popular network management protocol in the TCP/IP protocol suite.**
- **It is a simple request/response protocol that communicates management information between two types of SNMP software entities: SNMP *applications* (also called SNMP *managers*) and SNMP *agents*.**

SNMP lets TCP/IP-based network management clients use a TCP/IP-based internetwork to exchange information about the configuration and status of nodes. The information available is defined by a set of **managed objects** referred to as the SNMP Management Information Base (MIB). The subset of managed objects that make up the TCP/IP portion of the MIB is maintained by each TCP/IP node. SNMP can also generates trap messages used to report significant TCP/IP events asynchronously to interested clients.

SNMP applications run in a network management station (NMS) and issue queries to gather information about the status, configuration, and performance of external network devices (called *network* elements in SNMP terminology). For example, HP Openview software is an example of a network management station, and a Cisco 4500 Router with its SNMP agent enabled could be considered an example of a network element. Shown below is a (very) basic diagram illustrating this concept.

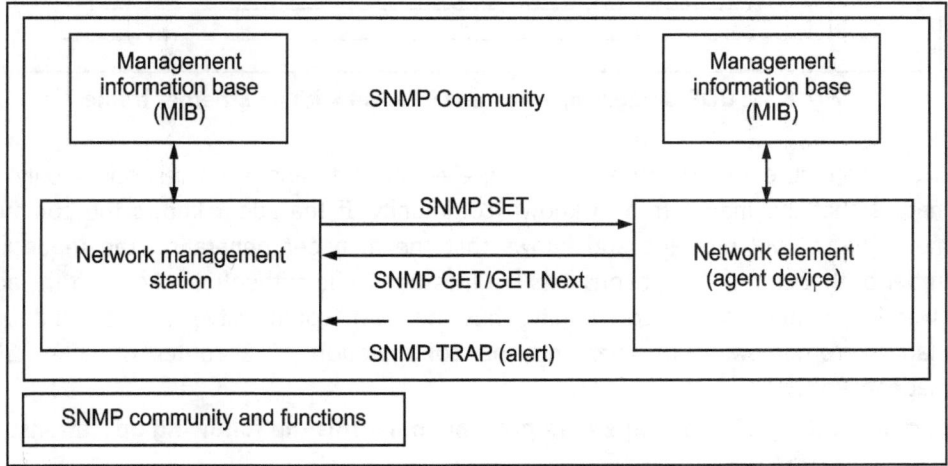

Fig. 6.30: Basic diagram illustrating concept of use of SNMP

SNMP agents run in network elements (for example, in the Cisco 4500 router) and respond to NMS queries (GETs) (for example, from HP Openview, or MRTG). In addition, agents send unsolicited reports (called *traps*) back to the NMS when certain network activity occurs. These traps can spawn events such as email alerts, automatic pages or network server parameter modifications.

For security reasons, the SNMP agent validates each request from an SNMP manager before responding to the request, by verifying that the manager belongs to an SNMP *community* with access privileges to the agent.

An SNMP community is a logical relationship between an SNMP agent and one or more SNMP managers. The community has a name, and all members of a community have the same access privileges: either read-only (members can view configuration and performance information) or read-write (members can view configuration and performance information, and also change the configuration).

All SNMP message exchanges consist of a community name and a data field, which contains the SNMP operation and its associated operands. It is embedded within a UDP Datagram, inside an IP Packet within an Ethernet frame (see below).

Fig. 6.31: UDP Datagram, inside an IP Packet with an Ethernet frame

You can configure the SNMP agent to receive requests and send responses only from managers that are members of a known community. If the agent knows the community name in the SNMP message and knows that the manager generating the request is a member of that community, it considers the message to be authentic and gives it the access allowed for members of that community. Thus, the SNMP community prevents unauthorized managers from viewing or changing the configuration of a router or other SNMP manageable device.

In summary, the SNMP Management program performs the following operations:
- The **GET** operation receives a specific value about a managed object, such as available hard disk space from the agent's MIB.

- The **GET-NEXT** operation returns the "next" value by traversing the MIB database (tree) of managed object variables.
- The **SET** operation changes the value of a managed object's variable. Only variables whose object definition allows READ/WRITE access can be changed.
- The **TRAP** operation sends a message to the Management Station when a change occurs in a managed object (and that change is deemed important enought to spawn an alert message).

An Introduction to SNMP:

Simple Network Management Protocol (SNMP) is an application protocol offering network management services in the Internet Protocol suite. SNMP is defined in several RFCs published in beginning. During the last few years, SNMP has been adopted by numerous vendors of network equipment as a main or secondary management interface.

SNMP defines a client/server relationship. The client program (called the network manager) makes virtual connections to a server program (called the SNMP agent) executing on a remote network device. The data base controlled by the SNMP agent is referred to as the SNMP Management Information Base (MIB), and is a standard set of statistical and control values. SNMP additionally allows the extension of these standard values with values specific to a particular agent through the use of private MIBs.

Directives, issued by the network manager client to an SNMP agent, consist of the identifiers of SNMP variables (referred to as MIB object identifiers (OID) or MIB variables) along with instructions to either get the value for the identifier, or set the identifier to a new value.

Through the use of private MIB variables (OIDs), SNMP agents can be tailored for a myriad of specific devices, such as network bridges, gateways, and routers. The definitions of MIB variables supported by a particular agent are incorporated in descriptor files, written in Abstract Syntax Notation (ASN.1) format, made available to network management client programs so that they can become aware of these MIB variables and their usage.

The OID naming scheme is governed by the Internet Engineering Task Force (IETF). The IETF grants authority for parts of the name space to individual organizations such as Microsoft, Novell or Cisco. For example, Microsoft has the authority to assign the OIDs that can be derived by *branching downward* from the node in the MIB name tree that starts with 1.3.6.1.4.1.311. Novell's OIDs branch down from 1.3.6.1.4.1.23. and Cisco's OIDs branch down from 1.3.6.1.4.1.9. You can see this structure in the diagram below.

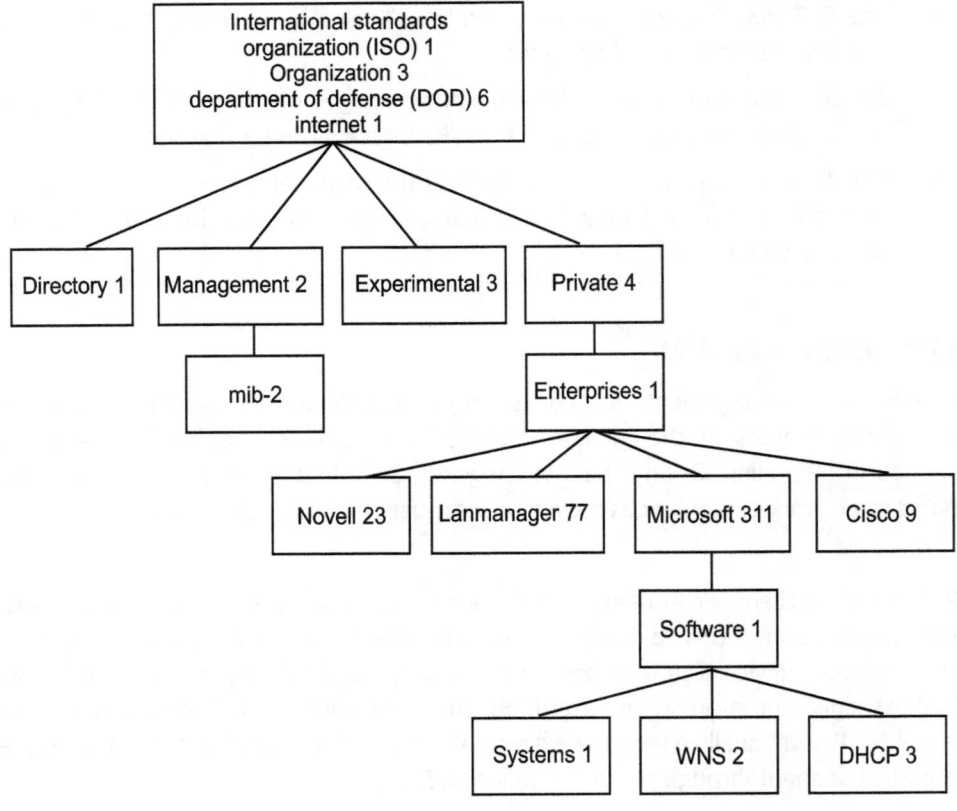

Fig. 6.32: OIDs structure

SNMP uses the OID to identify objects on each network element (i.e. router/computer) that can be managed using SNMP. For example, in order to get information about the free disk space on a Windows NT Server, the Network Management Station makes a request to the network element using the fully qualified OID that represents the variable containing the number representing the free disk space. In Microsoft's world, that would be .1.3.6.1.4.1.311.1.1.3.1.1.5.1.4.0. or something very similar, depending how the MIB for that object was created (i.e. perfm.bat). A Cisco 4500 router's CPU usage is accessed by targeting the OID .1.3.6.1.4.1.9.2.1.56.0. *Note how bolded text matches the tree above!*

Strengths and Shortcomings of SNMP:

SNMP has several strengths. Its biggest strength is arguably its widespread popularity. SNMP agents are available for network devices ranging from computers, to bridges, to modems, to printers. The fact that SNMP exists with such support gives considerable credence to its reason for existence; SNMP has become interoperable.

Additionally, SNMP is a flexible and extensible management protocol. Because SNMP agents can be extended to cover device specific data, and because a clear mechanism exists for upgrading network management client programs to interface with special agent capabilities (through the use of ASN.1 files), SNMP can take on numerous jobs specific to device classes such as printers, routers, and bridges, thereby providing a standard mechanism of network control and monitoring.

Several weaknesses of SNMP can be identified. Despite its name, (i.e. "Simple" Network Management Protocol), SNMP is a highly complicated protocol to implement. By the admission of its designers, a more apt name might be "Moderate Network Management Protocol", although even this seems generous in light of SNMP's highly complicated encoding rules.

Also, SNMP is not a particularly efficient protocol. Bandwidth is wasted with needless information, such as the SNMP version (transmitted in every SNMP message) and multiple length and data descriptors scattered throughout each message. The way that SNMP variables are identified (as byte strings, where each byte corresponds to a particular node in the MIB database) leads to needlessly large data handles that consume substantial parts of each SNMP message.

The above complaints, while fair, cannot reasonably be used to detract from the aforementioned strengths of SNMP. While complicated encoding rules frustrate programmers who must deal with them, it is easily argued that end users of the protocol are not concerned with the complexity of the algorithms that decode their data. As for complaints about SNMP efficiency, it has been shown to work well enough, given the nature of network administration activities.

The Greatest Criticism of SNMP:

One criticism of SNMP cannot be dismissed so easily: SNMP has generally lacked focus on why it is useful. Neither the governing RFC's nor other explanatory references describe why SNMP is better than more traditional network management tools such as "ping", "rsh", and "netstat". Consider: the design of SNMP agents is difficult. Equally difficult is the administration of these many agents and their managers, which typically entail individual configuration and possible maintenance. Why is SNMP all that much better than, say, telnet protocol? Does the elaborateness of SNMP justify its usefulness? Or can simple telnet driver programs, which periodically log into network devices to gather statistics and apply control, achieve the same end?

In part, this criticism has been aggravated by SNMP management program vendors, who create systems where SNMP is merely an alternative to remote shells rather than a new way of analyzing and managing networks. *Many SNMP vendors seem to see network management activities in terms of GUI's with point and click controls instead of automated systems for configuring devices, gathering data, and conduct corrective procedures on large networks.*

The Argument for SNMP:

Faced with the above criticism of SNMP, one tendency is to admit that there are alternatives to SNMP, but these alternatives are supplanted by the general popularity and interoperability of SNMP. This tendency should be rejected in favor of a much better argument for SNMP; a point made by the remainder of this paper is that there ARE NO current alternatives to SNMP, at least for certain types of network administrative functions.

6.7.7 SNMP - Simple Network Management Protocol in Detail

Introduction

1. Since it was developed in 1988, the Simple Network Management Protocol has become the de facto standard for internetwork management.
2. Because it is a simple solution, requiring little code to implement, vendors can easily build SNMP agents to their products.
3. SNMP is extensible, allowing vendors to easily add network management functions to their existing products. SNMP also separates the management architecture from the architecture of the hardware devices, which broadens the base of multivendor support.
4. Perhaps most important, unlike other so-called standards, SNMP is not a mere paper specification, but an implementation that is widely available today.

This Section will cover the following issues:
- Network Management Architectures
- Structure of Management Information
- Management Information Base
- SNMP Protocol
- Underlying Communications Protocols

6.7.7.1 Network Management Architectures

1. Network management system contains two primary elements: a manager and agents.
2. The Manager is the console through which the network administrator performs network management functions.
3. Agents are the entities that interface to the actual device being managed. Bridges, Hubs, Routers or network servers are examples of managed devices that contain managed objects.
4. These managed objects might be hardware, configuration parameters, performance statistics, and so on, that directly relate to the current operation of the device in question.

5. These objects are arranged in what is known as a virtual information database, called a management information base, also called MIB. SNMP allows managers and agents to communicate for the purpose of accessing these objects.

The model of network management architecture looks like this:

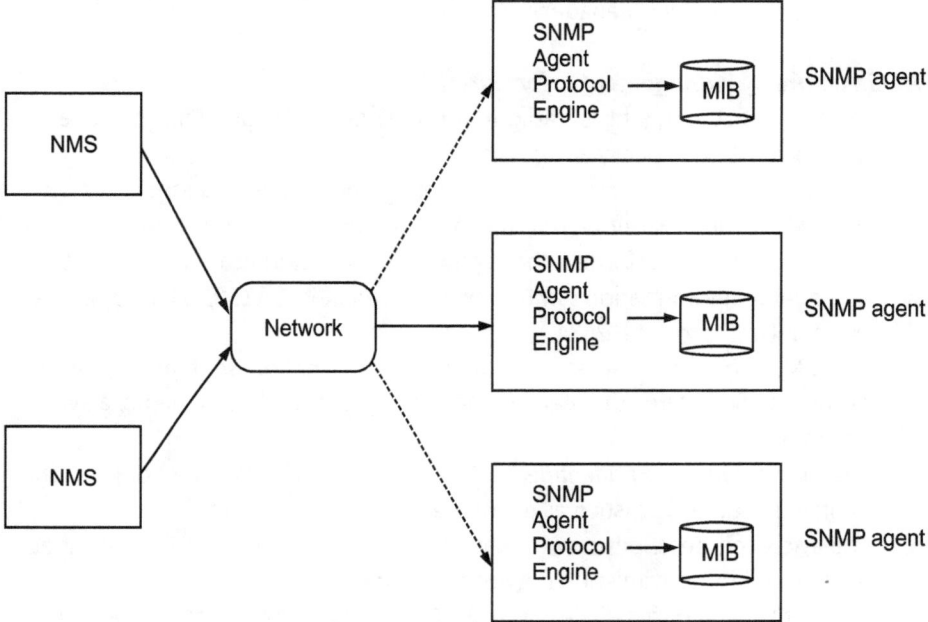

Fig. 6.33: Model of network management architecture

A typical agent usually:
- Implements full SNMP protocol.
- Stores and retrieves management data as defined by the Management Information Base.
- Can asynchronously signal an event to the manager.
- Can be a proxy for some non-SNMP manageable network node.

A typical manager usually:
- Implemented as a Network Management Station (the NMS).
- Implements full SNMP Protocol.
- **Able to**
    - Query agents.
    - Get responses from agents.
    - Set variables in agents.
    - Acknowledge asynchronous events from agents.

Some prominent vendors offer network management platforms, which implement the role of the manager:
- Dec PolyCenter Network Manager
- Hewlett-Packard OpenView
- IBM AIX NetView/6000
- SunConnect SunNet Manager

6.7.7.2 Structure of Management Information
1. In the Manager/Agent paradigm for network management, managed network objects must be logically accessible.
2. Logical accessibility means that management information must be stored somewhere, and therefore, that the information must be retrievable and modifiable.
3. SNMP actually performs the retrieval and modification. The Structure of Management Information (SMI), which is given in RFC 1155, is based on the OSI SMI given in Draft proposal 2684.
4. The SMI organizes, names, and describes information so that logical access can occur. The SMI states that each managed object must have a name, a syntax and an encoding.
5. The name, an *object identifier* (OID), uniquely identifies the object. The syntax defines the data type, such as an integer or a string of octets.
6. The encoding describes how the information associated with the managed objects is serialized for transmission between machines.
7. The syntax used for SNMP is the Abstract Syntax Notation One, ASN.1. The encoding used for SNMP is the Basic Encoding Rules, BER. The names used are object identifiers. Later we will see how the MIB uses these names.
8. ASN.1 is used to specify many RFCs (and not just the SMI), for example the Internet standard MIB and SNMP. ASN.1 is used widely in OSI for specification purposes. ASN.1 used for defining SMI and MIBs is a subset of the ASN language given by OSI. ASN.1 does specify in itself
    - Object instances (protocol specific).
    - Message transmission format (BER).
9. Each object whether it is a device or characteristics of a device, must have a name by which it can be uniquely identified.
10. That name is the *object identifier*. It is written as a sequence of integers, separated by periods. For example, the sequence 1.3.6.1.2.1.1.1.0 specifies the system description within the system group, of the management subtree.

6.7.7.3 Management Information Base
1. Management information bases (MIBs) are a collection of definitions, which define the properties of the managed object within the device to be managed.
2. Every managed device keeps a database of values for each of the definitions written in the MIB.

3. It is not the actual database itself - it is implementation dependant. Definition of the MIB conforms to the SMI given in RFC 1155.
4. Latest Internet MIB is given in RFC 1213 sometimes called the MIB-II. Click here to see MIB architecture. You can think of a MIB as an information warehouse.

Criteria and Philosophy for standardized MIB:
- Objects have to be uniquely named.
- Objects have to be essential.
- Abstract structure of the MIB needed to be universal.
- For the standard MIB, maintain only a small number of objects.
- Allow for private extensions.
- Object must be general and not too device dependant.
- Objects can not be easily derivable from their objects.
- If agent is to be SNMP manageable then it is mandatory to implement the Internet MIB (currently given as MIB-II in RFC 1157).

Naming an Object:
- Universal unambiguous identification of arbitrary objects.
- Can be achieved by using an hierarchical tree.
- Based on the Object Identification Scheme defined by OSI.

MIB
The Registered Tree

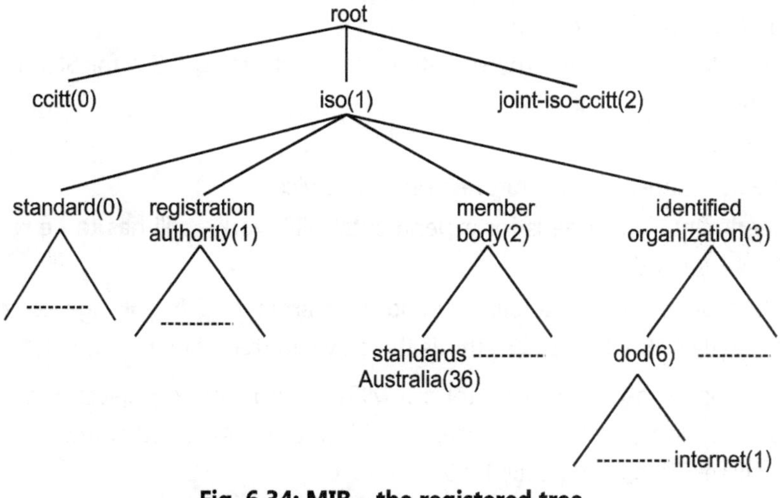

Fig. 6.34: MIB – the registered tree

Object Identifiers:
- Object name is given by its name in the tree.
- All child nodes are given unique integer values within that new sub-tree.
- Children can be parents of further child sub-tree (i.e they have subordinates) where the numbering scheme is recursively applied.

- The Object Identifier (or name) of an object is the sequence of non-negative Integer values traversing the tree to the node required.
- Allocation of an integer value for a node in the tree is an act of registration by whoever has delegated authority for that sub tree.
- This process can go to an arbitrary depth.
- If a node has children then it is an aggregate node.
- Children of the same parent cannot have the same integer value.

Object and Object Identifiers:
- Object is named or identified by the sequence of integers in traversing the tree to the object type required.
- This does not identify an instance of the object.
- The Object Identifier (OID) is shown in a few ways with a.b.c.d.e being the preferred.
- OIDs can name many types of objects:
  Standard documents (e.g. FTAM)
  people (e.g. Tax file numbers in Sweden are OIDs)
  Organizations (e.g. RAD or LANNET)
  Computing network nodes (e.g. workstations)
  Dumb devices (e.g. toasters)
  ... in fact anything at all ...
- For SNMP it is the Internet sub-tree for constructing OIDs for SNMP manageable agents.

The Internet Sub-tree
- Directory sub-tree if for future directory services.
- Experimental sub-tree is for experimental MIB work - still has to be registered with the authority (IESG).
- Mib sub-tree is the actual mandatory Internet MIB for all agents to implement (currently MIB-II RFC 1156 - this is the only sub tree of management).
- Enterprise sub-tree (of private) are MIBs of proprietary objects and are of course not mandatory (sub-tree registered with Internet Assigned Numbers Authority) for example: Cisco router OID: 1.3.6.1.4.1.9.1.1.
- SNMP management nearly always interest in MIB and specific enterprises MIBs.

MIB-II Standard Internet MIB:
- Definition follows structure given in SMI.
- MIB-II (RFC 1213) is current standard definition of the virtual file store for SNMP manageable objects.

- Has 10 basic groups
  - system
  - interfaces
  - at
  - ip
  - icmp
  - tcp
  - udp
  - egp
  - transmission
  - snmp
- If agent implements any group then it has to implement all of the managed objects within that group.
- An agent does not have to implement all groups.
- Note: MIB-i and MIB-II have same OID (position in the internet sub-tree).

MIB-II

The MIB Sub-tree

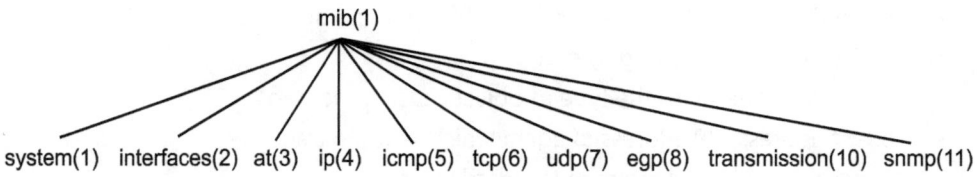

system(1) interfaces(2) at(3) ip(4) icmp(5) tcp(6) udp(7) egp(8) transmission(10) snmp(11)

Fig. 6.35: The MIB Sub-tree

6.7.7.4 SNMP Protocol

1. SNMP is based on the manager/agent model. SNMP is referred to as "simple" because the agent requires minimal software.
2. Most of the processing power and the data storage resides on the management system, while a complementary subset of those functions resides in the managed system.
3. To achieve its goal of being simple, SNMP includes a limited set of management commands and responses.
4. The management system issues Get, GetNext and Set messages to retrieve single or multiple object variables or to establish the value of a single variable.
5. The managed agent sends a Response message to complete the Get, GetNext or Set.

6. The managed agent sends an event notification, called a *trap* to the management system to identify the occurrence of conditions such as threshold that exceeds a predetermined value. In short, there are only five primitive operations:
- get (retrieve operation).
- get next (traversal operation).
- get response (indicative operation).
- set (alter operation).
- trap (asynchronous trap operation).

SNMP Message Construct:

Each SNMP message has the format:
- Version Number.
- Community Name - kind of a password.
- One or more SNMP PDUs - assuming trivial authentication.

Each SNMP PDU except trap has the following format:
- request id - request sequence number.
- error status - zero if no error otherwise one of a small set.
- error index - if non zero indicates which of the OIDs in the PDU caused the error2.
- list of OIDs and values - values are null for get and get next.

Trap PDUs have the following format:
- enterprise - identifies the type of object causing the trap.
- agent address - IP address of agent which sent the trap.
- generic trap id - the common standard traps.
- specific trap id - proprietary or enterprise trap.
- time stamp - when trap occurred in time ticks.
- list of OIDs and values - OIDs that may be relevant to send to the NMS.

Outline of the SNMP Protocol:
- Each SNMP managed object belongs to a community.
- NMS station may belong to multiple communities.
- A community is defined by a community name which is an OctetString with 0 to 255 octets in length.

  Each SNMP message consists of three components.
  - version number.
  - community name.
  - data - a sequence of PDUs associated with the request.

Security levels with basic SNMP:
Authentication:
- trivial authentication based on plain text community name exchanged in SNMP messages.
- authentication is based on the assumption that the message is not tampered with or interrogated.

Authorization:
- Once community name is validated then agent or manager checks to see if sending address is permitted or has the rights for the requested operation.
- "View" or "Cut" of the objects together with permitted access rights is then derived for that pair (community name, sending address).

Summary
- Not very secure.
- SNMP version 2 is addressing this.
- Extended security is possible with current protocol (example: DES and MD5).
- Does not reduce its power for monitoring

What does SNMP access:
- SNMP access particular instances of an object.
- All instances of an object in the MIB reside at the leaf nodes of the MIB tree.
- SNMP Protocol access objects by forming an Object identifier of form

  x.y, where x is the "true" OID for the object in the MIB, and y is a suffix specified by the protocol that uniquely identifies a particular instance (e.g. when accessing a table).
- For primitive single instance leaf objects, use y = 0, for example: sysDescr (OID: 1.3.6.1.2.1.1.1) would be referenced in the SNMP protocol by 1.3.6.1.2.1.1.1.0 (i.e. sysDescr.0).
- For single instance of columnar leaf objects (i.e one instance from a table type of object), use y = I1.I2.I3.... (Ii are table indexes).

6.7.7.5 Underlying Communication Protocols
1. SNMP assumes that the communication path is a connectionless communication subnetwork.
2. In other words, no prearranged communication path is established prior to the transmission of data.

3. As a result, SNMP makes no guarantees about the reliable delivery of the data. Although in practice most messages get through, and those that do not can be retransmitted.
4. The primary protocols that SNMP implement are the *User Datagram Protocol* (UDP) and the *Internet Protocol* (IP). SNMP also requires Data Link Layer protocols such as Ethernet or TokenRing to implement the communication channel from the management to the managed agent.
5. SNMP's simplicity and connectionless communication also produce a degree of robustness. Neither the manager nor the agent relies on the other for its operation.
6. Thus, a manager may continue to function even if a remote agent fails.
7. When the agent resumes functioning, it can send a trap to the manager, notifying it of its change in operational status.
8. The connectionless nature of SNMP leaves the recovery and error detection up to the NMS (Network Management Station) and even up to the agent.
9. However keep in mind that SNMP is actually transport independent (although original design was connectionless transport function, which corresponds to the UDP protocol) and can be implemented on other transports as well:
   - TCP (Connected approach)
   - Direct mapping onto Ethernet MAC level
   - Encapsulation onto X25 protocol
   - Encapsulation onto ATM Cell
   - and so on.....

Fig. 6.36 describes the Transport Mechanism used in SNMP over UDP:

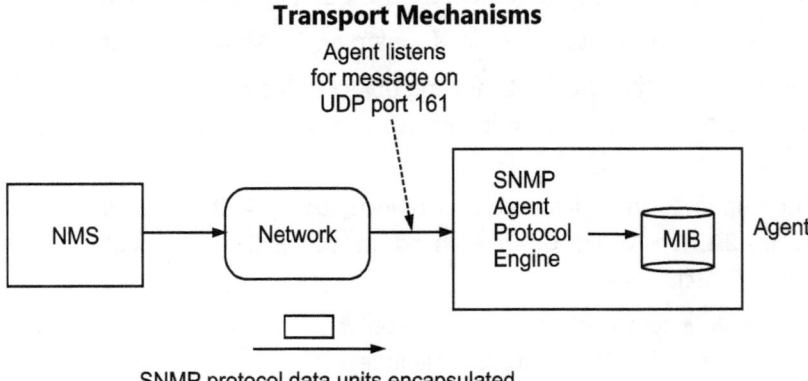

Fig. 6.36: Transport Mechanisms

UDP Transport:
- Agent listen on UDP port 161.
- Responses are sent back to the originating NMS port from a dynamic port, although many agents use port 161 also for this target.

- Maximum SNMP message size is limited by maximum UDP message size (i.e. 65507 octets).
- All SNMP implementations have to receive packets at least 484 octets in length.
- Some SNMP implementation will incorrectly or not handle packets exceeding 484 octets.
- Asynchronous Traps are received on port 162 of the NMS.
- UDP more suitable than TCP when dynamic route changes occur often (e.g. when there are problems in the network).
- UDP packets minimize the demands placed on the network (no resource tied up as with connection mode).
- Agent and NMS are responsible for determining error recovery.

The following diagram shows the architecture of UDP transport.

UDP Transport

Normal Send – Response Exchange

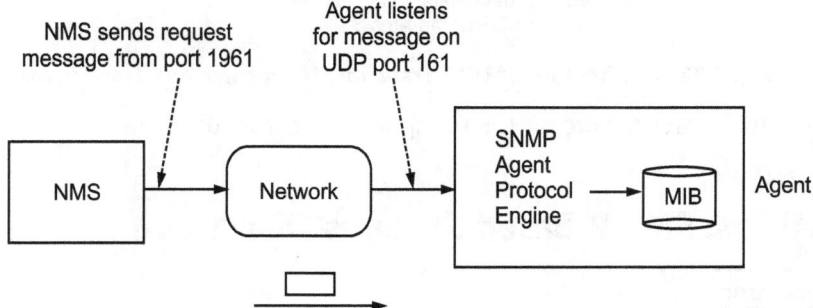

(a)

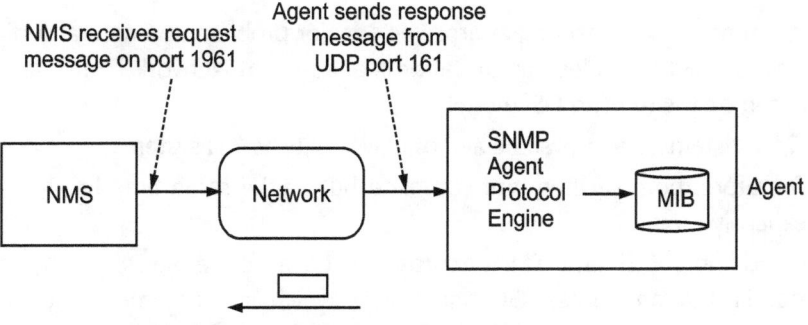

(b)

Fig. 6.37

Fig. 6.37 (a) and (b) show the architecture of UDP transport (Normal Send-response exchange).

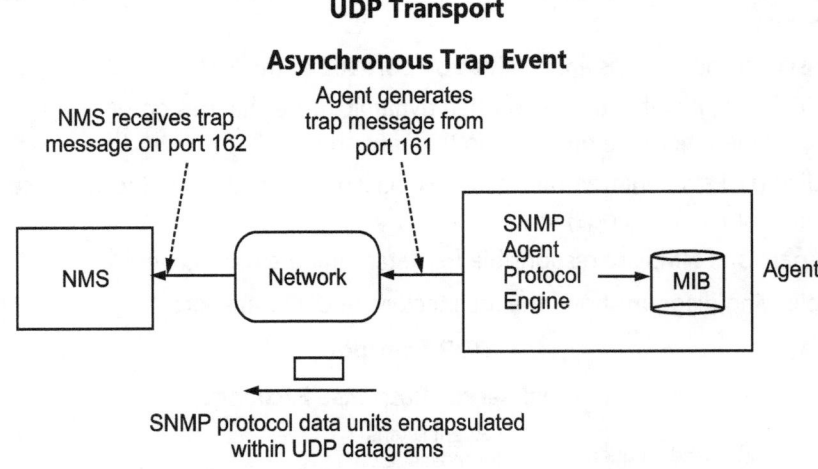

Fig. 6.38: Architecture of UDP Transport (Asynchronous Trap Event)

Fig. 6.38 shows the architecture of UDP transport (Asynchronous trap event).

6.8 TMN vs. SNMP Based Systems Discussion

1. Introduction

1. The OSI (Open System Interconnection) model has been a successful framework for protocol architecture in some environments. Academically oriented systems or high-end communication networks had taken advantage of its wide goals and generous features.
2. When network management arose as a major problem, the natural "official" answer was to build the Telecommunication Management Network (TMN), an architecture based on the existing OSI model.
3. TMN systems have the same aim of universality as OSI systems.
4. Therefore, both of them are complete but at the same time heavy, complex and expensive solutions.
5. In addition, OSI and TMN approaches have to be approved by international standardization bodies (ISO and ITU-T), which implies time-consuming efforts a drawback in today's rapidly changing communications world.
6. On the other hand, to cope with the OSI drawbacks, the TCP-IP and related protocols have become a *de facto* standard for many applications.

7. Most computer networks, both in academic or industrial environments are based on TCP-IP. Internet is also a TCP-IP based network.

8. This model uses quite simple but useful protocols to communicate computers.

9. It does not provide full support for every possible feature but its lack of functionality is far overcome its availability and almost universal extent.

10. According to this philosophy, in the Internet-like networks a much easier and informal approach has been adopted. Its kernel is the SNMP (Simple Network Management Protocol), which is widely supported and easy management of multivendor networks.

This section will address and compare the main characteristics of TMN and SNMP based systems. We will try to discuss the reasons for choosing either of the two systems, considering not just technical performance but also taking into account economic and commercial considerations.

2. Network Management Models

1. The problem of managing communication networks emerges in a double realm: managing computer networks and managing telecommunication networks.

2. In the field of computer networks, a standardized solution has been developed by ISO (international Organization for Standardization) in the context of the OSI model.

3. According to this solution, the network management task is carried out mainly by the application layer entities and is highly coupled to the OSI model structures.

4. That is, the ISO network management model is very ambitious, having many functionalities, but on the other hand, it can turn out to be excessively heavy and complex.

5. The complexity of the ISO network management model, its difficulty to follow technological progress and the lack of commercial products, make it necessary to look for an alternative for managing computer networks: the Internet model.

6. In this model the management tasks are carried out by means of very simple structures and protocols, which allows for a fast and easy implementation of the appropriate management systems.

7. This solution, considering its limited design aims, is not able to solve the problem of managing heterogeneous networks with the same powerful capabilities shown by the ISO network management model.

8. However, for many real-life computer networks, its functionality is considered satisfactory.

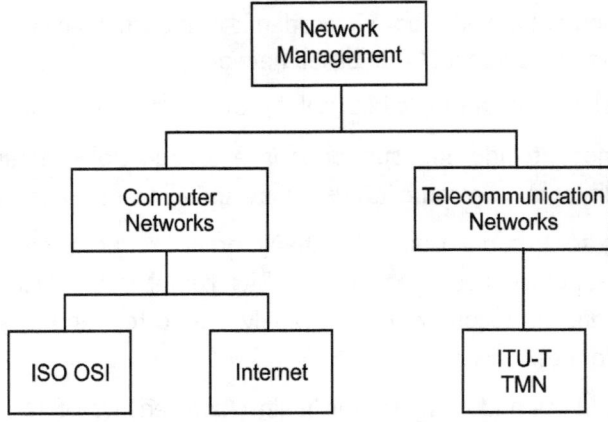

Fig. 6.39: Network Management Classification

Finally, in the much more specific area of telecommunication networks, the integrated network management problem emerges as well. To cope with this situation ITU-T approves the TMN model benefiting from most of the concepts and standards defined by the ISO model. This results in a very powerful model, although it has the same heaviness and slowness of the ISO model. In the next paragraphs, each model will be described.

3. OSI Model

1. The ISO network management model is based on three basic elements: the structure of management information, the protocols and the functions.

2. The structure of management information is based on an object-oriented model where every sort of device is modeled by means of an object class including its associated attributes, notifications and actions.

3. The objects are organized according to a tree of hierarchical dependency while the object classes are arranged following an inheritance tree.

4. The set of managed objects makes up the MIB (Management Information Base).

5. A standard language, called GDMO (Guidelines for the Definition of Managed Objects) has also been defined, allowing a non-ambiguous definition of every object class characteristics.

6. The resulting information model has a great describing capacity and easily permits to deal with every particular situation which can arise when managing actual networks.

7. To solve the problem of communicating with the network elements, the ISO model depicts a layered structure (OSI model) where the management functions can be found in every layer, but mainly in the application layer.

8. In that layer, a set of management service modules (SMASE: Systems Management Application Service Elements) are grouped, and the communication tasks associated to all management functions are carried out.

9. Each one of these modules is supported by the services provided by application layer conventional protocols, such as FTAM, ACSE and ROSE and, mainly, by CMIP (Common Management Information Protocol), the specific ISO network management protocol.

10. The CMIP can support the complex MIB information structures defined by ISO, and allows for a network management in a distributed platform environment.

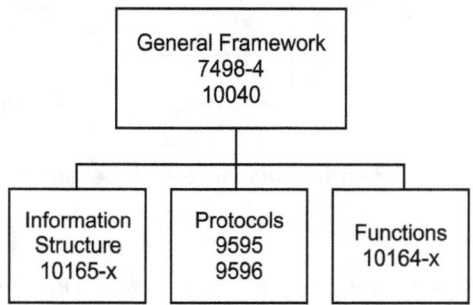

Fig. 6.40: General Framework Consideration

11. The last basic element of the ISO network management model are the functions. There are many management functions which can be classified into five functional areas: configuration management, fault management, performance management, accounting management, and security management.

12. The functions in the configuration area deal with the problem of evaluating the current state of the network, and of bringing it to a proper state where the system management requirements can be fulfilled.

13. The fault functions face the problem of processing the network devices alarms, making a diagnosis of their probable cause, locating and, eventually, repairing the faults.

14. The performance functions measure the efficiency of the network devices and the quality of service provided to the users, suggesting procedures to improve those performances.

15. In the accounting area, we can find those functions related to the administrative aspects of the network, such as the devices and services usage metering, the cost allocation and the invoicing.

16. Finally, the functions in the area of security deal with the problems related to establishing and maintaining a network security policy.

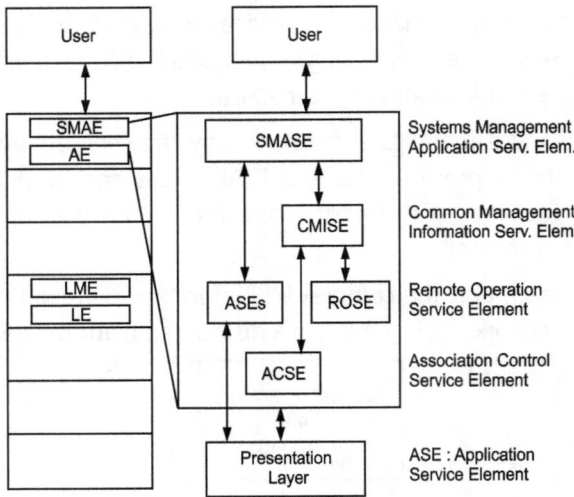

Fig. 6.41: ISO Network Management Model are the Functions

4. TMN Model

1. The ITU-T management model, formally called TMN (Telecommunication Management Network), is highly based on the OSI model which leads to a structure relying on three basic elements (structure of management information, protocols and functions).
2. Additionally, the TMN model takes advantage of and adopts many ISO management standards.
3. Using this ISO kernel, the TMN model expands in two directions: on the one hand it widens the concepts and functions in order to fit the telecommunication networks features: and, on the other side, it establishes a set of specific standards for each particular technology.
4. So, for instance, there are specific standards to manage technologies such as SDH, ISDN, ATM etc.

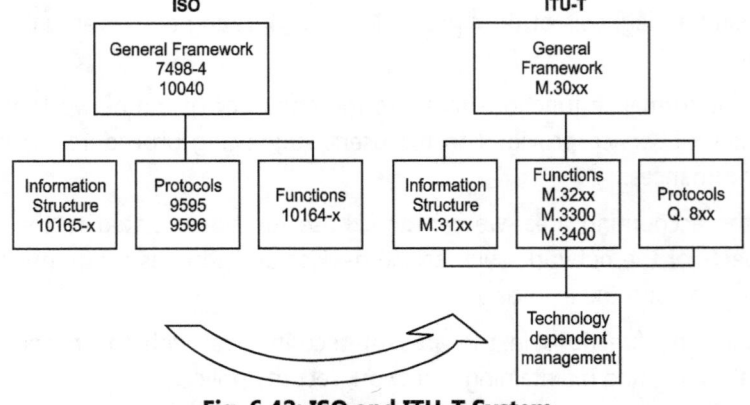

Fig. 6.42: ISO and ITU-T System

5. The TMN management information follows the patterns set in the ISO model but they are expanded to offer a catalogue of object classes adapted to the specific modelling needs found in the telecommunication network elements.
6. Particularly relevant in this structure of management information are those object classes related to the topological specification of the network.
7. On the other hand, the standardized protocols, specified as a part of the Q.3 interface, use the layered ISO structure where the CMIP plays the main role as the management protocol.
8. The functions in the TMN model follow, in some way, the organization in five basic functional areas defined in the ISO model.

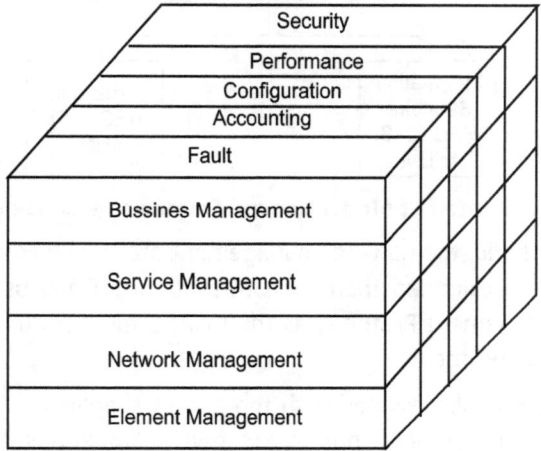

Fig. 6.43

9. But, on the other hand, each one of these functions is structured in four layers: element management, network management, service management and business management. So, for instance, the configuration functions of a PABX (Private Automatic Branch Exchange) can be considered from four different levels:
   (a) Determining states and parameters as a single device (element management);
   (b) Considered as part of a network which has to be configured as a whole (network management);
   (c) As a device which is able to provide different kinds of services to the users (service management) and
   (d) As an element of business where economic, working and technical aspects (business management) have to be considered.

5. Internet Model

1. The Internet Model for managing communication networks is based on a very simple set of protocols and structures of information.
2. The structure of information follows the object oriented model but introducing many simplifications with regard to the TMN model.

3. This situation makes the modelling of complex devices, networks and services more difficult but, on the other hand, it makes the management applications considerably easier.

4. While an Internet MIB can always be described according to the TMN model, the opposite is not true. Many features modelling objects in TMN have no translation to the Internet management model.

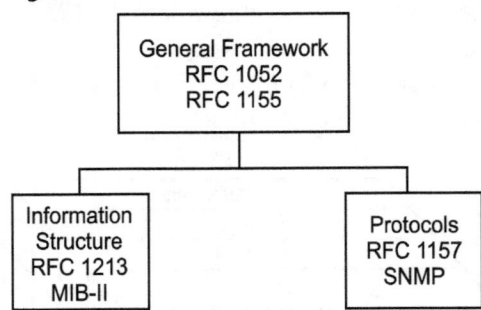

Fig. 6.44: Internet Model General Frameworks Consideration

5. On the other hand, the network management protocol follows the layered structure of Internet (more limited than the OSI model of TMN) using the SNMP (Simple Network Management Protocol) as the management protocol, usually on top of a stack of TCP/IP protocols.

6. The SNMP protocol, designed with the aim of simplicity, is able to manage many features of many devices, but it has severe limitations for managing complex objects or a structure of objects.

7. The limitations of the Internet model are, at the same time, an advantage and a drawback.

8. On the one hand it is clear that it limits the capabilities of managing the network.

9. But, on the other hand, its simple design permits an easy development of agents and managers, functions and management platforms.

10. This situation has led to a fast commercial expansion.

11. There are many devices supporting the SNMP management protocol, while only the high-end systems support the CMIP standard.

12. Additionally, many vendors provide management platforms based on SNMP, with similar functions and performances and at very attractive prices.

13. The greater simplicity of the Internet model, its greater market share, and the greater number of competitors make a situation of lower prices possible.

14. On the other hand, TMN management platforms support many functionalities and can describe and manage almost every particular aspect of a telecommunications network.

15. However, the number of communication devices which are able to interface in a Q.3 way is even lower. For this reason, the prices of TMN management systems are remarkably higher than their SNMP equipments, where a 10 to 1 price ratio, or higher, is not uncommon.

6. Conclusions

1. In this section three different models for network management and its main features have been shown.
2. From our point of view, in small networks with limited management functions, SNMP-based management systems are the best solution considering the balance between price and performance.
3. Nevertheless, in middle and large size networks, and when these networks require a wide range of management functions, using SNMP-based systems can be a hindrance for the present and a risk for the future.
4. In ever particular case we must consider the convenience of relying on a TMN-based management system, which can guarantee a full functionality and a proper system scalability.

6.9 Summary of Open Approaches for Management

Thus following are the different common approaches are used for system management:

1. **Manager-Agent Model**
   - ISO/ITU-T OSI Management (CMIP)
   - IETF Internet Management (SNMP)
   - X/Open XMP/XOM API
2. **Object-Oriented Management Model**
   - OMG's CORBA
3. **Specific Management Domain**
   - ITU-T TMN
   - DMTF's DMI
   - OSF's DME

Where;

ISO - International Organization for Standardization

ITU - International Telecommunication Union

OSI - Open System Interconnection Reference Model

CMIP - Common Management Information Protocol (CMIP)

IETF - Internet Engineering Task Force

XMP: X/Open Management Protocol;

XOM: X/Open OSI-Abstract Data Manipulation;

API: Applications Programming Interface

OMG's CORBA - Object Management Group's Common Object Request Broker Architecture-Middleware Specification for Distributed Real-time and Embedded Systems First two adopted profiles;

ITU-T TMN - International Telecommunication Union Telecommunications Management Network;

DMTF's DMI - Distributed Management Task Force and Desktop Management Interface;

OSF's DME - Open Software Foundation's Distributed Computing Environment and Distributed Management Environment.

6.10 CMIP vs. SNMP

CMIP	SNMP
GDMO	Internet SMI
Object-Oriented	Object-Based
7 Service Primitives	5 Messages
Connection-oriented	Connectionless
Event-Oriented	Polling
Scoping/Filtering	GetNext
Global Naming (X.500)	Local Naming (OID)
Security Mechanism	Community Name
OSI Seven Layers	Internet TCP/IP

6.11 Network Operation and Maintenance

1. **Network management** refers to the activities, methods, procedures, and tools that pertain to the operation, administration, maintenance, and provisioning of networked systems.
    - **Operation** deals with keeping the network (and the services that the network provides) up and running smoothly. It includes monitoring the network to spot problems as soon as possible, ideally before users are affected.
    - **Administration** deals with keeping track of resources in the network and how they are assigned. It includes all the "housekeeping" that is necessary to keep the network under control.

- **Maintenance** is concerned with performing repairs and upgrades—for example, when equipment must be replaced, when a router needs a patch for an operating system image, when a new switch is added to a network. Maintenance also involves corrective and preventive measures to make the managed network run "better", such as adjusting device configuration parameters.
- **Provisioning** is concerned with configuring resources in the network to support a given service. For example, this might include setting up the network so that a new customer can receive voice service.

2. A common way of characterizing network management functions is FCAPS—Fault, Configuration, Accounting, Performance and Security.
3. Functions that are performed as part of network management accordingly include controlling, planning, allocating, deploying, co-ordinating, and monitoring the resources of a network, network planning, frequency allocation, predetermined traffic routing to support load balancing, cryptographic key distribution authorization, configuration management, fault management, security management, performance management, bandwidth management, Route analytics and accounting management.
4. Data for network management is collected through several mechanisms, including agents installed on infrastructure, synthetic monitoring that simulates transactions, logs of activity, sniffers and real user monitoring. In the past network management mainly consisted of monitoring whether devices were up or down; today performance management has become a crucial part of the IT team's role which brings about a host of challenges—especially for global organizations.

6.11.1 Technologies and Solutions

1. A large number of access methods exist to support network and network device management. Access methods include the SNMP, command-line interface (CLIs), custom XML, CMIP, Windows Management Instrumentation (WMI), Transaction Language 1, CORBA, NETCONF, and the Java Management Extensions (JMX).
2. Schemas include the WBEM **(Web-Based Enterprise Management)**, the Common Information Model, and MTOSI **(Multi-Technology Operations System Interface)** amongst others.
3. Medical Service Providers provide a niche marketing utility for managed service providers; as HIPAA legislation consistently increases demands for knowledgeable providers.
4. Medical Service Providers are liable for the protection of their clients confidential information, including in an electronic realm. This liability creates a significant need for managed service providers who can provide secure infrastructure for transportation of medical data.

6.12 SNMP Traps and Network Management

1. SNMP is a computer network protocol and stands for "Simple Network Management Protocol". Of course, most network managers complain that it is anything but "simple". This protocol is a method of communication that systems, routers, switches and other various network equipment running SNMP agents, use to transfer and broadcast critical information about their status, happenings on the network, and whatever else may be concerning them. Typically, these agents are listening on a couple different UDP ports, namely 161 for standard SNMP queries, and 162, for SNMP Traps. When a system sends an SNMP message in the form of a trap, it doesn't matter which port it sends it out on, but because the remote listener is usually always listening on port 162, it must always send to 162. This is a reserved port for SNMP Traps in the list of assigned ports on the IANA website.

2. SNMP Traps are a crucial part of an entire network management solution. The traps utilize a push method of communication, i.e. they send unsolicited information to a network manager about themselves, in the form of an SNMP message called a Trap, Notification, or Inform. This information is then used by the manager to glean what possible happenings in the network can affect the business.

3. Fault management primarily consists of these traps, and because of that, it is a reactive type of technology. On the other hand, Performance management (a practice that does not capture traps), consists of polling or "proactive" monitoring, in which case a polling process contacts a list of agents in the manager's configuration, talks to them on port 161, and queries these agents for information related to statistics that the manager is interested in. Both of these have their advantages and disadvantages, but what we want to talk about more here is the SNMP protocol and how it relates to these trap messages.

4. The Trap message has several different components. Here we will discuss only the SNMP version 1 trap. Please note that there are other versions, including version 2 and version 3, but that is beyond the scope of this article. The easiest way to see these components is to use a protocol analyzer (also known as a sniffer), and capture these SNMP messages on the wire. Once captured, the observer can see that the protocol data unit (PDU) is broken up into several parts, including the enterprise, agent address, generic and specific trap values, a time-stamp, and a list of variable bindings.

5. The Trap Enterprise field gives information in the format of an Object Identifier (OID), about the vendor of the equipment or agent that the trap originated from. This allows a network manager an easy way of looking up the information and cross-referencing with other events and/or faults. The agent address contains information about the originator (the sender) of the trap. This address, in the form

of an Internet Protocol (IP) address, is not always from the sender, especially in the case that the trap was forwarded through an intermediary system. The Generic and Specific Type fields give the fault manager software an exact idea of the type of trap that is being sent. The timestamp specifies the exact time that this message was created and sent out on the wire. And finally, the variable-bindings include additional, detailed information that is specific to this event and that the manager can use to determine more about the event.

6. So, to sum up, the SNMP Trap PDU is not so simple, but luckily for us we have smart network monitoring programs and algorithms that know how to identify, decipher and act quickly on this information.
7. SNMP traps enable an agent to notify the management station of significant events by way of an unsolicited SNMP message.
8. In this diagram, the setup on the left shows a network management system that polls information and gets a response. The setup on the right shows an agent that sends an unsolicited or asynchronous trap to the network management system (NMS).

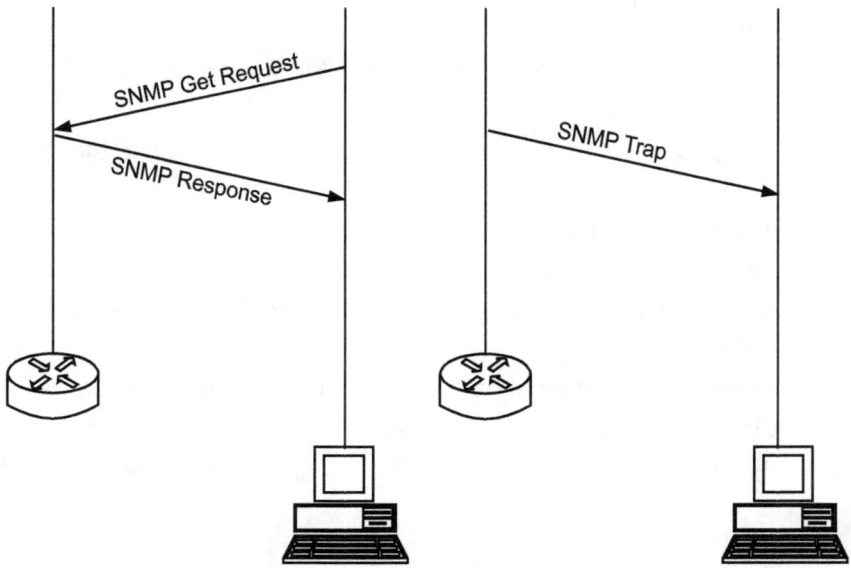

Fig. 6.45: Typical communication in network management system (NMS)

9. SNMP provides the ability to send traps, or notifications, to advise an administrator when one or more conditions have been met. Traps are network packets that contain data relating to a component of the system sending the trap. The data may be statistical in nature or even status related.
10. SNMP traps are alerts generated by agents on a managed device. These traps generate 5 types of data:
    - Coldstart or Warmstart: The agent reinitialized its configuration tables.

- Linkup or Linkdown: A network interface card (NIC) on the agent either fails or reinitializes.
- Authentication fails: This happens when an SNMP agent gets a request from an unrecognized community name.
- egpNeighborloss: Agent cannot communicate with its EGP (Exterior Gateway Protocol) peer.
- Enterprise specific: Vendor specific error conditions and error codes.

6.12.1 How Traps are generated

1. Traps are generated when a condition has been met on the SNMP agent. These conditions are defined in the Management Information Base (MIB) provided by the vendor.
2. The administrator then defines thresholds, or limits to the conditions, that are to generate a trap. Conditions range from preset thresholds to a restart.
3. After the condition has been met the SNMP agent then forms an SNMP packet that specifies the following:
   - SNMP Version: v1 or v2
   - Community: Community name of the SNMP agent (defined on the agent)
   - PDU TYPE: SNMPvX Trap (4)
   - Enterprise: Corporation or organization that originated the trap, such as .1.3.6.1.4.1.x.
   - Agent Address: IP address of the SNMP agent
   - Generic Trap Type: Cold Start, Link Up, Enterprise etc.
   - Specific Trap Type: When Generic is set to Enterprise a specific trap ID's identified.
   - Timestamp: The value of object sysUpTime when the event occurred.
   - Object x Value x: OID of the trap and the current value.
4. The above packet is sent to the SNMP trap host, or manager, through UDP port 162.

Packet Format:

| Version | Community | TRAP PDU | |

Trap PDU Format:

| PDU Type | Enterprise | Agent IP | GEN Trap | Spec Trap | Time Stame |

| OBJ 1 Val 1 | ...... | –Variable Bindings– |

Note: The Trap PDU format above is all one packet and has been wrapped for readability.

Fig. 6.46: Typical Packet and Trap PDU Format

6.12.2 Where is all of this information stored?

1. All of the values that SNMP reports are dynamic and are not stored in any file or registry key.
2. However, the information needed to get the specified values is stored in the Management Information Base (MIB).
3. This information ranges from Object IDs (OIDs) to Protocol Data Units (PDUs).
4. The MIBs must be located at both the agent and the manager to work effectively.

EXERCISE

1. Explain the general relationship of a TMN to a typical telecommunication network with proper diagram.
2. Explain the functional architecture of TMN in detail.
3. Explain the physical architecture of TMN in detail.
4. Explain the information architecture of TMN in detail.
5. Draw and explain the TMN functional model.
6. Write a detail note on "The Standard Interfaces and classes of application for TMN".
7. Explain the "Logical Model of TMN".
8. Write a detail note on TMN Cube.
9. What are the different aspects for support environment for TMN?
10. Explain the concept of "Detailing functional components and requirements" in TMN.
11. What are the needs for fault management?
12. Draw and explain the architecture for fault management system.
13. Explain accounting management in detail.
14. Draw and explain the performance management architecture in detail.
15. Explain the different functions of configuration management.
16. Draw and explain the architecture of security management.

17. What are the different issues involved in –
    (a) Lower layer protocol requirements?
    (b) Higher layer protocol requirements?
18. Write a detail note on "SNMP".
19. What are the different strengths and shortcomings of SNMP?
20. What are the different security levels with basic SNMP?
21. Write the transport mechanism concept in SNMP based system.

***